The Archaeology of Ancient Greece

The Archaeology of Ancient Greece provides an up-to-date synthesis of current research on the material culture of Greece in the Archaic and Classical periods (1000–300 BC). The rich and diverse material culture of ancient Greece has always provoked admiration and even wonder, but it is seldom analysed as a key to our understanding of Greek civilisation. Dr Whitley shows how the material evidence can be used to address central historical questions for which literary evidence is often insufficient. He also situates Greek art within the broader field of Greek material culture, providing an historically more accurate perspective on both, a significant contr⋯ ⋯ ⋯haeological and art historical evidence.

JAMES WHITLEY is Se⋯ ⋯ ⋯ ⋯ ⋯ ⋯ ⋯ ⋯ ⋯ ⋯ ⋯ ⋯ ⋯ Archaeology, Cardiff University. His ⋯ ⋯ ⋯ ⋯ ⋯ ⋯ ⋯ ⋯ ⋯ ⋯ ⋯ *ociety in Dark Age Greece* (1991) as we⋯

CAMBRIDGE WORLD ARCHAEOLOGY

Series editor
NORMAN YOFFEE, *University of Michigan*

Editorial board
SUSAN ALCOCK, *University of Michigan*
TOM DILLEHAY, *University of Kentucky*
STEPHEN SHENNAN, *University College London*
CARLA SINOPOLI, *University of Michigan*

The Cambridge World Archaeology series is addressed to students and professional archaeologists, and to academics in related disciplines. Each volume presents a survey of the archaeology of a region of the world, providing an up-to-date account of research and integrating recent findings with new concerns of interpretation. While the focus is on a specific region, broader cultural trends are discussed and the implications of regional findings for cross-cultural interpretations considered. The authors also bring anthropological and historical expertise to bear on archaeological problems, and show how both new data and changing intellectual trends in archaeology shape inferences about the past.

Books in the series

RAYMOND ALLCHIN AND BRIDGET ALLCHIN, *The Rise of Civilization in India and Pakistan*

CLIVE GAMBLE, *The Palaeolithic Settlement of Europe*

CHARLES HIGHAM, *Archaeology of Mainland South East Asia*

SARAH MILLEDGE NELSON, *The Archaeology of Korea*

DAVID PHILLIPSON, *African Archaeology* (second revised edition)

OLIVER DICKINSON, *The Aegean Bronze Age*

KAREN OLSEN BRUHNS, *Ancient South America*

ALASDAIR WHITTLE, *Europe in the Neolithic*

CHARLES HIGHAM, *The Bronze Age of Southeast Asia*

CLIVE GAMBLE, *The Palaeolithic Societies of Europe*

DAN POTTS, *The Archaeology of Elam*

A. F. HARDING, *European Societies in the Bronze Age*

NICHOLAS DAVID AND CAROL KRAMER, *Ethnoarchaeology in Action*

JAMES WHITLEY, *The Archaeology of Ancient Greece*

CAMBRIDGE WORLD ARCHAEOLOGY

THE ARCHAEOLOGY OF ANCIENT GREECE

JAMES WHITLEY

School of History and Archaeology
Cardiff University

CAMBRIDGE
UNIVERSITY PRESS

PUBLISHED BY THE PRESS SYNDICATE OF THE UNIVERSITY OF CAMBRIDGE
The Pitt Building, Trumpington Street, Cambridge, United Kingdom

CAMBRIDGE UNIVERSITY PRESS
The Edinburgh Building, Cambridge CB2 2RU, UK
40 West 20th Street, New York, NY 10011–4211, USA
10 Stamford Road, Oakleigh, VIC 3166, Australia
Ruiz de Alarcón 13, 28014 Madrid, Spain
Dock House, The Waterfront, Cape Town 8001, South Africa

http://www.cambridge.org

First published 2001

Printed in the United Kingdom at the University Press, Cambridge

Typeface Trump Medieval 10/13pt   *System* QuarkXPress™ [SE]

A catalogue record for this book is available from the British Library

Library of Congress Cataloguing in Publication data

Whitley, James.
  The archaeology of ancient Greece / James Whitley.
    p.   cm. – (Cambridge world archaeology)
  Includes bibliographical references and index.
  ISBN 0 521 62205 0 – 0 521 62733 8 (pb.)
    1. Excavations (Archaeology) – Greece. 2. Greece – Antiquities.
  3. Greece – History – To 146 BC. I. Series.
  DF77 .W537 2001
  938–dc21   2001018438

ISBN 0 521 62205 0 hardback
ISBN 0 521 62733 8 paperback

For CHRISTINA

CONTENTS

FIGURES

The following abbreviations are used in giving photographic credits and museum numbers.

Acr.   Acropolis Museum, Athens
ASCS Athens   The American School of Classical Studies at
                     Athens
BM London   The British Museum, London
BSA   The British School at Athens
DAI Athens   Deutsches archäologisches Institut, Athens
DAI Rome   Deutsches archäologisches Institut, Rome
EFA   Ecole Française d'Athènes
Hirmer   Hirmer Verlag, Munich
Inv.   Inventory Number
KER   Kerameikos, DAI photo number
Met. Mus.   Metropolitan Museum of Art (New York)
Neg. nr.   negative number (or photo number)
NM Athens   The National Museum, Athens (sometimes
                     Athens NM)
TAP   Tameion Archaiologikon Poron (Archaeological
                     Receipts Fund, Ministry of Culture, Greece)

TABLES

PREFACE AND ACKNOWLEDGEMENTS

As the title indicates, this book is concerned with the archaeology of ancient Greece. Any book with such a title could cover a very wide span of time and space. However, the Aegean Bronze Age has been covered by another book in the Cambridge World Archaeology series (Dickinson 1994), and this book begins precisely where Dickinson stops. Chronologically it covers the period 1000 to 300 BC, that is, the periods known as the Early Iron Age, the Archaic and the Classical. I touch on the very beginning of the Hellenistic period, but do not discuss that period in any detail. After Alexander the Great, the Greek world widens to well beyond the confines of the Mediterranean, and its material culture changes too. In many ways Hellenistic archaeology has more in common with Roman archaeology than with the material culture of Archaic and Classical Greece. Geographically, the book concentrates on the Aegean, that is the area of modern Greece and the western coast of modern Turkey. The Greek settlements in the Sea of Marmara and the Black Sea I do not discuss at all – my only excuse for this neglect being my complete ignorance of these areas. I glance at developments in the west (that is south Italy and Sicily) in the eighth and seventh centuries in particular for the simple reason that one cannot understand the 'Orientalising' phenomenon in Greek history and archaeology without reference to Greek and Phoenician activity in the western Mediterranean. The actions of Greeks, Phoenicians, Etruscans and other Italians in the western Mediterranean comprise a topic that undoubtedly deserves a book of its own in the Cambridge World Archaeology series, but I am not the one to write it.

No one writes a book (or no one ought to write a book) without a purpose and without a readership in mind. This book has two main purposes and is intended for two principal groups of readers. One purpose is to introduce students and others to the material evidence from Greece which dates to these periods – that is, to Greek archaeology and Greek art. In this sense, the book seeks to answer the question, what kind of evidence does Greek archaeology provide? But the book's principal purpose is to show how this material can be used to address a whole range of questions which are, in the broadest possible sense of the term, historical. To put it another way, what is the evidence that Greek archaeology provides evidence *for*? When I use the term historical I do not mean to suggest that the questions we ask should be determined by our literary sources – far from it. Nor do I wish to endorse the belief that, because we have written sources, Greek archaeology is simply another kind of 'historical' archaeology. The relationship between written and material evidence is invariably more complex than it first seems. Both kinds of evidence are equally mute unless we have a question or interest we wish to pursue. In Classical studies recently there has been a convergence of interest between historically minded archaeologists and archaeologically minded historians. Both groups are asking sophisticated questions of the material evidence, regarding such topics as trade, cultural exchange, urbanism, gender, mortuary practices, state formation and the relationship between domestic, civic and sacred space. The true historical potential of Greek archaeology is at last being realised.

These two purposes relate directly to the two main groups of readers for whom this book is written. In one sense this is a textbook for advanced undergraduates and beginning postgraduates. This does not mean it is a suitable introductory text for first-year students in universities in Britain, North America or Australia (though I hope they will find it a useful supplement). Such students will undoubtedly be better served by some of the many introductory books on Greek art and archaeology already available. If one simply wants a general impression of what Greek art looks like, and the main stages of its development, then it would be wise to turn first to those books written by William Biers, John Boardman, Robin Osborne, John Pedley, Martin Robertson, Nigel Spivey and Susan Woodford. But if one wants to know what Greek archaeology is good *for*, then this may be the book for you.

The second audience I had in mind was what might be called a general archaeological readership: that is, archaeologists who work in other parts of the world (Anglo-Saxon England, Jomon Japan or the Hopewell cultures of Ohio and Illinois, for example) who may want a reasonably up-to-date synthesis on this period and area. Those familiar with the Cambridge World Archaeology series should therefore expect a summary description of the relevant material, and of past and present avenues of research, and some general historical conclusions. I have indeed attempted something like this, but it seems to me that a straightforward synthesis of the Greek material is impossible. This is not simply because the quantity of material is now quite beyond the grasp of most individual scholars (it is certainly beyond me). It is rather that the material record of Greece is not simply just another material record, no different in principle from any other to be found in India, Nigeria or the Southwestern United States – or at least no different from other kinds of 'historical' archaeology, such as the archaeology of medieval Europe or colonial America. The archaeology of ancient Greece comes to us with a whole package of interests, values, preconceptions and metanarratives, which have given the subject its particular character. The archaeology of ancient Greece is the least innocent of all kinds of archaeological endeavour.

One of the features that distinguishes Classical Archaeology in general and Greek archaeology in particular from the archaeologies of other times and places is the proportion of its material record that has been called 'art'. There are, for example no fewer than five books in the Thames and Hudson 'World of Art' series on Greek painted pottery (all relevant to the period covered by this book). It has long seemed that the *archaeology* of ancient Greece is just there to provide a kind of backdrop for its *art*. But as more and more Classical archaeologists have engaged in field survey, petrography or quantitative analyses, such a view has seemed less and less tenable. Recently there has been an attempt to rescue the traditional subjects of Classical Archaeology from their dangerous proximity to such low-status activities by coining the term 'Classical art history'. Classical art historians can continue to study sculpture and 'vase painting' without having to take a close interest in broken pottery from survey or excavation, or bothering overmuch about the contexts in which such art was found or used. This book takes the opposite position. Archaeology is the study of material culture. All art is material culture, though not all material culture is art. Classical art history therefore is archaeology or it is nothing.

Like Caesar's Gaul, this book is divided into three parts. It is arranged by theme rather than by period or class of material. Part I deals with the history and character of the subject, and tries to get the technical matter of chronology out of the way as soon as possible. Part II deals with the major themes and problems in the study of Archaic Greece, and Part III with those of Classical Greece. My reason for choosing this arrangement is that the book is there to be read, rather than just consulted. A textbook (however good its index) is not an encyclopaedia. It should have a narrative thread, a series of arguments that engage the reader's interest. Of course, like everyone working in Classical studies, I know that there can be no generalisation without an equal and opposite qualification. But I have allowed myself the luxury of being a little glib at times, and tried to confine my qualifications to the footnotes. A further principle I have tried to adhere to throughout is that objects must be understood in context: that is, in the social context in which they were originally used and the archaeological context in which they were found. For every major object or class of objects I discuss I have then tried to give the original publication which states where it was found. This has resulted in a much longer bibliography than some might find suitable, but at least this enables the sceptical reader to check up any facts about which she/he may be (perhaps justifiably) suspicious.

This book has its distant origins in the time I was a student at the British School at Athens, where Hector Catling introduced me to dimensions of the subject I had never encountered before. It seemed strange then that there was no comprehensive book on the subject (this seems less strange now). Some parts of this book were first aired as seminars in Oxford, Cambridge, London or Cardiff, and many of the themes have been tried out on several cohorts of Cardiff students. But this is not in general a reworking of material I have published elsewhere. It was written in the numerical order of the chapters, beginning with chapter 1 and ending with chapter 15. Sue Alcock is primarily responsible for getting me started on this enterprise, and for gaining the approval of the Cambridge World Archaeology

Board. A grant of study leave for 1997 to 1998 by my home institution Cardiff enabled me to start work on this book, leave which I took in Cambridge. The departments of Classics and Archaeology in Cambridge gave me the status of Visiting Scholar for the academic year 1997–8. The libraries of the Faculties of Classics and of Archaeology and Anthropology have been essential, and I would like to thank the staff in both libraries for dealing with my often difficult requests. Access to the Ashmolean Library, Oxford has made the work of revision much easier than it would otherwise have been, and I am grateful to John Bennet for help in this regard.

For help and advice in obtaining illustrations and photographs I would like to thank Ian Jenkins, Robin Osborne and Anthony Snodgrass and the Museum of Classical Archaeology, Cambridge. I am grateful to the following for allowing me to reproduce photographic images: the British School at Athens; the British Museum, London; the Fitzwilliam Museum, Cambridge; the Ashmolean Museum, Oxford; the Centre for Ancient Documents, Oxford; the American School of Classical Studies at Athens (in particular the Agora Excavations and the Alison Frantz archive); the Metropolitan Museum of Art, New York; the Ecole Française d'Athènes; the Musée du Louvre, Paris; the Musée de Boulogne-sur-Mer; Hirmer Verlag, Munich; Antikesammlung, Staatliche Museen zu Berlin (Preussischer Kulturbesitz); the Deutsche Archäologische Institut, in both Rome and Athens; the Ny Carlsberg Glyptotek, Copenhagen; the Tameion Archaiologikon Poron (Archaeological Receipts Fund), Ministry of Culture, Athens; and Dr Herbert Hoffmann. I would also like to thank those who have given me permission to reproduce plans and drawings: Professor John Camp and the Agora Excavations; Dr Ian Jenkins and the British Museum, London; Drs M. Popham and J.J. Coulton, Oxford; Professor J.N. Coldstream, London; Professors W. Hoepfner and E.L. Schwandner (Berlin and Munich); Professor John Cherry, Ann Arbor; Professors Ian Morris and M.H. Jameson, Stanford; the editors of *Hesperia*; Professor A.M. Snodgrass; and Dr Ruth Westgate.

Many of the ideas in this book have been developed through conversations with a number of scholars, more indeed than I can remember. I would however like to thank those who have sent me offprints or unpublished drafts of their work: Sue Alcock; Stelios Andreou; Carla Antonaccio; John Bintliff; J.N. Coldstream; M. Cuozzo; Brice Erickson; Jonathan Hall; Herbert Hoffmann; Sanne Houby-Nielsen; Sally Humphreys; Irene Lemos; Ian Morris; Oswyn Murray; Lucia Nixon; A.M. D'Onofrio; Robin Osborne; F. de Polignac; David Ridgway; A.M. Snodgrass; Nigel Spencer; and Ruth Westgate. The text as it exists now has benefited from the advice and criticism of those who have read parts of it in draft form, in particular Ian Morris, Robin Osborne and Ruth Westgate. I have benefited too from the comments of CWA's anonymous referees, and that of the series editor, Norman Yoffee. It is Anthony Snodgrass however whom I must single out for special thanks. He has read the whole of it more or less as I wrote it, and whenever a chapter was sent out, helpful comments would be returned to me within the week. Lastly, I would like to thank my wife, Christina Hatzimichael. Despite having a thesis of her own to complete, she too has read it all in draft, and offered invaluable advice on many points. She has also, of course, supported me in countless ways, both small and large, from when I began to write the book until I finished it. This book is dedicated to her.

All this is not to excuse any of the manifest failings of this book that may result from my not taking the excellent advice of all those who have helped me. As another scholar once wrote, any omissions of this kind should be put down to 'obstinacy, and not to ingratitude'.

A note on the spelling and transliteration of Greek names

The transliteration of Greek names has always caused difficulties. Modern Greek presents few problems – phonetic transliteration is usually straightforward (though phonetic transliteration can be a very misleading guide to the original Greek spelling – 'i' in English can stand for eta, iota or any diphthong involving iota). Ancient Greek names are an entirely different matter. These have come down to us first through Roman writers such as Pliny and Vitruvius, who employed their own forms of transliteration, and then via Renaissance scholars. Ancient Greek names have often first been latinised and then (in some cases) anglicised. So, for example, Athinai became Athenae and then Athens; Korinthos became Corinthus and then Corinth. Since the nineteenth century there has been a reverse trend, to transliterate into English directly from the ancient Greek; Korinthos has made a comeback (in, for example, Shanks 1999).

Those with a Classical education can usually find their way through all this, but those without (including many students of Greek archaeology) often find the whole business baffling. This is especially so when writers are themselves inconsistent. Readers may think that they have a right to expect consistency from writers of textbooks. I am sorry to disappoint them. Here are my reasons.

If consistency is a virtue, ostentatious pedantry is a vice – and one that I have been keen to avoid. So, while I have in general used modern transliterations of ancient Greek names (Olynthos not Olynthus; Herodotos not Herodotus; Selinous not Selinus), some anglicised forms have become so familiar (e.g. Syracuse for Syrakousai) that it would be absurd to drop them, 'without the appearance of pedantic precision, or affected singularity' (Dodwell 1819a: v). The same applies to many latinised forms (e.g. Mycenae not Mykenai; Aeschylus not Aischylos; Euboea not Euboia). Other 'purer' forms of transliteration are just ugly; I sincerely hope that Thoukydides will never supplant Thucydides.

A note on bibliographic conventions

It is a version of the Harvard system of referencing that, as with all other volumes of this series, has been used in this book. The Harvard system has the advantages of logic, clarity and consistency; it is also the system with which most students and most scholars (at least, those outside of Classical Studies) are most likely to be familiar. Ancient texts lie somewhere outside the purview of the Harvard system proper, and I have used the standard conventions for referring to books of the *Iliad* or of Herodotos' *Histories* (conventions which do not depend upon edition or page number). Readers can therefore consult the Loeb editions, Oxford Classical Texts or Penguin translations as they please. Traditionally, however, Classical Archaeology has employed its own system of referencing, one that makes extensive use of footnotes and standard abbreviations. Those who delve into some of the works cited in this book are likely to come across references which take forms such as '*BSA* xxxix (1938–39), 52–64' or '*AM* lx/lxi (1935–6), pl.84' (Boardman 1961: 84). The former refers to the *Annual of the British School at Athens* vol. 39 (1938–9), pages 52–64; the latter to *Mitteilungen des deutschen archäologischen Instituts, athenische Abteilung* (or *athenische Mitteilungen*) vol. 60–61 (1935–6), plate 84. Like many others who have come to Classical Archaeology from prehistory, I have never entirely rid myself of the suspicion that the reason Classical scholars have held on to their own system for so long is that it helps to keep outsiders out. Mastery of abbreviations, like mastery of the Classical languages, is, after all, the mark of a true scholar. For those still baffled by all this, a full list and explanation of all standard abbreviations (bibliographic and otherwise) in use in Classical Archaeology is given in the *American Journal of Archaeology* 95 (1991), 1–16. It is a sign of the times perhaps that this journal too has now gone over to its own version of the Harvard system, without entirely dispensing with abbreviations and footnotes.

PART I

APPROACHES TO GREEK ARCHAEOLOGY

CHAPTER I

INTRODUCTION: CLASSICAL ARCHAEOLOGY AND ITS OBJECTS

1.1 Two objects

Classical Archaeology is pre-eminently an archaeology of objects. Much of what Classical archaeologists write has been concerned with the description and interpretation of certain classes of artefacts, artefacts of a very particular kind. Such objects are often striking and sometimes beautiful. They may even be considered art. Let us take a look at two of them, taken from two quite different periods in the Greek archaeological sequence.

Figure 1.1 shows a pot (Athens NM 1002) now on display in the National Museum of Athens. It is a large vessel, about 1.22 m (or 4 feet) high, known as the Nessos amphora, after the scene on the neck of the pot, which shows the hero Herakles slaying the Centaur Nessos. It was found in 1890 in the course of rescue excavations while building work was taking place in the Piraeus street area of modern Athens. In Antiquity this area was known to be a part of the Outer Kerameikos, a region which lay outside the city walls to the west of the ancient city.[1] It is conventionally dated to the end of the seventh century, and the general style of the pot can be called 'Late Protoattic' or 'Early Black-Figure'.[2] The painting on the surface of this pot, like a painting you might see hanging in one of the great galleries of Western Europe, has been 'attributed' to a particular craftsman or artist, named after the pot (or vase) itself, the 'Nessos painter'.[3]

To describe something in a certain way is also to begin to interpret it. I have listed above a number of facts or circumstances pertinent to our understanding of this pot. But before we describe or interpret something we have to have some idea of what we wish to learn from it; that is, we have to have some notion of what kind of evidence it is, and what it is evidence for. This is what archaeologists mean by the problem of approach, and it raises the question of how Classical archaeologists have traditionally looked at such objects. Which of these facts (some of which, to be truthful, are inferences) have been thought most important? And what role does this object play in the various stories scholars have wanted to tell us, stories about the art and archaeology of early Greece? Do we, for example, know the function of this pot? What it was actually used for is

---

[1] Kavvadias 1890: 4–5; Stais and Wolters 1891: 46.
[2] Early Black-Figure according to Beazley 1951: 14–15 (1986: 13–14); 1956: 4–5. Protoattic according to J.M. Cook 1935.   [3] Beazley 1944; 1956: 4–5.

1.1 Nessos amphora

unclear; it was found, like its near contemporary the Kynosarges amphora,[4] broken in many parts and associated with bones and ash. It has often been said that this vase, like its Geometric predecessors, served as a grave marker.[5] Indeed its findspot, close to a known cemetery area of Late Geometric graves referred to at the time as the 'Dipylon', is consistent with this view. The excavator, Kavvadias, thought that it served as a container for a cremation.[6] Kavvadias' description is, however, equally consistent with another interpretation; it could have come from what German excavators in the Kerameikos were later to call an 'Opferrinne' or offering trench, since the bones and ash of animals have been found associated with broken fineware pottery of similar date in offering

[4] For the Kynosarges amphora, see Smith 1902; for its context see Droop 1906.
[5] For example Robertson 1975: 54; R.M. Cook 1972: 71. Both here seem to be following Beazley 1951: 14–15.
[6] Kavvadias 1890: 4–5; Stais and Wolters 1891: 46. See now comments by Osborne 1998b: 18–20.

trenches. These 'Opferrinnen' were often filled with the bones and ash of animals used in sacrificial meals.[7]

Soon after its discovery, however, the function of this pot swiftly became a matter of secondary importance. Once restored, its context became the National Museum of Athens, where it can be seen today alongside other vases of late seventh-century date. Here its style and iconography can be closely scrutinised. It stands with its decorated face open to view, its rear being covered with a few large strokes of the brush. On the lip is a frieze of ducks; below this, on the neck, a scene familiar to students of Greek literature: the hero Herakles slaying the Centaur Nessos (or Netos). Indeed there can be little ambiguity about the subject, as these images are accompanied by dipinti (painted labels) telling us exactly who is who.[8] Beside the neck, on the handles, are some owls, and below them runs a frieze of palmettes. On the main body of the vase, Gorgons with wings, their tongues sticking out, stare out at the modern museum visitor. Below this a frieze of dolphins, and below that a cable pattern, can still faintly be discerned.

The careful reader may well ask, what is the point of this detailed description? Can we not see all this for ourselves? Descriptions not unlike this one, of objects not unlike this one, form a large part of many books on Greek archaeology and art. Such descriptions may form a prelude to an interpretation, as if interpretation flows naturally from description. And the careful reader (and viewer) may well be asking, what can this combination of images mean? Here we have to remember that the ancient viewer would have been familiar with the relevant myth or myths. One of the earliest versions of the story of Herakles and Nessos is to be found in Sophocles' play, *The Women of Trachis* (lines 555–81). Here Herakles' wife, Deianeira, recalls how Herakles killed Nessos (in this version, with an arrow) because the Centaur had tried to rape her. On the point of death, however, Nessos tells Deianeira to keep safe his blood. He tells her that if she ever finds that Herakles has fallen in love with another woman, she can, by making him wear a shirt dipped in the blood of Nessos' wound, return Herakles to her affections. Naively, Deianeira believes him, and the 'shirt of Nessos' proves the means by which Nessos, through Deianeira, contrives the death of Herakles. In the scene that we see here, Herakles kills Nessos. But an ancient viewer might also know that Nessos was to have his posthumous revenge.

The myth of Perseus slaying one of the Gorgons, Medusa, is in a sense the inverse of this.[9] In the Gorgon's case, her ability to turn anyone who looks at her to stone is used by Perseus himself to good (or bad) effect, when he shows the severed head of the Medusa to Polydektes, a man who had attempted to force

---

[7] For seventh-century Opferrinnen in the Kerameikos cemetery with deposits of ash and bones (probably the bones of animals from some kind of ritual meal) see Kübler 1959: 25, 29, 31 and 42.

[8] For the painted labels, see Boeghold 1962; Immerwahr 1990: 20; Jeffery 1990: 76 no. 6a. The names are written retrograde (right to left), and 'Nessos' is spelt 'Netos'.

[9] There are many versions of the Perseus myth. But we do know that one version at least was in circulation in neighbouring Boeotia in the years around 700 BC. The poet Hesiod mentions Perseus 'the Gorgon-slayer' several times (Hesiod, *Shield* 216–48; *Theogony* 280).

Perseus' mother, Danae, to marry him against her will. A viewer familiar with both myths might see the common theme that connects these two images as one of the inevitability of vengeance.

The difficulty with this interpretation is that we have to imagine an ancient viewer who can, as it were, read between the lines – that is, can supply the end of the story which the images leave out. Another possible answer to the question 'what do these images mean?' is that they are simply two scenes of violence: Herakles slays Nessos; whilst Perseus (who cannot be seen, but whose presence somehow has to be inferred) slays the Gorgons. The friezes of ducks and dolphins are there to provide some kind of narrative context. These images may then be plausibly related to others on Protoattic pots with funerary associations, such as the Polyphemos amphora from Eleusis (fig. 9.4). On this vase the neck shows another violent scene, one well known from book IX of the *Odyssey* (*Odyssey* IX.322–86): Odysseus and his companions blind Polyphemos. On the shoulder, one animal attacks another; and on the lower body, Gorgons stare out to 'freeze' the viewer. Both context and image suggest a common theme: death as deprivation of the senses. This linking theme has in turn been used as evidence to indicate that a certain kind of 'funerary ideology' existed in seventh-century Athens.[10]

There are many versions of Greek myths however. None of the images shown above conforms precisely to those known from literary sources, which are often much later than the myths to be seen on the surfaces of Greek pots. It is always possible to put forward other interpretations, and it is perhaps for this reason that most commentators have avoided detailed interpretation of the 'meaning' of the image or of the pot. Most attention has been given to the *style* of the Nessos amphora. Style was one of the principal interests of Stais and Wolters, the first to describe the pot in detail and, in so doing, admit it to the canon of Greek Art.[11] This status was confirmed, and its role in the history of Greek art carefully defined, by a number of later scholars, principally J.D. Beazley. By style is meant two things: the overall manner and technique of drawing and painting; and the individual style of the painter, that which distinguishes his hand from that of others. For Beazley, 'black-figure' is a technique where figures in black are drawn on a clay ground, their features being outlined by incision. It was Beazley who grouped this pot with others he believed to be by the same painter, a painter called (by other scholars) after this vase, the 'Nessos painter'.[12] In Beazley's eyes its significance is twofold: it exemplifies the style of a particular individual; and it comes to play a pivotal role in the development of Greek art and narrative composition. For this pot is pregnant with as yet unrealised possibilities. As Beazley put it:

---

[10] For this interpretation, see Osborne 1988: 1–6; for criticisms see Whitley 1994a: 63–5. For the publication of the pot, see Mylonas 1957. For the latest discussion of this image, see Snodgrass 1998: 90–100.   [11] Stais and Wolters 1891.

[12] Beazley 1944; 1956: 4–5. Beazley actually attributes this pot to the 'Nettos [sic] and Chimaera painter'. Most other scholars, while agreeing with Beazley's attributions, have preferred to use the term the 'Nessos painter'; see Boardman 1974: 15.

At the end of the seventh century, the black-figure takes the place of the outline technique in Attica: the exuberant ornament is reduced, the animals are powerfully stylized; the eccentricity disappears. The change is partly due to influence from proto-corinthian art. The chief example of this stage is the Nessos amphora in Athens, where the group of Herakles and the Centaur yields to fine proto-corinthian work in deftness, surpasses it in force. Other works by the same painter have been preserved: he is perhaps the earliest Greek artist whose *personality* we can grasp [emphasis mine].[13]

After Beazley, unanimity descends upon British Classical archaeologists. For Robert Cook, the style of fig. 1.1 is 'carefully chosen and admirably executed' and 'Attic art has gained in compactness and unity, and in subtlety too';[14] for Martin Robertson, the vase shows that 'patterns of form and meaning are beginning to crystallise, which keep their character through the archaic age and beyond'.[15] American commentators too have tended to follow Beazley's lead; for Hurwit, this pot shows that 'after a period of idiosyncrasy, experiment and whim, Athenian image making is once more subjected to the rigors of schema and type'.[16]

There seem to be a number of features common to all of these accounts, chief amongst which is a tendency to round off an empirical description with a kind of abstract, almost metaphysical claim. My argument in this chapter is that Greek archaeology, at least as it has traditionally been practised up until the early 1970s, is characterised by certain commonalities in the description of its preferred objects. If so, similar features may also be evident in the commentary on another example of Greek art I want to examine, the Delphi Charioteer (fig. 1.2). This can be seen today in the museum of Delphi, close to where it was found by French excavators in 1896. It is one of the few original bronze statues we possess, cast in several pieces by a version of the lost wax method.[17] It was discovered just to the north-west of the temple of Apollo itself, where it had been buried in rockfall.[18] The statue was almost immediately recognised as being part of a bronze chariot group of a kind described by the Greek travel writer Pausanias, who wrote a sort of 'Guide to Greece' in the second century BC.[19] Two inscriptions were found in close association. One, found much closer than the other to the statue itself, reads in part 'P]olyzalos m'anethek[e', Polyzalos dedicated me; the other, less clearly

---

[13] Beazley and Ashmole 1932: 11. I have presumed here that the style of writing indicates Beazley's rather than Ashmole's 'scholarly personality'.   [14] Cook 1972: 71.   [15] Robertson 1975: 54–5.
[16] Hurwit 1985: 178.
[17] For its technique, see Mattusch 1988: 4, 126–35. The lost wax method is the one most widely used by Greek craftsmen when making large, hollow statues in bronze. It requires first a clay model to be made, over which the features of the statue are modelled in wax. A clay covering is placed over the whole, and, when the molten bronze is poured in, the wax melts away, and, as the molten bronze cools, it takes on the wax's shape.
[18] For the circumstances of its discovery, see Chamoux 1955: 7.
[19] See for example Pausanias X.13.5; X.10.3. Neither of the chariots so described is a dedication after a victory in the chariot race. They are rather dedications of bronze chariot groups erected after military victories, and the subjects are legendary heroes rather than contemporary figures. Pausanias, in his description of Delphi, for the most part disdains to list all the athletic victors' statues, as he had done for Olympia.

1.2 Delphi Charioteer

associated, gives the name of a sculptor, Sotades.[20] The historical record of the time tells us of a certain Polyzalos who may plausibly be associated with this statue (Diodoros [Diodorus Siculus] XI.48.3–6, 8). He was one of the sons of Deinomenes who was, for a time, tyrant of Gela in Sicily. The inscriptions and the context allow us to say with some certainty what the sculpture was for: it was a monument intended both to commemorate Polyzalos' victory in the chariot race in the Pythian games and, simultaneously, to stand as a thank offering to the god Apollo. Since we know when Polyzalos and the sons of Deinomenes held power in Sicily, and since we know that the Pythian games were held every four

---

[20] For the inscriptions, see Chamoux 1955: 26–31 and 19 fig. 1. The inscription is, in fact, a bit more complicated than this. There seems to have been an erasure, and it is only the second inscription that mentions Polyzalos. An earlier inscription seems to mention Gela. See discussion by Jeffery 1990: 266, 275 no. 9 and plate 51. Like most inscriptions, it is far from complete, and there is no interpretation without some degree of restoration.

years, the statue can be dated, with some precision, to just after 478, 474 or 470 BC.[21] Soon after its discovery it was proclaimed a masterpiece of Greek art, a supreme example of the early Classical or Severe style in Greek sculpture. French archaeologists were particularly proud of their find. J. Charbonneaux exclaims, 'Before the Charioteer, one cannot but feel the presence of genius, asserting itself both in the overall conception and in the inventive multiplicity of detail' and goes on to encapsulate the essence of the work: 'Everything in the figure of the Charioteer simultaneously suggests immobility and movement, rhythm and symmetry, life and design.'[22] British scholars have often (though not always) agreed with this estimation. At the end of a long description, Martin Robertson boldly states that the Charioteer has 'architectural strength and simplicity, but infused with life'.[23]

As with the Nessos amphora, there is a distinct tendency for scholars to describe works in terms of abstract qualities which transcend that object's original function or purpose; as too with the Nessos amphora, there is an urge to search for a personality, the painter behind the pot and the sculptor behind the bronze.[24] Some commentators, who have a wider interest in cultural history, have been more ambitious. At least one has tried to relate the abstract principles they discern in this work to ideas current at the time of its creation. Here J.J. Pollitt attempts to discern the ethos (the 'character') within the Delphi Charioteer: 'Not only does it celebrate, like the Pythian odes [of Pindar], a victory won at the festival games, but the ethos which it conveys is a manifestation of Pindaric *arete* . . . the "innate excellence" of noble natures which gives them proficiency and pride in their human endeavors before the gods.' Pollitt goes on to describe the abstract qualities which both inhere in the work, and which sum up for him the spirit of the age: 'In the Charioteer we are confronted with a definable ethos which is neither aloof, as the High Classical period will often be, nor remote and neutral like the Archaic, but rather, like the early Classical era, simultaneously proud and vulnerable.'[25]

This is not the place to dispute the interpretations, nor to question the judgement of these writers. Whether or not either of these objects is a work of art (and what we may understand by this term); whether they possess qualities which transcend the original purposes for which they were made and the contexts in which they were used; these are, strictly speaking, not archaeological questions at all, but questions of an art-historical or even philosophical kind. But Pollitt's remarks do raise other important issues, issues which archaeologists and

[21] For a discussion of the sons of Deinomenes (the Deinomenidai) see Barrett 1973. For a recent attempt to place the Charioteer more firmly in its historical context (and a reconsideration of the date), see Rolley 1990.   [22] Charbonneaux *et al.* 1972: 106.

[23] Robertson 1975: 189. Other English-speaking scholars have however been far less complimentary; see Stewart 1990: 149; Boardman 1985a: 52.

[24] For attempts to identify the sculptor of the Charioteer, see Chamoux 1955: 74–5; Robertson 1975: 189. Ridgway (1970: 34) however makes no real attempt at attribution, content to see the sculpture as a good example of the style (and spirit) of the age.   [25] Pollitt 1972: 48.

historians have to addrress. It has often been said that Classical Archaeology differs from prehistoric and other archaeologies because it is historical, and that the art and material culture of ancient Greece must be understood primarily in a literary context. In the case of the Nessos amphora, all that the literary context can provide is the means of recognising the myth depicted; it cannot, in and of itself, produce an interpretation of the images that are shown. With the Delphi Charioteer on the other hand, Pollitt's ambition to link the art with the literature of the period may seem more reasonable. For we can identify the dedicator, and so place the object in its historical context. Direct historical context is however not Pollitt's principal concern. His interest lies rather in the sense conveyed by two words – *ethos* and *arete*. Ethos is a term used in discussions of art in Greek literature from the fourth century onwards. There is no positive evidence that it was used in this way in the first quarter of the fifth. With arete Pollitt is on firmer ground. Arete is a word much used by the poets Pindar and Bacchylides, who were very much this sculpture's contemporaries. Pollitt's suggestion that chariot groups like the Delphi Charioteer were analogies, in bronze, to the epinician odes composed and sung to celebrate some famous athletic victory is an attractive one. Here art and literature do genuinely illuminate one another, and contribute to a broader cultural history. But this approach does have its limitations. Cultural history of this kind can be written from works such as this one which we can date with some precision, and whose context is of a kind described in our ancient sources (in this case Pausanias). But the vast majority of objects even from such a well-documented period as the fifth century do not have accompanying inscriptions that are quite so helpful; nor do they come from sites which are quite so well known; nor can their purpose be so easily compared to that of a literary genre. That species of cultural history that turns itself into an elevated conversation between high art and high literature is necessarily limited in scope. Cultural history of this kind must perforce restrict itself to a narrow range of well-known objects, a small canon of great works.

But it is exactly the description, discussion and reinterpretation of such objects which has, in the past, been the traditional subject of Classical Archaeology. Such an archaeology necessarily puts objects before contexts, and prefers personalities to technique. Such an archaeology has rarely, if ever, seen its task as being one of providing a worm's eye view of the 'banausic' (that is commonplace, or 'common') realities of Greek life. Historical or anthropological knowledge of a comparative kind has not been its primary objective. Rather the archaeology of ancient Greece, like Classical studies in general, has seen its role as one of celebration as much as of study. The numerous books cited above are, in a sense, so many epinician (victory) odes to the enduring appeal of Classical art, and to the values that art represents. The task of Classical Archaeology has been one of a custodian of traditional values, of what the European aristocratic societies of the eighteenth, nineteenth and twentieth centuries most prized in ancient Greece.

1.2 The objects of Classical Archaeology

It is for all these reasons that the material, archaeological and artistic record of Greece cannot simply be viewed as just another body of material, material which can be studied according to the same principles and using the same methods that have been used in any other part of the world. Or rather, the Greek archaeological sequence may in fact be no different to the unprejudiced Asian or African eye, but it has not been treated as such by the vast majority of European, North American and Australian scholars. The material record of Greece reaches the modern student with a whole series of values attached. Hence the significance of the word 'Classical'. The archaeology of Greece in this period is not simply archaeology – it is Classical Archaeology. The term 'Classical Archaeology' does not merely indicate the archaeology of the so-called Classical period in Greece (479–323 BC). Objects from the Archaic and Hellenistic periods have traditionally enjoyed a status similar to those from the Classical. There is more Art in Classical Archaeology than in other archaeologies, and that Art has been more highly regarded than art from other times and places. The objects of Classical Archaeology have assumed canonical status, and this status has had a kind of 'trickle down' effect on the material record of Greece as a whole. All objects from Greece, however humble (such as terracottas), are in the eyes of many scholars considered 'Classical'.

The Classical Archaeology of Greece has thus had very different objects from other archaeologies – and I mean objects in both senses of the word. Classical Archaeology has been not merely the study of a different class of objects (or objects of a different class, one might say). It has also had a quite different set of objectives. Again, it is not simply that Classical Archaeology is the study of an historical period, and that its practitioners are thus more reliant on (and familiar with) texts than prehistorians; or that Classical archaeologists have a strong liking for art-historical modes of expression. It is rather that the practice of archaeology in Greece has been closely tied to the study of the Classics, with all that that fact implies. Not so long ago, the Classics played a central role in the elite education of most Western countries. All prestigious universities had Classics departments, and new and aspiring universities sought to acquire them. The Classics, as a university subject, was chiefly the study of the language, literature, history and philosophy of the Greek and Latin speaking world in Antiquity. Teachers of Classics were also much concerned with the transmission of the values contained within ancient literature and philosophy to future generations. Archaeologists of ancient Greece could enjoy a similar (if slightly lower) status to their literary colleagues if they could prove their philological credentials. Archaeologists were also concerned to show that the study of the material record of the ancient world, and especially of its art, had a role to play in the transmission of Classical values. Art, like poetry and philosophy, could be, in the words of the Latin poet Horace, a *monumentum aere perennius*, a monument more lasting than bronze. The values which Classical art embodied transcended its mere physical presence.

But the status of the Classics as a subject is not what it was. In Britain there are more departments of archaeology than there are of Classics, and in the United States archaeologists in anthropology departments considerably outnumber those attached to departments of Classics. Nor do the values which 'the Classics' were once held to represent enjoy the cultural authority they once did. The question that seems most urgent now is not, perhaps, can something as 'banausic' as archaeology be Classical, but is Classical Archaeology archaeology at all? It may be helpful (at least rhetorically) to consider Greek archaeology from an outsider's point of view – in fact from the point of view of a prehistorian.

1.3 Childe and Beazley: a conflict of paradigms

Many prehistorians dislike Classical Archaeology. It is not simply that they exhibit a perfectly understandable preference for their own area of prehistory; nor that they have a well-developed aesthetic preference for the rough-hewn, the rude and the primitive; nor even that there may be some lingering resentment of the prestige that Classical Archaeology once enjoyed. Many prehistorians (at least many who work in Britain) simply do not see the point of Classical Archaeology. From these prehistorians' point of view, Classical Archaeology is not archaeology at all but a rarefied and dilettantish pursuit, whose connexions to the art market are rather too close for comfort. This attitude is not new, as a brief historical excursus should show.

V. Gordon Childe was one of this century's most distinguished prehistorians. He is responsible for some of the most influential syntheses of European and Near Eastern prehistory ever written, and remains a major influence on the course of archaeology's intellectual development. It is not often remembered that he was first educated at Oxford as a classicist, and then, for a time, as a Classical archaeologist. He was in fact taught by J.D. Beazley, but his experience as a pupil was (in later recollection at least) not a happy one. Childe was bemused as to why bronzes, terracottas and painted pottery should be 'respectable', whereas stone and bronze tools were 'banausic'.[26] Childe devoted much of his life to the idea of the unity of archaeology, in the belief that archaeology was a universal science of humankind whose aims and methods where everywhere the same. Nowhere was his advocacy more passionate than in a paper he delivered in 1943. Childe did not, like many contemporary prehistorians, simply ignore Classical Archaeology. Rather he chided classicists for their myopia, and gave no quarter to his old teacher Beazley: 'It is absurd that students should be trained to distinguish between the several masters of Attic vase-painting and the different schools of sculpture, but given no inkling of even the typological significance of unpainted wares, safety-pins

[26] Childe 1958: 69.

[fibulae] and swords.'[27] This paper was delivered at a conference in London on the 'Future of Archaeology'. This conference can now be seen, in retrospect, as one of the most important occasions for the setting of intellectual agendas in archaeology in the twentieth century. It defined British (and, to a large extent, North American and Australian) ambitions for a World Archaeology, a science of Everyman Everywhere. It explicitly rejected a German philological model of a prehistory of peoples and nations, which had been tainted by Nazism. It outlined a new rationale for this project, which others later called 'ethnographic humanism'.[28] Such humanism was based on a concept of humankind derived from ethnographic observation and anthropological theory. A humanism so defined was necessarily distinct from the earlier kind, which Western thought had inherited from the Renaissance, and which placed a particular value on the Western inheritance from the Classical World. As such, ethnographic humanism was a direct challenge to the authority of the Classics. The 'World Archaeology Project' that this conference inaugurated was, for the next thirty years at least, undoubtedly a success. Its rationale underpinned major comparative projects in the study of the social and political evolution of Mesoamerica and Mesopotamia; it breathed fresh life into European prehistory; it justified the extension of archaeological interest into every corner of the globe; and the extraordinary series of discoveries relating to early hominid evolution were, in no small part, the result of its ambition.

J.D. Beazley was present at this conference. Together with J.L. Myres, he represented Greek and Roman archaeology. Myres clearly appreciated the conference's importance, and understood its implicit agenda. He pointed out that, if British archaeologists were to engage in fieldwork across the globe, they should display a greater understanding of local sensitivities than they had in the past. How would British scholars react, he argued, if the (admittedly hypothetical) 'Ruritanian Academy of Sciences' applied for a permit to dig Stonehenge or Offa's Dyke? Beazley by contrast limited himself to a few modest suggestions. Students of archaeology at universities should learn to draw, and learn to appreciate that much material remained in museum collections which could be studied with profit. Excavation was often as unnecessary as it was expensive.[29] Whatever the merits of this advice, it hardly rose to the challenge of outlining the 'Future of Archaeology'.

Childe and Beazley were both emblematic (if hardly representative) figures in twentieth-century archaeology. But, while Beazley showed absolutely no interest in prehistory, Childe was far from indifferent to the fate of Classical Archaeology. He regarded the Greek Achievement as a crucial threshold in human history, one where democracy began to replace monarchy, and reason to replace superstition. As a Marxist however Childe believed that this achievement was predicated on certain material conditions. It was these 'material conditions of life', the 'banausic' realities of the Greeks' everyday existence, as well as their art and architecture, that it

---

[27] Childe 1943: 25. Childe 1964 is the clearest articulation of the principles that informed his work.
[28] See in particular Clark 1943 for the clearest articulation of these ambitions, and comments by Marchand 1996: 373.   [29] Myres 1943; Beazley 1943.

was the archaeologist's principal task to understand. That is why, while obliquely criticising Beazley, Childe singled out the American excavators of Olynthos, a Classical city in northern Greece, for praise. Olynthos is the Skara Brae of Classical Greece.[30] It is a city preserved for us by its destruction by Philip of Macedon. The destruction had the effect of preserving numerous houses, houses which were laid out on a strict grid plan. The excavators, D.M. Robinson and J.W. Graham, had paid particular attention to defining the Greek Classical household, to understanding material conditions in their most fundamental sense. In recent years there has been a great revival of interest in this field.[31] One could say that a properly 'Childean' Classical Archaeology is at last being born. The question then arises. Why has it taken so long for the potential of this avenue of research to be realised?

For the majority of Classical archaeologists have, in the post-war period at least (1945–75), largely followed Beazley rather than Childe. With some important exceptions, they have confined their interest to matters exclusively Greek or Roman, and have preferred to study art rather than look closely at the 'material conditions of life'. They want no part in 'World Archaeology'. But things could have developed otherwise. Even within the narrow compass of British Classical Archaeology, there were other currents of thought in the 1930s and 1940s. Humfry Payne, Alan Blakeway and T.J. Dunbabin all had a particular interest in what archaeology could tell us about the growth and nature of trade, and the expansion of the Greek world in the eighth and seventh centuries BC. Each of these scholars had been active in the field. Their excavations at Knossos and Eleutherna in Crete, and at the sanctuary of Perachora near Corinth, had revealed a multitude of new finds of Archaic date. But this line of enquiry was brought to an abrupt close by the premature death of all three scholars. The final publication of Payne's excavations at Perachora was left to another scholar, Martin Robertson.[32]

Robertson's publication of Perachora was, in every respect, conscientious and thorough, a suitable act of piety to Dunbabin and Payne. But the virtues of Robertson's final publication are those of Beazley. Robertson displays a scrupulous attention to detail, particularly to those details which may reveal different workshops or individual craftsmen; and an engaging prose style, uncluttered by jargon. There is a clear principle in the organisation of the volume, and it is a

[30] See again Childe 1943, commenting on work already published by Robinson (1930; 1933a; 1933b; Robinson and Graham 1938; Robinson and Angel 1942).
   Skara Brae may be unfamiliar to many readers who may have only a passing acquaintance with British prehistory. This is a Neolithic village in the Orkney islands, excavated by the British Ministry of Works under Childe's supervision in the 1930s. Since it had been covered with wind-blown sand after having been abandoned, its several stone-built houses have been remarkably well preserved. Walls, stone hearths and 'dressing tables' can all still be seen.

[31] Robinson and Graham 1938; Robinson 1946; Mylonas 1946. Studies on houses continued in the 1950s, 1960s and 1970s; see in particular Jones *et al.* 1962; 1973; Jones 1975. For recent work in this field, see Jameson 1990a; 1990b; Hoepfner and Schwandner 1994; Nevett 1999.

[32] For Payne's and Blakeway's investigations in and around Knossos, see Payne 1928; Brock 1957. Payne's excavations at Eleutherna were never published, except in very preliminary form. For excavations at Perachora, see Payne 1940; Dunbabin 1962. Payne is now chiefly remembered for his ground-breaking study of Corinthian art and archaeology, *Necrocorinthia* (1931).

traditional one. Objects are listed by material and type. But just as Robertson shows he shares many of Beazley's strengths, so he exhibits the same blindspots. The historical questions that originally motivated the excavation of the site are played down. No attempt is made at a statistical analysis of the provenance or purpose of the numerous bronzes and other votives found at the site. The experience Robertson gained here nonetheless proved fundamental when he came to write his 'definitive' history of Greek art, very much in the Beazley manner.[33]

It is thus a matter of more than passing interest why it is that the 'Beazleyan' paradigm prevailed over the 'Childean' in the postwar years. The period 1945–75 was, in many respects, the heyday of 'World Archaeology'. Classical archaeologists, for the most part, remained unmoved. Such indifference cannot be explained by some prescience on the part of classicists to the suspicion that many nowadays feel, in these post-colonial, post-imperial times, towards a grand, universalising project of this kind. It was, rather, an indifference born of a belief in the self-sufficiency of Classics as a discipline (and of Classical Archaeology's status within it) and of its absolute separation from prehistory. Such indifference was not however intellectually or politically astute. It was prehistorians who were to write the history books of archaeology, and in such histories Classical Archaeology (and Greece in particular) was for the most part simply left out of the picture.[34] Classical archaeologists were conspicuous by their absence in the major theoretical debates that took place from about 1945 to 1980. When reading general books on the history of archaeological thought, students can be forgiven for believing (wrongly) that Classical archaeologists had no ideas, or at least no ideas worth writing about. This impression has been reinforced by the fastidious habits of many Classical archaeologists, their conviction that matters of fact must be settled before matters of interpretation can begin, and their settled belief that there is no real difference between a new theory and a passing fad.

In recent years however this picture has changed out of all recognition. From the late 1970s onwards there has been an explosion of interest in a whole range of issues, issues which have a direct bearing on the 'material conditions of life' of ancient Greece. Regional studies have flourished, revealing how much various parts of Greece differed from the Classical, Athenian 'norm'. The iconography of painted pottery has been studied, not in order better to understand the 'style' of the painter or the period, but to reveal inadvertent truths about the 'mentalities' that conditioned their making. The quantitative revolution in the social sciences has arrived with a vengeance. Burials and whole cemeteries have been analysed in order to address questions of social structure and political ideology. Intensive field surveys have been undertaken all over Greece, so redressing the longstanding bias

---

[33] The second volume of Perachora has Dunbabin as the author (1962), but it was brought to publication by Martin Robertson some years after Dunbabin's death. This experience proved invaluable when Robertson came to publish his *History of Greek Art* (1975).

[34] As for example in Trigger 1989, where Classical Archaeology after Winckelmann is more or less ignored.

towards the study of sanctuaries and cities; and the excavators of Olynthos have been vindicated by a host of new work on urban and domestic space. In all these studies, greater emphasis has been laid on the context of the manufacture and use of objects, and less attention has been given to 'art'. A 'Childean' Classical Archaeology of Greece is at last being born.

All these innovations have not however led to a new orthodoxy within the field. Far from it. New approaches rub shoulders with old. There continues to be vigorous, often heated, debate over everything from the utility of field survey to the interpretation of the Parthenon Frieze. The vigour of these debates is in no small part due to the tenacity with which older views on the character and purpose of Classical Archaeology are held. In these (often oblique) exchanges the idea is often put forward that extraneous 'theory' should be tempered by traditional 'common sense', and that evidence should be examined free from any preconceptions or prior expectations. The supposition, however, that Classical Archaeology is (or indeed ever was) a theory-free zone is not one that I myself support. Traditional Classical Archaeology did have theories; in fact it had a complete theoretical paradigm which has justified its singular attention on objects, and its relative neglect of context, landscape and environment. This traditional theoretical paradigm has been called 'Hellenism', and for years it served Classical Archaeology perfectly well.[35]

---

[35] For 'Hellenism' see in particular Morris 1994a. Marchand (1996) describes in detail the German genealogy of this theoretical paradigm. For other recent criticisms of the current state of Classical Archaeology in Greece, see Snodgrass 1987 and Shanks 1995.

CHAPTER 2

GREAT TRADITIONS: CLASSICAL SCHOLARSHIP AND CLASSICAL ARCHAEOLOGY

2.1 Rome and the Renaissance

The National Archaeological Museum in Athens, designed by Th. Hansen and E. Ziller, and completed in 1889, is in many ways a typical museum of its kind.[1] Like, for example, the National Archaeological Museum in Dublin, it contains some particularly fine examples of the country's glorious past. The museum is filled with pottery, sculpture and bronzes taken from the soil of Greece. It houses some particularly fine examples of Classical sculpture, such as the bronze Zeus lifted from the sea off Cape Artemision. Its architecture is Neoclassical, similar to many other contemporary public buildings in Athens. Nothing, it seems, could be more appropriate for a Greek National Museum. Only one feature jars. For, on entering the museum, the visitor may notice that the façade is topped by copies of Classical sculpture. These are not, as one might think, copies of the great Classical originals that may be seen in the museum itself. The Apollo Belvedere and the Doryphoros of Polykleitos (or Polyclitus) are, to be precise, Roman sculpture, Roman versions of Greek originals, a 'post-Classical' pastiche of Greek sculpture adapted to suit Roman taste. Their status as great works of Greek art owes more to Western European scholars of the Renaissance and the Enlightenment than it does to an autonomous Greek tradition of scholarship. Their presence on the top of a Greek National Museum is, in a sense, an act of homage to a Western European canon of taste and to Western European ideas of the Classical. Nothing could better symbolise the degree to which Greeks have been dependent on foreign ideas in the construction of their past, and the degree to which Greek archaeology is enmeshed in wider currents of thought and taste.

For the history of Greek archaeology begins in Italy. Though Greek historians had made some use of material evidence, no antiquarian tradition developed in Greece in Classical times.[2] The Romans were the first foreign people consciously to prize, study and collect Greek art. Some Romans developed antiquarian interests that went beyond mere aristocratic self-aggrandisement. The elder Pliny's

---

[1] See Kokkou 1977: 239–46. Though a National Archaeological Museum was on the cards almost as soon as the Greek state came into being (the famous German Neoclassical architect, Leo von Klenze, was initially commissioned to design this building) its design and construction were bedevilled by financial, aesthetic and political problems; see Kokkou 1977: 201–58.

[2] For the early uses of material evidence by the fifth-century Greek historians Herodotos and Thucydides, see Schnapp 1996: 43–51; Cook 1955.

Natural History discusses, if only *en passant*, numerous works of art in Roman collections, and Vitruvius' study of architecture depends crucially upon a knowledge of Greek examples. Such Roman interests clearly affected the Greek writer Pausanias, who wrote a guide to the sanctuaries of Greece (and the art therein) in the second century AD. Pausanias described buildings, works of art and cult practices that were already ancient, and did so partly with an educated Roman audience in mind. Interest in Greek art (as we understand it) lapsed during the Late Antique period and the Middle Ages, when pagan cults and pagan representations became (to say the least) unfashionable. Knowledge of the antique past was not entirely lost however, and was spectacularly revived in the cultural movement we know as the Renaissance.

Renaissance means 'rebirth', and the Italian Renaissance was, in many ways, a conscious attempt to restore the values and the culture of the ancient world. The period witnessed a 'rebirth' of antique architectural and decorative forms. This was a logical consequence of an attempt to restore Roman virtue; with Roman ideals came the Roman esteem for Greek art, and such art again became 'collectable'. The Renaissance required antique examples of architecture and art to copy, and this demand led to the first excavations in Rome in the sixteenth century. Figure 2.1 shows the Laocoön, a piece of very late Hellenistic sculpture. It was unearthed in excavations in 1506 near the church of Santa Maria Maggiore, and is now in the Vatican museum. Laocoön was a Trojan priest, who, in legend, had expressed apprehension at the appearance of the Trojan horse, and the trickery of the Greeks 'even when bearing gifts'. He was punished for his presumption by being strangled by snakes, together with his two sons. Pliny records that a marvellous marble statue of the death of Laocoön and his children could be seen in the palace of the Emperor Titus, the work of the Rhodian artists Hagesander, Polydorus and Athenodorus.[3] The identification of this statue with the one noted by Pliny is, perhaps, inevitable and natural, but it is a sign of the times in which the statue was found that little note was taken of its context. Connoisseurs tended to concentrate on its artistic qualities, and the question of authenticity. The Laocoön was only one of a whole host of works thought to be Greek unearthed in Rome in the course of the sixteenth and seventeenth centuries, works which came to grace the houses of such great families as the Farnese, Medici and Ludovisi, families who were in the business of supplying the Roman Catholic Church with its popes and cardinals. Through assiduous collection and excavation, these families established a canon of antique works, which, when studied, were often pronounced to be by the hand of one of the Greek masters praised by the elder Pliny.[4] As the ideals of the Renaissance spread beyond Italy, so did the aristocratic practice of collecting and studying ancient art. Francis I of France made a particular point of acquiring some to adorn his new Renaissance palace at

---

[3] The story of Laocoön is recounted by Vergil, *Aeneid* II, lines 40–53 and 199–231. The statue in the palace (or house) of Titus is described by Pliny, *Natural History* XXXVI.37.

[4] See Haskell and Penny 1981: 7–15, 23–30.

2.1 Laocoön

Fontainebleau.[5] Painters such as Rubens studied the Laocoön (in preference to human models) because it provided a truly imposing version of the human figure. By the seventeenth century, this habit of aristocratic collecting had spread to England. Thomas Howard, Earl of Arundel (1585–1646) went to considerable lengths to acquire sculpture from Italy and Asia Minor (modern Turkey). Though his collection was dispersed after his death, much of it came into the possession of Oxford University, and is now housed in the Ashmolean Museum.[6]

At the beginning of the eighteenth century a knowledge of antique art slowly came to be regarded as one of the accomplishments of a gentleman. Collecting coins, gems and antique sculpture became a fashionable pursuit for the well-heeled. The century was the heyday of the Grand Tour, when aristocratic young men visited the principal sites in Italy, frequently with a draughtsman or painter in tow. Often these painters contrived to paint their patrons against a background of some really imposing ruin or particularly celebrated sculpture. In 1734 some of these young men formed a club to further their antiquarian interests, called the Society of Dilettanti.[7] The Grand Tour was perhaps less grand than its title suggests – until the end of the eighteenth century touring was limited to Italy. But at least it had by this time incorporated some of the sites of southern Italy where Greek (rather than Roman or Etruscan) remains were to be found. The Doric temples of Poseidonia (Paestum) could not fail to impress those who came to visit after 1760, if only because they differed markedly from true Roman examples.[8] In the eighteenth century it became apparent that antiquity was not a seamless whole, and that in many respects Greek art differed profoundly from Roman.

2.2 Winckelmann and the invention of Hellenic archaeology

We tend to think of the eighteenth century as the Age of Reason, a century of philosophical rationalism and increasing scientific knowledge. Thought in general, and science in particular, depended less and less on the authority of ancient Greek philosophers, and more and more on direct observation and the application of reason. Eighteenth-century rationalism increasingly undermined the Renaissance project of restoring all aspects of antiquity. Yet, if anything, interest in Greek art increased by leaps and bounds during the course of the eighteenth century. This paradoxical development is the result of a number of factors: the possibility of actually visiting Greek monuments in Greece; the successful revaluation of Greek pottery as 'art'; and the growth of museums. But it is due in no small part to the work of one man: J.J. Winckelmann.

J.J. Winckelmann (1717–68) was once regarded as the 'father of archaeology'. He may indeed still deserve this title – at least in the narrow sense of the word

---

[5] Haskell and Penny 1981: 1–6; Stoneman 1987: 37–42.
[6] For the Earl of Arundel's collection, see Haynes 1968; Stoneman 1987: 42–55; Michaelis 1882: 6–43.
[7] For the beginnings of the Grand Tour and of the Society of Dilettanti, see Michaelis 1882: 56–65; Stoneman 1987: 120–2.   [8] Pedley 1990: 168–73.

'Archäologie' as it is used in Germany. Winckelmann, like the gentlemanly anti-quarians who preceded him, worked principally in Rome and never visited Greece. His magisterial *Geschichte der Kunst des Altertums* (History of Art in Antiquity, 1764) is based on close study of the material available,[9] principally on a number of famous antique sculptures like the Laocoön.[10] The amount of new material he studied was small – principally the Stosch collection of gems.[11] He, of course, knew that excavations at Pompeii were turning up more antique art; he visited Paestum in 1760, and was struck by the temples there; and he was aware that black- and red-figure pots, once thought to be Etruscan, were probably Greek (see below). But these new kinds of evidence played only a minor role in his account. His achievement was more theoretical than empirical. He imposed order and system on the chaos of antiquarian scholarship, which had been more concerned with details of iconography and authorship than with the overall development of Greek art. This is not to say he was indifferent to aesthetic ques-tions – far from it, since much of the History is given over to extended, lyrical descriptions of such famous works as the Laocoön, the Apollo Belvedere and the Niobe.

Winckelmann was not the first to suspect that there were stylistic differences between Etruscan, Greek and Roman art, and that these differences could be made to yield an overall chronological development. Nor was Winckelmann's interest in stylistic evolution from primitive beginnings to flowering and eventual decline entirely new – the Comte de Caylus had proposed a similar model some years before.[12] Winckelmann's reliance on Pliny was moreover completely in the tradi-tion of post-Renaissance antiquarian scholarship. Winckelmann's originality lay in bringing all these strands together into a new and highly influential synthesis. His scheme divided the evolution of Greek art into four successive stages: an archaic phase, where sculpture was 'straight and hard'; an early Classical phase, associated in particular with the sculptor Pheidias, where art was 'grand and square'; a third, late Classical phase, associated with the works of the sculptors Praxiteles and Lysippos, that was 'beautiful and flowing'; and finally a phase where art was imi-tative and decadent.[13] Winckelmann associated these stylistic phases with stages in the spiritual, cultural and political development of ancient Greece. The best Greek art, the art of the high Classical period, was produced in the years after the Persian wars, when Greece had freed herself from the threat of subjugation by an Oriental despot, and when democracy flourished in Athens. The later, beautiful style was the product of the less perfect conditions of the fourth century BC, when Greece was threatened by a new, Macedonian despotism but when the spirit of

---

[9] Winckelmann 1764. English translations of this work are hard to find. I have consulted a partial translation by G. Henry Lodge (Winckelmann 1850).

[10] On the Laocoön, see Winckelmann 1764: 169–71; Pollitt 1986: 120–2; Potts 1994: 136–44.

[11] Jenkins and Sloan 1996: 94–6; Winckelmann 1764: 215.

[12] On the Comte de Caylus, see Schnapp 1996: 238–47; Potts 1994: 76–81.

[13] Potts 1982; 1994: 67–72.

Greek liberty, for a time, lived on.[14] Liberty was, for Winckelmann, a necessary condition for the achievement of the Greek ideal of a 'noble simplicity and calm grandeur' (*eine edle Einfalt und eine stille Grosse*), an achievement which came as close to perfection as was humanly possible.[15] This association between political liberty and artistic perfection was an idea which was to have momentous consequences.

Winckelmann however was neither a true revolutionary nor a real romantic. Though he had argued that Classical Greek art was the product of particular historical conditions, and was subject to inevitable decline when those conditions changed, he left open the question of whether people in later times might equal or surpass the Greek achievement. Winckelmann remained true to the Enlightenment ideal of universal standards in taste, reason and judgement. Historicism – the idea that the works of past cultures were the products of particular historical conditions that could never be restored, and that the art and culture of past societies could only be understood and judged in terms of the values prevalent at the time – was a problem for Winckelmann's Romantic intellectual successors, not for Winckelmann. Winckelmann was none the less a theorist and something of a polemicist. His ferocious cataloguing of the inaccuracies of previous scholarship is uncannily reminiscent of recent debates in archaeological theory.[16] His four-stage scheme was, to say the least, underdetermined by the data – for the earliest, Archaic phase he was entirely dependent on coin evidence, since no actual examples of Archaic sculpture had yet been found.[17] The dates he proposed for sculptures on which he lavished his most evocative descriptions are, in the light of later scholarship, just plain wrong.[18] His scheme was not arrived at inductively (he was unable to make grand generalisations from a mass of empirical facts) but hypothetically, through the adoption of a model of rhetorical types and then applying these types to a chronological series of material objects. Winckelmann was quite explicit in acknowledging his dependence upon conjecture:

I have ventured certain thoughts which may not appear to be proved adequately: perhaps, however, they can help others who research into the art of the ancients to go further; and how often has a conjecture become truth through later discovery. Conjectures, or those that are least attached by a thread to something solid, are no more to be banished from a work of this kind than hypotheses from natural science. They are like the scaffolding of a building, indeed they become indispensable if, owing to the absence of knowledge about the art of the ancients, you do not wish to make huge leaps over empty spaces.[19]

---

[14] For Winckelmann's interest in liberty as a condition for the flowering of Greek art, see Winckelmann 1764: 130, 224; but see Potts 1994: 54–60, 182–221.

[15] Quoted in Potts 1994: 1: with references listed in p. 256 n.1 (Winckelmann, *Kleine Schriften* 1755: 43).

[16] Winckelmann 1764: ix–xxiii. Winckelmann's attitude towards the shortcomings of his antiquarian predecessors has something of the vehemence of the younger Lewis R. Binford (one of the leading lights of American 'New Archaeology' in the 1960s), who never failed to find fault with his teacher, James B. Griffin (see Binford 1972).   [17] Potts 1994: 81–96; Winckelmann 1764: 214–15.

[18] Potts 1994: 113–81.   [19] Winckelmann 1764: xxiv; translation by Potts 1994: 41.

If Winckelmann did indeed seek 'to explain a culture by its works of art',[20] his systematic history of those works depends as much on conjecture as on facts. Later archaeologists were to retain the overall framework of his stylistic scheme while, in the process, disproving his particular stylistic attributions. The Laocoön, for example, is now normally dated to the early Imperial period, not to the late Classical. But in 1768 at least, at the time of Winckelmann's death, the scheme was very much in need of empirical evidence in its support. This was to be supplied from an apparently unlikely quarter.

2.3 Pots into vases: the beginnings of ceramic connoisseurship

It was only in the latter part of the seventeenth century that any attention was given to the numerous painted pots which could be found in ancient graves in Italy. Coins, medals, gems and sculpture had formed the principal objects of antiquarian interest. In the early eighteenth century such pots began to attract notice. Many had turned up in northern and central Italy, and in Tuscany in particular, and it was perhaps for this reason that Tuscan scholars such as Buonarroti believed them to be Etruscan.[21] Antiquarians who lived in southern Italy, in the Kingdom of the Two Sicilies whose capital and whose cultural centre was Naples, had by this time formed their own collections of ancient pots, all acquired locally. Southern Italy had been colonised by Greeks in ancient times, and indeed was known to the early Romans as *Magna Graecia* ('Great Greece'). Neapolitan scholars were thus disinclined to agree with Buonarroti's Tusco-centric interpretation. A.S. Mazzochi argued, entirely logically, that since many of these pots had Greek inscriptions painted on them, their manufacturers must also have been Greek. The matter however remained unresolved until foreigners intervened in this Italian family quarrel.[22]

In 1764 William Hamilton arrived in Naples as British Ambassador. Hamilton was, in many ways, not untypical of his generation of gentleman scholars. His interest in natural history was as great as his passion for the ancient world, and Naples provided an opportunity for him to indulge both.[23] He was, however, unusual for an antiquarian connoisseur of his generation in lavishing his attention more on pots than on gems or sculpture. Through purchase of other collections, acquisitions on the Neapolitan art market and his own excavations he rapidly amassed one of the largest collections of vases – as pots of this kind were henceforth to be called – ever assembled by a private individual. He was proud of his collection, and engaged an enterprising Frenchman who styled himself the Baron d'Hancarville to publish it.[24] The effect of these several volumes published between 1767 and 1776 was twofold: they confirmed that vases were respectable items of antiquarian interest, so respectable indeed that painted vases became

---

[20] Shanks 1995: 56.   [21] Cook 1972: 287–90.
[22] Cook 1972: 290; Jenkins and Sloan 1996: 51–2, 151.   [23] Jenkins and Sloan 1996: 40–64.
[24] Jenkins and Sloan 1996: 46–61, and 149–55.

2.2 Red-figure hydria, name vase of the Meidias painter

necessary props in portraits of aristocratic German and British Grand Tourists;[25] and their publication brought empirical weight to bear in favour of such vases being Greek rather than Etruscan. It was not, however, d'Hancarville's publication alone that made these vases respectable and Greek – indeed his wild and eccentric interpretations were seen by later scholars as something of an embarrassment. Winckelmann managed to study some of the pots in Hamilton's collection before his sudden death in 1768. One in particular, figure 2.2, the name vase of the Meidias painter, he pronounced 'the finest and most beautiful drawing in the world'.[26] Winckelmann's intervention was decisive. After Hamilton sold his first collection in 1772, he found that assembling a second was a much more

[25] Jenkins and Sloan 1996: 52, 176–7.
[26] On d'Hancarville's eccentricities, see Jenkins and Sloan 1996: 96–8; on Winckelmann's intervention, see *ibid.*, 180–1 and Burn 1987: 1 n.6.

expensive business than assembling his first. Vases had become collectable *objets d'art*, examples of that pure Greek spirit which Winckelmann had described so evocatively. The publication of Hamilton's second collection between 1793 and 1803 merely confirmed these trends.[27]

From now on Greek vases were to appear in increasing numbers in both Greece and Italy. They were acquired, first by individual collectors and connoisseurs, and increasingly by public museums. The British Museum had led the way through its purchase of Hamilton's first collection in 1772. So valuable indeed did vases become that excavation became a profitable business for enterprising landowners. Napoleon Bonaparte's brother Lucien, who happened to own land around the ancient Etruscan city of Vulci (just north of Rome) was a particular beneficiary of the new value placed on ancient vases. After excavations began there in 1828, Vulci yielded over 3,000 painted pots, now dispersed in the major museums of Europe and America.[28] Sometimes excavators destroyed some of the pots they excavated from Etruscan graves in order to maintain the market value of the rest. It was vases as they were arranged in museums and private collections, not pots whose original context had been carefully recorded by conscientious scholars, that were to provide German scholars such as E. Gerhard with the material they needed to sort out the chronological development of Greek pots and the various centres of their production.

2.4 Imperial Romanticism: British, French and German antiquarians in Greece 1750–1870

Before the eighteenth century, it was quite difficult for scholars and travellers from Western Europe to visit the eastern Mediterranean. With the exception of the Ionian islands (and, until 1649, Crete), what is now Greece was part of the Turkish Ottoman Empire, a Muslim power ideologically opposed to all Christian enterprise. Renaissance scholars were forced to confine their interests to Italy. There were, of course, notable exceptions, in particular Cyriac of Ancona.[29] In the seventeenth century the occasional English or French traveller managed to reach Athens, and some important antiquarian studies (such as Jacques Carrey's drawings of the Parthenon) were undertaken before Morosini's disastrous bombardment of the Acropolis of Athens in 1687.[30] Still, conditions for Western study were not favourable until the decline in Turkish power made the Ottoman authorities increasingly dependent on the goodwill of Western powers. It was in these new circumstances that the Society of Dilettanti sponsored the expedition of Stuart and Revett.

James Stuart and Nicholas Revett were artists, not gentleman connoisseurs. They brought an artist's professionalism to their study of the monuments of

---

[27] Jenkins and Sloan 1996: 53, 186.   [28] Cook 1972: 293–7.
[29] For Cyriac of Ancona, see Stoneman 1987: 56–83; Schnapp 1996: 110–14.
[30] For Spon, Wheeler and then Morosini, see Stoneman 1987: 56–83.

Athens, which they undertook between 1751 and 1753. Their *Antiquities of Athens*, published in four volumes between 1762 and 1816, surpassed all previous antiquarian studies in accuracy and thoroughness.[31] They produced an informed, scholarly and lavishly illustrated account of all the major (and many minor) ancient monuments in Athens. Their aims, however, were strictly speaking not archaeological, but architectural. They strove, not for a better understanding of the Greek past, but for the improvement of British taste. Their illustrations were intended to enrich the repertoire of forms then available to architects. They were none the less unapologetic Hellenists, unashamedly preferring things Greek to things Roman. As they put it: 'as Greece was the great mistress of the Arts, and Rome, in this respect, no more than her disciple, it may be presumed, all the most admired Buildings which adorned that imperial city, were but the imitations of Grecian originals'.[32] The impact of Stuart and Revett's work was straightforward but profound. Henceforth scholars, antiquarians and travellers would look to Greece for examples of that Hellenic ideal that Winckelmann had championed. From the 1750s onward Athens joined Rome as one of the destinations of the Grand Tour, and it was during this period that various bits and pieces of the Parthenon found their way out of Athens and into various private collections.[33] It was at this point that the course of Greek archaeology was (not for the last time) affected by outside events.

The French Revolution of 1789 eventually brought Britain and France to war, a war both longer and bloodier than earlier eighteenth-century conflicts. The war accentuated growth in national feeling in both Britain and France. A cultural rivalry developed between these two imperial powers that would have been unimaginable in the more settled aristocratic world fifty years before. By 1800 both countries had created national cultural institutions. When founded in the earlier part of the century the British Museum was more library than museum. It was only with the acquisition of the Hamilton collection in 1772 and George Townley's collection of antique marbles in 1805 that it came to resemble a national museum of antiquities.[34] In the 1790s and 1800s Napoleon was to transform the former royal palace of the Louvre into a showcase for French imperial grandeur. To this end he arranged for the transfer of some of the more celebrated antique marbles, including the Apollo Belvedere and the Laocoön, from Rome to Paris.[35] Hitherto museums had hardly existed as separate institutions. They had, for the most part, been little more than adjuncts to royal palaces or aristocratic country houses. Henceforth they were to become public space, and the focus of national pride. This new cultural rivalry was to affect events in Athens, where

---

[31] Stuart and Revett 1762; 1787; 1794; 1816. See also Stoneman 1987: 116–30.
[32] Stuart and Revett 1762: i.   [33] St Clair 1967: 56–60.
[34] For the acquisition of the Townley marbles, see Jenkins 1992: 102–6; for the Hamilton collection, see Jenkins and Sloan 1996: 40–64.
[35] See McClellan 1994: 119–23. The convoy of loot conveying both the Laocoön and the Apollo Belvedere arrived in Paris in 1798; this was a propaganda move intended to enhance Napoleon's political career.

from around 1780 the Frenchman Fauvel had more or less cornered the local market in antiquities (many of which subsequently found their way to the Louvre). It is in this context that we must understand the actions of the most notorious collector of them all: Lord Elgin.

In 1799 Lord Elgin was made British Ambassador to the Sublime Porte, as the Turkish Government was then called. Turkey was at that time at war with France, and French troops had occupied Egypt. In 1801 British forces succeeded in forcing the French to surrender. A month or so later Lord Elgin received his firman (permit) to 'excavate and remove' marbles from the Athenian Acropolis.[36] Elgin's intentions seem originally to have been very similar to Stuart and Revett's. Accurate casts and drawings of Classical Greek sculpture would lead to the improvement of the arts in Britain. He was also well aware of the traditional Turkish indifference to antiquities. Some of these had completely disappeared between 1750 and 1800, most notably the small Ionic temple by the Ilissos which Stuart and Revett had taken such trouble to describe.[37] Furthermore, like any other aristocrat of the time he wanted to add to his collection. These circumstances (together with the ambiguous wording of the firman) may not however be enough to explain the scale of the removals then undertaken. Elgin's men did not confine themselves to removing parts of the Parthenon that had fallen down and were buried in the ground – they took away much of the architectural sculpture that had survived *in situ*: the pedimental sculpture, many metopes and large parts of the frieze.[38]

The scale of Elgin's acquisitions (which bankrupted him) was unprecedented, and encouraged others to act in a similar manner. Open season was declared on Greek architectural sculpture. In 1811–12 an enterprising group of German and British antiquarians, including C.R. Cockerell, excavated and then removed sculpture which had fallen from the pediments of the temple of Aphaia on Aegina. They then turned their attentions to the temple of Apollo Epikourios at Bassai in Arcadia, which they excavated and from which they removed the frieze. These were then sold to the Crown Prince of Bavaria and the British Museum respectively.[39] The British Museum also purchased Elgin's marbles in 1816, after a long period of controversy about their date, authenticity, artistic quality and the legality of their removal.[40] When the Louvre was forced, after 1815, to return sculptures to Rome, the French consoled themselves with the acquisition of the Venus de Milo, hailed at the time (1820) as one of the works of Praxiteles.[41]

---

[36] St Clair 1967: 87–98; Smith 1916.
[37] For general destruction in Athens between 1750 and 1800, see St Clair 1967: 97; for Lord Elgin's expressions of concern, see Smith 1916: 189: 336, 346. For the temple on the Ilissos, see Stuart and Revett 1762: 7–11.
[38] For the removal of the sculpture, see St Clair 1967: 99–120; Smith 1916: 189–256; Stoneman 1987: 168–9. Elgin's men also removed a caryatid and an Ionic column from the Erechtheion, which are both now in the British Museum.   [39] Stoneman 1987: 179–201.
[40] St Clair 1967: 218–29, 250–62; Smith 1916: 294–348; Stoneman 1987: 168–79.
[41] Stoneman 1987: 201–6; Haskell and Penny 1981: 325–8.

This frenzy of activity had filled the new national museums of Munich, Paris and London with Greek art. Winckelmann's conjectural scheme could now be substantiated by actual examples from Greece. The sculptures from the temple of Aphaia were the first that could confidently be attributed to the Archaic phase of Greek art. The 'Pheidian' marbles from the Parthenon seemed living proof that the fifth century was the high point of Greek artistic achievement. And one had to go no further than the Venus de Milo to see what a Praxitelean (that is a 'beautiful and flowing') style truly was (the inscription that indicated that this sculpture was by an artist unknown to Pliny was conveniently lost).[42] Large-scale acquisitions of celebrated Greek works continued throughout the nineteenth century. Unsurprisingly perhaps the lion's share went to the leading imperial power of the time, Great Britain. A commentator of a slightly later age was to look back on it as the 'Golden Age' of Hellenic exploration. As he put it:

Never again can we [British] hope to see our national collections enriched by such spoils as those of the Parthenon or the Mausoleum [of Halicarnassos] . . . when Sir Charles Newton, with a Firman in his pocket, a Company of Royal Engineers and Sappers at his back, and a British man-of-war lying at a handy distance in a convenient bay, was able to rifle at his will the half-hidden treasures of Cnidus and Halicarnassus.[43]

By 1820 many of the elements of Hellenist archaeology were in place. Greece had displaced Rome as the model of the Classical ideal. Winckelmann had provided a conjectural framework, for which later British, French and German antiquarian scholars had provided the material facts. Thanks to William Hamilton, A.S. Mazzochi and other Neapolitan scholars these facts now included vases as well as sculpture and architecture. Cultural and political rivalry between France and Britain had produced the impetus behind the creation of national museums and the rash of acquisitions to fill them. The foundations had been laid for the world's first imperialist archaeology.[44] Yet to enumerate these circumstances is perhaps to miss the essence of early Hellenist archaeology, for it is to miss out the crucial element of Romanticism. If Winckelmann was the first to speak eloquently about the Greek ideal, it was French and British travellers and poets who were to relate this ideal, not to a vanished past accessible only through literary texts, but to a real present which could be glimpsed through the land and monuments of Greece.[45] While Lord Byron might deplore his fellow Scot's depredations of the Parthenon, his poetry and his enthusiasm for both ancient and modern Greece lent Greece and Greek art a lustre it had never held before. Greek objects became invested with Romantic values. German poets and philosophers echoed Byron's sentiments, and added a particular Romantic gloss to Winckelmann's

[42] Haskell and Penny 1981: 325–8; Stoneman 1987: 201–6.
[43] Asquith 1900: 136–7. For an account of Charles Newton's activities on the coast of Asia Minor, see Stoneman 1987: 216–24; Jenkins 1992: 168–95; Newton 1862a; 1862b; 1863.
[44] As defined by Trigger 1984: 363–8. Trigger's distinctions between nationalist, imperialist and colonialist archaeologies are clear and useful. It is simply inaccurate (and misleading) to describe the work of foreign archaeologists in Greece as 'colonialist' (e.g. Shanks 1995: 15).
[45] Stoneman 1987: 136–64; Tsigakou 1981.

writings. Rather than simply representing a universal (and universally realisable) human ideal, German thinkers began to see the Greek achievement as the product of peculiar historical circumstances and the unique genius of the ancient Greeks. This was an achievement it was difficult, if not impossible, for others to emulate, unless of course there was some underlying spiritual kinship between an ancient and a modern people. For contemporary Greeks this Romantic European idealisation of their ancient ancestors was to have profound political and cultural consequences.[46]

2.5 Archaeology for the Greek nation, 1800–1922

Demoralised and subject peoples do not make the best custodians of their own past. This is not to say that the Greek population of, let us say, Attica or the Troad in the years around 1800 had no regard for antiquities. English travellers record a number of curious beliefs which Orthodox Christian Greeks held about statues and inscriptions, beliefs whose effect was largely to help preserve certain remnants of the ancient world.[47] When, for example, E.D. Clarke tried to remove a 'statue of Ceres' from Eleusis in 1801, he encountered strong opposition from the local population, who attributed the statue with magical powers.[48] Antiquarians like Clarke, however, tended to hold local populations in low regard. Many who had come to idealise ancient Greece could not but compare modern Greeks unfavourably with the ancients. Ancient virtues seemed to be conspicuous by their absence in areas under Ottoman rule. Some, like Leake, attributed these failings to Turkish oppression. After all, the martial spirit of ancient Sparta lived on in the remote fastnesses of the Mani. With the coming of Liberty, the Greek spirit would surely be rekindled.[49] Others saw contemporary Greeks as being irredeemably tainted by Oriental customs. It did not occur to these travellers that there might be something a little ludicrous about their own idealisation of Classical Hellas. Rather the reverse. Their observations encouraged a belief amongst many Westerners that it was they, rather than modern Greeks, who were the true spiritual heirs of ancient Hellas.[50]

These patronising attitudes affected Greek intellectuals, and one in particular. A. Korais was a Greek from Smyrna who settled in Paris and established himself as a noted Classical scholar. He devoted his life to making his fellow Greeks aware of their Classical past. Korais seems to have internalised both foreign idealisation of the ancients and their low esteem for modern Greeks. He came up with a novel solution to the problem. Korais argued that Greeks could only be worthy of the liberty the ancients had enjoyed when they had purified their culture and language from the taint of Byzantine obscurantism, Ottoman oppression and Oriental custom. Korais advocated a cultural programme at the

[46] See Morris 1994a: 20–3; Shanks 1995: 53–91; Herzfeld 1987.
[47] Smith 1916: 182–3, 347; Stoneman 1987: 174–5.   [48] Stoneman 1987: 153–4.
[49] Leake 1830a: 268; Tsigakou 1981: 44.   [50] See generally Herzfeld 1987; Tsigakou 1981.

heart of which was the katharevousa, an artificial 'purified' version of modern Greek. If modern Greeks were taught this rather than the demotic, they would be brought closer in spirit to their Classical forebears. Korais' ideas had more impact on the émigré Greek community of merchants and intellectuals than it did on those Greeks still under direct Ottoman rule.[51] On many it had little impact at all, since, around 1800, Greeks did not regard themselves as Hellenes but as Romans (Romii), heirs not to the Athens of Pericles but to the Christian Empire of Constantine the Great. Greeks defined themselves as much by their orthodox religion as by language. 'Hellenes', in the folklore of the time, were a lost race, responsible for some marvellous buildings whose remains could still be in the country around.[52] Events were to bring about a change in these attitudes.

In 1821 a series of risings in the Peloponnese developed into a full-scale war of independence against Turkish rule. Simple resentment of an arbitrary and alien regime rather than any direct inspiration from ancient Greece was probably the immediate cause of the revolt. Ultimate success however depended in part upon the effective propaganda of classically educated foreign philhellenes such as Lord Byron, propaganda which played an important role in enlisting the reluctant support of the Great Powers: Russia, Britain and France.[53] The price of independence from Turkey was a constitution acceptable to those powers, and Otho of Wittelsbach (the younger son of Ludwig who, as Crown Prince, had acquired the Aegina sculptures for Bavaria) was duly installed as king of Greece. The king's patronage of philhellenic Germans and the fact that many (though not all) in the Greek intelligentsia had been captivated by Korais' ideas ensured that, during Otho's reign at least, it was Korais' cultural programme that was carried out. Greece initiated her own renaissance, with her eyes firmly focussed on the glories of Periclean Athens. In 1834 Athens was chosen as the capital of the new kingdom.[54] Archaeology was to play an important role in this process of cultural renewal and nation building. So closely indeed were Classical monuments and Greek liberty associated that, standing on the Athenian Acropolis, I. Rizos-Neroulos could exclaim: 'these stones, thanks to Pheidias, Praxiteles, Agoracritos and Myron, are more precious than diamonds or agates: it is to these stones that we owe our political renaissance'.[55] These words were spoken at one of the first meetings of the Greek Archaeological Society, which had been founded the year before in 1837. The setting, the Acropolis, was also entirely in keeping with the spirit of cultural renewal. One of King Otho's first acts had been to appoint Ludwig Ross, a fellow German, as head of the National Archaeological Service. Ross' first

---

[51] Clogg 1992: 28–9, 216–17; Morris 1994a: 22–3. See also Herzfeld 1987: 51–3 and his remarks p. 19: 'Greece may be unique in the degree to which the country as a whole has been forced to play the contrasted roles of Ur-Europa and humiliated oriental vassal at one and the same time.' Though see Hamilakis and Yalouri 1996 for a different view of the 'Helleno-Romaic dilemma'.

[52] Kakridis 1978; Herzfeld 1987: 101–4.   [53] Clogg 1992: 33–46; Tsigakou 1981: 46–62.

[54] Clogg 1992: 47–61; Stoneman 1987: 237–55; Hamilakis and Yalouri 1996: 121–3.

[55] Quoted in Tsigakou 1981: 11.

task was the Acropolis. Before excavation could take place, the site was cleared (or perhaps we should say purified) of its Byzantine, Frankish and Ottoman remains. Excavation was followed by the restoration of buildings of Classical date, such as the temple of Athena Nike by the Propylaia.[56] Later Ross was to embark on a programme of survey and excavation of numerous sites within the boundaries of the new state, including numerous sites in the Peloponnese, such as the so-called Menelaion near Sparta.[57]

But Greek archaeology could never be an archaeology conducted by and for Greeks, or even, like other nationalist archaeologies, mainly for the Greek nation. Though it was the Classical past (and, until the late nineteenth century, no other period) that was regarded as essential to Greek national identity, it was precisely this past to which other countries had already laid claim. Because of earlier depradations, the export of antiquities had been expressly prohibited by law. Greece was none the less a small country dependent on the goodwill of the Western powers. These powers had to be humoured. The French, for example, were allowed to establish a School for Classical Studies in Athens in 1846.[58] It would be wrong however to suppose that the establishment of the foreign Archaeological Schools, the most important of which (apart from the French) were founded between 1872 and 1886, was simply a sign of Greek weakness. It was in fact a shrewd piece of cultural politics, especially on the part of the modernising Greek prime minister Trikoupis. By allowing schools to be established and large-scale foreign excavations to take place, philhellenic sentiment in Western countries was reinforced. No further antiquities were lost to foreign museums, and the activities of foreign scholars could be closely regulated. Moreover well-publicised excavations emphasised the common heritage of the Classical past, and made Greece seem more European in French, German or British eyes.[59] Some Western politicians (such as Bismarck) regarded the terms under which the Schools were to work as distinctly disadvantageous. As one, referring to British work, lamented:

In these later times [i.e. the 1890s], when, as we are told by the newspapers, we are all Imperialists, the British explorer proceeds upon his task with a humbler mien. There is no longer pride in his pick or defiance in his spade. If he wishes, as Mr Hogarth and his friends have been doing, to unearth the suspected treasures which might or might not exist in the Island of Melos, he must first conciliate the local demarch, and pay full compensation for disturbance to the peasant proprietor.[60]

[56] Stoneman 1987: 240–5.
[57] For the Menelaion, see Catling 1977: 24; Ross 1861: 72–142. Despite Ross' interest in these and other sites in the Peloponnese, it was the Acropolis that was to remain the principal object of Greek archaeological endeavour throughout the nineteenth century. Major excavations were continued under the auspices of the Archaeological Society, from 1885 onwards; see Kavvadias and Kawerau 1906.   [58] Etienne 1996: 5–9.
[59] For Trikoupis generally, see Clogg 1992: 67–70. For details of his negotiations with foreign powers on archaeological matters (in particular the French, and the deal whereby the French were allowed to dig at Delphi in exchange for a relaxation of the French tariff on currants), see Amandry 1992.
[60] Asquith 1900: 136–7; for Bismarck see Marchand 1996: 85–6.

It is still widely believed that foreign archaeologists brought new, higher, scientific standards to Greek archaeology from the 1870s onwards. This may be true of the Germans (see below), but it would be wrong to imagine that archaeologists such as Kouroniotis or Stais were any less competent than their foreign colleagues. They were just poorer. This situation led to some understandable resentment at the degree to which foreigners had managed to acquire concessions to some of the more important Classical sites. The Archaeological Society was particularly annoyed when the French were given permission to dig at Delphi.[61] Despite this, the years from 1880 to the beginning of the First World War were productive ones for both the Archaeological Society and the Archaeological Service. Major excavations at important Classical sites such as Sounion, Eleusis and Eretria were undertaken.[62] More statues came to grace the National Museum. With the opening up of Greek prehistory, first by Schliemann and then by Tsountas, Greek archaeology began to lose its exclusively Classical emphasis. Greek history began to be seen as a continuum, where the Bronze Age and Byzantium both had their due. But to understand the process by which the Classical had been dethroned, and why so much emphasis from 1870 onwards was placed on 'big digs', we have to look at the impact of the Germans.

2.6 The impact of the Germans, 1820–1941

During the course of the nineteenth century German scholars transformed Classical studies from being an amateur pursuit for clergymen and gentlemen into a professional, university-based 'science' – *Altertumswissenschaft* or the 'science of antiquity'. Throughout the century German scholars led the way in all Classical fields, including archaeology. Yet there was a fundamental inconsistency at the heart of this imposing academic edifice.[63] It had been the German Romantics who had been the most ardent followers of Winckelmann, and who had believed most fervently in the ideals of Classical Greece. The study of antiquity, which they championed, was to be no dry academic exercise but a form of humanistic self-cultivation and self-realisation (as the German term *Bildung* is cumbersomely translated). In practice however this Romantic devotion to the Hellenic ideal went hand in hand with the development of Classical studies as a professional academic discipline. Professionalisation was in part the result of state intervention. Prussia in particular had led the way in turning the university of Berlin into an internationally renowned centre for research, where knowledge was increased by the application of positivist science. Positivism regarded facts (rather than hypotheses) as the bedrock of all scientific endeavour. There was a direct and simple relationship between an increase in facts and the growth of knowledge. Classical studies, especially Classical philology, was infected by this

[61] Dassios 1992.
[62] For excavations at Sounion, see Stais 1917; for excavations at Eretria, see Kouroniotis 1903; 1913.
[63] Marchand 1996: 3–77.

positivist spirit, which led to the instigation of the first collaborative research projects. The *Corpus Inscriptionum Graecarum*, the Corpus of Greek Inscriptions, instigated by A. Boeckh, was the first of many attempts to assemble all the evidence concerning antiquity.[64]

It would be wrong, however, to think that positivist science simply replaced romantic Hellenism. They were in fact two sides of the same coin. Classical philology developed its own pedantic habits, underpinned by an unquestioned set of Romantic assumptions. It was also supremely successful. The rigours of academic philological training made it possible for linguists to discover that Sanskrit, Greek, German and Latin were languages with common roots and common structures. Indo-European studies were born at this time, studies which were later to provide some areas of German archaeology with a theoretical model for the historical development of material culture. But, just as philological rigour made such studies possible, devotion to the unique achievements of the ancient Greeks ruled out any kind of comparative studies.[65]

Professionalisation, however, developed only gradually, and affected archaeology last of all. In the early years of the century the main centre for German Classical archaeology was still Rome. In 1823 a number of scholars of various nationalities formed a club to pursue their common interests. By 1829 however E. Gerhard had persuaded the Prussian state to provide some financial support, and, though remaining international in composition, the 'Hyperboreans' became the Institut für archäologische Korrespondenz.[66] The institute dedicated itself to the scientific study of all the material aspects of Classical antiquity. Gerhard himself concentrated principally on the (now recognisably) Greek pots which were turning up in increasing numbers from excavations at Vulci (see above, section 2.3). Whereas sculpture was rare, fragmentary and difficult to date, the 3,000 or so pots from Vulci all came from graves which could be placed in a series. This fact allowed Gerhard to describe the history of Greek art in the Archaic and Classical period in much greater detail.[67] This institute in Rome was to become the prototype of the bureaucratic, state-supported organisations devoted to the scientific study of the past which were to proliferate thereafter. After the formation of the German Reich in 1870, German scholars began to look to Greece itself. In 1872 the institute in Rome formally became a cultural arm of the German state, the Deutsches archäologische Institut, of which a branch was established in Athens.

The new German state craved cultural prestige. Some argued that Germany should try to build up museum collections to rival those in London and Paris. Others frowned on British-style archaeological treasure hunting (though such disapproval did not prevent the acquisition of the Pergamon frieze at a slightly later date). The distinguished scholar Ernst Curtius had for some time been

---

[64] Boeckh 1828; Marchand 1996: 42–3.   [65] Marchand 1996: 43–51.   [66] Marchand 1996: 51–65.
[67] Marchand 1996: 56–8; Cook 1972: 294–7; Gerhard 1831.

pressing for a different kind of project. Olympia was the foremost panhellenic sanctuary of ancient Hellas, a place where the agonistic spirit of Classical Greece manifested itself in the quadrennial festival games. Winckelmann himself had once expressed a wish to explore the site. What project could better display the superiority of German Classical scholarship than an excavation at Olympia? How better to honour the 'father of archaeology'? And how better to demonstrate that, unlike other nations, Germans were animated by the pure spirit of disinterested scientific enquiry than to refrain from taking anything of value from the soil of Greece?[68] Curtius' lobbying was successful. The German and Greek governments entered into negotiations, and in 1875 digging began in earnest.

The Olympia excavations (1875–81) were the first of the 'big digs' in Greece, and were to set an example for others to follow. The excavation was on an unprecedented scale, involving 500 workers at any one time. Study and publication of the finds moreover required a specialised division of scholarly labour. Curtius allocated much of the important work to two young scholars who, more than anyone else, were to bring philological rigour to Classic Archaeology, A. Furtwängler and W. Dörpfeld.[69] At the start of the excavations it was hoped that much ancient sculpture would be found at Olympia, since Pausanias had recorded numerous statues there. Whilst the 'Hermes of Praxiteles', the Nike of Paionios of Mende (fig. 11.4) and the pedimental sculpture from the temple of Zeus (fig. 11.1) were hardly trivial additions to the corpus of Classical sculpture, what strikes one about the early Olympia publications is the amount of attention given to *Kleinfunde* (small finds) often of distinctly non-Classical appearance. These small finds were given to Furtwängler to publish, who notes that he had described and catalogued 14,150 bronzes and 4,643 terracottas.[70] There is little attempt here to look at the finds stratigraphically, by deposit or context; instead they are treated as minor works of art, to be described principally by material and type. Furtwängler was setting a precedent for other publications, which have always put classification by date and material first and context second. None the less Furtwängler, by his work at Olympia and later by giving the same attention to Classical gems, demonstrated that it was the spirit of scientific positivism rather than Romantic Hellenism that was now dominant.[71]

The Olympia excavation was a great success. The German example was soon to be imitated by others. The French, not to be outdone, undertook their own *grande fouille* at Delphi between 1892 and 1903.[72] First the Americans (in 1884) and then the British (in 1886) established their own archaeological schools in Athens. The Americans began large-scale excavations at Corinth and the Argive

---

[68] On the Olympia negotiations, see Marchand 1996: 77–87; Stoneman 1987: 256–64. On Pergamon, see Marchand 1996: 92–103; Stoneman 1987: 284–91.

[69] Adler *et al.* 1897; Marchand 1996: 87–91.   [70] Furtwängler 1890: vii–viii.

[71] For a discussion of the crisis of faith caused by the success of scientific positivism, see Marchand 1996: 75–7, 104–18.   [72] Radet 1992; and more generally Picard 1992.

Heraion soon after.[73] Increasingly, Greek archaeologists too modelled themselves on the Germans. Co-operation between Greek and German scholars was particularly close at this time. Kavvadias' excavations on the Acropolis were published in great detail in several lavish volumes, with parallel text in Greek and German.[74] The German institute was even allowed to take over the excavation of the Kerameikos in Athens in 1913. When excavations resumed there in 1926, Karl Kübler was to set new standards in the stratigraphical recording of finds and deposits, and was instrumental in introducing physical anthropology to the study of cemeteries.[75]

In one sense, however, German archaeology in Greece was undermined by its own success. Archaeologists had, for the most part, first been trained as philologists, educated to see Classical Greece as the pinnacle of human 'spiritual' achievement. The reading of Classical texts and the contemplation of Classical sculpture were part of a disinterested, aesthetic and moral education of the 'whole man'.[76] Excavation demanded different qualities, chiefly the ability to synthesise large amounts of information. Scholarship became a kind of industry, a production line of more and more facts. Since Classical scholarship was now a professional career, and since one's career depended on the patronage of elderly professors, Classical philology and archaeology became very conservative fields of study. New facts were, more often than not, fitted in to a developmental framework based ultimately on Winckelmann's conjectural scheme. Increasingly, however, excavation revealed information about periods which were far from Classical, for which literary sources were little help, and which seemed at the time to have little aesthetic appeal. German scholars none the less diligently catalogued and studied material of Bronze Age, Protogeometric, Geometric and Orientalising date.[77] But, by the 1920s and 1930s, partly under the influence of Friedrich Nietzsche's philosophy, many educated Germans had lost faith in Romantic ideals. For some, racial theories and the idea that there was a racial as well as a spiritual affinity between ancient Greece and modern Germany, began to fill the gap. It was partly a new interest in race that had prompted the introduction of physical anthropological techniques into the study of the Kerameikos cemetery.[78] National prestige was soon to displace Romantic idealism entirely. When, in 1936, excavation at Olympia was resumed, it was done so on Hitler's orders specifically to celebrate the 1936 Berlin Olympics. Excavation had become

---

[73] For early American excavations at Corinth from 1896 onwards, see Lord 1947: 89–90, 92–4; for excavations at the Argive Heraion (or Heraeum), see Lord 1947: 78, 84; Waldstein 1902.

[74] Kavvadias and Kawerau 1906.

[75] Kraiker and Kübler 1939; Knigge 1991: 166–7. For physical anthropology, see Breitinger 1939a; 1939b.   [76] Marchand 1996: xvii–xxiv, 3–35.

[77] For disillusionment with 'big science', see Marchand 1996: 75–7. For early German work on the Geometric and Orientalising periods, see Cook 1972: 300–6. The works of Wide (1899; 1900) and Schweitzer (1917; 1918) were fundamental breakthroughs in the study of Geometric pottery.

[78] Marchand 1996: 110–11. For examples of racial ideas in archaeology, see Kraiker and Kübler 1939; Breitinger 1939a; 1939b.

more a useful symbol of pride in German scientific achievement than a disinterested act of homage to the Hellenic ideal.[79]

Still, even in the 1930s, German Classical Archaeology could find enthusiastic imitators. In 1933 the American School successfully negotiated for the sale of land in the centre of modern Athens, an area which was thought to correspond to the location of the ancient Agora. The world's greatest modern democracy was to embark on the excavation of the civic centre of the greatest democracy in the ancient world. The excavation was generously funded by, amongst other donors, the Rockefeller Foundation.[80] As at Olympia, the Agora excavations were to be published as a series of specialist monographs, with the finds being described by material and type. Unlike the German excavations however, Americans were to find a rationale for the examination of even the smallest and meanest pieces. For one could never tell what kinds of evidence (such as the inscribed potsherds known as ostraka) might be relevant to our understanding of the workings of Athenian democracy. Like their American colleagues working at Olynthos, the excavators of the Agora showed a new interest in the more mundane aspects of ancient Greek life. But excavations at Olynthos and the Athenian Agora were the last of the 'big digs' to be initiated by any of the foreign schools. Conditions were changed by the Second World War and its aftermath, from which German academic prestige was never fully to recover. It was left to scholars of other nationalities to carry the torch of Romantic Hellenism.

2.7 Beazley and the re-formation of the Hellenic ideal

Of all the foreign nationalities who worked in Greece, the British had been least inclined to adopt the German model. In Britain the tradition of the amateur gentleman scholar had lived on. The British preferred to work on smaller sites and in smaller teams. The only 'big dig' undertaken by the British School, Sparta (Knossos being the private preserve of Sir Arthur Evans), was, in comparison with French, German and American efforts, chaotic.[81] Nevertheless British Classical scholars could not fail to be impressed by German standards and German achievements. In the 1880s German scholars had made great strides forward in the study of Greek pottery. They had tried to isolate particular vase painters on the basis of signatures, or rather painted labels which told us such facts as 'Amasis made me' (*Amasis mepoiesen*) or 'Exekias drew me' (*Exekias megraphsen*). From 1900 onwards A. Furtwängler and K. Reichhold embarked on a lavish publication of the

---

[79] Wrede *et al.* 1937: 1–5.
[80] Lord 1947: 177–8: 200–2, 231–45; Morris 1994a: 34–5. On Rockefeller's donation, see Lord 1947: 255. For an account of the Agora excavations generally, see Camp 1992. In order to accommodate the volume of material uncovered by the Agora excavations, the Americans began to publish a new annual archaeological journal, *Hesperia*.
[81] The majority of the results of the extensive excavations in Sparta have only ever been published as articles in the *Annual of the British School at Athens*. Apart from the report on the sanctuary of Artemis Orthia (Dawkins 1929), no other final reports have ever seen the light of day.

most celebrated Greek vases, Furtwängler writing the text and Reichhold drawing the pictures.[82] It was this publication that impressed one British scholar in particular, J.D. Beazley.

J.D. Beazley (1885–1970) devoted his life to the study of Greek vases, principally vases from Attica (the territory of ancient Athens).[83] He attempted to isolate – and in his eyes and in the eyes of most of his contemporaries he succeeded in isolating – the individual hands of the painters of these pots. Beazley did not, for the most part, work with pots from known contexts in Athens itself. The bulk of Greek pottery had been found in Italy, and came mostly from hastily excavated Etruscan graves. These vases were now scattered throughout the major museums of Europe and America. Beazley's identification of hands and workshops relied upon a new approach derived from the study of the Italian Renaissance, called Morellian connoisseurship. Giovanni Morelli had argued that it is possible to identify and group the works of an individual painter through the isolation of that painter's style.[84] Style – or as Beazley put it 'a peculiar system of renderings through which a certain conception of the human form found expression'[85] – cannot be grasped through the study of signatures, or by appraising the overall effect of the work, or looking only at larger features such as its composition or iconography. Such things can be imitated. Individual style is apparent most clearly in those apparently unconscious tricks of draughtsmanship used in the rendering of the smaller parts of the human anatomy, that is in the drawing of eyes, noses, ears, hands and feet. It is on the attention to such apparently insignificant details that the isolation of individual style depends. Carlo Ginzburg has argued that this attention to 'significant details', details more likely to have been unconsciously produced than consciously intended, is part of a new paradigm in the historical sciences that crystallised in the late nineteenth century.[86] It is at this time that the 'science' of graphology is invented and detective fiction appears. Sherlock Holmes is only the most famous fictional character whose application of deductive logic and attention to apparently minor facts leads him, inexorably, to the truth. In such stories criminals, in a sense, betray themselves by leaving unconscious clues behind, clues which eventually lead to the identification of the personality of the perpetrator.[87]

Whether or not Beazley was consciously aware of these influences is unimportant. His advocacy came through example, not through manifesto. His breakthrough came in the isolation of painters who had left no signatures. His articles on the Berlin painter (named after a vase in Berlin (fig. 11.12)) and the Kleophrades painter (named after a potter with whom the painter seemed to have worked (fig 9.6)) established his method.[88] Beazley was eventually to attribute about one-third

---

[82] Furtwängler and Reichhold 1900. For earlier German work, see Cook 1972: 298–9, 316–27.

[83] For Beazley's life, see Ashmole 1970. For his Oxford context, see Boardman 1985b.

[84] Morelli 1892. On Morelli's influence on Beazley, see Kurtz 1985a; Beazley and Kurtz 1983: 11–47; Whitley 1997a.   [85] Beazley 1922: 90.   [86] Ginzburg 1990.

[87] Ginzburg 1990; see also Shanks 1995: 37–41.   [88] Beazley 1911; 1918; 1922.

of all known Attic pots (which can be numbered in the tens of thousands) to particular hands or workshops, which were published as lists called *Attic Black-
Figure Vase Painters* and *Attic Red-Figure Vase Painters*.[89] These books trace the
influence of 'Master' painters from one generation to the next. Beazley tended to
employ a hierarchical terminology to describe the relationship between painters,
schools and workshops: 'I make a distinction between a vase by a painter and a
vase in his manner; and that "manner", "imitation", "following", "school",
"circle", "group", "influence", "kinship" are not, in my vocabulary, synonyms.'[90]
This is a very similar terminology to the one that had been used to describe the
workshop practice of the Italian Renaissance. It is an analogy that runs through
Beazley's work. In trying to sum up the differences between the Berlin painter and
the Kleophrades painter, he says of the latter that 'he may be said to play a kind
of Florentine to the Berlin painter's Sienese'.[91] Such remarks are by no means
insignificant details. The Renaissance analogy gave coherence to his overall
scheme for the development of Greek vase painting and, by extension, of Greek
art. For Beazley managed to reconcile three main strands in Classical archaeological thought: a humanism derived from Renaissance scholarship that sought to
find the individual behind the work of art; the 'scientific' practice of archaeological philology with its scrupulous attention to detail; and Winckelmann's conjectural scheme, which outlined the growth of Greek art from primitive beginnings
in the Archaic, to a high point in the Classical and then decline in the Hellenistic.
Beazley's lists demonstrated that the development of Greek art was not an impersonal process of stylistic evolution, but depended crucially on individuals
working within a tradition and passing on their skills from master to pupil. In this
light the Greek miracle, the achievement of a fully naturalistic artistic idiom,
came to resemble the Italian Renaissance.

Though Beazley's method was new, the ideas that gave coherence and structure
to his lists were not. It is possible, on reading or using Beazley, still to believe in
the uniqueness of the Greek achievement, to suppose that the Greeks had
attained artistic standards of universal validity. The problems of historicism, cultural relativism or hermeneutics can be sidestepped. The beliefs of Romantic
German Hellenism could be supported by the authority of scientific fact.
Positivism could, at last, be seen to serve a purpose.[92] To be sure, Beazley identified the high point in Greek art earlier than had Winckelmann – the painters he
most highly esteemed he placed in the late Archaic or early Classical.[93] This was
to locate the pinnacle of vase painting earlier than the pinnacle of achievement in
sculpture, an anomaly that could be explained away by saying that, from the 480s
onwards, wall painting became the principal vehicle for non-sculptural artistic
achievement. In this way the metanarrative of Greek Classical Archaeology could
be retained.[94]

[89] Beazley 1956; 1963.   [90] Beazley 1956: x.   [91] Beazley 1918: 40–1.
[92] As I argue in Whitley 1997a.   [93] Beazley and Ashmole 1932: 29–32, 41–2.
[94] For metanarratives, see Shanks 1995: 53–91; Morris 1994a; Whitley 1997a.

It is none the less important to emphasise that Beazley's approach was that of an archaeologist not an art historian. He examined every scrap of evidence, regardless of quality (to which, however, he was by no means indifferent).[95] Beazley indeed is the most influential Classical archaeologist of the twentieth century. His most positive legacy was the indirect inspiration he gave to several generations of British and American scholars to attempt archaeological synthesis on a grand scale. Gisela Richter's studies of Archaic sculpture, for example, manage to reconcile the isolation of individual hands with an overall scheme in which sculptors approach a Classical, naturalistic ideal, and Humfry Payne's *Necrocorinthia* remains fundamental to the study of Archaic Corinthian art.[96] However Beazley's example also had less positive effects. It became a truth universally acknowledged that a painter defined by Beazley was in need of a scholarly monograph. This species of monograph had many illustrations and numerous footnotes, but, with some honourable exceptions, possessed nothing approaching a serious academic argument.[97] In this particular academic genre, a painter's *œuvre* is sometimes fleshed out with pseudo-biographical details: 'Smikros wanted to sneak himself into this high-life circle where Euphronios excelled . . . Smikros may have succeeded in his social ambitions.'[98]

Excesses like this have led, inevitably, to a reaction. Critics of Beazley (or at least of 'Beazleyism') have appeared, most notably Michael Vickers and David Gill. Vickers and Gill have argued that it is wrong to think of vase painting as an art, and of vase painters as artists.[99] No famous potters are recorded in the literary sources. Vases have been valued as 'art objects' only because of d'Hancarville, whose publication of Hamilton's collection was a 'marketing ploy' designed to increase its value.[100] They point out that vessels in gold, silver and bronze were always most highly valued in antiquity, and gold vessels were several thousand times more expensive than pots. Pottery was in comparison ridiculously cheap. Since pottery tends to survive, whereas most valuable metal vessels have been melted down, pots have assumed an importance they do not merit.[101] 'Trade' in pottery, in Gill's eyes, is an insignificant by-product of other kinds of economic and cultural exchange.[102] Vickers has gone further. Since pots are cheaper than metal vessels, potting and pot painting must be consider the humbler craft.[103] It is a universal law of human culture that humbler crafts will take their cue from major arts – in this case metalworking. Pots are, for the most part, skeuomorphs,

---

[95] Boardman 1978: 8; see also Robertson 1985.

[96] Richter 1968; 1970; Payne 1931. Other scholars who benefited from Beazley's inspiration were Desborough (1952), on Protogeometric pottery, and Jeffery (1990) on Archaic inscriptions. Beazley's indirect influence has been far more fruitful than the emulation he has inspired amongst students of 'vase painting'.

[97] One honourable exception being Burn 1987. See also Whitley 1997a: 44–5.

[98] Frel 1983: 150.   [99] Vickers 1985; Vickers and Gill 1994.

[100] Vickers and Gill 1994: 1–32; Vickers 1987. For a different view, see Jenkins and Sloan 1996: 40–64.

[101] Vickers and Gill 1994: 33–76; Vickers 1990.   [102] Gill 1988a; 1988b; 1994.

[103] Vickers 1985; Vickers and Gill 1994: 105–204; Gill and Vickers 1990.

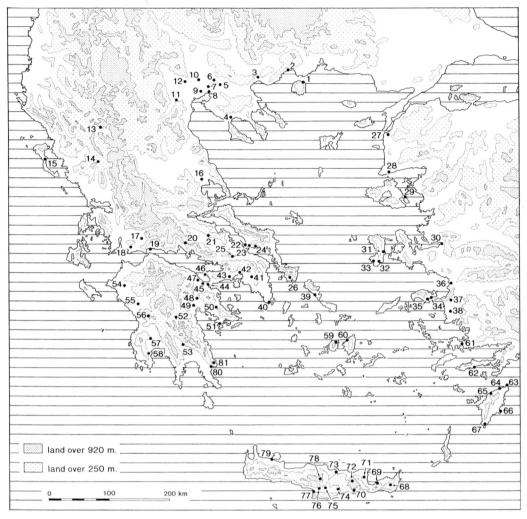

land over 920 m.

land over 250 m.

0   100   200 km

1. Thasos town	19. Naupaktos	37. Priene	52. Tegea	67. Vroulia
2. Kavala	20. Delphi	38. Miletos	53. Sparta	68. Praisos
3. Amphipolis	21. Kalapodhi	39. Zagora on	54. Elis	69. Kavousi
4. Olynthos	22. Chalkis	Andros	55. Olympia	70. Kato Symi
5. Langadas	23. Lefkandi	40. Sounion	56. Bassai	71. Dreros
6. Assiros	24. Eretria	41. Athens	(Phigeleia)	72. Karphi
7. Derveni	25. Thebes	42. Eleusis	57. Messene	73. Knossos
8. Thessaloniki	26. Karystos	43. Megara	(Ithome)	74. Afrati
9. Sindos	27. Troy	44. Isthmia	58. Nichoria	75. Phaistos
10. Kastanas	28. Assos	45. Corinth	59. Paros,	76. Gortyn
11. Vergina	29. Mytilene	46. Perachora	Koukounaries	77. Kommos
12. Pella	30. Smyrna	47. Sikyon	60. Naxos, Grotta	78. Idaean Cave
13. Vitsa Zagoriou	31. Chios town	48. Mycenae	61. Halikarnassos	79. Kydonia
14. Dodona	32. Emborio	49. Argos	62. Knidos	80. Epidauros
15. Kerkyra (town)	33. Kato Phana	50. Epidauros	63. Rhodes town	Limera
16. Pherai	34. Samos (town)	(sanctuary of	64. Ialysos	81. Zarax
17. Thermon	35. Samos (Heraion)	Asklepios)	65. Kameiros	
18. Kalydon	36. Ephesos	51. Halieis	66. Lindos	

2.3 Map of Greece, showing major sites

their shapes taken from metal prototypes. Further, figured gold appliqué decoration found on silver vessels in some Bulgarian tombs must provide the prototype for the technique of red-figure, if we allow that much of the silver would have been tarnished almost to blackness.[104] Like many Classical scholars, Vickers is a literary platonist, for whom the red-figured pots surviving in the archaeological record are but shadowy copies of the true metal vessels, now lost from the material world and accessible to us only through the close reading of ancient authors.

It may seem odd to end this chapter with a summary of what, in other archaeologies, must seem a minor controversy. In this field, however, Vickers' criticisms are far from unimportant. In criticising Beazley the traditional practice of the whole of the subject is threatened. The 'Vickers' controversy is symptomatic of wider changes taking place within the Classical Archaeology of Greece. Classical Archaeology began as the antiquarian study of works of art thought to be both ancient and Greek. When national museums were created, and 'vases' joined sculpture as examples of ancient art, collecting such examples became a matter of social and national prestige. Winckelmann provided a conjectural history of this art, which later German scholars were to fill out with empirical facts. It was the Germans who turned Classic Archaeology into a discipline, into the material arm of an overall 'science of antiquity' devoted, almost exclusively to the Greek and Roman past; and it was Germans who directed the tools of philological scholarship to hitherto neglected areas of the material record. Beazley managed, for a time, to unite these various strands and so to produce a distinctly 'Hellenic' archaeology. He, more than any other scholar, has shaped the discipline in the twentieth century. But, in developing primarily as a branch of Classical philology, Greek archaeology has found itself isolated in the field of archaeology as a whole, an isolation which Beazley's temporary success has reinforced. It is this sense of isolation, and in particular a feeling of distance from the anthropological and evolutionist roots of other archaeologies, that has been the proximate cause for the appearance of what may be called dissident Classical archaeologies in Hamburg, Paris, Naples and Cambridge.[105] It is this very same feeling that has also encouraged the importation of techniques of field survey into Greek archaeology. Of all the new methodologies, field survey has had the biggest impact in recent years. It would be wrong, however, to see field survey as a largely extraneous approach. It has its own history.

---

[104] Vickers 1985. For criticisms, see Boardman 1987; Robertson 1985.

[105] Separate 'schools' of dissenting Classical Archaeology have emerged in all these places. Herbert Hoffmann has founded the journal *Hephaistos*, which is based in Hamburg; Bruno d'Agostino and Anna Maria D'Onofrio have been instrumental in creating a distinctive Italian school in Naples, whose discussions are published in *Annali di Archeologia e Storia Antica*; the Paris 'school' is best represented by the work of Alain Schnapp and F. de Polignac, and is shown to its best advantage in Bérard *et al.* 1989.

CHAPTER 3

MODERN ARCHAEOLOGIES OF GREECE

3.1 Archaeologies of orthodoxy and dissent

If a date has to be put on the appearance of a modern archaeology of ancient Greece, 1977 would be it. That year saw the appearance (quite independently of one another) of two short monographs whose aims and methods mark a decisive break with the usual concerns of Classical archaeology. The first of these was Herbert Hoffmann's *Sexual and Asexual Pursuit.*[1] This was a self-conscious attempt to apply the methodology of structural analysis, derived via social anthropology from linguistics, to the study of the imagery (or the iconography) of a particular class of Athenian fifth-century red-figure pottery, the askoi. Nothing could be further from the dry academic chore of cataloguing and then attributing vases than Hoffmann's bold attempt to discern the underlying cultural logic in the decoration of these pots. In the same year Anthony Snodgrass published *Archaeology and the Rise of the Greek State.*[2] Snodgrass' concerns are quite distinct from Hoffmann's, and he draws his inspiration from quite different sources. Snodgrass sought to determine which kinds of archaeological evidence are relevant to the question of the date and nature of the process of state formation in Archaic Greece. Snodgrass was as much concerned to determine the conditions that made the 'rise of the state' possible as with the more obvious material symptoms of that process. He used simple quantitative methods to argue that it was an increase in population that underpinned the great transformation of the eighth century BC. His interest in state formation, and his use of quantitative methods, aligned him clearly with the dominant themes of a theoretically informed, comparative world archaeology (his debts to David Clarke in particular are explicit). Apart from a shared awareness of anthropological debate, Hoffmann's and Snodgrass' works have little in common. Hoffmann was directly inspired by anthropological structuralism;[3] Snodgrass by new or 'processual' archaeology. They are alike only in one respect, in their dissent from the traditional concerns and the traditional story of Classical archaeology.

Here I should perhaps qualify the title of this chapter. All forms of contemporary archaeological practice now used in the study of ancient Greece are, by definition, modern. It is just that some of these current forms of practice make their

---

[1] Hoffmann 1977.   [2] Snodgrass 1977.   [3] Hoffmann 1977: 1–3.

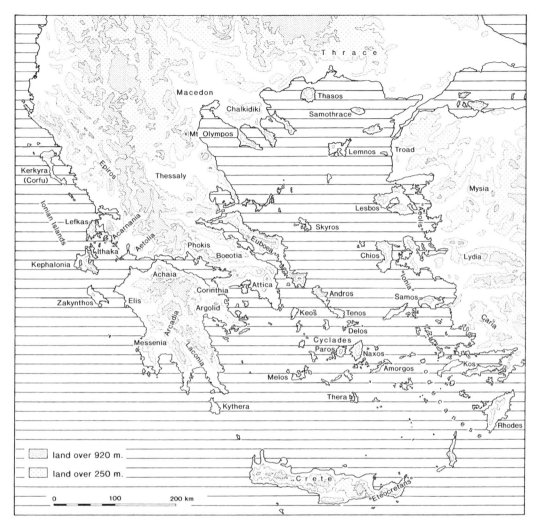

3.1 Map of Greece, showing relief and regions

dissent from traditional concerns (and from the traditional narrative that
Classical archaeology has been inclined to tell) more obvious than others.
Dissenting Classical archaeologies have appeared in different places, at different
times and for different reasons over the past thirty years or so. There is no unified
school of 'new' Classical archaeology, still less a discernible development away
from traditional through processual and on to post-processual approaches.[4]
Instead of one new school there are a number of schools, a number of attempts to
move the subject in new directions and to place Classical archaeology closer to

[4] See Morris 1994a; 1994b; 1994c for arguments for a plurality of approaches. Shanks (1995: 119–82)
 argues that Classical archaeology is going through a 'processualist' phase which must inevitably be
 followed by a 'post-processualist' one. I disagree.

the lively debates that have taken place in the humanities and human sciences in recent years. The purpose of this chapter is to describe some of these 'dissident' archaeologies, and the kinds of directions the archaeology of ancient Greece may be taking in the near future. Of course there is a danger here: in drawing attention to the more vociferous forms of innovation I may be neglecting more subtle, less spectacular but equally important changes that may be taking place in the mainstream of Classical archaeology. But to deny that there have been signs of dissatisfaction with traditional Classical archaeology, and that these signs have become more frequent in recent years, would be obtuse.

3.2 Travellers and topographers

Of all the modern archaeologies of Greece, surface survey has undoubtedly been the most successful. Ancient historians in particular have turned to survey to establish facts about rural settlement and demography that are simply not available in the written sources. This success may seem odd, since survey is perhaps the most defiantly unclassical (or rather uncanonical) methodology currently in use in the study of ancient Greece. Indeed its emphasis on the mundane and the fragmentary seems the very reverse of the priorities of traditional Classical archaeology, devoted to the explication of great works. What, it may be asked, does the fieldwalker, clicker in hand, walking determinedly in a straight line over the fields and scrublands of Greece, picking up fragments of sherds whose decoration has, more often than not, been completely effaced, have in common with the refined museum scholar engaged in the re-assignation of all the works attributed to the Pan painter? The answer is, of course, that the fieldwalker depends on the museum scholar for the precise dating of his surface finds (see below). But another factor behind the ready acceptance of survey methods is that survey has respectable 'Classical' antecedents, to which the publishers of major survey projects frequently allude:[5] the tradition of travellers and topographers.

Travel literature was not a genre in which the ancient Greeks themselves excelled. The most celebrated (and meticulous) traveller of ancient Greece, Pausanias, provides us with the minimum of information concerning the country he travels through, unless he comes upon a spring, grove or sanctuary whose poetic or historical associations are too well known to ignore. Most of his attention is given to towns and major sanctuaries, and to the (already ancient) works of art to be found within them. Strabo provides us with some two-dimensional cross-references but little more detail, as does Herakleides Kritikos.[6] Early modern travellers to Greece too concentrated on major cities, and on the ruins or inscriptions they encountered there. Little attention was paid to landscape. This was to change after 1750, when more and more Western visitors came to Greece.[7]

---

[5] E.g. McDonald 1972a: 9–13; Cherry 1982.   [6] Snodgrass 1987: 67–92.
[7] Stoneman 1987: 136–64.

A new Romantic interest in the picturesque made many travellers more attentive to the country they were passing through on their way to visit the more celebrated ruins of antiquity. This interest is particularly evident amongst British travellers, the most numerous in the years after 1800, who were as captivated by the romance of ancient landscapes as they were by the picturesque effect of ancient ruins. 'Romanticism', however, is an insufficient explanation for this new combination of interests, since the Romance of ancient Greece tended to go hand in hand with more practical and scientific interests. Indeed it is this tension between the romance of contemplating the past through the veil of the present on the one hand and a straightforward scientific curiosity on the other that lends this literature its distinctive character.[8] A fairly representative example of an early nineteenth-century traveller is Edward Dodwell, whose explorations of Greece took place between 1801 and 1805.[9] Dodwell is, superficially at least, a Romantic:

In these volumes the present state of Greece is described, in order to illustrate the ancient, and to add new interest to modern localities and customs, by identifying them with the events or manners of a more early period. The reader must never forget, that a classic interest is breathed over the superficies of the Grecian territory; that its mountains, its valleys, and its streams, are intimately associated with the animating presence of the authors, by whom they have been immortalized. Almost every rock, every river, is haunted by the shadows of the mighty dead. Every portion of the soil appears to teem with historical recollections; or it borrows some potent but invisible charm from the inspirations of poetry, the efforts of genius, or the energies of liberty and patriotism.[10]

This sense of the whole landscape being infused with an 'animating presence' is new. It goes beyond anything in Pausanias, or in early modern travellers. Dodwell is not simply interested in those places which have a particular historical interest, nor even simply in picturesque effects. Even though he is clearly at the more Romantic end of the spectrum of nineteenth-century travellers, he is as interested in the manners of the present inhabitants as he is in ancient ruins. He even manages to collect some Corinthian pots, and is only about one hundred years wrong in his dates.[11] A more interesting feature of Dodwell, however, is his attitude to written sources. Like any other traveller interested in topography, and the correct identification of ancient sites, he is dependent on Pausanias, Strabo and various ancient historians. His visit to the imposing remains of Mycenae prompts the following reflections:

Diodorus Siculus [B.11.c.25] says that the Argians destroyed Mycenae, *tas Mykenas kateskaphsan*, and adds that it remained deserted to his time. Diodorus, in speaking of the destruction of sites, generally uses the word *kateskaphsan*, which supposes a complete

---

[8] By practical interests I mean here primarily politics. W.M. Leake for example was no disinterested traveller. His various works on the Peloponnese (Leake 1830a; 1830b; 1830c) and on northern Greece (1835a; 1835b) are of course still of immense value to the scholar. But they were prompted by political interests, chiefly the need for good military intelligence which had hitherto been entirely lacking in that part of the world. See Stoneman 1987: 155–62.

[9] See Dodwell 1819a; 1819b; Stoneman 1987: 147–51.   [10] Dodwell 1819a: iv.

[11] Dodwell 1819b: 196–200.

razing; many of the cities, however, which he thus destroys, still exhibit considerable ruins, but long prior to his time. Livy is the destroyer of Italian cities, as Diodorus and Strabo are of those of Greece; but many of those which he [Livy] represented as 'sine vestigiis,' still retain their walls, gates, and towers, in a state of high preservation.[12]

To scrutinise visible, standing remains to test the authority and veracity of the ancient sources is a new approach. Hitherto most writers had treated the ancients as 'authorities', not as sources to be treated with a certain critical scepticism. Dodwell, however, shares with his contemporaries a complete dependence on these authors for the identification of the sites he visited. Topography was a major interest of all these travellers. Topographical identification required a good knowledge of ancient authors, since one had to try to reconcile what little information was contained therein with one's own personal observations of the site, its general situation, and the surrounding landscape. It is these scientific interests that are most apparent in the work of William Martin Leake. Leake was certainly the most thorough (if not the most readable) of all early nineteenth-century travellers. He made great efforts to reach remote and uncelebrated places. He appreciated the importance of detail. He makes numerous shrewd comments on botany and agriculture, combined with topographical descriptions and observations on the customs and manners of the current inhabitants. Given that his original brief was to spy out the lie of the land for the British government (in case Napoleon extended his conquests of Ottoman territory), politics form an inevitable backdrop to his observations. But this does not explain his thoroughness when it came to antiquities. Both Leake and Dodwell travelled to the Argolid, and both seem to have reached the vicinity of the Argive Heraeum (or Heraion). Dodwell notes that there must have been an ancient sanctuary nearby, but has no idea of what sanctuary it was, or where exactly it was located.[13] Leake by contrast produces elaborate arguments, based on the ancient sources and his own observations, for correctly placing the Argive Heraion (Heraeum) close to Prosymna.[14]

By 1840, then, a new archaeological genre had developed. Travel literature combined the study of architecture and inscriptions, observations on landscape and the picturesque, and topographical identifications, with accounts of the manners and customs of the inhabitants. Antiquarianism, ethnography, history and geography all shared a place. The British traveller attempted to be a jack of all these trades; when the French tried their hand, in the Expédition Scientifique de Morée, they divided the task, in properly scientific fashion, amongst a number of specialist savants.[15] It was the British tradition however that, for the time being, was to

---

[12] Dodwell 1819b: 243.   [13] Dodwell 1819b: 244–5.   [14] Leake 1830b: 387–94.

[15] The Expédition Scientifique de Morée was partitioned into the physical and the cultural realms of 'science'. The physical sciences (which included geography, botany and zoology) were published by Bory de St Vincent (1835; 1836). The 'cultural' sciences comprised the traditional Classical subjects of architecture, sculpture, inscriptions and *vues* by Blouet *et al.* (1831; 1833; 1838). *Pace* McDonald 1972a: 10, there is no real attempt to integrate these two branches of knowledge. Blouet's work is very much in the tradition of exact description of Classical architecture established by Stuart and Revett.

prove the more tenacious. Though by the middle years of the nineteenth century the demand for travel literature of mainland Greece had waned, the same was not true for the study of ancient Crete. Pashley and Spratt are to Crete what Dodwell and Leake had been to the Morea.[16] In their works too, archaeology, epigraphy, topography, ethnography and general descriptions of the landscape have their place. Indeed when Crete became an object of general archaeological interest in the late nineteenth century, pioneers of excavation such as Halbherr, Demargne and Evans took care to travel through the island first.[17] The habit of travelling was ingrained in the pioneers of Minoan archaeology, and, when excavations at Knossos, Mallia and Phaistos provided Crete with a reliable ceramic chronology, this information could be used to date the sites they had visited from their surface remains. Pendlebury is the first archaeologist, to my knowledge, to put this information to good use. He collated the information from all known sites in Crete from the Neolithic to the Roman. Often, sites were dated simply from surface finds, brought back by him or by other members of the British School who were based at Knossos.[18] This tradition was continued in the post-war years by other members of the British School, usually with Bronze Age interests, who conducted 'surveys' of this kind in Crete and on the mainland.[19] It was from this tradition that modern survey emerged. So what distinguishes survey of this kind from modern surveys? The chief difference lies in whether or not a survey can be considered intensive.

3.3 From extensive to intensive survey

There are many reports of surveys in Greece published in the early 1960s. Though many individual scholars (notably Eugene Vanderpool of the American School, who managed to explore every nook and cranny of Attica) continued the tradition of individual topographical investigation, these surveys differed from the work of early travellers in having a specifically archaeological focus. In 1965, for example, Hugh Sackett and others conducted a survey of the island of Euboea.[20] The purpose of the survey was to find sites, to date them through 'sherding' (i.e. from their surface finds, particularly pottery), to list sites in a catalogue, and then to pick out one or two of them that might be suitable candidates for excavation. (It was in this way that excavations were begun at Lefkandi.) This relaxed attitude to survey, however, was one that could only survive in an academic climate insulated from the example of World Archaeology. While the study of Archaic and Classical Greece was to remain a world unto itself for some time to come, a number of younger Aegean prehistorians (notably William McDonald and Colin

---

[16] Pashley 1837a; 1837b; Spratt 1865a; 1865b. [17] Brown 1993: 35–85; Pendlebury 1939: 16–19.
[18] Pendlebury 1939. Pendlebury makes it clear that the determination of a site's date is not his work alone. The names of Miss Eccles and Miss Money-Coutts appear frequently, as having helped first to identify a site and then to date it from its surface remains.
[19] See for example Hood *et al.* 1964; 1966. [20] Sackett *et al.* 1966.

Renfrew) began to see their work in a wider, comparative perspective. The Bronze Age Aegean could be seen to exhibit processes, such as state formation and collapse, comparable to those that took place in other times and places, such as in Fourth- and Third-Millennium Mesopotamia or in the Formative and Classic periods of Mesoamerica.[21] Large-scale surveys (of the Diyala and Tehuacan valleys respectively) had been undertaken in both these regions by the mid-1960s, and these surveys had succeeded in providing a diachronic (that is, period-by-period) picture of rural settlement pattern, so placing the major city sites of the area into some kind of wider perspective. These surveys were to provide the inspiration for what was later to be regarded as the first real survey project in Greece: the Minnesota Messenia Expedition.[22]

Though it developed almost haphazardly, the Minnesota Messenia Expedition self-consciously defined itself as an interdisciplinary endeavour with a set of well-defined goals, making use of the skills of environmental scientists, historians, geographers, ethnographers and geomorphologists as well as archaeologists. The overall aims were twofold: to provide the settlement history of an entire region from earliest prehistory to the present; and to determine those particular factors (be it climate or historical circumstance) affecting the population, settlement and political structure of this whole area of the south-west Peloponnese. The scale of the project was unprecedented, and, despite a formal nod of acknowledgement to the Expédition Scientifique de Morée, so was the attempt to combine different kinds of evidence and different scientific approaches. In field methods, however, the Expedition was in some ways conservative. Their objectives were, like those of the Euboea survey, to find sites, and to this end they used their experience of the topography of known sites to predict the locations of new ones. Their only innovation lay in the use of aerial photography.

The interests of most of the archaeologists who participated in the project lay firmly in the Bronze Age, particularly in the period in which the 'Palace of Nestor' at Pylos had flourished. Is it then really surprising that they had their greatest success in finding new Bronze Age sites? Could the numbers of sites found for each period be trusted as a representative sample of all the sites that had once existed? Did not the overall approach of the Messenia Expedition, with its emphasis on finding more sites of known character, automatically preclude the discovery of sites which (for particular historical reasons) may have been located in unlikely places? It was such questions that were to preoccupy the next generation of archaeological surveyors in Greece, in particular the organisers of the Melos survey, Colin Renfrew and John Cherry.[23] This survey adopted a particular method of sampling (systematic sampling by transect) in the expectation that this would yield a representative (if not total) proportion of sites belonging to particular periods. It also employed a more intensive method of survey in the field.

[21] Renfrew 1972.
[22] For the Diyala valley survey, see McAdams 1981. For the Minnesota Messenia Expedition, see McDonald and Rapp 1972.   [23] Renfrew and Wagstaff 1982.

Instead of making predictions about likely site locations, and testing these predictions through visits, the Melos survey adopted a method of fieldwalking in teams. Groups of fieldwalkers would walk through the landscape, maintaining a constant interval of 20 m between them, and record any sites they came across.[24] Cherry argued that a more intensive method of survey would lead, not simply to the discovery of more sites, but to the discovery of a representative proportion of those sites. Valid comparisons could then be made between the number and density of sites from different periods. Statistics seem to bear out Cherry's contention.[25] Cherry later extended his interests to other islands, notably Kea (or Keos), whose survey was conducted with even greater regard for sampling problems (and with a greater degree of intensity) than that of Melos.[26]

Until 1980, most directors of large field surveys in Greece had been prehistorians. It was not long, however, before the potential of field survey for revealing diachronic change in settlement pattern was exploited by archaeologists whose main interests lay in the Archaic and Classical periods. The Southern Argolid survey, for example, partly grew out of Michael Jameson's investigations at the Classical city of Halieis.[27] Similarly it was the importance of the whole region of Boeotia in the historical period that prompted John Bintliff and Anthony Snodgrass to begin work there.[28] The new Classical emphasis in survey brought with it new questions and new methodological innovations. Survey revealed that many (though by no means all) areas of rural Greece were covered with what could only be described as a carpet of ancient sherds, sherds which for the most part seemed to be of Classical or Hellenistic date. Two questions arose: first, what mechanism could have produced such a 'carpet', and second, if much of Greece is covered with sherds, and if it is the presence of sherds that indicates the presence of a site, how should sites be defined? Should we not define sites by the density of sherds relative to the underlying 'background noise' of 'off-site' distributions?[29] These methodological issues have provoked considerable debate, and have encouraged Classical archaeologists to pursue quantitative methods with a sophistication and rigour that, a few years ago, would have seemed unimaginable.[30] Another, paradoxical, effect of the rise of rural survey is a renewed interest in examining urban sites through their surface remains. If survey is sufficiently intensive, if sampling is rigorous and if the local ceramic chronology is sufficiently well defined, it should be possible to produce a history in phases of a particular settlement through time. 'Urban surveys' have now been produced for a number of medium-sized city sites in Greece, notably Phleious (Phlius) and Thespiai, with interesting results.[31]

Survey is now an integral part of the archaeological investigation into Archaic and Classical Greece. Indeed, for some parts of Greece, big digs have been replaced

[24] Cherry 1982. For criticisms of some of the methods, see R. Catling 1984.   [25] Cherry 1983.
[26] Cherry *et al.* 1991.   [27] Jameson *et al.* 1994.   [28] Bintliff and Snodgrass 1985.
[29] Gallant 1986; Cherry *et al.* 1991: 20–8.   [30] Cherry *et al.* 1991: 13–54; Alcock *et al.* 1994.
[31] Alcock 1991; Bintliff and Snodgrass 1988.

by big surveys. Practitioners of survey tend to be more aware of (and sympathetic to) the agenda of World Archaeology than more traditional scholars. They have not been ashamed to borrow widely from elsewhere. Nothing, it would seem, could be further from the aesthetic contemplation of Greek sculpture than the quantitative and ethnoarchaeological arguments that have arisen over the extent to which manure was used in rural Greece, and whether it is the practice of manuring that is largely responsible for the widespread 'off-site' distribution of ancient sherds across the Greek countryside.[32] It would be a mistake, however, to think that, for this reason, survey archaeologists are any less Classical than their museum-based colleagues. As Fotiadis has reminded us, there is a certain romance to the study of the Greek countryside, and it is this romance of Hellenism that the fieldwalker shares with the student of Greek sculpture.[33] Moreover it is hardly a coincidence that survey projects in Greece have, for the most part, been conducted by scholars from English-speaking countries, since survey in part derives from a largely British tradition of topographical exploration. Exponents of field survey have, for polemical reasons, to some extent exaggerated the innovative character of their approach. Field survey thus forms an instructive contrast to other new approaches, no less quantitative or scientific, which have insinuated themselves into the fabric of Greek archaeology with much less fuss.

3.4 The impact of petrology

By the early 1960s many archaeologists working in Greece had acquired an extensive and intimate knowledge of the various regional pottery styles of the Archaic period. Though the precision that Beazley had arrived at with Attic black-figure could rarely be equalled in the study of other regions, scholars such as F. Villard, R.M. Cook and John Boardman could normally distinguish between pottery made in eastern Greece, in the Cyclades or in the Argolid, and could arrive at probable dates to within a quarter century or so.[34] None the less there were some pot styles whose origin remained somewhat mysterious. Were, for example, the numerous cups or chalices which British excavators had turned up at the site of the Greek colony of Naucratis in Egypt of local manufacture, or were they imports from the 'mother city' of Chios?[35] Even more puzzling was a group of Orientalising amphoras, numbers of which had turned up on the Cycladic island of Melos. Were these amphoras actually 'Melian'? Melos had been in recent geological times a volcanic island, and it was this vulcanism that was responsible for the vast quantities of obsidian (volcanic glass) still to be found there. The absence of inclusions from

---

[32] Alcock *et al.* 1994; Snodgrass 1994.   [33] Fotiadis 1995.
[34] See in general Cook 1972. R.M. Cook had been in the forefront of characterising and dating 'East Greek' pottery (see now Cook and Dupont 1998). Boardman had successfully characterised Euboean in a series of articles (Boardman 1952; 1957) besides making major contributions to the study of Archaic Chios (e.g. Boardman 1967), Archaic Crete (Boardman 1961) and elsewhere.
[35] Boardman 1956; 1967; Lemos 1991.

volcanic rocks in the rather coarse fabric of these vessels seemed to make Melos an unlikely source for Melian vases.[36] In any case, it became clear that the original production centre for these pots could not be determined by style, context or provenance alone. A new approach was needed.

So-called scientific studies (i.e. studies which relied on techniques borrowed from the natural sciences) had made considerable advances in archaeology during the 1950s. Many such studies focussed on the chemical properties of archaeological objects, the aim being to trace the origins of, for example, bronze axes through their trace elements. In the late 1950s and 1960s a number of archaeological laboratories were established to continue these lines of research. One such was the Research Laboratory for Archaeology and the History of Art at Oxford. Thanks to Beazley, Oxford had a great reputation as a centre for the study of Greek pottery, and it was natural that co-operative ventures between archaeologists and archaeological scientists should develop to address problems that, at the time, seemed insoluble by traditional means. Might not a closer, scientific look at the fabric of some of the pots tell us something new? Archaeologists had long been accustomed to making macroscopic identifications of fabrics, often making observations on the colour of the (fired) clay, the density of inclusions and on their size and number. Petrological (or petrographic) approaches to the study of fabrics by archaeological scientists represented a refinement of these techniques, with the addition of new microscopic methods such as the use of thin sections. Petrological analyses were better suited to coarse wares, whose inclusions were generally larger (and therefore more amenable to geological characterisation). For fine wares, which constituted the bulk of the material whose origin was sought, different methods were needed. It should be possible to distinguish fabrics on the basis of their chemical composition, in particular through the determination of trace elements characteristic of particular clay beds. To this end techniques were developed to analyse the chemical composition of samples from sherds.[37] Ideally the results of chemical analyses should be compared with the chemical composition of samples from certain identifiable clay beds, using the same techniques in both cases. This required an extensive programme of 'petrological' survey, to identify and characterise clay beds from all over Greece and build up a 'databank' of regional clays.[38] By these means is should be possible to determine the origin of most Greek fabric groups.

Though a number of chemical analyses were made in the 1960s, it was only during the 1970s that studies really took off. A landmark was the article by Boardman and Schweizer in 1973, which made use of the technique of optical emission spectrography.[39] The results, though in general positive, served more to confirm existing hypotheses than to open up new avenues of investigation. None the less the overall approach seemed promising, and in the 1970s new laboratories

---

[36] Hopkinson and Baker-Penoyre 1902; Jones *et al.* 1986: 643–59.   [37] Jones *et al.* 1986: 15–56.
[38] Jones *et al.* 1986: 31, 50–3.   [39] Boardman and Schweizer 1973.

opened in Athens dedicated, in part, to this line of research.[40] New technical advances were made, in particular the development of atomic absorption spectroscopy (AAS).[41] The new technique, together with more extensive knowledge of clay beds, proved much more effective. For example, Callaghan and Jones were able to prove beyond reasonable doubt that the Hadra hydrias used as cremation urns in Hellenistic Alexandria were not manufactured locally but produced in central Crete.[42] By far the most elaborate and informative of the new chemical analyses is that produced on the hundreds of Early Iron Age and Orientalising pots from the North Cemetery at Knossos, which has helped sort out regional groupings in a much more sophisticated manner.[43]

Chemical and petrological analyses of fabrics have now become a part of common archaeological practice in the study of ancient Greece. These techniques have helped to sort out problems that traditional archaeology was interested in but could not resolve. Petrology has developed with the help and support of traditional ceramic specialists, and it should surprise no one that most attention has been given to finewares. It may be that petrology will have a more revolutionary effect when more attention is paid to coarse wares, whose relative lack of aesthetic appeal may have hindered appreciation of their archaeological importance. None the less analyses of this kind have certainly changed the institutional structure of Greek archaeology. There are now a number of established centres for archaeological science working on ceramic problems. This relative success in the institutional sphere may be contrasted to other new approaches whose advocates have made their dissent from traditional ceramic studies more obvious and more vociferous.

3.5 New iconographies

'The majority of those who have described themselves as Classical archaeologists have tended to think of their subject as a specialised branch of art history which could be divorced from the wider sociological investigations of the society in which that art was developed.'[44] So wrote the anthropologist Edmund Leach in 1977, describing, from an outsider's point of view, the situation in traditional Classical archaeology. Leach was writing a foreword to Herbert Hoffmann's *Sexual and Asexual Pursuit*, in which he applied structuralist ideas to analyse the images to be found on a class of fifth-century Athenian pots, the so-called askoi.

Structuralism is (or was) an approach that sees all forms of cultural expression, be they pots or burial practices, as resembling a language. Just as a language has rules (grammar) which determine which utterances do or do not make sense, so

---

[40] In particular the Fitch Laboratory, attached to the British School at Athens, and the Demokritos Laboratory, attached to the University of Athens.

[41] See Jones *et al.* 1986: 16–22. In the 1960s and 1970s Optical Emission Spectroscopy had been the principal method in use.   [42] Callaghan and Jones 1985.   [43] Liddy 1996.

[44] E.R. Leach in Hoffmann 1977: v.

each culture has underlying rules (structures) which govern what kinds of images make sense within that society. These rules apply to all forms of cultural production, and determine not only what can be made but what can be understood within any particular culture. Often these rules take the form of paired binary oppositions, governed by the ultimate biological division between male and female. Hoffmann's aim was quintessentially structuralist. It was to uncover the cultural logic governing the universe of forms that appeared on these pots.[45] Askoi were ideal for his purpose, since they were decorated with antithetical, almost heraldic scenes. These scenes more often than not involved either pursuit or confrontatation, and contrasts seem to be built into the very structure of the images. Structural analysis allowed Hoffmann to argue that these images were linked by themes of sexual and other kinds of pursuit, and that these themes could be conveyed most conveniently by a series of binary oppositions. In this way certain features particular to the society of the time could be highlighted, features which were not necessarily evident in the literature of the time. Cultural ideas could be read out of iconography, and a kind of cultural ethnography produced from largely archaeological evidence.

Hoffmann's remains a very provocative paper, even after the passage of more than twenty years. Unsurprisingly perhaps Hoffmann encountered a degree of critical scepticism.[46] In order to promote his and others' unorthodox ideas, he was instrumental in founding a new journal, *Hephaistos*, dedicated as much to discussions of a theoretical nature as to more empirical studies. In this journal he advanced the view that, after Beazley, the study of vase painting had reached an impasse, and that in future more emphasis should be placed on interpretative studies than on attribution, classification or description.[47] However Hoffmann might well have remained an isolated figure, were it not for developments elsewhere.

France is the home of the approach to language and culture we call structuralism. But for a long time French Classical studies, like Classical studies everywhere, remained very conservative during the heyday of structuralism in the 1960s and early 1970s. With the exception of maverick figures such as Louis Gernet, there was very little interest in anthropological questions. Nevertheless Gernet managed to inspire a younger generation of French Classical scholars. J.P. Vernant and M. Detienne have been in the forefront of advancing new interpretations of Greek cultural practices, interpretations that have made considerable use of structuralist ideas. Vernant and Detienne in turn have encouraged others to view the images that survive from Archaic and Classical Greece in anthropological terms. The study of images, it is argued, should help to reveal more about underlying cultural patterns in ancient Greek society, and help us to highlight those ways in which Greek culture differed from our own.

---

[45] The classic statement of anthropological structuralism in Lévi-Strauss 1973. For the application of structuralist ideas to archaeology, see Hodder 1982; Whitley 1991a: 19–23; and in Classical archaeology now Shanks 1999. [46] Boardman 1979; 1981. [47] Hoffmann 1979.

That Greek culture was a culture of images, and that these images in turn provide oblique insights into Greek culture, is the principal theme of the major work to date of the Paris school: *La Cité des images*.[48] Archaeological arguments are produced to show that hunting, sacrifice and initiation are intimately linked in Classical Athenian culture;[49] or that, in the Archaic period, hunting is symbolically associated with the conventions of homoerotic courtship.[50] These arguments are not quite so explicitly (or, one might say, dogmatically) structuralist as Hoffmann's,[51] but they are informed by the same climate of thought. Such intellectual undercurrents are also apparent in a number of other French studies not directly concerned with iconography, such as F. de Polignac's theories on the origins of Greek states and the appearance of sanctuary sites at the beginning of the Archaic period. Here, binary oppositions between the wild and the sown, and between urban centre and rural periphery, are seen as underlying the spatial logic in the location of early Greek sanctuaries.[52]

Structuralism, or more precisely the Paris and Hamburg schools, has certainly changed the face of iconographic studies. The difficulty with all structuralist approaches, however, is that they inevitably take a synchronic view; that is, structural analysis tends to describe society or culture as a system, and a system in which there is no obvious potential for change. Moreover, the kind of structuralism that prevailed in the 1970s often gave the impression that a correct portrayal of a particular cultural world could be arrived at, and so a culture adequately characterised, by a set of underlying binary oppositions. But this variety of 'high structuralism' was rarely advocated in Classical studies. The appearance of structuralism fortunately coincided with a more general turn away from attribution and towards iconography, that is towards the study of the range of images that a society produces. General studies, of images of Zeus in the Classical period or of Dionysos in the Archaic, were often much more empirical in their approach.[53] Sceptical empiricism and a background of structuralist ideas could sometimes prove to be a very fruitful combination. A case in point is Lucilla Burn's interpretation of three white-ground cups by Sotades, one of which is shown in fig. 13.22. Burn shows that the myths depicted on these cups are linked by common themes (honey, death and rebirth), but does not try to arrive at a correct interpretation of what these images mean.

the Sotades painter . . . was not deliberately setting a puzzle with one correct solution. Rather it would seem that in the same way as Greek tragedy . . . the Sotadean cups explore a problem to which there is no one answer. Through mythological paradigms they suggest various approaches to death, and life after death, in full awareness that the mystery is insoluble.[54]

Structural analysis still has a useful role to play in the interpretation of the material culture of ancient Greece. The Paris school in particular has inspired

---

[48] Bérard *et al.* 1984. This was later translated into English as Bérard *et al.* 1989.
[49] Durand and Schnapp 1984; 1989.   [50] Schnapp 1984; 1989.
[51] Hoffmann 1977 is rigidly structuralist, Hoffmann 1997 much less so.
[52] De Polignac 1984; 1995.   [53] E.g. Carpenter 1986; Arafat 1990.   [54] Burn 1985: 104.

other scholars in their attempts to interpret aspects of Archaic and Classical Greek culture which rely primarily on archaeological evidence.[55] None the less an approach that, inadvertently perhaps, tends to treat a dynamic cultural process as a static cultural system does have inherent limitations. Furthermore, approaches which confine themselves to a universe of images and of cultural forms, while not taking much account of the contexts in which these images were used and the archaeological contexts in which they were found, are likely to give us a partial and unbalanced view of Greek culture. It is slightly troubling, for example, to realise that one of the chief pieces of visual evidence commonly used in discussions of Greek sacrifice is a hydria manufactured in the Etruscan city of Caere (Cerverteri).[56] Many images used to illustrate aspects of Athenian life and culture actually come from pots found in Etruscan graves. Structuralist approaches have often pushed discussion of archaeological context into the background. It is time to take a closer look at a number of approaches more explicitly concerned with both context and process.

3.6 Social and contextual archaeologies

One of the principal interests of World Archaeology in the 1960s and 1970s (when the term 'New Archaeology' was in vogue) lay in the question of how and why complex societies, and specifically states, emerged from less complex agricultural or tribal communities. Colin Renfrew had explored some of these ideas in relation to the Aegean Bronze Age.[57] Renfrew was an advocate of social archaeology, an archaeology explicitly concerned with answering the question of how past societies could be reconstructed by archaeological means. Renfrew championed the view that the answer to such questions as state formation lay in an examination of internal processes. He rejected what was called diffusionism, that is the proposition that advanced, civilising ideas necessarily have one point of origin, and have a natural tendency to spread from that one source. For Renfrew, diffusionism did not really try to explain innovation; mere proximity to the Near East could not in and of itself account for the emergence of civilisation in the Aegean at the close of the third millennium BC.[58] But if the appearance of states in the Aegean Bronze Age still seemed to be a bit of a mystery in the early 1970s, this was no less true of developments in the Early Iron Age. In 1971 Anthony Snodgrass had argued strongly that Aegean palace societies had effectively collapsed at the end of the Bronze Age, and that there was little or no continuity in politics or culture between Bronze Age and Archaic Greece.[59] After 1100 BC Greece had entered a Dark Age, where society and culture had more in common with the rest of barbarian Europe than with the literate civilisations of the Near

---

[55] For example, Shanks 1993; 1999.   [56] See Durand and Schnapp 1989: fig. 74.
[57] Renfrew 1972.
[58] Renfrew 1972: 3–44, 225–307. See also Renfrew 1973 for a definition of 'social archaeology'.
[59] Snodgrass 1971.

East. In 1977 he tried to show that the sudden emergence of polis (state) societies in the eighth and seventh centuries BC was due in part to large-scale internal developments. He argued, on the basis of the number of graves found in Attica and elsewhere, that there was a major demographic explosion, a sudden and revolutionary increase in population in the eighth century BC.[60] This central demographic fact lay behind the rise of the Greek state. Quantitative methods had arrived in Greek archaeology.

Snodgrass and (later) Renfrew were both based in Cambridge, and Cambridge began to attract graduate students who sometimes were more familiar with 'theory' than with the traditional subjects of Classical archaeology. One such was Ian Morris, who developed Snodgrass' interest in demography. Morris' *Burial and Ancient Society*, however, while it shares many of Snodgrass' historical and methodological interests, takes issue with Snodgrass' thesis.[61] Morris showed that there are serious methodological and practical objections to taking a simple measure of the number of graves as a direct index of a rise or fall in overall population. He argued that patterns in the archaeological record are skewed by the depositional practices characteristic of particular kinds of society. In the Athenian case, he argued, the number of burials at any particular time is affected by an ideology which effectively 'rations' visible burial. Sophisticated quantitative approaches to the elucidation of long-term historical processes have also been undertaken by other Snodgrass students. Cathy Morgan (with Todd Whitelaw) attempted to determine to what extent the distinctiveness in the decoration of Early Iron Age pottery found at various localities in the Argolid could be correlated with the degree of local political autonomy.[62] Did style express cultural or political differences within the region? Did, for example, pots found at Tiryns become more distinctive from those found at Argos during the eighth century BC, at a time when individual small states emerged elsewhere in Greece? These questions demanded that standardized means be found to measure and compare the 'styles' found at different sites. Other quantitative approaches have paid more attention to archaeological context. My own work, for example, attempted to assess the degree to which the decoration to be found on Protogeometric and Geometric pots found in graves in Athens was related to other features of the grave assemblage, chiefly the grave goods associated with the deceased.[63] I argued that at times there were very strong correlations, and from this fact I inferred that art was not an autonomous practice divorced from social life, but directly responsive to various social demands.

These scholars, all of whom had worked in Cambridge with Anthony Snodgrass, have been called a 'school' by some.[64] Many of Snodgrass' students have since gone on to topics of little direct relevance to the question of state formation, and

---

[60] Snodgrass 1977; a thesis elaborated in Snodgrass 1980: 15–48.   [61] Morris 1987.
[62] Morgan and Whitelaw 1991.   [63] Whitley 1991a.
[64] For varied reactions to recent developments in this field see Shanks 1995: 119–55; Boardman 1988c; Papadopoulos 1993; Cuozzo 1996.

some, such as Sue Alcock, have in any case concerned themselves principally with later periods.[65] Still, in so far as these scholars share similar interests, particularly in theory, the term 'school' is an accurate one. But if the term is meant to imply that everyone concerned shares the same views and doctrines it is extremely misleading.[66] The 'school' has provoked a hostile reaction in many quarters, and this in turn has revealed deep cracks in the once smooth face of Classical archaeology. The façade of disciplinary unity, a unity based on a set of shared assumptions going by the name of 'common sense', has been broken.

The archaeology of Archaic and Classical Greece is now a very diverse field, diverse not only in the subjects of archaeological enquiry but in the approaches employed in these investigations. Old and new approaches exist alongside one another in a kind of disciplinary pluralism. Many of the new approaches originated in anthropological or prehistoric archaeology. It is curious then that one of the chief concerns of prehistory – an interest in environmental and economic change – has had virtually no impact on the Classical field. It is time to consider the reasons for this apparent blind spot.

3.7 'Marble doesn't float': the absent environment

There is an anecdote – perhaps apocryphal – which may help to explain why it is that past environments have not been of much interest to Classical archaeologists. A few years ago a committee of one of the major foreign schools in Athens was trying to plan its excavation strategy for one of its flagship sites. It so happened that this site had many wells which had been filled in with debris dating to the Early Iron Age and Archaic periods. These wells were dug down to some considerable depth, well below the water table. They were waterlogged, and had been lined with planks at their base. One of the members of the committee suggested that these waterlogged deposits were ideal for environmental investigation. Flotation methods could be used to recover samples of pollen, samples which could be dated both by the pottery in the well and by dendrochronological dates obtained from the wood. Others on the committee were not impressed by this suggestion. The site was, after all, Classical. A senior member overrode the proposal by pointing out that 'marble doesn't float'.

Marble, of course, had been the traditional subject of Classical archaeology since Winckelmann. Many early excavations, such as those at Olympia, had been undertaken to find more marble, preferably marble sculpted by the famous. To archaeologists concerned with great works an interest in environmental detail must appear 'banausic'. None the less it is still remarkable that such attitudes persisted into the 1970s, a time in which 'science' had become much more widely

---

[65] Alcock 1993; Alcock *et al.* 1994.

[66] Almost every one of Snodgrass' students has taken issue with him on some key archaeological or historical question; Whitley (1988) on hero cults and (1997b) on literacy; Morris (1987) on demography.

accepted within Greek archaeology. One possible reason for this reluctance to adopt an environmental perspective may be that, just as Winckelmann turned Greek marbles into the expressions of a Classical, aesthetic ideal, so other scholars have idealised the Greek landscape. Oliver Rackham has argued that many scholars have tended to see the real landscape of both ancient and modern times through the prism of landscape painting. Claude, Poussin and the German Romantics are largely responsible for our unconscious ideas of what the Greek landscape ought to be.[67] Of course, if Claude had had a real model for his landscapes, that model was Tuscany and not Greece; and one may ask why it is that anyone should have associated these paintings, with their baroque detail, with the reality of ancient Greece. One has to remember that the serious exploration of Greece by Western travellers only really began in the nineteenth century, and that nineteenth-century conceptions of ancient Greece remained tied to literature and Romantic artifice.[68] Rackham argues that this idealisation of the landscape of ancient Greece has had two consequences. First it has simply inhibited any kind of empirical enquiry into real landscapes; and second it has helped to construct a false view of what the ancient landscape was like. Rackham calls this the 'Ruined Landscape Theory'. Observant nineteenth-century travellers and later scholars did not fail to notice that there was a certain disparity between what they had been led to expect from paintings and what they actually saw. This disparity did not, however, lead them to question their idealisation of Classical Greece, since scattered literary reference could be found which seemed to indicate that many trees had indeed been cut down in antiquity, and goats left to graze at will. Overgrazing goats and the felling of forests were thought to be responsible for the Classical landscape's fall from grace.[69] Though the growth of field survey has made this view less and less tenable, this idealisation of the landscape (and an excessive trust in literary sources) has inhibited proper environmental enquiry.

Of course conditions in Greece are not ideal for many kinds of environmental investigation. Most methods have been developed in Northern Europe, which is wetter and colder than Greece, and where there are many ponds, fens and peat bogs in which pollen evidence had been preserved. Greece for the most part lacks these waterlogged conditions, and the pollen record for the Aegean is poor at best. What pollen evidence we do have does give us some clues as to the climate in the Bronze Age, but provides little or no help when it comes to later periods.[70] We simply cannot place developments in Archaic and Classical Greece into any kind of environmental context, unless we are prepared to assume that the modern environment differs little from the ancient. There has been an equal reluctance to

[67] See Rackham 1983; 1990; Rackham and Moody 1996. See also Snodgrass 1987: 93–7.
[68] Tsigakou 1981.   [69] Rackham 1983; 1990.
[70] See Rackham and Moody 1996: 123–7; Rackham 1990: 99–100. There has been a fair amount of palynological work, but the interests of palynologists tend to lie more in the direction of the 'origins of agriculture' than in the reconstruction of a Classical environment. Most work has also taken place in northern Greece, which is marginal to the history of the Archaic and Classical periods. For pollen diagrams, see Greig and Turner 1974; Bottema 1979; 1982; Wright 1972.

explore the potential for economic archaeology (I am using the term in the sense employed by Eric Higgs, as being an archaeology explicitly concerned with sub-sistence). Studies of animal bones and plant remains from archaeological deposits of Archaic and Classical date have been rare.[71] It is still maintained in some quarters that, since we have scattered literary references as to what ancient Greeks said they ate, we know what it is that they ate. This is to forget that it is one of the tasks of archaeology to explore the differences between what people say they do and what they actually do. Literary references are no substitute for hard archaeological data. Environmental and economic archaeology remain the principal blind spots in the contemporary archaeology of ancient Greece. Whereas certain kinds of 'science', such as the chemical analysis of pottery, have been readily accepted within the field, others, such as environmental approaches, have not. A certain reluctance to use 'science' has also been apparent in one area where, one would have thought, it would be readily agreed it was most necessary, an area which remains the bedrock of all archaeological investigation: chronology.

---

[71] The only bone reports I know of are from the Early Iron Age sites of Kavousi in Crete (Klippel and Snyder 1991) and Nichoria in Messenia (Sloan and Duncan 1978). Recently there has been much more extensive work on bone deposits from sanctuaries, particularly sanctuaries of Demeter; see Jarman 1973 (for Knossos); and Bookidis *et al.* 1999 (for Corinth).

CHAPTER 4

CHRONOLOGY AND TERMINOLOGY

4.1 Some terms

Chronology is essential to archaeology. This is no less true of historical archaeologies, archaeologies which try to relate archaeological evidence to written sources, than it is to prehistory. Precise terminology is also essential to historical enquiry, and readers are entitled to expect some consistency amongst scholars. In Classical archaeology the terms used for archaeological periods have a historical basis. The Classical period (479–323 BC) is defined in both historical and archaeological terms. Historically it covers the time when Greece was a mosaic of independent states, freed from the threat of foreign domination after the Persian wars and (before the death of Alexander) not yet fully subject to the whims of Macedonian potentates. This historical period is also characterised by a particular artistic style we call 'Classical' (see chapter 11 below).[1] Historical and archaeological criteria combine to form a picture of a particular cultural epoch, where ideas like 'naturalism', 'balance' and 'proportion' have their place.

The Archaic period is more difficult to define on historical grounds. The Archaic is simply the period which precedes the Classical and which made the Classical possible. That the Archaic is simply a forerunner, or a less fully realised form of Hellenism, is an old idea that still retains a certain grip on scholarly minds. Historically it is less well known, and consequently it is difficult to decide when the Archaic began. Some take a narrow definition, on the basis of the earliest written testimony; for them the Archaic extends from 700 to 480 BC. Others choose to define the Archaic more broadly, and include the eighth century; yet others split the difference, and define the Archaic as lasting from 750 to 480 BC.[2] Archaeologists tend to be more precise. For them the Archaic begins not earlier than 700 BC. But even here there is a certain amount of confusion. Attempts to define the Archaic period in stylistic terms work best for the late Archaic period.[3] For the earlier part, for the seventh century BC, the term 'Orientalising' is in common use. The seventh century is thought to be the time when Greece was most influenced by Near Eastern and Egyptian culture. 'Orientalising' is an example of how an archaeological, stylistic term can come into general use to

---

[1] For a definition of Classical, see Pollitt 1972: 11–14.
[2] For definitions of the Archaic, see Snodgrass 1980: 11–14.
[3] For attempts to define the Archaic stylistically, see Hurwit 1985: 15–32; Robertson 1975: 34–180.

describe a period of Greek history. Within the Archaic period various terms have been used to describe the material culture, and in particular the pottery. Orientalising is one, to be followed by black-figure and then red-figure (which extends into the Classical period). These last terms have not, however, come into general use as cultural markers – no one speaks of a 'black-figure' period in Greek history.

For periods before the Archaic the terminology is exclusively archaeological, with one important exception. The era between *c.* 1100 and *c.* 700 BC (the terminus varies) is often referred to as the Dark Age of Greece.[4] The term has a historical basis. Dark Ages are not so much historical periods in their own right as intervals between periods whose history is illuminated by written records. Where empires have fallen, civilisations have collapsed and literacy has been lost, and where therefore there can be no written records, there is darkness.[5] There are, however, several archaeological alternatives to this rather loaded term. One is to make the Greek sequence conform to the 'Three Age' system. Thus the Dark Age becomes the Early Iron Age. Another is to define periods by ceramic styles, as with 'Orientalising'. So the earlier part of the Early Iron Age is sometimes called 'Protogeometric', and 'Geometric Greece' has come into common use as a term covering both the ninth and the eighth centuries BC.[6] One must remember here that a pot style is not a period, and that the Geometric style was not universal in 'Geometric Greece' in the ninth century BC.[7] Figure 4.1 provides an illustration of these terms, and their ambiguities.

4.2 Chronology: some principles

So-called scientific techniques of dating are not much used in Greek archaeology; or rather, they have been widely used for prehistory and for the Bronze Age, but not for later periods. There are a few scattered radiocarbon dates, mainly for the Early Iron Age.[8] There are several reasons for this relative neglect of radiocarbon. One is that the radiocarbon calibration curve is so erratic after about 1000 BC as to make many C14 determinations very imprecise; another is that many practitioners believe that standard methods of cross-dating and style yield more precise dates. As for other scientific dating methods, Professor Peter Kuniholm of Cornell University has for some time been trying to build up a complete dendrochronological sequence for the whole of the Aegean, extending back from the present into the Bronze Age.[9] This may in time prove a useful check or corrective to the established chronology. As yet, however, there are too many gaps in the sequence, and too few 'dendro' dates from the Aegean proper to serve this purpose.

[4] For the definition of Dark Age, see Snodgrass 1971: 1–25; Morris 1999: 77–106.
[5] On the general phenomenon of collapse, see Tainter 1988. [6] For example Coldstream 1977.
[7] Again, see Coldstream 1977: 25–106; Snodgrass 1971: 24–105. [8] E.g. Wells 1983: 28.
[9] See for example Kuniholm 1987.

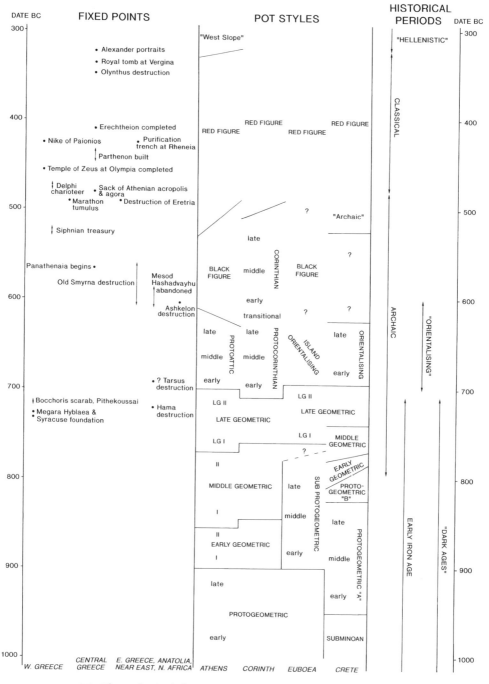

4.1 Chronological chart

Traditional chronology relies on tried and tested methods of sequencing, stylistic analysis and cross-dating. The first task of the chronologist is to establish a relative sequence, either from grave groups or from stratified deposits from settlements or sanctuaries. For the earlier periods fairly detailed relative sequences have now been built up for Athens, Knossos, Argos, Euboea and Corinth. Relative sequences can also be built up through attribution. By grouping pots according to painters, by estimating the degree of stylistic overlap between painters and by reckoning the length of a craftsman's working life, a fairly precise relative sequence can be built up. Such a sequence does not rely primarily on stratified deposits or closed groups, though the good chronologist will seek to use both kinds of evidence. Good relative chronologies for Attic black- and red-figure have been provided by Beazley, and good chronologies for Protocorinthian and Corinthian have been constructed by Payne.[10] Having established a local relative sequence, the next step is to determine whether there are any synchronisms between them. Weak synchronisms can be arrived at by general stylistic similarity, but it is the presence of imports in closed contexts that provides the real key. For example, in the Early Iron Age Attic pottery was exported to both Knossos and Lefkandi, where it has been found in graves. In Lefkandi Early Geometric II pots have been found in Subprotogeometric graves; we can thus peg the Lefkandiot on to the Attic sequence.[11] Such cross-dating between relative sequences does not, of course, yield an absolute date. But cross-dates do substantially reduce the elasticity of any particular sequence, making attempts either to stretch them over several centuries or to compress them into one appear less plausible.

None the less, relative sequences, however well the phases within them may be defined, are not in themselves sufficient to establish a chronology. Relative sequences have to be pegged by fixed points, whose calendar date we can be reasonably sure of. Archaeological sequences have to be related to a number of historical events. Fixed points come in several varieties. The most useful are destructions by fire, usually the result of some invading army sacking a city, a sack which is recorded in the historical record. Destructions often provide a layer of fired debris, and the historical date of such destruction should then provide a *terminus ante quem* (terminus before which) for all the material beneath this destruction horizon and a *terminus post quem* (terminus after which) for all the layers above it. Other kinds of material have also been thought to provide absolute dates. Certain imports, for example Egyptian scarabs with a cartouche of a Pharoah the dates of whose reign are known, can tie a deposit down to a very narrow range of dates. A third type of fixed point is the foundation date. Foundation dates are given for a number of so-called Greek colonies in Sicily by the historians Thucydides, Diodoros and Eusebios. Foundation dates provide, at

[10] Beazley 1956; 1963; Payne 1931. For a summary of Payne's chronology, see Dunbabin 1954; for a summary of the earlier part of Beazley's, see Boardman 1974: 193–5, 234.
[11] Popham *et al.* 1980: 350–4; Coldstream 1977: 63–5.

best, a *terminus post quem* for the earliest (Greek) material from a site.[12] Lastly we have a number of historical sources which provide dates for the erection of certain famous buildings (such as the Parthenon) and of certain celebrated statues.

There are, all in all, quite a number of fixed points for the Classical period, but far fewer for the Archaic, and fewer still for the Early Iron Age. Consequently chronology becomes less and less reliable as we go back in time. Estimating or 'dead reckoning' the intervals between fixed points, or the duration of phases within a particular local sequence, plays a large part in the chronology of Greek archaeology. Readers should beware of the archaeologist's habit of estimating in quarter centuries. Dates such as '825–800 BC' are rarely proper historical calendar dates, but rather archaeological ceramic phases translated into rough calendar terms. They are, as it were, uncalibrated.

4.3 The fixed points

To return to absolute chronology: it would be misleading to suggest that all chronological problems had been solved. Chronology has in recent years become a controversial field in itself. Most of the fixed points have their own ambiguities and uncertainties. Recently E.D. Francis and Michael Vickers have, in a series of articles, ruthlessly exposed the weak links in the traditional chronology. For this reason I will discuss the basis for each of the principal fixed points in some detail, omitting only the fixed points for the beginning of the Early Iron Age and the end of the Bronze Age.[13] I begin with the Near East and the Aegean.

Near Eastern synchronisms

Early Greek pots, in the Protogeometric and Geometric styles, have been found in a number of stratified deposits in Palestine (or Israel), Syria and south-east Turkey. In a site known as Tell Abu Hawam in Palestine some Subprotogeometric pots, probably from Euboea, were found in stratum III, the stratum immediately below a layer of material of Persian date.[14] Some Euboean Late Geometric material has also been found in stratum V at Megiddo.[15] These synchronisms with the Palestinian sequence, however, do not provide absolute dates, since absolute dates are the very thing that archaeologists working in Palestine themselves dispute. There are none the less two destruction deposits which should provide more useful information. We know from Assyrian records that the Assyrian king Sargon II destroyed the city of Hamath (modern Hama) in 722–720 BC. Once destroyed, the city appears not to have been reoccupied until very much later. A number of

---

[12] Foundation dates are given in Thucydides VI.3–5. The best discussion of the literary evidence is still Dunbabin 1948: 435–71; but see now Vallet and Villard 1952: 291–325 and Coldstream 1977: 233–7; Graham 1982a: 89–91.

[13] These are discussed by Snodgrass 1971: 107–13; and Desborough 1964: 237–41.

[14] Hamilton 1935: 23–4; Heurtley 1935.   [15] Clairmont 1955: 99.

Euboean Subprotogeometric pendent semi-circle skyphoi and one Middle Geometric II Attic krater were found in the destruction horizon; a number of unstratified Late Geometric sherds were also found.[16] We also know from Assyrian records that the Assyrian king Sennacherib destroyed the city of Tarsus in south-eastern Turkey in 696 BC. This city has been excavated, and a number of Euboean Subprotogeometric pots, Rhodian 'bird bowls' and one Early Protocorinthian aryballos have been found in closed contexts below the destruction fill.[17] These two destruction horizons thus provide *termini ante quos* for the appearance of all these types of Greek pottery.

The western colonies

Both the fifth-century historian Thucydides and the later chronographer Eusebios have provided us with absolute dates for the establishment of the first Greek settlements in Sicily. Though there is no exact agreement between these two historians as to precise calendar dates, they agree on the sequence of events and differ little in their absolute figures. It is not quite clear how either of these historians arrived at these dates. Thucydides in particular may have used a kind of 'dead reckoning' of generations, checked against the traditions of important Sicilian families such as the Deinomenidai.[18] Other sources inform us that the Sicilian colonies were not the first in the western Mediterranean. They had been preceded by Cumae (Kyme), and by a little-known island colony called Pithekoussai.[19] Pithekoussai (modern Ischia in the bay of Naples) has been thoroughly investigated since 1952, and we now have a good local sequence of grave groups, some with imported Euboean and Corinthian Geometric and Protocorinthian pottery. In one of these graves (325) two children were buried with (amongst other things) two globular early Protocorinthian aryballoi (perfume flasks; see below chapter 6) and a scarab bearing the cartouche of the Pharaoh Bocchoris (718/7–712 BC).[20] This effectively provides us with a *terminus ante quem* for the earliest phase of occupation on Pithekoussai.

For Sicily, Thucydides' dates in particular provide us with, at best, *termini post quos* for the earliest Greek occupation (though not for the earliest Greek contact

---

[16] For the finds from Hama, see Johansen 1957: 106–8; Francis and Vickers 1985. For a general discussion of all Near Eastern synchronisms, see Coldstream 1968: 302–13. I have not discussed the material from Samaria (Crowfoot 1957: 210–12) as the Greek finds are unstratified and so useless for dating purposes.

[17] For Tarsus see Hanfmann 1963: 127–30; Coldstream 1968: 320–1. I am at a loss to understand Boardman's (1965) objections to Hanfmann's arguments and dates.

[18] See again Thucydides VI.3–5 and discussion by Dunbabin 1948: 435–71; Gomme *et al.* 1970: 198–210; Graham 1982a: 89–91; Osborne 1996a: 119–27.

[19] The literary evidence for the foundation of Pithekoussai is Strabo V.4.9; Livy VIII.22.5–6: discussed by Ridgway 1992: 31–7.

[20] For the grave with the Bocchoris scarab (grave 325), see Buchner and Ridgway 1993: 378–82; and more generally Ridgway 1992: 65–7; for the scarab, see de Salvia 1993: 777–80. The two aryballoi are also discussed by Neeft 1987: 372–80.

with the native Sicels). We have good archaeological evidence for three colonies in particular: Syracuse, Megara Hyblaia and Selinous. There is little to distinguish the earliest material from Syracuse and Megara Hyblaia: both have material of Corinthian Late Geometric and Early Protocorinthian date from settlement deposits; Syracuse has largely Early Protocorinthian from the Fusco cemetery.[21] The foundation dates of 732 (Syracuse) and 728 (Megara Hyblaia) can thus be taken as useful fixed points for these phases of the Corinthian sequence. There is more disagreement between ancient authorities over Selinous, and consequently more uncertainty over the chronological significance of the earliest finds there. However, most scholars agree that the site must have been founded around 628 BC. Given the almost total absence of Protocorinthian finds, and allowing for a decade or so for the colony to become established, the finds from Selinous allow us to fix the transition from Late Protocorinthian to Corinthian to the years around 610 BC.[22]

Eastern Greece, North Africa and Palestine

The next set of fixed points come from eastern Greece, North Africa and Palestine. They comprise both foundation dates and dates of destruction and abandonment. Though geographically disparate, they serve to link the Corinthian and East Greek ceramic sequences, and so have been considered together.

The first of these fixed points concerns the Greek colonies established in North Africa, in that part of modern Libya known in Antiquity as Cyrenaica. The fifth-century historian Herodotos describes the events that led to the foundation of all the North African colonies. Though Herodotos does not provide an absolute date, it is clear from his narrative that the events he describes (or rather the traditions he recounts) must have taken place in the late seventh century BC, and probably around 630 BC.[23] Unfortunately for archaeology, one of the earliest colonies established, Aziris, is known only from surface finds, and it seems that the earliest levels in the major colony, Cyrene, have not yet been found.[24] The best that can be said is that the earliest finds from one of the later, daughter-colonies, Taucheira (modern Tocra), are consistent both with Herodotos' narrative and with the standard chronology for Greek ceramic development.[25] Similar difficulties have been

---

[21] For Syracuse, see Vallet and Villard 1952: 329–35; Payne 1931: 13–14, 26–7. For Megara Hyblaia, Vallet and Villard 1952: 335–40. The slight stylistic differences in the finds from the two sites are not enough, in my view, to alter the established chronology. See also Coldstream 1968: 322–7; Graham 1982a: 103–9.

[22] There are two conflicting dates for the foundation of Selinous; Diodoros XIII.59.4 gives a date of 651/50; and Thucydides VI.4.2 a date of 628. Most historians prefer Thucydides' date (though Vallet and Villard 1952 prefer Diodoros'). For the archaeological evidence from Selinous, see Payne 1931: 22–7; Vallet and Villard 1952: 325–8; 1958; Graham 1982b: 167–8. For the circumstances of the colonisation of Selinous, see de Angelis 1994.

[23] Herodotos IV.150–71. See discussion by Osborne 1996a: 8–15.

[24] For a general discussion of the archaeological evidence from North Africa: see Boardman 1966: esp. 150–2 for Aziris. For the earliest finds from Cyrene, see Schaus 1985.

[25] For Taucheira (Tocra), see Herodotos IV.171. For the finds from excavations here, Boardman and Hayes 1966; 1973.

encountered with the earliest finds from the Greek *emporion* (trade colony) at Naucratis in Egypt. Here the date that Herodotos gives for its foundation is in conflict with the archaeological evidence,[26] a problem that will be considered below.

There are however two (or three) fixed points that are of much more use. We know from historical records (principally the Old Testament) that in the late seventh and early sixth centuries BC, there was war in southern Palestine. The end result of these wars was for the Babylonian king, Nebuchadnezzar, to bring the small Hebrew kingdom of Judah to an end, deporting the people of Jerusalem to Babylon.[27] We know from Babylonian records that the city of Ashkelon was sacked in 604 BC. Ashkelon then lay abandoned until the Persian period, and 604 BC is thus a secure *terminus ante quem* for all the imported finds there. Some East Greek 'Middle Wild Goat II' pots and some Transitional Corinthian pottery have been found in the Iron Age destruction levels from this site.[28] The pottery from Ashkelon is clearly of the same character, and certainly from the same horizon, as the finds of imported Greek pottery from the small fort of Mesad Hashadvayhu. We do not know when this site was abandoned, but we do know that it was occupied for only a short period of time, and the presence of Hebrew inscriptions makes it extremely unlikely (if not impossible) that the site could date from the Babylonian period. A date of between 609 and 587 seems most likely for its abandonment.[29] Broad confirmation of these dates, at least as regards the development of Corinthian, comes from the destruction levels of Old Smyrna on the coast of modern Turkey. We know from Herodotos that the Lydian king Alyattes (607–560) seized Old Smyrna, and Herodotos' narrative suggests that this took place early in his reign.[30] Late Protocorinthian, Transitional and Early Corinthian aryballoi (perfume flasks) and kotylai (cups) have been found in the destruction horizon.[31] This destruction cannot realistically be dated after 580 BC, and it seems more probable that it took place earlier, around 600 BC. Again, the evidence from Old Smyrna is, at the very least, consistent with the established chronology for Corinthian pottery.

Greece and the Persian wars

For most of the sixth century we have very few fixed points. The beginning of the Panathenaic games in Athens in 566 BC perhaps provides a *terminus post quem* for the production of black-figure Panathenaic amphoras.[32] We have to wait till the end of the century for more precise correlations. Herodotos records that the

[26] The key passage is Herodotos II.178–9. For a lucid discussion of the archaeological evidence from Naucratis, see Boardman 1980: 117–33; but see also Bowden 1991.
[27] II Kings 22–5; II Chronicles 34–6.   [28] Waldbaum and Magness 1997.
[29] Waldbaum and Magness 1997; Naveh 1962. For the kinds of East Greek pottery referred to, see now Cook and Dupont 1998.
[30] Alyattes' career is described by Herodotos I.16, I.2 and I.86. See discussion of the literary evidence by Kaletsch 1958.   [31] Anderson 1959; Cook 1985.
[32] Beazley 1951: 88–100; Langlotz 1920: 9–11.

4.2 Siphnian treasury, front view

people of Siphnos, who became suddenly rich through the discovery of silver mines, dedicated a 'treasury' at Delphi, and his narrative suggests that this took place sometime in the late sixth century BC (*c.* 525 BC) (fig. 4.2).[33] Delphi has been thoroughly investigated, and the only plausible candidate for this undoubtedly imposing marble treasury is the one so identified by French archaeologists.[34] The next set of dates we owe to the Persians, for whose activities we again have to rely on Herodotos. After the Ionian revolt they took Miletos in 494 BC (Herodotos VI.18–19). Unfortunately the archaeological deposits associated with this sack have never been published. The Persians then mounted a punitive expedition against those two states, Eretria and Athens, which had helped the Ionians in their revolt. The Persians took Eretria in 490 BC and burned its temples.[35] They went on to engage the Athenians at Marathon, where they were defeated. The 192 Athenians who fell in the battle were buried on the battlefield in a great soros or

---

[33] Herodotos III.57–8. The Siphnian treasury is also described by Pausanias X.11.2.

[34] See Daux and Hansen 1987; Langlotz 1920: 17–23; Amandry 1988; *pace* Francis and Vickers 1983: 54–67 and Vickers 1985b: 9–12.

[35] Herodotos VI.101.2–3. For the evidence from the temple of Apollo Daphnephoros, see Auberson 1968. See also Francis and Vickers 1983: 49–54.

tumulus, which has been plausibly identified and excavated. In it was found a cremation tray with some late Attic black-figure lekythoi (oil flasks).[36]

When the Persians returned to Athens ten years later they took the Athenian Acropolis and burnt it. The Acropolis has been thoroughly excavated. There is, however, no clear destruction horizon across the site, more a number of pits filled with material gathered from Athenian cleaning up operations after their return.[37] None the less the destruction of the Acropolis remains one of the key fixed points in Greek archaeology, providing a general *terminus ante quem* for the Archaic period as a whole. In the pits were found numerous examples of late Archaic marble sculpture (and some thought to be early Classical) and numerous fragments of late Archaic red-figure pottery, as well as a considerable quantity of earlier material. These deposits cannot, however, really be seen as sealed or closed; or, if closed, only sealed by the Periclean building operations which began in 447 BC. The possibility remains that some later material has been mixed with this *Perserschutte*. A year later the Persians returned, to ransack and loot Athens.[38] Excavators in the Athenian Agora have noted that at least ten wells, in use during the Archaic period, were filled in with dumped material, material which included a quantity of architectural debris. The pottery from these wells was remarkably homogeneous, including both black-figure and red-figure sherds, and clearly comes from the same horizon. The only plausible historical event that can be associated with this horizon is the second Persian sack of Athens, and the subsequent 'clearing up' operations.[39]

The fifth century

The next fixed point for the general development of Archaic art is the Delphi Charioteer (fig. 1.2), which, for reasons given above, cannot have been erected later than 470 BC. It provides a secure terminus for the development of the early Classical style.[40] A votive inscription, recorded by Pausanias, gives us a *terminus ante quem* for the erection of the temple of Zeus at Olympia of 457 BC.[41] We know from a variety of sources that the Parthenon was begun in 447 BC, and that the building (together with its decoration and cult statue) was completed in

---

[36] For the battle, see Herodotos VI.110–17; for the burial, Thucydides II.34.5; the soros is described by Pausanias I.32.3. For the excavation of the soros see Stais 1893; for a more recent discussion, see Shear 1993: 406–11.

[37] For the capture and burning of the Acropolis by the Persians, see Herodotos VIII.52–3. For the 'Perserschutte', see in particular Graef and Langlotz 1925: i–xxxv; 1933: v–viii; and Langlotz 1920: 98–100.

[38] Herodotos IX.13.2. The ruinous state of Athens after the Persians' departure is described by Thucydides I.89.3.

[39] For the archaeological evidence relating to the second Persian destruction and clearing up operations afterwards, see Shear 1993 *contra* Francis and Vickers 1988.

[40] See references in chapter 1 notes 20 and 21.

[41] Pausanias V.10.4. The votive concerned was a gold shield, commemorating and giving thanks for the Spartan victory over the Athenians at Tanagra (Thucydides I.108.1).

432 BC.[42] A *terminus ante quem* for the phases in the development of Attic red-figure pottery is provided by the purification trench on the island of Rheneia. We know from Thucydides that the Athenians 'purified' (i.e. cleared) the sanctuary of Delos in 425 BC, and placed all the material they found (much from earlier graves) into a trench on the nearby island of Rheneia, which French archaeologists have since excavated.[43] The marble Nike, sculpted by the artist Paionios of Mende (fig. 11.4) and discovered by German archaeologists at Olympia, must, on Pausanias' testimony, have been dedicated shortly after the Athenian and Messenian victory at Sphakteria in 424 BC.[44] Finally, inscriptional evidence provides details of work on the Erechtheion on the Acropolis in 408/9 BC.[45]

The fourth century

There are fewer fixed points for this period. The information given by Pausanias and the elder Pliny for famous fourth-century artists, such as Praxiteles, do not furnish us with precise dates, especially since we do not know that we have any original works (as opposed to Roman copies) of these sculptors (see chapter 11, section 11.2). The first real archaeological datum is the date of the seizure of the town of Olynthos in Chalkidiki by the Macedonian King Philip II in 348 BC, after which the town remained deserted for some centuries.[46] If we could be sure that the tomb of Philip II so identified by Manolis Andronikos is indeed his final resting place, we would have a secure terminus of 336 BC for the finds in one of the royal tombs of Vergina, and a fixed point in the development of Greek wall painting.[47] Though we only have Roman versions or copies of the famous portraits of Alexander sculpted during his lifetime by the artist Lysippos (e.g. fig. 15.7), Alexander's death in 323 provides a fairly secure terminus for the originals.[48] Finally, the habit of inscribing the names of archons on late Panathenaic ampho-

---

[42] The main literary account for the 'Periclean building programme' is Plutarch, *Pericles* 12–13. More information concerning the stages of the construction of the Parthenon is given by various inscriptions, for which see Dinsmoor 1913a. Since these inscriptions give the name of the archon for that year they can be related to the Athenian yearly archons recorded by Diodoros and the Marmor Parium. A *terminus ante quem* for the completion of the Parthenon is given by Thucydides (II.13.5) at the beginning of the Peloponnesian war.

[43] For the purification of Delos and the removal of material to Rheneia, see Thucydides I.8.1; III.104.1–3. For the red-figure from the Rheneia purification trench, see Dugas 1952: esp. 3–5.
   I have not discussed the finds from the polyandrion at Thespiai (Lullies 1940: 8–10) since their relation to historical events is far from clear.

[44] For the Athenian/Messenian victory at Pylos and Sphakteria, see Thucydides IV.37–41. The Nike itself is described by Pausanias V.26.1. For the sculpture itself, and the circumstances of its discovery, see Treu 1897: 182–94; for the accompanying inscription (no. 259), see Dittenberger and Purgold 1896: 378–83.

[45] For the Erechtheion we again rely on epigraphic (inscriptional) evidence; see Dinsmoor 1913b.

[46] The siege and capture of Olynthos is described by Diodorus Siculus (XVI.53) and alluded to (sarcastically) by Demosthenes (*Philippic* III.26 = *Orationes* IX.26). For the finds, see in particular Robinson 1933; 1950. For a lucid discussion of the chronological issues, see Rotroff 1997: 18–20.

[47] For the tomb of Philip at Vergina, see Andronikos 1994: 226–33.

[48] For portraits of Alexander, see Pollitt 1972: 178–84; 1986: 20–2.

ras (between 379 and 312 BC) means that we can determine the end of the Attic red- and black-figure pottery sequence with some precision.[49]

From these fixed points we can establish an overall chronology by relating them to local sequences. For the earlier part of the period our chronological yardstick is the sequence of Attic and Euboean Protogeometric and Geometric pottery, as established by Coldstream and others.[50] For the late eighth, seventh and early sixth centuries we rely principally on the sequence of Corinthian Late Geometric, Protocorinthian and Early Corinthian pottery, as determined by Dunbabin and Payne.[51] For the rest of the sixth century we again have to depend upon the Attic sequence as established by Beazley, and the Attic/Cycladic sequence of Archaic sculpture as arrived at by Richter.[52] Stylistic relations between late Archaic sculpture and vase painting, tied to the fixed points, were worked out by E. Langlotz at the beginning of the twentieth century.[53] For the Classical period as a whole we are for the most part reliant on the Attic sequence, principally on Beazley's groups of pot painters and on a sequence of stratified deposits from excavations in the Athenian Agora and Kerameikos.[54] For the last sixty years or so it was widely believed that the fixed points and the local sequences together yielded a reliable overall chronological scheme. There have however in recent years been attempts to overturn the established chronology, from two very different quarters.

4.4 Orthodox and alternative chronologies

The chronology of the Early Iron Age has always been a subject of dispute, as there is such a long interval between the fixed points at the beginning of this period and those of the eighth century BC. Recently there has been an attempt to compress the 'Dark Ages' from about five centuries into two.[55] This attempt relies principally on a radical reinterpretation of the so-called Sothic system of Egyptian chronology, based on calendrical calculations. The effect of this is to move the 'fixed points' at the beginning of the Dark Age up by a few centuries. I am not really competent to deal with the question of Sothic chronology, but I can say that their attempt to abolish the Early Iron Age is partly based on a misconception – namely that this is a period where the archaeological evidence is sparse in the extreme. There are in fact a number of fairly deeply stratified deposits which date to the Early Iron Age, and, while it would obviously be a mistake to try to estimate the length of a period based on a notional annual rate of natural or cultural deposition, this fact makes the attempt to down-date the Early Iron Age sequence wholesale considerably less plausible.

---

[49] Beazley 1951: 88–100.
[50] Coldstream 1968; 1977; see also for Crete, Brock 1957; for Euboea, Popham *et al.* 1980.
[51] Payne 1931: with modifications by Dunbabin 1954. For recent discussions of the Corinthian sequence, see Amyx 1988: 397–434; Neeft 1987: 363–71.
[52] Beazley 1956; 1963; Richter 1968; 1970.   [53] Langlotz 1920.
[54] Beazley 1963. See also the Agora reports, or at least the evidence as summarised by Camp 1992.
[55] James *et al.* 1991a. See also discussion, James *et al.* 1991b.

A more serious challenge to the traditional chronology has been mounted by
E.D. Francis and M. Vickers. In a series of articles they have argued that the chronology of Greek archaeology needs to be down-dated by about sixty years or so.
While they have paid some attention to Near Eastern synchronisms, most of their
efforts have been directed at the chronology of the late Archaic period. Here they
have attempted a wholesale down-dating of late Archaic architecture, vase painting and sculpture. They have tried to show that many of the 'fixed points' are illusory. In their first (and best) article they tackle the fixed points provided by the
temple of Apollo Daphnephoros at Eretria (which should have been destroyed by
the Persians in 490 BC) and the Siphnian treasury at Delphi (which traditionally
has been dated to 525 BC).[56] The temple of Apollo at Eretria has been extensively
studied by Swiss archaeologists. We know that there were at least four temples
here. The earliest are two apsidal temples, traditionally assigned to the eighth
century BC; over the larger of these a wooden temple was built, to be succeeded
by the last and largest temple in stone. It is the marble pedimental sculptures from
this temple which are conventionally dated to before the Persian destruction in
490, and it is these sculptures that have usually been thought to be contemporary
with other late Archaic examples. To down-date these is thus to down-date late
Archaic sculpture.[57] Francis and Vickers rightly point out that, if we accept this
traditional interpretation, it is exceedingly odd that a later Roman general
managed to remove seemingly Archaic sculptures from Eretria. If it is the latest,
stone temple that the Persians destroyed, where was the temple from which the
general L. Quintius Flaminius removed 'signa priscae artis'? Here Francis and
Vickers have exposed a genuine flaw in the traditional chronology. They then go
on to argue that, since the 'so-called' Siphnian treasury is similar in style, so too
must it be similar in date; and that, since the Eretria temple must be dated to
around 470 BC, so too must the 'Siphnian treasury'.[58] This leaves them with the
difficulty of explaining away the testimony of Herodotos and Pausanias. One solution (the first they adopted) is to accept the identification of the Siphnian treasury proposed by its French excavators, but to argue that Herodotos' words do not
necessarily imply that the Siphnian treasury was built in the late Archaic period,
even though Herodotos only mentions the treasury in the course of describing
events that took place several decades before the Persian wars.[59] This solution is
clearly unsatisfactory, so later Vickers tries another line of attack. He argues that

[56] Francis and Vickers 1983. A general account of their overall chronological scheme is provided by
Vickers 1987b. Other important articles include Francis and Vickers 1985; 1988. A general
summary of all their points is also given by R.M. Cook (1989).
[57] For the temple of Apollo Daphnephoros, see Auberson 1968. For their discussion of this evidence,
see Francis and Vickers 1983: 49–54. Their argument hangs on an interpretation of Livy's words
'signa tabulae priscae artis ornamenta eius generis plura quam pro urbis magnitudine aut opibus
ceteris inventa' (Livy XXXII.16.17). If 'priscus' means 'ancient' or 'archaic', then Flaminius must
have carried off much 'ancient' sculpture as booty. Nowhere however does Livy explicitly say that
any booty was taken from the temple.
[58] For the Siphnian treasury, see Amandry 1988; Daux and Hansen 1987. On its overall stylistic relation to other works, see Hurwit 1985: 292–307.   [59] Francis and Vickers 1983: 54–67.

the French have been mistaken in their identification of the Siphnian treasury;
the so-called Siphnian treasury is in fact a treasury as yet unidentified and which
Pausanias somehow neglected to mention. He does not suggest any alternative
candidates for the treasury that Herodotos mentions. Vickers goes on to argue that
the 'Siphnian' treasury cannot be put before 480 BC, since all caryatids must, on
the basis of a passage in the first-century Roman author Vitruvius, date to after
the Persian wars.[60]

Francis and Vickers have reminded us that chronology is not a matter about
which any archaeologist should be complacent. They have exposed serious weak-
nesses in the orthodox scheme, and so have put forward a new, low chronology
for Archaic and early Classical Greece. But it is not enough to show that an established scheme has flaws. It is also incumbent on them to demonstrate that their
new system accommodates all known facts, that it is internally coherent and
contains no major inconsistencies – in brief, that it is comprehensively better
than its traditional alternative. New schemes should not needlessly multiply
hypotheses, nor should they prefer late to early literary testimony. For we are
dealing with 'fixed points' not in isolation, but in relation to an overall chronological scheme. In this light Francis and Vickers have failed – and this failure is
much more than a failure simply to convince the majority of their colleagues. It
is a failure of reasoning. They have simply ignored evidence that does not suit
their scheme – there are only oblique references to the Marathon tumulus, and
there is no mention at all of the Delphi Charioteer. They have needlessly multiplied hypotheses – we are asked to believe, for example, that it was the 'Ephialtic
cultural revolution' (an event unknown to the fifth-century historians Herodotos
and Thucydides) that was responsible for the destruction of aristocratic monuments on the Athenian Acropolis, and that it is the remains of this event in the
460s that earlier archaeologists have mistaken for the Persian destruction level.[61]
Their scheme also has consequences which they have clearly not thought
through. Francis and Vickers do not question the relative stylistic sequence of
Greek archaeology, and so, like everyone else, rely on Beazley's attributions of
black- and red-figure pottery. We have numerous signatures, apparently of
potters, on numerous black-figure pots which allow us to trace sons succeeding
fathers in the same workshop in at least three cases. So it is surely a major difficulty for their scheme that their chronology would compress a working life of
fifteen years in the traditional scheme to one of seven or so in theirs. We are
forced to choose. Either we reject all of Beazley's work concerning families and
workshops, or we reject Vickers' chronology.[62]

There are then sound methodological grounds for rejecting the Francis/Vickers
chronology. Recently it has been shown that their scheme fails on empirical
grounds as well. They seem to have misinterpreted the evidence from Palestine.[63]

---

[60] Vickers 1985b: 9–12.   [61] Suggested in Vickers 1987.
[62] Boardman 1988d. For a review of the Francis/Vickers chronology, see Cook 1989.
[63] Waldbaum and Magness 1997: *contra* Francis and Vickers 1985.

The final publication of the graves from Pithekoussai has not helped their case.[64] A re-examination of the Agora deposits has made it much more difficult for them to spirit this evidence away.[65] To be sure, the style of the pediments from the temple of Apollo at Eretria remains something the traditional account fails to explain, if at least we are to continue to suppose that sculptural style evolves at a constant rate and in a uniform manner. If however we allow for the possibility of the existence of alternative styles, some more archaic-seeming than others, then this difficulty disappears. The one major anomaly that remains in the traditional picture is the date of the foundation of Naucratis, but it would perhaps be wise to await the publication of the finds from this site (now underway) before passing judgement.

For all these reasons I have preferred to stick with the traditional chronology. This is not due to some ingrained academic conservatism. It is because the traditional scheme is better. It accommodates most (if not all) of the available evidence, it is internally coherent, and it contains no major inconsistencies. The traditional scheme, with the fixed points, is outlined in fig. 4.1. It may be, of course, that future work in dendrochronology or radiocarbon will upset this picture. But, for the time being, all dates given are traditional dates, and it is these dates I will use when it comes to describing, interpreting and explaining the evidence. It is to these tasks that we now turn.

[64] Buchner and Ridgway 1993.   [65] Shear 1993.

PART II

ARCHAIC GREECE, 1000–479 BC

CHAPTER 5

EARLY IRON AGE GREECE, 1000–700 BC

5.1 The end of the Aegean world

If the Archaic period is what made Classical Greece possible, the Early Iron Age is in turn the crucible of Archaic Greece. Changes that took place during this time were to affect the path along which Archaic Greek society would later develop. But the Early Iron Age, or Dark Age, begins with a catastrophe: the collapse of Mycenaean civilisation, and the disappearance of the culture that had grown up with it.

Around 1200 BC all the major palace centres of the Mycenaean kingdoms were destroyed. Though a recognisably Mycenaean culture continued for another hundred years or so (the so-called Late Helladic IIIC (LHIIIC) or Late Minoan IIIC (LMIIIC) period), the political and economic superstructure of Mycenaean states was effectively brought to an end. Palaces, once destroyed, were not rebuilt, and ceased to function as political and administrative centres. Linear B literacy, whose use had in any case been the preserve of a small number of scribes, was lost with the palaces; and the craft skills which had been employed to embellish these centres of power also abruptly disappeared. No more wall paintings were produced, sealstones having ceased to be made some time before 1200 BC.[1]

If the centres of Mycenaean power collapsed abruptly, Mycenaean culture lingered on. In mainland Greece and in the Cyclades, a recognisably Mycenaean style of pottery continued to be manufactured and used, and the Mycenaean practice of multiple interments in chamber tombs was maintained. There are some surprisingly large cemeteries in LHIIIC, such as the one at Perati in Attica.[2] In Crete a slightly different picture emerges. The major palace centre of Mycenaean Crete, Knossos, had probably ceased to function at a much earlier date than the mainland palaces,[3] but coastal towns, such as Palaikastro in eastern Crete, continued to flourish after this, maintaining recognisably Aegean (that is Minoan or Mycenaean) urban culture for a further century. However, some time before 1200 BC, these coastal towns begin to be abandoned, and smaller settlements appear in the most unlikely places. So-called refuge settlements appear from about 1250 BC onwards,

---

[1] See Chadwick 1976: 188–93; Snodgrass 1971: 304–13; Desborough 1964; 1972. For the general phenomenon of 'collapse', see Tainter 1988.   [2] Iakovidis 1969.
[3] See now Driessen 1997 and Popham 1997 for the latest views on the date of the final destruction of Knossos.

located in remote, rocky, defensible positions, often at altitudes in excess of 500 m above sea level. These settlements maintain Minoan (that is local Cretan) traditions in house forms and in most other aspects of material culture (such as pottery) as well as in cult. The best known of these refuge settlements is Karphi, located in a prominent position close to the upland plain of Lasithi. This settlement, spread out as it is over three adjoining hills and covering an area of over 3.5 hectares, is large enough to be called a town.[4] Associated with the town are two cemeteries, on the east and west slopes of the surrounding hills. Here too older traditions are maintained. The cemeteries consist of rows of tholos tombs, tombs constructed with a dromos leading to a central corbelled chamber. Such tombs are best seen as modifications of earlier chamber tombs found at Knossos, since chambers of this kind cannot easily be cut into the hard, karst limestone of the uplands of Crete.

Karphi is by no means an isolated example. For some years now the Polish scholar K. Nowicki has been undertaking an island-wide search for more of these sites. We now know of more than a hundred of them. Some of those located in upland regions, like Karphi itself and Kypia above Kalamafki, are large, measuring almost 4 hectares in extent.[5] Most are considerably smaller, sometimes consisting of little more than one or two dwellings perched on a rock. Some 'refuge settlements' are not to be found inland at all. Vrokastro in eastern Crete, for example, is positioned on a steep cliff just above the sea.[6] Though some of these 'refuge settlements', such as the site of Kavousi Kastro, continue in use until the seventh century,[7] many begin to be abandoned at around 1000 BC. It seems that at Karphi, for example, the settlement is relocated a little further down, at the site of Ayios Georgios Papoura.[8]

In Crete at least the transition to the Early Iron Age was, despite major changes in settlement pattern, gradual. Older traditions were maintained, and there does not seem to have been a major reduction in population. In this respect the situation in Crete differed profoundly from that in mainland Greece.

5.2 Disruption and discontinuity: the coming of a 'Dark Age'

Though, on the mainland, Mycenaean culture persisted for a century or so, there was an abrupt change around 1100 BC. The practice of interring successive generations in chamber tombs was suddenly abandoned in many areas of central Greece, such as Attica and the Argolid. Individual burial replaces collective interment. In a number of new cemeteries, such as the new Pompeion cemetery in the Athenian Kerameikos, the dead were buried in stone cists or trenches.[9] In some areas of Greece, cremation is introduced. House forms too change. In Mycenaean

---

[4] Pendlebury *et al.* 1938; Nowicki 1987a; Desborough 1972: 120–9.
[5] On Kypia, see Whitley *et al.* 1999: 238–44. On 'refuge settlements' generally, see Nowicki 1987b.
[6] Hayden 1983.
[7] On Kavousi Kastro, see Coulson 1998; Mook 1998; Gesell *et al.* 1985. For the nearby settlement at Vronda, see Gesell *et al.* 1986.   [8] Watrous 1980: 270–1.   [9] Kraiker and Kübler 1939.

times, most houses and domestic complexes had been rectilinear; after about 1100 or 1050 BC older mainland designs, in particular apsidal houses with porches and oval houses, become more common. Around 1100 too, other, subtler changes that had been gathering speed since the fall of the palaces become more evident. In the late palatial period (LHIIIB) pottery was very homogeneous, there being very little difference between the shape and decoration of pottery found at Mycenae, for example, and at Pylos. During LHIIIC certain regional styles become apparent: the 'close style' and the 'Granary style' in the Argolid; an 'octopus style' in the islands; and some remarkable oddities in western Greece.[10]

After 1100 BC regionalism becomes harder to detect. In Attica the local style is called Submycenaean (best viewed as a local variant of LHIIIC). Its chief characteristic is that it is bad – it has a narrower range of shapes and decorative motifs, and it is much more poorly made than other LHIIIC styles.[11] Though something like 'Submycenaean' seems to have existed in the Argolid and in Euboea, it becomes much harder for the archaeologist to assess the degree to which eleventh-century local styles differed from one another. This is because the eleventh century appears to be a low point in the material record of mainland Greece, particularly in those regions of central Greece where Mycenaean civilisation had flourished and which were later to play a prominent role in Greek history: Attica, Euboea, Boeotia, the Corinthia and the Argolid.[12] In 1971, Anthony Snodgrass came up with some figures for the number of known sites from the mainland and the Cyclades; 320 sites were known from the thirteenth century BC, 130 from the twelfth and only 40 or so from the eleventh.[13] He argued from these figures that there must have been a severe decline in population after the fall of the palaces, a decline particularly marked around 1050 BC. The information from intensive surveys undertaken since 1971 seems to bear out this picture. Surveys in Laconia, in northern Keos, in the southern Argolid and on Melos had great difficulty in locating any sites at all from the Early Iron Age, finds from the eleventh century being particularly hard to find.[14] If Snodgrass' figures exaggerate to some degree the extent of the decline, the case for an overall fall in population seems inescapable. But what had brought this about? And how is this decline related to the other dramatic changes of the eleventh century BC?

The most extensive treatment of these changes remains that of Vincent Desborough. Desborough noted that one of the changes in fashion that seems to take place in the eleventh century is a change in dress. Long bronze (and later iron) dress pins, used for fastening cloaks and, perhaps later, an item of female dress known as the peplos appear in a number of graves.[15] Both pins and the peplos were,

---

[10] Desborough 1964: 1–28.   [11] Desborough 1972: 30–48; Snodgrass 1971: 28–40; Mountjoy 1988.
[12] Desborough 1972: 64–105.   [13] Snodgrass 1971: 364–5.
[14] For Melos, see Cherry 1982. For Keos, see Cherry *et al.* 1991: 245–7. For Laconia, see Cavanagh *et al.* 1996: 31–89. For the southern Argolid, see Langdon 1995 and Jameson *et al.* 1994: 228–48, 372–81.
[15] Desborough 1964: 53–8. For pins generally, see Jacobsthal 1956; and for early Peloponnesian pins, Kilian-Dirlmeier 1984: 66–83.

in later Greek tradition, associated with the Dorians, and the Dorians in turn have been identified with the Herakleidai, whose return in legend marks the end of the Greek Heroic Age. Desborough was inclined to associate these and other 'intrusive elements' together, implying that a change in culture was brought about by a change in population. Desborough tried to locate the origin of many of these 'intrusive traits' in northern Greece, whence the Dorians were supposed to have come, and whence Doric dialects spread from northern Greece into the Peloponnese. In this he was not entirely successful.[16] More recently there have been attempts to revive the theory of the 'Dorian invasion'. Hector Catling has noted a peculiar kind of pottery known as 'Barbarian ware' that seems to occur consistently in association with the period just after the destructions of palaces and other sites at around 1200 BC.[17] 'Barbarian ware' is however a century too early for Desborough's cultural change. Catling has also argued that certain Subminoan warrior burials in Knossos are both markedly different from what had gone before, and remarkably similar to other 'warrior graves' in mainland Greece, implying that cremation with weapons was an idea spread by the Dorians.[18]

I should state here that I am not myself convinced by migration theories. Abrupt culture change can have causes other than an abrupt change in population. Recent scholarship has shown that the relationship between ethnic groups and archaeological 'cultures' is far from clear cut. Material culture may serve as what Jonathan Hall has called the 'indicia' of an ethnic group – or it may not.[19] In any case, the traits that come to make up the distinct cultural package of the eleventh century have in fact diverse points of origin, cremation for example beginning in 'Eteocretan' east Crete rather than 'Dorian' northern Greece.[20] This is not to deny that there may well have been movements of people in the less settled conditions which followed the fall of the Mycenaean palaces. It is rather to assert that we cannot necessarily 'track' these movements by looking at changes in fashion, burial or dress. Still, one fact stands out: the culture had changed, and changed abruptly and decisively. A pattern of life had been set that was to endure until at least 800 BC. One of the key elements in this new pattern was a new technology, a technology that gives the period its name: iron-working.

5.3 The Age of Iron

Working iron is a quite different technology from working bronze. Most bronze objects in the Late Bronze Age were cast in moulds, few items being produced by a combination of hammering and annealing. Early iron technology did not involve

---

[16] Desborough 1972: 106–11; see also Snodgrass 1971: 311–13; Morris 1999: 198–207.
[17] Catling 1981.   [18] Catling 1995.
[19] On 'ethnicity' in the Early Iron Age generally, see Hall 1995b. On the question of archaeological 'cultures', Clarke 1978; Hodder 1982.
[20] Snodgrass 1971: 187–90; Popham 1986. On the material attributes of 'Eteocretans' in these early periods, see Whitley 1998.

casting, but rather smelting and then working the metal by hammering in a hot and semi-liquid state. Production of effective iron tools and weapons (as opposed to trinkets) involves a number of other sophisticated processes, such as carburisation, quenching and tempering. Some at least of these techniques have to be mastered if iron tools and weapons of a standard equivalent to those in bronze are to be produced. Introducing iron technology is thus a major step. The investment in new skills is considerable.[21] What then were the incentives that encouraged Greeks to adopt this new technology?

One advantage that iron has over bronze is that the raw material is much more common. Copper sources are rare in Greece and not that common elsewhere in the eastern Mediterranean; tin is rarer still. Iron ores of various kinds are widely distributed. In 1971 Anthony Snodgrass suggested that the chief incentive behind the adoption of iron was a shortage of bronze.[22] In the Mycenaean palace system, supplies of copper and tin were secured by long-term trade agreements, and ships carrying ingots of both metals sailed from Cyprus and the Levant to Greece. In the disturbed conditions following the fall of the palaces, these trade links were disrupted, and supplies of copper and tin dried up. Bronze can, of course, be recycled, but there is a limit to how often this can be done without catastrophically reducing the quality of the items produced. Eventually, the resulting shortage of bronze led to a desperate search for an alternative technology. This in turn resulted in the wholesale adoption of iron-working in Greece.

There are however serious difficulties with our accepting this explanation. First metallographic study of a number of bronzes from Early Iron Age Greece does not seem to indicate that these bronzes were poor in tin, which is what we would expect if there were a 'bronze shortage'.[23] Second, iron technology in Greece is an imported technology. It was invented in Anatolia, and developed and refined in the twelfth and eleventh centuries in north Syria and especially in Cyprus.[24] Though iron finds in Greece itself are often too corroded for serious scientific study, a comparison of finds from the Levant and Etruria seems to indicate that this new technology had reached a level of considerable sophistication relatively early in its development. Comparisons of weapon types moreover show that the technology was introduced, in a developed form, from Cyprus.[25] Cyprus was the very island from which the Mycenaean palaces imported their copper. If trade relations had been disrupted, how is it that iron technology passed so easily from Cyprus to the Aegean?

Perhaps we should look at the evidence for early iron in Greece in greater detail. A number of small iron objects have been found in Late Bronze Age contexts in the Aegean, but they do not seem to indicate anything more than abortive experiments with an exotic metal.[26] Objects found in twelfth-century BC contexts are for the most part small.[27] In the eleventh century however a greater range of iron

---

[21] Snodgrass 1971: 213–17; 1989.   [22] Snodgrass 1971: 237–9.   [23] Catling *et al.* 1983: 282–3.
[24] Waldbaum 1978.   [25] Snodgrass 1971: 213–17; 1983; Sherratt 1994; Maddin 1983.
[26] Varoufakis 1983.   [27] Snodgrass 1971: 217–21.

Table 5.1 *Metal objects from Early Iron Age graves in central Greece (after Morris 1999: 211, fig. 6.2)*

Period	Number of graves	Number of metal objects	Iron	Bronze	Gold	Silver
SM	376	354	6%	89%	4%	1%
PG	390	446	41%	48%	11%	0%
EG/MG	392	778	27%	45%	27%	1%
Total	1158	1578	26%	55%	18%	1%

Notes:
Key: SM = SubMycenaean (*c.* 1150–1025 BC)
     PG = Protogeometric (*c.* 1025–900 BC)
     EG/MG = Early Geometric to Middle Geometric (*c.* 900–770 BC)

objects is found, including knives (often with bronze rivets) and a few daggers, examples of which have been found in both Knossos and Tiryns.[28] In the tenth century BC the number and range of iron items increases dramatically. Long swords, and iron ornaments such as dress pins and fibulae, have been found in some quantities from grave contexts in Athens, Lefkandi and Knossos. Catling, Snodgrass, Waldbaum and Morris have provided statistical breakdowns of all these finds, and it is clear that their deposition peaks towards the end of the tenth century (table 5.1).[29] Finds from the so-called Areopagus warrior grave in Athens (fig. 5.1) illustrate the range of iron tools and weapons that Greeks were producing around 900 BC: a sword; a horse-bit; two spearheads; an axe; a knife; and a chisel.[30]

By 900 BC many regions of Greece had fully embraced iron technology. There is however considerable debate as to the reasons for this transformation, and its long-term consequences for Greek society. The quality of most iron products in Greece is rarely superior to those in bronze produced at the end of the Bronze Age, and this fact has led Waldbaum to argue that it was not so much a bronze shortage (since links with copper-rich Cyprus were maintained throughout) as a tin shortage that brought on a metallurgical crisis in Greece. Iron was the only possible alternative to tin bronze.[31] Others have pointed out that the reasons so far put forward for the adoption of iron have been narrowly technical. The fact that the first large objects to appear are weapons, particularly daggers and swords, items indelibly associated with masculine prowess, would suggest that there is a symbolic and social dimension to this transformation.[32] Be that as it may, it is the consequences rather than the causes of iron-working that have provoked the most

[28] Snodgrass 1971: 219–28; Catling 1996.
[29] Waldbaum 1978: 31–5; Catling and Catling 1980; Catling 1996; Snodgrass 1996; Morris 1999: 210–18.   [30] Blegen 1952.   [31] Waldbaum 1978: 67–73.
[32] Morris 1989; 1999: 208–18; Sherratt 1994.

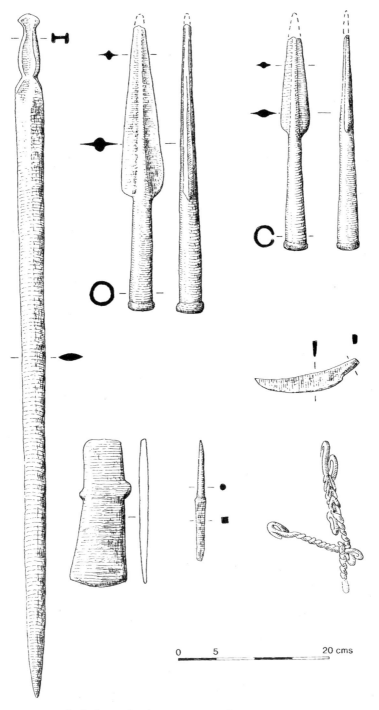

5.1 Iron finds from the Areopagos warrior grave

heated debate. Long ago Childe argued that iron-working was the most momentous and most democratising of technological innovations.[33] There were two strands to his argument. First the relative ubiquity of iron made it for the first time much easier to produce metal tools in some quantity. Iron tools thus considerably increased the productive forces of agrarian societies in Europe and the Near East in the first millennium BC. Second, Childe argued that, whereas Bronze Age palace states had, in part, retained their authority through control over the supply, production and redistribution of bronze objects, the same trick cannot be achieved with iron. Sources of copper and tin are rare; iron is found almost everywhere. Iron-working thus favours a more dispersed pattern of production, and so of political power.

Let us consider these hypotheses in turn. We encounter two difficulties with regard to the effect of iron on the 'productive forces' of Greek society. The first is that there is little positive evidence for iron tools (though there are some). Of course, most of our iron finds are from graves, and this may have led to an overrepresentation of 'status' items such as weapons in the archaeological record. Second, if increased iron tool production led to an increase in 'productive forces', these effects were by no means obvious in Greece for several centuries after 900 BC. Settlements remained dispersed and population low. There are also major empirical difficulties with our accepting Childe's 'democratic' hypothesis. Archaeology and literary sources both seem to indicate that considerable social stratification existed in both European and Near Eastern societies in the first millennium BC. The Assyrian Empire, for example, was a power that made very effective military use of the new technology, without exhibiting any major democratic tendencies. The best that can be said for Childe's suggestion is that the introduction of iron probably made a revival of the particular state structures of the Mycenaean palaces that much more difficult to achieve. None the less there is still something attractive in Childe's suggestion. Democracy did (eventually) appear in Greece, and hierarchy is considerably less evident in the tenth and ninth centuries BC than it had been in the Bronze Age.

5.4 Settlement and society

During the Early Iron Age most settlements in Greece were small. If there is a typical mainland Dark Age settlement, Nichoria in the south-west of the Peloponnese (modern and ancient Messenia) is it.[34] There had been a Bronze Age village here, and, after what appears to have been a brief period of abandonment, a new settlement arose. Instead of the rectilinear structures arranged in rows of streets characteristic of the Late Bronze Age settlement, Dark Age settlement consisted of scattered house plots, placed at odd angles to one another. Buildings of the first phase at Nichoria, such as Unit IV.1 (datable to the tenth century BC),

---

[33] Childe 1964: 190–2, 199–200.   [34] McDonald et al. 1978; 1983.

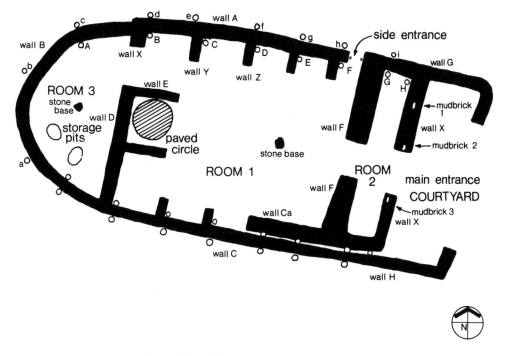

5.2 Plan Unit IV.1 at Nichoria

seem to have been rectangular in shape. The walls of this house were built of mud brick on a stone socle, and the thatched roof was supported by a timber frame – a type of construction absolutely typical of Dark Age Greece. Gradually the apsidal shape began to predominate, and the houses grew in size (fig. 5.2). Unit IV.1 is about 8–10 m in length, whereas its eighth-century successor, Unit IV.5, measured about 16 m.[35] The material culture of this community appears to have been poor. There was some, extremely local, wheelmade pottery. There were a number of bronze ornaments, some trinkets and some iron, again produced from within the region. There was one gold object. There were no imports.[36]

In one respect however Nichoria is rich. Unusually, the excavators took the trouble first to record and then to study the seed and bone evidence. Though the results of the seed analysis were disappointing, analysis of the animal bones reveals that many more cattle were being eaten in the Dark Age than in the Bronze Age.[37] This fact, it has been argued, indicates that there was a switch away from a reliance on cereal agriculture and pulses and towards herding of cattle. Though cereal and pulse cultivation was not abandoned, the rearing of cattle became much more important to the overall diet. Herding may have been a more practical economic

---

[35] Coulson 1983a; see also Mazarakis-Ainian 1997: 174–80.
[36] Coulson 1983b; Catling *et al.* 1983.
[37] Sloan and Duncan 1978; Shay and Shay 1978; see also discussion in McDonald *et al.* 1983: 189–210.

strategy when labour is short but land is plentiful, that is at a time when population appears to have been low.[38] But to what extent can we generalise from this to other Dark Age sites?

At least one other site presents a completely different picture. In a study of the animal bones from Kavousi Kastro and Kavousi Vronda, ovicaprids (sheep/goat) dominated the assemblage. Sheep and goat accounted for over 70 per cent of the bones which could be identified (838 from Vronda, and 2164 from the Kastro). Cattle and pig by contrast accounted for between 5 per cent and 8 per cent of the identifiable bones.[39] Of course, the uplands of eastern Crete have been heavily grazed by goats to this day, and so the result is perhaps not so very surprising. It may none the less indicate the variety of subsistence strategies pursued by Early Iron Age communities in different parts of Greece.

Still, neither the evidence from Nichoria nor that from Kavousi contradicts a picture of Dark Age communities being both poor and isolated. The same however cannot be said of the site of Lefkandi, which lies on the southern shores of the island of Euboea, between what were to become the cities of Eretria and Chalkis. Lefkandi, like Nichoria, appears to have been a loose collection of households, scattered over the neighbouring hills of Xeropolis and Toumba. Lefkandi is by now probably the best known Dark Age site, and one that has consistently managed to surprise its excavators. From Xeropolis there is evidence that the 'lost wax' process for casting bronze was already being used by 900 BC.[40] The cemeteries of Lefkandi, in particular the rich Toumba cemetery, have revealed a rich series of exotic goods. Pottery was imported from nearby Attica; gold ornaments were found in abundance, as were objects in bronze and faience whose origins can be traced to Phoenicia and Egypt (see below, chapter 6).[41] But even finds such as these did not prepare the excavators for the discovery, in 1981, of an extraordinarily large apsidal building on the Toumba hill, whose construction was of a sophistication once thought impossible in tenth-century Greece. The building is over 40 m in length, and is constructed of dressed stone as well as mud brick (figs. 5.3 and 5.4). It also appears to be peripteral i.e. it has an outer colonnade of post-settings to support the roof.[42] Its interpretation remains controversial, especially since the building was unfinished and rich burials have been found beneath its floor. Even the sequence of events, especially the question of whether the burials preceded the building or the building the burials, remains a subject of heated

---

[38] The hypothesis that the Dark Ages witnessed a large-scale shift away from the cultivation of crops and towards herding is put forward by Snodgrass 1987: 189–210. It should be emphasised however that no one has ever argued that agriculture was abandoned during the Dark Ages, or that Dark Age society was wholly pastoral.

[39] See Klippel and Snyder 1991. To be more precise about the data: 7,620 animal bones were recovered from Vronda, 9,990 from the Kastro, of which only 16 per cent and 28 per cent respectively were identifiable. Sheep/goat accounted for 70 per cent (838) of the identifiable specimens from Vronda, and 77.9 per cent (2,164) from the Kastro. For the environmental conditions that make a heavy dependence on ovicaprids a viable strategy, see Rackham and Moody 1996.

[40] Popham et al. 1980: 93–7.   [41] Popham et al. 1980: 109–97, 217–30, 248–51.

[42] Coulton 1993.

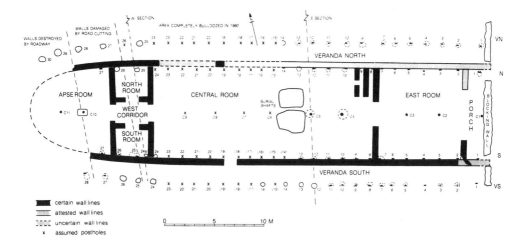

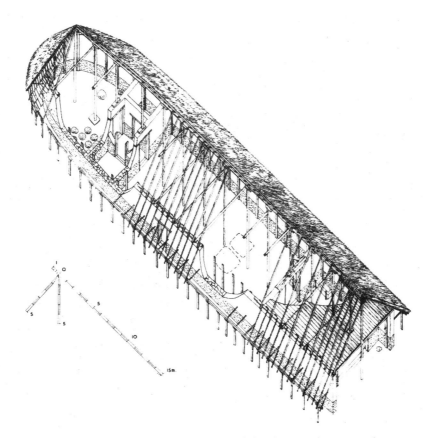

5.3 Lefkandi, plan of the large building at Toumba (the 'heröon')

5.4 Lefkandi, Toumba, reconstruction of the 'heröon' by J.J. Coulton

debate. It is not clear whether it is a house, a communal feasting-hall, a proto-temple or a hero shrine, or whether the building in some way performed a combination of these functions.[43]

Regarding Lefkandi, three things are certain. First, this was no isolated community, but one well connected to the outside world (see chapter 6). Second, whatever the function of the Toumba building, Lefkandi was not a densely packed settlement. Like Nichoria, it appears to have been a loose cluster of households and hamlets, scattered over a wide area. Within this area settlement seems to have moved around a little. The Toumba hill seems to have been used entirely for burials after the destruction of the large building there, and settlement seems to have moved to Xeropolis. Lastly, whatever their relative degree of material wealth, the populations of both Nichoria and Lefkandi appear to have been low. In 1983 Anthony Snodgrass came up with some calculations for the size of the community at Lefkandi, calculations based on the assumption that the excavated burials were a representative sample of those that had once existed.[44] On this basis the population of Lefkandi can hardly have exceeded a few hundreds. But were small settlements such as these typical in Dark Age Greece?

Certainly there were some larger settlements, but larger settlements about which we will probably never know very much in detail. Both Athens and Argos have been built over continuously since Antiquity, and not much survives from their earlier phases. Though we have few, if any, houses from either site, what we lack in houses is made up for in various kinds of indirect evidence, chiefly the fills from disused wells. Athens appears to have been a large, loose settlement – like Lefkandi an agglomeration of individual households and hamlets, each with its own cemetery area, but much bigger.[45] Argos was perhaps more densely settled.[46] Knossos, another site that was important throughout Antiquity, was denser still.[47] But then large settlements are, almost by definition, untypical in any period. We need to take a regional perspective. We need to look at an area, and then at the pattern of settlement within it.

There has been only one considered study of settlement pattern in Dark Age Greece, Donald Haggis' report on his investigations in the Kavousi area of eastern Crete.[48] Haggis tried to understand the settlement system of the Kavousi area through an historical analogy with nineteenth- and twentieth-century settlement patterns. In both times, Haggis argues, there were distinct settlement clusters, that is a collection of small settlements of one or more households. Settlements within a cluster were both socially and economically linked, there often being complementary upland and lowland locations. Within the clusters individual settlement

[43] Popham *et al.* 1982a; Calligas 1988; Whitley 1991b; Mazarakis-Ainian 1997: 48–57.
[44] Snodgrass 1983b: 167–9.
[45] For estimates of the size of Athens, see Desborough 1972: 135–7; Coldstream 1977: 132–7; Morris 1987: 62–9.   [46] Hägg 1982.   [47] Coldstream 1984.
[48] Haggis 1993; 1996: 408–15. For the excavated evidence from sites in the Kavousi area, see Coulson 1998; Gesell *et al.* 1985; 1986.

locations would be periodically abandoned and then reoccupied. The clusters themselves, however, would remain a stable unit. None the less it is not clear to what extent Haggis' model can be applied outside this small area of eastern Crete. Even 40 or so kilometres away, on the Lasithi plain, the settlement pattern seems utterly different. Here, instead of a number of 'settlement clusters' we have two large settlements that succeed one another. Papoura replaces Karphi as the large, nucleated centre of the Lasithi region.[49]

Still, it would not be unreasonable to say that, in general, Dark Age settlements were small; that such that existed were often scattered across the landscape; and that the population was, compared to later periods, low. What kind of social and political organisation is consistent with this pattern? Discussion of Early Iron Age social and political organisation has in the past been dominated by the question of 'Homeric society'. That is the idea, formulated by Moses Finley, that Homer's world is essentially the Greek world of the tenth and ninth centuries BC. Finley argued that too little of the background detail we find in Homer is consistent with what we know of Late Bronze Age palace society, and that nothing in the poems betrays any hint of the political structure we know of as the polis or city-state. Homer's world seems a simple one. Many of the institutions (e.g. gift exchange) and many of the social patterns (e.g. the relationships between lords and commoners) we glimpse in the poems are only consistent with a time when states, of any kind, did not exist, and when the major organising principle of society remained the ties of locality and kin. The only period when life was this simple and whose customs might have been familiar to a poet composing in the eighth century BC is the so-called 'Dark Age'.[50] Many archaeologists, however, doubt whether 'Homeric society' has any reality outside of the poems themselves.[51] Whatever one's view, the relationship between Homer and the social patterns of the Dark Age is far from straightforward.[52]

There are in any case numerous possible ethnographic analogies for what appears to be the slightly unstable settlement system we can see in both Kavousi and Lasithi. It may not be sensible to expect that one single model or analogy will suit all cases, and this is one reason for being suspicious of the very notion of 'Homeric society'. What does seem clear is that the political organisation can hardly have been very complex. A society composed of household or kin groups of more-or-less equal size fits more comfortably with what American anthropologists have termed a ranked society rather than a stratified one.[53] That is, there would certainly have been inequalities of wealth and status, but such inequalities had not become a permanent feature of the social hierarchy. Hierarchies existed,

---

[49] Pendlebury *et al.* 1938; Watrous 1980: 270–1.
[50] For Finley's arguments, see Finley 1979 (first published 1954). For more recent attempts to gain a picture of Early Iron Age society from Homer, see Murray 1980: 38–68. The most recent discussion of the problem is by Osborne 1996a: 137–60.
[51] For example Snodgrass 1974. See also Morris 1986.
[52] For recent discussions of this question, see Donlan 1985; Qviller 1981; Morris 1986; Crielaard 1995; Raaflaub 1998.   [53] Fried 1967.

but shifted constantly, and status was achieved rather than being ascribed.[54] Whoever the *basileis* of Homer and Hesiod were, they were not kings, but men of lesser power (if equal pretension).

Still the study of settlements alone may not be sufficient to answer these questions. I have presented Nichoria and Lefkandi as two extremes, but the difference between them is chiefly one of overall material wealth. If we add Athens, Knossos, Argos and the Kavousi area into the equation, then there seems to be more diversity in settlements than can be accommodated within a single model of social organisation. Settlement diversity is perhaps even greater than I have indicated. Some settlements in the Cyclades, such as Zagora on the island of Andros, do appear to have been densely packed with houses. Furthermore, this settlement was fortified, and many of the houses within it laid out in what appear to be rectangular plots. There seems to have been an overall plan in the layout of Zagora, something conspicuously lacking in other ninth-century settlements.[55] The question then arises: is this range of settlement types reflected in any other kind of evidence? Is 'diversity' a universal feature of Dark Age Greece? And how can we, by scrutinising the archaeology of the period, begin to understand the social and political systems of the Early Iron Age?

5.5 Hierarchy and diversity: pot styles and burial practices

Not so long ago the sequence of Dark Age pottery styles seemed clear. The Late Helladic and Late Minoan IIIC styles were succeeded by 'Sub'mycenaean and 'Sub'minoan respectively. These styles in turn gave way to the Protogeometric, a style first established in Athens whose distinguishing characteristic was the use of compass drawn circles and semi-circles, an example of which is shown in figure 5.5.[56] This severely aniconic (that is, non-representational) style was in turn succeeded, again first in Athens, by the Geometric, whose characteristic motif was the hatched maeander. Figure 5.6 shows an example, a belly-handled amphora datable to the end of Early Geometric found in the Kerameikos cemetery in Athens. The Geometric in turn developed from a predominantly dark-ground style, where most of the body of the vessel was covered in lustrous black paint, to one where, in Middle and Late Geometric, almost the whole of the vessel was covered with geometric designs and 'geometricised' representations of humans, ships and animals (see figs. 6.6, 6.8, 8.6 and 9.3).[57]

Since about 1960, however, it has become apparent that this neat evolutionary scheme only really applies to one region of Greece: Attica. Only in neighbouring areas of central Greece, and in Corinth and in the Argolid in particular, do similar evolutionary developments take place, and in both of these regions Late Geometric styles take a markedly different turn from the Attic.[58] Elsewhere idiosyncrasy

[54] As I argue in Whitley 1991b.   [55] Cambitoglou *et al.* 1971; Cambitoglou *et al.* 1988.
[56] Desborough 1952; 1972: 29–63, 133–58.   [57] Coldstream 1968: 8–90; 1977: 25–81.
[58] Coldstream 1968: 91–147; Courbin 1966.

5.5 Protogeometric neck-handled amphora from Athens, Kerameikos grave 17

5.6 Middle Geometric belly-handled amphora from Athens, Kerameikos (from grave 41, KER 4288)

reigns. On the island of Euboea, principally at the site of Lefkandi, the local Protogeometric style is succeeded in the ninth century by a style called 'Subprotogeometric'.[59] This style retains many of the features of Protogeometric, with a few added local idiosyncrasies. Chief amongst its peculiarities is the retention of the use of compass-drawn circles and semi-circles, principally used to decorate a particular type of drinking cup, the pendent semi-circle skyphos, an example of which is shown in figure 5.7.[60] In western Greece (that is the Ionian Islands, Elis, Achaea, Messenia and Laconia) styles develop which, though clearly Early Iron Age in date and character, owe little to Athenian examples. These are 'Protogeometric' styles without the chief distiguishing feature of Protogeometric, the use of compass drawn circles and semi-circles. For this reason W.D.E. Coulson has classified these styles as 'Dark Age', without further qualification except to divide them into phases.[61] It is these local 'Dark Age' styles that were in use in Nichoria.

Turning to Crete, it seems that pottery from the west of the island is both similar to these 'Dark Age' styles from Messenia and Laconia and also quite distinct from that to be found in the centre.[62] Knossos has perhaps the oddest ceramic sequence in all of Greece.[63] A local Subminoan style is succeeded by a local variant of Protogeometric, one with a repertoire of shapes (such as the krateriskoi and the local varieties of kraters and pithoi) quite different from that of Athens. Knossian Protogeometric is less disciplined than Athenian, and more inclined to make use of figured scenes. In the late ninth century, Protogeometric is succeeded by what should really be called an early Orientalising style, Protogeometric B, whose motifs are borrowed extensively from metal-working (see fig. 6.8 and chapter 6.3 below). Only in the eighth century is there a return to Attic norms of decoration, in the Early, Middle and Late Geometric styles. Even here, local rather than Attic shapes remain predominant.

It is difficult to generalise about other regions of Greece. The Cyclades is not a distinct cultural area at this time, as it had been in the Bronze Age. Thessaly and Skyros seem to follow a Euboean lead.[64] Macedonian sites such as Assiros and Kastanas maintain 'Balkan' traditions of unpainted bucchero pottery, as does the Aeolic island of Lesbos.[65] The Dodecanese seems to follow a broadly Attic pattern of development. What is clear, however, is that it is only in the eighth century that Geometric styles are to be found throughout the Aegean, and that all of these styles show marked regional variations.[66] This regionalism in pot styles is mirrored in burial customs. Every region of Greece has its own distinctive practices. In Attica, from Protogeometric times until the eighth century, adults are cremated, then

[59] Desborough 1980.   [60] Kearsley 1989.   [61] Coulson 1983b; 1985; 1991.
[62] Andreadaki-Vlasaki 1991.
[63] Brock 1957; Desborough 1952: 236–50; 1972: 225–34; Coldstream 1968: 234–55. See now Coldstream 1996 and Catling 1996a for the North Cemetery.
[64] Desborough 1972: 188–202; Coldstream 1977: 40–5, 87–92.
[65] For Assiros, see Wardle 1980: 253–61; 1987: 313–29; 1988: 376–80; 1989: 448–55. For Kastanas, see Becker 1986; Hochstetter 1987; Hänsel 1989.   [66] Coldstream 1968; 1977: 107–292; 1983a.

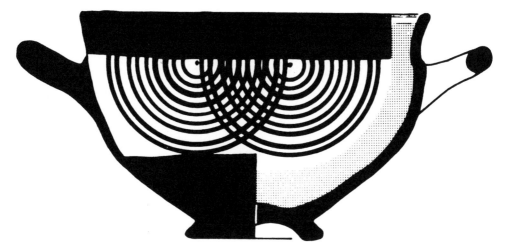

5.7 Subprotogeometric pendent semi-circle skyphos from Lefkandi, Skoubris grave 59

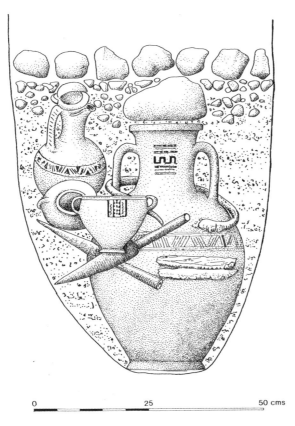

5.8 Section through trench-and-hole cremation burial in Athens (Areopagus Warrior Grave D 16.4)

placed in urns. Men are generally interred in neck-handled amphoras (fig. 5.5), women in belly-handled amphoras (fig. 5.6). The urn is then placed inside a circular pit inside a rectangular trench (see fig. 5.8). Remains of broken pots and animal bones, perhaps from a funeral feast, have been found in these trenches. Children however are treated differently, their unburnt bodies being laid out fully extended in cists or trenches.[67] In the Argolid by contrast, cremation was only practised in the earlier period. Almost all burials were inhumations. Large stone cists or trenches were used for the multiple inhumation of adults. Children's bones seem to be found inside painted or unpainted vessels, mainly to be found in trenches.[68] In the cemeteries of Lefkandi, actual bodies are hard to come by. Cremation in urns (whether bronze or ceramic) seems to have been reserved for adult males. Many tombs appear to be cenotaphs, often large cists with grave goods carefully placed around the 'ghost' of a body, represented by a few token pieces of bone.[69] In Crete (as in Thessaly) tholos and chamber tombs continue to be used. In Knossos both inhumation and cremation were practised, though cremation predominated. All human remains however, whatever the rite involved, were placed in urns, sometimes kraters, but usually a variety of pithos such as the 'straight-necked' or the 'ovoid necked'. There are both plain and painted varieties of these shapes, and burials are to be found in both. These urns, with a few personal items, were then placed in the chamber or dromos of either a chamber tomb or a tholos.[70]

One obvious fact ought to be stressed here: these patterns are regional. Athenian pot styles and burial practices are to be found throughout Attica, and it is the Argolid, rather than the individual communities of Argos, Tiryns or Mycenae, that shares similar burials and pot styles.[71] Regions seem to share what can only be described as a common culture, in Childe's sense of that term. Are there then any traits which are super-regional, which are to be found across the whole Aegean world? Painted pottery in both the Protogeometric and Geometric styles is certainly confined to the Aegean region, excluding the northern islands of Imbros, Samothrace, Lemnos and Thasos. Such pottery is rarely to be found in Macedonia, though it does turn up on sites in the Chalkidiki, such as Torone.[72] Geometric styles of one kind or another are a defining feature of the Aegean world in the eighth century BC. In burials too there appears to have been a degree of shared symbolism. Burials with weapons and (more rarely) armour accompanying male graves are a feature common to many areas of Greece. One of the earliest examples of these 'warrior graves' is the adult male cremation in an antique bronze urn, accompanied by weapons, that was found beneath the large building at Toumba in Lefkandi (see fig. 5.9).[73] Inurned cremation with weapons seems to

---

[67] Morris 1987: 57–62, 76–82; Whitley 1991a: 87–162; Kraiker and Kübler 1939; Kübler 1943; 1954.

[68] Hägg 1974; 1983; Courbin 1957; 1974. Neither Courbin nor Hägg believes that there was any special manner for the treatment of children at burial, but I think both have misinterpreted the evidence (see Whitley 2000). For the hard, osteological facts behind this disagreement, see Charles 1958; 1963.   [69] Popham *et al.* 1980: 196–216.   [70] Brock 1957; Cavanagh 1996.

[71] Morgan and Whitelaw 1991.   [72] Papadopoulos 1996.

[73] Popham *et al.* 1993; see now discussion in Morris 1999: 218–38.

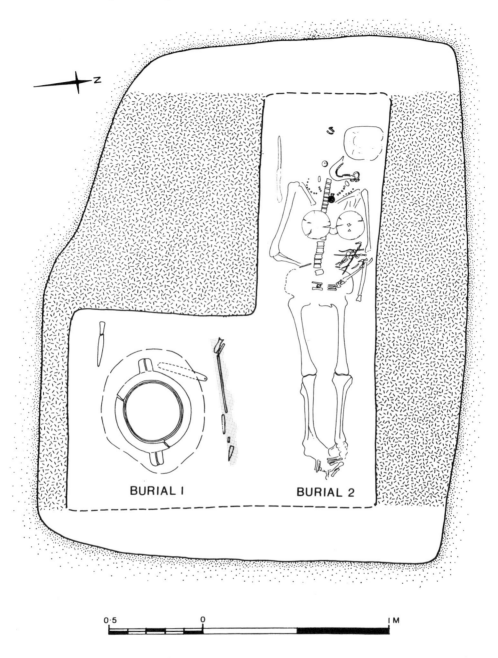

5.9 Plan of male cremation and female inhumation at Lefkandi, Toumba

have remained a male privilege in Euboea from the tenth century until the early seventh. In Eretria, a spectacular set of (apparently male) cremations in bronze urns, accompanied by weapons, has been found near to the West Gate of that city.[74] In the Argolid, male burials with arms was a common practice which, in the eighth century, developed into the spectacular 'cuirass tombs', where warriors are interred with a full panoply of armour (fig. 8.8), together with iron weapons, oboeloi (spits) and firedogs.[75] In Knossos, cremation in urns accompanied by weapons was a frequent occurrence from the eleventh century onwards. In the eighth century, iron oboeloi and fire dogs, similar to the Argive examples, also occur in a number of (presumed) 'warrior graves'.[76] In Athens too, warrior graves are to be found, such as the well-known example from the Areopagus (figs. 5.1 and 5.8). Here, adults males are interred in painted amphoras, their weapons 'killed' and placed around the neck or belly of the vessel.[77]

The only other general rule that seems to apply to the whole of Greece is that children are always treated in a different way from adults. Children are rarely if ever cremated. Child inhumations are either placed in trenches or pits, or their disarticulated bones are placed in painted or plain vessels.[78] It is more difficult to generalise about adult female graves. Rich, but not particularly distinctive, graves of adult women are to be found in both Argos and Lefkandi.[79] Only in Athens, however, do we have a distinct manner of burying important women. In the tenth century, we have numerous cremations of women, accompanied by simple ornaments such as bronze or iron dress pins. In the ninth century, inurned cremation inside belly-handled amphoras (e.g. fig. 5.6) becomes the preserve of a certain class of rich women, now buried with gold jewellery and bronze fibulae (safety pins) as well as pins.[80] Though there is a general switch to inhumation for most adults during the course of the eighth century, some women continue to be buried in a distinct manner with a distinct range of grave goods, of which the horse pyxis is the most characteristic.[81]

This survey of burial types inevitably raises the issues of gender, status and society in Early Iron Age Greece. The existence of a 'panhellenic' form of warrior grave suggests, at the very least, a shared symbolic order where masculinity and warfare are closely connected. With the exceptions of Lefkandi, Toumba and the cuirass tomb at Argos, none of these warrior graves was spectacularly rich. The near ubiquity of this grave type, and its restriction to adult males, suggests that being a warrior was a status that any adult male in Dark Age Greece could achieve. This fact, and the markedly different treatment of children, has led some to

---

[74] For later 'warrior' graves at Lefkandi, see Popham and Lemos 1995; for the Eretria graves, see Bérard 1970.
[75] See especially Courbin 1957; 1983. There are more 'cuirass' graves other than this one in Argos.
[76] Snodgrass 1996.   [77] Blegen 1952; see also Whitley 1991a: 130.
[78] Snodgrass 1971: 143–59.
[79] Examples being the so-called 'queen' of Lefkandi (Popham et al. 1993) and grave T.23 from Argos (Courbin 1974).   [80] Coldstream 1977: 55–63; Smithson 1968; Whitley 1991a: 133–7.
[81] Bohen 1988; Freytag 1974; Young 1939; see also Whitley 2000.

suggest that something like an 'age-grade' system, common to many African societies, was characteristic of Dark Age Greece.[82] But perhaps we should be wary of interpreting 'warrior graves' in too literal a manner, as if grave goods provided us with biographical facts about what a person did and suffered in life. Studies of other cultures with 'warrior graves', such as those conducted by H. Härke on graves from Early Anglo-Saxon England, indicate that burial with weapons, far from representing a status that an individual has achieved in life, is rather a metaphorical way of indicating high status in a society where 'being a man' and 'being a warrior' are closely associated with one another.[83]

However we may wish to interpret warrior graves, there do seem to be few if any lavish, male 'princely' graves in Early Iron Age Greece. There is nothing comparable to the royal tumulus burials at Gordion in Phrygia, nor to the 'princely' graves of seventh-century Etruria.[84] Indeed the nearest we come to 'princely' graves are some collective tombs in Knossos and the rich female graves in Athens, which are considerably richer than their male counterparts. A literal-minded interpretation of the Athenian evidence might be that Dark Age Athens was a kind of matriarchy, a hypothesis which on other grounds (chiefly the relatively low status of Athenian women in the Archaic period) must be considered unlikely. Certainly gender differences in Dark Age Athens were represented in a manner distinct from any other region of Greece. If the vessels used to inter the dead or act as grave markers are anything to go by, men (whose graves were marked by kraters (fig. 8.6)) were strongly associated with wine, whereas women (whose graves were marked by belly-handled amphoras (e.g. fig. 6.6)) were associated with water.[85] The most that can be inferred from this fact is that regional variations in the representation of gender probably indicate a certain regional diversity in social forms. Still, the fact that even the richest graves in the Aegean cannot compare with the rich graves of Phrygia or Etruria, and the fact that the rich female graves we find are all of middle-aged women, are all consistent with a picture of a ranked rather than a stratified society. Status differences existed, but not elaborate, rigid hierarchies. We can, I think, exclude the possibility that many communities in Early Iron Age Greece were 'chiefdoms', that is societies with the kind of elaborate ceremonial and hierarchical structure that anthropologists have said were characteristic of Polynesia.[86] But can we be more precise?

One possible analogy for the kind of ranked society that may have existed in Dark Age Greece is Nuristan, a mountainous region now divided between Afghanistan and Pakistan.[87] This is a society partly agricultural, partly pastoral pagans, composed of patriarchal households of more or less equal size. Here, as

---

[82] Sallares 1991: 160–92 (see also Whitley 1991a: 97–137).   [83] Härke 1990.

[84] For the graves at Gordion, see Young 1981; for 'princely' Italian graves of the seventh century, see Rathje 1979.   [85] Boardman 1988e.

[86] Whitley 1991b. For a description of how Polynesian chiefdoms work, see Sahlins 1963. The concept of 'chiefdom' has been increasingly subject to criticism in recent years; see Yoffee 1993.

[87] Jones 1974. The idea that Dark Age Greece might have much in common with Nuristan was first put forward by Oswyn Murray 1980: 38–68.

perhaps in Dark Age Greece, 'being a warrior' is a prerequisite for 'being a man'. Men compete for honour, first through prowess in hunting and battle, then, later in life, as skilled negotiators or mediators. Wealth, and family position, is necessary to achieve honour, but is by no means a guarantee of individual success. Such a society is not 'acephalous', it is not without leaders; it is one where positions of leadership are temporary, and where neither birth nor wealth offers any guarantee of recognition, status or success.[88] One particularly striking feature of Nuristani society is their use of material culture. The geometric designs which the Nuristani use on many items in the household, and particularly on their clothing, represent the statuses which the head of a particular household has achieved in his life. 'Inflation' in the use of unearned symbols is tightly controlled. I have argued elsewhere that this fact in particular makes Nuristan a very good analogy for the situation in ninth-century Athens.[89] But perhaps this point should not be pressed too closely. What does seem incontrovertible is that the level of social and political complexity to be found in Early Iron Age Greece has much more in common with that of 'Barbarian' Europe in the Late Bronze and Early Iron Age than it does with contemporary, state societies in the Near East and Egypt. This was to change during the course of the eighth century.

5.6 The eighth century: revolution or renaissance?

The eighth century is widely seen as a turning point in Greek history. It was at this time that Greece left the Dark Ages behind, and that Greek society and culture took on a recognisably 'Archaic' character. Many changes took place during this century, changes whose significance is hotly contested. Some see what took place as little short of a revolution, the overturning of an older Dark Age aristocratic social order, and its replacement by a new kind of political structure based on the idea of citizenship: the polis.[90] Others are more inclined to see the transformation in purely cultural terms, as a revival of images, ideas and craft skills which had been current in the Late Bronze Age.[91] For these scholars, the eighth century represents a renaissance, a rebirth of civilisation. Other scholars see both processes at work. But, it may fairly be asked, what were these changes whose significance is so widely disputed?

1. An increase in population (see chapter 8.1 below). In 1977 Snodgrass argued that the rise in the number of burials to be found in both Attica and the Argolid during the eighth century was proof of nothing less than a demographic explosion. The population increased enormously, doubling in size in the course of a century

---

[88] For arguments that the political systems of Dark Age Greece were relatively complex, see Foxhall 1995: 244–50. No one, however, not even Donlan (1985) or Qviller (1981), has suggested that Dark Age Greek communities were 'acephalous'.   [89] Whitley 1991a: 191–4; 1991b: 352–61.
[90] For arguments to this effect, see Snodgrass 1977; 1980a: 15–48; Morris 1987; 1997.
[91] See articles in Hägg 1983b; see also Benson 1970.

(see fig. 8.10).[92] Studies undertaken in other large cemeteries, in particular the North Cemetery at Knossos, reveal that this increase is not confined to central Greece.[93] Other scholars have expressed serious reservations as to whether numbers of burials can ever be an exact reflection of a living population, since burials reflect the level of mortality, rather than the number alive at any one time. Other factors, such as famine or disease, may be responsible for such increases.[94] Peculiar burial practices, or forms of social exclusion, may affect the number of burials visible to the archaeologist. Certainly the burial record of Attica appears to be very bizarre if it is treated as a straightforward index of demographic change. Even so, it would be difficult to explain the rate at which the number of interments rises without positing some increase in population, particularly when there is a concomitant rise in the number of occupied sites in Attica in the eighth century as compared to the ninth.[95] More striking perhaps than the evidence from burials are the results of recent surveys. In islands such as Melos or northern Keos, there seems to have been an increase in the number of rural sites, if not in the eighth, at least in the seventh century BC.[96] In the southern Argolid, the increase in rural sites throughout the course of the eighth century is even more dramatic.[97] That there was a general increase in population throughout the Aegean world in the course of the eighth and seventh centuries, subject of course to local and regional variation, seems undeniable.

2. The appearance of sanctuaries and votives. Whether there were particular localities reserved for cult, with their own altars and temples, during the Dark Ages in mainland Greece is a complex question, which I will return to later (see chapter 7.1 below). Equally controversial is the question of 'continuity of cult' from Bronze Age times. What cannot be denied is that many more sanctuaries were established in the eighth century than in either of the two preceding centuries. More significant perhaps is the enormous increase in votive offerings that takes place at this time.[98] Objects which can have had no function other than as dedications to gods or heroes are to be found in much larger numbers in the eighth century than they were in the ninth (see tables 7.1, 12.1 and 12.2). Moreover, during the course of the eighth century it is sanctuaries, rather than graves, which become the principal context for the disposal of valuable objects, particularly bronzes.

3. Increasing contact with the Mediterranean world beyond the Aegean. It is certain that the first Greek colonies, whether these were trading posts or permanent new communities, were established in the eighth century and not before. It

---

[92] Snodgrass 1977; 1980: 20–4; see now also Tandy 1997: 19–58; Sallares 1991: 44–293.

[93] Cavanagh 1996.   [94] Camp 1979; but see also Snodgrass 1983b: 169–71.

[95] For the Athenian burial record generally, see again Morris 1987. For the increase in the number of settlements in eighth-century Attica, see *ibid.*: 156–67; Osborne 1996a: 74–81.

[96] For Melos see Cherry 1982: but also the comments of R. Catling (1984). It may be that a number of sites attributed to the 'Geometric' period were so dated on the basis of 'Subgeometric' pottery, and so should be down-dated to the seventh century BC. For Keos see Cherry *et al.* 1991: 245–8, 328–37.

[97] Langdon 1995; Jameson *et al.* 1994: 228–48, 372–81.

[98] Snodgrass 1980a: 52–4; Osborne 1996a: 92–5.

is more difficult, however, to assess the extent of trade and exchange with the outside world in the eighth century as compared to earlier periods. Colonisation may simply be the culmination of a longer process (see chapter 6 below).

4. Changes in artistic practice (see chapter 9.1 and 9.2 below). During the course of the eighth century scenes with figures, both human and animal, became a more important feature of the decoration on Geometric pots and contemporary metalwork. The Geometric gradually became less Geometric, to be replaced by the 'Orientalising' styles of the seventh century.[99] Some of these artistic innovations seem to have been inspired by examples from the Near East and Egypt (though some scholars see in these same examples signs of a Mycenaean revival). This artistic revolution is thus connected to a wider cultural process we call the Orientalising (see below chapter 6). In this light, to see the eighth century as the crucial period in the transition from Geometric to figured styles is to take a narrowly Athenocentric perspective. Figured styles had developed earlier elsewhere, notably in north central Crete, and for many art historians the key innovations took place in the seventh century. Neither revolution nor renaissance seems the right term for these changes, except for those scholars who see Mycenaean prototypes for every new figure to be seen in eighth-century art.[100]

5. The recovery of literacy. Linear B had fallen into disuse after the end of the Mycenaean palaces. In the eighth century we find the first epigraphic (that is inscriptional) evidence for the use of the alphabet in Greece, a good example being 'Nestor's cup' from Pithekoussai (fig. 6.12). There can be no doubt that the Greek alphabet is inspired by the Phoenician, and that the adoption of the alphabet is another feature of that long-term process we call the Orientalising (see chapter 6.5 below).

6. The rise of the polis (see chapter 8 below). The other changes I have listed have, in a sense, all been archaeological, straightforward empirical generalisations based directly on the material record. The 'rise of the polis' is different in that it is both an interpretation based on these phenomena, and, in part, an explanation for them. None the less one necessary condition for the rise of a 'city-state' (polis) is the rise of cities or towns, and there is some evidence to suggest that some communities (such as Athens and Eretria) grew tremendously during the course of the eighth century. However, the phrase 'the rise of the polis' implies that a major social and political transformation also took place. This transformation, it has been argued, involved both the creation of state sanctuaries and the invention of a new concept, the citizen. How the idea of citizenship can be inferred from archaeological evidence is hardly a straightforward matter. One aspect of citizenship in later Archaic and Classical times seems to have been participation in the military class known as hoplites. If so, changes in armour, weapons and tactics may provide indirect indications of this transformation.

[99] Cook 1972: 13–160.   [100] E.g. Benson 1970.

It has become clearer in recent years that many of these changes have their roots in periods earlier than the eighth century. The increase in trade with the Levant was underway perhaps as early as the tenth century, and other things we associate with the 'Orientalising revolution', such as experiments with figurative art, took place during the ninth. The Orientalising was thus a long-term process, a process which cannot be distilled into a complex of near contemporaneous events in the eighth century. The same is true of the emergence of sanctuaries, since sanctuaries existed on the mainland long before the eighth century. Even the demographic revolution has its roots in earlier times. Snodgrass has argued that the eighth-century increase in population can only have been made possible through a change in subsistence practice. Only agriculture, that is intensive cultivation of cereals, pulses, olives and vines, could have supported the populations of the eighth and seventh centuries. Herding is a strategy for low populations where land is plentiful; herding and population increase are incompatible. In this area too there is evidence that changes in subsistence practice were underway in the ninth century. It is, after all, in rich ninth-century graves in Athens that we find models of granaries being deposited as grave goods. To equate wealth in general with wealth in grain implies not merely a shift in subsistence practice, but also a new social importance attached to agriculture and the ownership of land.[101] New settlements were also being established in the ninth century, Zagora on Andros being only the largest of those to be founded in the Cyclades.[102] Surveys moreover have shown that, in some areas, an increase in rural settlement was already underway by about 800 BC. In the southern Argolid, for example, the most dramatic rise in settlement numbers takes place between the Early and Middle Geometric periods.[103]

Many would argue that, despite all of this, the eighth century should still be regarded as a watershed. A watershed is, even allowing for a certain mixing of metaphors, not a revolution. It may still count as a renaissance, but the evidence for any kind of Mycenaean 'revival' is very slim. Perhaps another metaphor is more appropriate, that of a crossroads. The eighth century was when the cumulative effect of various long-term processes of transformation began to be felt. The looser, more fluid patterns of life and settlement that had prevailed in the Dark Ages could no longer be sustained. It remains to look at these longer-term processes in more detail, beginning with that cultural transformation we call the Orientalising.

---

[101] Smithson 1968; Snodgrass 1980a: 35–6.   [102] Cambitoglou *et al.* 1971; Cambitoglou *et al.* 1988.
[103] Jameson *et al.* 1994: 237–8, figs. 4.18, 4.19 and 4.20.

CHAPTER 6

THE AEGEAN, THE LEVANT AND THE WEST: THE ORIENTALISING PHENOMENON

6.1 Defining the Orientalising

Figure 6.1 shows an aryballos, a flask for perfumed oil, manufactured in Corinth around the middle of the seventh century BC, and now in the Pergamon museum in Berlin. The vessel is small but elaborately decorated. Its ornament is a rich mixture of curvilinear motifs and human and animal figures, arranged in several registers: on the handle there is a guilloche, a kind of elaborately interlaced cable; on the shoulder, a palmette; on the belly, a frieze of men, horses and chariots; and below this another frieze, showing goats and lions. I am not concerned here with interpretation, with establishing the meaning of these scenes; nor do I wish to modify its attribution (to someone connoisseurs call the 'Ajax painter').[1] I am rather concerned with its lineage. This aryballos is (rightly) regarded as a specimen of an Early Orientalising style of pot painting, whose local manifestation, in Corinth, is called Protocorinthian. This Orientalising style marks a decisive break with the local Corinthian Geometric, which had been particularly strict in its rejection of the human figure and the Levantine motif.[2] The very term 'Orientalising' suggests that this change came about through Oriental (that is Levantine or Near Eastern) 'influence'.

There are three areas in which the vessel's overall design is indebted to the East. First, in its shape: the idea of a perfume flask, particularly one with a wide, flat lip, can be traced back to Cyprus in the ninth century BC.[3] Second, in the elements of its decoration: both the guilloche and, more significantly, the palmette, have a distinguished ancestry in Oriental and Egyptian metal- and stonework; and human and animal figures not dissimilar to these have been found in 'Phoenician' bronze bowls recovered from Greek contexts (e.g. fig. 6.2).[4] Lastly, its Oriental ancestry is betrayed by its decorative technique: the figures (horses, humans, lions and goats) are first painted in black, and then the details of eyes, hair, manes and bridles are outlined by incision with some pointed instrument. This combination of black paint with outlining in incision is called black-figure, and was first developed in

---

[1] Benson 1995; 1989: 43–4.   [2] Benson 1989: 11–17; Coldstream 1968: 98–111.
[3] Coldstream 1984b.
[4] Markoe 1985: 162–9, 203–9. There have been thirteen such bowls found in Crete, and twelve from the rest of Greece. For new finds from Lefkandi, see Popham *et al.* 1989; Popham 1995; Popham and Lemos 1996.

6.1 Protocorinthian aryballos – Pergamon Museum Berlin no. 3319

Corinth. Incision is not found on Cypriot or Phoenician pottery, but is common on Levantine metalwork, particularly on 'Phoenician' bronze bowls mentioned earlier.[5] Herein lay the Greek craftsman's genius for innovation: in the application of a technique proper to metal-working to a new medium, pot painting, to new and brilliant effect.

That, in essence, is the Orientalising phenomenon: the transformation of Levantine ideas, techniques and images to suit new, Greek purposes. That Greece owed much, if not everything, to the Near East is not in doubt. No one would deny that one of the principal factors in the transformation of Greek culture, politics and society in the eighth and seventh centuries BC was the adoption of a whole host of ideas, images and technologies from Egypt and elsewhere in the Near East. The adoption of the Greek alphabet, the development of figurative art styles, and the beginnings of Greek colonisation in the western Mediterranean and the Black Sea were all, in part, due to this stimulus from the East. But is this a simple case of cause (the Orient) and effect (the Orientalising)? Can we still be satisfied with Robert Cook's explanation for 'Orientalising' innovations in pot decoration, when he states that 'the growing exhaustion of the Geometric style . . . opened the way to new influences, and Oriental models were handy'?[6] The Orientalising is still too frequently seen as a phase or an episode, something without which Greek culture would not have developed in the way it did, but not something that has to be explained in its own right. Renewed contact inevitably follows a period of relative isolation; with contact comes trade, and a flow of ideas, images and technologies.

[5] Markoe 1985: 9–12.   [6] Cook 1972: 41.

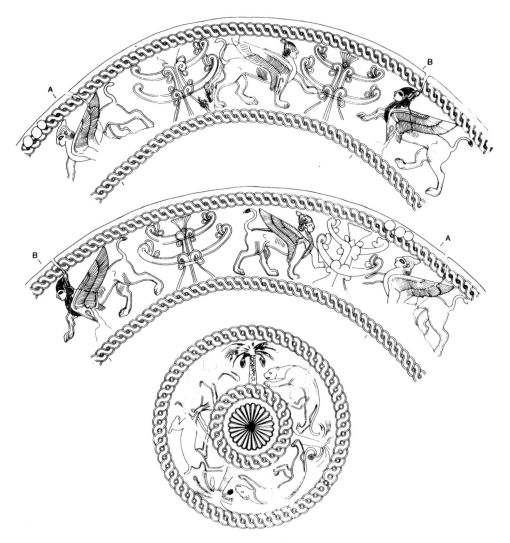

6.2 Phoenician bronze bowl (T.55,28) from Toumba grave 55 at Lefkandi

Contact between an advanced civilisation (the Near East and Egypt) and a more primitive culture (Dark Age Greece) leads inevitably to the less advanced society borrowing extensively from the civilisation with which it has been in contact. In this view of things, the role of the less advanced culture is passive; it is simply a grateful recipient of the fruits of civilisation.[7] In this diffusionist perspective,

---

[7] This attitude is, unfortunately, constantly reinforced by the unthinking use of the term 'influence' to describe the relationship between two cultures when one borrows extensively from the other. 'Influence' is a term that encourages bad thinking. As Baxandall (1985: 58–9) puts it: '"Influence" is a curse . . . because of its wrong-headed grammatical prejudice about who is the agent and who is the patient; it seems to reverse the active/passive relation which the historical actor experiences and the inferential beholder will wish to take into account.'

contact is both a necessary and a sufficient condition for a change in culture. The Orientalising was a phenomenon simply waiting to happen; it does not have to be explained.[8]

All this is not to say that the Orientalising phenomenon is not controversial; far from it. The publication of Martin Bernal's *Black Athena* has made the relationships between Greece, Egypt and the Near East a very hot topic indeed.[9] Bernal maintains: (a) that Greek culture owes much more to the Near East and Egypt than any scholar has hitherto been willing to admit; (b) that Near Eastern and Egyptian influence (and, at times, political control) was largely responsible for shaping Greek culture in the Bronze Age; (c) that it was this Bronze Age culture that, in turn, shaped Iron Age and Archaic Greece; and (d) that there is a kind of academic conspiracy to conceal these facts from the wider public. More recently other books have appeared seeking to document in great detail the degree of Greece's indebtedness to the Near East. Walter Burkert's *The Orientalizing Revolution* is concerned to demonstrate the revolutionary character of the Orientalising innovations of the eighth and seventh centuries BC.[10] Sarah Morris' *Daidalos* is a rich concoction of literary and archaeological facts, tracing many aspects of Archaic and Classical Greek culture to an Oriental source.[11] Morris does not care to be too precise about when and how certain traits were transmitted. She deliberately blurs the distinction between, for example, 'Minoan' and 'Daedalic' Crete.[12] This is unfortunate, as it fails to make use of the chief merit of archaeological as opposed to literary evidence in a protohistoric period, namely that we can be much more precise with the former. It may be possible to say, for example, that many elements in Hesiod's tales have Near Eastern antecedents, but we will never be able to tell how and when these elements were transmitted from north Syria to Greece. Were they part of a Bronze Age oral tradition that Hesiod inherited, or do they signify a period of literary transmission in Hesiod's own time? It is impossible to say.[13] It is otherwise with archaeology. The sheer quantity of archaeological information, and the fact that many artefacts can be dated with some assurance to within a quarter century, enables us to be very precise about which aspects of 'Oriental' material culture were adopted by Greek communities, and when. Archaeology enables us to trace the effects of Oriental ideas in particular media (pot painting, say, or metalwork) and in different parts of the Greek world.

Bernal and Morris differ from more traditional scholars in placing the beginning of the Orientalising at a much earlier date. But they agree with traditionalists in one fundamental respect; they both believe that there is little here to be explained. For Morris this is because Greek culture was Oriental in all essential respects.

[8] Diffusionism, that is the notion that the ideas, techniques and culture of an advanced civilisation simply spread or diffuse naturally among that civilisation's more backward neighbours, is rarely something for which explicit arguments are put forward when scholars discuss the relationship between the Near East and Greece; it is simply assumed to be the case.

[9] Bernal 1987. For criticisms of Bernal, see Marchand and Grafton 1997; Shanks 1995: 86–91.

[10] Burkert 1992.   [11] S.P. Morris 1992.   [12] S.P. Morris 1992: 150–94.   [13] Walcot 1966.

This may, in a broad sense, be true, but it does little to account for the manifest change in culture that took place in Greece between 950 and 650 BC. For if neither Bernal nor Morris quite believes that either Greek or Near Eastern culture is a stable essence, their language at times comes close to endorsing such an assumption.[14] For them, an Oriental trait remains Oriental, however it may be reconfigured in a new cultural matrix. Or, to put it another way, if culture is a quilt made up of the 'shreds and patches' of other cultures, it is enough for the historian to identify the origin of the individual patches. The overall design, whence the quilt (or the culture) derives its coherence, is none of their concern. Both fail to understand that culture and culture change are processes. There never was a stable or homogeneous 'Oriental' culture, nor was there ever, except in Romantic retrospect, a stable Greek one. Both Greek and Oriental culture were subject, albeit to different degrees and at different rates, to constant change. What we have to explain is how, when and why Oriental ideas, images and technologies were adopted. What local circumstances made such adoption useful and propitious? What kinds or degrees of selectivity were there in the adoption of these Oriental traits? And what were the consequences, locally or more widely, of such adoption? To do this we have to look at the Orientalising phenomenon in different regions of Greece: Athens, Crete, Euboea and Corinth. But perhaps to do this is right away to look at the problem from the wrong end of the telescope. Who were these 'Orientals', after all, and what interest did they have in Greece?

6.2 Phoenician traders and Levantine craftsmen

The terms 'Oriental' and 'Near Eastern' are far from precise. Inevitably for Westerners, they conjure up images of luxury, despotism and caprice, and their continued use (as Said has argued) implies that the essential character of Near Eastern culture remains unchanged over several millennia.[15] But the Near East in the first millennium BC was a culturally diverse region, a mosaic of small and large states constantly under pressure from Assyria. The area was divided into several cultural and linguistic zones (see figs. 6.3 and 6.4). Working from south to north, these were:

1 Egypt, whose culture (despite political divisions) continued with little change throughout the early first millennium BC. For much of this time the Egyptian capital was at Tanis. Egypt continued to produce numerous artefacts that reached Greece, and Egyptian art was to have a major impact on Greek.

---

[14] By this I mean that both Bernal and Morris are cultural historians who see cultures as being made up of the accidents, or the 'shreds and patches', of history. Cultures are like magpies; they just pick things up and keep them. For cultural historians of this stamp, there is no underlying logic – symbolic, economic or social – to any particular culture, and so no point in employing perspectives which seek to discern the system (or the structure) behind the culture. For these scholars, anthropological approaches, whether functionalist, structuralist or processualist, are all equally useless.

[15] Said 1995.

2 Philistia, the land of the Philistines. This was a region of the Levantine coast corresponding to the Gaza strip and modern Israel as far north as modern Tel Aviv. Ashkelon (Ascalon) and Gaza were its principal cities. There was little contact between the Aegean and Philistia.

3 Israel and Judah: first one, then two kingdoms in the hills behind Philistia, corresponding to most of modern Israel and Palestine. The principal cities were Jerusalem and Samaria. Despite the rich Hebrew literary tradition, there are few signs of extensive cultural exchange between Israel and the Aegean.

4 Aram or Aramaea. This corresponds to the bulk of modern Syria, to the east of the mountains of the Lebanon. Its principal cities were Hama (or Hamath) and Damascus. Aramaean became an important language in this period, inscriptions in Aramaic being quite common in the Near East and the Mediterranean. The Aramaeans were not seafarers however, despite the fact that they (intermittently) controlled the coast of northern Syria.

5 Phoenicia. The Phoenicians were undoubtedly the most important traders in the first half of the first millennium BC. Phoenicia was a coastal area, corresponding to modern Lebanon. It extended from Mt Carmel in the south to Arvad in the north, bounded on the east by the mountains of the Lebanon. The principal cities of Phoenicia in the Iron Age were Tyre and Sidon, though Byblos and other Bronze Age Canaanite centres remained important. Like the Aramaeans and the Hebrews, the Phoenicians were one of the first Semitic peoples to employ a version of the consonantal alphabet that had been invented in this area towards the end of the Bronze Age. The Phoenicians also produced a sophisticated, if eclectic, art style, numerous examples of which have been found in Greece.

6 North Syria. This is an ill-defined area, extending from the coast by the mouth of the Orontes to the banks of the Euphrates. Its principal cities were Unqi (Tell Tayinat), Aleppo and Carchemish. It was however home to an influential school of bronze-working and ivory-carving.

7 Cyprus. Cyprus was a multicultural island, most of whose inhabitants spoke Greek, but where there were important minorities of 'Eteocypriots', particularly at Amathus, and (later) of Phoenicians at Kition. Many of the Levantine artefacts that later found their way to the Aegean were produced in Cyprus.

8 Cilicia, a 'Neo-Hittite' region, whose principal city was Tarsus.

The Greeks, of course, had other neighbours to the east. In Anatolia (modern Turkey) both the Phrygians (whose capital was at Gordion) and the Lydians (whose principal town was Sardis) were to have some impact on Greek history and culture. But both these and other Anatolian peoples (such as the Carians and the Lycians) were, broadly speaking, at the same cultural level as Aegean Greeks throughout the first half of the first millennium BC. There is little to suggest that Lydian or Phrygian ideas, images or technologies had any major effects on Greek culture.[16]

[16] Boardman 1980: 84–102.

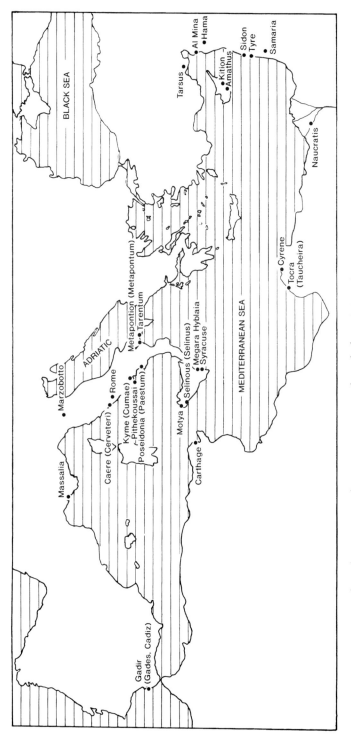

6.3 Map of Mediterranean, showing major Greek and Phoenician sites

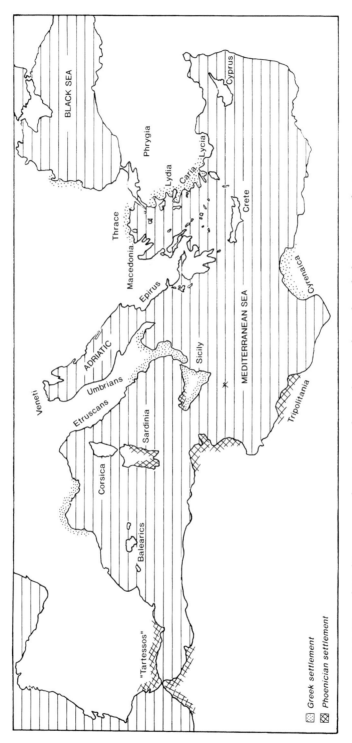

6.4 Map of Mediterranean, showing peoples and areas of Greek and Phoenician colonisation

BLACK SEA

Phrygia

Cyprus

Lydia

Caria

Lycia

Thrace

Crete

Macedonia

Epirus

Cyrenaica

Veneti

ADRIATIC

Umbrians

Sicily

MEDITERRANEAN SEA

Etruscans

Sardinia

Tripolitania

Corsica

Balearics

"Tartessos"

Greek settlement

Phoenician settlement

As for Assyria, Babylonia and the mountain kingdom of Urartu, the effect of these cultures was felt indirectly, particularly through the pressure that Assyria exerted on north Syria and Phoenicia.

Of all the peoples of the Levant, the Phoenicians were by far the most important, at least as far as Greeks were concerned. The Phoenicians were the trading people *par excellence* of the early first millennium BC, and Phoenician bronze, silver and ivory work are to be found all over the Mediterranean world. North Syria too was an important centre of bronze-working and ivory-carving.[17] It is Cyprus however that seems to have been the chief centre of craft production in this period. Cyprus had had a particularly rich bronze-working industry in the Late Bronze Age (thirteenth to twelfth centuries BC). This industry was responsible for some striking objects. Two in particular stand out: the wheeled stand and the rod-tripod.[18] The distribution of these objects is wide. They have turned up in Cyprus, Crete, the Greek islands and the Greek mainland, and in Sardinia and central Italy. They are also often to be found in contexts much later in date than their supposed date of production.[19] If we accept Catling's dating, the bronze rod-tripod found in an eighth-century grave in the Pnyx must have been over 400 years old by the time it was deposited.[20] Considerations such as these have led some scholars to suppose that production of, and trade in, these objects must have been continuous from 1200 to 800 BC.[21] Still, for the basic design of an artefact type produced by twenty generations of craftsmen to remain fundamentally unchanged would be a remarkable feat, and for this reason I prefer to retain Catling's dating.

Two things can be inferred from the distribution, in space and time, of these two classes of artefact. First, even during the disturbed conditions of the twelfth and eleventh centuries BC, the Levant in general, and Cyprus in particular, maintained regular contacts with Sardinia. The reason for this was undoubtedly Sardinia's rich deposits of metalliferous ores, particularly iron and tin.[22] To reach Sardinia by sea from the Levant one is obliged to travel via Crete. It is not then surprising that archaeologists have detected a Levantine presence there. By the harbour of Kommos on Crete's southern coast, J. Shaw has excavated an early shrine, founded around 900 BC. This shrine is clearly not Greek. The three pillars in particular are reminiscent of contemporary Canaanite (that is Phoenician) cult places.[23] Equally remarkably, Sardinian artefacts have been found in Knossos, and it is difficult to see how they got there unless they were carried in Levantine ships.[24] These Levantine seamen do not seem to have been particularly interested in the Aegean as such; Knossos and Kommos were simply ports of call on the journey to the western Mediterranean.

[17] Winter 1976; 1988.   [18] Catling 1964: 191–223; Matthäus 1985: 299–316.
[19] Catling 1964: 191–223; 1984.   [20] Brueckner 1893.
[21] Matthäus 1985: 299–316; 1988; on Cretan rod-tripods see now discussion in Hoffman 1997: 116–20.
[22] For the Sardinian connection, see Ridgway and Ridgway 1992; Gale and Gale 1992; Lo Schiavo *et al.* 1985.   [23] Shaw 1989; but see now comments by Hoffman 1997: 172–6.
[24] Vagnetti 1989.

To return to our Cypriot bronzes: the difference between the time of their manufacture and the time of their deposition implies that we are dealing here with the circulation of *antiques*. These items must have been in use for (sometimes) hundreds of years before they were finally used to furnish the graves of important men.[25] How can we explain this unusual practice? Here both Homer and ethnography can provide some insights. In *Iliad* XXIII.740–9, Achilles offers a silver krater as a prize in the funeral games of Patroklos. The poet, in an aside, describes both the krater and its history. It was made first by Sidonian craftsmen, brought over the sea by Phoenicians and given as a gift to Thoas (king of Troy). Then it was given as ransom for one of Priam's daughters whom Achilles had captured.[26] Circulation of high-status goods of this kind is called 'gift exchange' by anthropologists.[27] Such exchange normally takes place between persons of high but equivalent status who come from different communities. In such systems objects acquire prestige as much through their history of exchange, their 'biography' as it were, as through the value of the materials or the quality of the craftsmanship.[28] This hypothesis seems to be confirmed by archaeology. The practice of burying important men with rich antiques goes back to the very beginning of the Early Iron Age. The cremated remains of the 'hero' of Lefkandi were interred in a Cypriot bronze urn manufactured about one hundred or so years earlier.[29] Other Levantine objects seem to have played an important role in this international system of aristocratic exchange, for example the 'Phoenician' bronze and silver bowls (see fig. 6.2). These objects turn up in funerary and then sanctuary contexts in Greece from about 900 BC onwards.[30] Both their date of manufacture and their origin are difficult to establish (many of the bronze examples may in fact have been made in north Syria).[31] But if, as their contexts suggest, they were part of the same system of aristocratic gift exchange, they too, like the Cypriot tripods and wheeled stands, may have been antiques at the time of their deposition. The same may be true of the north Syrian and Phoenician ivories that begin to be found in the Aegean from the ninth century onwards.[32] If so their contexts in Greece provide, at best, a *terminus ante quem* for the date of their manufacture.

Rod-tripods excepted, what marks all these objects out is that they are all decorated with figured scenes. The bronze bowls in particular demonstrate the skilled rendition of human and animal figures using the techniques of repoussé and incision (see fig. 6.2). They thus stand out from most Greek material culture of the period, where figures were largely eschewed. This generalisation is as true for

---

[25] Catling 1964: 191–223.   [26] See discussion in Aubet 1993: 102–13.

[27] For the utility of the concept of gift exchange in early Greece, see Finley 1979: 61–6, 145–6.

[28] Kopytoff 1986.

[29] Catling 1993; on Lefkandi, Toumba see generally Popham *et al.* 1993; I. Morris 1999: 218–21; for the Cypriot parallels for this bronze amphora, see Catling 1964: 156–61; Matthäus 1985: 228–32.

[30] Markoe 1985: 203–9.

[31] This may well be true of the 'Phoenician' bronze bowl found in the Athenian Kerameikos (no. G1 in Markoe's (1985: 203) catalogue). For arguments to this effect, see Winter 1988.

[32] Winter 1976.

bronzework as it is for pottery. In most regions of Greece, the decoration of bronze, gold and ceramics remained resolutely aniconic until the eighth century BC. If it was high-status objects of this kind that were to provide the models for Greek Orientalising art in the seventh century BC, why did it take so long for Greek craftsmen to catch on? One answer might be that the particular aristocratic associations of such objects made them unsuitable objects for imitation or inspiration, particularly when applied to the humbler arts such as pot decoration. It is interesting that Phoenician, or Cypro-Phoenician, pottery was, for the most part, no less 'Geometric' in its decoration than Greek.[33] Of course it could be argued that the Greeks needed a greater stimulus than could be provided by one or two items. It was only in the eighth century that objects like this began to reach Greece in large numbers, a supposition supported by the observation that most 'Phoenician' bronze bowls have been found in sanctuaries.[34] Certainly, more Levantine goods, such as the ivory 'Lyre-player' seals, reach Greece in the eighth century than in the ninth.[35] It is reasonable to associate increased movements of goods of this kind with the great Phoenician expansion that began just before 800 BC. The Phoenician colony of Kition in Cyprus was founded around 820–810 BC; soon after this we find the first signs of Phoenician trading posts being established in southern Spain.[36] By the end of the eighth century BC (and perhaps earlier) Phoenicians had established outposts in Sardinia, North Africa, Sicily and Morocco. It is worth pausing to consider the character of this 'colonisation': that is, both its purpose and its effects.

The coastal cities of Phoenicia were economically strong but politically weak. Cities such as Tyre were simply not large enough to resist Assyrian pressure to provide the Assyrian Empire with the silver and other metals its expansionist policies required. In the ninth century, Phoenician enterprise seems to have been confined to the eastern Mediterranean. The distribution of Phoenician metalwork in Greece (Athens, Lefkandi) and the various indications of Phoenician activity in Crete probably define the extent of Phoenician commercial interest. Some contact with Libya was likely (if only as a stop on a return journey), but if contact with Sardinia was maintained during this period, such contact seems to have been sporadic. It was in the eighth century that Assyrian demands increased, and it was these demands that drove the Phoenicians westwards in search of new sources of metal. (Sardinia was known to be rich in metal ores.)

Southern Spain was less well known (if it was known at all), and so the number of Phoenician trading posts established there in the eighth century is all the more remarkable. Two kinds of settlements were founded here. The first are the remarkable series of 'trading posts' located on the Malaga coast, spaced only a few kilometres apart. Every river mouth seems to have had one. Toscanos is typical of such settlements. It is small, and at its centre was not a temple, but a warehouse.

---

[33] Coldstream 1984b.   [34] Markoe 1985: 203–9.   [35] Boardman 1990b.
[36] For the foundation of Kition, see Aubet 1993: 42–5.

These places (they cannot be called communities) seem to have flourished as an indirect consequence of the trade in metals with Atlantic Spain. Currents in the straits of Gibraltar are notoriously difficult to negotiate, and ships bound further west had to have safe havens where they could wait for conditions to improve. These small places were never autonomous, and did not long survive the disruption in trade that took place in the sixth century BC.[37]

The Phoenician city of Gadir (Roman Gades, modern Cadiz) could not be more different (see figs. 6.3 and 6.5). This was a large settlement located on an offshore island. Though it retained close connections first with Tyre and then with Carthage throughout its history, it was genuinely autonomous. Temples, such as the famous temple of Melqart (the 'Phoenician Herakles'), seem to have been established here from the time of its earliest foundation. Its *raison d'être* was the trade in metals. It was located a day's journey by sea from Huelva (close to the silver, zinc and copper mines of Rio Tinto) and within easy reach of the Guadalquivir, a broad river navigable many miles upstream. Its position offshore had two advantages. From the point of view of its Phoenician inhabitants, it provided a considerable degree of security should relations with the locals turn sour. From the point of view of the various native communities of the region, it provided a neutral zone where different interests could be accommodated. It was sufficiently distant from the actual sources of metal not to be seen as a threat. In all these respects it was a classic example of what the economist Karl Polanyi has called a 'port of trade', an outpost or community intended to promote trade between two very different peoples, while at the same time minimising cultural friction between two 'regimes of value'.[38] Other Phoenician settlements in the central Mediterranean, notably Motya in the west of Sicily, seem to have followed Gadir's example.[39] Phoenician settlement in the central Mediterranean seems to have been directed at controlling these all-important trade routes to the West.

How did all this Phoenician activity affect Greece? It is questionable whether the Phoenician drive westwards increased the flow of Levantine goods into the Aegean itself. Indeed, it could be argued that there had been more direct trade between Phoenicians and Greeks in the ninth and early eighth centuries than there was in the late eighth and early seventh. Phoenicians were simply too few in number to maintain major trading interests in both places. Of course, the same is not true for other Levantine peoples, and the Aegean may well have been a haven for some north Syrian craftsmen in the eighth as well as the ninth centuries. Still, the degree of 'Orientalisation' in Greece in no way correlates directly with the degree of contact with the Orient itself. The significance of Phoenician activity lies elsewhere. The Phoenicians had shown the Greeks what it was possible for an enterprising trading people to accomplish. They had opened up the western Mediterranean, and indeed the Atlantic, for trade. Some (but not all)

---

[37] Aubet 1993: 249–76. For another view of the nature of Phoenician colonisation, see Niemeyer 1990.
[38] Aubet 1993: 220–47.   [39] For Motya, see Aubet 1993: 200–3.

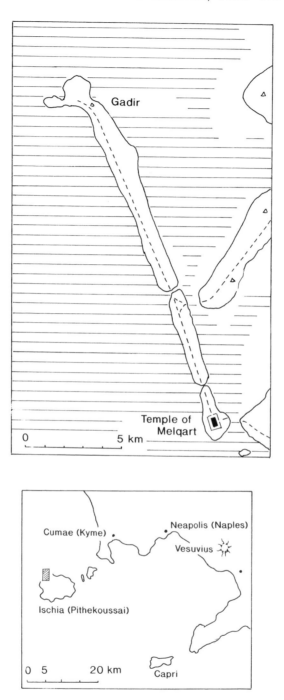

6.5 Position of Gadir and Pithekoussai compared

Greeks were to follow their example. Quite how and why, say, Euboeans did one thing and Cretans another is, however, a question that can only be addressed by looking at the evidence from each region in some detail.

6.3 Responses to the Orient: Athens, Euboea, Crete and Corinth

Athens

Figure 5.6 shows a belly-handled amphora, a large vessel used in Athens in the ninth century to contain the ashes of important women. The decoration on this vessel, which was almost certainly produced locally, is uncompromisingly Geometric. Most of the metal objects from this grave, such as fibulae and pins, also derive from a local tradition of craftsmanship that owes little to the Levant. The same is true of another contemporary grave whose urn was almost identical to this one and also contained the cremated remains of a middle-aged woman. Here too almost all the ceramic vessels are decorated in a strictly Geometric style. But this 'Tomb of a Rich Athenian Lady' also contained some gold earrings, whose manufacture required craft skills which, at this time, were only available in the Levant. It is a moot point whether the style of these earrings is 'Oriental'; but it is certain that granulation and filigree were techniques then only current further east.[40] This grave (datable to around 850 BC) is a near contemporary of grave G42 in the Kerameikos, the contents of which were again mainly Geometric pots, but which also contained a Phoenician bronze bowl, similar to the one illustrated in fig. 6.2.[41] These finds show that Athens was not an isolated community in the ninth century. Indeed aristocratic Athenians were able to acquire Oriental goods, and had access (at however distant a remove) to Oriental craft techniques. None the less, Oriental metal-working had no discernible effect on the local tradition of pot decoration.

Such indifference to the potential applications of Oriental metal-working remains evident throughout the ninth century. It is only in the eighth century that things begin to change, and when they do, they do so subtly and by degrees. Figure 6.6 shows a large belly-handled amphora, Athens NM 804, used as a grave marker and datable to around 760 BC. The bulk of the decoration on this pot, including the figured scenes which form the central frame, is Geometric: battlements, maeanders and double-maeanders. On the neck, however, there are two friezes: one of grazing animals, the other of goats 'regardant'.[42] Such friezes may have been 'influenced' by the example of figures of animals worked in repoussé on gold diadems, which are found in rich eighth-century graves in Athens and Eretria.[43] It

[40] For the context of the Kerameikos graves, see Kübler 1954: 209–56. For the 'tomb of a rich Athenian lady', see Smithson 1968; Coldstream 1977: 55–8; for the jewellery itself, see discussion by Higgins 1969.

[41] Markoe 1985: 203 no. G1; for its context, see Kübler 1954: 209–56 (grave 42) and Coldstream 1977: 58–60.   [42] Coldstream 1968: 29–41.

[43] For the diadems, see Ohly 1953. Repoussé is also a technique found on the ubiquitous 'Phoenician' bronze bowls; see Markoe 1985: 9–12.

6.6 Athens NM 804, a Late Geometric I belly-handled amphora from the 'Dipylon' cemetery in Athens

is only towards the end of the eighth century that Oriental metalwork is consciously imitated in clay.[44] Direct copying of this kind is confined to a small class of bowls or skyphoi. Even in Protoattic, Athens' 'Orientalising' style, Oriental motifs are added slowly. The works of the Analatos painter, an Early Protoattic craftsman, have more in common with Late Geometric than with contemporary Protocorinthian.[45] In the so-called Black-and-White style (Middle Protoattic; see fig. 9.4), decoration is dominated by large scenes with human or animal figures.[46] The effect of Oriental metalwork here is indirect. To be sure, the very fact that human and animal figures appear at all is due to Oriental inspiration. But it is only in the so-called raptor scenes, where a carnivore attacks a herbivore, and in the

[44] Borell 1978; Markoe 1985: 117–27.   [45] Cook 1972: 65–9.
[46] Cook 1972: 69–73; S.P. Morris 1984.

choice of subsidiary ornament, that a direct derivation from Oriental metalwork can be traced. Certainly the techniques of metal-workers, in particular incision, have to wait until the end of the seventh century (the time of the Nessos amphora (fig 1.1)) to appear.

'Orientalising' styles such as Protoattic rarely simply supplanted the local Geometric. The Protoattic style owes as much to a local tradition of fashioning large vessels for graves as it does to Oriental metalwork. Moreover, as elsewhere in Greece, Protoattic co-exists with a class of vessels where the tradition of Geometric principles of design persists. Such 'Subgeometric' pots continue to be manufactured and used throughout the seventh century and beyond. In general Attica was a region that seems reluctant to 'Orientalise'. Athenians had acquired some Oriental goods and made some use of Oriental craft skills in the ninth century, but widespread Oriental 'influence' is only apparent in the seventh. Of course, one could argue that Levantine finds are few and far between in Geometric Athens. Had exposure to Oriental material culture been greater, so too would be the local willingness to 'Orientalise'. It would then surely be appropriate to look at another region whose contacts with the Levant were so much more extensive than Attica's: Euboea.

Euboea: Lefkandi and Eretria

The community of Lefkandi was, in a sense, never out of touch with the Levant. The tenth-century 'hero's burial' in Toumba (fig. 5.9) was, after all, an interment in a thoroughly Levantine piece of metalwork, and the quantity of gold buried with the hero's 'queen' speaks volumes about this community's ability to secure a supply of precious metals from further east.[47] Early Oriental 'influence' may even be detected in the decoration of the krater which may have served as a grave marker for these burials (fig. 6.7). The 'tree-of-life' is a motif common in Near Eastern art, and it is still a little surprising to find it on a tenth-century Greek Protogeometric pot.[48] This early experiment in 'Orientalising' design was not followed up however, a fact which cannot be due to any lack of Levantine or Egyptian imports. The Toumba cemetery in particular is rich in these. Egyptian faience and Egyptian bronze jugs, Phoenician bronze bowls and Phoenician 'Egyptianising' scarabs and seals all turn up in quantities hardly paralleled in contemporary Greek contexts.[49] It is striking how little 'influence' such metalwork had on the local tradition of pot decoration and even bronze-working.[50] Protogeometric and then Subprotogeometric styles persisted throughout the tenth and ninth centuries and

[47] Popham *et al.* 1982a; 1993.   [48] Catling and Lemos 1990: 25–31 and plate 54 (Crater 327).
[49] For the Toumba cemetery in Lefkandi, see Popham *et al.* 1980: 168–96; 1982b; 1989; Popham and Lemos 1995; 1996; Popham 1995; for discussion of the finds, see Catling and Catling 1980; Popham *et al.* 1980: 217–30. It is particularly striking that two Phoenician bronze bowls have been found here.
[50] For the Lefkandi bronzework, see Catling and Catling 1980; for the pottery see Desborough 1980; Catling and Lemos 1990.

into the eighth (indeed, one class of that characteristic Euboean drinking cup, the pendent semi-circle skyphos (fig. 5.7), may last into the late eighth century[51]). There are, to be sure, odd experiments in figured decoration, but these owe little to the East. As in Athens, the example of Oriental metal-working was followed up only in small particulars. On that masterpiece of Euboean Late Geometric art, the Cesnola krater, Attic-inspired Geometric decoration predominates (see fig. 6.8). It is only in the central panel, where two goats frame a tree (of life?), that any Levantine influence can be detected.[52] Even in seventh-century Euboean pottery, motifs directly inspired by Oriental prototypes are few and far between.

As far as pot decoration is concerned, Euboea went her own way when she was not following Athens'. As in Athens, Euboean use of Oriental motifs is highly selective. The same is not true of the Euboean attitude to other aspects of Levantine culture – trading, for example. Just as Levantine goods reached Lefkandi from an early date, so Euboean pottery reached Tyre in some quantity from the tenth century onwards.[53] Euboean pottery, in particular drinking vessels, seems to have been quite popular throughout much of the Levant in the tenth to eighth centuries BC.[54] Who were the carriers of these goods? It has long been believed that such exchanges were due as much to Euboean as to Phoenician enterprise. Arguments in favour of Euboean enterprise rest on negative as well as positive considerations. Lefkandi seems an unlikely port of call for Phoenicians, even if there is evidence that the nearby region of Laurion in Attica was producing silver from an early date.[55] The Euboeans are even thought to have been responsible for the first Greek *emporion*, the trading post of Al Mina established on the mouth of the river Orontes in north Syria in the ninth century BC.[56] Certainly, a lot of Euboean pottery has been found there, but so has Euboean pottery elsewhere in the Levant. There is no necessary correlation between Greek pottery and the 'Greekness' of the settlement, and it is probably rash to draw quantitative conclusions from such a biased sample.[57] Everything else about the settlement, particularly the architecture, seems to derive from local traditions. As J. Luke has convincingly demonstrated, Al Mina was probably a 'port of trade', set up by and serving the interests of the local north Syrian state of Unqi (Tell Tayinat).[58] Al Mina was in no sense a Euboean colony, though some Euboeans may have settled there.

Ninth-century Euboean commercial activity has then probably been exaggerated. This is not to say that it did not exist; it is rather to emphasise that it was the Phoenicians who had the greater incentive to expand their trading horizons, and that the Euboeans probably followed the Phoenician example rather than the

---

[51] Kearsley 1989.
[52] For the Cesnola krater, see Coldstream 1968: 172–6 and plate 35; Coldstream 1994.
[53] Coldstream and Bikai 1988.   [54] Luke 1994: 109–53.
[55] As suggested by Coldstream 1977: 70–1. Coldstream's arguments would apply as well to Lefkandi as to Athens.   [56] Boardman 1980: 39–46.
[57] For opposing views on Al Mina, see Boardman 1990a; Graham 1986.
[58] Luke 1994: 17–22, 36–8, 49–108.

6.7 Protogeometric krater (no. 327) from the 'heröon' at Lefkandi, Toumba

6.8 Cesnola krater, a Euboean krater found in Cyprus,
New York Met. Mus. 74.51.965

Phoenicians the Euboean. In one case it is clear that Euboeans followed where Phoenicians had first led, in the establishment of the first of the western colonies. The choice of Pithekoussai, an offshore island, is inconceivable without the precedent set by the Phoenicians in Gadir and Motya (see below).[59] Similarly, prolonged Euboean contact with Phoenicia and north Syria is a major factor in the precocious Euboean adoption of the alphabet. These are broad claims, which I will attempt to justify below. What should be emphasised here is that following a Levantine example in one sphere (trading or the use of the alphabet) need not entail following a Levantine example in another (the creation of 'Orientalising' art styles). This point can best be illustrated by the third of our regional examples, Crete.

Crete

Crete, or more precisely Knossos, is the findspot of the earliest Phoenician inscription to be found in Greece: the inscribed bronze bowl from Tekke tomb J, datable to around 900 BC.[60] This bowl was only one of many Levantine imports that found its way to Knossos during the Early Iron Age. Cypriot tripods and wheeled stands are soon followed by Egyptian bronze jugs, Egyptian faience, Phoenician bowls and, lastly, Cypro-Phoenician flasks and aryballoi.[61] Here at least, Oriental examples did have a direct effect on Cretan art. From about 840 BC onwards, motifs whose origin seems to lie in Oriental metal-working, such as the guilloche and the cable, are to be seen on the surfaces of Knossian pots. These motifs jostle with Attic-derived Protogeometric and Geometric decoration to create an eclectic, effectively Early Orientalising style known as 'Protogeometric B' (see fig. 6.9).[62] Why was the impact of Oriental art so much more immediate in Knossos than it was in Athens or Lefkandi? One possible answer is that, whereas other regions of Greece were the recipients merely of Oriental goods, Crete also received immigrant craftsmen from the Levant itself. There was, as Boardman has argued, in Crete a school of Levantine (more specifically north Syrian) craftsmen who worked there over several generations.[63] This 'school' was responsible in the first instance for the gold jewellery found in the Khaniale Tekke tholos tomb, and the elaborate bronze quiver found in Fortetsa tomb P.[64] The descendants (whether as sons or apprentices) of these craftsmen went on to produce the votive bronze shields or tympana (e.g. fig. 10.6) which have turned up in the major sanctuary sites of eighth-century Crete, the cave of Zeus on Mt Ida and the temple of Dictaean Zeus at Palaikastro.[65]

---

[59] See again Aubet 1993.   [60] Snycer 1979; Hoffman 1997: 120–3.
[61] Brock 1957; Catling 1996c; Coldstream 1984b. For an up-to-date list, see now Hoffman 1997: 19–151.   [62] Brock 1957: 143; Coldstream 1968: 235–9.
[63] Boardman 1961: 129–59; 1967b; but see the comments of Blome 1982 and Hoffman 1997: 153–89.
[64] Brock 1957: 134–6; Boardman 1967b; but see recent reassessment by Hoffman (1997: 191–245) of the evidence from the Khaniale Tekke tomb.
[65] Boardman 1961: 129–59; Kunze 1931; Blome 1982. See also Markoe 1985: 110–17.

In this light, it is perhaps less surprising that Oriental motifs remained an important part of the repertoire of Cretan pot decoration well into the seventh century BC. In the so-called Early, Middle and Late Geometric phases of the sequence at Knossos, the 'Oriental' guilloche and cable accompanied the 'Attic' maeander and zig-zag throughout the eighth century.[66] As in Athens and Euboea, the ornate polychrome Cretan 'Orientalising' style of the seventh century (e.g. fig. 6.10) has its plain, linear counterpart.[67] But in Crete at least it would be wrong to call any of the 'plain' pithoi decorated simply with concentric circles, such as we find in tomb P in the Fortetsa cemetery, 'Subgeometric'. For one thing, concentric circles are essentially a Protogeometric feature, not a Geometric one; for another, the immediate precedents for such decorative schemes are not Greek at all, but rather the concentric circles to be found on Cypro-Levantine aryballoi which had been finding their way into Knossos from the ninth century onwards.[68] In this sense, the linear pithoi are every bit as 'Orientalising' as the ornate polychrome examples.

In art-historical terms, the Orientalising begins in the ninth century and continues, with some modifications, into the seventh. Crete is unique in Greece in the length of its Orientalising period. Crete's receptiveness to Oriental figurative art and motifs inspired from metalwork is, however, balanced by its passivity and conservatism in other areas. Cretans were clearly in contact with literate Phoenicians from at least 900 BC, but the earliest Cretan alphabetic inscriptions date to only just before 700 BC.[69] Nor did the presence of Phoenician traders in south Crete and in Knossos encourage Cretans to make their own trading ventures overseas. Cretans were late and half-hearted colonists. So, again, despite the presence of Oriental craftsmen in their midst, Cretans, like every other Greek, were selective in what they took from their eastern neighbours. It is just that what Cretans chose to take from the Levant (artistic inspiration) was exactly the opposite of what the Euboeans were to take (overseas trading and the use of the alphabet). Cretans were moreover more conservative in their artistic use of what the Levant had to offer than other Greeks. Cretans adopted motifs and figures from metalwork, but made little change to their techniques of figured decoration. The use first of white paint and then of polychromy were their sole technical innovations, and in most respects Cretan pot painters painted in the same way from the late ninth century until the seventh. Perhaps relations with the Levant were simply too close to provide any real stimulus. It is time to return to a region that, in many respects, had kept the Orient at arm's length throughout the 'Dark Ages': Corinth.

Corinth revisited

Having undertaken this *tour d'horizon* of various regional responses to the Orient, let us look again at the pot with which we began this chapter (fig. 6.1).[70] Here the

---

[66] Coldstream 1968: 239–55; 1996.   [67] Brock 1957: 149–52; Moignard 1996.
[68] Coldstream 1984b.   [69] Johnston in Jeffery 1990: 468 no. 8a.   [70] Benson 1995: 342–5.

6.9 Drawing of Protogeometric 'B' straight-sided pithos, flattened view
(no. 107.178 from the North Cemetery at Knossos)

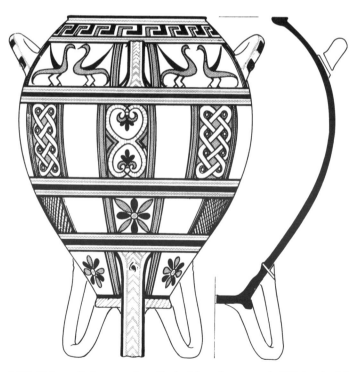

6.10 Orientalising two-handled pithos from tomb 285 in the North
Cemetery of Knossos (no. 285.27)

painter has taken a technique from metal-working (incision) and applied it to the decoration of a pot. The pot in question is a perfume flask, a shape, like the decoration, of Oriental inspiration. The figured decoration itself, the two friezes of humans and animals, is reminiscent of the complex, narrative scenes we find on Phoenician bronze bowls and other metalwork. Indeed to a Greek viewer familiar with the Homeric tradition of story telling (which antedates Homer) it would be difficult to look at this pot, particularly at its upper frieze showing humans, chariots and animals, and not to think of the stories evoked by the metalwork so elaborately described in the Homeric poems. This is not to say that we can decipher the scene, in the sense of telling exactly which story it alludes to. That is not the point. This was a very small pot with very large pretensions, pretensions to be on a par with those works in gold, silver or bronze which Homer describes. It was (somewhat cheekily) claiming equality of attention with those objects, such as the silver bowl described in *Iliad* XXIII.740–9, which had had a considerable pedigree within the sphere of aristocratic gift exchange. This is not to say that anyone could ever have been deceived into thinking that this flask could ever have been the 'social equal' of such silver bowls. Many however might have appreciated the allusion, and the joke. It may have been a very naive little pot, but many may have been amused by its presumption.

Highly decorated pots like this one were very much in a minority. Most Protocorinthian is in a plain or linear style. Such linear pots were by no means carelessly decorated. Protocorinthian linear pots retain the clear patterns and outlines of their Late Geometric antecedents. It is difficult then to see linear pots as inferior versions of their ornate counterparts. What exactly was the relationship between these two styles? There was, first, no difference in the shapes employed. Examples of shapes used to contain scented oils (aryballoi and alabastra) and of shapes used for pouring (olpai and oinochoai) or drinking (the deep cup or kotyle) are to be found both in Orientalising figured and in plain, linear styles.[71] Of course, it may be that some kind of analysis of the contexts in which these two styles are to be found will reveal more about the relationship between them. But, in the absence of such analysis,[72] one thing is clear. Corinthian production of both styles (in all shapes) was geared towards an 'export' market. It may be that the elaborate Orientalising vessels functioned as a kind of advertisement for the qualities that were supposed to inhere in all vessels of this shape.

Corinth was, in purely art-historical terms, the city that made the most innovative use of what the Near East had to offer. But, though Corinthians were major participants in the colonising movement and no laggards in their adoption of the alphabet, they did not lead in either field. Here the Euboeans were in the forefront of developments. Colonisation and the adoption of the alphabet

---

[71] For a discussion of Protocorinthian and Corinthian pottery generally, see Payne 1931; Amyx 1988; Rasmussen 1991.

[72] Shanks (1993; 1999: 169–94) does attempt some contextual analysis. But he does not seem interested in counting the proportions of linear versus figured pots.

are innovations of such revolutionary importance that they require extensive treatment.

6.4 Trade and colonisation

The term 'colony', in ordinary English, is used as a portmanteau word for two terms the Greeks used to describe their own settlements overseas. The first of these is *apoikia*, a 'home away from home'. Apoikiai were settlements which were, from the time of their very foundation, always destined to be new communities in their own right, with their own territory and urban centre, their own citizens and laws. In theory at least, every apoikia had a mother city in the Greek homeland, a community from which the majority of its settlers (and, most importantly, its founder or oikist) had originally come. 'Mother cities' (*metropoleis*) and colonies usually maintained reasonably close ties, and an apoikia could sometimes appeal to the mother city for help in times of crisis.[73] In direct contrast to the apoikia was the *emporion*. An emporion (from which the English word 'emporium' derives) was a settlement devoted first and foremost to trade, a settlement whose primary purpose was to facilitate exchanges between Greeks and foreigners (whom the Greeks unselfconsciously referred to as 'barbarians').[74] Such were never intended to be autonomous political communities, and did not necessarily have a 'mother city'. Their inhabitants, being traders, were more diverse and cosmopolitan than those living in apoikiai. Emporia survived and prospered for as long as they were sustained by active trade. In practice, of course, the distinction between apoikia and emporion was not so clear cut. Naucratis in Egypt, for example, seems to have begun as a trading post, an emporion, and its very existence depended on the Egyptian need for Greek goods and Greek mercenaries. But Naucratis was, after a while, granted a degree of autonomy by the Pharaoh, and in practice functioned like any other Greek polis overseas (though one without its own territory, or chora).[75] So a settlement could begin as an emporion and develop into a city-state (polis) in its own right.

Considerations such as these have led some scholars to question the validity of the terms 'colony' and 'colonisation'. A review of the tales the Greeks told about their early settlements in the West showed that these tales are closer to myth than to history. We cannot take stories of intrepid bands of men setting sail and settling a new land as direct historical truth.[76] Moreover, if colonisation is meant to

---

[73] Corinth, for example, maintained close links with her colony, Syracuse, arranging for aid from the Peloponnese when Syracuse was attacked by Athens during the Peloponnesian war. Relations between colony and mother-city were not always amicable however. Corinth and her colony of Kerkyra (Corfu) were often at loggerheads.

[74] 'Barbaroi' in Greek, however, does not have the same connotations as 'Barbarian' in English. 'Barbaroi' were not necessarily uncivilised, merely foreign. Greeks referred both to the sophisticated Egyptians (whom they clearly admired) and the unsophisticated Celts and Scythians as 'barbaroi'.   [75] Boardman 1980: 118–33.

[76] Compare, for example, Dunbabin 1948: 1–47 with Dougherty 1993.

imply the deliberate settling and setting up of new communities then some Greek settlements abroad cannot be accounted 'colonies' at all. Colonisation may have entailed not only a much longer, more gradual process of settlement and movement of people than scholars had previously thought, but also a more complex negotiation of identities between Greeks and 'natives' than anyone had previously imagined.[77]

Nevertheless, we have to call this process something, and colonisation is as good a term as any. Moreover the distinction between emporion and apoikia remains a useful one, as it directs our attention to the motivation behind the Greek expansion overseas. Did Greeks venture abroad primarily in pursuit of trade and wealth? Or were there other pressing reasons for expanding the frontiers of the Greek world by exporting people overseas? To use Alan Blakeway's phrase (thinking of the history of the British expansion abroad) did the 'flag' follow trade, or did trade follow the 'flag'?[78]

Colonisation certainly expanded the Greek world, and did so very rapidly. Beginning with the first colonies in Italy and Sicily in the eighth century BC, it gathered momentum in the seventh with more colonies in Italy and Sicily, an expansion northwards into the north of the Aegean, the sea of Marmara and the Black Sea, and an expansion southwards towards Libya. The last major Greek colony, Massalia (modern Marseilles), was founded around 600 BC in the far west of the Mediterranean, in southern France.[79] With many of these colonies, commercial interests seem to have been slight. Metapontion (Metapontum) in the 'heel' of Italy (established as a polis around 600 BC) is not situated close to any particular trade route. Its harbour is not particularly good, nor does it lie within easy reach of any natural resource (such as metals) that the Greeks might have needed or coveted.[80] It does however lie near good agricultural land (in later times it chose an ear of wheat as an image for its coins). It is the agricultural potential of the area that first seems to have attracted its earliest Greek settlers. So some eighth- and seventh-century Greeks seem to have wanted more agricultural land. Does not then the rise in population in the Greek homeland, so well documented in the archaeological record, provide an adequate explanation for the Greek movement overseas? Was not the pressure of population on the available arable land a sufficient reason for this expansion? One difficulty with this kind of explanation is that we have no clear evidence for 'overpopulation' in those areas of the Greek mainland from which, according to historical tradition, the bulk of Greek colonists seem to have come. No intensive surveys have been undertaken in the Megarid, the Corinthia, Achaea or Euboea.[81] Other areas of Greece, such as Attica and the Argolid, which have provided the best evidence for a rise in population in

---

[77] As argued by Osborne 1998c.   [78] Blakeway 1933.   [79] Boardman 1980: 217–24.
[80] See Carter 1994; see also discussion by Osborne 1996a: 237–9.
[81] Of course, extensive survey has been undertaken in Euboea (Sackett *et al.* 1966), and a smaller survey has been conducted in the area around Karystos by a Canadian team in recent years. But no major intensive survey of Euboea (or any part thereof) has been published so far.

the eighth century, sent out no colonies.[82] 'Agricultural' colonies such as Metapontion are, for the most part, later in date than the earliest Greek colonies overseas. 'Land hunger' may have been as much a consequence as a cause of the colonising movement. To discover the original motivation behind the colonisation we have to look at the archaeological evidence from the earliest Greek settlements abroad. Fortunately two of these (Pithekoussai and Megara Hyblaia) have been excavated to a very high standard.

Until Giorgio Buchner's excavations began in the 1950s, Pithekoussai (the modern island of Ischia in the bay of Naples) was a site lost to history. Only odd references in Livy and Strabo gave any indication of its original importance.[83] Since 1952, excavations have taken place in the Valle di San Montano and in other areas adjacent to the ancient acropolis of Monte di Vico, just by the modern town. Excavations in the Valle di San Montano have revealed over one thousand graves, the first interments dating to around 750 BC.[84] Other important early finds have come from the so-called 'Acropolis dump'. Many of these finds from here, such as the Middle Geometric chevron skyphoi, attest to some kind of connection with Euboea, as do the burial customs. As in late eighth-century, early seventh-century Eretria, important adult males seem to have been cremated, whereas the unburnt bones of children were placed in amphoras of some kind.[85] The bulk of the pottery found in the cemeteries is, however, not Euboean but Corinthian, including drinking vessels (kotylai) and perfume flasks (aryballoi). There are other indications that Pithekoussai was not simply a daughter community of Chalcis or Eretria. There are indications, for example, that some Levantines lived there. There are a number of north Syrian 'face aryballoi', and a number of Semitic inscriptions.[86]

A Phoenician presence would go a long way to explaining how it was that Pithekoussai was established in the first place. First consider its position: like many Phoenician 'colonies' further west (Gadir and Motya, for example), Pithekoussai is a small, offshore island (fig. 6.5). It was about one or two days' sailing away from major sources of copper, tin and other metals in northern Etruria (modern Tuscany). The Euboeans here seem to be following a Phoenician model in setting up a trading post within striking distance of a valuable resource: close enough for trade, but isolated enough for security. Like earlier Phoenician settlements, Pithekoussai has a decent (if not exceptional) harbour, but its agricultural potential is not great. Pithekoussai's location is striking for another reason: it is very, very far from Greece. Indeed, before the founding of Massalia, Pithekoussai and Cumae (Kyme) must count as the most distant of Greek colonies from Greece itself. It is difficult to see how early Greek navigators could have

[82] Snodgrass 1977; 1980: 22–4; I. Morris 1987: 156–67; Jameson *et al.* 1994.
[83] Livy VIII.22.5–6; Strabo, *Geography* V.4.9. Both Livy and Strabo were writing towards the end of the first century BC, and must have relied on earlier sources (now lost) for their information.
[84] Buchner and Ridgway 1993; Ridgway 1992: 45–82.
[85] Ridgway 1992: 49–51. For Eretria, see Bérard 1970.
[86] Ridgway 1992: 111–18; Docter and Niemeyer 1994.

come upon this site purely by chance. Equally, memories (if that is what they were) of earlier Mycenaean voyages can hardly have been reliable guides for early traders or colonists. The Euboeans had to have had inside information, and this can only have been supplied by the trading people who seem to have maintained contacts with the central Mediterranean (particularly Sardinia) throughout the first part of the first millennium BC: the Phoenicians.

Though Pithekoussai was clearly a populous settlement for the seventy or so years of its existence, it never seems to have become a proper polis. After the foundation of Cumae (Kyme) on the Italian shore opposite around 725 BC, it began to lose residents. Few continued to live there during the seventh century. Pithekoussai was always primarily a trading post. But Cumae did become a polis, and this was because by the end of the eighth century the idea of a political community was taking root in Greece itself. To gain some insight into this new type of settlement, we must take a look at Sicily, and at Megara Hyblaia in particular.

Megara Hyblaia (a daughter community of Megara in central Greece) was one of the earliest colonies in Sicily, founded sometime around 728 BC. Its location, not far from good agricultural land but with a poor harbour, was the result of both positive and negative factors. The negative factor was rivalry with Corinth and its colony, Syracuse. Syracuse, founded (according to Thucydides) a few years earlier, was located on an ideal 'colony' site, of a kind a Phoenician might have considered ideal: an offshore island (Ortygia) at the mouth of one of the best harbours in the Mediterranean.[87] The arable land around Syracuse was by no means poor. The positive reason for Megara Hyblaia's location was that the agricultural land in its vicinity was more extensive than that close to Syracuse. Trade then cannot have been the primary reason for the setting up of this colony, which seems to have been more apoikia than emporion. Megara Hyblaia was a planned community, a 'new town' of the late eighth century BC.[88] The houses seem to have been laid out in some kind of grid system. From at least the seventh century onwards, public space in the form of an agora or marketplace was set aside. Care was taken to demarcate the space for the living (houses) from the space assigned to the dead (the cemeteries), anticipating a pattern which we find only much later in communities in the Greek homeland. Whilst the founding of Pithekoussai would have been an impossible venture without the Phoenician example and Phoenician help, Megara Hyblaia owed little to the Levant. Greek colonisation was by now taking a very different form from the example set by the earliest Phoenician traders, and Phoenicians and Greeks increasingly found that their interests clashed as the seventh and sixth centuries progressed. The Greeks however never quite forgot that they were indebted to Levantine pioneers. They never forgot that it was to the Phoenicians that they owed their most useful technology: the alphabet.

[87] Boardman 1980: 172–4; see also Dunbabin 1948: 13–18; Vallet and Villard 1952.
[88] See especially Vallet *et al.* 1976; 1983: 144–9; Dunbabin 1948: 18–20. See also discussion in Osborne 1996a: 239–42; Danner 1997. On 'overpopulation' as a possible cause for Megara Hyblaia's founding of Selinous, see de Angelis 1994.

6.5 Literacy and the alphabet

The Greek alphabet, from which both the Cyrillic and Latin alphabets are derived, is not the only means of representing the Greek language in written form. Linear B, which was a syllabic script using a variety of signs for both vowel/consonant combinations and a number of ideograms, had functioned perfectly well for administrative purposes in the Late Bronze Age. The Greek speakers of Cyprus, it seems, continued to make use of a syllabic script (the Cypriote syllabary) until the third century BC. This script may well have been in use during the earlier part of the Iron Age, but if so Greek visitors to Cyprus from the Aegean showed no interest in it.[89] Instead, Aegean Greeks of the eighth century BC chose as the model for their new alphabet a script devised for a language totally unrrelated to Greek: Canaanite or Phoenician.

At the end of the Bronze Age, the Phoenicians and other Semitic-speaking peoples of the Levant had devised a script of twenty-two letters. This script was entirely phonetic, and dispensed with both ideograms and vowels. For this reason it has been called a consonantal alphabet by some, and a consonantal syllabary by others.[90] It was this Phoenician script that was adapted by Greeks to represent their own language. The Greeks, however, made one crucial innovation. They dropped from their new alphabet those Phoenician signs for which there was no consonantal equivalent in Greek (such as the Phoenician aleph) and used them instead for vowel sounds (a, for alpha)[91] (fig. 6.11). They thus invented an alphabet that could, for the first time, accurately represent speech. It is difficult to overestimate this achievement. Whereas syllabaries and logographic (or pictographic) systems bore only an oblique relation to spoken language, the new Greek alphabet could accurately transcribe speech. Early Greek writing does not then resemble modern English, which has a host of archaic spelling conventions which bear almost no relationship to the actual sounds used, and which do not vary from one dialect of English to another. If eighth- and seventh-century Greeks never quite wrote and spelt as they spoke, they came as close as any people, before or since, to doing just that.[92] If, in their local dialect, they pronounced the Greek for sea as 'thalassa', rather than 'thalatta', that is what they wrote down. Writing and speech were thus brought much closer together. Moreover, the number of signs in the

---

[89] See Powell 1991: 89–101. The Cypriot syllabary is generally thought to have been derived from the 'Cypro-Minoan' scripts used in Cyprus during the Bronze Age. The earliest inscriptions in the Cypriot syllabary proper date to the late eighth or early seventh century BC (Petit 1999: 112–14), but, because of this script's great similarity to 'Cypro-Minoan', it is inferred that some kind of Cypriot syllabary must have been in continuous (if restricted) use throughout the 'Dark Ages'.

Recently doubts have been cast on the distinctiveness of the 'Eteocypriot' Amathus as against the rest of Cyprus in the Archaic period. But, *contra* Given 1998: it is clear (Petit 1999) that inscriptions in the Cypriot syllabary are in a language distinct from either Greek or Phoenician, and that at least six of these inscriptions are Archaic in date.

[90] For discussion of the Phoenician script and its relation to early Greek alphabetic scripts, see Jeffery 1990: 1–42, 425–8; Powell 1991: 5–12, 101–6.   [91] See Jeffery 1990: 23; Powell 1991: 32–42.

[92] On the idiosyncratic nature of early Greek literacy, see Powell 1991: 115–17.

	Hypothetical Phoen. name	Hypothetical Phoen. sound	9th–8th cent. Phoen. shape	shapes from epichoric varieties 8th–5th cent. (all forms from right to left)	Greek sound	Greek name	in 4th cent. Koinē left to right	printed Greek shape
	a.	b	c.	d.	e.	f.	g.	e.
1	ʾalf	ʾ ˣ	𐤀	(shapes)	a	ἄλφα	A	A α
2	bēt	b ˣ	(shape)	(shapes)	b	βῆτα	B	B β
3	gaml	g ˣ	(shape)	(shapes)	g	γάμμα / γάμμα	Γ	Γ γ
4	delt	d ˣ	(shapes)	(shapes)	d	δέλτα	Δ	Δ δ
5	hē	h ˣ	(shape)	(shapes)	ě	εἶ, ἒ ψιλόν	E	E ε
6	wau	w ˣ	(shapes)	(shapes)	w	ϝαϋ	–	–
7	zai	z ˣ	(shape)	(shapes)	dz, zd	ζῆτα (from sādē?)	I Z	Z ζ
8	hēt	ḥ ˣ	(shape)	(shapes)	h, ē	ἦτα	H	H η
9	tēt	ṭ ˣ	⊗	(shapes)	th	θῆτα	θ ⊙	Θ θ
10	yōd	y ˣ	(shape)	(shapes)	i	ιῶτα	I	I ı
11	kaf	k ˣ	(shape)	(shape)	k	κάππα	K	K κ
12	lamd	l ˣ	(shape)	(shapes)	l	λάμβδα	Λ	Λ λ
13	mēm	m ˣ	(shapes)	(shapes)	m	μῦ, μο	M	M μ
14	nūn	n ˣ	(shape)	(shapes)	n	νῦ	N	N ν
15	semk	s ˣ	(shape)	(shapes)	ks	ξεῖ	(shapes)	Ξ ξ
16	ʿain	ʿ ˣ	O	O O	o	οὖ, ὄ μικρόν	O	O o
17	pē	p ˣ	(shape)	(shapes)	p	πεῖ	π	Π π
18	sādē	ts ˣ	(shapes)	(shapes)	s	σάν (from zai?)	–	–
19	qōf	q ˣ	φ	φ φ	q	ϙόππα	(shapes)	–
20	rōš	r ˣ	(shape)	(shapes)	r	ῥω	P	P ρ
21	šin	sh ˣ	(shape)	(shapes)	s	σῖγμα (from semk?)	(shape)	Σ σ s
22	tau	t ˣ	(shape)	┬ T	t	ταῦ	T	T τ
23	see wau above			(shapes)	u	ὖ	Y	Y υ
24	(? ϙ [qof] >)			φ ⊕	ph	φεῖ	φ	Φ φ
25	(? ×, + [tau] >)			X +	ks, kh	χεῖ	X	X χ
26	(? [kaf] >)			(shapes)	ps, kh	ψεῖ	Ψ	Ψ ψ
27	o [ŏ μικρόν] >			(shapes)	ō	ὦ, ὦ μέγα	Ω	Ω ω

6.11 The Greek and Phoenician alphabets compared

new system were few enough to make writing a skill which, in principle at least, could be made available to all.[93] In the Near East and in the Late Bronze Age palace states of the Aegean, writing had, for the most part, been the preserve of a class of specialists: the scribes. In Greece the potential was there for all this to change.

When did this revolution take place? The archaeological evidence points to a transmission sometime in the eighth century BC. The earliest Greek inscriptions are graffiti incised on pots and potsherds, whose style or whose context allows them to be dated with some precision. The graffiti from Lefkandi and Eretria, the 'Dipylon oinochoe' from Athens and 'Nestor's cup' from Pithekoussai (fig. 6.12) all date to the decades just before 700 BC.[94] No earlier inscriptions have been found, and it seems eminently reasonable to conclude that the alphabet had been developed a little earlier than this.[95]

But direct archaeological evidence may not be the only consideration. Recently Semitic scholars have argued that the transmission must have taken place earlier, as the letter forms used on the earliest Greek inscriptions more closely resemble those on early Phoenician inscriptions than they do those current in the eighth century BC.[96] Writing must have existed on some kind of perishable material (parchment or papyrus) before it is to be found on bronze, stone or pot. They point out that the absence of evidence is not always positive evidence of absence, and that we must, for example, postulate that the Cypriote syllabary was used on perishable materials if we are to explain its evident derivation from the Cypro-Minoan scripts of the second millennium BC.[97]

There are several counters to these arguments. First, we are not, in the case of the Aegean and Cyprus, exactly comparing like with like. In Cyprus there seems to have been a continuous use of essentially similar scripts by people using the same language over hundreds of years.[98] In Greece, the change from syllabary to alphabet is abrupt (if not sudden), and the users of the alphabet seem to have had no awareness that an earlier script had ever existed.[99] Second, the letter form argument is far from decisive. We have far fewer Phoenician inscriptions than Greek. The fewer the inscriptions, the greater the temptation to arrange those that we do have in a neat, evolutionary series, and the more difficult it is to discern variation in contemporary letter forms. But as more inscriptions (both Greek and Phoenician) are discovered, it seems that there is greater variety in contemporary letter forms than was previously suspected.[100] The 'letter form' problem is an illusion, caused by the relative paucity of a certain class of evidence. Finally, proponents of an earlier date for the transmission make no attempt to address questions of how and why the alphabet was adopted, and then adapted to suit Greek needs.

---

[93] See the arguments of Goody and Watt 1963.   [94] Johnston 1983.

[95] See arguments in Jeffery 1990: 12–21, 426–7; Carpenter 1933; Powell 1991: 18–20.

[96] Naveh 1982: 175–86; 1988; Bernal 1987.   [97] Powell 1991: 90.   [98] Powell 1991: 89–101.

[99] Legends, of course, existed concerning the 'Kadmeian' (i.e. Phoenician) derivation of the Greek script. Homer was dimly aware of the existence of some form of writing, but does not seem to be familiar with its use. See *Iliad* VI.167–70 and discussion by S.P. Morris (1992: 106).

[100] See Johnston 1983; Johnston in Jeffery 1990: 426–7.

Once literacy has been lost (and there are almost no signs of Linear B literacy in Greece after 1200 BC[101]), it takes a considerable leap of imagination to appreciate the potential of a foreigner's script. Considerable interaction between Greeks and Phoenicians, sustained over a number of generations, is thus a necessary condition for such a cultural exchange. Such interaction is more than the contact that can be traced back to the tenth century BC, and can only have come about after the expansion in both Greek and Phoenician horizons that took place in the late ninth. Coldstream has gone further than this, and argued that the alphabet can only have been invented by someone who was truly bilingual in both languages and knew how the Phoenician script was used.[102] The Greek alphabet was thus the child of one or more mixed marriages, marriages that were more likely to take place at the frontiers of the Greek world.

For all these reasons, it seems safest to stick with a date for the transmission of some time after 800 BC. But the question remains: why was the alphabet adopted? Or, to put it another way, what did Aegean Greeks first use the alphabet for? And why was the Phoenician script better suited (as, at least, a prototype) to their needs than, for example, the Cypriote syllabary or cuneiform? Late Bronze Age Aegean scripts seem to have been used mainly for records and accounting. The Phoenicians may have used their script for similar purposes, but also used writing to mark property, and to record the names of their kings on their tombs, and the names of dedicants on votive objects.[103] Some of the earlier Greek inscriptions seem to serve similar functions. A graffito on a pot from Phaistos in Crete marks it as the property of a certain Erpetidamos.[104] Most of the numerous seventh-century graffiti from the sanctuary of Mt Hymettos in Attica were dedicatory inscriptions.[105] But there are no early Greek inscriptions which are, by any stretch of the imagination, administrative. Some early Greek inscriptions are, in Near Eastern terms, quite unusual. Both the 'Dipylon oinochoe' and 'Nestor's cup' from Pithekoussai are inscribed with several lines of verse, written in hexameters.[106] The inscription on Nestor's cup (fig. 6.12) appears to make an allusion to Homeric poetry.[107] Both these inscriptions are on vessel forms which are related in some way to the consumption of wine. Both therefore appear to be connected to a Greek institution better known in later Archaic times: the symposion, or male drinking club.[108] In the symposion, competitive verse- (and joke-)making are an integral part of the occasion. Other scholars have seen in the hexameters a more direct connection to Homer. Barry Powell has argued that the alphabet was invented specifically with the intention of recording in writing the *Iliad* and the *Odyssey* in their original form.[109] Powell argues that, since Greek alphabetic writing was the

---

[101] Nothing has appeared since Snodgrass wrote in 1971 to show that Linear B was used at all after the great destructions of *c.* 1200 BC.   [102] Coldstream 1993.   [103] Naveh 1982.

[104] Powell 1991: 138.   [105] Langdon 1976.

[106] For these inscriptions generally see Powell 1991: 158–67; Coldstream 1977: 295–302; Jeffery 1990: 66–78, 235–41.

[107] For the 'Nestor's cup' inscription in particular, see Buchner and Ridgway 1993: 212–23; Russo 1993; Murray 1994; Ridgway 1992: 55–7.   [108] Murray 1994.   [109] Powell 1991: 67, 187–237.

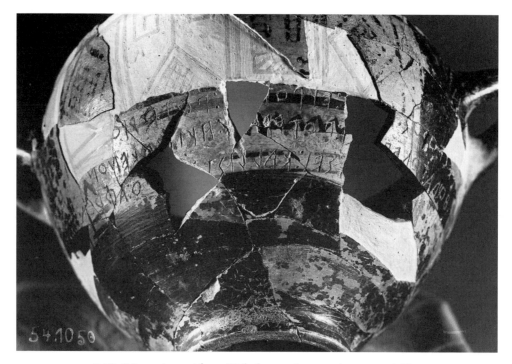

6.12 'Nestor's cup' from Pithekoussai cremation grave 168

only system where writing bears a direct relation to speech, it was ideally suited to such a purpose. Only a true alphabet can record the vowels and the quantities necessary to Homeric verse.

Though this is in many respects an attractive hypothesis, it is not without its difficulties. For one thing, the early alphabet, an alphabet where the long vowels eta and omega were not yet in use, is hardly the perfect instrument for recording the quantities of Homeric verse.[110] What is clear, however, is that the distribution of the earliest Greek inscriptions corresponds closely to the Euboean sphere of trading interests. It is surely remarkable that one of these, Nestor's cup, was found in the first Greek colony, Pithekoussai.[111] The bulk of the other early inscriptions have been found in Lefkandi or Eretria, or in regions immediately adjacent to Euboea, such as Attica.[112] That it was a Euboean who first adapted the alphabet, specifically for Euboean cultural reasons, seems highly likely. From Euboea, the alphabet must then have been diffused to Athens, Corinth, Rhodes and Crete.

The alphabet is the key innovation of the Orientalising revolution. Though Greeks continued to 'Orientalise' throughout the Archaic period (and beyond) no other 'orientalising' development can compare to this one. It demonstrates both

[110] See discussion in Powell 1992.   [111] Powell 1991: 12–18; Ridgway 1992: 55–7.
[112] For Euboean inscriptions, see Jeffery 1990: 79–89, 433–4; Johnston 1983; Johnston and Andreiomenou 1989; Jeffery in Popham *et al.* 1980: 89–93.

Greece's indebtedness to the Near East, and its ability to turn a Levantine 'technology of the intellect' to very different purposes. Phoenician inscriptions in the Levant are few in number, and restricted in type.[113] In both the quantity of inscriptions they produced, and the variety of purposes to which writing was put, the Greeks far surpassed the Phoenicians. Greek inscriptions appear on stone and bronze, and as graffiti (incisions) and dipinti (inscriptions in paint) on pots. Greek writing was not simply used to record property or to commemorate the dead on tombstones; writing became a means of jesting and boasting, about matters ranging from drink to buggery. Art, narrative and writing became interdependent parts of the sympotic occasion, and in this way Greek literacy became an integral part of Greek art, culture and life. By far the commonest use of writing was votive: to record the name of the dedicator and of the god to whom a humble pot or an ostentatious bronze tripod might be dedicated. Archaic Greek literacy was thus intimately connected to Greek religion, or rather to the social, performative practice of that religion as it became institutionalised in the eighth and seventh centuries BC.

[113] See remarks in Powell 1991: 103, with references. Only sixty or so Phoenician inscriptions are known from the Levant, dating from the time of the Phoenician script's invention to its eventual disappearance.

CHAPTER 7

GODS, HEROES AND SACRED PLACES

7.1 What makes a sanctuary?

It is impossible to imagine ancient Greece without its sanctuaries. The Parthenon, floating effortlessly above the modern city of Athens, remains an icon of all that 'Greece' stands for in the popular mind. This view is not misplaced; sanctuaries were essential to ancient Greek life. It is perhaps more difficult for us, living in a secular age where, whatever one's private religious views, church and state, art and politics are conceived of as being entirely separate spheres, to imagine quite how central sanctuaries were to ancient Greeks. Greek sanctuaries were not, like modern mosques, churches or synagogues, places where a minority of devout believers practise rites that seem more and more removed from the secular world around. Sanctuaries in ancient Greece were places in which every citizen and his family had a stake. Sanctuaries were the places where all that was best in Greek art and architecture was to be found. Sanctuaries moreover played an important political role, whether as the principal centres for state cult (as in the Acropolis of Athens) or as the locations for major, panhellenic festivals (such as Delphi and Olympia).

Still, the popular icon of the Greek temple as an image of what Greek sanctuaries were is in some ways a little misleading. This is not simply because many temples of the Archaic period were built, not of stone, but of wood; nor is it simply that sanctuaries with imposing temples are, in many ways, unrepresentative of the variety of cult sites that existed in ancient Greece. Rather it is because the temple was not the central feature of a sanctuary. Indeed, temples were not, strictly speaking, needed at all, and many of the mountaintop shrines to Zeus never acquired a temple.[1] For the principal, ritual activity that marked out a place as sacred to the gods was the act of animal sacrifice, and for this one needed, not a temple, but an altar. Altars were not necessarily of stone; one of the most celebrated altars in antiquity, the altar of Zeus at Olympia, was made out of the remains of bones and ash from hundreds of years of sacrifices to Zeus, held together with clay. By the time it came to be described by Pausanias in the second century AD it was over 22 feet (about 7 m) high (fig. 7.1). Not a trace of it was found by the German archaeologists who excavated Olympia; its position on modern plans is entirely conjectural.[2]

[1] M.K. Langdon 1976; 1997. Burkert 1985: 85–7.   [2] Pausanias V.xiii.9. See also Rupp 1983.

7.1 Reconstruction of the altar of Zeus at Olympia

Normally, each deity worshipped in any sanctuary had his or her own altar. After the altar, the next most common feature in a sanctuary is its votives. These are the gifts set up as offerings to the gods, which are to be found in huge quantities in both major and minor sanctuaries. Indeed most of what is considered 'art' in standard textbooks was originally a votive offering. By the time the archaeologist comes to excavate a votive deposit, the finds have usually been moved from their original position, and have often been reused as fill for later terraces or buildings.[3] It is thought however that, even if redeposited, votives were never removed from the temenos of a sanctuary. A temenos is that area of the land reserved for the god (the god's property, as it were), and could be defined either by a wall or by boundary (*horos*) stones. Certainly, where sanctuaries do have a clear wall (as at Delphi) votives are not found outside it, but it is not so evident that all sanctuaries (particularly smaller ones) were so well defined.[4] Most important sanctuaries also had temples, where votives were displayed and the cult image of the god was housed. These 'houses of the gods' were usually aligned in such a way as to make the altar visible to the image of the god inside (gods were thought to take a personal interest in the sacrifices made to them).[5] Sanctuaries might also have various amenities, more for the convenience of those attending festivals or visiting the shrine to make offerings than for any other reason. Such amenities might include stoas (open colonnades which provided shade); a good supply of water from springs or wells; small buildings for cult equipment, called treasuries; an imposing entranceway, or propylon; and, very much later, and only in some sanctuaries, built stadia or theatres.

But to list such amenities is to conjure up an image of the sanctuary of the Classical era, a time when there is no real difficulty in determining what is and what is not a sanctuary. In the Archaic period, the question of how, when and why sanctuaries first developed is at the forefront of most scholars' minds, and for the Archaic period the evidence is much more ambiguous. Early sanctuaries are rarely smaller and simpler versions of Classical ones. Temples only became architecturally distinct from houses in the course of the Archaic period. An item chosen as a gift for a god may be identical to those used as grave goods. Further to complicate matters, the question of the origins of sanctuaries is necessarily connected to the question of 'continuity' in cult practice from Bronze Age times. Can the early history of sanctuaries be seen as a gradual process of evolution from Bronze Age antecedents? Or is the early Greek sanctuary, with its emphasis on animal sacrifice and the ostentatious giving of gifts to gods, something that marks a sharp break from Bronze Age practice?

---

[3] On the original position of votive offerings, see Alroth 1988; Burkert 1985: 68–70, 92–5.
[4] On the early Greek temenos, see Bergquist 1967; Burkert 1985: 85–7.
[5] By this I do not mean to imply that every altar was aligned exactly on the principal axis of the temple it faced. Many were 'off centre'; see again Bergquist 1967.

7.2 The origins of sanctuaries and the question of continuity

There is no real doubt that Greek religion, as practised in the Classical period, owes something to the religion of the Greek Bronze Age. Many of the names of deities mentioned in the Linear B tablets (Dionysos, for example) are the same as the Classical Olympians.[6] But continuity in the deities venerated by the Greeks does not necessarily entail continuity in religious practice. It is cult practice, rather than belief, that determines the form that sanctuaries, and sanctuary architecture, are to take. What then were the material manifestations of Bronze Age cult?

Shrines in Late Bronze Age Greece are not conspicuous structures. Often, like the shrine at Mycenae or at Phylakopi, they are little more than small rooms filled with objects that may have been images of the deity, votaries or cult equipment.[7] Small shrines of this type do not come to an end with the fall of the palaces. The 'Shrine of the Double Axes' at Knossos is, for example, clearly post-palatial in date. However, during the LMIIIC/LHIIIC period, the pattern on the Greek mainland and in the islands begins to diverge from the pattern in Crete. On Crete, 'bench temples' such as the 'Shrine of the Double Axes' continue to be built and used, an example being the LMIIIC/Subminoan 'temple' at Karphi.[8] Bench temples like these seem to have remained in use throughout the LMIIIC and 'Subminoan' periods. Their use therefore almost overlaps with the earliest Cretan 'hearth' temples, of which temple A at Kommos is the earliest example.[9] On Crete moreover, votive deposits from the mountain/spring shrine at Kato Symi continue without a break from the Late Bronze Age until well into the Hellenistic period, and the same may be true of the votive deposits in the 'Cave of Dictaean Zeus' near Psychro.[10] Crete, it seems, witnessed a gradual evolution in the material manifestations of cult from the twelfth century until the seventh. Is the same true of the mainland and the islands?

Unlike their Cretan counterparts, the small shrines at Mycenae and Phylakopi have no obvious successors. There are few signs of cult in and around the old palace centres in the earlier part of the 'Dark Age'. However, in a corner of rural Phokis, at the site of Kalapodhi, a sanctuary of some kind was established in the LHIIIC period. Early activity seems to focus on a very early altar. Here a continuous series of deposits, apparently votive in character, can be traced from the twelfth century until the seventh.[11] Elsewhere on the Greek mainland, in the

---

[6] Chadwick 1976: 84–101; Burkert 1985: 43–6.

[7] For the shrine(s) at Mycenae, see French 1981; for the shrine at Phylakopi, see Renfrew 1981. See also Burkert 1985: 19–46.

[8] For these bench temples, see Peatfield 1994. For the shrine at Karphi, Rutkowski 1987.

[9] For the earliest temples at Kommos, see Shaw 1989.

[10] For Kato Symi, see Bergquist 1988; Lebessi 1985. This site has been excavated for many years by A. Lebessi, who has produced regular reports in the *Praktika tis Archaiologikis Etaireias*. For the cave of Dictaean Zeus, see Hogarth 1900; Boardman 1961: 1–75.

[11] For Kalapodhi generally, see Felsch 1987; 1996. For evidence of early cult and the earliest altar, see Felsch 1981; 1991. For the earliest pottery deposits, see Jacob-Felsch 1996.

eleven and tenth centuries, sanctuary architecture is hard to come by. Instead of architecture what we find at a number of sites (which we know were sanctuaries in later times) are deposits of some kind; masses of one-handled cups at Isthmia;[12] pottery at the sanctuary of Zeus on Mt Hymettos and at the sanctuary of Artemis at Mounychia;[13] bronze animal figurines at Olympia.[14] The earliest levels of these deposits seem to be of tenth-century date, though some can be traced back to the eleventh. What do they represent?

The most economical explanation is that these are early votive deposits, accumulations of offerings to the gods we know were later worshipped at these sites. If so, cult of a recognisably Greek kind goes back to the tenth century, with hardly any hiatus between the Bronze and the Early Iron Ages. But the evidence is perhaps not quite so straightforward as it seems. Are accumulations of objects in sanctuaries necessarily votive? Could not the one-handled cups at Isthmia, for example, be rather the result of some kind of ritual drink or meal? This whole problem has been complicated by two rival theories about cult in the so-called Dark Ages.

The first of these is a thesis elaborated by François de Polignac.[15] De Polignac argues that, while various beliefs in the gods may have undergone a slow process of evolution from the Bronze Age through the Iron Age and into the Archaic period, the cult practices of these three periods differed profoundly from one another. The Classical pattern of altar, temenos, temple and votive offering only really establishes itself in the Archaic period, and can be traced back no earlier than the ninth century. Cult in the Early Iron Age was focussed not on sacred places but on sacred practices. Cult followed a pattern which can be illustrated from the *Odyssey*. In book III.5–6, Telemachos' shipmates make a sacrifice of bulls to Poseidon, as a thank offering for their safe arrival in Pylos. The sacrifice takes place on the beach – and there is no suggestion that the beach is a sacred place, just a convenient one for a large gathering and a large sacrifice.[16] For de Polignac, the absence of sacred architecture, in particular altars, is evidence for the relative 'spatial indeterminacy' of cult practice during the Early Iron Age. It is only from the eighth century onwards, after all, that we have unambiguous evidence for the construction of altars. At the Heraion of Samos a series of seven increasingly monumental altars were constructed between 800 and 600 BC (fig. 7.2).[17] It can be no coincidence too that seventy or so sanctuaries can be identified for the eighth century BC, but fewer than ten for the earlier part of the Early Iron Age.[18]

[12] Morgan 1994: 113–24; 1999a; Gebhard 1993: 156–9. Morgan (1999a: 340) thinks that a shrine was established at Isthmia in the Protogeometric period.

[13] For Mt Hymettos, see Langdon 1976; for the Mounychia sanctuary, Palaiokrassa 1989.

[14] For figurines from Olympia, see Heilmeyer 1972; 1979; and discussion in Morgan 1990: 30–9; 1993.

[15] De Polignac 1984; 1994; 1995.   [16] *Odyssey* III.5–6; see also discussion in de Polignac 1995: 16.

[17] For the earliest evidence for altars generally, see Rupp 1983; Coldstream 1977: 317–27; de Polignac 1995: 11–21. For the sequence of altars at the Heraion of Samos, see Buschor and Schleif 1933.

[18] Estimates from Coldstream 1977: 318–20. There were probably more sanctuaries than these during the eighth century, and more sanctuaries of earlier date. I doubt however whether the proportion of Dark Age to eighth-century sanctuaries will change very much in the future.

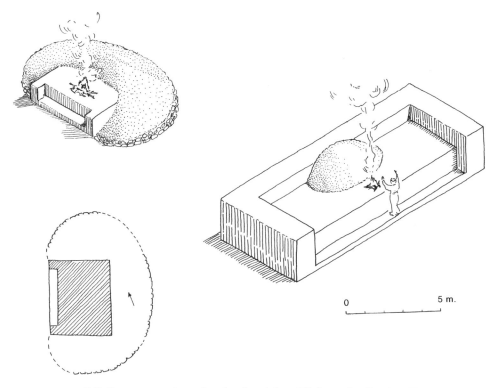

7.2 Reconstruction of early altar (altar III) from the Samian Heraion

A parallel argument has been put forward by A. Mazarakis-Ainian.[19] Mazarakis-Ainian has noted that the earliest temples are identical in plan to the larger houses of the Geometric period. He goes on to argue that the origin of not only the form but the function of early temples must be found in these large house structures. These houses were houses of 'chiefs' or basileis, and so must have had a public and ritual function that transcended their role as residences. These functions were subsumed by the temple when chiefs' houses were turned into gods' houses. But at no point does Mazarakis-Ainian try to relate these houses to the practice of animal sacrifice, except in so far as these buildings may have served as centres for communal dining. Sacrifice to the gods and the sacred functions of chiefs' houses were not clearly associated with one another in the Dark Ages. It is only from the ninth century onwards that the pattern of altar, votive, temenos and temple begins to emerge. It is this distinctive pattern of cult (rather than any distinct pattern of belief) whose origins we seek to trace. Both early altars and early temples, however, are, for different reasons, difficult to detect in the archaeological record. It is hard to distinguish temples from houses; and altars were rudimentary structures made up of a few stones at best. Only votive deposits can provide

---

[19] Mazarakis-Ainian 1988; 1997.

us with a reliable means of detecting, and dating, early sanctuaries. But this raises another fundamental question: what is a votive?

7.3 Votives: gifts to the gods

A votive offering is a gift to a god. Anything dedicated by a mortal, which, once dedicated, becomes the inalienable property of that god, and so is retained within the god's temenos, is a votive. It is not for archaeologists to delve into the psychology of giving to beings whose existence, as the Greeks themselves were inclined to admit, was unclear.[20] It is unlikely, however, that the motives were as crude (or as straightforward) as the Latin phrase 'do ut des' (I give you something so that you will give me something) would suggest. Votives were not simply bribes for divine favour, or offerings of thanks for favours already received.[21] Votive offerings were also outward and visible signs not only of the wealth but also of the piety of the dedicator. The social and spiritual value of piety in ancient Greek society is not to be underestimated. Still, the anthropological concept of reciprocity, of a cycle of exchange between men and gods, is not irrelevant here. Ancient Greeks were interested not in private devotion, but rather in public acts which demanded public recognition. Nothing could be more public than to dedicate a bronze statue, or a marble pillar, or a whole ship in a sanctuary frequented by others.

What kind of object then could be used as a votive? In theory, almost anything could. Later literary accounts tell of whole ships captured in battle being dedicated by the victors as a thank offering to the god.[22] Both the small 'treasuries', such as the Siphnian treasury at Delphi (fig. 4.2), and the bronze statues set up to commemorate victory in the games, such as the Delphi Charioteer (fig. 1.2), were votive offerings.[23] Most Greek art is votive. This does not quite mean that everything found within a sanctuary's temenos is a gift to the god. Sanctuaries often kept equipment, such as libation vessels, reserved for use in cult, and it would be stretching the definition of the term to call these 'votives'. How then can we distinguish between votives proper and cult equipment?

In the Archaic period many votives were inscribed. Sometimes the inscription just gives us the name of the deity to whom the object is dedicated. Often, however, a particular formula is followed: the dedicator's name, followed by the verb 'set up' (anetheke), followed by the name of the deity in the dative case. An example of such an inscription is shown in figure 7.3.[24] This was a marble

---

[20] Burkert 1987. For votive offerings generally, see Rouse 1902. For an essential discussion of the 'psychology of giving' and votive offerings, see Van Straten 1981.

[21] The whole problem of what Greeks actually believed is a complex one. Greek religion was not theologically consistent, since there was no mechanism for enforcing orthodox belief, but this does not mean that Greeks did not have beliefs. It was easier, in the ancient world, to enforce uniformity of practice rather than belief.   [22] For ship dedications, see Rouse 1902: 105; Herodotos VIII.121.

[23] For the Delphi Charioteer, see Chamoux 1955; for the Siphnian treasury, see Daux and Hansen 1987.

[24] Lewis 1981: no. 487; Raubitschek 1949: no. 3; see discussion in Kron 1996: 160–2 (esp. p. 161 fig. 14).

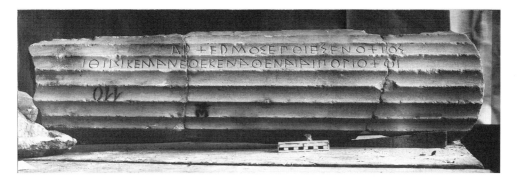

7.3 Sixth-century marble votive column from the Acropolis

column, probably the base for a statue, set up in the Athenian Acropolis towards the end of the sixth century BC. In the second line it reads '*Iphidike m'anetheken Athenaiai Poliochoi*', that is 'Iphidike set me up to Athena, protectress of the city.' Dedications are often referred to in this way, and are often called 'anathemata', i.e. things set up. Another term in common use is agalma, an adornment. Both words (neither of which corresponds to the English word 'dedication') attest to the public character of votive offerings; the act of dedication was something which was in itself worth commemorating. By the end of the Archaic period, most of the more ostentatious votives, and many humbler ones, were routinely inscribed in this way. Inscriptions do then give us some indication of the kinds of objects dedicated to gods. Caution, of course, is necessary in earlier periods, before the widespread adoption of alphabetic scripts. None the less, even for these periods, it is possible to divide votives into the following categories.

1 Dedications of personal objects. For women these may have included such things as pyxides, spindle whorls and the near ubiquitous bronze dress pins (fig. 7.4). Men are more likely to have been responsible for the dedications of arms and armour found in many sanctuaries, such as those found at the sanctuary of Poseidon at Isthmia.[25]

2 Purpose-made votives, objects which could not really have served any other purpose. Such objects may have included hand-made and then mould-made terracotta figurines, or the small figurines of bronze horses on stands which turn up in large numbers from the eighth century BC onwards (fig. 7.5).[26] Sometimes objects seem to have been made specifically with one divinity, or even one sanctuary, in mind. Examples of this type include the clay 'imitation cakes' found at the sanctuary of Demeter and Kore at Corinth.[27]

[25] For dedications of pins, see Jacobsthal 1956; Kilian-Dirlmeier 1984: 84–292. For dedications of armour, see Jackson 1991; 1999. For dedications of armour at Olympia, see Bol 1989.
[26] For bronze horse figurines, see Zimmermann 1989.   [27] For these, see Bookidis 1993.

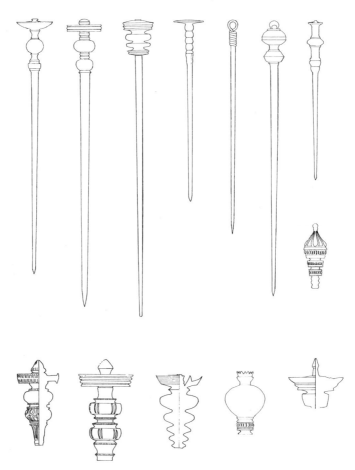

7.4 Bronze dress pins used as votives, from the sanctuary of
Hera Limenia at Perachora

3 Objects which, in other circumstances, would have been considered appropriate as gifts within the eastern Mediterranean sphere of aristocratic gift
exchange. Oriental objects with figured decoration, such as the Phoenician
bronze bowls found at Olympia and the bronze relief for the forehead of a horse
found at the Samian Heraion, fall into this category.[28]

Olympia indeed provides us with the most abundant evidence for early votives,
and for changes in votive practice during the Archaic period. Though there are
major difficulties with dating finds by stratigraphic means at this site, it is clear
that the votives were being dedicated at a date much earlier than the traditional

---

[28] For Phoenician bronze bowls, see Markoe 1985; for Orientalising cauldrons at Olympia, see
Herrmann 1966; 1979. For a discussion of the origin of this type of cauldron, see Muscarella 1992.
For Oriental objects found at the Samian Heraion, see Kyrieleis 1979; 1993; Kyrieleis and Röllig
1988. For a discussion of Oriental finds in sanctuaries generally, see Strøm 1992.

7.5 Bronze votive horse, probably of Corinthian manufacture

founding date of the games of 776 BC. Many of the bronze and terracotta animal figurines must, on stylistic grounds, date to the tenth and ninth centuries. But by far the greatest number of these objects belong to the eighth century.[29] From the ninth century onwards, both the quantity and the range of votive objects increases. There are substantially more bronze dress pins, tripods and other bronze objects which date to the eighth century than to any earlier period.[30]

Of these new kinds of votive perhaps the most interesting are the large bronze tripods. These seem to date to the eighth century. It is clear however that tripods have a longer history than this. Clay tripods (very similar in form to later bronze examples) have been found in Protogeometric grave contexts in the Kerameikos cemetery in Athens, and the ambiguous 'moulds deposit' from Lefkandi, which is datable to around 900 BC, seems to have some connection

[29] For the chronology of the Olympia figurines see Heilmeyer 1979: 19–28. For the increase in figurines in the eighth century, see *ibid.*: 24–7; Snodgrass 1987: 206 fig. 64. There appear to be over 4,042 bronze figurines, most of which date to the eighth century. For the terracottas, see Heilmeyer 1972.

[30] New kinds of votive which become popular in the eighth century at Olympia include pins and jewellery (Philipp 1981: 30–63) and tripod figurines (Maass 1978). See also Snodgrass 1980a: 53; Kilian-Dirlmeier 1985: 230–5.

with tripod production.[31] Tripods are frequently mentioned in Homer, where they are used for such things as prizes in funeral games, or circulate more generally in a network of aristocratic exchange.[32] Early tripods found at Olympia had cast legs and small handles, and were rather squat. By the end of the eighth century techniques had improved, leading to the magnificent tall tripods with hammered legs and elaborate handles, often crowned by a small horse figurine (fig. 7.6). Some scholars argue that tripods like these found at Olympia were originally prizes in the games, only later dedicated to a god by victors in the various athletic competitions. But if 'their social value depended upon their previous role as gifts or exchange items within an elite exchange network',[33] then their appearance in sanctuaries takes on an added significance. Tripods become a part of an exchange network with the divine. Such factors may help explain the equally sudden appearance of Oriental and Orientalising objects, such as the bronze cauldrons with human, siren, bull or griffin protomes, in sanctuaries at the end of the eighth century BC (fig 7.7).[34] Oriental metalwork had long been a staple of aristocratic gift exchange. What is new is that the gods were now a part of this elite exchange network.

Whatever criterion you choose, the eighth century remains the crucial threshold for the development of the practice of giving ostentatiously to the gods. It is not simply that the number of votive offerings increases dramatically. It is also that this increase in numbers coincides with an increase in the range of possible items that can be dedicated, and with other changes in depositional practice. Objects which in earlier times had been deposited in graves, such as the ubiquitous dress pins and fibulae found in many Early Iron Age female graves, or the armour that has turned up in eighth-century 'warrior' graves in Argos, were in future to be deposited almost exclusively in sanctuaries. By the end of the eighth century, the sanctuary has replaced the funeral as the principal arena for aristocratic competition and display, display now sanctioned by and mediated through the gods.[35]

For the archaeologist, votives are the most conspicuous feature of sanctuaries in the Archaic period. Some indication of the scale of offerings is given in tables 7.1 (for Peloponnesian pins) and 12.1 (for dedications at Isthmia). The sheer quantity of bronze pins, figurines, tripods, cauldrons, shields and greaves dedicated at Olympia alone is staggering, and has understandably attracted most of

---

[31] For tripods at Olympia generally, see Willemsen 1957; Maass 1978. For the evolution of the type (including tripods in clay), see Schweitzer 1971; Maass 1981. For the mould deposit from Lefkandi, see H.W. Catling in Popham *et al.* 1980a: 93–7.

[32] Tripods in Homer were often used as prizes, for example in the funeral games of Patroklos; *Iliad* XI.700; XXIII.262–5.

[33] Morgan 1990: 46. For sanctuaries as arenas for aristocratic competition and display in the eighth century, see S. Langdon 1987; de Polignac 1996b.

[34] For Oriental and Orientalising cauldrons, see Herrmann 1966; 1979; Muscarella 1992.

[35] For deposits of eighth-century armour in graves, see in particular Courbin 1957 (cuirass tomb in Argos). For deposits of armour in Olympia, see Kunze 1991 (greaves) and Bol 1989 (shields). The deposition of armour in sanctuaries seems to peak in the sixth century BC.

7.6 Reconstruction of hammered tripod from Olympia, zu 201

7.7 Griffin protome from Kameiros on Rhodes in the British Museum, London

the interest of German archaeologists working there.[36] This quantity cannot be explained simply as a mechanical result of the end of the Dark Age 'bronze shortage'.[37] Votives are to be found in all materials, not only bronze. Nor are large numbers of votives confined to panhellenic sanctuaries. At the sanctuary of Pherai in Thessaly – hardly a place which was ever at the centre of the Greek world – 3,739 votives, mainly bronzes, were dedicated during the eighth and early seventh centuries BC.[38] At Perachora, so many Archaic bronze votives were found that the excavators stopped counting – but they estimated that there must have been over 2,000.[39] At the shrine of Artemis Orthia near Sparta, over 100,000 lead figurines were recovered by British archaeologists, the bulk of which must have been dedicated in Archaic times[40] (see table 12.2). The production of such votives has rightly been called an industry. Production was on a large scale, requiring industrial methods of mass production such as moulds to

---

[36] The arrangements for publication of finds from Olympia, in the Olympische Forschungen, remain strictly by type of object and material, not by context or deposit.

[37] For this hypothesis, see Snodgrass 1971: 275–86.

[38] For votives from Pherai, see Kilian-Dirlmeier 1985: 216–25.

[39] Payne 1940: 123–84; see also Kilian-Dirlmeier 1984; 1985: 225–30.

[40] Wace 1929. For a revised chronology, see Boardman 1963b.

Table 7.1 *Pins found in Peloponnesian sanctuaries (after Osborne 1996a: 92, table 3; information from Kilian-Dirlmeier 1984)*

Sanctuary	Submycenaean and Protogeometric (c. 1080–850)	Early to Late Geometric (850–700)	Late eighth and early seventh centuries (725–650)	Archaic (700–500)
Perachora	0	38	9	78
Argive Heraion	2	699	279	388
Lousoi	0	3	5	23
Olympia	7	58	29	225
Tegea	0	273	243	50
Artemis Orthia	0	133	926	403
Menelaion	0	2	17	41

make hundreds of figurines of terracotta, bronze and lead. Traditional Classical archaeology has in the past laid great emphasis on the study of such objects, perhaps at the expense of asking questions of a more fundamental character. What makes a place the focus for such ostentatious deposition? What is it about Olympia, on the junction of the Kladeos and Alpheios rivers, or the Argive Heraion, at the edge of the Argive plain, that makes such places numinous? It is little more than a tautology to point out that votives are deposited in places hallowed by successive acts of sacrifice. For what was it about the place that made it hallowed in the first place?

7.4 Sacred place and sacred space

What makes a place holy? Modern visitors to Delphi are often struck by the beauty of its setting. It is easy, at Delphi, to believe in the numinous quality of certain places, to which the establishment of a sanctuary might seem a natural response. But, to those acquainted with other Greek sanctuaries, it is clear that aesthetics can only be part of the answer. The sanctuary of Artemis Orthia near Sparta is set in an unprepossessing location, among reeds close to the river Eurotas. An anthropologist might be more inclined to disregard aesthetics and turn instead to the concept of liminality. Anthropologists talk of liminal occasions and liminal places, times or places which stand 'betwixt and between' one stage, or one world, and another. Liminal occasions are those times, such as birth, the passage to adulthood, marriage or death, which are times of transition, during which members of the community sometimes have to undergo 'rites of passage'. Certainly we know that some Greek sanctuaries served as places where such rites took place. Young Athenian girls, at (or rather just before) the onset of puberty, took part in a ritual at the sanctuary of Artemis at Brauron where they pretended they were little bears;[41] adolescent Spartan boys had to undertake a strange rite of transition at the sanctuary of Artemis Orthia where they were required to steal cheeses, having first to run the gauntlet of the whips of their elders.[42]

Sacred places are often also liminal places, places which in some way stand between one world and another. Mountain peaks are where the earth meets the sky; caves where the world above meets the world below; and springs where running water appears mysteriously from solid rock. Such places may seem to be naturally hallowed, particularly in a mountainous country like Greece where, in summer, water is particularly scarce. But such considerations can take us only so far. To be sure, altars of Zeus are frequently to be found on the tops of hills and mountains.[43] But the most celebrated shrine of Zeus is at Olympia, a site as far removed from mountains as it is possible to imagine. In Crete, many caves were used as shrines, the most celebrated example being the cave of Zeus on Mt Ida. Such caves received vast quantities of votives during the Archaic period.[44] But in mainland Greece, caves were rarely treated as sacred places before Classical times, when (in Attica at least) a number of mountain caves became shrines to Pan. Spring shrines too are rarer than one might think. Certainly great efforts were made to ensure that important sanctuaries were well supplied with water, but the natural springs often associated with major sanctuaries rarely became the focus of cult. The most famous of all springs in ancient Greece, the Castalian spring at Delphi, lies outside the temenos of each of the sanctuaries there. The concept of liminality can take us only so far.

But perhaps the location of a sanctuary may be related to the character of the god that was worshipped there. After all we know that certain gods favoured certain kinds of sacrifice. Recent faunal analyses have confirmed that pigs were indeed the animals regularly sacrificed to Demeter, bulls, sheep and goats being generally preferred for other deities.[45] Might not the same principle apply to the location of sanctuaries to particular deities? Is it not appropriate that Zeus, the Sky-God, is worshipped on mountain peaks? The most systematic attempt to link the attributes of a deity to the place in which that deity's sanctuary is set is Vincent Scully's *The Earth, the Temple and the Gods.*[46] Scully argues that sanctuaries of Hera, such as the Argive or the Samian Heraion, or the two temples of Hera at Poseidonia (Paestum) in Italy, are found mainly in lowland locations; sanctuaries of Apollo, such as that of Apollo Epikourios at Bassai in Arcadia or the sanctuary at Delphi itself, are, more often than not, set amidst dramatic mountain scenery (though never actually on a mountain's peak).[47] There is something to Scully's arguments.

---

[41] Simon 1983: 83–8; Kahil 1977; Aristophanes, *Lysistrata*, lines 641–6.

[42] Dawkins 1929: 399–407; Pausanias III.xvi.7–11; Burkert 1985: 262. Of course, the literary evidence for these rites is late – nothing is attested earlier than Pausanias. It is an open question whether they went back to the Archaic period.   [43] M.K. Langdon 1976; Scully 1979: 132–54.

[44] For the Idaean cave, see Kunze 1931; Boardman 1961: 79–88; Sakellerakis 1988. For the Dictaean cave, see Hogarth 1900; Boardman 1961: 1–75.

[45] On the faunal evidence from sanctuaries of Demeter, see Jarman 1973 (Knossos) and Bookidis *et al.* 1999 (Corinth). On other kinds of sacrifice to other deities, see Van Straten 1988.

[46] Scully 1979.   [47] Scully 1979: 41–69 (Hera) and 100–31 (Apollo).

But much of what he says depends upon unsubstantiated hypotheses concerning Aegean religion in the Bronze Age, and his whole approach relies on the assumption that Greek polytheism was a theologically consistent belief system. This cannot have been the case. The origins of most cults were specific and local. The Artemis venerated at Sparta, Artemis Orthia, had little in common with the Artemis of Ephesos. Scully is on firmer ground when he tries to relate the placing of sanctuaries to specific features of the landscape, and describes the ways in which the architecture of a shrine evokes particular aspects of its setting. In this respect, Scully anticipates some of the recent 'phenomenological' approaches to the prehistoric landscapes of Britain.[48]

That there is a spatial dimension of cult, and that sanctuaries have a setting in a landscape, seems undeniable. Of course, archaeologists and topographers who wish to understand 'sacred landscapes' have to work with the bare bones of the country as it exists today. Many of the ancient features that made a place sacred (such as particular trees or groves) have gone forever, and Greek archaeology still lacks the means to reconstruct past environments in a scientific manner. Still, in recent years there has been renewed interest in this spatial dimension of cult, stimulated by the work of François de Polignac.[49] De Polignac relates the origins of cult to landscape and to politics, as well as to religion. He sees the appearance of sanctuaries as being intimately linked to the development of early states, particularly to poleis. Establishing authority over sanctuaries was a means of marking out a community's territory. His paradigm is Argos, or more precisely the relationship between the town of Argos itself and the principal sanctuary of the Argive state, the Argive Heraion. The Argive Heraion is situated on the northeastern fringes of the Argive plain (see fig. 7.8), on the opposite side from Argos itself. It is much closer to Mycenae (an independent polis for much of the Archaic period) than it is to Argos. De Polignac argues that Argos established its control over the Heraion in the eighth century BC, and did so in order to assert its territorial claim to the Argive plain as a whole. Certainly, the floruit of the sanctuary dates from the late eighth century BC.[50] Argos was the paradigm of the 'bipolar' city-state, whose axis was defined by its urban centre (Argos) and its principal sanctuary (the Heraion). De Polignac goes on to argue that the location of the Heraion is also significant in symbolic terms. The Heraion lies in a 'liminal' location, at the very edge of the plain (the area suitable for arable farming) and just below the wild maquis and garigue of the mountains (where wild beasts lurk and only goats can graze). Hera was a goddess, if not of the hearth, then certainly of the house, of the settled community and the sedentary way of life. The city of Argos and the Heraion effectively established the limits of this sedentary existence. The Heraion thus marks the symbolic as well as the territorial limits of the early polis.[51]

---

[48] See Tilley 1994.   [49] De Polignac 1984; 1995.
[50] For early finds from the Argive Heraion, see Strøm 1988; Waldstein 1902; 1905.
[51] De Polignac 1995: 33–45, 52–3.

7.8 Map of central Greece, showing position of major cities and

De Polignac has argued that a similar pattern can be seen in other areas of Greece. On Samos, the Heraion, which was again the principal sanctuary of the polis, is located at some distance from the city (if not on the opposite side of the island). The sanctuary of Hera at Perachora is located by a small harbour on a headland directly over the sea from Corinth itself (see figs. 7.8 and 12.1).[52] Corinth, as a maritime state involved in trade and colonisation from an early date,

52 Morgan 1994: 129–35; de Polignac 1994; 1995: 51–2.

had an interest in controlling the seaways and harbours in its vicinity. By making Perachora into a Corinthian sanctuary Corinth established its territorial boundaries, and denied this harbour to its neighbour, Megara. The line between Corinth and Perachora establishes a maritime axis equivalent to the one established between Argos and its Heraion.

De Polignac's arguments have attracted much criticism. It is not clear how sanctuaries could establish borders in Greek colonies at a time when there were no borders, only frontiers.[53] It is far from certain that the Argive Heraion was the principal sanctuary of Argos from the eighth century onwards. Some have argued that the Heraion served as a regional shrine for the whole of the Argolid, and only became exclusively 'Argive' in the sixth century or later.[54] We do know that in western Greece sanctuaries were not associated with major early city-states. Delphi itself was little more than a village with an important sanctuary, whose independence was guaranteed by a league of protecting powers. The sanctuary of Apollo at Thermon served the whole of Aetolia, a region which consisted of a mosaic of small communities such as Kalydon.[55] Furthermore the landscape in which these early sanctuaries were placed was neither pristine nor entirely natural. It was a landscape already shaped by generations of human endeavour, generations whose imposing remains could still be seen. It is not too fanciful to see, in our mind's picture of eighth-century Greece, a ruined, almost romantic landscape, one full of powerful associations of an earlier, more heroic age. Eighth- and seventh-century Greece was a country that had once been inhabited by earlier races and by heroes. It had a past which exerted a gravitational pull on both the sites and the occasions of early Greek cult.

7.5 The uses of the past

Greeks have always had a variety of views concerning their own past. Before the Classical period, Greece remained a society where collective memory was primarily oral. In such societies accurate knowledge about what happened long ago does not extend further back than four, sometimes five, generations.[56] In oral societies, the past has to be imagined, or rather envisioned. One vision of a heroic past is contained in Homer's *Iliad* and *Odyssey*. Homer sings of heroes who quarrelled, fought, lived and died in some (unspecified) time long, long ago. Another vision is given to us by the Boeotian poet Hesiod, who tells of a world that had once been inhabited by successive races: the races of gold, then silver, then bronze, then of heroes and finally his most miserable race of iron.[57]

---

[53] Malkin 1996.   [54] Strøm 1988; Hall 1995a.
[55] For Thermon, see Soteriadis 1900; Rhomaios 1916.
[56] For Greece as a partially 'oral' society, see Thomas 1992: esp. 15–28.
[57] Hesiod, *Works and Days*, 109–201; see comments in Whitley 1995. There is, to me, a remarkable similarity between the attitude of Hesiod to previous races and to modern Greek folk ideas about 'Hellenes' as recorded by Kakridis 1978.

7.9 Early terrace wall at the Argive Heraion

There were however plenty of reminders in the eighth- and seventh-century landscape of Greece of what the heroes, gods, giants (Cyclopes) or previous races of men might have done. Impressive 'Cyclopean' masonry can still be seen even today in many parts of Greece, particularly in the Argolid and Boeotia, and must have been much more impressive in Archaic times than it is now. Such remains seem to have been a factor in the location of many early sanctuaries. The earliest temple of Athena on the Athenian Acropolis was set within the area enclosed by fairly substantial Mycenaean fortifications.[58] The earliest signs of cult at the sanctuary of Poseidon at Isthmia seem to be located very close to a surviving piece of 'Cyclopean' masonry.[59] More striking is the establishment of an early temple at Mycenae almost directly over an earlier Mycenean megaron.[60] So important indeed was the appearance, if not the reality, of earlier 'Cyclopean' structures for any self-respecting sanctuary that, if it was not there already, it had to be created. Such at least is one interpretation of the massive 'pseudo-Cyclopean' terrace built for the earliest temple at the Heraion of Argos (fig. 7.9).[61] At the Heraion moreover there are other signs of interest in a Bronze Age past. Many of the Mycenaean chamber tombs in the Prosymna cemetery close by contain offerings of pottery

[58] For the 'Bronze Age' landscape, see Antonaccio 1994. For earlier buildings on the Athenian Acropolis, see Nylander 1962.   [59] Gebhard 1993: 156–9; 1999.

[60] For Mycenae, see Klein 1997. It was once thought that the smaller, later megaron inside the earlier one at Tiryns was constructed in the eighth century as a temple of Hera (Frickenhaus 1912). Though there is no doubt that there was a temple of Hera at Tiryns, associated with some eighth-century votive shields, recent investigations in the second, smaller megaron have shown conclusively that it was constructed in the twelfth century BC.

[61] As argued by Wright 1982. For criticisms, see Antonaccio 1992.

and bronze, offerings which seem, for the most part, to date to the late eighth and the seventh centuries BC.[62] Similar offerings have been found in tholos and chamber tombs at both Argos and Mycenae, and, more sparsely distributed, in other regions of Greece.[63] What could such offerings represent?

There are in fact two questions here: what does the distribution of such offerings represent? And what 'god, man or hero' was the object of such veneration? Concerning the distribution of finds many hypotheses have been put forward. Nicolas Coldstream has suggested that this new practice was prompted by the spread of epic poetry. Offerings in Mycenaean tombs only appear in those areas of Greece whose eighth-century funerary customs were markedly unlike those of the Mycenaean period, and this marked Mycenaean tombs as different, and so appropriate for heroes.[64] Anthony Snodgrass by contrast notes that there is nothing in epic poetry to link the heroes of epic with Mycenaean tombs. Mycenaeans tended to practise inhumation, placing several generations in the same collective tomb. Heroes in the *Iliad*, such as Hector or Patroklos, are cremated, and their remains placed within a metal urn over which a tumulus is then raised up. Snodgrass notes that such 'tomb cults' appear in the eighth century, and are concentrated in those regions of Greece where population appears to have risen sharply at that time. For Snodgrass, offerings in Mycenaean tombs represent the actions of colonising peasant agriculturalists, who were both propitiating the previous owners of the land (represented by the impressive Mycenaean funerary architecture) and establising their title to land that they would then farm.[65] But the distribution of tomb cults is not as markedly rural as this explanation would lead us to expect. In the Argolid, offerings in Mycenaean tombs are strongly associated with sanctuaries and urban centres. It is not too far fetched to see this practice as being linked to the politics of cult in this area of competing early poleis.[66]

Theories about the distribution of tomb cults tend to avoid the tricky question of what beings Archaic Greeks were making offerings to. One answer is that these are ancestor cults, offerings to real or imagined forebears, perhaps heroic ones. Carla Antonaccio has argued that something along these lines may have been taking place in Archaic Greece. Antonaccio argues that the popularity of such tomb cults in the eighth and seventh centuries has obscured the fact that their origin is much earlier. Eighth-century tomb cults represent the continuation of a practice of ancestor cult that runs throughout Early Iron Age Greece.[67] Still, the evidence for such continuity is rather thin, and it is odd that 'tomb cults' were so very popular around 700 BC. Other explanations are possible. One is that the objects of such veneration were heroes. But if so, it is curious that there are no votive inscriptions among the eighth-, seventh- and sixth-century offerings in these tombs. The richest of the 'tomb cults', the series of offerings at the

[62] Blegen 1937; Antonaccio 1995: 53–65.
[63] Morris 1988; Antonaccio 1995: 11–143; for the Argolid, *ibid.*: 12–65.
[64] Coldstream 1976; 1977: 344–8.   [65] Snodgrass 1980: 37–40; 1987: 160–4.
[66] Whitley 1988: 178–81; de Polignac 1995: 138–43.   [67] Antonaccio 1993; 1995: 245–68.

Mycenaean tomb at Menidhi in Attica, contains one inscription, but it is a dipinto by the painter Sophilos, and has nothing votive about it.[68] There is nothing to link these offerings to the heroes of epic. The only clue as to the identity of the beings venerated (whether they were ancestors, or heroes, or one of Hesiod's four races) comes from an early Classical graffito on a plain cup from above Grave Circle A at Mycenae, which reads simply '*tou heroos eimi*' 'I am of the hero'.[69] Whoever they were, these beings maintained strict anonymity.

This lack of any direct link with the heroes of epic may seem rather surprising, particularly in the Argolid, an area with rich potential for assocations with the heroic age. But cults to named heroes, that is to heroes known from epic poetry, are rather rare in the Archaic period. Indeed there is only one shrine where we have direct, epigraphic evidence that 'epic' heroes were venerated before 500 BC: the heröon of Helen and Menelaus (the so-called Menelaion) at Therapne near Sparta.[70] Though there are votive offerings at the Agamemnoneion at Mycenae and the Polis cave on Ithaca that date to the eighth, seventh and sixth centuries, there is no concrete evidence that either shrine was linked with Agamemnon or Odysseus until the Classical or Hellenistic periods.[71] Of all the epic heroes, only Herakles seems to have been widely venerated in Archaic times, and Herakles was as much god as hero.[72]

Heroes of epic, however, are only a part of the picture. Other kinds of hero existed. Almost nothing, for example, is known from our literary sources about 'Akademos', whose shrine near Athens is attested from the late Archaic period onwards.[73] Akademos was a hero with a purely local following. In Classical Attica there were also a number of anonymous heroes, nameless but none the less strongly associated with a particular locality, such as the 'hero of the saltmarsh.'[74] It was also possible that the recently dead might receive heroic honours. The founders, or oikists, of colonies may well have been honoured in this way. The best archaeological example of such a posthumous cult is the heröon at the West Gate of Eretria. Here a large, stone triangular structure was erected over a number of male 'warrior' cremation graves in the early seventh century BC.[75]

But non-epic heroes such as these do not appear to be important to the writers of the early fifth century. Pindar likes to link his victors to the epic heroes associated with his victors' locality, and epic heroes such as Herakles feature prominently in Herodotos' narrative. The impression one gains from these authors is

---

[68] Wolters 1899; Antonaccio 1995: 104–12.
[69] Antonaccio 1995: 49–53; Jeffery 1990: 174 no. 6; Whitley 1995: 55–6.
[70] Wace *et al.* 1909; Catling 1977; Catling and Cavanagh 1976; Antonaccio 1995: 155–66.
[71] For the Agamemnoneion, see Cook 1953; Antonaccio 1995: 146–52. For the Polis cave on Ithaca, see Benton 1935; Antonaccio 1995: 152–5. Recently a hero shrine of the 'Seven against Thebes' has been discovered in Argos. There are no finds as such, and the shrine is dated by the letter forms on its horos stone to the sixth century BC; see Pariente 1992.
[72] For late Archaic cults to Herakles in Attica, see Woodford 1971.
[73] For Akademos, see Antonaccio 1995: 187–9. In my view, the 'cult house' is something of a mirage, but the horos stone is genuine enough.   [74] Kearns 1989: 144.
[75] Bérard 1970; see also discussion in de Polignac 1995: 129–38.

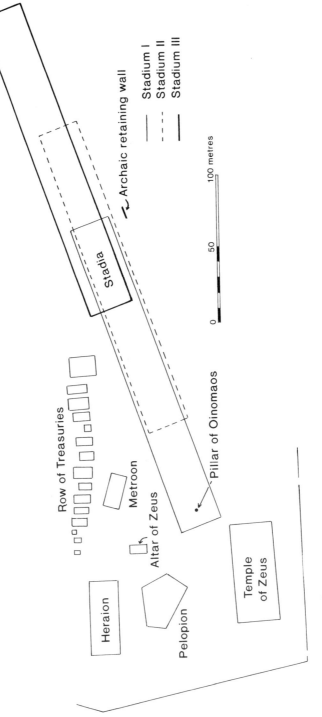

Row of Treasuries

Metroon

Heraion

Altar of Zeus

Pelopion

Temple
of Zeus

Pillar of Oinomaos

Stadia

Archaic retaining wall

Stadium I
Stadium II
Stadium III

0   50   100 metres

7.10 Sketch plan of early buildings at Olympia, showing position of earliest stadium

that heroes were everywhere in late Archaic and early Classical Greece. Certainly many major Classical sanctuaries had shrines to heroes as well as gods. Archaeologists of the last century were, understandably, inclined to believe that such hero cults went back to the very beginnings of cult at these sanctuaries. The German archaeologist Dörpfeld, for example, undertook extensive excavations at the Pelopion at Olympia. The Pelopion was the shrine of Pelops, the local hero *par excellence* of Olympia, whose chariot race to win Hippodameia for his bride was the event that established a legendary precedent for the whole Olympic games.[76] The Pelopion, the tumulus and grove of Pelops, was indeed a prominent feature of the Classical sanctuary, pointed out to many later travellers such as Pausanias.[77] But Dörpfeld's excavations of what he thought was a Bronze Age tumulus uncovered a tumulus without a tomb. There is indeed no sign of any Bronze Age or Early Iron Age activity in what seems to be a small natural rise in the ground. Later scholars have argued that the earliest activity here was the construction of a small boundary wall of marker stones in the late Archaic period. There are no unambiguous signs of early cult.[78] The Pelopion seems to be an example of the 'invention of tradition', part of a pattern of the establishment of hero cults that took place in the late Archaic period.

Such inventions, or reinterpretations, of ancient monuments continued in later times. One of the minor features of the sanctuary that Pausanias notes is a small structure, or tetrapylon, built over an old wooden column or post. Pausanias was told that this was the only surviving column of the house of Oinomaos, a legendary contemporary of Pelops.[79] Now historians of Pausanias' time were unanimous in placing both Pelops and Oinomaos in what we would call the Late Bronze Age (the thirteenth or fourteenth century BC), in which case the pillar seen by Pausanias would have survived for well over a thousand years. This seems highly improbable. Eric Brulotte has presented us with a more plausible alternative.[80] The 'pillar of Oinomaos' was in fact the westernmost turning post of the original stadium, laid out sometime in the eighth or seventh century BC. As the Olympic games became more important, successively larger stadia (stadia II and III) were built further east, so as to remove the crowds of spectators from the area of cult activities close to the Altar of Zeus (fig. 7.10). The original function and identity of the post was forgotten. But the column survived, and, as it was obviously ancient, had to be incorporated into the heroic history of the sanctuary. Hence the story of its being the only surviving column from the house of Oinomaos.

The ways in which Archaic Greeks appropriated the remains of earlier ages, and the use that they made of their past(s), underwent several stages of development. In the eighth and seventh centuries the presence of Mycenaean ruins seems to

---

[76] The whole of Pindar, *Olympian* I is devoted to the legend of Pelops. References to the 'tymbos' or 'sama' (tomb or grave) of Pelops are given in Pindar, *Olympian* I.88–98; IX.24.
[77] Pausanias V.xiii.1–7.   [78] Dörpfeld 1935: 118–24; Antonaccio 1995: 170–6.
[79] For early references to Oinomaos, see Pindar, *Olympian* I.76: 88; X.51. For a description of the 'pillar' see Pausanias V.xx.6–8.   [80] Brulotte 1994.

have been a factor in the location of early sanctuaries, and Mycenaean tombs received votive offerings. But these activities seem to have little, if anything, to do with the heroes of epic. Hero cult, in the strict sense, is found only at the Menelaion. It is only in the late Archaic period that epic heroes become important objects of cult, and it is only from this time that major sanctuaries acquire shrines to heroes as well as gods. It was gods, not heroes, who received most attention. Much energy was directed towards the construction and embellishment of their 'houses'. The evolution of the temple is perhaps the most striking achievement of Greek architects and builders. How and why did this happen?

7.6 The first temples

How do we recognise a temple? This may at first sight seem a foolish question. Late Archaic temples, such as the temple of Aphaia on Aegina, or the temple of Apollo in Corinth, could not really be mistaken for anything else. But identifying an eighth-century temple is much harder. Early temples resemble large houses. For example, in Eretria there appear to be two early, eighth-century temples to Apollo, which have been excavated underneath the late Archaic one. The earliest, the Daphnephoreion, is little more than an apsidal hut built to hold a cult image. We may get some idea of what it looked like from the votive temple model found at Perachora. If so, it would have had a high-pitched, thatched roof, and a small portico with two columns in antis[81] (fig. 7.11). The second temple is a much larger apsidal structure, little different in overall plan from the large house or 'heröon' at Lefkandi, Toumba. Only the fact that its east end lies open, facing the altar, identifies this building as a temple, and distinguishes it from contemporary oval structures in Eretria.[82] It is this ambiguity, or indeterminacy, that has led Mazarakis-Ainian to suggest that early temples derive their function as well as their form from late Dark Age 'chiefs' houses'. Mazarakis-Ainian argues that these houses were not merely residences, but places where rituals of importance to the community at large were carried out.[83] If Mazarakis-Ainian is right, we cannot really tell when temples as such begin to be constructed. Their development fits seamlessly into the history of early Hellenic domestic architecture.

To be sure, in the second temple at Eretria there are slight intimations of a temple as a distinct architectural form. It is an unusually long building, and one that is apsidal rather than oval in plan. None the less, like other buildings in Eretria, it is built on a stone socle, with a timber frame and walls of mud brick supporting a thatched roof. For the next steps in the development of the temple we have to go to the Heraion on Samos. At some time in the eighth century, a long temple was built, rectilinear rather than oval in plan. The cult statue stood at the

---

[81] On the Daphnephoreion see Auberson 1974. The Perachora and Heraion models are discussed by Payne (1940: 34–51).
[82] On the temple of Apollo generally, see Auberson 1968. Eighth-century structures at Eretria are discussed by Mazarakis-Ainian (1987; 1997: 58–63).   [83] Mazarakis-Ainian 1988; 1997.

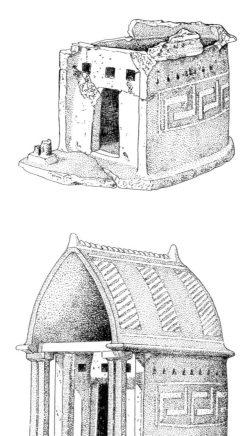

7.11 Reconstruction of Perachora temple model A

west end, the entrance facing east towards the altar. This is one of the first examples of a hekatompedon (or hekatompedos), a long temple with a standard length of 100 feet (fig. 7.12).[84] A standardized ground plan need not require any special roofing arrangements. The row of internal columns in this temple suggests that it had a thatched roof. Soon after its construction however it was embellished in a rather significant way. The Samians constructed an external colonnade, a peristyle or peristasis, which set it apart from any other building in the vicinity.[85] The overall impression was still of a long building, having seventeen columns along the flanks and seven along the front. This design still had one major drawback. The internal row of columns obscured any view of the cult statue from the

---

[84] Buschor 1930: 10–20. This first temple seems to have been built after Altar II but before Altar III; see Buschor and Schleif 1933.   [85] Buschor and Schleif 1933.

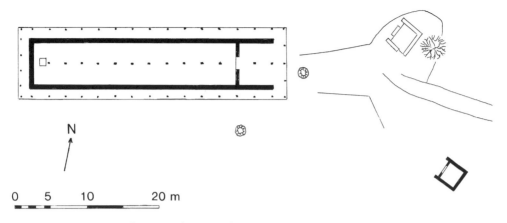

N

0   5   10   20 m

7.12 Hekatompedon 1 at the Samian Heraion

entrance. This problem was solved in the design of the second hekatompedon. In this, the single row of columns was replaced by a double row of engaged columns, and the façade was adjusted, now having two rows of six columns in the front (fig. 7.13). The effect of these changes was not merely to make the view of the cult statue from the entrance easier. The second hekatompedon had a more complex series of spaces through which one approached the interior of the temple, and the cult statue within. This architectural complexity is paralleled in the sanctuary as a whole. The middle of the seventh century witnessed the construction of a large stoa, of yet more monumental altars, and of a gateway or propylon which marked the entrance to the temenos itself.[86]

To trace the next stages in the evolution of Greek temple design we have to turn to the Peloponnese, and in particular to the Corinthia. It was here that a number of technological advances were made that enabled Greeks to transcend the limitations of wood and mud brick. The first of these was the ceramic roof tile. Ceramic tile made thatch redundant, and so removed the need for a high-pitched roof. The earliest tile comes from the Corinthia, specifically the first temple of Poseidon at Isthmia, dating to the first half of the seventh century BC.[87] This was a temple with an exterior colonnade of seven by nineteen columns. The columns were of wood, standing on a base of cut and shaped stone, or stylobate, which had by now replaced the crude stone socle of small stones of earlier times. It seems that the walls too were largely of stone, though the upper superstructure (or entablature) supporting the roof (or pediment) would still be of wood.[88] Like the second hekatompedon at Samos, this temple had a deep and imposing entrance, or pronaos. One approached the temple first through the peristyle, and then through

[86] Buschor 1930: 21–48; Buschor and Schleif 1933; for dating evidence see Eilmann 1933. For recent redating, see Kyrieleis 1993.
[87] Broneer 1971: 40–53; Gebhard 1993: 159–63. For the earliest examples of roof tiles generally, see Winter 1993: 12–18.   [88] Broneer 1971: 3–56, esp. 53–5.

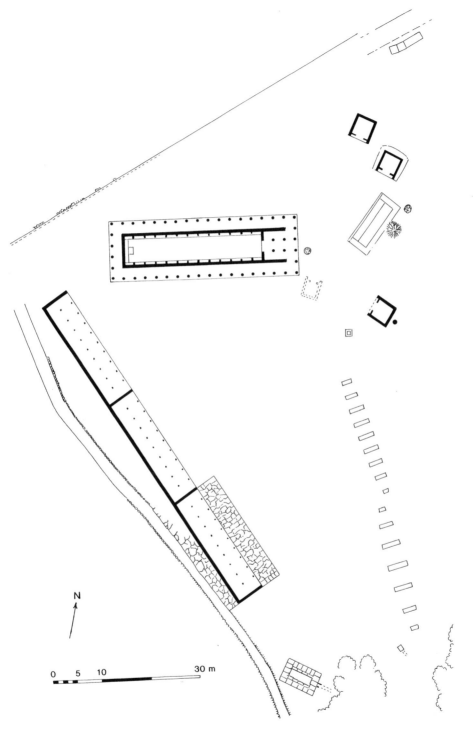

7.13 Hekatompedon 2 at the Samian Heraion

N

0   5   10   30 m

a porch with three interior columns. This was a building whose function could not be mistaken.

The new ceramic technology also offered new possibilities for the decoration of temples. Tiles could be painted, and ceramic plaques and antefixes added to the wooden superstructure. We know little or nothing of the decoration of the temple of Poseidon, except that some fragments of early wall paintings (probably from the interior or cella) have been found there.[89] But in nearby Aetolia, a region very much under the cultural influence of Corinth, there are signs that craftsmen were putting this technology to good use. At the sanctuary of Apollo at Thermon, which in later times served as a meeting place for the Aetolian league, several successive temples seem to have been built. The second temple was constructed with wooden columns on a stone stylobate a little after 640 BC.[90] Here Greek excavators in the early years of the twentieth century found numerous ceramic antefixes and ceramic metopes, both painted in a polychrome (i.e. multicoloured) style reminiscent of late Protocorinthian vases. The antefixes, often in the form of human heads, were used to decorate the junction of the roof with the entablature below. This roof also had a simple gable, or pediment, over the entrance to the cella. The metopes contained scenes from myth, often with human figures, and often with helpful accompanying inscriptions. They were, in all probability, used to decorate the entablature. The (hypothetical) arrangement of metopes, antefixes and tiles is shown in figure 7.14.[91] We have here an early example of the Doric order, one of the later 'standard designs' for both the plan and the decoration of a Greek temple. This would suggest that temples were beginning to be conceived as 'sculptural wholes', where overall design and exterior decoration were conceived as one. But the design of Thermon (as of the temple of Poseidon) is, as yet, far from standardised. It still has an internal row of columns, obscuring the view of the cult statue. Moreover, to say that the temple at Thermon anticipates features of the Doric order is to impose a retrospective, or rather teleological, view on the evidence. The term 'Doric' was only formulated much later, and it is doubtful whether seventh- or sixth-century Greek architects saw things in these terms.

Still, later seventh- and early sixth-century Peloponnesian architects do seem to be consciously trying to improve on their designs. The single row of interior columns created difficulties that required a solution. In the early sixth-century temple of Hera at Olympia this solution has been found. The temple has two

---

[89] Broneer 1971: 33–4.

[90] On Thermon generally, see Soteriadis 1900; Rhomaios 1916. For a full discussion of the earlier temple, 'Megaron B', see Bundgaard 1946. For a discussion of the impact of recent excavations by J. Papapostolou, see Mazarakis-Ainian 1997: 125–35; Morris 1999: 222–8.

[91] On the Thermon metopes, see Kawerau and Soteriadis 1908; on their date, Payne 1926. On the roof, antefixes and tiles, see Winter 1993: 112–15. The roof seems to have had a pediment (and raking sima) only over the entrance. The rear of the temple had a hipped roof, like earlier temples at Corinth and Isthmia. It should be remembered, however, that there is no actual architecture to go with these terracottas. The stone foundations of 'Temple C' seem to date to the Hellenistic period (see Mazarakis-Ainian 1997: 134–5). The Archaic temple must therefore have been a structure of timber and mud brick.

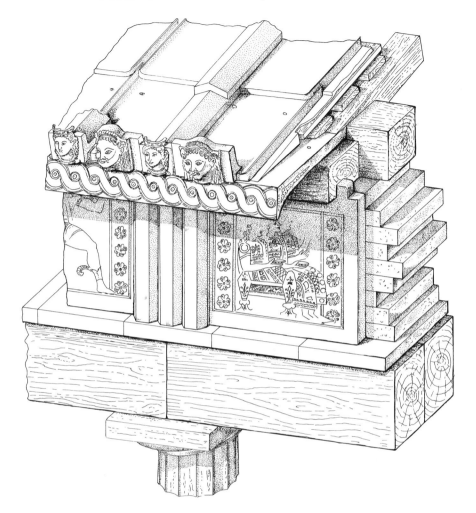

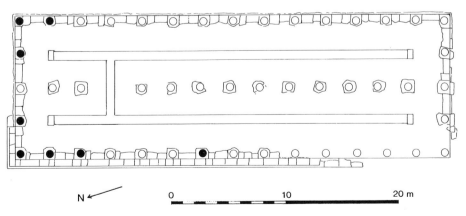

7.14 Reconstruction of the entablature of the temple of Apollo at Thermon, showing metopes

7.15 Columns from temple of Hera at Olympia

interior rows of bays and columns; its façade has six, allowing for an unimpeded view from the entrance of what lies within.[92] This solution, of course, is one arrived at earlier by the Ionian architects of the hekatompedon at Samos, but it may here none the less have been reached independently.

This temple is also of interest for other reasons. Certain refinements in the roof have been made. The temple has a gable or pediment at both ends, decorated in the Laconian (or Arcadian) rather than the Corinthian manner. Over the entrance, the pediment was surmounted by a remarkable polychrome disc acroterion.[93] It was moreover described in some detail by Pausanias, who provides us with important clues as to its original construction. The surviving parts of the temple, including its columns, are entirely of stone. But on close observation it becomes clear that the individual columns are of different proportions. In particular the echinus of the capital (that is, the top of the column) is markedly more splayed in some, and has a sharper, more angular profile in others (fig. 7.15). These differ-

[92] Dörpfeld 1935: 125–214.   [93] Winter 1993: 134–7.

ences in the profiles of the capitals are usually taken to indicate that columns are of different dates.[94] How could this be so? When Pausanias visited the site in around 173 AD, he remarked that all the columns were of stone, but one, in the opisthodomos, was of wood.[95] The natural inference from this is that originally all the columns were wooden, but, as each column decayed, it was replaced in stone – but at different times, hence the differences in the profiles of the Doric capitals.

It may seem, from these examples, that there can be no doubt that the Doric temple in stone derives from the Doric temple in wood. Certainly many features of later sixth-century Doric temples would seem to support this idea. The surviving columns from the temple of Apollo in Corinth are long limestone shafts, covered with plaster. These columns are fluted, a practice which seems more appropriate for woodworking than stone-carving. The columns resemble nothing so much as carven tree trunks, shaped mistakenly in stone. But this straightforward derivation of stone temples from wooden ones is complicated by several factors. For one thing, the sixth-century temple of Apollo was not the first stone temple on this site. There seems to have been an earlier, late Geometric stone temple, about which we know, admittedly, very little.[96] The walls of the first temple of Poseidon at Isthmia also seem to have been largely of stone.[97] Moreover, as Carpenter has pointed out, though the forms of the various elements of the Doric order (taken individually) may seem to imitate timber construction, 'no construction of wooden beams, planks and pegs was ever put together in any sort of correspondence with the detail . . . of the Doric order'.[98] The Doric order is not then derived directly from a wooden prototype. It is rather an ingenious synthesis of apparently wooden forms, expressed in stone. Its genealogy is complex, and may not fit into simple evolutionary schemes.

Such technicalities may, however, miss the point. By the middle of the sixth century, it would have been impossible to mistake a temple for a large house. A special architectural language had developed, reserved exclusively for the dwellings of the gods. By the middle of the sixth century, moreover, the centres of many Greek cities were adorned with monumental temples in stone, a mark as much of the solidity of the institution of the polis as of the Greeks' devotion to their gods. The temple of Apollo is, to be sure, by no means the last word in Greek monumental architecture, nor is the existence of the polis a sufficient reason for its being there. A full explication of the factors behind the sixth-century trend

---

[94] Dörpfeld 1935: 164–72, 190–7. See also discussion by Hurwit (1985: 179–185).
[95] Pausanias V.xvii.1.
[96] For early temples at Corinth, see Robinson 1976; Morgan 1994: 138–9. On the early evidence for tile, see Roebuck 1990; Winter 1993: 12–16. For the precocious development of stoneworking in Corinth, see Brookes 1981.   [97] Broneer 1971: 12–33, 53–5.
[98] Carpenter 1970: 177–80, esp. 179.

towards monumental architecture is the subject of another chapter. It is the connection between temples and the polis that is contentious. For if there was a Late Geometric predecessor in stone to this sixth-century temple, was such architecture used to embellish an area that was already recognisably urban? Can we then infer that a Corinthian state had emerged in some recognisable form by the end of the eighth century BC?

CHAPTER 8

THE CITY, THE STATE AND THE POLIS

8.1 The polis: city or state?

The typical Greek state of the Classical period was the polis: this at least has become the accepted wisdom among both ancient historians and Classical archae-ologists. That a Classical polis such as Athens was a state seems undeniable. A polity which could mobilise a fleet of over one hundred triremes and still field an army of several thousand conforms to most of the organisational criteria that political scientists usually apply. (Archaeologists, of course, tend to be more impressed by the capacity of Classical Athenians to create so many enduring public monuments.) Athens is, as always, an exception. But Classical states such as Sparta, Corinth or Thebes were clearly in the same league. Historians and archaeologists of Archaic Greece have, not unnaturally, concerned themselves with how, when and why this kind of state developed. The 'rise of the polis' may seem to be a straightforward example of 'state formation', a process which can be paralleled in many other times and places. But the question 'how, when and why did the polis emerge' is not, in truth, straightforward at all. It is a question clouded by misconceptions. There are several reasons for this unsatisfactory state of affairs.

First of all, the term *polis* is itself ambiguous. Polis in Greek can mean one of two things: the actual urban centre of a community, its principal city; and the political community itself, the state and its citizens. Of course, there is another word in Greek – *asty* – that means simply city or town, and sometimes (as in *Odyssey* VI.175–9) a distinction is made between asty and polis. But, more often than not, no distinction is made, and polis means both 'community' and 'town'. Therefore the question 'When did the polis rise?' is in fact two questions. When did that particular kind of state we call polis emerge? And when do cities arise in Greece?[1] Now it may be thought that the former necessarily entails the latter. Polis is usually translated as 'city-state' in English, as if at the centre of every Greek state was a city, every city having its own land or territory. Not all Greek states however were 'city-centred' states of this kind. In western Greece another kind of polity – the *ethnos* – prevailed. Ethne (plural of ethnos) were federal states,

---

[1] For various ways of defining 'state', 'city' and polis see Morris 1991a; 1997b; Davies 1997; Snodgrass 1980a: 31. For the significance of the *Odyssey* passage, see Hurwit 1985: 73–85. The question 'When did the Polis rise' was first asked explicitly by Ehrenberg (1937).

states made up of a number of large villages or small towns. The largest town in the ethnos of Aetolia was probably Kalydon, but this was in no sense its capital. Federal decisions were made at the sanctuary of Apollo at Thermon.[2] Even 'city-centred' states like Argos, Corinth and Athens were less urban than the term 'city-state' might imply. In the early Archaic period, their principal towns were hardly urban at all, if by urban we mean a large settlement whose inhabitants made their living, not from the land, but from secondary activities such as trading, retailing, craft production, holding priesthoods or political office and administration. The processes of urbanism and state formation are in fact separate.[3] As Runciman has pointed out, the term polis has been misconstrued: 'a polis is a type of society for which the proper label is not "city state" but "citizen state". It does not have to have an urban centre dominating a rural hinterland (which would exclude Sparta).'[4] It follows from this definition that, in Greece at least, state formation represents the development of a particular ideology, an ideology of citizenship. If so, what kinds of theory would help us to understand this process?

State formation theory is very diverse. Oddly enough, even in the heyday of diffusionism, few suggested that the Greek polis was modelled on a Near Eastern prototype. More recently, however, Bernal has noted that Greek and Phoenician cities share common features. Both the Greek polis and a Phoenician city-state such as Tyre have urban centres, a central sanctuary dedicated to a patron deity, and small rural hinterlands. Both societies made use of alphabetic scripts.[5] But, with the exception of fourth-century Carthage, no Phoenician state was a republic, still less a 'citizen-state'. Monarchy prevailed throughout most of the Levant, including Phoenicia. Other scholars have looked elsewhere in the Mediterranean for analogies to the Greek polis. Renfrew based his 'Early State Module' principally on Etruria. Etruscan city-states do appear to come in a more or less uniform size, each having an urban centre and a territory of around 1500 km^2.[6] None the less, Renfrew's model conspicuously fails to accommodate the Greek case. Early Greek poleis could be either very much larger (as in the case of Sparta) or very much smaller (as in the case of Phleious, in the north-west Peloponnese) than Renfrew's model would predict. Similarly, the concept of 'peer-polity interaction' may help us to explain why early states in a given cultural sphere (or civilisation) assiduously borrowed ideas and art styles from one another, but tells us little about the origins of a particular political system.[7]

Most archaeological theory concerning state formation has been developed by American scholars, and has been applied principally to the (historically) unrelated but (anthropologically) analogous cases of Mesopotamia and Mesoamerica. Such theories have tended to see urbanism as a necessary corollary of state formation. Urbanism requires craft specialisation; an increasingly differentiated

---

[2] For Aetolia generally, see Lang 1996: 17. For approaches to the question of the formation of the ethnos, see Morgan 1991; 1997.   [3] Morris 1991a.   [4] Runciman 1990: 348.
[5] Not directly discussed in Bernal 1991: but alluded to in Snodgrass 1980a: 32.
[6] Renfrew 1975: 12–21.   [7] Renfrew 1986; Snodgrass 1986.

economic system requires a hierarchy of decision making, that is administration (a system which, perforce, usually has recourse to writing of some kind); a hierarchy of decision-makers in turn requires a stratified social order, and a structure of power to enforce decisions; hence states arise.[8] As many have pointed out however, urbanism and state formation may not always be so closely connected. Medieval historians have often argued that towns arose independently of the state in Western Europe in the eleventh century AD. Indeed, if urbanism depends on trade, and trade depends on the mobility of persons as well as goods, then urbanism and the development of a polis ideology – one that stresses the obligations of citizenship and belonging to a particular community – may pull in opposite directions.[9] Few material facts in Archaic Greece conform to the American checklist. Administration was the last, not the first, use to which writing was put. There is little to suggest that Archaic Greek society became more hierarchical, more stratified through time. Indeed if we think of the polis as a citizen-state rather than a city-state, then what we should be looking for is not a measure of different degrees of social stratification, but rather a means of detecting different kinds of hierarchy.[10]

The emergence of the polis, it would seem, provides a number of counter-factuals to various anthropological generalisations about state formation. But this is to assume that we do know when the state or polis did emerge, and to accept that it did so at the beginning of the Archaic period. It is to associate the early polis with the cluster of innovations that took place around 700 BC.[11] Is this a case of circular reasoning, or is there some independent confirmation for this view? In 1937 Victor Ehrenberg demonstrated that the earliest literary evidence we have for magistracies, constitutions and laws in Archaic Greece dates to the latter part of the seventh century BC. These constitutional arrangements presuppose a certain earlier period of development. On these grounds the polis most probably rose in the course of the eighth century.[12] One possible objection to this inference is that an early polis is not necessarily a state, and that it is only in the fifth century that we have the full panoply of attributes that American anthropological theory predicts. If so, state formation would be a gradual process of evolution that took place throughout the Archaic period, rather than a sudden revolution in the eighth century. Still, many scholars prefer to see the eighth century as at least a crucial watershed in the formation of Greek states. Snodgrass has emphasised the role that sanctuaries and early monumental temples may have played in this process. For, if the early hekatompeda at Eretria and the Samian Heraion, and the earliest temple of Apollo at Corinth, were not polis sanctuaries, then what were they? What other corporate body could have provided the necessary manpower

---

[8] For a discussion of these approaches, see Wright 1977.   [9] See Purcell 1990.
[10] For criticisms of this whole school of thought, as applied to the Greek case, see Morris 1997b.
[11] As argued principally by Snodgrass 1980a: 15–24. But for other lists of symptoms of eighth-century state formation, see Hurwit 1993; Whitley 1991a: 39–45.
[12] Ehrenberg 1937; see discussion in Snodgrass 1991.

and organisation to construct them?[13] Equally, de Polignac has shown that it is in those areas of central Greece where the polis did emerge that we find major state sanctuaries located on the borders of that (later) state's territory. Monumental construction in such sanctuaries seems to have been undertaken in the years around 700 BC. That sanctuaries were used to 'stake out' a state's territory would seem a plausible inference. Panhellenic sanctuaries, by contrast, are found in those areas of western Greece where poleis were few and the ethnos prevailed.[14]

Questions of state formation and the origins of urbanism must then be kept separate. If the polis was a 'citizen-state', then it is to the emergence of a citizen ideology that we should direct our attention. Archaic Greek warfare depended on hoplites, heavily armed infantrymen who fought not as individual champions but together in tight, disciplined formations. Hoplite warfare has, not unnaturally, often been seen as a symptom of this new 'citizen ideology'. More recently, the burial record has been scrutinised to see how the collective representations of Greek society in death change through time. Such idealised representations may yield information, not about how things really were, but how they ought to have been; burials are in this sense profoundly ideological. To understand urbanism on the other hand we have to assess both the overall size of settlements, their density and their structure. Since urban (as opposed to village) life depends on specialised activity, we also have to estimate the degree of craft activity, specialised production and exchange. Towns depend on trade, the material evidence for which has to be assessed. But let us first turn to a simpler question: what did early Archaic settlements look like?

8.2 Houses, settlements and urban space

Not so long ago, scholars knew what a typical early Greek town looked like. British and Turkish excavations at Old Smyrna (in ancient Ionia, on the coast of modern Turkey) had revealed a settlement that had become well established by the ninth century BC. The town had been surrounded by a fortification wall from a very early date. Settlement was concentrated in the area within. By the end of the seventh century BC the town was furnished with a temple, impressive walls, a public supply of drinking water and (less certainly) an agora or marketplace. British excavators produced a reconstruction.[15] The implication is clear. Here was Aristotle's polis in embryo – a smaller and simpler version of Classical Priene, Olynthos or Athens.

Reconstructions are seductive. The past restored is a past we no longer have to think very much about. As a reconstruction of Old Smyrna before Alyattes' sack, this picture still has much to recommend it. But as an icon of the early Greek polis it is profoundly misleading. It suggests that most urban centres of most early

---

[13] Snodgrass 1980a: 52–65; Hurwit 1985: 73–85.   [14] De Polignac 1994; Morgan 1990; 1997.

[15] J.M. Cook 1959: 15 fig. 3. For Old Smyrna generally, see Nicholls 1959; 1983; Cook and Nicholls 1998; Akurgal 1983.

poleis were nucleated: concentrations of human habitation with civic amenities. Archaeological exploration since the 1950s has undermined this view. Not all nucleated settlements were (or were to become) the urban centres of poleis, and not all early urban centres of poleis were nucleated settlements. Eighth- and seventh-century Corinth is a case in point. Corinth has one of the earliest stone temples in ancient Greece, which is often taken as a symptom of early urbanism. But early settlement seems to have been dispersed within a wide area contained within the later enceinte. To be sure, there was a concentration of houses near the temple hill and close to the springs of Peirene and Glauke.[16] But this settlement area was, in truth, no larger than a village during the eighth and seventh centuries BC. Elsewhere within the enceinte there were other small hamlets, each of which in the eighth century had its own cemetery. One such was the so-called 'Potters' Quarter' in the west of the city.[17] The enceinte which (most probably) was built around Corinth towards the end of the seventh century BC therefore enclosed a wide area (some 4 km^2), but an area that was probably very thinly settled. Before the construction of these walls, the Acropolis (or Acrocorinth) had probably served as a place of refuge in times of danger. This pattern – that of a large settlement, consisting of a number of hamlets or villages, loosely grouped around an acropolis – can be paralleled elsewhere in central Greece. Argos may have been more densely settled, but it too had its acropolis.[18] Athens too, judging by the indirect testimony of well groups and cemetery areas, seems to fit the 'Corinthian' model.[19] It is these 'loose' settlements that seem to have been the largest. Morris estimates that Athens in the late eighth century must have had around 7,000 inhabitants, a population which begins to approach the urban.[20]

It is from Eretria however that we gain our clearest impression of what such settlements must have been like (fig. 8.1). Much of the town has been excavated by Swiss and Greek teams, who have uncovered a number of house plots.[21] More precisely, individual houses are exactly what they have found. There seems to be no underlying principle behind their arrangement. There is no common orientation, no obvious street plan. The impression is one almost of individual homesteads, whose only relation to one another is that of proximity. The only focus of the community was the temple of Apollo, which, in the eighth century at least, was little different from the houses around it. This arrangement (or lack of it) has been called an *Einzelhaussiedlung* – a settlement of individual houses – by Lang.[22] This is the most common arrangement in those settlements which were later to form the urban nuclei of the major Greek poleis. This must strike most people as odd. For is it not a basic principle of polis organisation that every citizen owes his allegiance

---

[16] Roebuck 1972; Williams 1982; Lang 1996: 165–72.
[17] Stilwell 1948; 1952; Stilwell and Benson 1984.   [18] Hägg 1982; Lang 1996: 174–6; Hall 1997.
[19] Morris 1987: 62–8; Lang 1996: 152–63.
[20] Morris 1987: 101. The argument Morris puts forward here is complex, but consistent. It is based on the number of burials combined with estimates of the settled area. It is, necessarily, imprecise.
[21] Mazarakis-Ainian 1987; Krause 1982; Vink 1997.   [22] Lang 1996: 58–9.

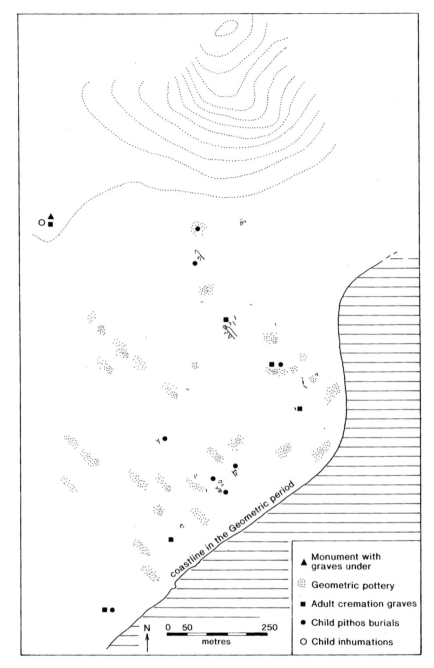

8.1 Plan of eighth-century Eretria

principally to the community as a whole, rather than to his family or homestead? The subordination of the individual house to an overall community plan, usually in the form of a grid, is the guiding principle of Classical cities, seen at its most extreme form at Olynthos. What is even odder is that we do find something akin to a grid plan in some early settlements. The houses in Area H in Zagora on Andros, for example, were arranged, if not on a grid, at least on a single axis. But Zagora was a small settlement, whose inhabitants cannot have numbered more than a few hundred, and was abandoned by the early seventh century BC.[23] Still, a number of other island settlements seem to have followed an axial plan. One such is Vroulia, on the very southern tip of the island of Rhodes. Here individual rectangular house plots were laid out in two parallel rows behind a fortification wall sometime after 700 BC (fig. 8.2).[24] It is an early example of what Lang has called a *Reihensiedlung* – a settlement in rows.[25] The settlement had its own sanctuary and cemetery, the latter placed outside the walls. Vroulia was clearly a community, and a planned one. But it was small (it can only ever have had a few hundred inhabitants) and it was short lived. By the early decades of the sixth century it too had been abandoned.

Early grid plans of this type are not quite confined to small settlements. Megara Hyblaia in Sicily seems to have had houses laid out on an overall grid almost from the time of its foundation.[26] But planned communities of polis size are, in the Archaic period at least, confined to the 'colonial' world of the western Mediterranean. This is not to say that important changes did not take place in 'Old Greece'. For one thing, there is a definite evolution of house forms. Oval and apsidal houses, so characteristic of the Early Iron Age, cease to be built in the course of the seventh century. At Old Smyrna, for example, individual oval houses had been replaced by groups of rectilinear structures by about 600 BC.[27] In general there is a move away from the single-room, 'megaron' house and towards house complexes with many rooms. Multi-roomed house complexes, often grouped around a courtyard, are to be found on Zagora in the eighth century BC.[28] Such courtyard houses become much more common during the seventh and sixth centuries, one example being building F in what was later to become the Athenian Agora (fig. 8.3).[29] There is an evolution too in the size of settlements. By this I do not simply mean that large settlements get larger. Many small settlements were abandoned at the beginning of the sixth century BC. This seems to affect small settlements of all types – both *Reihensiedlungen* (row settlements) such as Vroulia and *Einzelhaussielungen* (single-house settlements) such as Emborio on Chios.[30] One explanation put forward for their abandonment is a

[23] Cambitoglou *et al.* 1971; 1988; Vink 1997.
[24] Kinch 1914. For a recent analysis of the cemetery (and the settlement) at Vroulia, see I. Morris 1992: 174–99. Vroulia has also been the subject of a very interesting architectural study by Alexandra Coucouzeli, which, alas, remains unpublished.   [25] Lang 1996: 60–2.
[26] Vallet *et al.* 1976; 1983.   [27] Lang 1996: 235–43; Akurgal 1983.
[28] Lang 1996: 78–116; Morris 1998a.
[29] See Thompson 1940: 15–33; and discussion in Lang 1996: 154–7.
[30] For Emborio, see Boardman 1967a; Morgan 1990: 230–2.

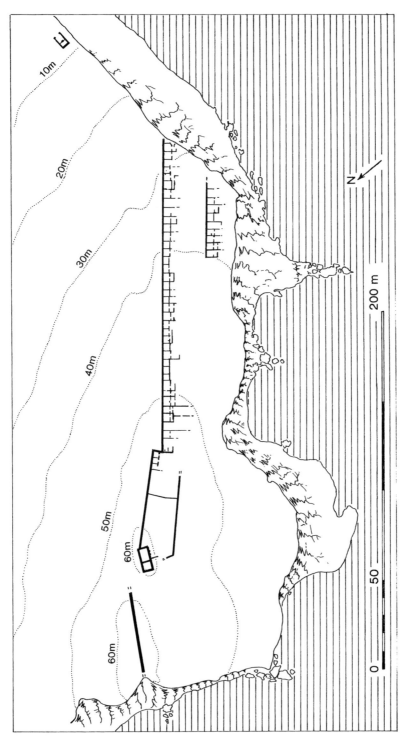

8.2 Plan of Vroulia on Rhodes

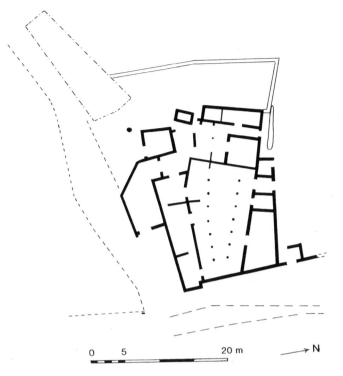

8.3 Building F in the Athenian Agora

change in trade patterns. But there is no reason to believe that trade with Egypt and the Levant (on which Vroulia in particular is supposed to have depended) less-ened to any degree at the end of the seventh century. There were other reasons why small coastal settlements of this kind ceased to be viable. One clue may lie in Emborio's architecture and plan. The excavator, John Boardman, interpreted the 'megaron' on the top of the hill as the residence of the local chief or basileus, dominating the settlement below.[31] The abandonment of small settlements thus yields a political interpretation: small, autonomous communities run by basileis were no longer viable in the sixth century, a time when larger settlements man-ifestly prospered as never before.

Large settlements certainly grew larger. Urban surveys of Haliartos and Thespiai in Boeotia and Phleious in the north-west Peloponnese have shown that surface material of Archaic date is generally more abundant than Geometric.[32] Ian Morris estimates (chiefly on cemetery evidence) that if Athens had 7,000 inhabi-tants in 700 BC it must have had close to 20,000 by the end of the sixth century.[33] Athens and Corinth faced the problem of accommodating a larger population to a

[31] Boardman 1967a: 250–1; Mazarakis-Ainian 1997: 197–8.
[32] For Haliartos and Thespiai, see Bintliff and Snodgrass 1988; for Phleious (Phlius), see Alcock 1991b.
[33] Morris 1987: 100–1. I have extrapolated from Morris' raw figures to some extent.

plan of houses, roads, sanctuaries and water-sources that had grown up organically (that is haphazardly) over the decades. The scale of Corinth's fortification wall can then partly be explained by a need to accommodate an existing pattern of settlement. Redesigning the city from scratch, creating a new town on a grid plan, was never a serious proposition. None the less these large settlements do display a greater interest in public amenities in the sixth century than they did before. It was in this century that the Peirene and Glauke springs at Corinth become proper 'fountain houses' for the first time, and the south-west fountain house was constructed in the Athenian Agora.[34] In Eretria, the stream that in the eighth century ran through the urban area is channelled in the seventh.[35] Other changes too seem to betoken a new, community identity. In both Corinth and Athens in the eighth century, small settlement areas seem to be associated with their own burial plots. In the course of the seventh and sixth centuries, burials are progressively removed from areas of habitation and placed outside the city's limits.[36] Spatial differentiation of the living from the dead can be seen most clearly at Corinth, where the North Cemetery, established in the eighth century, gradually became the principal necropolis for the city as a whole.[37] When Corinth's great enceinte is built around 600 BC, it encloses houses, workshops, sanctuaries and (presumably) fields or gardens. But its necropolis, the North Cemetery, lies clearly beyond its bounds.

Urban space was created during the Archaic period, not before it. At its beginning, most large settlements consisted of individual house plots, almost randomly distributed. The only focus for the community was the central sanctuary, which may, in the early period, have looked little different from the houses around it. Settlements organised on some underlying principle, such as a common axis, become more common in the seventh century. Such 'new towns', however, were sometimes little more than 'new villages', planned communities which ultimately failed. In the larger settlements of Old Greece principles of urban design had become apparent by the end of the sixth century BC. A city now had to have walls, temples and public supplies of water. Space for the dead had to be firmly separated from space for the living. Still, a town has to be more than a comfortable residential area, however impressive its civic centre. After all, many of the political functions of Greek states could equally well take place in a sanctuary. A town is also a centre for specialised production and exchange.

8.3 Urbanism: production and trade

Greeks of the Archaic period were very accomplished producers of pottery. The quality of Greek painted pottery was unequalled in the Mediterranean and the Near East, which may account for its wide distribution. Pottery production too was widespread in the Aegean. Regional styles attest to the number and variety

---

[34] Camp 1992: 42–4; Thompson and Wycherley 1972: 197–203.   [35] Lang 1996: 124; Krause 1982.
[36] Young 1951.   [37] Blegen *et al.* 1964.

of local production centres. Even relatively new foundations such as Thasos (founded *c.* 650 BC) took the trouble to set up their own kilns, some of which (at Phari, on the south-west part of the island) have recently been examined by French archaeologists.[38] Archaic pottery kilns are found all over the Aegean, and in the seventh century they seem to be geared principally to local production. The Archaic kiln recently discovered at Knossos, for example, seems to have been dedicated to the production of pottery whose 'market' was entirely local.[39] In the seventh century, only Corinthian wares seem to have been produced largely for export.

Pottery is, of course, what survives best from the ancient world. Pottery, as Brian Sparkes has pointed out, was the plastic of antiquity. It was cheap, and it could be turned to virtually any use.[40] Pots were used for everything: for cooking; for storage of corn, wine and oil, in the form of large thick-walled vessels called 'pithoi'; as containers for transport over long distances; and as fine tableware for eating and drinking. Pottery's high rate of survival tempts us to exaggerate its economic importance *vis-à-vis* other commodities, commodities which will remain invisible to the archaeologist for a long time to come. Metal vessels of all kinds tend to be recycled, and we will probably never gain a clear picture of the textile trade in the ancient world.[41] Most trade in antiquity was probably in such invisibles, most particularly agricultural products such as olives, olive oil, wine and grain.[42] Still, the movement of agricultural goods does leave a trace in the archaeological record, since such products were normally carried in special transport amphoras. An amphora would normally only be used for one product: once an amphora had been used to carry oil or olives, it really could not have been used for anything else. The distribution of certain amphora types, for example the 'SOS' amphora manufactured in Attica and Euboea, gives us some idea of the range of those cities' trading interests in the seventh century. Unfortunately, the distribution of Archaic amphoras does not enable us to reconstruct Archaic trade patterns in any detail as yet.[43]

In any case, the scale of amphora production is dwarfed by comparison with the quantity of fine pottery Greece produced. It is to this fine pottery that we should turn for clues concerning production and trade. This is not because pottery was an intrinsically valuable commodity. Gill and Vickers have convinced almost everyone that pottery was very much less valuable than any vessel in bronze,

---

[38] Blondé *et al.* 1992; for the foundation of Thasos, see Graham 1978.
[39] Coldstream and MacDonald 1997: 197–9.   [40] Sparkes 1991: 1–2.
[41] On metal vessels, see Vickers and Gill 1994: 55–76. On textiles, Keuls 1983. Most of our information for textile production comes from iconography.
[42] On trade in 'invisibles' (i.e. perishables), see Foxhall 1998. It may be that analysis of traces of lipids inside transport amphoras may one day help to pin down trade in invisibles more precisely, but little is as yet being done in this field.
[43] On the 'SOS' amphora, see Johnston and Jones 1978. On transport amphoras generally see Whitbread 1995. On other Archaic, chiefly East Greek, amphoras, see Cook and Dupont 1997: 142–90.

silver or gold. But trade in pots may very well have been a profitable activity.[44] We do have some later (Classical) epigraphic evidence for prices: a few inscriptions give us prices in drachmas or obols for batches of fineware vessels.[45] Price seems to vary according to the size of the pot (a krater or mixing-bowl is much more expensive than a lekythos or oil flask) and to its decoration. Decorated (painted) pottery was more expensive than plain, and the more ornate the pot, the higher the price.[46] Such prices made the export of pottery a worthwhile enterprise. The wide distribution of Greek pottery throughout the Mediterranean world confirms that pots were more than 'saleable ballast', particularly when there is evidence for specialised production and directional trade.

A case in point is the workshop of Nikosthenes, a potter-cum-entrepreneur who worked in Athens in the latter part of the sixth century BC. We can reconstruct this workshop partly from epigraphic evidence (Nikosthenes' helpful habit of signing his works) and through Beazley's attributions. Nikosthenes' workshop seems to have employed at least four people, two potters, Nikosthenes and Pamphaios, and two, perhaps three pot painters.[47] This workshop specialised in a range of shapes, in particular the 'Nikosthenic' amphora which cannot be paralleled elsewhere in Attic pottery or indeed in Greece (see fig. 8.4). The antecedents of the 'Nikosthenic amphora' are instead to be found in Etruria.[48] Etruria indeed is where most of Nikosthenes' products turn up. The conclusion seems clear. Nikosthenes' workshop is specialising in pottery for the Etruscan market. His was by no means the only specialised workshop. Some potters and painters in Archaic Chios seem to have been engaged in producing chalices with 'bespoke' inscriptions, to be used specifically by named dedicants to named deities.[49] Robin Osborne has taken this line of reasoning further, and argued that there were distinct regional preferences for distinct types of Attic pottery. Not only did consumers in, let us say, Thasos in the northern Aegan prefer different Attic shapes to those in Caere (Cerveteri) in Etruria, they also tended to prefer the products of distinct Attic potters and painters.[50] This degree of interdependence between Attic producers and Thasian and Etruscan consumers is remarkable, and has been taken as proof that interdependent markets had developed in the Mediterranean world by the end of the Archaic period.

Talk of interdependent markets invites discussion of a market economy, which would be a true test of urbanism. Such questions demand that we look into the

---

[44] For arguments against the high value of pottery, see Vickers and Gill 1994: 77–104. For the overall profitability of the pot trade, see Boardman 1988a; 1988b; *contra* see Gill 1988a; 1988b; 1994. See now Salmon 2000.   [45] Johnston 1978.

[46] As argued again by Boardman 1988a; see also Johnston 1991 and Sparkes 1991: 126–35 for a discussion of prices.

[47] Beazley 1956: 216–37; 1963: 122–35; 1971: 104–9; Tosto 1999: 173–92. Apart from the potters Nikosthenes and Pamphaios, three painters (the BMN painter, painter N and the painter of Louvre F117) seem to have worked regularly for Nikosthenes, only two of whom (judging by their output) can be regarded as 'full-time'. Other painters, such as Lydos, seem to have worked on a casual basis. See Beazley 1989b for further discussion. Tosto (1999: 193–206), however, argues that Nikosthenes' workshop was very much smaller than this.   [48] Spivey 1991; Rasmussen 1985.

[49] Cook and Woodhead 1952.   [50] Osborne 1996b.

8.4 Nikosthenic amphora, *c.* 530 BC

scale of production in the Archaic period. How many people did the pottery 'industry' employ? And how many were engaged in other craft activities? By the mid-sixth century Athens had overtaken Corinth as the principal centre for the production of fine pottery in the Mediterranean. We can estimate the numbers of painters and potters working at any one time from Beazley's lists. If we include painters, potters and their assistants, we arrive at a figure of about 200 or so.[51] There may have been 100 or so more engaged in making storage vessels, cooking pots and transport amphoras, and in other kinds of coroplasty (that is, working in clay). This would be a generous estimate, to say the least. As for other crafts, we have some direct evidence from Athens for metal casting in the form of a casting pit in the Agora.[52] But, as Mattusch has argued, bronze casting of statues was likely to have been undertaken by itinerant craftsmen; it is not relevant to the question of urban production.[53]

---

[51] Information from Beazley 1956; 1963; 1971. Calculated on criteria defined by R.M. Cook (1972: 270–4).　[52] Mattusch 1977: 343–7; 1988: 54–8.　[53] Mattusch 1988.

We can none the less arrive at an estimate of the proportion of skilled potters/painters to other skilled craftsmen by counting the number of signatures. From inscriptions, we know the names of no more than nine sculptors from sixth-century Athens, whereas we know of at least sixty-three potters and painters.[54] So, on this basis, other craft skills such as gem engraving, jewellery and metal-working of all kinds would have provided employment for no more than 100 people. This yields a figure of 400 or so engaged in specialised craft production. If we assume that most of these craftsmen were resident in Athens (and certainly the name of the deme Kerameikos (Potters' Quarter) would indicate as much), then this can represent no more than 2 per cent of the population of Athens in the late sixth century, assuming my previous estimate of Athens' population is correct. Of course, given the scale of public works undertaken in late sixth-century Athens, 400 men may well have been engaged in building of some kind. But public works are a consequence of urban development, whereas craft special-isation and trade have, to some extent, been seen as its cause. Craft production can have engaged only a small proportion of Athens' population at any one time during the Archaic period.

Still, craft production in Archaic Greece was not simply work that was special-ised and skilled; by the end of the sixth century it was also, to some degree, indus-trialised. The Potters' Quarter in Corinth was the equivalent of the Athenian Kerameikos, an area devoted to pottery production and coroplasty of all kinds. Excavations here in the 1940s uncovered what could only be described as a large workshop or small factory for clay figurines, which were produced in large numbers using stone or clay moulds.[55] Similar techniques seem to have been used in the production of Corinthian 'head' vases.[56] Great skill was needed to make the moulds, but much less to make the individual terracotta figurine or head vase. This represents an elementary application of the principle of mass production, a principle that was to become much more widespread in the Hellenistic period (when mould-made pottery appears in quantity). Of course, the production of ter-racottas was economically of even smaller importance than the production of pottery, and pot production remained a craft skill based around the small work-shop until the end of the Classical period.[57]

Craft production and long-distance trade can, then, only ever have been a sec-ondary factor in the growth of towns. Could it be that cities grew up as much for social, cultural and political as for economic reasons? Though the 'consumer city' is a concept which has been much used in discussing ancient urbanism, it is

---

[54] Information for painters and potters (dipinti), Beazley 1956; 1963; 1971; 1989b. For sculptors' 'sig-natures', see Viviers 1992; Jeffery 1962b: 151–3.

   I am assuming here that the work of sculptors would have been more highly esteemed than that of potters or painters, and so that sculptors would have had even more reason to add their names to their works than craftsmen in either of the humbler trades.

[55] Stilwell 1948: 3–62, 82–113; 1952. Twenty-two moulds of Archaic date were recovered from the 'factory'.   [56] Biers 1994.

[57] On pottery production in Corinth generally, see Arafat and Morgan 1989; Shanks 1999: 37–72.

scarcely relevant to the Archaic period. A 'consumer city' is a residential area for a leisured elite, who can afford to spend their incomes from agricultural production on ostentatious luxuries. Consumer cities tend, then, to be full of well-appointed, richly decorated houses. This we do not find, nor do we find any other obvious archaeological trace of a leisured elite residing in Archaic towns.[58] Could it be that settlements grew into cities for *political* reasons? Towns, after all, were the centres of poleis, and the polis was a centre of power.

8.4 Hoplites, cemeteries and citizens

The city (polis) was its citizens – that at least was the theory as propounded in Classical times.[59] Can we trace the origins of this idea – the male-only citizen-state – in the archaeological record? Not so long ago it was widely believed that we could, and that the origins of the idea of citizenship were, in part, military. In Classical times participation in a city's navy or army was one of the principal conditions of citizenship. Sparta's 'citizens' – the Spartiatai – formed the elite core of her hoplite army, whereas in Athens (with its wider franchise) even the poorest citizens could serve their city as rowers in her triremes. There thus seemed to be a strong correlation between the type of warfare practised by a state, that state's constitution and the extent of its political franchise. In the fifth and fourth centuries, the most effective hoplite armies were fielded by oligarchies such as Sparta or Thebes. An oligarchy is a more restricted, and so perhaps more primitive, form of citizen-state than a democracy like Athens. Might not the origins of citizenship then be found in the development of this kind of warfare? After all, in the hoplite phalanx men fight together as a unit, each depending on the other, each equal to his neighbour, and this experience might be held to foster a sense of equality, common purpose and common identity (at least amongst those able to afford the equipment)? Such an identity would cut across ties of kinship, and so help to foster that sense of 'organic' solidarity that a primitive state needs. Moreover, if political power derives from military participation, then the development of the hoplite might indeed herald the appearance of the polis.[60]

We can certainly track the development of hoplite equipment in the archaeological record, and do so with some precision. Late Archaic and Classical hoplites were armed with a close-fitting bronze helm, a bronze cuirass (or breastplate), an iron-tipped spear, a large, round bronze shield, an iron sword and bronze greaves. A hoplite was a heavy infantryman, and hoplite tactics in the late Archaic period demanded that men fight in close formation *en masse*. Figure 8.5 shows a plate

[58] The nearest we come to a well-appointed town house in the Archaic period is Building F in the Agora of Athens. See Thompson 1940: 15–33; Morris 1998: 27–36.
[59] An ideology that can be reconstructed from fifth-century speeches, such as those of Pericles (Thucydides II.35–47).
[60] As argued by Snodgrass 1965; see also Snodgrass 1999: 48–88; Salmon 1977.

8.5 Plate from Kameiros on Rhodes, showing hoplites duelling

from Kameiros on Rhodes with a picture of two warriors. The warriors – Menelaus and Hector – seem to be duelling, as heroes were wont to do, but are equipped with the full panoply of a hoplite. The date of this plate (*c.* 600 BC) may then be taken as a *terminus ante quem* for the development of hoplite equipment.[61] Moreover, many of the items shown here are not to be found in the Early Iron Age. To be sure, iron weapons, chiefly swords and spears, turn up in numerous 'warrior graves', such as the one on the Areopagus in Athens, and the types of swords (Naue II) found in such graves differ little from those used in Archaic times.[62] But armour is something of a rarity. Some kinds of armour clearly existed in the Dark Age – there are some isolated finds of helmets and greaves, and small circular shield bosses (often with a central spike or knob) are common enough in the Kerameikos and other cemeteries.[63] There is nothing here to contradict the

[61] Snodgrass 1964: 10. The plate is known as the 'Euphorbus plate'.
[62] On the grave itself, see Blegen 1952. On early sword types, see Snodgrass 1964: 93–113; on spears, *ibid*.: 115–39.   [63] On shield bosses, see Snodgrass 1964: 37–51.

impression that, in the Early Iron Age, warfare consisted of 'loose, disorganized skirmishing'.[64]

This impression is, if anything, reinforced by a preliminary examination of fighting scenes on Middle to Late Attic Geometric pots.[65] The earliest such fighting scene, on a skyphos from Eleusis, seems to depict just such a skirmish.[66] Fighting seems to be a matter of duels between individual warriors. But we may here be in danger of making a cardinal error – of reading images as a direct reflection of reality. The painters of these images may have intended simply to portray scenes of individual combat. If so, what they portrayed may have been what they had seen, experienced or heard about. But they may equally well have been trying to portray scenes from myths, where, as in the Kameiros plate, it is in the nature of a hero to fight man-to-man. Or the painter may not have been very good at depicting more complex fighting scenes, constrained as he was by the artistic conventions of the time (see below, chapter 9). For Middle to Late Geometric pots do show something else which apparently contradicts the 'skirmishing' hypothesis – files of warriors, all seemingly equipped in the same manner. Figure 8.6, a Middle Geometric II krater, shows just such a scene.[67] By the late eighth century, as depicted on at least one Late Geometric II amphora, these warriors seem to be armed with round shields, not dissimilar to those worn by hoplites.[68]

Still, we should be wary of any plain reading of scenes like these. This is not merely because these scenes are governed by conventions we do not fully understand; it is also because it is often not at all clear what is actually being represented. Some images – in particular the 'Dipylon shield' – defy easy interpretation.[69] Scholars too are often inconsistent. Those who are willing to treat eighth-century images as providing important clues for eighth-century infantry warfare are equally reluctant to see the chariot scenes as evidence that 'Homeric' chariot warfare was still being practised in the eighth century. More concrete evidence for changes in arms and armour comes from finds in graves and sanctuaries. The late eighth-century 'warrior' grave T.45 from Argos, for example, is furnished not only with weapons but with some magnificent bronze armour (fig. 8.7). The cuirass in particular seems almost identical to depictions in seventh-century vase painting. This form was to remain virtually unchanged throughout the Archaic period.[70] The helmet, however, is very odd. For one thing, its high crest means that it could never have been used in battle – it is top heavy. The

---

[64] Snodgrass 1964: 189. For a discussion of the literary evidence concerning early warfare, see Van Wees 1992; for another review of the material evidence for pre-hoplite warfare, Snodgrass 1999: 35–47.   [65] As collected by Ahlberg 1971b.

[66] Eleusis 741; for its context see Coldstream 1968: 26–8.

[67] For discussion, see Ahlberg 1971b; Hurwit 1985b.

[68] Athens NM 894; for discussion see Whitley 1991a: 164; Coldstream 1968: 58–64.

[69] On the 'Dipylon shield' see Snodgrass 1964: 58–60; 1980a: 74–5; 1980b; Boardman 1983; Hurwit 1985b.

[70] On the grave itself, see Courbin 1957; on the cuirass, Snodgrass 1964: 72–84; 1971: 271–3.

8.6 Middle Geometric krater from Attica

helmet itself is of a type which turns up also in Olympia – the Kegelhelm – and which does not seem to outlast the eighth century.[71] Soon after this, the true hoplite's helmet, the close fitting Corinthian helm, is developed, examples of which turn up in sanctuary deposits in Delphi and elsewhere from the early seventh century onwards (fig. 8.8).[72] However, we have to wait until the seventh century is well underway before either greaves or round hoplite shields turn up in Olympia in any quantity.[73] It was the large round shield in particular that was

---

[71] On the Kegelhelm, see Snodgrass 1964: 13–16; Kunze 1958: 118–25; 1967: 111–16.
[72] Snodgrass 1964: 20–8; Kunze 1961: 56–128.
[73] For the hoplite shield itself, see Snodgrass 1964: 61–7; Kunze 1956: 35–68; 1958: 74–117. For the later 'Argive' shield, see Bol 1989. For greaves, see Snodgrass 1964: 86–8; Kunze 1991. For the contexts of dedications of weapons and armour at Olympia, see Kunze and Schleif 1938: 67–103; 1939: 76–118.

8.7 Helmet and cuirass from tomb T.45 from Argos, the 'Argos warrior grave'

8.8 Early seventh-century Corinthian-style helmet from Olympia

necessary for hoplite tactics to develop. Its absence before 700 BC thus provides an indispensable *terminus post quem* for the emergence of the hoplite phalanx.[74]

For any clues as to tactics we have to return to images on pots. Early seventh-century images, such as that on a Middle Protocorinthian aryballos from Lechaion, seem to show that individual combat and 'disorganised' skirmishing were still the norm. Neither the warriors' equipment nor their tactics seem to have been standardised.[75] The mid-seventh century, however, provides us with a powerful icon of the hoplite phalanx in the form of the Chigi vase (fig. 8.9).[76] Here ranks of men in full hoplite gear are depicted as not only advancing but also fighting in a disciplined formation that looks very like a phalanx.[77] Some kind of hoplite tactics had emerged by 650 BC. None of this contradicts the old theory that the 'hoplite reform' was a major catalyst of political change in the seventh century. That all the new forms of armour are to be found first in the

[74] Snodgrass 1964: 197; 1965; Salmon 1977.   [75] Snodgrass 1964: 197–200.

[76] Rome, Villa Giulia 22697. This is a Middle to Late Protocorinthian olpe known as the 'Chigi Vase'. On this vase's attribution to the Chigi painter, see Amyx 1988: 31–3; Benson 1989: 56–8. *Contra* Dunbabin and Robertson 1953: 179–80, who attribute this vase and the 'Macmillan aryballos' to the Macmillan painter.

[77] For discussion of its imagery and figured style, see Payne 1931: 94–8. Protocorinthian images of hoplite warfare are intelligently discussed by Salmon (1977: 85–92).

8.9 Protocorinthian olpe known as the Chigi vase

Argolid and Corinthia, or in sanctuaries frequented by Argives and Corinthians;
that 'hoplite tactics' are represented first on Corinthian pots; and that a political revolution took place in Corinth in the seventh century; all this is too much
of a coincidence to be lightly dismissed. The objection that something like
hoplite tactics – or at least fighting in ranks – occurs in the *Iliad* is moot.[78]
There is, for one thing, no agreement on the date of the *Iliad*. If it was composed
principally in the seventh century, then it is largely contemporary with the
'hoplite reform' itself, and so the intrusion of certain aspects of a seventh-
century social reality is hardly surprising. It is none the less difficult to accept
that the emergence of hoplite tactics was an immediate cause of constitutional
change. The experience of fighting with one's equals in the phalanx may indeed
have helped to foster a notion of 'equality' amongst members of the same

[78] See general discussion in Van Wees 1992.

hoplite class – but can it really have been the sole or principal cause of such a transformation?

Another quite different kind of evidence has been brought in to show that ideas of equality (or at least of 'equal rights', *isonomia*) were current from a very early date in Greek history: burials and cemeteries. Cemetery evidence can be looked at from any number of perspectives, but only two are relevant here. First, we can roughly estimate the wealth of graves (whether measured in terms of grave goods or the total energy expended in the construction of the grave), and so the degree of disparity between the wealth of the very richest and the very poorest graves.[79] Second, we can assess the degree to which the persons buried in graves archaeologists have excavated are representative of the population as a whole. A representative cemetery is one that includes all the dead of all ages and sexes, in proportions that would be consistent with the probable rates of mortality in pre-modern times.[80] Of course the surviving burial evidence from Athens has reached us by various, sometimes haphazard means. But the sheer quantity of rescue and other excavations over the past forty years or so has made it much more likely that we do indeed have a representative sample of at least the more archaeologically visible forms of interment.[81]

Ian Morris has argued that Athenian cemeteries were very unrepresentative of the population as a whole during much of the Early Iron Age and then during the seventh and early sixth centuries BC. In his calculation of the numbers of burials per annum (fig. 8.10) there are two peaks: one in the late eighth century, and one at the end of the sixth and the beginning of the fifth.[82] A commonsense explanation for this might be that the peaks directly reflect fluctuations in Athens' population (see chapter 10 below). But it is difficult, for all sorts of reasons, to see eighth-century Athens as being a larger place than the Athens of Peisistratos, which is what these figures would seem to indicate.[83] Moreover it is odd that the rate at which children are buried varies so much. Children's graves almost disappear during the ninth century BC, and this cannot have been because the rate of child mortality was then particularly low.[84] Morris proposes a different explanation: in certain periods (the seventh century for example) both custom and ideology dictated that certain persons be effectively excluded from formal burial.[85] In

[79] For arguments that an 'ideology of equality' existed in Greece from the eighth century onwards, see Morris 1999: 109–91. The literature on how best to interpret mortuary practices (especially in social terms) is vast. The discussions by Binford (1972) and Tainter (1978) on 'energy expenditure' are fundamental, but should be taken with a heavy dose of scepticism. For the relevance of such approaches to Classical archaeology see Morris 1987: 29–54; 1992: 1–30; Whitley 1991a: 23–34. On other 'anthropological' approaches to mortuary patterning in the Classical world, see Humphreys 1980.

[80] On burials and demography, see Morris 1987: 57–71; 1992: 70–102.

[81] On sampling, see Morris 1987: 101–4.   [82] Morris 1987: 73 fig. 22.   [83] Morris 1987: 99–101.

[84] For ninth-century Athenian burial practices (and the small number of children's graves), see Morris 1987: 18–20, 61–2, 72–3; Coldstream 1977: 30; Whitley 1991a: 116.

[85] Morris 1987: 104–9. By 'formal burial' Morris means burials that archaeologists are more likely to pick up. He does not mean to imply that others were not properly interred, but that the relatively informal manner in which they were is unlikely to leave traces which the archaeologist can easily pick up. Both the number and the quality of grave goods, and the various ways in which the body can be treated after death are likely to skew the archaeological record in various ways.

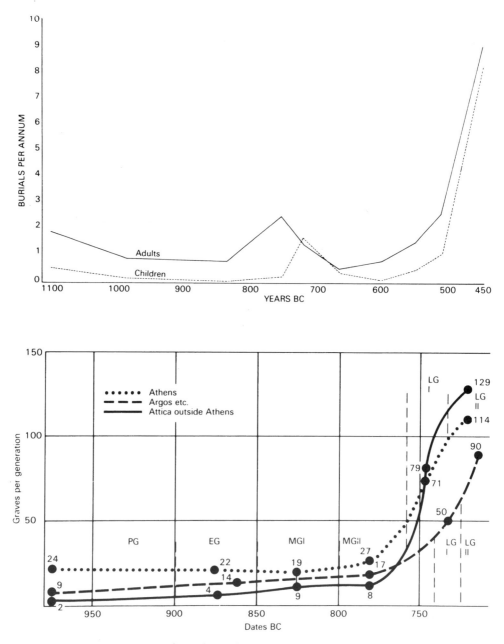

8.10 Diagram of numbers of graves in Attica

these times, certain burial forms (such as cremation beneath tumuli) were reserved for more important people. At other times, burial practices were more inclusive. Children as well as adults were embraced within the community of the dead, and all age and sex classes are represented in the surviving burials. The second peak in the 'inclusiveness' of formal burial coincides, remarkably enough, with the period just after the democratic reforms of Kleisthenes. Might inclusiveness then be a symptom of democracy, or at the very least of an ideology of equality? Morris goes on to observe that in both the late eighth century and the early fifth there was much less disparity in the wealth of graves than in other periods. Ostentatious marble grave markers were a feature of the sixth century that do not persist into the fifth.[86] Elaborate ceramic grave markers (e.g. figs. 6.6 and 8.6) and rich funerary accoutrements, such as gold diadems, were a feature of the earlier part of the eighth century. Such aristocratic graves become less common in the Late Geometric II period, when most adult graves are inhumations, furnished principally with pots.[87]

Morris goes on to argue that the burial record in late eighth-century Athens provides a model for the early appearance of a polis ideology in other places. In this pattern, all age and sex classes are represented in the burial record; children are included, but there is usually a separate custom for children's burials (usually interment in pithoi); and there are no great disparities of wealth in adult graves, which are generally inhumations. Certainly, the North Cemetery in Corinth seems broadly to fit this pattern. Late eighth- and seventh-century graves here are generally inhumations, and generally poor, and children are well represented.[88] But this pattern is also one that can be discerned in the cemetery of Vroulia on Rhodes. Morris' 'strong principle of equality' may well have been in operation in this community too, whose architectural layout anticipates the city plans of Classical Greece.[89] Vroulia however was too small and too short-lived to be considered a polis, and many Archaic Greek states seem to have been perfectly effective power structures without having to observe any such 'democratic' principle.

Still, the burial record may yield clues about the formation of the polis in other ways. One of the major features of Early Iron Age burial practices was the 'warrior grave' – a male interment with weapons. This 'burial weapon ritual' disappears with remarkable rapidity from central Greece during the eighth and early seventh centuries. The deposition of weapons in graves declines first in Athens, at a time when it remain common in Argos.[90] Seventh-century Argive warrior graves,

---

[86] Richter 1961; see also Jeffery 1962b. It was also in the sixth century that kouroi and korai came to be used as grave markers.

[87] Ohly 1953; Whitley 1991a: 137–62, 183 table 11. By my calculations there are seven diadems which date to the ninth century, five or six which can be dated to MGII to LGI, and only two or three to the LGII period. The ambiguity in numbers depends partly on how we date Kerameikos grave G72 (Kübler 1954), which belongs to an intermediate stylistic phase. It is striking that, just as the number of overall interments goes up, so the number of diadems drops.

[88] Blegen *et al.* 1964: 13–64; see also Morris 1998: 19.   [89] Kinch 1914: 34–90; Morris 1992: 174–99.

[90] Whitley 1991a: 183 table 11, 189–91; Van Wees 1998: 338–43.

however, are hard to find. The last 'warrior graves' in central Greece are those to be found near the West Gate in Eretria, dating to no later than 680 BC.[91] The 'weapon burial ritual' persists in other areas of Greece, particularly in areas where other political forms (the ethnos or the territorial monarchy) are to be found[92] (see chapters 10 and 15 below). Moreover, the disappearance of 'warrior graves' in central Greece coincides with a decline in the fashion of bearing arms in public in that region. Depictions of men carrying swords are common in eighth-century Attic vase painting. They are considerably less common in seventh-century depictions, and by the mid-seventh century men are represented as holding a single spear, but no sword. The spear remains an essential item of men's attire until the mid-sixth century, from which time men are represented as carrying a single staff, or, less frequently, an elaborate parasol. Hans van Wees has argued that these changes indicate how arms were progressively removed from civil life in central Greece during the Archaic period.[93] Bearing arms came to be seen as not being in keeping with a civil, leisured way of life. Outside of the hoplite phalanx, bearing arms in public and the civilisation of the polis did not mix.

All this is to suggest that the development of a 'civil society' was a gradual process that culminated in the sixth century. Rather than suddenly rising in the eighth, the polis emerged slowly during the course of the Archaic period. Is this gradualist view really justified? And is it borne out by the final piece of evidence to be discussed, namely inscriptions, the material evidence for the uses of writing in the service of the polis?

8.5 Written laws and minted coins: the polis and the agora

When Greeks first adopted the alphabet, sometime before 750 BC, they put this new technology to many uses. Short, jokey poems are incised on pots; homo-erotic sexual boasts appear on the rockface outside of the principal settlement (Sellada) on Thera;[94] graffiti are used to mark property; dedications are made to gods, naming both deity and dedicator; and, from the mid-seventh century onwards, painted labels (dipinti) are used to clarify the narrative scenes on painted vases (see chapter 9 below).[95] All these inscriptions are personal; names are rarely absent, and many inscriptions seem to engage in a kind of dialogue between one aristocratic individual and another. It takes one hundred years for there to be any sign that writing was used in the service of the polis. The first archaeologically attested Greek law comes from Dreros in Crete (fig. 8.11). It was found in what is thought to have been a public space (agora), close to the temple of Apollo, and, with a number of other near-contemporary inscriptions, dates to around 650 BC. It is inscribed in a manner known as boustrophedon, where the

[91] Bérard 1970.   [92] Morris 1998a: 36–55.   [93] Van Wees 1998.
[94] For the Thera inscriptions, see Powell 1991: 171–80; Jeffery 1990: 316–20, 323.
[95] For early inscriptions, see Johnston 1983; Powell 1991: 119–86.

8.11 Dreros law code

words are incised as the ox ploughs the field, alternately left to right and then right to left.[96] The law's content is simple: it regulates the term of office of the principal magistrate of this small town, the *kosmos*, and prevents any one individual from serving a successive term until at least ten years have elapsed. It is an eminently republican document, and an impersonal one. No names are mentioned; it is institutions that are important. The Dreros law provides concrete evidence that something like a republican constitution (*politeia*) was already in existence in many cities in Greece by the seventh century BC.

Until relatively recently, it was widely believed that law and literacy together were jointly responsible for putting Archaic Greece on the road to democracy.[97] The alphabet made writing a skill, in theory at least, accessible to all. Writing down laws put law in the public domain, and made law something which a literate public would be able to criticise, amend and improve. But recent scholarship has cast doubt on this simple relationship. It is unclear why some laws were

---

[96] Demargne and Van Effenterre 1946a; Jeffery 1990: 306–16, esp. 315 no. 1a. On the boustrophedon system, *ibid.*: 43–50.
[97] See for example Snodgrass 1980a: 83–4; Murray 1980: 96; Goody and Watt 1963. For criticisms, see Whitley 1997b: 635–40.

written down, and others apparently remained unwritten.[98] Early written laws seem principally to be concerned with matters of procedure, procedures that could only have affected the elite minority which was eligible for public office.[99] Crete, the island where the bulk of early legal inscriptions have been found, is moreover a region whose development takes a decidedly odd turn in the sixth century BC (see chapter 10 below).[100] To appreciate the wider significance of written law we have to look elsewhere in the Greek world.

Another early law is to be found inscribed on a stone from Chios, and dates to around 575–550 BC.[101] It has no clear archaeological context. Like the Dreros law, however, this inscription is concerned with defining (and limiting) the powers of magistrates. Its subject is judicial procedure, and it mentions a court of appeal chosen by the people, the demos. It is thus procedural, outlining how things are to be done, not what is to be done.

Mention of the demos invites discussion of democracy, a political form which developed in Athens (and perhaps elsewhere) in late Archaic times. We know from literary evidence that various laws had been written down in Athens by the late seventh century BC. Drakon's (Draco's) law on homicide was followed by various laws of Solon, which he, as he says himself, wrote down.[102] But the axones and kyrbeis – the original material form of these laws – do not survive, though Drakon's homicide law was reinscribed sometime in the late fifth century BC.[103] Judging by the number of informal inscriptions that survive, sixth-century Athens was one community where the skills of literacy seem to have been widely diffused. Here, if anywhere, written law should have had a democratising effect. Maybe it did, but if so it is odd that Athens did not care to monumentalise its laws until the very end of the sixth century. It is only after about 520 BC that public inscriptions of any kind are to be found in Athens. These include a few laws and decrees, but also other kinds of inscription such as horos or boundary stones.

Two of these are of particular interest, as they mark the boundaries of a new kind of public space, the agora. Two say quite plainly 'I am the boundary of the agora' (*horos eimi tis agoras*) (fig. 8.12).[104] The new agora necessitated the clearing away of older domestic structures, a process well underway by the middle of the sixth century at the latest (fig. 8.13). In it, or rather round its edges, were some of Athens' principal public buildings: the law courts; the prytanikon, a reused building F; the Council house or bouleuterion; and a stoa for one of the three archons, the basileus (literally 'king'). The agora also had its own water supply (the south-east fountain house), and its own shrines, principally the temple of Apollo Patröos, the shrine of

---

[98] As argued in particular by Thomas 1992: 65–73; 1995; Hölkeskamp 1992; Whitley 1997b.
[99] Gagarin 1986: 81–97.   [100] Whitley 1997b: 649–660; Stoddart and Whitley 1988.
[101] Jeffery 1956; 1990: 336–8, 343 no. 41.
[102] Solon fragment 36: lines 18–20 (West 1980: 179–80). For a translation, see Osborne 1996a: 218.
[103] Stroud 1968; 1979. *Inscriptiones Graecae* (3rd edition) I, no. 104 (i.e. Lewis 1981: 122–4) is the republication of Drakon's law.
[104] On early horos stones, see Lalonde 1991: 27: esp. nos. H25 and H26.

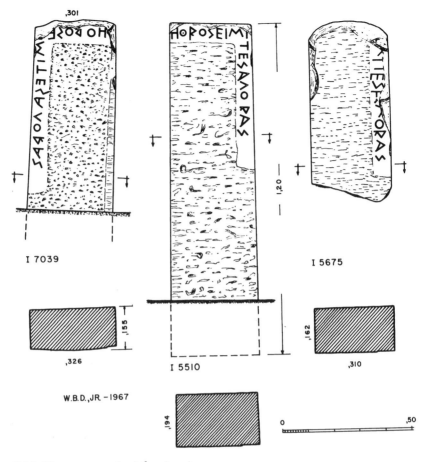

8.12 Horos stones in Athenian Agora

Zeus and the Altar of the Twelve Gods.[105] Smaller 'agoras' may have existed in the seventh century. The Dreros law was found near a small open space that may have served as an agora, and an earlier Athenian 'agora' may have once been located below the Acropolis. Nor is this the first consciously planned agora in the Greek world – that honour goes to Megara Hyblaia. But it is the first of any size among the older and larger cities of central Greece. The creation of an agora on this scale represents a conscious decision to create urban space. Previously the only areas within a settlement reserved for the community as a whole were its sanctuaries. The Athenian agora was to serve two functions that a sanctuary could not: as a civic centre, that is as a centre for public life and politics; and as a marketplace.

Markets are places where goods are bought and sold, preferably using a standard medium of exchange. It is quite likely that standard weights of silver and gold had

---

[105] On the Archaic Agora, see Wycherley and Thompson 1972; Camp 1992: 35–60.

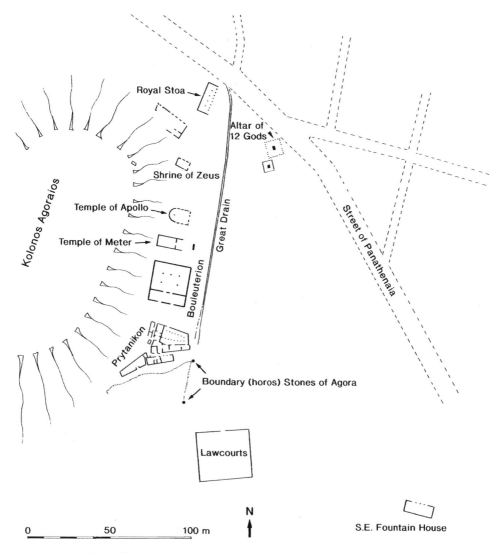

8.13 Plan of Athenian Agora around 500 BC

served such a role during much of the earlier part of the Archaic period. Early inscriptions mention fines of 'staters' which imply as much.[106] In the sixth century such weight standards took a new form: coinage. According to Herodotos, coinage was invented by the Lydians, who had formed a powerful kingdom in western Asia Minor. Herodotos' story was confirmed by the find of what seemed to be a foundation deposit of early coins discovered under the foundations of the late Archaic Artemision at Ephesos, whose construction began sometime around

---

[106] Von Reden 1997: 156–61.

8.14 Aeginetan stater, or 'turtle'

560 BC.[107] Lydian coinage must be an invention of the late seventh century BC at the earliest. These Lydian coins are of electrum, an alloy of silver and gold that occurs naturally in that region. The coins are in fact simple slugs with simple stamps. Such coins do not seem to have circulated widely, certainly not beyond the territory acknowledging the authority of the Lydian king. There is a reason for this. Within the king's domain, the stamp of his authority alone would have been a sufficient guarantee of a coin's value. Outside it however, where the king's writ no longer ran, it would have been impossible to estimate the relative proportions of silver and gold in the coin, and so to translate its value as coin into a value in standard weights.

When Greek cities, such as Phokaia in Ionia, start to mint their own coins they do so in silver. They tend to employ their own weight standards. Since value depends on weight rather on the city's stamp, coins could have been used as a medium of exchange between two cities which had different weight standards, provided one had a reliable set of scales to undertake the conversion. Still, the variation in weight standards, and the fact that (for the most part) coins were issued in large denominations, betrays a relative lack of concern with facilitating long-distance trade.[108] The invention of coinage did not lead to anything like a money economy in the Archaic period. None the less, by 480 BC most of the poleis in the Greek world (with the important exceptions of Sparta and Crete) were minting their own coins. Their designs are individual in the extreme. No one could be in any doubt that a 'turtle' was Aeginetan (fig. 8.14), an 'owl' Athenian, and that an 'Arethousa' hailed from Syracuse. It is hard to resist the conclusion that coins were more important as a badge of a city's identity and autonomy than as a medium for international exchange. Coinage is then undoubtedly a sign that

---

[107] Hogarth 1908: 74–93.   [108] Howgego 1995; Osborne 1996a: 250–9.

the polis had risen. But it remains more a potent symbol of a political idea – the autonomous citizen-state – than an indication of a new kind of urban society, based on a new kind of economic institution, the market.

Nevertheless the rapid spread of coinage among Greek cities in the late Archaic period is perhaps the clearest example of 'peer-polity interaction' that could be imagined. Rivalry between states also took more expensive forms – the late Archaic period is the heyday of the monumental temple. But it would be wrong to see monumentality as a simple effect of rivalry between states. Rather it is connected to other cultural forms, such as narrative art, which it will be our next task to examine.

CHAPTER 9

ART, NARRATIVE AND MONUMENTALITY

9.1 Visual cultures

Ancient Greece was a culture of images.[1] Had you been a visitor to, let us say, Athens in 520 BC, images would have confronted you at every turn. Naked marble male youths (kouroi), fully carved in the round, would have stared over you as you passed through the cemeteries on the outskirts of the city. Had you ventured further, into the city's principal sanctuary, Athena's Acropolis, yet more images could be seen. Painted maidens, or korai, set up as votive offerings by the well-to-do, would have stared past you as you approached one of Athena's two temples. In the pedimental spaces above the entrance to these two temples, more marble figures could be glimpsed.[2] Had you stayed longer in Athens, and been admitted to an aristocratic drinking party, or *symposion* (symposium), you would have seen more images, complex scenes of human, animal and monstrous figures painted on the surfaces of cups, water jars, wine pourers and mixing-bowls. Even if you were a foreigner, and relatively unacquainted with Greek aristocratic culture, you could not fail to notice that the subjects of these images were principally human and principally male. If you were a fellow-Greek, you would immediately be aware that many of the scenes you encountered, both on pots and on temple pediments, were scenes from myth, excerpts from stories of the Greek heroic past. You would have been able to recognise, for example, that the scene in figure 9.1 (an amphora painted, almost certainly, by Exekias) represented the suicide of Aias, one of the chief Greek protagonists in the Trojan war.[3] The images you encountered then were not merely figurative but narrative: picture making in the service of story-telling.

Greek art is still sufficiently familiar to many of us for few to be surprised by all this. For did not the Greeks see their gods in anthropomorphic terms, as larger, lustier and more powerful men and women? And were not Greek myths an integral part of Greek culture, so integral a part indeed that there is nothing odd about the desire to illustrate their myths on pots or temple pediments? This may seem a straightforward explanation, until one remembers that not all narrative art traditions are in the habit of narrating myths. The grand series of panels that once

---

[1] For some thoughts on why ancient Greece was a culture of images, see Hoffmann 1988; Schnapp 1994. [2] This information is all well summarised by Hurwit 1985a: 236–48.
[3] This vase is Boulogne-sur-Mer 558; see Beazley 1951: 69–70; 1956: 145 no. 18.

9.1 Amphora showing the death of Aias, attributed to Exekias

adorned the palaces of the Assyrian kings at Nineveh, Nimrud and Khorasabad, did tell elaborate stories in pictures. But they narrated recent events: the glorious exploits of the king in battle; the siege and capture of Lachish; and the king's invariably successful hunt of the lion.[4] The figurative art of Egypt performed a similar role. There are numerous reliefs and paintings that relate the exploits of Rameses II and his army at the battle of Kadesh.[5] There are far fewer illustrations of Egyptian myths, and none of the exploits of Egyptian heroes.[6] Still, Mesopotamian culture had its heroes, the most famous of whom was Gilgamesh. But there are few, if any, images which unambiguously portray Gilgamesh performing a particular feat from a particular story. There are, to be sure, images which could be interpreted in this way, but they are stock images. In seal engravings such as the one shown in figure 9.2, the hero always gets to fight with the lion.[7] But we do not know which hero he is, what lion he is fighting, or why. There is nothing in this image that anchors it to a particular story.

Greek images of the late Archaic period are not like this. They portray particular men, gods, monsters or heroes in particular situations (or at least situate them in particular myths). But it had not always been thus. Greek art had not always been predominantly figurative, still less narrative. Athens in particular had been the home of the Geometric style, a relentlessly non-figurative art form, and had you come here 230 years earlier (that is in 750 BC) you would have been confronted

[4] Powell 1997: 166–70; Russell 1993.   [5] Powell 1997: 160–6; see also Boardman 1983.
[6] Powell 1997: 166–70.   [7] Hurwit 1985a: 115–17.

9.2 Small ivory plaque from Nimrud, showing a hero or god with a rampant lion

by a very different visual environment. In some of the cemeteries around the city, you would, to be sure, have encountered funerary monuments, but these took the form of monumental kraters or amphoras. One of these, Athens NM 804 (fig. 6.6), was probably set up over a woman's grave.[8] Most of the decoration on this vase is rigorously aniconic, that is non-representational. It is dominated by variations of one single motif, the maeander, running round the pot in a series of bands.[9] To be sure, there is one frieze of grazing animals, and the central panel has human figures, but not figures involved in any known myth. They consist instead of mourners grouped around the prothesis (lying in state) of a woman, presumably the woman whose grave this marks. The scene is generic, a stock scene. It is not attached to any time, place or story.

[8] Whitley 1991a: 137–62; Brueckner and Pernice 1893.   [9] Coldstream 1968: 29–41.

Attic Late Geometric art then is figurative in only a minimal sense. The human figure is more pictogram than picture, little more than a convenient visual short-hand for 'man' or 'woman'. There is no attempt to depict anatomy, or to distinguish one mourner from another.[10] The Geometric style however, a style in which human or animal figures are subordinate to principles of abstract design, was dominant in eighth-century Greece, even if some regions (Crete) had a more vigorous figurative tradition than others (Attica or the Argolid). Still, it cannot be held that figurative, narrative art was something that came naturally to Greeks, or was a natural outcome of Greek culture. Figurative and then narrative art developed from very unpromising beginnings. At the end of this development, in the Classical period, Greek art became what we would call naturalistic, producing images so close to nature that they could be mistaken for the real thing. This achievement is called the 'Greek revolution', and is usually considered as a single, all embracing transformation of visual culture and visual norms. But this characterisation tends to treat the 'Greek revolution' as inevitable, and so is, in some respects, misleading.

The Greek 'triumph of naturalism' is in fact the outcome of a number of separate if related changes, whose distinctions must be maintained. First, Greek visual culture went from being predominantly *aniconic* (non-representational) to *iconic*, that is from a culture of patterns to a culture of images. Human and animal figures gradually oust Geometric designs. Second, Greek figurative art gradually became *narrative*, that is primarily geared to 'telling stories in pictures'. Third, Greek sculpture gradually became more *monumental*, more accomplished at producing kouroi, korai and other kinds of sculpture 'in the round'. And finally, in the course of the Classical period, Greek art became truly naturalistic. Now these changes may relate to one another, and do so in a causal way. It has often been suggested, for example, that narrative art was a necessary condition for the emergence of naturalistic art. Gombrich has proposed that the development of naturalism depends not upon a straightforward 'imitation of nature', but on a more gradual process of 'making and matching', a progressive adaptation of inherited artistic conventions towards a more convincing rendering of natural, particularly human, forms. This process takes place, not through any overriding cultural imperative to show things 'as they are', but in order to create increasingly convincing artistic fictions. Telling a story in pictures (narrative art) thus provides a powerful stimulus for the development of naturalism[11] (see below). None the less, we should remember that not all figurative art is narrative, and not all visual narratives are naturalistic. Greek art could have developed otherwise. In Crete that is exactly what happened: a sophisticated figurative art developed that had no use for 'telling stories in pictures'.

We should bear these distinctions in mind in our search for the origins of figurative, narrative and naturalistic art. Such distinctions should, at least, discourage

---

[10] On 'Geometric anatomy', see the contrasting views of Coldstream (1968: 29–41) and Whitley (1991a: 139–41).   [11] Gombrich 1962: 99–125.

9.3 Attic Late Geometric II krater

an account that sees a simple progression from one stage to another. For Greek narrative art has its own peculiarities, which require a closer look.

9.2 Beginnings, and narrative art

In the beginning (the Dark Ages) Greek art had little use for images. In the ninth century we find the odd sketch of archers on a pot from a grave in Lefkandi; ships, fighting scenes and nature goddesses all put in an appearance in Knossos; and the occasional horse and mourning woman can be glimpsed in the remoter regions of Attic funerary vases.[12] Images were certainly not unknown – a fact which makes the question 'how and why did the Greeks rediscover the image' an unnecessary one. During the eighth century, images become more common, even in 'Geometric' Athens. Most of these images, however – fighting scenes on land or sea (fig. 8.6), or the *prothesis* and *ekphora* that represent lying in state and then the carrying out of the bier (fig. 6.6) – are generic.[13] There is nothing to identify the particulars of the persons or the occasion – all that is signified is a funeral or a fight. Yet not all Late Geometric scenes can be so categorised. Figure 9.3 for example shows a ship with rowers, and a man either taking leave of or greeting

[12] On images from Lefkandi, see Popham *et al.* 1980: 127–8. On images from Knossos, see Brock 1957: 11–15; Coldstream and Catling 1996: 7–8, 155. For Athens, see Benson 1970 and Whitley 1991a: 48.

[13] See Ahlberg 1971a; 1971b.

a woman.[14] Some have seen here an incident from Greek mythology – perhaps Menelaus taking leave of Helen. Certainly it is no stock image – it has no contemporary parallels. But there is nothing in the image itself that allows us to determine what, if any, myth it may refer to. Its meaning remains opaque – at least to us.

Throughout the eighth century however, it is the stock scenes, such as the prothesis, that predominate. Of course, there are regional variations. Scenes with a 'horse and rider', and horses generally, are much more common in the Argolid than they are in Attica.[15] Throughout the eighth century, moreover, all kinds of imagery had remained subordinate parts of an overall Geometric design. It took the dissolution of these Geometric principles for a fully figurative art style to flourish. It is only then that Oriental 'influence' (Crete excepted) is fully felt. In Corinth figured scenes become more and more common on small vessels as the seventh century progresses. The invention of the black-figure technique allows figures to be rendered in greater detail. Few scenes on Protocorinthian pots, however, can be described as narrative. There are numerous fighting scenes – some, as on the Chigi vase (figure 8.9), showing hoplites in battle (see above). But there is little to distinguish these scenes from the generic scenes of a century earlier, except that they show hoplite equipment. Corinthian painters also produced numerous images where humans and monsters are juxtaposed, as in figure 6.1. But juxtapositions are exactly what they remain. As with the fighting scenes, there is nothing to anchor them to a particular myth or story. We cannot tell whether they are indeed 'myths', or serve some other, quite different purpose.[16]

It may be helpful to look at this problem from the (hypothetical) artist's perspective. If you were required to turn a generic scene into a particular incident from a known story, how would you go about it? One way would be to pick an incident that only occurs in a particular myth. So we can be fairly sure that figure 9.4, for example, represents the blinding of Polyphemos by Odysseus and his companions. Or, to put it another way, how many other stories do you know of where several men come together to blind a Cyclops with the burnt tip of a giant tree trunk? There is only one. Another method might be to identify the characters in a story by their *attributes*. One of the attributes of Polyphemos in the story (*Odyssey* IX.345–402) is that he gets drunk. In the picture this attribute – his drunkenness – is conveyed by the cup he is holding. Still, there are several ways of conveying an attribute and of identifying characters in a tale. One is by piling on the iconographic particulars. In sixth-century Athenian vase painting, the 'figure of eight' shield was to become one of the defining attributes of two heroes in the Trojan cycle – Achilles himself and, more specifically, Aias (or Ajax). It is this visual clue, among others, that allows us to identify the hero in figure 9.1. In the seventh

---

[14] See Coldstream 1991; Snodgrass 1987: 166; 1998: 33–4; Fittschen 1969: 51–60.
[15] See Boardman 1983; for Argive Late Geometric pots generally, see Courbin 1966; Coldstream 1968: 125–47.
[16] On Protocorinthian images, see generally Benson 1989; 1995. For a different view, see Shanks 1993; 1999. I take a view diametrically opposed to Benson in what I write here.

9.4 The Polyphemos amphora from Eleusis

century, however, pot painters hit upon a simpler way of conveying the identity of the figure: just paint on a label (a dipinto).[17] This was the technique adopted by the Nessos painter (fig. 1.1), and later taken to extremes by the early sixth-century Athenian painters Sophilos and Kleitias (figs. 9.9 and 9.10).

So far we have been talking about myth scenes, as if to convey the whole of a story it is enough to show a single incident from it. Let us take a closer look at some of these images. In the Polyphemos scene, Polyphemos steadfastly holds on to a cup, while Odysseus and his companions blind him (fig. 9.4). In the *Odyssey* however

---

[17] On this question generally, see Snodgrass 1998: 101–26. A dipinto (painted label) may be deceptive. Often they do identify a figure in a picture. But they may also be doing something else. As Ferrari (1987) has convincingly argued, the dipinto 'Menelas' on a Protoattic stand found in Aegina is almost certainly not identifying one of the men holding spears as 'Menelaus'. It is, rather, a means of signifying the song or poem that these spear-carriers are collectively reciting.

(IX.367–402) Polyphemos is first offered wine, which he drinks neat. The wine (which is new to him) goes to his head, and he falls immediately asleep. Only then does Odysseus urge his companions to take the tree trunk, hold it in the fire, and plunge it into his single eye. It defies credibility that a drunk and sleeping Cyclops would have held on to his cup all the while. What we see here, surely, is two separate incidents compressed into one scene. Or rather, the cup functions as a visual epithet both of the drunken Polyphemos (the character) and the 'Polyphemos story' (the episode).[18] Similarly, on the Boulogne vase (fig. 9.1), it is a moot point whether the armour set to one side, the sword placed carefully in the ground, and the sombre palm tree are just props necessary for a single scene, or attributes of the whole myth, the 'suicide of Aias'. For do not the arms, in a sense, allude to the cause of the dispute, the quarrel over the arms of Achilles? And does not the placing of the sword in the ground anticipate (though it does not show) the actual moment of immolation itself? To those familiar with the myth itself, this image sums it all up. The painter, Exekias, has succeeded in telling a whole myth in one scene – provided, of course, you know the story, and are able to pick up all the visual clues.[19]

In a medium such as vase painting, visual clues are a necessity. For how do you go about 'telling a story in pictures'? In the modern world, the most popular form of narrative art (television and cinema aside) is the comic strip. Here a story is conveyed by a number of separate, chronologically successive frames or episodes, which usually run (like the conventions of our writing) from left to right. In such episodic narrative, scenes succeed one another in chronological order and at an even tempo. But ancient Greeks rarely, if ever, resorted to this 'episodic' technique of visual narrative. Even in large vessels with numerous complex scenes, such as the François vase (fig. 9.10), the scenes themselves are not really successive incidents from the same story, but episodes from separate myths linked together in a larger cycle. Most Greek narrative is 'monoscenic', as in the Boulogne amphora. Narrative is conveyed partly through an allusion to both what has happened and what is yet to happen. This fact has led to the view that the Greek visual representation of myth is 'synoptic'. The image shows the myth as a whole, not merely an incident from it. This interpretation gains in credibility if we look at another class of images. Figure 9.5 depicts a vessel by Lydos (now destroyed). Here two incidents from the sack of Troy are shown. Neoptolemos, son of Achilles, slays first the young Astyanax (son of Hector), and then Priam. In this image he slays them *at the same time*. The same conventions are used half a century later when the red-figure vase painter, the Kleophrades painter, depicts the same myth (fig. 9.6).[20] In surviving literary accounts, these incidents are separate. Scenes like these raise questions

---

[18] On this vase, see originally Mylonas 1957. For discussion see Morris 1984: 37–51; Osborne 1988a; Snodgrass 1998: 90–100.   [19] On this scene, see Hurwit 1985a: 271–2; Stewart 1987: 32–3.

[20] For discussion of these images in relation to the concept of 'synoptic narrative', see Snodgrass 1982; 1998: 12–39; Whitley 1993: 15–17. The notion of 'synoptic narrative' derives ultimately from the proposals of Himmelmann 1967. For another view on narrative, see Connelly 1993. For a recent classification of types of narrative, see Stansbury-O'Donnell 1999.

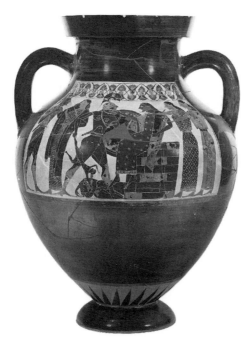

9.5 Scene showing Neoptolemos slaying both Astyanax and Priam on a belly amphora in Berlin, attributed to Lydos

9.6 Attic red-figure hydria attributed to the Kleophrades painter

about the nature of Greek narrative art. Is such 'synoptic' representation merely an artistic convention – a way of cramming all the incident into a single small space? Or does such a way of telling pictorial stories tell us something more fundamental about how Greeks conceived myth? Could it not be that Greeks had a synoptic view of myth? What mattered to them was not that successive incidents were portrayed in chronological order, but that all the attributes of a myth were present in the image. A myth existed in 'simultaneity'. In this view, the cup that Polyphemos holds and the two victims of Neoptolemos are attributes of the story, rather than of the characters. This seems to be the view held by the 'Paris' school of Classical scholars, and it has much to recommend it.[21]

By 580 BC myth had become an integral part of the visual culture of many of the regions of Archaic Greece. Athenian, Corinthian and Laconian vase painters were producing their own versions of Greek myths using the black-figure technique. Even in those regions of Greece which had lost interest in producing pottery with figured scenes (such as the Argolid), scenes from myth were produced in other media. Argive metal-workers decorated the inner straps of bronze-faced hoplite shields with scenes taken from mythology, sometimes, as in vase painting, using inscriptions to aid identification.[22] Narrative art pervaded Greek life, and there can be little doubt that this narrative impulse provided an added incentive to improve the drawing of the individual figures. The black-figure technique allowed for more detail than could be provided by the older 'outline' method of drawing. The limbs of both Odysseus and Polyphemos in figure 9.4 are portrayed with minimal fuss, but in figure 9.1 Exekias manages to convey the powerful musculature of his hero, Aias, by the careful use of incision. Black-figure had its limitations – no black-figure artist (Exekias included) managed to convey character wholly successfully. The black-figure technique enabled painters to show all the features of a story economically; it could not hope to provide a naturalistic illusion of a real event.

So far we have considered these images outside of any social or institutional setting – as if indeed narrative art developed naturally and inevitably. Yet, of course, such images appeared on pots which had a very specific function, and which were meant for a very specific occasion. The Boulogne vase is an amphora, intended for the holding of wine or water; the vase by the Kleophrades painter is a hydria, used for pouring water into a mixing-bowl. In the sixth century, such shapes are related to a very specific occasion: the symposium, or drinking party. It is time to give these images some context.

9.3 Shapes, images and the symposium

A symposium (or symposion) is a drinking party, often an all-male affair. Women may be present, but only as entertainers or temporary consorts. A symposium was

---

[21] Snodgrass (1987: 136–46) tries to summarise the position of the 'Paris School'.
[22] Bol 1989; Kunze 1950.

not a dinner party, and wives did not take part. The most complete picture we have of the symposium is the one on the painted walls of the 'Tomb of the Diver', discovered in 1968 near the Greek colony of Paestum (Poseidonia) in southern Italy. It dates to around 480 BC.[23] Here men recline, sometimes two together, on couches. On one couch, two men embrace and almost kiss; on another, two hold tortoiseshell lyres; on a nearby couch, one flicks his drinking cup – he may be playing a game called *kottabos*, whose aim was to hit a target with the dregs of one's wine. By each of the couches, slightly lower, is a table, on which the cups (and some food) may be placed. On one of the smaller of the tomb's panels, between the two depicting men on couches, is an image of the central object of the symposium – the krater or mixing-bowl, in which wine was mixed with water, as was the custom among the Greeks (and, as they believed, among all civilised peoples).

The symposium had evidently become an important institution throughout much of the Greek world by the end of the Archaic period. Indeed, if we look at the shapes of that most widely distributed of sixth-century Greek regional ceramic styles, the Attic, most seem to be designed for this occasion (fig. 9.7). First, there are the large cups, or kylikes, normally held by the base. Cups, however, came in a range of shapes, including the kotyle and the kantharos (a shape preferred by Etruscans and Boeotians). Then there are the vessels for holding liquids, such as the amphoras, and those specifically designed to help in the mixing of the water (the hydria or 'water jar') and the wine (the oinochoe or 'wine pourer'). Wine and water are mixed together in the krater or 'mixing-bowl'. The krater was central to the symposium in both a literal and a cultural sense. It was the vessel around which the participants, the symposiasts, whose numbers were rarely fewer than eight or more than twelve, were arranged. Kraters came in a variety of forms. Column kraters (fig. 9.8), bell kraters, calyx kraters (fig. 11.13) and volute kraters (fig. 9.10) all had to be placed on a small table; but the dinos (fig. 9.9) had its own stand.

In Athens around the time of our notional visitor in 520 BC, this institution was well established, as it was also in Corinth, Boeotia, much of Ionia, Sparta and many western colonies. But can we say with equal assurance that our earlier visitor, coming to Athens around 750 BC, would have encountered anything like it? This is not a trivial question, as the date of the emergence of this institution is very much in dispute. Of course, when we date its appearance will depend in part on what we mean by that term. The symposium is not just a feast followed by a drinking party. Rather, it is a largely private affair, a banquet for the better off, whose male participants seat themselves on couches around a krater. The symposium then has concrete material attributes, which should allow us to date its appearance with some precision. Our notional visitor to Athens would have

---

[23] On the 'tomb of the diver' ('Tomba di Tuffatore'), see Napoli 1970; Pedley 1990: 89–94. On the game of kottabos, see Lissarrague 1990a: 80–6.

Belly-amphora

Neck-amphora

Skyphos or Cup

Cup or Kylix

Aryballos

Kantharos

Dinos and Stand

Hydria

Calyx Krater

Volute Krater

Lekythos

Oinochoe

Pelike

Psykter

Kotyle or Skyphos

Stamnos

9.7 Outline drawing of various shapes of Greek pots, showing predominance of 'symposion' shapes

9.8 Early Corinthian column krater, from Caere, showing Herakles at the feast of Eurytios

9.9 'Erskine' dinos by Sophilos

found few of these in 750 BC. To be sure, drinking cups of all kinds had been a major feature of Greek material culture since Protogeometric times, and there were plenty of drinking vessels in eighth-century Athens. Hydriai, oinochoai and amphoras were also common enough.[24] But the central item of the symposium – the krater – is something of a rarity. Or rather, there are plenty of so-called kraters, over 1.4 m high, which were used as grave markers in the Kerameikos and Dipylon cemeteries, but their uncompromisingly funerary iconography and their size would have made them most unsuitable for a symposium (though not, perhaps, for a wake). Few eighth-century Attic kraters are of the right size and shape for a drinking party.[25] This dearth of kraters is less apparent in other regions of eighth-century Greece. The Argolid produced kraters of suitable size, whose iconography would not have been out of place in a symposium.[26] But Argive potters singularly failed to produce an appropriate range of shapes in succeeding centuries. Even in that most dynamic of seventh-century pottery industries, Corinth, symposium shapes are hardly in evidence. Corinthian potters had been making oinochoai and drinking cups for some time, and around 700 BC developed two new forms, the olpe (for pouring, of which the Chigi vase (fig. 8.9) is an example) and the kotyle (for drinking). But Protocorinthian remained a style best suited to small perfume flasks. Protocorinthian kraters are a rarity, to say the least. It is only at the very end of the seventh century that Corinthian potters produced kraters in any quantity, but when they do one theme dominates the decoration: the symposium itself.[27] Figure 9.8 shows groups of men seated on couches, with small tables (and dogs) beneath. Here all the items that make up a symposium are present – and if we cannot actually see a krater on this particular vase, they are to be found depicted on many like this one. At the same time as they were making these kraters, Corinthian potters were producing a new range of cups – Komast cups – with a new iconography, related specifically to drinking. A few years later, all these shapes were being enthusiastically copied by Attic potters.[28]

It is this kind of evidence that has led many scholars to conclude that the symposium only crystallised as an institution towards the end of the seventh century BC. The symposium, or 'banquet couché', was, in this respect, only one of the later borrowings from the Near East that had been the principal characteristic of that century. Certainly the habit of dining and drinking in a reclining position is a Near Eastern practice, and the furniture that goes with the 'reclining banquet' does not appear in the Greek visual record before 620 BC.[29] But there is a dissent-

---

[24] On symposium shapes, see Lissarrague 1990a; Boardman 1975a: 208–10; 1975: 208–10. On the names of pots/vases, see Richter and Milne 1935.

[25] On eighth-century Attic pottery generally, see Coldstream 1968: 21–90. On Kerameikos 290 (from grave G22), see *ibid.*: 21–3; Kübler 1954: 209–56. For a recent review of Geometric kraters from Athens, see Bohen 1997.   [26] See again Courbin 1966; Coldstream 1968: 125–41.

[27] On these vases, see Dentzer 1982: 76–87; Schmitt-Pantel 1992: 27–30. But on Protocorinthian, see Benson 1989.

[28] On komast cups, see Boardman 1974: 18; Beazley 1951: 19–21; 1956: 23–37; Brijder 1983.

[29] On the Oriental antecedents of the 'banquet couché', see Dentzer 1971; 1982: 51–69. On symposium furniture, see Boardman 1990c.

ing view. Oswyn Murray has argued that the symposium (or something like it) was a central institution in Greek society from at least the ninth century onwards.[30] He draws our attention in particular to cremation grave 168 from Pithekoussai.[31] Here a ten-year-old boy was buried with a drinking cup and a Geometric krater. On the surface of the cup (Nestor's cup) is one of the earliest Greek inscriptions, a joke about love (or rather sex) and drinking, with a possible allusion to Homer (fig. 6.12). Murray sees this as a quintessentially sympotic joke, akin to those that were later to appear as dipinti on Attic drinking cups, especially those we call 'Little Master cups'.[32] Certainly sympotic inscriptions of one kind or another are very common in early Greek writing.[33] Can Murray's position be reconciled with the other evidence?

I think it can, albeit not without a certain semantic sleight of hand. Murray has shown that feasting and drinking together had long been a part of the male bonding rituals that formed part of the social cement of early Greece. But male commensality of this kind need not entail an institution as elaborated as that of the symposium. In some regions of Greece, notably Crete, other forms of male communal dining seem to have persisted throughout the Archaic period, centred not on the symposion but on the andreion. It was a synthesis of these older traditions of commensality with a new style of 'couched dining' imported from the Near East that brought about the institution we think of as the Greek symposium. It was this 'synthetic' institution that brought about the conditions first for the creation of a certain range of appropriate vessel forms, and then for the development of a certain kind of visual literacy.

This last point requires some elaboration. By visual literacy I mean two things: first the skill required to read images in a narrative way; and second the ability to read the accompanying inscriptions. For, to quite a surprising degree in Archaic Greece, image and inscription went together. Image and inscription were equal partners in the joint task of telling stories in pictures. It would then be a mistake to try to define Archaic Greek culture in simple, bold terms such as 'oral', 'visual' or 'literate', or to imagine that Archaic Greek culture gradually became less oral and more literate. Orality, visual narrative and literacy were interdependent parts of a cultural whole. Archaic Athens in particular can justly be called an oral-literate-visual culture.[34] Oral performance, literacy and narrative art all came together in the symposium. Both inscriptions of vases and myth scenes proliferate after the 'sympotic synthesis' had been achieved sometime around 620 BC. For the symposium provided a social context for the recounting of myths and for visual literacy. The pots themselves provide the most striking evidence for this.

---

[30] As argued by Murray 1980: 199–203; 1983.

[31] Murray 1994. For this grave see also Buchner and Ridgway 1993: 212–23; Russo 1993; Ridgway 1992: 54–7.

[32] Murray 1994. For later 'symposiastic' inscriptions, see Beazley 1932; Lissarrague 1990a: 123–9.

[33] Powell 1991: 158–71.

[34] On the relationships between orality, literacy and imagery in early Greek culture, see Hurwit 1990; Lissarrague 1990a: 123–39; 1994; Whitley 1997b: 641–5.

Let us look at two kraters, the centrepiece of any symposium, different sides of which would have been seen by different participants in any dinner party. The first is a dinos by Sophilos (fig. 9.9).[35] It shows the marriage of Peleus and Thetis, and takes great care to show (and list) not only the bride and groom, but all the wedding guests. In case there is any ambiguity, all participants are marked out by a dipinto, or painted inscription. Now Archaic Greece knew little or nothing of silent reading:[36] to read something is to speak it aloud, and to read a name is to make that name, and so that person, present. Inscriptions are thus visual cues for the story being presented in the image.

The same is true of a much more elaborately decorated volute krater, the François vase, made by Kleitias and Ergotimos (fig. 9.10).[37] This vase is decorated in a series of parallel friezes, each containing a scene from myth. The two lowest friezes excepted, each character (and a character might be a dog or a boar) in each myth is named. Sometimes, in more crowded scenes, a name substitutes for an image. The vessel has two sides, each with a different series of myths. On one side, on the lip of the vessel, is the Kalydonian boar hunt; just below this is the funeral games of Patroklos, which in turn is set above the marriage of Peleus and Thetis, parents of Achilles, decorating the shoulder of the vessel. Below this, on the belly, is the scene where Achilles meets Troilos, and then kills him. Turning to the other side, the scene on the lip shows the triumphant return of Athenian youths and maidens, led by Theseus, to Athens; below this the battle between Lapiths and Centaurs, a battle which had broken out at the marriage feast of Perithöos; below this again, more of the marriage of Peleus and Thetis; and finally, on the belly, the return of the god Hephaistos to Olympia, an event overseen by both Zeus and Hera. Linking these two sides are the identical images on the handles, showing (above) Artemis, or the 'mistress of animals'; and (below), Aias (Ajax) carrying back the body of the dead Achilles. Obviously there are some common themes here – but what are we to make of them? What on earth can this collection of myths add up to? What, in short, does it 'mean'?

One theory has it that this is a visual representation of a particular poem or song – an equivalent in clay and paint of a lost work by a well-known lyric poet, let us say, Stesichoros.[38] It is the *Bild* (picture) that derives from the original *Lied* (song). In this view, all the images represent episodes from the poem, whose central theme must have been the deeds of Achilles. Other scenes – the Kalydonian boar hunt,

---

[35] On this vase, see Bakir 1981: 5–7; it is also intelligently discussed by Brownlee 1995: and the inscriptions by Immerwahr 1990: 21–2. On the centrality of the krater to the symposium, see Lissarrague 1990a: 19–46; 1990b.

[36] For arguments to this effect, see Svenbro 1993: 44–63. (See also Lissarrague 1990a: 123–39; 1994.) There may be compelling reasons to think that 'silent reading' was being practised in Classical times, at least by the end of the fifth century BC (Gavrilov 1997; Burnyeat 1997). It is harder to argue for the prevalence of silent reading before the appearance of long prose texts, which is a phenomenon of the fifth century (and not earlier).

[37] For useful descriptions of this vase, see Beazley 1956: 76–7 n.1; 1951: 26–37. For the inscriptions, see Immerwahr 1990: 24–5. For detailed illustrations of the whole thing, see Furtwängler and Reichhold 1904: 1–14, 55–62 and plates 1–2, 11–13.   [38] As argued by Stewart 1983.

9.10 Black-figure volute krater, 'the François vase', signed many times by Kleitias and Ergotimos, from Chiusi

the arrival of Theseus, the return of Hephaistos – represent incidents alluded to (or digressed upon). I myself think that this interpretation is too rigid. I doubt whether the images were intended to add up to a single, stable 'meaning' at all. Its meaning depended upon its context – and by this I mean its primary context of use in a Greek symposium, not its final resting place in an Etruscan grave. The meaning varied with the occasion, that is with each symposium in which it was used. The images provide, not a single, coherent tale, but a series of episodes related by a number of themes, and a number of talking points. Each participant would have seen a different side, and so a different set of episodes. Each side – the one side relating the life of Achilles, the other being linked by marriage and what results from marriage – would have provided a set of visual cues on which symposiasts would have been asked to improvise. Improvisation on a common theme (love) is after all the theme of our major literary account of a Classical symposium, Plato's dialogue of that name. Improvisation, of course, would have been constrained as much by the inscriptions as by the image, but one can still see how the scenes on this krater could have provided the raw material for an entertaining evening.

9.11 Tondo (i.e. interior) of cup signed by Exekias

But to suggest that the principal topic in a Greek symposium was the high culture of myth is a little misleading. The symposium involved drinking wine, and wine was the province of Dionysos. Dionysiac imagery blossomed in Attic vase painting during the course of the sixth century.[39] By Dionysiac imagery I do not simply mean images of Dionysos, as in figure 9.11. Dionysos had his follow-ers and companions, of whom the satyr was the most prominent. A satyr is a com-posite creature: mainly human, but with long hair, snub nose, tail and pointed ears. The activities of satyrs can be seen as a kind of ironic commentary on the symposium itself. Satyrs are creatures of excess, and their participation in 'Dionysiac' revelries is not governed by any civilised norms.[40] Whereas in the

---

[39] On Dionysiac imagery generally, see Carpenter 1986.
[40] On satyrs, see Lissarrague 1990a: 13–14, 37–40, 76–80; Stewart 1997: 156–71.

symposium, wine is mixed with water and drunk from cups, satyrs just guzzle straight from the amphora. A satyr's sexual urges are not governed by any etiquette of restraint; satyrs will copulate with anyone, as the fancy takes them. Satyrs then are a joke, and jokes – visual and verbal – were an integral part of the symposium. But images of satyrs also betray a certain visual sophistication. To depict a mythical creature like a satyr effectively you have first to be able to draw a man, for a satyr is little more than a bestial man. Satyrs attest, albeit indirectly, to the growing interest in human, particularly male, anatomy in the late Archaic period. But surviving Archaic satyrs are always painted, always in two dimensions. To understand the growing Greek obsession with the human (particularly male) body we have to turn to three-dimensional images – that is to sculpture.

9.4 Sculpture and the body

Of all the arts, sculpture is a field in which the Greeks excelled. Ancient writers like Pausanias and the elder Pliny pay the closest attention to great sculptors and their works. The most celebrated Greek sculptors worked in the Classical period, and it might be imagined that such sublime achievements must derive from a long sculptural tradition. In this one would be mistaken. There is no Minoan and little Mycenaean large-scale sculpture in either stone or bronze.[41] During the Dark Ages, some small-scale terracotta and bronze figurines were produced in some quantity, and by the eighth century bronzesmiths had taken to adding small human and animal figures to tripod cauldrons and similar objects.[42] Yet neither coroplasty (working in clay) nor bronze casting was to make great advances during the succeeding seventh century. The first impressive Greek sculpture was neither cast nor moulded, but carved.

It is rare for wood to survive well in Greece. It does not do so, except in water-logged conditions. Fortunately however, some sanctuary sites, such as the Heraion of Samos, are close to the sea and so have a high water table, and this has helped to preserve much wooden sculpture that would otherwise have been lost. Figure 9.12 shows one, a figure of a woman just under 30 cm high. Such statues as these may have been votives, but we know from literary accounts that many early cult statues (misleadingly referred to as xoana) were often of wood. One such stood in the temple of Hera in this sanctuary, and may have been life-size or even larger.[43] Seventh-century wooden statues such as this one are known as Daedalic, a style marked out by the high hat or polos and the wig-like coiffure.[44] When

---

[41] It may be objected that the artists of the Early Bronze Age Cyclades produced numerous marble figurines, some on a large scale. But there is no continuous tradition linking their achievements to Archaic Greece. The Mycenaeans only ever produced a few reliefs in stone, principally the 'lions' over the Lion Gate at Mycenae and the grave stelai over grave circles A and B.

[42] See in general Schweitzer 1971: 127–63; Stewart 1990: 103–4.

[43] See Kopcke 1967: 102–7; Ohly 1967; Stewart 1990: 44–6, 104–5.

[44] On the 'Daedalic' style see Jenkins 1936; Ridgway 1977: 17–39. 'Daedalic' is a conventional term. It has little to do with the legendary Daedalus (Daidalos); see Morris 1992: 238–56.

9.12 Wooden statue from the Samian Heraion

Greeks, in the mid-seventh century, begin to carve sculpture in stone, their work closely resembles these wooden carvings, both in style and in technique. Figure 9.13 shows Nikandre, the earliest large-scale stone sculpture in Archaic Greece. She is about 1.75 m tall, and was set up as a votive offering in Delos around 650 BC.[45] As Hurwit has noted, the stone here has been treated like a plank carved in low relief, something we can also observe on the slightly smaller, but better-preserved example of the so-called Auxerre goddess.[46] Nikandre is the first in the line of stone *korai* (singular *kore*), statues of young, unmarried girls ('maidens') in marble or limestone, usually life-size, and invariably clothed.[47] Bombarded as we are daily with images of young pretty girls (clothed and otherwise), one might expect that the kore could have been the subject of the kind of fetishistic interest

[45] On Nikandre, see Richter 1968: 26.
[46] Hurwit 1985a: 186–91; on the Auxerre goddess, see Richter 1968: 32.
[47] See generally Richter 1968; Ridgway 1977: 45–77.

9.13 Nikandre, dedication from Delos

that now characterises many fields of cultural studies. But in this one would be wrong. It is her male counterpart, the *kouros*, that has instead received most attention from Classical art historians

The kouros is a naked male youth, usually carved in limetone or marble, with stiff arms and left leg forward. The kouros has pride of place in the history of early Greek sculpture for two reasons: first, the type seems to have been inspired by Egyptian work; and second, because it is in (or on) the body of the kouros that progress towards naturalistic representation 'in the round' can most easily be traced. The first of these propositions is now the least controversial. For early kouroi, such as the colossal example dedicated at Sounion in the latter years of the seventh century BC (fig. 9.14) betray clear signs of their Egyptian origins. Not only the kouros' stance, with one foot forward, but also his proportions

9.14 Kouros from Sounion

derive directly from the Egyptian canon.[48] However, contacts between Greeks and Egyptians had been going on for several hundred years before Greeks became interested in this form of monumental sculpture. What exactly had changed?

Conditions in Egypt itself had changed. After 664 BC a new, strong native dynasty had unified the country, and had embarked on an ambitious building programme. But this dynasty was militarily weak, and had had to rely on the services of Carian and Greek hoplite mercenaries. Egyptian Pharaohs, in short, actively encouraged many Greeks to come to Egypt (many making their mark, literally, by scrawling their names all over the monuments of Abu Simbel), and it was partly to regularise this arrangement that Naukratis was formally established around

---

[48] On kouroi generally, see Richter 1970. On its Egyptian origins, see Hurwit 1985a: 192–7. On the Egyptian 'canon' and kouroi, see Guralnick 1978.

560 BC.[49] As more Greeks came to Egypt, they were exposed to Egyptian sculpture. Moreover the new building programmes which the Pharaohs initiated gave them a chance to witness Egyptian techniques of building and sculpting at close hand. The kouros is the indirect result of this new, intensive Egyptian–Greek interaction, but it was no slavish copy of Egyptian forms. To be sure, the stance, scale and proportions of the kouros might be the same as its Egyptian models.[50] But both the style and the form were different. Egyptian representations of males were not fully naked – they always retained their kilts, and they were not fully in the round. Egyptian tomb sculpture was sculpture in hard stone and in very high relief. The kouros on the other hand is a male nude – the first such – and is a truly three-dimensional form, carved from a single block. Its style moreover has more in common with contemporary Greek vase painting and metalwork than it has with its Egyptian sculptural inspiration. The modelling of the torsoes on the kouroi from Delphi (Kleobis and Biton?) (fig. 9.15), for example, resembles nothing so much as that to be found on the early cuirass from Argos (fig. 8.7).[51] The muscles are rendered in the same way, by incision, and with the same decorative, 'daedalic' effect. Indeed in many respects the early Greek kouros is less naturalistic than the Egyptian models which inspired it. Early kouroi entirely lack the soft modelling of the body in hard stone, once thought to be the hallmark of Greek naturalism.

This is odd, as one of the main motives for studying kouroi has been to trace the origins of Greek naturalism. The great American scholar Gisela Richter, who devoted much of her life to their study, made her reasons for doing so crystal clear:

> the inquisitive Greek reached out continually for greater knowledge and precision. And so we owe to him . . . the discovery of naturalistic art . . . The laboratory, so to speak, in which the Greek sculptor worked out this naturalistic art was the kouros type. Its careful analysis is therefore infinitely important. We can here study in a large number of examples the gradual evolution of Greek art during the archaic period. We can see developing before our eyes the conception of the figure as a whole and of its various parts – the skull, ear, eye, mouth, collar-bones, chest, abdomen, shoulder-blades, arm, knee, foot etc.[52]

Just as Beazley had done with the history of vase painting, Richter used strict anatomical criteria, such as the rendering of noses, tear-ducts, lips and muscles, not only to isolate workshops, hands and regional styles but to arrange kouroi in a chronological sequence, a sequence that led ineluctably from the less to the more naturalistic forms. She went so far as to argue that the search for a more naturalistic male form was one of the principal motivations of the sculptors themselves.[53] Few agree with her today. For the kouros was in fact a very conservative type. The basic elements of the kouros hardly changed at all between 650 and 500 BC. It is only amongst Attic kouroi of the latter part of the sixth century that any

---

[49] On Egyptian contact generally, see Boardman 1980; Hurwit 1985a: 179–85. On the Abu Simbel inscriptions, see Bernard and Masson 1957.   [50] Guralnick 1978.
[51] On Kleobis and Biton, see Richter 1970: 49–50; on their original context, Homolle 1909: 5–18. On the Argos cuirass, see Courbin 1957.   [52] Richter 1970: 4.   [53] Richter 1970: 5.

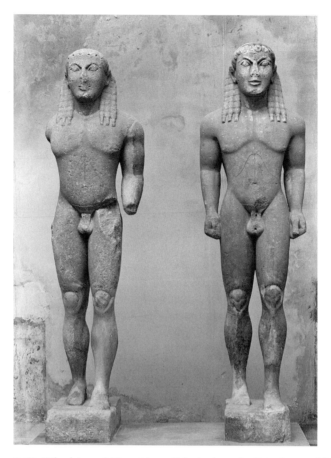

9.15 'Kleobis and Biton' (possibly in fact the Dioskouroi) from Delphi

movement towards naturalism can be discerned.[54] Naturalism may have been an indirect consequence of the development of the kouros type: it can hardly have been its cause. Scholarly interest has now shifted to the meaning of these images. What were kouroi for? And did form in any sense follow function?

Kouroi were put to many uses. Often, they were offered as votives (e.g. figs. 9.14 and 9.15). Large numbers have turned up in sanctuaries to Apollo, at Delphi, Delos and Mt Ptoion in Boeotia, and this once led to the belief that they were, in fact, representations of that god. Kouroi however were also dedicated in large numbers at the sanctuary of Hera on Samos, and at the sanctuaries both of Athena and of Poseidon at Sounion, so that explanation cannot hold.[55] Moreover, there is little to

[54] 'Naturalism' only really becomes apparent in two late Archaic kouroi from Attica; 'Kroisos', or the Anavyssos kouros (Richter 1970: 118–19 no. 136); and 'Aristodikos' from Mt Olympus (Richter 1970: 139 no. 165). On the conservatism of the kouros form, see Ridgway 1977: 45–77.

[55] On the kouroi from Mt Ptoion, see Ducat 1971; on those from Samos, see Freyer-Schauenburg 1974: 61–105; Kyrieleis 1996. On the old belief that a kouros represented Apollo, see Stewart 1986.

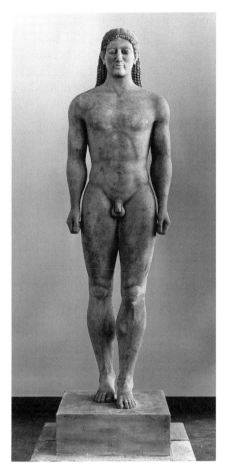

9.16 'Kroisos' from Anavyssos, the Anavyssos kouros

distinguish a kouros used as a grave marker, such as the Anavyssos kouros (fig. 9.16) from one used as a votive. As Ducat and others have pointed out, the kouros is 'polyvalent': it can mean anything. Its meaning depends on context, and on the inscription (votive or funerary) that accompanies it.[56] This does necessarily imply, however, that the kouros was a blank, to which any significance could be ascribed. Rather the kouros was a kind of meta-statement, whose import was subconscious and ideological. The kouros is a universal, aristocratic youth, eternally youthful and (in Greek eyes) eternally beautiful. More than a mere object of homoerotic appeal, the kouros embodied male aristocratic excellence (*arete*). The repetition of this type, its constant presence both in sanctuaries and over tombs, was a means of reaffirming those assumptions of natural superiority (*kalokagathia*) in which Greek aristocrats had come to believe. This at least is A. Stewart's argument, and

[56] Ducat 1971: 444–5.

certainly the kouros type seems to rise and fall with the aristocratic society of the sixth century.[57] Stewart goes further, and suggests that the distribution of kouroi corresponds to the area of the Aegean where aristocracies prevailed. For, as figure 9.17 shows, kouroi are common in Samos, southern Ionia, the Dodecanese, the Cyclades, Attica, Euboea, Boeotia and the Corinthia, but are hardly to be found in most of the Peloponnese, Thessaly, north-west Greece or Crete.[58] Still, it is hard to see why the societies of horse-mad Thessaly, or of Sparta, or of Crete, were any less aristocratic than the societies of Athens or Samos in the sixth century. Their distribution does, however, coincide with what Ian Morris has called the Central Greek culture area, in which case they must relate to forms of material practice whose roots go deeper than political structures or constitutions.[59]

If the kouros represents aristocratic arete, what of the kore? Like kouroi, korai were youthful and beautiful, and could serve equally well both as dedications and as funerary monuments. But korai were figures who were invariably clothed, and it is difficult to see them being objects of any direct erotic attention. Archaic Greeks were not entirely averse to representing erotically charged, female nudes 'in the round', but such representations in bronze, ivory, terracotta and stone were almost invariably on a small scale.[60] There does seem to have been a taboo preventing Greeks from depicting unmarried women (whether god or human) at life size in the nude. Moreover korai, unlike the kouros type, display considerable variation. Even if we, unlike Richter, confine our attention to single, free-standing figures, great differences in both dress and setting may be discerned. A nude kouros is a nude kouros, just as a rose is a rose is a rose; a kore on the other hand may be clothed in either a peplos (fig 9.18) or a chiton and chlamys (fig. 9.19). Clothing creates differences, and this allows specific aesthetic effects to be accentuated by the application of colour and paint. Regional differences too are sharper. The difference between an Attic and a Samian kouros is a subtle one, one of a regional manner or style. Korai on the other hand differ in both setting and form: in east Greece, especially at the Samian Heraion, full-figured, 'cylindrical' korai are set up on low bases, sometimes in groups; on the Athenian Acropolis, korai have a more 'masculine' form, and are often placed on the top of votive columns, where they could only be seen from below.[61] The kore then could hardly function as a kind of meta-statement. Korai are likely to have had more specific meanings. Nowhere is this clearer than in the case of Phrasikleia.

Phrasikleia ('fame-speaker') is a tomb statue, named after the woman it commemorates. It was identified through an inscription which originally stood at its base, which reads '*Sema Phrasikleias: kore keklesomai aiei/ anti gamou para theon touto lachos' onoma.*' A literal (and unpoetic) translation might read '[This

---

[57] Stewart 1986; 1990: 109–110; 1997: 63–70.
[58] Distribution map after Renfrew 1986: 12 fig. 1.10; information from Richter 1970.
[59] Morris 1998a: 10–36.   [60] Stewart 1997: 108–18, 231–4.
[61] On Samian korai, see Freyer-Schauenburg 1974: 13–61, 106–39. On the Acropolis korai, see Richter 1968: 40–1, 68–84, 99–104; Payne and Mackworth-Young 1950: 14–42.

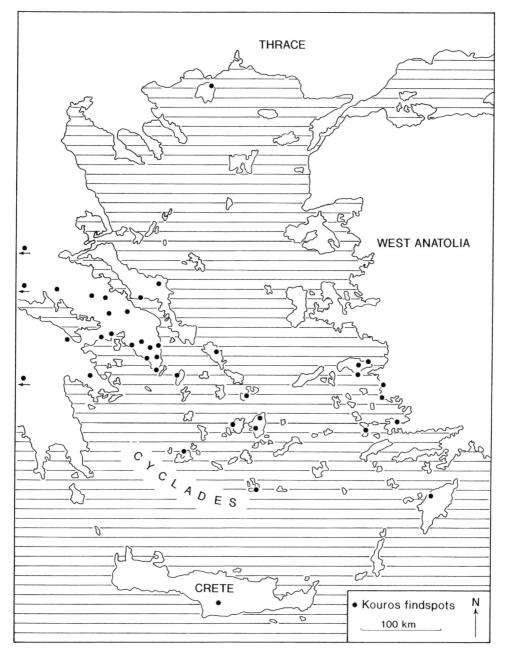

9.17 Distribution map of kouroi

9.18 The 'peplos' kore from the Athenian Acropolis, front view

9.19 Kore from the Acropolis, about 500 BC

is] the tombstone of Phrasikleia: I will always be called a kore [maiden], taking this name before marriage from the god.' The implication is clear: she will always be called a maiden because she died before she could marry. The statue has some rather odd iconographic features, such as the crown of lotus buds on her head, and the single lotus she holds in her hand. Jesper Svenbro has argued forcefully that this imagery continually refers back to phrases in the funerary inscription. The lotus alludes to the fire of the family hearth, a (metaphorical) fire that can be perpetuated only now through her *kleos*, her fame, embodied forever in both statue and inscription.[62] As in vase painting, there is here a play on both words and images. Image and inscription depend on one another and produce a range of

[62] For the statue itself, see Mastrokastos 1972. For the inscription, see Jeffery 1990: 78 and plate 3 no. 29. For discussion, see especially Svenbro 1993: 8–25. For a general discussion of Archaic epitaphs, see Humphreys 1980; Sourvinou-Inwood 1995: 140–296, esp. 29–50 for Phrasikleia.

meanings that are quite specific to the person represented. This is to say not that a kore was any less aristocratic than a kouros, but that the specificity of a particular kore's form made it a less effective vehicle for a generic 'aristocratic ideal'. The inscription beneath 'Kroisos', the Anavyssos kouros (fig. 9.16), is a straightforward reaffirmation of aristocratic martial valour; it would mean the same with or without its statue – and, one might say, the statue would mean much the same with or without its inscription.[63] Here image and inscription simply amplify one another. Our understanding of the Phrasikleia inscription, by contrast, has been radically changed by the statue's discovery, and we can never read tomb inscriptions in quite the same way again.

'Phrasikleia' dates to around 540 BC, by which time sculpture was becoming more varied and sculptors more adventurous. More types of free-standing sculpture appear, such as the equestrian votives (including the 'Rampin Rider') found on the Athenian acropolis.[64] The development of the lost-wax process enabled sculptors to produce bronze statues on a larger scale, and allowed them to experiment with pose.[65] Architectural sculpture in particular made new demands on both sculptors and viewers. The explosion of temple-building on a monumental scale provided sculptors with new genres with which to experiment: the panel or metope; the continuous frieze; and that triangular space left by the roof, the temple's pediment. Developments in sculpture then cannot reasonably be divorced from advances in architecture, to whose late Archaic history we now turn.

9.5 Temples and monumentality

Greeks had been building temples (some in stone) since the eighth century BC, and by the late seventh century the Greek temple had become a distinct architectural form. By the early sixth century, certain regional differences in temple construction and decoration had become apparent. In Lesbos and parts of Ionia, the 'Aeolic' style had developed. This order of column was used in the temple at Old Smyrna, destroyed around 600 BC.[66] In the Peloponnese, and in western Greece, the 'Doric' temple had emerged. Temples were then a common enough sight in Greece around 580 BC. But temples were not particularly large buildings (few were larger than the much earlier 'heröon' at Lefkandi, which was 40 m in length), and very few were built in stone. To be sure, some had been: the Doric temple of Artemis in Kerkyra (Corfu), dating to around 580 BC, even had limestone pedimental sculpture.[67] This however is very much the exception. The monumental stone temple – temples whose sheer size led them, in later times, to be counted

---

[63] On the Anavyssos kouros, see Richter 1970: 118–19; Hurwit 1985a: 253–4.
[64] On these sculptures from the Acropolis, see Payne and Mackworth-Young 1950: 43–54. On other genres of sculpture, see generally Ridgway 1977: 187–26.   [65] Mattusch 1988.
[66] Nicholls 1991; Cook and Nicholls 1998: esp. 17–27, 109–58. On the Aeolic style generally, see Betancourt 1977.   [67] Rodenwaldt 1939; 1940. See also discussion in Coulton 1977: 42–3.

amongst the wonders of the world – was a development of the sixth century, and a development moreover where the cities of eastern Greece took the lead. Such monumental temples were ostentatious – and expensive. What factors lay behind such a striking cultural development?

One factor may again have been foreign contact (or 'influence'). We know from Herodotos that Greek visitors were very impressed by Egypt and its monuments. Greek contacts with Egypt had become much closer in the years after 664 BC. Egyptian buildings showed what an accomplished group of artisans and workers could achieve in stone. Still, though Greeks may have been inspired to emulate Egyptian achievements, they did not imitate them.[68] No Greek temple, even the largest, is a direct copy of an Egyptian one. There is in any case a time-lag of about eighty to a hundred years between the establishment of close contacts between Greece and Egypt and the construction of the first truly monumental Greek temple.

A more significant factor may be technology. Up until the middle of the sixth century (at the very earliest), Greeks, in common with most Mediterranean peoples, had relied on ramps and levers to manoeuvre large stones. By 500 BC, however, Greeks had discovered a new technology – the pulley hoist. This new technology made it easier to lift a block into place, without having to construct ramps (which were almost as much trouble to demolish as they were to build). But, with a winch, there is a limit to how heavy a block of stone you can lift before the rope breaks. After 515 BC temples were, with increasing frequency, constructed using much smaller units.[69] Blocks were held together with metal clamps, usually made of iron covered with lead to prevent corrosion. The effects of this new technology can best be appreciated by comparing two late sixth-century temples. The temple of Apollo at Corinth (see above), dating to around 540 BC, has columns made of single limestone shafts, whose wooden origins are only too apparent. Such columns must have been levered into place. When architects began to construct the second stone temple of Aphaia on Aegina, they had a new technique to experiment with.[70] Though the majority of the columns were still limestone monoliths, some were composed of column drums, which must have been lifted into position (fig. 9.20). (Some of the blocks in the temple of Aphaia have U-shaped holes, into which ropes could be inserted for lifting.) If blocks and column drums can be lifted with a pulley hoist, so too can sculpture. The temple of Aphaia possesses some of the finest pedimental sculpture in the history of Greek art. It is the first in a long line of Doric temples constructed out of units of more or less equal weight, if not of identical shape. Such structures cannot be improvised; they have to be planned meticulously in advance. Architecture had here become more than a vernacular craft. It took detailed mathematical knowledge to construct temples such as this one.

[68] See again Hurwit 1985a: 179–84.   [69] Coulton 1974; 1977: 46–50.
[70] On the earlier temple of Aphaia, see Furtwängler et al. 1906; Schwandner 1985. On the late Archaic temple, Furtwängler et al. 1906: 174–365; Bankel 1993.

The temple of Aphaia on Aegina has, rightly, been seen as a triumph of late Archaic architecture. Its arrangement (with some modifications) became a standard design for fifth-century architects. It showed how a temple could become both a vehicle for elaborate sculpture and an essay, or poem, in solid geometry. But it was by no means the first, nor the largest, monumental temple in Greece. Indeed, its overall dimensions (13.8 m by 28.8 m) put it in the third division of Archaic Greek temples, at least as far as size is concerned (fig. 9.21). The truly monumental temples are earlier in date, and come from Ionia. The first is probably the so-called Rhoikos temple of Hera on Samos, built around 560 BC.[71] This replaced the so-called second hekatompedon, but did so on an unprecedented scale. Its stylobate (base) measured 48.33 m by 93.45 m. It was a dipteral temple, that is it had two rows of exterior columns, and a much smaller cella. Indeed its 'forest of columns' (eight at the front, twenty-one along the flank) led to its being called a 'labyrinth' in later times.[72] None of the columns survives, but there is good reason to believe that they were over 12 m high. Not to be outdone, the Ephesians began the construction of their own monumental temple soon afterwards. The fourth Artemision, temple D, was built on the same general plan as the 'Rhoikos' Heraion, but on an even larger scale. Its stylobate measures 55.1 m by 109.2 m.[73] When the 'Rhoikos' Heraion was destroyed by fire, Polykrates, tyrant of Samos, ordered the construction of a yet more magnificent temple, with a larger stylobate (57.7 m by 117.6 m), and an even denser forest of columns (eight along the front, and twenty-four along the flanks) (fig. 9.22).[74] All these temples were constructed without the aid of any new technology. Though both the successive Heraia on Samos and the fourth Artemision at Ephesos are poorly preserved, it is clear that they were both constructed of individual blocks which would have been far too heavy to lift. One piece of the architrave from the Artemision weighed 41.25 tons.[75] They were built on an Egyptian scale, and with the time-honoured Egyptian techniques of lever and ramp. The labour costs of such an enterprise would have been tremendous, and it is hard to see citizens willingly devoting their time to its construction. It is surely more likely that many were compelled to work on these projects. If so, slavery may already have become widespread in Greece by the end of the Archaic period.

The association between grandiose projects and autocracy is one deeply ingrained in the historiographic tradition of the English-speaking world. An inclination to moralise on the ultimate political failure of, for example, that grandest

[71] Buschor 1930: 49–94; Walter 1990: 120–52. Rhoikos is supposed to have been the architect of this first enormous Heraion. Herodotos' words however (III.60.4) suggest that Rhoikos was a contemporary of Polykrates – patron of the later Heraion.

[72] Pliny, *Natural History* 34.83; 36.90. See also Pollitt 1990: 181.

[73] On the Artemision at Ephesos ('temple D'), see Hogarth 1908: 247–92; Bammer 1984: 212–29; 1998; Schaber 1982. The precise plan of the temple is still disputed.

[74] Buschor 1930: 94–9; Walter 1990: 154–87. For a good overview of all these grandiose Ionic temples, see Lawrence and Tomlinson 1996: 90–7 (whence I have derived my figures).

[75] Coulton 1974: 18–19.

9.20 Plan showing method of construction of temple of Aphaia on Aegina

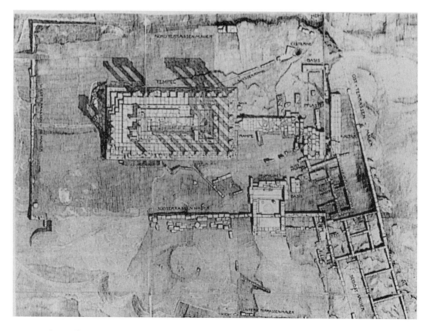

9.21 Plan of temple of Aphaia on Aegina

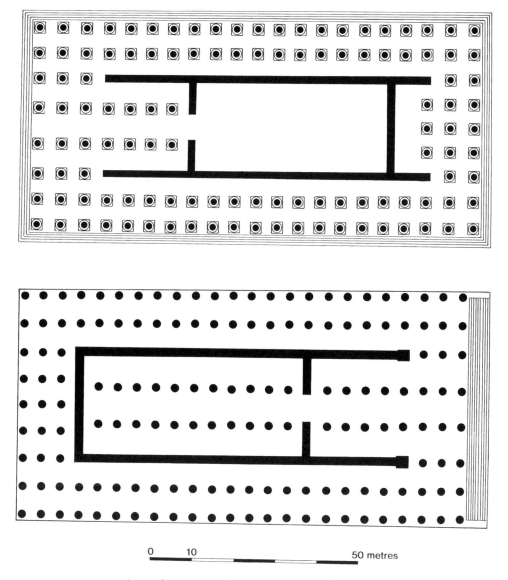

0   10   50 metres

9.22 Plans of Ionic temples: (a) the temple of Artemis at Ephesos, *c.* 550 BC; (b) the fourth temple of Hera on Samos, *c.* 530 BC

of kings and grandest of architectural patrons, Louis XIV, is sometimes impossible to resist. Such an association may not be entirely warranted here. To be sure, the second gigantic temple of Hera was instigated by Polykrates, and the late Archaic Artemision completed with the help of the Lydian king, Croesus (Kroisos). But we do not, in fact, know very much about the political circumstances under which such enterprises were first undertaken around 560 BC. Oligarchies and democracies can be every bit as oppressive as autocracies. It is perhaps best to see these building programmes as extreme examples of that spirit of rivalry between states that goes by the name of peer-polity interaction.[76] Such competition seems to have reached a peak in the sixth century, which saw an epidemic of temple-building. Construction was begun on over fifty stone temples in the Greek-speaking world between 580 and 480 BC, even if some of these temples were to take centuries to complete.[77]

The monumental temples of eastern Greece are usually classified as the first temples of the Ionic order, a type quite distinct from its 'Aeolic' predecessor. On closer examination however, such Vitruvian terminology appears to be a mirage. That defining feature of the Ionic order – the Ionic capital – is something of a rarity. Some capitals survive from the great Archaic Artemision at Ephesos; and canonical Ionic columns and capitals were probably used in the final phases of the Polykratean Heraion on Samos.[78] This is to say not that Ionic capitals are not to be found, but that their setting is, as often as not, not primarily architectural. Many surviving sixth-century Ionic columns and capitals were used as supports for votive offerings, such as the column of the Naxians at Delphi, an Ionic capital surmounted by a sphinx. Moreover, the gigantic 'Ionic' temples of Ephesos and Samos lack that other crucial feature of the Ionic temple of Classical times – the exterior frieze. Yet the architectural frieze is one of the crucial artistic innovations of the late Archaic period. Fully to appreciate its importance we have to turn to the smallest kind of 'temple' there was in Archaic Greece – the treasury.

At least fifteen treasuries were built at the panhellenic sanctuaries of Delphi and Olympia between 600 and 480 BC. It is not entirely clear what a treasury was for; presumably to store the valuables of the city which had commissioned it. Perhaps it is best to see such buildings as votive offerings in their own right, offerings that would reflect creditably on the cities which had paid for their construction. Of all the treasuries, the one built by the people of the small island of Siphnos at around 525 BC is of the greatest artistic importance. Though it housed no cult image, it is built like a small temple 'in antis', with two caryatids (korai) in place of columns. It is made entirely of (Siphnian?) marble, constructed out of small blocks fitted together with 'butterfly' clamps.[79] Sculpture in the round adorned the pediments (fig. 4.2). But its most striking feature is the frieze, which

---

[76] Snodgrass 1986.   [77] Osborne 1996a: 262–4.
[78] Hogarth 1908: 247–92; Walter 1990: 154–87. There are however other, smaller Ionic temples in sixth-century Greece. One, at Iria on Naxos, has produced some true Ionic column capitals; see Lambrinoudakis and Gruben 1987.   [79] Daux and Hansen 1987.

9.23 Detail of part of the north frieze of the Siphnian treasury at Delphi

runs around the building below the gable, just above the level of the eye (fig. 9.23). The frieze was carved in low relief, and both the background and the figures were painted. Two artists seem to have worked on the frieze, the more accomplished one being responsible for the two principal surviving sections: the east frieze, depicting the gods in council, and a battle scene from the Trojan war; and the north frieze, showing the original battle between gods and giants.[80] The frieze is, in one sense, a more vivid, polychrome version of those visual narratives that had been the mainstay of Attic black-figure vase painting. Indeed, the mêlée of overlapping figures in the north frieze resembles nothing so much as those crowded scenes we find on the François vase or on Sophilos' dinoi. As in vase painting, so here, the individual figures are identified by a painted inscription, a dipinto.[81] As in vase painting too, the continuous frieze is not used (as it could be) to convey a sense of a successive series of events related in strict chronological order. Rather, each side has its own scene, its own 'synoptic' narrative, whose relation to the other side is thematic. Still, in one respect this frieze represents a significant advance over what vase painters had achieved. The artist has here sculpted a complex group of overlapping figures, and has succeeded in conveying a sense of action. This is much harder to accomplish in low relief than on the surface of a pot.

The Siphnian treasury is one of the gems of late Archaic art. It displays a level of technical and artistic accomplishment that anticipates the achievements of Classical times. In this, however, it was not untypical of its times. The late Archaic period witnessed many such innovations. In vase painting the principal one was the invention of the red-figure technique. This technique was more painterly than black-figure, which had relied very much on the metal-worker's trick of incision. In red-figure, lines were drawn, and could be painted (with different effects) either in a bold black or in a thinner, brown wash. Details could be conveyed with greater precision. The new technique allowed painters to explore the contours of the human body with greater subtlety. It is no coincidence that anatomically accurate

---

[80] On the frieze, see Watrous 1982; Hurwit 1985a: 295–300.   [81] Brinkmann 1985.

renderings of the (male) human body only appear after the time of its invention, *c.* 530 BC.[82]

All these innovations are well documented, and, in sum, may seem to validate a claim that late Archaic Greek art was already well along the path that leads to naturalism. But to make such a claim is also to impose a teleological structure, a set of expected outcomes, on our exploration of Archaic material culture. It may be true that the Archaic period made the Classical achievement inevitable.[83] To sustain such a view, however, we have to pick and choose from the enormous cultural variety of Archaic Greece; we have to select only those elements that best fit the grand narrative of Classical art history. This is to set aside some other, perhaps equally interesting features of the period. For Archaic Greece was a cultural domain – or rather, in David Clarke's terms, a 'culture group' – characterised by very different regional traditions and art forms.[84] Outside of central Greece, artistic development could take some very strange turnings. These regional patterns surely deserve a closer look.

---

[82] Williams 1991.   [83] As argued by Snodgrass 1980a: 201–18.   [84] Clarke 1978: 245–327.

CHAPTER IO

REGIONAL ARCHAEOLOGIES

10.1 The persistence of regionalism

Figure 9.4 shows the Polyphemos amphora, an Athenian (or Attic) pot, whose surface is covered with Orientalising motifs. It is of about the same date as the Protocorinthian pots shown in figures 6.1 and 8.9, and its decoration derives from the same Near Eastern sources. But no one with even the slightest acquaintance with Greek Archaic pottery could possibly suppose that the aryballos (fig. 6.1) was manufactured in Attica, or the amphora in Corinth. Protoattic, the Athenian Orientalising, is big and splashy, 'a style seen at its best only on large surfaces'; Protocorinthian is a field in which the miniaturist excelled.[1] Protocorinthian and Protoattic are two distinct local styles. Regional differences in pot styles had become apparent in the Late Geometric period. Such differences seem to be more than local aesthetic preferences. In the eighth century local pottery styles correlate closely with regional differences in burial customs.[2] Regional styles persist into the sixth century, even when most production centres (chiefly Attica, Corinth and Laconia) had adopted the 'black-figure' technique. What are the reasons for the persistence of these regional variations?

One explanation we can rule out. Attica and the Corinthia are hardly isolated from one another. Indeed, they are sufficiently close for there to have been no physical barrier to the exchange of styles, especially in the seventh century when 'Orientalising' ideas travelled easily the length of the Mediterranean. They were different, in part, because they chose to be. Athens, Corinth and Sparta (Laconia) were the leading states of Archaic Greece. They were communities which took pride in their differences as much as in anything else. But it would be a mistake to see regionalism of this kind as a simple outcome of political rivalry between states. In some regions, such as the eighth-century Argolid, there existed a variety of independent political units (Argos, Tiryns, Mycenae), but they all (with the possible exception of Asine) seemed to use the same 'Argive' pottery, and practised very similar burial customs.[3] Equally, while we can perhaps isolate a Chian (or

---

[1] For Protoattic, see Cook 1935; S.P. Morris 1984. The quotation is from Coldstream 1968: 87. For Protocorinthian and Corinthian, see Payne 1931; Amyx 1988; Benson 1989.

[2] For late eighth-century regional pottery styles, see Coldstream 1968; 1983a. For regional patterns in burial customs, see Snodgrass 1971: 147–76.

[3] For the eighth-century Argolid, see Courbin 1966; 1974; Coldstream 1977: 140–56. For a succinct examination of the problem of relating political units to style zones in the eighth century, see Morgan and Whitelaw 1991.

Chiot) school of pottery production, most 'East Greek' pottery styles seem to have been manufactured in a number of centres, and were certainly in use all over Eastern Greece.[4]

Regional differences are apparent in virtually all areas of material culture. Pottery styles are the most obvious, and the easiest to quantify. But styles of architectural terracotta (that is different kinds of tiled roof) are perhaps equally significant. Architecture is a communal enterprise, and also one where form must, to a degree, follow function. Archaic Greeks, however, seemed unable to agree on the best way of constructing a temple roof.[5] The variety of roofing styles in Archaic Greece is therefore an interesting cultural fact, one of far greater political importance than different schools of pottery or gem-engraving. But even here however it is difficult to find an exact correlation between roofing traditions and political units. It is the regions which, again, appear to be important. The same observation applies to the varieties of local scripts which begin to be used in the Archaic period. It is easier to discern the general similarity of Peloponnesian or Cretan scripts than it is to isolate what made Argive script distinct from Corinthian, or the script of Gortyn different from that of Knossos.[6]

These differences then were regional and cultural, but not political – at least not in the narrow sense of marking out distinctions between autonomous polities. If regionalism is then cultural, should we not be looking at the broader cultural zones of Archaic Greece rather than at those exceptional regions (Attica or the Corinthia) whose boundaries happened to coincide with political units? Cultural regions of this kind would be defined in traditional archaeological terms as a set of interlinked material practices, or set of recurrent assemblages.[7] By 'interlinked material practices' I mean such things as the habit of making and erecting marble kouroi and korai; or of investing heavily in gifts to the gods rather than gifts to the dead; or the practice of burying men with arms; or of writing one's name on every available surface; or the conventions governing arrangement of rooms within a house. Ian Morris has used criteria such as these to divide the Aegean into four broad cultural regions: Central Greece; Western Greece; Northern Greece; and Crete. These terms may require a little explanation. By Central Greece he means the eastern mainland (southern Euboea, Boeotia, Attica, the Megarid, the Corinthia and the Argolid), the Cyclades, the Dodecanese and Ionia; by Western Greece, most of the Peloponnese, the Ionian islands, and the lands north of the Corinthian gulf (Acarnania, Aetolia, Locris and Phokis); by Northern Greece, Epirus, Thessaly and (modern) Macedonia.[8] These broad 'macro-regions' exhibit

[4] For Chiot pottery, see Lemos 1991; for East Greek pottery generally, see Cook and Dupont 1998.
[5] For architectural terracottas, see Winter 1990; 1993.
[6] On different kinds of script in the north-eastern Peloponnese, see Jeffery 1990: 114–74, 440–5.
[7] On the concept of an archaeological 'culture', see Clarke 1978: 245–327. It cannot be emphasised too much that an archaeological 'culture' in this (and Childe's) sense is not necessarily to be identified with an ethnic group or with a political unit. Culture and ethnicity are not the same, though they may be related (see Hall 1995b).
[8] On these 'macro-regions' or cultures, see I. Morris 1997a; 1998a.

deep structural differences. Warrior graves, for example, persist in the west and the north long after they have disappeared in Central Greece, and sanctuaries of any kind are much rarer in the north than elsewhere. Such macro-regions do not correspond with political units as such. Rather there seems to be a correlation between different cultural zones and different kinds of political structure. Evidence for the early polis is most easily found in Central Greece; in Western Greece, larger, federal states known as ethne prevailed; whereas in the north the large territorial monarchies of Macedonia and Epirus are to be found. Such correlations are not, of course, exact. Sparta was a polis (albeit an odd one), even though her material culture has more in common with other areas of Western Greece than with its neighbouring region, the Argolid.

Does the existence of these macro-regions mean that other levels of regional difference were not important? Attica and the Corinthia remained distinct cultural as well as political entities throughout the Archaic period. What might be the significance of this fact? To answer such a question with any precision would entail, at the very least, a detailed examination of, and comparison between the material practices of both communities. This has not been done. However scholars have been quick to notice that there is much more coming out of Corinth in the seventh century than there is from Attica, whereas this situation seems to be reversed in the succeeding period. Corinth appears to have been more prosperous early on – at the very least, Corinth appears to have produced more of what the archaeologist is most likely to recover, namely pottery. But does this mean that seventh-century Attica was necessarily the poor, the less populous relation? There are a number of other gaps (or troughs) in the material record at other times and places in Archaic Greece. The almost complete absence of any evidence from Crete in the sixth century is only the most glaring example of its kind. Such gaps have led some scholars to suggest that some natural disaster had set the region (whether Attica or Crete) back for the period of a hundred years or so. Certainly the absence of any evidence at all is the most striking aspect of Greek regionalism. Here I want to make a rash claim: it is through our attempting to explain such absences that we can begin to understand the social and political conditions that made the material cultures of Archaic Greece so distinct. Let us begin with the now notorious case of Attica in the seventh century BC.

10.2 The strange case of seventh-century Attica

In the eyes of many scholars, Attica was the most innovative region of the Aegean in the eighth century. Certainly Middle Geometric II and Late Geometric Attic pots were, if not widely exported, widely copied. There is no lack of such pottery, mostly from good contexts (chiefly graves) in Attica itself.[9] The century witnessed

---

[9] For Attica in the late eighth century BC, see Coldstream 1977: 109–39; Snodgrass 1977; 1980: 21–4; Whitley 1991a: 162–80.

an increase in the number of both sites and individual burials. The increase in burials in particular has been seen as providing the strongest indications of a rapid rise in population.

In taking burials as a direct index of demographic change (that is, as a snapshot, inevitably delayed by mortality, of a once-living population), we are left with some explaining to do when it comes to the seventh century. For, as figure 8.10 shows, the number of both child and adult interments declines dramatically after 700 BC.[10] The first scholar to notice that there was something amiss was John Camp, who looked at the evidence from the Athenian Agora. Here, there is a rapid increase in children's graves around 700 BC, and there are very few graves of any kind thereafter. Camp noted that child mortality is a very sensitive indicator of environmental stress. If there is famine, it is the children who will die first, not the adults.[11] Sarah Morris has gone further. There is a decline in Attic pottery production after 700 BC. Middle Protoattic in particular – the so-called Black-and-White style, dated to the middle of the seventh century – is very rare, even in Attica itself.[12] On purely material grounds, seventh-century Attica seems a very backward place. There are few attempts at monumental temple architecture. The votive deposits at the major sanctuaries (Sounion excluded) are not particularly rich, especially if compared to the votives found in sanctuaries in the Corinthia such as Perachora. In general, the region seems to have been less prosperous and less populous than before. All this has led John Camp and Sarah Morris to conclude that some natural disaster, possibly a drought, perhaps exacerbated by a war with neighbouring Aegina, may have been responsible for Attica's decline.[13]

This view has the merit of accounting for the available evidence in a straightforward way. Still, to see Attica in the seventh century as simply a less prosperous region of central Greece is to overlook certain other peculiarities of its material record. Attic sanctuaries are very odd. This is not just because the Acropolis lacks any monumental architecture to rival that of Corinth, or that the richest votive deposit from seventh-century Attica (Sounion) cannot really compare with the finds from Perachora or the Argive Heraion.[14] It is rather that the kinds of small sanctuary common in seventh-century Attica have few parallels elsewhere (fig. 10.1). These sanctuaries are of two kinds. There are the peak sanctuaries, altars to Zeus located on the tops of hills or mountains, the best known of which is the sanctuary on the summit of Mt Hymettos.[15] Finds from these sites are hardly rich, consisting for the most part of plain or 'Subgeometric' pottery. Then there are the tomb cults, deposits of offerings in or over Mycenaean or Dark Age tombs. The richest of these deposits is at the Mycenaean tomb of Menidhi, whose dromos was filled with masses of Late Geometric, Orientalising

---

[10] Morris 1987: 72–5.   [11] Camp 1979.   [12] S.P. Morris 1984: 37–90.
[13] Camp 1979; S.P. Morris 1984: 104–19.
[14] For finds from seventh-century Attic sanctuaries generally, see S.P. Morris 1984: 9–12, 99–100, 104–7. For Sounion, see Stais 1917; for Perachora, Payne 1940; Dunbabin 1962; for the Argive Heraion (Heraeum), Waldstein 1905.   [15] M.K. Langdon 1976; 1997.

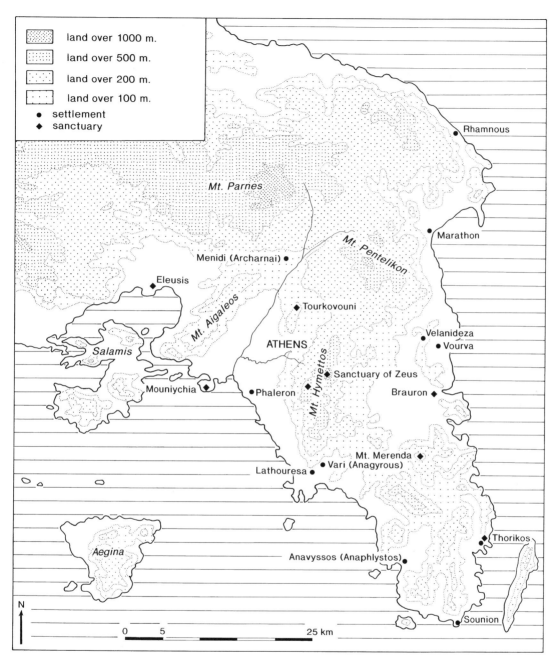

10.1 Map of Attica, showing sites in use in the seventh century BC and later pottery. The quantity of finds here is much greater than those found in contemporary tomb cults from the Argolid, for example.[16] All this suggests that Attic votive practices were, in some fundamental sense, different not only from those of Corinth but also from anywhere else in central Greece. It is not necessarily evidence for the inhabitants of Attica being poorer.

The second peculiarity lies in the burial record itself, which has been taken as the most dramatic indicator of the fall of Attica in the seventh century and its rise in the sixth (fig. 8.10). There are certainly very few 'visible' burials, particularly in mid-century. But burials remain relatively sparse during the sixth century as well, a period which, on other grounds, appears to have been relatively prosperous. This fact alone should make us suspicious of the idea that burials provide us with a direct reflection of past demographic reality, for two reasons. First it is difficult to find any historical analogy that would mirror such dramatic fluctuations in a region's population. The second reason is more complex. If we assume that the burial record is representative (as proponents of the drought hypothesis must), then it should be possible to arrive at an estimate of the total population by simple multiplication. We know from literary evidence that the population of Classical Athens must have been around 35,000 or so. We have numerous burials from the period, but even so only sufficient burials to account for 1.7 per cent of the population. If we take this ratio as a constant (allowing for the hazards of survival), and we apply it to sixth-century graves, then the population of sixth-century Athens must have numbered only 4,000 or so. This is too low a figure for the Athens of Peisistratos, a time when major temples were erected, when the Athenian pottery industry flourished, and when much expense was lavished on ostentatious votives on the Athenian Acropolis.[17] The most likely explanation for the relative rarity of burials is not that the population rose, fell and then rose again quite so dramatically, but that the burials we actually pick up are less representative of the population as a whole during the sixth century. If this holds for the sixth century, it also, *a fortiori*, must be true for the seventh.[18] Many scholars are understandably reluctant to accept this conclusion, but the alternative seems to create even more difficulties. The seventh-century decline is more a decline in archaeological visibility than it is in overall prosperity or population.

But this inference immediately raises a further question: why should the burial record of seventh-century Attica be so uniquely unrepresentative of the population as a whole? What social, ideological or ritual mechanisms selected which individuals were to receive the kind of burial – that is burial with quantities of recognisable grave goods, located in an identifiable place – that archaeologists are most likely to uncover? But before we try to identify the mechanisms at work, perhaps we should look in more detail at the pattern. Which few individuals were buried with grave goods? Burials seem to be of two kinds. First there are graves

---

[16] For the Menidhi tholos, see Wolters 1899; Antonaccio 1995: 102–9; Whitley 1994b: 222–6.
[17] See arguments put forward by Morris 1987: 99–101.   [18] Morris 1987: 99–109.

Table 10.1 *Child and adult graves from the seventh-century Kerameikos cemetery in Athens (simplified after Whitley 1994a: 54, table 3.2, chiefly from information contained in Kübler 1959; 1970)*

	Adult graves	Children's graves	Total
Cremations	24	3	27
Inhumations	5	13	18
Total	29	16	45

Table 10.2 *Pottery found in children's cemeteries in Attica (simplified after Whitley 1994a: 56, table 3.4)*

	Phaleron	Eleusis	Thorikos	Kerameikos (children's graves)	Total
Type of pot					
Protoattic	12	2	3	13	30
Protocorinthian and Corinthian					
Linear decoration	40	2	?	6	48
Protocorinthian and Corinthian					
Orientalising	5	0	?	3	8
Attic					
Subgeometric	75	11	42	8	136
Coarse wares	9	10	12	9	40
Other	10	0	7	0	17

of children. Sometimes, as at Phaleron, whole cemeteries seem to be devoted to children.[19] Children's graves were mostly inhumations in trenches. The accompanying pottery is, for the most part, Subgeometric rather than Orientalising (see tables 10.1 and 10.2).[20] Adult graves are quite different. Some tomb complexes in the Attic countryside, such as Vourva, seem to have been reserved especially for adults, but our best evidence for seventh-century adult graves comes, naturally enough, from German excavations in the Kerameikos (fig. 10.2).[21] Here the

[19] For Phaleron, see Young 1942. For children's cemeteries generally see Whitley 1994a: 54; Houby-Nielsen 1995: 146–50; I. Morris 1987: 61–9.
[20] There are however the odd, spectacular exceptions, such as the child interred inside the Polyphemos amphora (see Mylonas 1957). For discussion, see Whitley 1994a: 63–5; Osborne 1988.
[21] For Vourva, see Stais 1890. For grave complexes generally, see Morris 1987: 82–7, 103; Houby-Nielsen 1995: 152–63; for the Kerameikos, see Kübler 1959; 1970; Houby-Nielsen 1992; 1995.

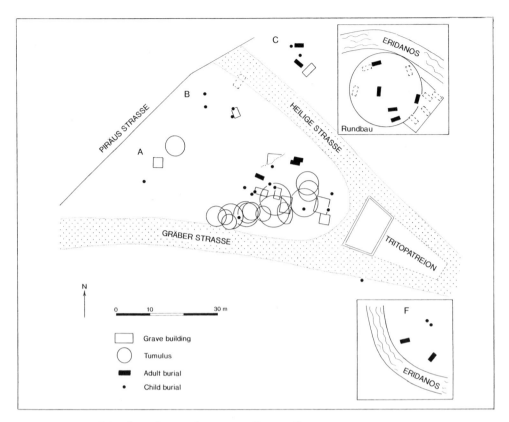

10.2 Plan of seventh-century Kerameikos cemetery

cremated remains (we do not know whether they are of men or women) are placed in a trench beneath a tumulus, which in turn is often crowned by a ceramic grave marker (fig. 10.3).[22] Cremation beneath a tumulus is one of the key features of a hero's burial in the *Iliad*, and it may be that this Attic custom is intended as a deliberate allusion to honour the aristocratic dead.[23] The graves themselves have few, if any, grave goods (see table 10.3). Such grave goods as exist are found in the so-called offering trenches (or Opferrinnen), a double trench divided by a ridge and lined with clay. It is from these trenches that most of the Orientalising pottery from known contexts in Attica comes. Some of this pottery – in particular the clay figures of mourning women – can only ever have been used in funerals (or in whatever ceremony actually took place in these offering trenches). Much of it, however, has a more conventional kind of Orientalising decoration – such as the representations of duelling warriors on the 'Kerameikos mugs' (fig. 10.4).

[22] Kübler 1959: 80–94.
[23] Whitley 1994b; Houby-Nielsen 1992. The relevant passages in the *Iliad* are XXIII.249–57 and XXIV.790–803: the funerals (respectively) of Patroklos and of Hector.

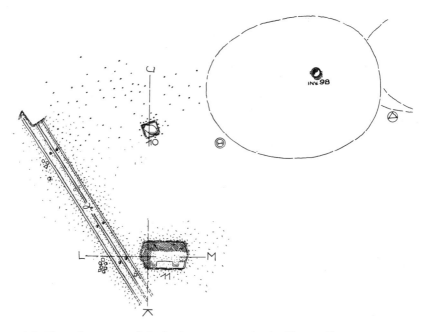

10.3 Plan of graves and Opferrinne gamma in the Kerameikos

10.4 Beaker or mug (one of the 'Kerameikos mugs') from the Kerameikos cemetery

Table 10.3 *Breakdown by context of types of pottery found in various contexts in the Kerameikos cemetery (simplified after Whitley 1994a: 57, table 3.5)*

	Opferrinnen, Opferplatzen, etc.	Adult graves	Grave markers	Children's graves	Total
Protoattic	52	9	7	13	81
Protocorinthian and Corinthian Orientalising	17	2	0	6	25
Protocorinthian and Corinthian Linear decoration	7	2	0	3	12
Subgeometric	0	2	0	8	10
Other	3	2	0	0	5

Tables 10.1, 10.2 and 10.3 summarise the information from Attic graves. Taken together, Attic seventh-century ritual deposits (whether votive or funerary) seem to exhibit strong patterning. Subgeometric pottery was used in peak sanctuaries and children's graves; Protoattic in graves of adults and in association with tomb cults. If we were to adopt a rigidly structuralist perspective, we could end up with a set of binary oppositions that would look like this:

adult:child
burnt:unburnt
exotic:local
tomb (heroes/ancestors):peaks (sky gods).

This is perhaps to push structuralism too far. Such an interpretation can be criticised for assuming that Orientalising pottery did have exotic connotations, whereas Subgeometric was thought of as local – that is, of assuming what it is attempting to demonstrate. This is, to be sure, the interpretation that I prefer: Orientalising pottery stirred up associations of a rich world beyond the horizons of seventh-century Attica, whereas Subgeometric pottery was safer, more local, more homely, if less prestigious.[24]

One way to test this hypothesis might be to compare the finds from ritual deposits with those from settlements. Unfortunately, seventh-century Attic settlements are not at all well documented. There are a number of seventh-century finds from the settlement of Thorikos, but there is very little stratified material that is of much use.[25] Then there is the enigmatic site of Lathouresa, whose plan is well known but whose finds remain unpublished and inaccessible.[26] The only

[24] This is my argument in Whitley 1994a.   [25] Bingen *et al.* 1967: 9–19.
[26] Lauter 1985; Mazarakis-Ainian 1997: 235–9.

Table 10.4 *Pottery types from the
Agora well deposits (simplified
after Whitley 1994a: 55, table 3.3)*

Protoattic	83
Protocorinthian and Corinthian Orientalising	4
Protocorinthian and Corinthian Linear decoration	27
Subgeometric	182
Terracottas	59
Coarse wares	53
Stone objects	6
Other	19

'domestic' deposits with finds of any quantity are the fills of wells in the Athenian Agora which fell into disuse during the seventh century, into which much domestic rubbish was (apparently) dumped. Here most of the fineware pottery seems to have been Subgeometric rather than Protoattic, which would lend some support to the idea that Subgeometric was 'homely', and Protoattic something special (see table 10.4). Such observations led the publisher of these finds, Eva Brann, to conclude that Protoattic was a ceremonial ware.[27] But the evidence from graves and sanctuaries indicates that such a straightforward dichotomy between 'ceremonial' and 'domestic' is unwarranted, since Orientalising pottery was used in some ritual contexts, but not in others.

The explanation I prefer for this curious state of affairs is that pottery with exotic connotations – that is Orientalising – was rationed. Material which hints at a wider, richer world beyond local horizons often has connotations which are as much negative as positive. The wider world has an exotic allure, but it is also dangerous; it has the potential to disrupt stable patterns of hierarchy and status. So its use has to be carefully controlled. By confining Orientalising pottery to liminal occasions, to those rituals which honoured the 'heroised' dead and those beings (heroes, ancestors or a previous race) thought to inhabit Mycenaean tombs, its positive, status-enhancing qualities could be used to maintain a stable aristocratic social order, and its disruptive, 'foreign' connotations could be kept well away from everyday life.[28]

Whatever you think of this interpretation, one thing is certain. There is here a particular, robust pattern in how material culture was used that requires some kind

[27] For the Agora deposits generally, see Brann 1962. For the well deposits, see also Brann 1961; Young 1938; 1939: 139–94. The finds from a seventh-century house in the Agora (Brann 1962: 110) are too meagre to be worth considering.

[28] As I argue in Whitley 1994a. For criticisms see S.P. Morris 1997.

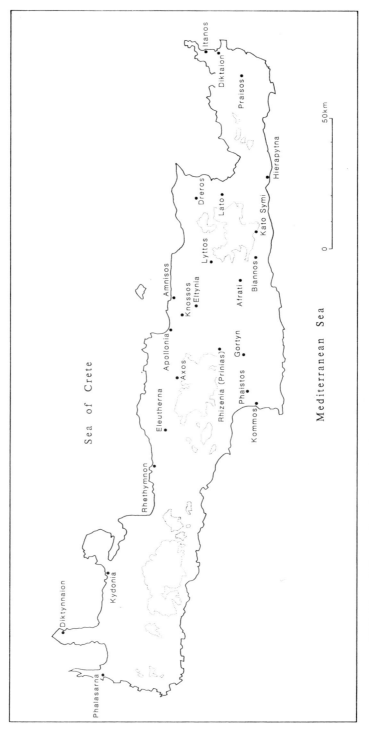

10.5 Map of Crete, showing major sites

of explanation. That some kind of rationing mechanism was in operation would, in turn, help to explain why there is so little of anything from seventh-century Attica. Alternative accounts are, of course, possible, but any such account would have to address both phenomena at once; that is, why it is that material 'poverty' is accompanied by such strong patterning in the use of Orientalising and Subgeometric pottery. The explanation of one phenomenon should help to explain the other. At present, the alleged 'drought' is little more than a hypothetical *deus ex machina*, wheeled on to the stage around 700 BC, and then departing, leaving Archaic Greece to resume its natural progressive course towards democracy and Classical art.

Attica in the seventh century has perhaps attracted too much scholarly attention of late.[29] The history of Athenian society and Athenian politics has, perforce, to be a major part of any account of Archaic Greece, so seventh-century Attica is an anomaly that can hardly be ignored. But it is not the only case of its kind. There is, for example, a curious dearth of burials in the Argolid at around the same time. Even though Argive votive deposits are nothing if not rich, here too the same drought that supposedly devastated Attica (but not, apparently, Aegina or Corinth) has been held responsible.[30] But at least both Attica and the Argolid have some (albeit ambiguous) finds from the seventh century; it is not as if the archaeological record fails us completely, as it appears to do in sixth-century Crete.

10.3 Laws without cities: sixth-century Crete

Crete has never fitted comfortably into any standard narrative of Archaic Greece (fig. 10.5). The cultural history of the island has a habit of taking unexpected turns. Cretan Orientalising begins a full one and a half centuries earlier than elsewhere in Greece, starting with the Protogeometric B phase in metal-working and pot decoration at Knossos and continuing with the remarkable series of eighth-century bronze shields found in the Idaean Cave and the temple of Dictaean Zeus at Palaikastro.[31] A tradition of figurative art was never entirely lost in Crete, and some of the scenes on the shields from the Idaean Cave are of a complexity that deserves to be called narrative (fig. 10.6).[32] Cretans moreover made precocious use of the alphabet. Dreros in east-central Crete is the city where the earliest written laws have been found (fig. 8.11).[33] Seventh-century Crete has every appearance of being a flourishing island. The votive material from the cave sanctuaries on Mt Ida and Mt Dicte are as rich as any in Archaic Greece.[34] Temples in stone were built, and sometimes,

---

[29] As well as the works mentioned above, there are also the synthetic articles by Robin Osborne (1989) and Anna Maria D'Onofrio (1997).   [30] Foley 1988.

[31] For 'Protogeometric B', see Brock 1957: 143; Coldstream 1968: 235–55; 1996: 416–17. For Cretan bronze votive shields, see Kunze 1931. For an overview of ninth- to seventh-century Cretan art, see Boardman 1961: 129–59.

[32] In particular the Hunt Shield from the Idaean Cave, see Kunze 1931: 8–12 no. 6.

[33] Demargne and Van Effenterre 1937; see also discussion in Jeffery 1990: 309–16.

[34] For the Idaean Cave sanctuary, see Sakellarakis 1988; Kunze 1931. For the Dictaean Cave, see Boardman 1961: 1–75; Hogarth 1900. Other seventh-century Cretan sanctuaries have equally rich bronze votives; for Kato Symi Viannou, see for example Lebessi 1985.

10.6 Idaean Cave shield, the so-called Hunt Shield

as at Prinias (Rhizenia), these temples were decorated with sculpture in relief. All over the island there are numerous votive deposits, rich in terracotta figurines of the 'Daedalic' style.[35] The richness and variety of seventh-century Cretan material culture can most easily be glimpsed in the finds from the large 'Orientalising' cemeteries of Prinias, Afrati and Knossos.[36] It remains a mystery therefore why, after about 630 BC, these cemeteries simply ceased to be used. Central Crete around 550

[35] For the temples at Prinias, see Pernier 1914. For a particularly rich votive deposit of seventh-century date from Gortyn, see Rizza and Scrinari 1968.

[36] For Knossos, see principally Brock 1957; Coldstream and Catling 1996; Coldstream and Huxley 1999. For the Afrati cemetery, see Levi 1929. The material from Prinias has not yet been properly published.

BC is an archaeological desert. The picture is at its starkest at Knossos. Here there are no domestic deposits (that is, either house floors or filled-in wells) datable to between 590 and 525 BC; there is only one terracotta from all the Knossian sanctuaries that could date to the sixth century; and there are no burials at all that can be dated to between 630 BC and the very end of the sixth century.[37] It is only after 525 BC that we have any finds at all from north-central Crete.[38] For most of central and western Crete the sixth-century gap is equally stark.[39]

Now someone could argue this picture of Crete in the sixth century is merely a 'blip' in the archaeological record, due to nothing more significant than certain objects falling into and then out of fashion. Stephen Hodkinson has argued that this is exactly what happened in fifth-century Sparta, and it is caused by nothing more than some kinds of material expression being replaced by others.[40] Another possible analogy would be the situation in the Argolid in the seventh century, where the rich eighth-century ceramic and burial records do not continue into the seventh. All that seems to have happened here is that the focus of material expression has switched from graves to sanctuaries. The seventh century is the richest period for votives from the Argive Heraion.[41] However, the short duration of a particular craft tradition (such as Laconian black-figure) is not an adequate explanation when we come to sixth-century Crete. In most other regions of Greece, when some kinds of deposit become unfashionable, the shortfall is made up from finds from other contexts; when some craft tradition falls from favour, artefacts are produced in some other medium. Nowhere else does the archaeological record actually disappear from view.

There has been no lack of explanations for this curious phenomenon. Sixth-century Crete appears to have suffered from a catastrophe. Some natural disaster must be responsible. Might not the Theran drought of *c.* 630 BC, which was the proximate cause for the colonisation of Libya, have been the cause? Herodotos (IV.151.1–2) records that 'After this it did not rain in Thera for seven years, in which time all the trees on the island, save one, shrivelled away.' Just as there is a break in the Knossian record, so the sequence of burials in Thera seems to come to an end around 630 BC.[42] Thera lies more or less opposite north-central Crete, and both areas may have been subject to the same climatic fluctuations. Drought is here a local explanation for a local phenomenon. We encounter serious difficulties however if we try to invoke drought as the principal cause for an island-wide

---

[37] For domestic deposits from Knossos, see Coldstream 1973; 1992; Coldstream and Sackett 1978; Callaghan 1992: 90–3. The only sixth-century votive from Knossos is a small terracotta from the sanctuary of Demeter; see Higgins 1973: 59 no. 11.

[38] The earliest known Knossian burial after 630 BC is an interment in a plain pithos found in Fortetsa tomb V, associated with an imported black-figure cup (Brock 1957: 27 no. 238). Other late sixth- or early fifth-century finds from north central Crete include the inscription from Agia Pelagia (Jeffery 1990: 468 no. H) and other scattered finds (see Boardman 1962).

[39] There are, however, many more finds of sixth-century date from eastern Crete, particularly in the 'Eteocretan' territory of Praisos; see Bosanquet 1902; Whitley 1998.   [40] Hodkinson 1998.

[41] Waldstein 1905; see also Hall 1995a.

[42] Coldstream 1984; Huxley 1994: 128–9. Coldstream and Huxley (1999: 301–4) review the 'drought' hypothesis.

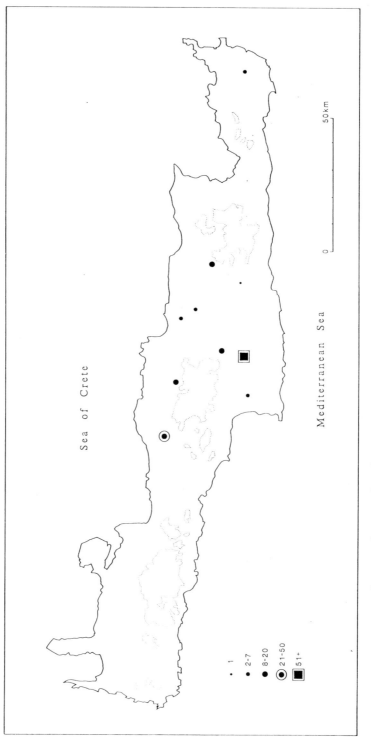

10.7 Map of Crete, showing distribution of major sixth-century legal texts

decline. First it strikes me as inherently implausible that drought has been used to explain gaps in the record of large regions of Greece which have reasonably high relief and therefore a better chance of regular rainfall. Drought has been used as an explanation for the relative decline of Attica *vis-à-vis* Aegina in the seventh century. It is however unlikely that a small island like Aegina would be relatively unaffected by a drought that devastated nearby Attica, as Aegina's rainfall is inherently less reliable. It is the ecosystems of small islands that are most vulnerable to small fluctuations in rainfall, not those of large islands such as Crete.[43] Thera is a small island that nowadays has to bring in much of its drinking water by ship; Crete is large and mountainous. There is no suggestion in Herodotos' narrative that the drought which forced the Therans' hands had any major effect on Crete – despite the fact that two Cretan cities (Oaxos and Itanos) are mentioned in his tale. It is moreover extremely improbable that any natural disaster could set a whole region back for very much longer than a decade, and wildly unlikely that a single drought could be responsible for a century-long gap in the record.

Other explanations have to be sought. Some might say that Crete has not been as thoroughly explored as some other regions of Greece – or that too much attention has been paid to the Bronze Age compared to other periods. The sixth-century gap has none the less engaged the attention of a number of distinguished scholars for some time. Knossos at least has been thoroughly explored. Might not Cretans have adopted a more mobile way of life in the sixth century, or come to prefer a more dispersed pattern of settlement? A more mobile way of life might have led to fewer traces in the archaeological record, and there has certainly been a marked urban bias in the study of Archaic Crete. Recent surveys have, however, begun to improve our understanding of rural settlement. In the western Mesara (in south-central Crete, near Phaistos), thirteen or so 'Orientalising to Archaic' sites have been identified, a number which represents a marked increase over the Early Iron Age. Many of these small settlements seem to have a sixth-century phase of occupation.[44] The Vrokastro and Kavousi surveys have by contrast revealed almost nothing that could be assigned to the sixth century. The Mesara evidence is impressive, but it does not add up to positive evidence for a more dispersed pattern of settlement throughout sixth-century Crete. The absence of evidence from surveys further east might, if anything, be taken as an indication that settlement was more nucleated in late Archaic times.[45]

One thing we do know is that cities were not completely abandoned. They continued to function as the political and cultural centres of their communities, since sixth-century legal inscriptions have been found in most of the major cities of the island[46] (figs. 10.5 and 10.7 and table 10.5). Even if cities ceased to be truly urban,

---

[43] Cherry 1981.   [44] Watrous *et al.* 1993: 229–30.

[45] This at least is the conclusion drawn by the Vrokastro and Kavousi survey teams; for Vrokastro, see Hayden *et al.* 1992: 329; Hayden 1995; for the Kavousi survey, Haggis 1996: 414–15. The situation further east, around Praisos (Whitley 1998; Whitley *et al.* 1999: 247–53) seems to be quite different.

[46] For a summary of this evidence, see Jeffery 1990: 308–16, 467–9.

Table 10.5 *Archaic Cretan inscriptions (simplified after Whitley 1997b: 649–51, tables 5 and 6)*

Date range BC	Dedications (including inscribed armour)	Graffiti	Inscribed tombstones	Laws (minimum number of)	Separate legal fragments
750–650	0	5	0	0	0
650–600	15	2	1	3	8
600–550	0	0	0	7	38
550–500	2	4	1	16	85
500–450	2	2	3	12	34

and continued to function largely as ceremonial centres, we would expect to find some indication of where they had moved to. We should pick up some sign of rural dispersal. The Mesara excepted, this we do not find.

Others still might argue that the problem is purely one of chronology. Much that is dated to the seventh century in Crete in fact belongs to the sixth. Still, whatever doubts we may have about the overall chronology of Archaic Greek pottery, the relative sequence itself seems to be secure. Cretan pottery is dated by good synchronisms with the Attic and Corinthian sequences, since Attic and Corinthian pottery turn up in well deposits in Knossos and elsewhere.[47] Mid-sixth-century pottery from Attica or Corinth simply does not find its way to Crete. While it may be possible to assign many of the smaller terracotta figurines to a 'sub-Daedalic' style that spans much of the earlier part of the sixth century, the same trick cannot be played with monumental sculpture. Only with bronze-work (particularly armour) would the argument for stylistic conservatism hold any water, and even here individual pieces (e.g. fig. 10.8) can only be down-dated by a few decades or so. We cannot engage in a full-scale down-dating of Cretan art that will fill the sixth-century gap.

It is in one respect an exaggeration to say that we know nothing about sixth-century Crete. For there are plenty of inscriptions. It is the rarity of pots and the abundance of inscriptions that make sixth-century Crete stand out from any other region of Archaic Greece. The almost total absence of pottery is very odd. In the ancient world, pottery is multi-purpose, cheap and normally ubiquitous. It is wildly improbable that any Mediterranean society would simply stop using pottery. In fact we do have some evidence that pottery production continued in Crete during the sixth century. Some fineware pottery found at Tocra in Libya (Cyrenaica) has been identified as Cretan on petrological as well as stylistic grounds (fig. 10.9).[48] There are other indications that a Cretan ceramic tradition

---

[47] See again discussion in Coldstream 1992: 84–7; Callaghan 1992: 90–3; Coldstream and Huxley 1999.
[48] Boardman and Hayes 1966: 78–80; 1973: 36–8; Boardman and Schweizer 1973: 280.

10.8 Helmet from Afrati, no. H2

10.9 Sixth-century Cretan hydria from Tocra

persisted throughout the sixth century. The seventh-century Cretan one-handled cup appears to be the ancestor of the Hellenistic tulip cup.[49] It is just that the missing stages that might link the former to the latter have not yet been properly documented. Some plain and coarse vessels from some small rural sites in Lasithi also appear to be sixth century.[50] Monochrome or plain fineware vessels and coarse functional pottery are less likely to attract the attention of ceramic specialists, and may well have been missed by survey teams. Recent (unpublished) studies of stratified deposits from Eleutherna, Kato Symi and Afrati have begun to fill in the missing stages of the Cretan sequence. Sixth-century Cretan fineware pottery does exist, but it is very plain – so plain indeed that it can be identified only by its shape, not its decoration.[51] Why then do sixth-century Cretans appear to have preferred plain pottery, when their contemporaries elsewhere in Greece were avid consumers of elaborately painted vessels? The reason must be a cultural one. For clues we must turn to the only real body of evidence we have: inscriptions.

Public inscriptions which, on the basis of their letter forms, have been dated to the sixth century have been found in most of the major cities of the island. These inscriptions are usually on stone, and usually legal in character. Praisos has two; Lyttos seven; Prinias (Rhizenia) fourteen; Knossos two; Gortyn forty-two; Phaistos one; Axos (Oaxos) twelve; and Eleutherna twenty-four (see figs. 10.5 and 10.7 and table 10.5).[52] These 104 legal fragments are by no means small, having been carefully incised in large letters by skilled masons. They concern themselves with legal matters; with procedures, with politics and with fines, in short with all the concerns of a relatively complex society. They are not what one would expect from an island that had been depopulated. Cities must have remained centres of civic, legal and political authority throughout the century. One might have thought that such a quantity of legal inscriptions would be accompanied by a variety of inscriptions (graffiti, dedications and dipinti) of other kinds, since societies that rely so much on written law must be both literate and sophisticated. In fact there is very little evidence for the kind of informal literacy that existed elsewhere in Greece.[53] As table 10.5 shows, there are almost no graffiti and few dedicatory inscriptions, little that would indicate that the population at large regularly practised these skills. Literacy seems to have been limited to public purposes. Indeed one celebrated Cretan inscription, the contract of the scribe Spensithios, indicates that public scribes played a much bigger role in Crete than they did else-

---

[49] For discussion, see Callaghan 1978: 6–11.   [50] Watrous 1980: 275–8.

[51] I am most grateful to Mr Brice Erickson for sending me drafts of his Ph.D. thesis, soon to be submitted at the University of Texas at Austin. The finds from Eleutherna (excavated by P. Themelis, Th. Kalpaxis and N. Stambolidis) and from Kato Symi and Afrati (excavated by A. Lebessi) are not fully published, but are apparently stratified. For contemporary bronzes from Kato Symi, see Lebessi 1985.

[52] Figures from Whitley 1997b: 649–60. These figures are principally derived from information in Guarducci 1935; 1939; 1942; 1950.

[53] These are the arguments put forward in Whitley 1997b; Stoddart and Whitley 1988.

where in Greece.[54] Literacy seems to have been the almost exclusive preserve of a scribal class; public inscriptions were made to impress rather than to inform.

In Crete, then, literacy seems to have been divorced from those institutions (and I am thinking here in particular of the symposium) in which it was elsewhere enmeshed. There are no dipinti from Archaic Crete, no inscriptions that form a part of any narrative in art. It cannot be emphasised enough how odd this is. Narrative art and inscriptions accompany one another almost everywhere else – dipinti accompany scenes from myth on pots manufactured in Attica, Corinth, Laconia, Ionia and the Cyclades from the late seventh century onwards. Even in those regions of Greece which did not use pottery as a medium for narrative, attempts at depicting scenes from myth are, as often as not, accompanied by an inscription. The Argive *Schildbänder* (shield bands) found at Olympia, for example, frequently have inscriptions in their myth scenes, and the sculptors of the Siphnian treasury at Delphi took care to accompany their low reliefs with the names of the protagonists shown.[55] Narrative art and literacy appear to be connected in some fundamental way in most of Archaic Greece – except in Crete. Indeed Crete is alone among the regions of Archaic Greece in that it is possible to detect a move away from narrative art and towards less ambitious forms of figuration. The best candidates for Cretan narrative art are the earliest in date. The Hunt Shield from the Idaean Cave, with its interconnected scenes of humans and animals, seems to be trying to convey a story (though we have no idea what story it is) (fig. 10.6).[56] By the seventh century, however, scenes of such complexity are hard to come by. There are figured scenes (usually individual birds) from the Orientalising urns from Knossos, and some human figures from pots from Afrati.[57] The scene on the Rethymnon mitra could conceivably be part of a story.[58] It is, in Cretan terms, very much an exception. Most of the mitrai, corselets or helmets produced towards the end of the seventh century, in particular those looted from Afrati early in the 1960s (fig. 10.8), are decorated with simple antithetical animal figures. Cretan figurative art had dwindled into a kind of heraldry, with no ambition to tell a story in pictures.[59]

One clue as to why this should be so may be found in Plato. In the *Laws* (680 b–c), the Athenian stranger quotes from the *Odyssey*. Kleinias the Cretan seems, however, to be unfamiliar not merely with the passage, but with Homer altogether. For most of Plato's 'characters', familiarity with Homer was an integral part of being cultured. The number and variety of myth scenes on pots used in the symposium testifies to the centrality of the Epic cycle in aristocratic life and culture. Whereas elsewhere in Greece the Epic cycle, narrative art and informal literacy seem to go together, all are absent in Crete. Crete produced almost no

[54] Jeffery and Morpugo-Davies 1970; see again discussion in Whitley 1997b: 656–60.
[55] For Argive Schildbänder, see Kunze 1950; Bol 1989.   [56] See again Kunze 1931: 8–12 no. 6.
[57] For scenes on pots from Knossos and Afrati, see Moignard 1996; 1998; Levi 1929.
[58] For the Rethymnon mitra see Poulsen 1906; for discussion see Boardman 1961: 141–3; Hoffmann 1972: 25–6.   [59] Hoffmann 1972: esp. 34–40.

symposium pottery. Kraters and dinoi, which had been common earlier, were becoming rarer in Knossos during the seventh century. The principal drinking vessel, the one-handled cup, is usually painted monochrome black.[60] What little we do know of sixth-century Cretan pottery indicates that it was very plain; the hydrias from Tocra (e.g. fig. 10.9) are decorated only with lines.[61] This is not to say that Archaic Crete did not have forms of all-male commensality – the andreion seems to have been an institution of this kind. But the region does appear to lack material signs of that social gathering that brought together eating, drinking, partying, story telling and informal literacy, the symposium. Crete moreover seems to lack any evidence for competitive aristocratic display. Whereas a rich Athenian or a successful Spartan athlete would think nothing of dedicating a marble column or perirrhanterion to a god, taking care to have his name inscribed on the dedication, little activity of this kind seems to have taken place in Crete.

Crete seems to have lacked those institutions and practices which elsewhere were central to Archaic Greek aristocratic culture. Indeed Cretan society seems to have deliberately taken a different path, one that led to a society one could call traditionalist. Cretan poleis did not merely seek to conserve the past as much as possible; rather they sought to portray their own communities as stable and unchanging, as societies rooted in laws and customs extending back to mythical founders and lawgivers. The written laws which in Crete are so abundant are as much a means of making this idea concrete to the inhabitants of these communities as they are a simple record of the law itself. Activities which emphasised individual achievement rather than collective identity seem to have been frowned upon. One unintended side effect of this turn to traditionalism is to make Crete well nigh invisible to the archaeologist. Traditionalism of this kind, however, can only be established in societies where the idea of the polis as the ideal form of Greek community has already taken root. In this light, it may be instructive to contrast Cretan material behaviour with that from a region where the polis idea never took hold – namely Macedonia.

10.4 Archaic Macedonia

Macedonia has always had a slightly uneasy relationship with the rest of the Aegean world. The character of ancient Macedonian culture is widely believed to have some bearing on the region's political status in the modern world. The geographical extent of Macedonia and what is implied by the term 'Macedonian' have become sensitive topics.[62] Here I should define what I mean by these terms. For my purposes, Macedonia is the core area of the ancient kingdom, extending north

---

[60] For one-handled cups from Knossos, see Brock 1957: 166–7; Moignard 1996: 457–9.
[61] Boardman and Hayes 1966: 78–80; see also note 51 above.
[62] See for example the fuss that has surrounded the publication of Karakasidou 1997. See also Karakasidou (1997: 31–5) on local interpretations of local antiquities, often maintained in defiance of the relevant archaeological evidence.

from Thessaly and Mt Olympos to the valleys of the Aliakmon and the Axios, and east from what is now Thessaloniki to the Strymon valley, excluding most of Chalkidiki. By 'Macedonian' I mean a particular set of material practices associated with this region. Ethnicity and culture are not the same, and however ancient Macedonians viewed themselves, Macedonian material culture had little in common with that of central Greece.

Differences are apparent from a very early date. Whereas surveys in southern Greece indicate, if anything, that Early Iron Age sites are few and far between, the reverse appears to be the case in Macedonia. Preliminary results from the Langadas survey show a dramatic increase in the number of sites in the years after 1000 BC. Traditional tell sites are supplemented by new sites on small hills.[63] In domestic architecture, however, there is no clear break. Bronze Age Macedonian houses had been built of mud brick, wattle and daub, a style of construction which tends to result in the creation of tells. In the Early Iron Age many houses continued to be built in the same way and on the same tells. Occupation at Assiros, for example, spans both periods, and only ends around 700 BC.[64] Kastanas, in the Axios valley north of Thessaloniki, has eight major phases, four of which postdate the Bronze Age. Occupation here lasts well into the sixth century BC.[65] The inhabitants of these sites continued to use a style of 'Balkan' pottery that has little in common with Greek painted wares throughout the Archaic period, even though towards the end of that period they were clearly becoming more open to influences from the south.

It is however not so much in their domestic architecture and household wares as in their depositional practices that ancient Macedonians differed from Greeks further to the south. Macedonians chose quite different occasions on which to display and destroy their wealth than their southern cousins. In Crete, central Greece and much of the western area, sanctuaries had become the major context in which valuable objects were deposited. Macedonian sanctuaries, on the other hand, are few and far between. They are not particularly rich in finds, and Archaic Macedonian votive offerings are almost unknown.[66] There is nothing to compare with the rich Geometric and Archaic votive deposits from sanctuaries in Thessaly, immediately to the south.[67] Macedonians did not choose to waste their wealth on expensive dedications to the gods. Instead, metals and other valuables went into graves.

Now, of course, in the Early Iron Age, Macedonia is hardly unique in this respect. The Iron Age burials at Vergina, for example, are not noticeably richer

---

[63] Andreou and Kotsakis 1994; 1995; forthcoming. I am most grateful to Stelios Andreou for supplying me with this information.   [64] Wardle 1980; 1987; 1988; 1989.

[65] Hänsel 1989; see also Morris 1998a: 46–7. A recent survey of the evidence from eastern Macedonia (Koukouli-Chrysanthaki 1993) has underlined the 'Balkan' character of the material culture here.

[66] See Gergova 1993; and discussion in Morris 1998a: 45–6. Votive deposits, such as the one at Sani (Votokopoulou 1993), are only found in areas of modern Macedonia settled, or colonised, by Greeks from central Greece.

[67] For Thessalian votive deposits, see in particular Kilian-Dirlmeier 1985: 216–25 (Pherai).

than contemporary burials further to the south.[68] Nor could Macedonian burial customs be considered at all odd. The custom of burying some (male?) individuals with weapons, particularly swords, was widely practised throughout Greece during the ninth and eighth centuries BC. What is perhaps more significant is that Macedonians continued their weapon burial ritual when those in central Greece and Crete are steadily abandoning this practice. Few, if any, weapons are found in central Greek graves after 600 BC, but Macedonian 'warrior graves' continue to appear.[69] Macedonian mortuary practices come to be sharply divergent from those in use further south. Nowhere is this divergence clearer than at Sindos.

Sindos, close to Thessaloniki, is a large cemetery with over 100 graves. Unlike earlier cemeteries, the individual interments can be closely dated by imports of Attic and Corinthian black-figure pottery to the late sixth and early fifth centuries BC.[70] These pots have often been taken to indicate the progressive hellenisation of Macedonia during late Archaic times. But, if Macedonians were beginning to make use of some central Greek objects, they were otherwise sticking to their peculiar Macedonian ways. The Sindos tombs are extraordinarily rich by central Greek standards. Grave 20, an adult female grave, for example, contained seven gold items, ten of silver, four of bronze, as well as other objects of iron, faience, electrum and glass.[71] One of the gold items was a 'death mask', of a type that would not be out of place in the shaft graves of Bronze Age Mycenae. At least five such masks have been found at Sindos, and two others elsewhere in Macedonia.[72] In male graves, such as graves 25 and 115, these death masks are often accompanied by helmets of 'Illyrian' type (fig. 10.10). Burial with weapons and arms – the 'warrior grave' – was still a potent symbol in late Archaic Macedonia.[73]

Nothing could better illustrate the cultural difference between Macedonia and central Greece. Contemporary burials in Athens and Corinth are very sparing in their use of grave goods, which for the most part consist of little more than pottery. Warrior graves are almost unknown. In Crete, sixth-century burial practices are parsimonious to the point of invisibility. Macedonian burials are by contrast extravagant. Real or imagined differences in status, role, gender or wealth are emphasised, rather than played down. This was not because Macedonians were more prone to competitive display than their neighbours to the south, but rather that they preferred the funeral to the sanctuary as their chosen arena for such display. Athenians, Argives and Corinthians preferred to show off their piety, as well as their wealth, by putting up expensive dedications to the gods. Still, this fact cannot quite account for what must remain the major cultural differences between Macedonians and other Greeks. There are few, if any, Archaic inscriptions in Macedonia, and none dating to before 500 BC. Macedonian inscriptions

---

[68] For Vergina, see Andronikos 1969 and summary in Snodgrass 1971: 160–3.
[69] Morris 1998a: 43–5.   [70] For the Sindos cemetery, see Votokopoulou *et al.* 1985.
[71] Votokopoulou *et al.* 1985: 80–1, 86–103; Morris 1998a: 44–5.
[72] Votokopoulou *et al.* 1985; for the gold death masks, see now Theodossiev 1998.
[73] Votokopoulou *et al.* 1985: 120–7, 152–73; see comments in Morris 1998a: 49–52.

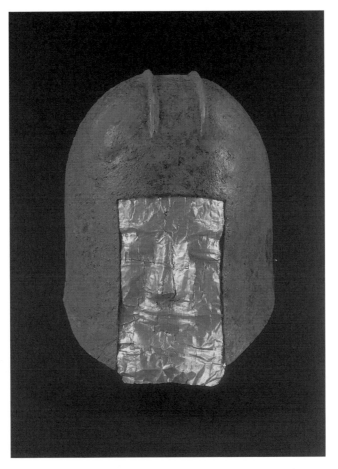

10.10 Gold mask and helmet from grave 115 at Sindos,
in the Museum of Thessaloniki

appear at the same time as the first Macedonian coins.[74] Macedonians may not
have been completely illiterate, but their use of the alphabetic 'technology of the
intellect' was certainly limited, especially when we compare their behaviour with
that of their contemporaries further south. Nowhere is this contrast starker than
with sixth-century Athens.

10.5 Athens and the end of the Archaic period

If, to us, Attica in the seventh century appears backward when compared to
Corinth, it was in step with its near neighbour in at least one respect. Inscriptions

[74] The earliest Macedonian inscriptions appear to be on coins (Jeffery 1990: 364–5 and 369 nos. 16–21),
and can be dated no earlier than 500 BC. It is only by the middle of the fifth century that other
inscriptions appear (Jeffery 1990: 479 no. F).

are numerous in seventh-century Attica. Inscriptions come in many forms; informal, and indeed obscene, graffiti scratched on potsherds; dedications to the gods written on stone, bronze or pot; and, in the later part of the century, dipinti added to explain a scene from myth on a vase.[75] In the sixth century all signs of material 'backwardness' in Attica (if that is what it was) disappear. As the material record becomes richer, so inscriptions become more various and more numerous. Epigraphic practices are good indications of the kinds and degrees of literacy that must have existed. Together with the study of mortuary practices, votive habits and iconography they can reveal much about what was distinctive about Archaic Athenian culture. Such a statement, however, is making a claim about 'culture' that many may find contentious, and it is not this approach that has found favour with most scholars interested in the period. Sixth-century Attica has been viewed as a fully historical period, and scholars have, naturally enough, tended to follow an agenda framed by our literary sources.

The sixth century was certainly a formative period in all kinds of ways. Many if not most Athenian cults which flourished in later times seem to have begun in the sixth century. Such at least is Alan Shapiro's argument and, though the evidence is often circumstantial, there can be no doubt that the century witnessed the erection of numerous public buildings. Temples in stone were constructed in the Agora and on the Acropolis.[76] Often the sculptural decoration of these temples required prodigious amounts of marble. Indeed, under the Peisistratids, the Athenians attempted to emulate the great Ionic temples of Samos and Ephesos by beginning work on a massive structure dedicated to Olympian Zeus (a temple not completed until the reign of the Roman emperor Hadrian).[77] Scholars have tried to date these buildings very precisely, suggesting they were related to particular historical events (such as the founding of the Panathenaia), more precisely indeed than the archaeological evidence warrants.[78] Some have gone even further, and tried to link the iconography found on Athenian pots with particular political regimes. Images of Herakles in particular have been seen as 'propaganda' for the Peisistratid tyranny.[79] It is not clear to me how an image, painted by a craftsman on a pot whose ultimate destination was Italy, could have functioned in any meaningful sense as propaganda. Convincing an Etruscan or Campanian of the merits of Peisistratid rule can hardly have been an effective policy, even if the Etruscan consumers of these vessels could pick up all the nuances. One would have had to suppose that the Attic pottery that reached Etruria came there indirectly, and that all Athenian pots with images of Herakles were intended primarily for home consumption. This seems far fetched. The best one can say for this idea is that the images may have been produced in a political climate that encouraged the association between Peisistratos and Herakles.

---

[75] Immerwahr 1990: 9–14, 20–3.   [76] See discussion by Shapiro 1989; Hurwit 1985a: 234–48.
[77] On the worship of Olympian Zeus, see Shapiro 1989: 112–17.
[78] See discussion by Shapiro 1989: 18–47.
[79] On Peisistratos and Herakles, see Boardman 1972; 1975b; and discussion by Shapiro 1989: 157–63.

Table 10.6 *Archaic Athenian inscriptions (after Whitley 1997b: 641, table 1)*

Date range BC	Inscribed dedications	Graffiti	Dipinti	Inscribed tombstones	Legal texts
750–650	2	49	2	0	0
650–600	8	64	6	2	0
600–550	35	63	45	12	0
550–500	101	32	531	66	4
500–480	249	32	174	2	4

The idea that iconography can be linked directly to politics, that art functioned as propaganda, is a mistake. It is a mistake that is the direct result of an expectation. It is often said of the sixth century that it is a fully historical period, one where the literary record should take primacy over the archaeological. Just as archaeology is expected to illustrate history, so art must illuminate politics. This expectation depends upon a very optimistic view of our literary evidence, one that underestimates how fragmentary, haphazard and selective such evidence in fact is. Art tells us little about politics, but archaeology can tell us quite a lot about culture.[80] One of the striking cultural facts that is apparent from table 10.6 is how extensively Athenians made use of their alphabet, and how much their writing was concerned with naming individuals. Athenians wrote out their names when putting up ostentatious votive offerings. Each of the Archaic marble korai found on the Acropolis is accompanied by an inscription beneath it, giving the donor's name.[81] Athenian families arranged to have the names of their dead relatives inscribed on the bases of their grave stelai, sometimes adding the names of the family members who had arranged for the funeral marker to be put up.[82] Athenian craftsmen too seem to be the most name-conscious in all of Greece. We know the names of sixty-three potters and painters and six sculptors who worked in Archaic Athens, all from the pots or sculptures that they themselves produced.[83] Athenian potters and painters were responsible for the bulk of material intended for the symposium in the Archaic world, and it is on the surfaces of these vases that we find the closest relation between image and inscription. It is not merely that mythological characters are named, or that sometimes, as on the François vase (fig. 9.10), inscriptions take the place of images.[84] Inscriptions on Athenian pots make quite subtle sympotic jokes, which it would have required a fairly literate

---

[80] I do not here want to enter into a discussion of what is meant by culture. My use of the term is largely anthropological; for a recent discussion of this notoriously tricky concept, see Sahlins 1999.

[81] On inscriptions from the Acropolis, see Raubitschek 1949; on the korai see Payne and Mackworth-Young 1950.

[82] On funerary epitaphs, see in particular Jeffery 1962; Willemsen 1963; and discussion in Humphreys 1980; Sourvinou-Inwood 1995: 147–91; Whitley 1997b: 640–5.

[83] On craftsmen's names: for potters and painters, see Immerwahr 1990: 24–80; Whitley 1997b: 640–5; Beazley 1932; 1956. For craftsmen, see Viviers 1992.   [84] Immerwahr 1990: 24–9.

audience to appreciate. On Athenian vases, more often than not, image and inscription work together.

It is this broad, aggregate picture derived from hundreds of small pieces of evidence that tells us most about Athenian culture at this time, not the detail to be found on one or two pots. The same holds true for burials. Attempts have been made, for example, to identify Mound G (Grabhügel G) in the Kerameikos as the tomb of the Athenian statesman Solon (see figs. 10.11, 10.12 and 10.13).[85] The immense grave tumulus is certainly impressive, but there are several difficulties with this interpretation. The only supporting literary sources are late. There is no inscription identifying the mound as that of Solon, and it seems very odd that a legislator who was in part responsible for laws prohibiting excessive funerary display should have been buried in a manner that is quite so ostentatious.

Instead of trying (vainly) to make archaeology fit into a historical narrative shaped by our literary sources, we should be looking at the totality of our burial evidence. Between the seventh and sixth centuries there are few changes in burial customs, none of them dramatic. Cremation ceases to be the norm for adult burials. Offering trenches become less common, and graves again become the primary receptacles for grave goods. Grave goods consist, for the most part, of inexpensive pots. Ceramic grave markers more or less disappear, to be replaced by various alternative forms of commemoration. One such were the painted clay funeral plaques, of which we have several examples.[86] Stone markers of various kinds become much more common. These include funerary kouroi and korai, and ornate marble stelai, often painted, carved in low relief. Such stelai have a low base and a main relief, and are often crowned with marble sphinxes in the round. Figure 10.15 shows an example of one such, the stele of one Ariston, found at the site of Velanideza in Attica and dated to around 530 BC (see fig. 10.14).[87] This particular stele shows Ariston as a hoplite, an image that might be thought of as emphasising the civic virtues of the warrior/citizen.[88] Stelai of this kind were almost invariably accompanied by an inscription. At least seventy-eight funerary inscriptions are known from sixth-century Attica.[89] Such inscriptions vary in length from a simple name (as here) to short epigrams of four or so lines, which sometimes invite a passer-by to pause and remember the man or woman whose tombstone they are walking past.[90] Archaic inscriptions should not be thought of as the equivalents of modern or nineteenth-century gravestones. They were not meant for the general run of the population, that is for the many, but for the few. To go by Ian Morris' statistics, the Attic burial record is hardly more representative of the population as a whole in the sixth century than it was in the seventh, and tombs with gravestones are but a small fraction of those graves that do survive.[91]

---

[85] Kübler 1973; 1976: 5–21.   [86] Boardman 1955.   [87] Richter 1961: 47 no. 67.
[88] As argued by D'Onofrio 1982; 1988.
[89] Jeffery 1962; Willemsen 1963; for exact figures, see Whitley 1997b: 644 n.47.
[90] Examples include Jeffery 1962: 118–19, 132–3. See discussion by Humphreys 1980: 103–4; Sourvinou-Inwood 1995: 147–91.   [91] See again Morris 1987: 72–4, 97–109.

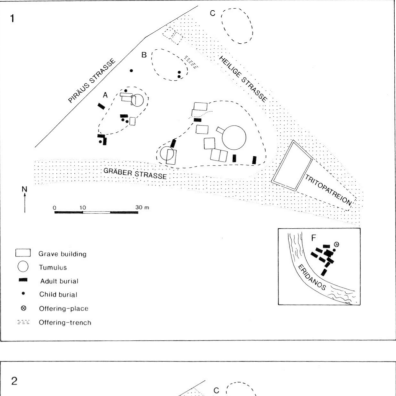

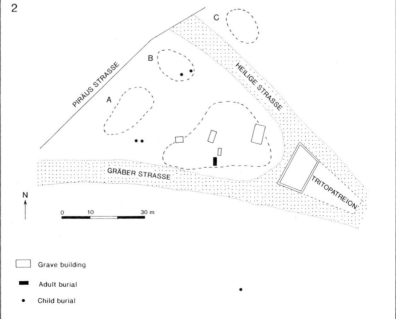

10.11 The development of the Kerameikos cemetery, from 600 BC, phases 1 and 2

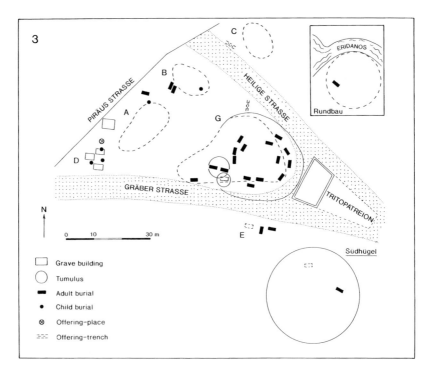

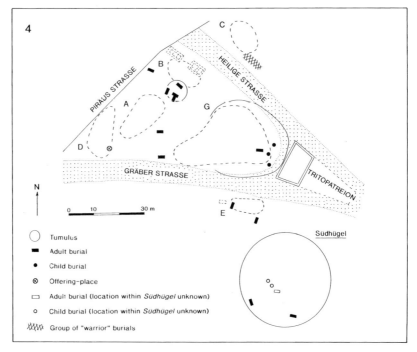

10.12 The development of the Kerameikos cemetery, phases 3 and 4

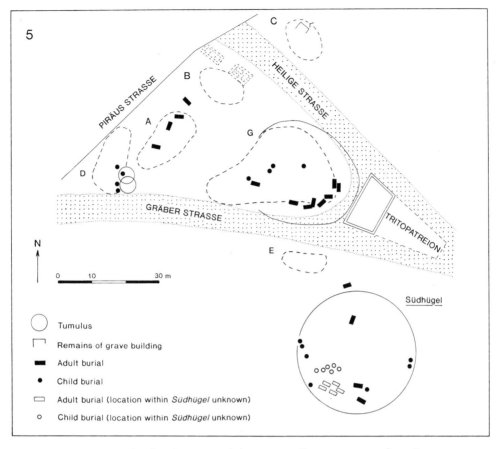

10.13 The development of the Kerameikos cemetery, phase 5

In so far as the context of these inscriptions can be reconstructed, they were intended to accompany either a grave stele or an imposing funerary kouros or kore – the most celebrated example of the latter being, of course, Phrasikleia herself (see chapter 9.4 above).[92] Funerary monuments and inscriptions are often found in association with a number of tumulus complexes in the Attic countryside, such as those at Vourva, Velanideza and Anavyssos (fig. 10.14).[93] Such tumuli are clearly the archaeological descendants of the mounds erected in the Kerameikos and elsewhere in the seventh century, but with one crucial difference: they are now very much larger. Nowhere is this clearer than in the Kerameikos itself, where mound G (Grabhügel G) and the 'South Mound' (Südhügel) were erected between 560 and 540 BC (figs. 10.12, 10.13 and 10.14).[94] These mounds contain

[92] Svenbro 1993: 8–25.

[93] For example the base of a kore found at Vourva; see Stais 1890a: 105–12; 1890b; Richter 1968: 58–9 no. 91; Jeffery 1962: 137. On these tumuli generally, see Houby-Nielsen 1995: 152–6.

[94] On these 'shaft graves' and tumuli, see Kübler 1976: 5–21 (Mound G); Knigge 1976: 60–85 (South Mound); and discussion in Houby-Nielsen 1995: 156–9.

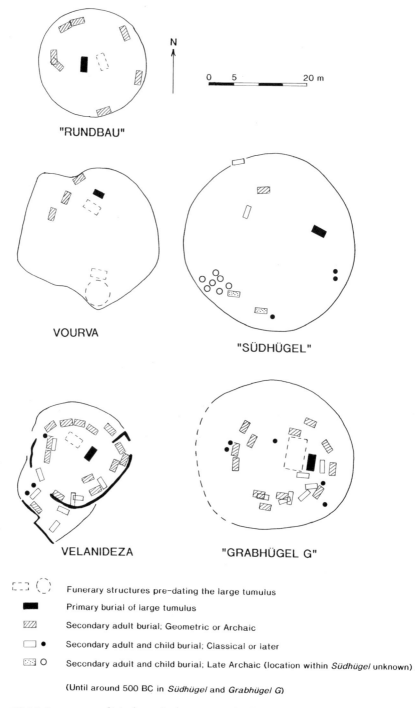

10.14 Large tumuli in late sixth-century Attica

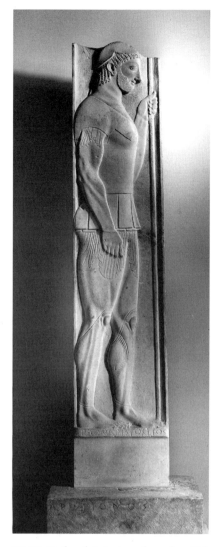

10.15 Stele of Aristion, found at Velanideza in 1839

huge primary burials in shaft graves. The goods placed around the body in these grave shafts are not particularly rich; they consist mainly of lekythoi (oil flasks) and flasks for exotic perfume, the so-called lydion. What makes these graves exceptional is the numerous ivory fragments which apparently come from the exterior decoration of a couch or kline, an item of furniture central to the symposium. Secondary burials are then often placed around the primary one in a series of concentric circles.

Who were the social groups that made use of such complexes? And what principles governed the membership of these 'burying groups'? Clearly we are dealing here with the upper stratum of the Athenian population, and the natural inference is that these are the tomb complexes of aristocratic families. Such an interpretation is certainly plausible for some of the smaller grave complexes in the Attic countryside, such as Vourva. But to associate such complexes with kinship groups may be to overlook certain important features of the evidence. Houby-Nielsen has argued that the number of individuals interred in each of the very large tumuli in the Kerameikos is too large for them all to be members of a nuclear family. It is difficult too to see them as the grave plots of extended families, as they seem to have been in continuous use for only one or two generations. Instead of kinship, Houby-Nielsen has suggested that the principle governing membership of these 'burying groups' was that of an aristocratic sodality, or symposiastic club.[95] Men who had drunk and perhaps fought together were buried together. There are several attractions to this proposal. First it might help to explain the underrepresentation of women in funerary imagery. Images on grave stelai are almost invariably of men, and Attic funerary kouroi outnumber korai by a factor of about two to one.[96] Second, it would help to explain why certain features of these grave assemblages (the kline in particular) have associations with the symposium. In any case, whatever one thinks of this interpretation, it is hard to see Athenian burial practices in the sixth century as being intimately linked with the ideology of the polis. Depictions of hoplites on grave stelai may have served to emphasise civic virtues, but it is hard to see how figures such as 'Aristion' (fig. 10.15) could have become resonant images before Athenian hoplites had undertaken any great service to the state. To be sure, Athenian graves were poorer than Macedonian, but this fact can be explained by the emphasis that Athenian burial practices laid on membership of a group. Whether it was kinship or the symposium, it was still institutions outside the polis that were the biggest social factors affecting the burial record. This was to change in the years after 507 BC.

To some it may seem perverse to have laid so much emphasis on inscriptions and burials. For many archaeologists, sixth-century Athens is the principal arena of all Archaic Greece in which great potters, painters and sculptors worked, quarrelled, competed and excelled. It did not, until very recently, seem at all odd to describe sixth-century Athens in terms of its great black-figure pot painters, Lydos, Exekias and the Amasis painter. Not so long ago a group of scholars published a book with the title *The Amasis Painter and His World*, its subject being Athens itself, as if the period is to be remembered chiefly through and because of its artists.[97] But to place Beazley's 'artistic personalities' at the centre of this world is, in my view, profoundly misleading. It leads to a kind of circular reasoning: the period is to be celebrated for its artists; the personality of these artists may be appreciated through their iconographic idiosyncrasies; the evidence for which is – those same idiosyncrasies. It is much more important to appreciate that these

---

[95] Houby-Nielsen 1995: 159–64.
[96] For Archaic Attic funerary reliefs, see Richter 1961. By my calculations there were nine kouroi used as grave markers, and a maximum of only four korai; figures from Richter 1968; 1970; Svenbro 1993: 8–25.   [97] See Von Bothmer 1985.

craftsmen were working within a tradition, a tradition which was in turn shaped by the demands of the society in which they were working.[98] Such demands may, indeed, be as much external as internal, as much those of the Etruscan consumers as of the Athenian producers. None the less, to study the shapes and images of Athenian pottery is to be struck by the centrality of the symposium in Athenian life (a fact borne out by close attention to their burial practices); and to study Athenian inscriptions is to come to understand how much more literate Athenians were compared to many of their contemporaries, and how much ordinary 'literacy' is bound up with a particular cultural capacity to read images. It was these cultural forces that shaped the Athenian pottery tradition, as much as external demand or the idiosyncrasies of individual craftsmen. In other respects, of course, Athenian material practices were much the same as their neighbours' elsewhere in central Greece. Athenians, like Corinthians, preferred sanctuaries to tombs as occasions for the ostentatious display of wealth. For expensive votives did not merely display one's wealth and piety for all to see; a man who set up a votive (particularly if inscribed) was much more likely to be remembered for years to come.

By the end of the Archaic period Athens has regained a certain cultural pre-eminence within the Aegean. Athens had rejoined the cultural mainstream, and Athenian culture began to be exported along with her products. The Archaic period as a whole had witnessed a whole range of technical advances which, in aggregate, improved the material standard of Greek life. Temples were now built in stone and covered with terracotta roof tiles; soon these innovations would be applied to public buildings and houses too. Both sculpture and pottery displayed much higher standards of craftsmanship than those of 150 years earlier. Towards the end of the sixth century, three new advances were made; temples were built out of smaller, more manageable parts, lifted with pulleys and cranes; the red-figure technique was developed in Athens; and gem-engravers, perhaps following a Phoenician example, mastered the use of the drill, which enabled them first to equal and then to surpass the standards set by the seal-engravers of the Bronze Age.[99] Most of the technical developments on which the Classical achievement depended were made in Archaic times. This fact has led some scholars to see the flowering of Greek art in Classical times as being, in a sense, inevitable.[100] But was it? And why, in any case, should we still regard the Classical period as 'Classical'?

[98] As argued for earlier periods in Athenian history in Whitley 1991a; 1994a.
[99] On late Archaic/early Classical engraved gems, see Boardman 1967c; on Phoenician influence, see *ibid*.: 9–12, 19–25. On changes in architecture, see Coulton 1974.
[100] See Snodgrass 1980a: 200–18.

PART III

CLASSICAL GREECE

CHAPTER 11

DEFINING THE CLASSICAL: CLASSICAL ART

11.1 Classic and Classical

In today's parlance, a classic is something which sets a standard. It does not matter, for the most part, in what field the standard is set. We are now used to sports commentators talking of a classic horse race, and the notion of 'rock classics' no longer seems as incongruous as it once did. So what does it mean to call a period and its art Classical? It is still widely accepted that the greatest achievements of the Greeks in literature and philosophy were made in the years between 479 and 323 BC. As with literature, so with art: it is Classical art that stands at the acme of what Greeks could do. Not too long ago, Classical Greek art did indeed set standards, universal standards by which what artists produced in both earlier and later times could be judged. The artistic worth of any work, from any time, any period or any place, could be estimated by the degree to which it equalled (for it could not surpass) the art of Classical Greece. Copying and drawing ancient sculpture formed part of the training of many a budding artist well into the early years of the twentieth century. Today, however, artists look elsewhere for inspiration. The belief that naturalistic art is inherently better than abstract seems ridiculous. Abstract art, realism and naturalism are merely different modes of expression, each more appropriate for some purposes and not for others. Even in that genre of modern art which is, as it were, inherently realist – namely photography – the influence of Classical Greek art is hard to discern.[1]

Modern art has turned its back on ancient Greece, and especially on the Classical. In the early years of this century, Archaic art was esteemed more highly, and if there is any 'post-modern' interest in Greek art, it focuses on the Hellenistic. This may, of course, prove to be a mistake, a product of an age whose only universal belief is that all values are relative, and each culture incommensurable. None the less, this abandonment of universal standards does make the appeal of Classical art harder for us to understand. For hundreds of years Classical art did set standards, even if much of what was once thought of as 'Classical' does not (in modern historical terms) deserve the name. In setting standards, Classical art also enforced certain ideas. One of these was that naturalism – albeit the naturalism of the ideal rather than the actual human form – was what every good artist should

---

[1] For the etymology of the word 'Classical', see Pollitt 1972: 1–2.

strive for. Another was that 'Classical' implied ordered, balanced and measured, as opposed to emotional, sensual and sentimental. Such ideas go back at least to Winckelmann, who distinguished between an earlier Classical art that was 'grand and square' and a later one that was 'beautiful and flowing'. This historical distinction however suggests that there is something inherently unstable in the Classical ideal. For how can a single work be both 'grand' and 'flowing' (see above chapter 2, section 2.2)?[2] Hence arose the Romantic notion that the Classical artistic achievement was necessarily transitory, the product of circumstances that could never be repeated. Classical order began to be contrasted with Romantic feeling.

Modern Classical scholars have never entirely abandoned these ideas. But, in a relativistic age, they cannot but be embarrassed by them. J.J. Pollitt, for example, tries to define Classical art in strict historical terms, as the art of the Classical period, and hence as the expression of the cultural ideals of the time. Pollitt seeks to define Classical by demonstration. Classical art is contrasted with the Archaic. The Archaic kouros is stiff; the Classical male figure on the other hand betrays a certain inwardness of feeling.[3] This historical view of Classical art has also encouraged some strictly historical explanations. Classical art is sometimes seen as expressing a new sense of freedom which came about through Greek victory in the Persian wars.[4] Definition through demonstration is perhaps the only course available to the modern scholar – and it is a course I will be following too. But such a definition requires some prior classification. It begs the question of what kinds of things constitute 'Classical art'.

Ancient authors, both Roman and Greek, were interested principally in three artistic media: sculpture, architecture and painting. The sculpture they admired was chiefly of bronze; the architecture that of temples and other public buildings; and the painting was that which adorned the walls of stoas and other public places. Sometimes they alluded to other art forms, such as mosaics. Modern scholars have tended also to treat gem engraving, pot painting and other kinds of metalwork as art of almost equal stature. Indeed in any full history of Classical art, such media should be given at least the same amount of space as pottery. But historically it is sculpture, architecture and painting – and in default of real painting, 'vase painting' – that have been most prized and most studied. Simply for the purposes of illustrating what other scholars have meant by the term 'Classical', there follow three brief histories of these three art forms.

11.2 Classical sculpture

Of all Greek art forms, sculpture was held in the highest regard. So too were Greek sculptors, and none more so than those of Classical times. It was, after all, the

---

[2] Winckelmann 1764: 224–35. Winckelmann talks about two Classical styles – the high style and the beautiful style. It should be noted, however, that Winckelmann never called any one piece both 'grand and square' and 'beautiful and flowing'. The instability arises from trying to combine both these styles into one, the 'Classical'.   [3] Pollitt 1972: 15–22; Hurwit 1985: 336–55.
[4] Pollitt 1972: 22–7.

works of Polykleitos, Pheidias, Myron, Skopas, Praxiteles and Lysippos that the educated Roman tourist of the early centuries AD came to Greece to see. Unfortunately for 'Classical art history' however, none of their celebrated works (with one doubtful exception) survives. Their most influential sculptures are known to us only through what Classical archaeologists optimistically call copies – later versions, usually in marble, of an original that was, more often than not, cast in bronze. We can never really know how faithful these copies were.[5] Fortunately, however, 200 or so years of collection, study and excavation have produced numerous original works, whose primary context can sometimes be reconstructed with some accuracy. This allows us to reconstruct the broad outlines of sculpture's stylistic development, albeit without the apparent intimacy of knowing the 'artistic personalities' involved.

The functions and genres of sculpture had been established by the end of the Archaic period. Free-standing sculpture – such as the 'Kritios boy' – was sometimes in marble, but more often in bronze. Much free-standing sculpture of early Classical date was votive. The Delphi Charioteer (fig. 1.2) is a good example (see chapter 1, section 1.1). Here the fixed stare, heavy chin, and regular folds of the drapery are utterly characteristic of the so-called Severe style. Another genre that had developed rapidly in late Archaic times was pedimental sculpture. The best early Classical examples come from the temple of Zeus at Olympia. The east pediment shows the beginning of the race between Pelops and Oinomaos; the west, the battle between Lapiths and Centaurs. The central figure here is Apollo (fig. 11.1), whose Olympian detachment from the mayhem around him has often been commented upon.[6] His heavy chin, the symmetrical treatment of the hair, and the simple linear folds of his drapery are reminiscent of the Charioteer, and characteristic of the Severe style as a whole. The limitations of this style are also evident on other figures from the east pediment. The Lapith women, even when being abducted, show no discernible signs of distress, and Lapith men (e.g. 'Q'), who are, we are to believe, engaged in a desperate fight with drunken centaurs, appear neither angry, nor grimly determined, nor calm – simply vacant. If inwardness was the aim, the sculptors here have failed. What in one context may be failings, however, in another can count as strengths. The detachment on the figures on the Olympia metopes, which depict all twelve labours of Herakles, is perhaps in keeping with its subject, though, since this is one of the few low reliefs we have from early Classical times, it is difficult to find a useful point of comparison.[7]

---

[5] Ridgway 1984; see also Boardman 1985: 15–18.

[6] In particular Ashmole 1972: 27–89; Ashmole and Yalouris 1967. For the original publication of the Olympia sculpture, see Treu 1897: 44–181. The arrangement of the statues on the east pediment in particular remains controversial; see articles in Herrmann 1987.

[7] On the Severe style generally, see Ridgway 1970; 1981. It has sometimes been maintained, notably by Ashmole (1962), that the apparent absence of feeling on the figures on the Olympia pediments (and elsewhere in early fifth-century sculpture) indicates something quite other than clumsiness on the sculptor's part. Such figures show emotion, but with Classical restraint; faces such as 'Q' or the so-called seer show 'restrained emotion'. I have to say I disagree with Ashmole's eloquent argument.

11.1 Apollo (figure L) from the west pediment of the temple of Zeus at Olympia

By the mid-fifth century however, the clumsiness evident on some of the Olympia figures had been overcome. Although now eyeless, the bronze Zeus from Artemision used to be the next important reference point, until, that is, the discovery of the Riace bronzes. These two statues were found in the sea off the coast of Calabria in southern Italy in the early 1970s.[8] They had probably been on their way to grace the villa of some Roman aristocrat when the ship was wrecked. These statues give a vivid impression of what Greek sculptors could achieve by mid-century. Especially in 'Warrior A' (fig. 11.2), Greek male athleticism is celebrated as never before. All of his anatomy, from muscles to hair, is rendered with minute attention to detail. The statue even manages to stand (and stand up) 'like a man',

---

[8] For the circumstances of the discovery of these statues see Borea 1984. For a good short account in English, Boardman 1985: 51–65.

11.2 Riace warrior A

with most of the weight on one foot. 'Ideal' realism has finally arrived. We do not, of course, know the original context of these sculptures. That they once formed part of a large group dedicated at a major sanctuary (Delphi or Olympia) seems likely.[9] But even if their context is lost, the sea has preserved the eyes and the copper mouth. It is a timely reminder that Classical sculpture, whether bronze or marble, was polychrome – multicoloured. 'Classical' white is a modern misconception.

To serve as a dedication of one kind or another was probably the original role played by most of the more celebrated mid-century sculptures – Myron's 'Diskobolos' (discus-thrower) and Polykleitos' 'Doryphoros' (spear-carrier) were also originally of bronze but are now known to us only through Roman copies. But to get an idea of what heights could be reached in High Classical times we have

---

[9] For the suggestion that their original context is Delphi, see Busignani 1981: 33–9. This is hotly contested by Rolley 1984.

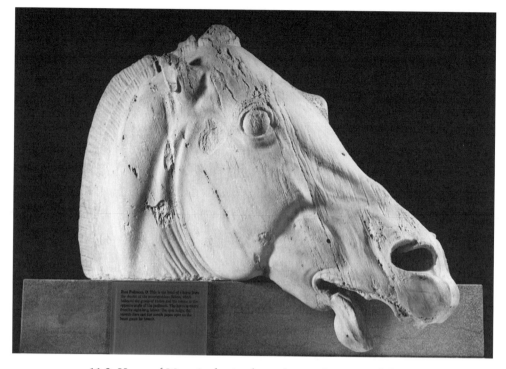

11.3 Horse of Moon's chariot from the north corner of the east pediment of the Parthenon, no. 303, O

to turn to Athens, where, from 446 BC onwards, artists and craftsmen had been engaged in the sculptural ornament of the Parthenon – pediments, metopes and frieze. Of course, the greatest (in every sense) of these sculptures – the chryselephantine (gold and ivory) statue of Athena by Pheidias, a companion piece to his Zeus at Olympia – is gone forever, known only through much smaller, and inferior, copies.[10] To what extent the Parthenon sculptures were executed by Pheidias himself must remain a mystery.[11] But certainly here we have the most complex sculptural programme in Greek art, a programme that must have had an original designer. The figures from the east pediment in particular have all the grandeur Winckelmann would have admired. Even when reclining, the Dionysos from the east pediment is an imposing presence; the horse in the far northern corner shows all the weariness of one who has had to drag the moon's chariot across the sky (fig. 11.3); and the drapery on the three goddesses twists and turns, and, in clinging, both reveals and conceals the bodies beneath. This new interest in the female body is characteristic of late fifth-century sculpture. It is evident in the Nike of

[10] For the relevant iconographic evidence for the lost statue of Athena, see Stewart 1990: 157–60; Brommer 1979: 59–61.
[11] For the elusiveness of the 'personality' of Pheidias, see Spivey 1996: 152–71. The literary sources for Pheidias' life and work are collected together by Pollitt 1990: 53–65.

11.4 Nike of Paionios of Mende

Paionios of Mende (fig. 11.4) found at Olympia – one of the few pieces whose sculptor (and date) we know. If the Caryatids of the Erechtheion still have some of the repose of earlier work, the 'Nike adjusting her (sandal) strap' from the balustrade of the temple of Athena Nike on the Acropolis (around 420 BC) shows the full erotic possibilities of 'clinging drapery'.[12]

Judging by the high standards set by Athens in the late fifth century, the surviving works from the earlier part of the fourth are something of a disappointment. The frieze from the temple of Apollo Epikourios at Bassai in Arcadia, showing the battle between Lapiths and Centaurs, seems a clumsy treatment of a hackneyed theme.[13] The accomplishment shown in the best of the horsemen and charioteers from the Parthenon frieze has not been maintained. There are

[12] For the Nike parapet itself, see Stewart 1990: 165. See also the proposals of Osborne 1994.
[13] On the Bassai frieze, see Madigan 1992. His views are not my views.

11.5 Roman copy (or version) of the Aphrodite of Knidos by Praxiteles

indeed no friezes from the fourth century that can compare with the Parthenon – even the Greeks and Amazons from the Mausoleum at Halikarnassos appear, in comparison, second best. Surviving fourth-century pedimental sculpture is little better. Some heads from the temple of Athena Alea at Tegea may, perhaps, betray a sense of pathos characteristic of the sculptor Skopas – or they may not.[14] Yet the fourth century is a century of great sculptors. Skopas, Lysippos and Praxiteles may not have been better than Pheidias (who can say?) but they were certainly more influential. Praxiteles was the principal innovator of the age. His greatest novelty (we cannot say it was his greatest work) was the cult statue of Aphrodite from Knidos. This only survives in the form of some rather poor Roman copies (e.g. fig. 11.5) which give little sense of its original appeal.[15] For, as our literary sources make clear, this was the most successfully erotic statue in

[14] On fourth-century sculpture, see Boardman 1995.
[15] For the archaeological context of the Knidia, see Love 1970: 154–5; 1972a: 70–6; 1972b: 402–5. The best recent discussion is by Spivey 1996: 173–86.

11.6 Half life-size bronze statue of a boy found off the coast at Marathon

all the ancient world. It was set up in its own circular temple, which allowed it to be viewed from every possible angle. If it was not the first Greek female nude, it was by far the most celebrated, and became the model for the depiction of women for centuries (indeed millennia) to come. Yet, for all his fame, not one original work by Praxiteles survives – with the possible but doubtful exception of the polished marble statue of Hermes and the infant Dionysos from Olympia, a statue found in the right place but made with the wrong tools.[16] Some idea of his effect on other contemporary sculpture can be grasped from some bronzes of around 330 BC, in particular the half life-size boy found off the coast at Marathon (fig. 11.6). The long straight nose and pursed lips are features found on much later

[16] For the discovery of this statue, see Treu 1897: 194–206. The studies of Adam (1966: 124–8) and Carpenter (1969) have, I think, shown conclusively that the carving technique employed has to be later than the fourth century BC. The Hermes therefore cannot be an original work by Praxiteles, though it may indeed be the statue that Pausanias saw (V.17.3). The ancient sources for Praxiteles are gathered together by Pollitt 1990: 84–9.

11.7 A 'portrait' of Socrates, Roman copy of a Greek
original of the fourth century BC

sculpture, key elements in a Praxitelean manner that many found useful to
imitate.

But what, it may fairly be asked, was all this sculpture for? Many things, of
course, but one thing they were not was portraits as we understand the term. Of
course, they were meant to represent gods, heroes and other generic figures (such
as 'The Charioteer'; fig. 1.2), but these could not, by definition, be likenesses.
They were idealised representations of how gods or heroes ought to appear, using
the language of realism without in any sense being realistic. There are, however,
a small number of Classical images that purport to represent real people. There
are a few 'portraits' of statesmen, such as Themistocles and Pericles, and later in
the fourth century a 'Socrates' type appears. Figure 11.7 shows an example, which
may well be a portrait but cannot be a likeness. To be sure, the features appear to
be based partly on literary accounts of how Socrates looked – that is, like a satyr.

But such 'portraits' only begin to appear some time after his death. It is a portrait of a philosophical satyr, not of Socrates.[17]

This brief account of Classical sculpture cannot begin to do justice to it. It is nothing more than a sketch, an outline of the main trends in its development. Certain genres – tomb sculpture, for example – have been entirely omitted. I have not attempted to interpret complex architectural ensembles, such as the Parthenon. I have barely touched on the important subjects of context and function. To begin to understand such matters we must take a broader view. It is time to look at what often provided the frame and the context for sculpture – architecture.

11.3 Classical architecture

Architecture is today a very controversial subject. Today's celebrated architects are innovators, whose skill in using new materials in new ways is highly prized. Architecture today embraces all kinds of buildings, from museums to municipal housing blocks. The ancients had a different view. Architecture was a term reserved for public and sacred buildings. Greek architects designed and then supervised the construction of temples, stoas and council houses. Classical Greeks had very clear ideas of what such structures were for, and how they should look.

Let us begin with an illustration. Sometime after 470 BC the citizens of Elis in the Peloponnese commissioned a local man, Libon, to supervise the construction of an entirely new temple to Zeus at the panhellenic sanctuary of Olympia. This was, if not to replace, at least to supplement the Archaic temple of Zeus and Hera constructed in the seventh century, but was to be built on a much grander scale. When completed it measured 27.68 m by 64.12 m. Its plan, however, was entirely traditional (figs. 11.8 and 11.9). It had thirteen columns along the flanks and six in the front, thus deviating by the addition of only one column from the standard Doric temple of a generation earlier, the temple of Aphaia on Aegina. But the fact that his design was traditional did not make Libon's task very much easier. For one thing, the temple was to be built, not on solid rock, but on alluvial soil by the river Alpheios. This entailed the cutting of large trenches to lay deep foundations made of large limestone blocks, which were then buttressed with an earthen ramp. Having completed the stylobate (the base), the architect was confronted with the choice of materials for the temple proper. Given its size, it is not really surprising that he opted for a local limestone, which was then covered with white stucco. Marble, which had to be imported over some distance, was reserved for the pedimental sculpture and the twelve metopes. In the construction of the temple he employed the techniques which had first been developed in the temple of Aphaia. The walls and columns are composed of units of more or less uniform

---

[17] On portraits see Richter and Smith 1984: esp. 24–7. On Socrates, see *ibid.*: 198–204.

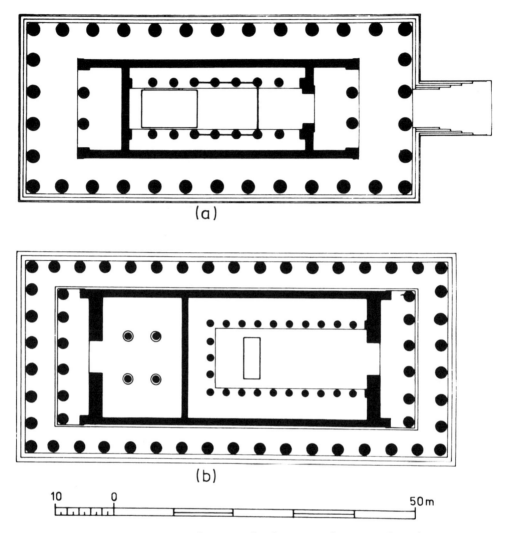

11.8 Comparative plans temple of Zeus at Olympia and Parthenon in
Athens

size, lifted into place with pulleys and cranes. This technique (which undoubtedly
contributed to the speed with which it was built) does, however, require the architect to make precise calculations as to the size of each block or column drum. The
architect had to be something of a mathematician. Libon seems to have been good
at his job, and the temple was completed in 457.[18]

Did this temple serve its purpose? Though later damaged by earthquakes, it certainly provided sufficient space to hold the chryselephantine statue of Zeus by

---

[18] On the German excavations of the temple of Zeus, see Adler *et al.* 1892: 4–27. For its sculpture, see
Treu 1897: 44–181. My account relies heavily on Ashmole 1972: 1–26.

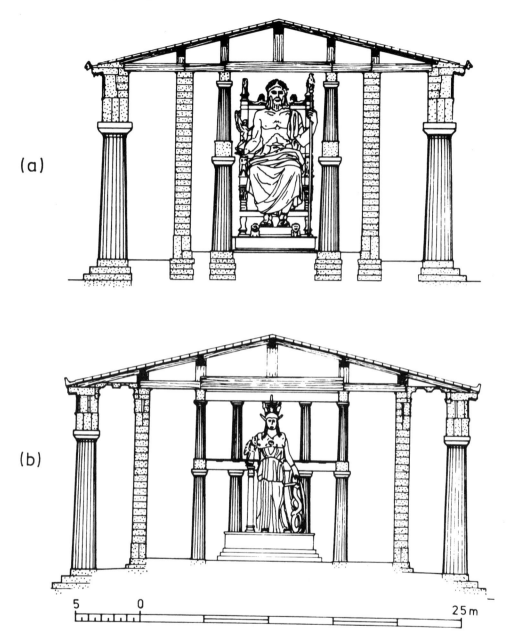

11.9 Comparison of interiors of the temple of Zeus at Olympia and the Parthenon, showing how both were designed to accommodate giant chryselephantine statues

Pheidias, later considered to be one of the wonders of the ancient world. Given its dimensions, it is difficult not to believe that the temple was constructed with some large statue in mind. As a setting for Pheidias' actual work, however, it leaves much to be desired. There is no architectural backdrop or 'frame' for the cult statue, which must have appeared more than a little cramped (fig. 11.9). The temple's interior does not seem to have been uppermost in the architect's mind. The exterior by contrast provides a fine setting for both the pedimental sculpture and the metopes, which were clearly integral to its overall design. If we bear this in mind, we can perhaps allow for the apparent failings in the detailed execution of the pedimental pieces. Such faults (if faults they are) would not have been apparent to a viewer looking at these painted sculptures from below. If we confine our view to the outside of the temple, then form does indeed follow function.

The temple of Zeus at Olympia set the pattern for other fifth-century Doric temples. The Hephaisteion above the Agora in Athens, the temple of Poseidon at Sounion and the so-called temple of Ares at Acharnai, which were all part of the energetic building programme undertaken by Athens after 449 BC, were all built on the same fundamental principles (see chapter 13, section 13.4).[19] To be sure, their dimensions are smaller, and their ornament is plainer, but in other respects they differ little from the temple of Zeus. The situation is a little different when we turn to the Ionic order. There are no successors, in the fifth century at least, to the huge temples of Ephesos and Samos. Ionic temples in Attica are generally small. The (now lost) structure by the Ilissos or the temple of Athena Nike on the Acropolis have only four columns in front, and none on the flank. Their effect depends upon their exquisite sculptural decoration, not their size.[20]

It was only towards the end of the fifth century that temples deviated at all from the traditional Doric template. In some exceptional cases, such as the Telesterion at Eleusis, a particular function dictated an unusual form, in this case a columned hall in which the Mysteries were played out. It is the Parthenon, however, that marks a real break with traditional design. Not only does it wed an Ionic frieze to an overwhelmingly Doric plan. More significantly, the Parthenon is the first building which seems to have been designed from the inside out rather than the outside in. The need to provide a suitably impressive setting for the chryselephantine statue of Athena seems to have determined the arrangement of the internal colonnade (see below pp. 346–8).[21] But for real experimentation we have to look further afield. The temple of Apollo Epikourios at Bassai in Arcadia has always

---

[19] The 'temple of Ares' refers to a temple found in the Athenian Agora, and obviously taken there from somewhere else in Roman times (see Dinsmoor 1940). This is now thought to be the temple of Athena at Pallene.

[20] A good brief discussion of Ionic temples is provided by Lawrence and Tomlinson 1996: 96–7, 117–24. The temple on the Ilissos was, of course, thoroughly examined by Stuart and Revett 1762: 7–11. For a brief overview of the Periclean building programme in Attica, see Lawrence and Tomlinson 1996: 129–32 (see also discussion in chapter 13).

[21] On how the design of the Parthenon differs from the temple of Zeus at Olympia, see in particular Coulton 1977: 111–17; 1984.

puzzled scholars. Literary testimony to the effect that its architect was Iktinos, who had been partly responsible for the Parthenon, seems to conflict with other indications of its date.[22] On the outside it seems to be a typically Doric structure. Indeed, in the eyes of nineteenth-century painters such as Edward Lear, it becomes the very archetype of the Romantic, ruined temple, standing alone in the desolate wilds of Arcadia. The interior, however, could not provide a greater contrast to its stark, grey exterior. There is, for one thing, an internal frieze, set between a number of engaged Ionic colums that support the roof. At the end of the cella, as a frame for the cult statue, there are three Corinthian columns, the first of their kind.

It was Bassai's example that was followed in the succeeding century. Though temples of standard Doric plan, such as the reconstructed temple of Apollo at Delphi, were still being built in the fourth century, this period sees renewed interest in experimentation. Both the new temple of Athena Alea at Tegea and the temple of Zeus at the panhellenic sanctuary at Nemea combine Doric exteriors with Corinthian and Ionic interiors. A combination of Doric with Corinthian can also be seen in the circular buildings or tholoi, a new type of structure which proliferates in the fourth century.[23] Both the tholos in the sanctuary of Athena at Delphi and the one to be found in the sanctuary of Asklepios at Epidauros unite an austere Doric exterior colonnade with an ornate Corinthian interior (figs. 11.10 and 11.11). The fourth century also witnessed other innovations in public architecture. The bouleuterion or council house, such as the one constructed at Priene in Ionia, becomes a recognisable type of structure. So too does the theatre. Little survives of the earliest theatres in Athens, but other fourth-century theatres have survived from other sanctuaries in Greece. The fifth-century example at Thorikos is probably the earliest. Like all Greek theatres, it exploits the natural slope of the hill to form an oval or semi-circle, in the midst of which was an orchestra or dancing floor. The degree of refinement that such simple structures had achieved towards the end of the fourth century can be seen at Epidauros. Here the auditorium is a semi-circle surrounding the perfect circle of the orchestra. Such is the acoustical refinement that a pin dropped in its centre can be heard in the very furthest reaches of the theatre.[24]

For all its refinements, Greek architecture remained wedded to simple techniques. It has often been remarked that Classical Greeks were great architects but poor engineers. Certainly, the Greeks developed and refined a narrow range of architectural forms. Once refined, these forms, such as the temple, were nearly

---

[22] On the temple at Bassai, see Cockerell 1860: 43–6; Coulton 1977: 116–17, 127–8; and the recent study by Cooper 1996b; 1996a: 131–353. Pausanias VIII.41.8–9.

[23] For general discussion of circular buildings, see Lawrence and Tomlinson 1996: 137–41. On fourth-century temples see *ibid*.: 143–50. For the circular building at the sanctuary of Athena at Delphi, see Homolle and Gottlob 1925. For the 'Thymele' at Epidauros, see Tomlinson 1983: 60–7.

[24] On theatres generally, see Lawrence and Tomlinson 1996: 205–8. On the theatre at Epidauros, see Von Gerkan and Müller-Wiener 1961.

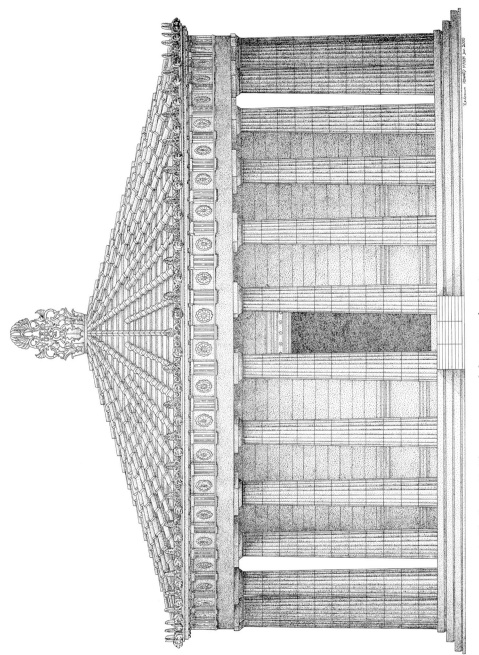

11.10 Tholos at Epidauros, restored drawing of exterior

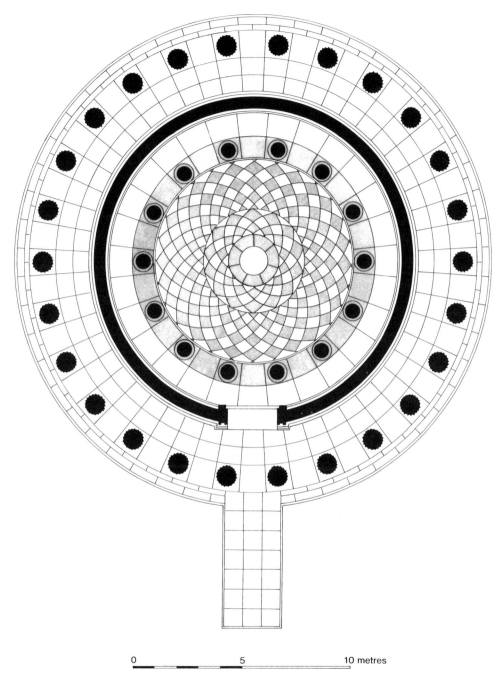

0   5   10 metres

11.11 Tholos (or Thymele) at Epidauros, restored plan

perfectly suited to their function, but could not easily be developed further. A temple, after all, should look like a temple. The engineering principles on which such temples were based were no more sophisticated than those achieved by the Egyptian architects of Karnak, indeed no different from those employed by the temple-builders of Neolithic Malta or the designers of Stonehenge. Classical Greek architecture is a sophisticated variation on the theme of the lintel block. If the Greeks knew of the arch in Classical times, they made very limited use of it. It was left to the ambitious, but far from perfectionist Romans to experiment with arches and vaults using their new materials of concrete and brick.

11.4 Classical vase painting

Besides sculpture, of all Greek art forms discussed by Roman writers painting was the most admired. Roman writers particularly prized a Greek painter's ability to imitate nature and deceive the eye – a trick Ernst Gombrich has called 'illusionism'. The elder Pliny records an anecdote concerning the painters Zeuxis and Parrhasios, both active in the early years of the fourth century BC. Zeuxis had painted a picture of some grapes so well that birds flew up to the scene, expecting (Pliny records) to find food. Not to be outdone, Parrhasios painted a linen curtain. Such was his skill however that, on seeing the painting, Zeuxis asked that the curtain be lifted so that he could see the painting beneath. Only then did he learn, to his chagrin, that his eye too had been tricked by his fellow artist, Parrhasios.[25] Artists such as Zeuxis and Parrhasios seem to have produced both paintings on wooden panels and frescoes on walls. But none of their works survives. We know of Polygnotos in the fifth century and Zeuxis, Parrhasios and Apelles in the fourth only from the admiring accounts of later writers. To be sure we can locate the physical remains of both the Knidian Lesche at Delphi and the painted stoa (the stoa poikile) in the Athenian Agora, both of whose walls were decorated by Polygnotos.[26] But only the foundations of these buildings remain. Any reconstructions of the paintings themselves have to rely largely on the surviving literary testimony. The only contexts in which actual wall paintings survive are the elaborate tombs from Macedon.[27] These give us some idea of what Classical painters had achieved by the end of the fourth century, but do not enable us to reconstruct the steps by which they reached that point.

Lacking the archaeological means to write a history of Classical painting as such, scholars have turned to the next best thing: painted images on pots. Of course,

---

[25] Pliny, *Natural History* XXXV.65–6. The literary evidence for Zeuxis and Parrhasios is gathered together by Pollitt 1990: 149–56.

[26] For Polygnotos and the Stoa Poikile, see Pliny, *Natural History* XXXV.58–9. For the foundations of the stoa, see now Shear 1984: 5–19. For a long description of the Knidian Lesche, see Pausanias X.25–31. For the remains of the building itself see Pouilloux 1960: 120–39. The most recent art-historical reconstruction of the Lesche is by Stansbury-O'Donnell 1989; 1990; 1999: 178–90. See also the discussion by Castriota 1992: 96–133.

[27] See for example the Tomb of Persephone at Vergina, Andronikos 1994b.

neither Roman nor Greek authors troubled to describe such objects, but they do have the merit of surviving in large numbers. German scholars of the earlier part of this century were apt to treat the history of vase painting as a pale, but true, reflection of the history of Greek painting in general. Beazley's work made this approach much more difficult to sustain. For one thing, Beazley showed that the red-figure technique was invented much earlier than 479 BC. For another, the 'high points' in painting and vase painting do not seem to coincide. Most of the painters most highly esteemed by later writers seem to have worked in the fourth century. But the 'vase painters' Beazley most admired – the Kleophrades painter and the Berlin painter (fig. 11.12) straddle the Archaic and Classical worlds. Moreover the points of contact between painting and vase painting are few and far between. To be sure, the scene on the name vase of the Niobid painter (fig. 11.13) is probably inspired by some larger mural. But such instances are rare, and the fact that many fifth-century Attic pot painters chose the name 'Polygnotos' serves only to confirm that, of the two crafts, 'vase painting' was the lesser. Indeed, in Beazley's view the illusionistic ambitions of wall and panel painters had a bad impact on their fellow artisans working on pots, since it encouraged them to attempt effects for which the medium was not well suited.[28] None the less, Beazley's chronology and attributions do allow us to write a history of Classical vase painting, albeit a traditional one that places 'artistic personalities' in the foreground.

The red-figure technique of outline drawing had been invented in Athens around 530 BC.[29] It was then developed in the succeeding decades by a group of craftsmen known collectively as 'the pioneers'.[30] The technique was perfected by the Berlin painter and the Kleophrades painter in the decades either side of 480 BC. Figure 11.12 shows a scene on an amphora attributed to the Berlin painter. In front, a satyr holds his lyre, or barbitos; a faun rears his head behind; and behind both is Hermes, with winged helmet, holding both a staff and kantharos in one hand and an oinochoe in the other. By anyone's standards, the calligraphy here is superb; the anatomy of the satyr's torso is sharply delineated, and the three figures are clearly distinguished in space. The surrounding decoration is restrained, avoiding any sense of clutter. It exemplifies in many ways what twentieth-century scholars have taken to be the Classical ideal of harmony and balance. Yet it is not exactly a Classical harmony or balance that we see here. The figures, though distinct, are not drawn in such a way as to give the impression of being in three-dimensional space. There is no attempt at perspective, nor do the figures convey any illusion of volume or rotundity. As the rendering of the eyes and noses show, the style here is still Archaic.[31]

---

[28] For Beazley's comments, see Beazley and Ashmole 1932: 41–2. On the name vase of the Niobid painter and its relationship to the decoration of the Theseion in Athens, see Robertson 1992: 180–5; Barron 1972.

[29] Robertson 1992: 7–14; Boardman 1975: 15–17. There is still disagreement as to whether its invention should be attributed to 'Lysippides' or the 'Andokides painter' (who may have been the same craftsman).   [30] Robertson 1992: 20–35; Boardman 1975: 29–36.

[31] On the Berlin painter, see Beazley 1922; Beazley and Kurtz 1983; Robertson 1992: 56–83.

11.12 Red-figure amphora of around 480 BC, name vase of 'Berlin painter'

11.13 Name vase of 'Niobid painter' (Beazley's attribution), calyx krater from Orvieto

This late Archaic style of vase painting persisted until around 460 BC. It survives not only in the works of the Kleophrades painter and the Berlin painter, and in their contemporaries who painted cups, the Brygos painter and Douris, but also in others who belong more firmly in the Classical world, such as the Pan painter.[32] Early Classical vase painting only properly begins around 460 BC with the Niobid painter (fig. 11.13; see above). As 'vase painting' developed, so did the art of shaping pots. In the workshop of Sotades Greek potters reached the highest standards. Sotades and his circle produced elaborate vessels, such as the Oriental-style drinking vessels we know as rhyta, which must have taken much trouble to produce.[33] This workshop attracted skilled painters, in particular the painter we know as the 'Sotades painter', one of whose works is illustrated in figure 13.22. The key figures of the next generation – the High Classical period proper – were the Achilles painter and the Phiale painter. As well as painting red-figure, these craftsmen also worked in a medium new to the fifth century – white ground. Drawing on a white background allowed them to make some use of colour, and to achieve a level of detail impossible in red-figure. On a white-ground lekythos by the Achilles painter we can see the bodies of both a woman and a warrior (her husband?). These images convey a sense of volume; their faces have recognisable expressions. We can share the illusion of seeing in their faces the feeling, the pathos, of the parting between a dear husband and his wife.[34] We are as close here to Gombrich's illusionism as we are ever to get in vase painting. Feeling too is present here, but its expression is restrained – thereby achieving the kind of balance that, once more, suits modern ideas of the Classical. Such restraint, however, is abandoned at the very end of the century. The painters who worked in the workshop of the potter Meidias (the Meidias painter among them) specialised in scenes full of pretty young women and (equally pretty) men. The men are nude, the women clothed only in that kind of clinging drapery that reveals as much as it conceals (see fig. 2.2).[35] It is an idealised view of happy youthful innocence, an ancient equivalent of the airbrushed Hollywood version of the American high school. In Beazley's stern view, true Classical beauty has here been supplanted by vacant pleasure-seeking.[36] Others have interpreted such scenes as a kind of 'escapism' from the difficult times Athens was experiencing as the Peloponnesian war came to a close.[37] Whatever interpretation you prefer, the Meidias painter is the last significant red-figure craftsman. The fourth century witnesses a precipitate decline, where even the best painters are undistinguished. On the pelike by the Marsyas painter shown in figure 11.14, new kinds of polychromy have been attempted. Though the standard of drawing is still good, the composition is crowded, and the treatment sentimental at best. Nothing better was

[32] For these painters, see Robertson 1992: 84–106, 143–52; Boardman 1975: 111–96.
[33] On the workshop of Sotades (and the 'Sotades painter'), see Robertson 1992: 185–90; Hoffmann 1997.   [34] On the Achilles painter, see Robertson 1992: 193–210; Oakley 1997.
[35] On the Meidias painter, see Burn 1987.   [36] Beazley and Ashmole 1932: 53.
[37] Pollitt 1972: 122–5 – though this is a view dismissed by Burn 1987: 15–25, 94–6.

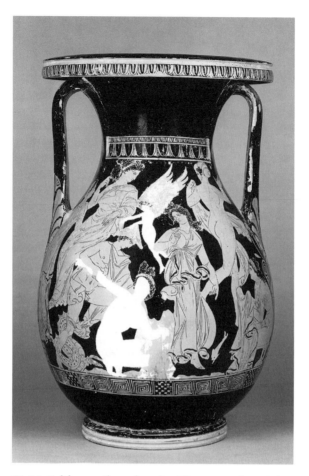

11.14 Pelike attributed to the 'Marsyas painter', from Kameiros on Rhodes

produced by Athenian workshops, and by the end of the century Athenian production of red-figure pottery had ceased entirely.[38]

This did not quite mean the end of red-figure vase painting. Production of red-figure had begun in various parts of Greece during the fifth century – indeed all the major Archaic production centres of mainland Greece (Corinth, Boeotia and Laconia) produced their own red-figure.[39] These centres, however, never really equalled Athens as a centre of ceramic production. It was only in southern Italy that Athens had any rival. Red-figure here was adopted around the middle of the fifth century, and by 400 BC the Apulian, Lucanian and other south Italian schools were in full swing.[40] These workshops produced elaborate vases, such as the

---

[38] On fourth-century 'vase painting' see Robertson 1992: 265–95; Boardman 1989: 190–4.
[39] See generally Cook 1972: 187–8. On Laconian red-figure, see McPhee 1986; on Corinthian, Herbert 1977; McPhee 1983; on Boeotian, Lullies 1940.
[40] On south Italian vases generally, see Trendall 1989; Cook 1972: 190–201. On Apulian, see Trendall and Cambitoglou 1978; 1982. On other south Italian and Sicilian styles, see Trendall 1967.

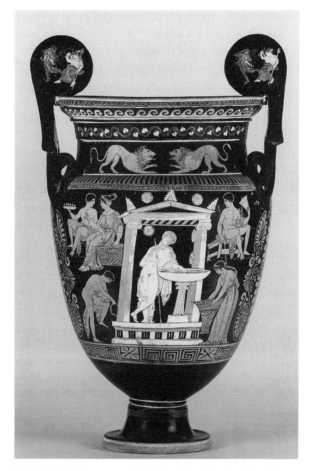

11.15 Red-figure south Italian (Apulian) volute krater, attributed to the Ilioupersis painter

volute krater shown in figure 11.15. 'Illusionistic' effects, such as shading and showing figures in three-quarters view, to give an effect of depth, were frequently attempted on these pots. Still, such ornate and indeed gaudy vessels do not sit easily with most scholars' conception of the Classical. Their floridity seems almost Hellenistic, even though most south Italian red-figure is firmly Classical in date.[41]

The above is a conventional view of red-figure vase painting – a kind of authorised sketch. It is a history of individual craftsmen working within an established tradition.[42] That we can write a history of 'vase painting' at all is, of course, simply a function of a pot's higher chances of survival in the archaeological record. We

---

[41] Even though Lucanian and Apulian workshops continued their output into the early third century, the vast majority of vases are fourth century (that is Classical) and not Hellenistic in date. See Trendall 1989: 15–17; Trendall and Cambitoglou 1978: liii; 1982: 1038–9.

[42] That is, a kind of précis of Robertson 1992: in turn based on the information given in Beazley 1963.

should not deceive ourselves and imagine that these pots really were 'works of art' in the eyes of fifth- or fourth-century Greeks. Nor should we succumb to either one of the two brands of art-historical platonism currently on offer: the one that sees images on pots as wall paintings in miniature; or the other, more recently put forward, that sees painted pottery as shadowy copies of the lost glories of metal-work.[43] Even in a conventional account such as the one given above the word 'Classical' appears less stable than one might have hoped for. For the Classical red-figure that scholars have, traditionally, most admired is, in style at least, not Classical at all. Red-figure vase painting peaks rather too early in the Classical period, too early indeed to coincide with the (inferred) high point in painting in general. Winckelmann's scheme, if it works at all, works best for sculpture. Defining the 'Classical' by demonstration has proven to be a difficult task, perhaps because much of what was most exemplary, most 'Classical', has simply been lost.

Defining the 'Classical' has then proved an elusive task. It is tempting perhaps to avoid for the time being all general definitions, and to accept the Classical as simply one period among others in Greek history, one in which certain kinds of houses were built, certain kinds of city plan emerged, and certain kinds of rebuild-ing took place in Greek sanctuaries. Perhaps then it may indeed prove possible to define the Classical by demonstration. But we cannot in truth simply abandon Winckelmann's aesthetic criteria, and simply take the 'Classical' out of Classical art. For was not the Classical, at the very least, a period of Athenian cultural heg-emony, a time when the city-states and other regions of Greece came to adopt many of the styles and conventions that emanated from Athens? And did not these artistic innovations best suit Athenian circumstances?

The answer to both of these questions must be a qualified 'yes'. Certainly many Classical sculptors were Athenian (Pheidias, Praxiteles), even if many others were not (Polykleitos). But even if we accept that Athens was the principal innovator of Classical Greece, the political and cultural community that played a leading role in creating the Classical 'style', it remains to be shown how Athenian culture and politics shaped the development of Athenian art. It was Winckelmann, after all, who first suggested that political liberty was the necessary condition for the Classical achievement. More recently, other scholars have tried to assess the extent to which political liberty might have helped to raise the status of the artist, and so contribute to notions of artistic autonomy.[44] But if art somehow expresses politics, then so too must other areas of material culture, which in turn must be investigated in some detail (see chapter 13 below).

Even if we accept the central role of Athens in the creation and dissemination of the Classical, we still have to explain why this 'Athenian style' was so influen-tial elsewhere. Certainly, wider factors were at work. Artistic patrons in the fifth

---

[43] For the platonism of lost paintings, see Pfuhl 1926; for the platonism of lost metal vessels, Vickers and Gill 1994.   [44] See the excellent discussion by Tanner (1999).

and fourth centuries were increasingly states, rather than individuals. The Archaic aristocrat who commissioned a bronze or marble dedication to a god, or a marble tombstone to a deceased member of his family, could afford to regard the artist as a mere artisan, there to carry out his wishes. The state that wanted to outdo its rivals in building a splendid temple, adorned with a complex group of marble sculptures, or the community that wanted to create a gold and ivory statue to its patron deity, necessarily had to treat the sculptor/designer with greater respect.[45] These new political relations of artistic production may in turn be related to other patterns we can discern in the archaeological record, such as changes in the number and type of votives deposited in sanctuaries. Such changes should in turn be most easily discernible in that key arena for ancient Greek competition, culture and display: the sanctuary.

[45] A point emphasised by Osborne (1994a).

CHAPTER 12

CITIES AND SANCTUARIES OF CLASSICAL GREECE

12.1 Sanctuaries and cities

To juxtapose sanctuaries and cities may strike many readers as odd. The image we have of the Classical Greek sanctuary – Delphi springs to mind – is of a temple and altar standing alone in rural Arcadia. No amount of scholarly effort will entirely erase this popular, Romantic misconception, which owes more to Western painting than it does to Greek reality. It is a picture the Greeks themselves would not have recognised. This is not because Greeks were insensitive to landscape and place – far from it. It is rather because sanctuaries were a part of the everyday. Sanctuaries, from simple altars to impressive temples, can be found in almost every public space. Sanctuaries were often placed in the very heart of cities – an example being the temple of Apollo at Corinth, which stands immediately over that city's marketplace or agora. Moreover, rural sanctuaries are sometimes not what they seem. To be sure, there are plenty of small rural shrines in Classical Greece, one such being the small temple of Zeus Messapeus at Tzakona near Sparta.[1] But many sanctuaries we think of as rural were nothing of the kind. Delphi is simply a small town with two large sanctuaries attached. We gain a romantic impression of the place because excavators have dug (and partly restored) the sanctuaries, not the town.

Furthermore, sanctuaries were, by the Classical period at least, entirely dependent upon cities. Most major shrines (such as the Heraion of Argos or the Heraion at Perachora) functioned as state sanctuaries – the festivals and sacrifices that took place having an intimate connection with the running of Argos and Corinth respectively. This was true even of panhellenic sites. Though many Greek states helped to embellish both Delphi and Olympia, it was Delphi and Elis respectively that were the communities responsible for maintaining these holy places. In many communities, participation in rituals that took place in state shrines was a condition of being a member of that community – that is, of citizenship. Sanctuaries cannot be neatly separated from cities. It is in looking at cities and sanctuaries together that we can see the most enduring architectural, social and political legacies of the Classical era.

---

[1] Catling 1990. It is unlikely that this is the sanctuary of Zeus Messapeus mentioned by Pausanias III.20.3.

By 479 BC most Greek sanctuaries had been around for hundreds of years. One could argue that all that changes in the Classical period is that we acquire more evidence than we had in the Archaic; that the picture becomes fuller, but nothing fundamentally new is added. Certainly, the iconographic evidence for matters such as sacrificial ritual becomes much more abundant than in earlier times, and such images may provide important clues for Archaic practices.[2] But perhaps it would be wiser to reserve judgement, and simply to look at how sanctuaries actually developed in Classical times. I shall consider three examples in some detail. Two of these (the Heraion at Prosymna, the 'Argive Heraion'; and the Heraion at Perachora) we have looked at before; the third, the sanctuary of Asklepios at Epidauros, we have not.

12.2 Three state sanctuaries

The Heraion at Perachora (figs. 12.1, 12.2 and 12.3) had, by 479 BC, long been in the hands of the Corinthians. In the late sixth century Corinth had gone to the trouble of replacing the original, apsidal temple by the harbour with a grander building in limestone and marble. A new altar was built opposite.[3] Though no more temples were built, the sanctuary was embellished considerably in Classical times. A number of stoas were erected, principally an unusual L-shaped example at the eastern end of the harbour, with two storeys, Doric below and Ionic above.[4] At the same time, the altar was surrounded by an Ionic colonnade.[5]

Additions such as these had been common enough in Archaic sanctuaries. More remarkable are the lengths that the Corinthians went to in order to supply the sanctuary with water. Perachora is in a dry part of the country, and there are no natural springs nearby. An artificial pool had been dug in Archaic times, but this was obviously felt to be insufficient. For around 450 BC the Corinthians constructed a double-apsidal cistern, lined with hydraulic (waterproof) cement, to collect and store rainwater (fig. 12.3).[6] An enigmatic 'circle', apparently of the same date, found on the hill above also seems to be for collecting water, and later, in the fourth century, an elaborate storage-tank and fountain house were built nearby.[7] Quite why the sanctuary needed so much water is unclear. Certainly, water would be needed in quantity with the arrival of visitors and pilgrims for any festival, but this would only have happened a few times a year, at most.

---

[2] E.g. Van Straten 1988; Himmelmann 1997.

[3] On the later Archaic buildings at Perachora, particularly the temple, see Payne 1940: 78–109. On the altar, see Payne 1940: 89–91; Plommer and Salviat 1966.

[4] Coulton 1964. On the stoa-like 'West Court', see Coulton 1967. On the relationship of these buildings to the development of the stoa in Classical times, see Coulton 1976: 39–54.

[5] Plommer and Salviat 1966.

[6] Tomlinson 1969: 157–64. On the date, see now Tomlinson 1988; 1990; Tomlinson and Demakopoulou 1985: 276.

[7] Tomlinson and Demakopoulou 1985. It is not clear whether the 'nymphaeum' (or fountain house) is fourth century or early Hellenistic in date; see Tomlinson 1969: 203–18.

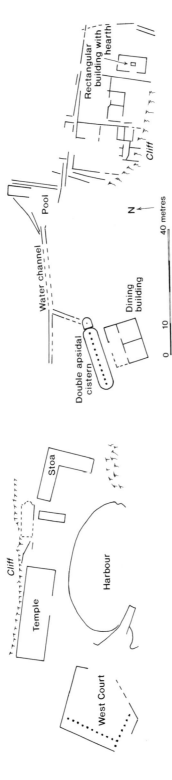

Rectangular
building with
hearth

Cliff

Water channel

Pool

Double apsidal
cistern

Dining
building

N

40 metres

0   10   40 metres

Cliff

Stoa

Temple

Harbour

West Court

12.1 General plan of the sanctuary at Perachora, *c.* 400 BC

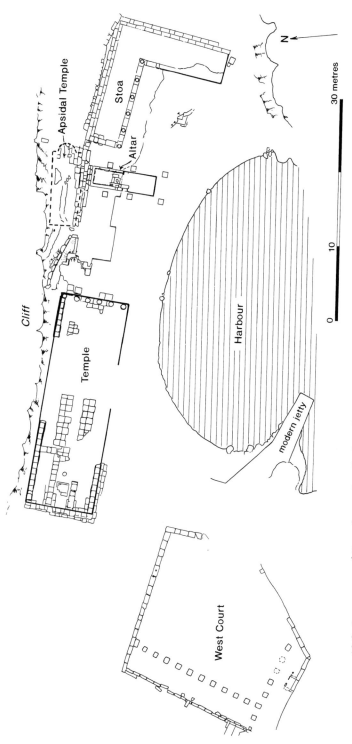

12.2 Sanctuary of Perachora, detail of Harbour area

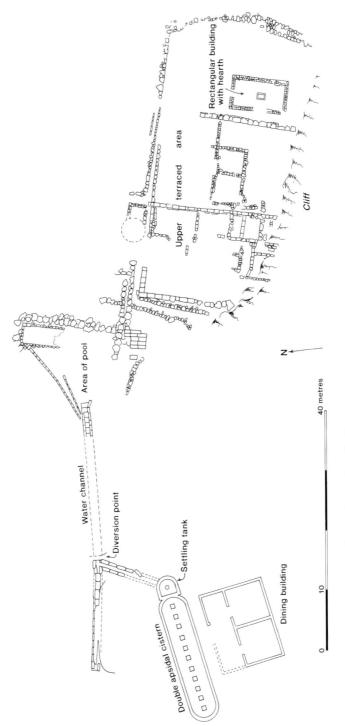

12.3 Sanctuary of Perachora, detail of western area

Double apsidal cistern

Settling tank

Dining building

Water channel

Diversion point

Area of pool

Upper terraced area

Rectangular building with hearth

Cliff

H

N

0   10   40 metres

Conceivably, large amounts of water might have been needed in some kind of purification ritual, but, if so, we might expect similarly elaborate water works in other sanctuaries of Hera. This does not appear to be the case.

But before we leave Perachora, there is one other architectural addition to note. Just by the double-apsidal cistern, and presumably contemporary with it, is a building with two more or less identical rooms (fig. 12.8). Both of these are furnished with eleven stone *klinai* or dining couches. This is the kind of room which pictures on Attic pots and Paestan tomb paintings suggest must have been used for some kind of dining or symposium.[8] It is not clear whether dining in these *hestiatoria* (dining rooms – modern Greek for 'restaurant') was in any way connected to the rituals surrounding the worship of Hera (such as the consumption of meat used for sacrifices), or was merely a facility provided for the wealthier visitors.[9] It may, however, be worth noting that an even grander building of this type was constructed at the Argive Heraion around 480 BC.[10]

The Heraion of Argos remains a subject of controversy, as much for its Classical remains as for its Archaic (see chapter 7 above). In either late Archaic or early Classical times it seems, according to at least one scholar, to have undergone some major embellishments, with the addition of a large hestiatorion, two stoas and a columned hall (fig. 12.4).[11] Further modifications were made to these buildings, and another stoa added, in the years after the Persian wars, a time during which Argos established a firm hegemony over the whole of the Argive plain. It is tempting therefore to see this building programme as reflecting Argive assertiveness, that is as a concrete affirmation that the sanctuary of Hera was now firmly linked to the Argive state.[12] Whatever the truth of the matter, the Argives do not at this time appear to have been in any way dissatisfied with the old, wooden temple of Hera that had stood there since the seventh century – not until, that is, this temple was burnt down in 423 BC through the negligence of Hera's priestess, Chryseis.[13] The temple that most later visitors, such as Pausanias, saw was a much more splendid stone, Doric structure, housing a huge chryselephantine (gold and ivory) cult statue of Hera made by the Argive sculptor Polykleitos. This statue was in every sense comparable to the images of Zeus at Olympia and Athena in the Parthenon made by Polykleitos' more celebrated contemporary, Pheidias.[14] It would be natural to conclude that this later, Classical temple simply replaced the older one that had burnt down in 423 BC, thus providing a convenient *terminus post quem* for its construction. Yet it is odd that the new temple was built, not on the site of the older one on the topmost terrace of the sanctuary, but on an entirely new site one terrace lower down. The old temple was neither

[8] Tomlinson 1969: 164–72.   [9] On 'hestiatoria' generally, see Tomlinson 1980.
[10] On the 'hestiatorion' at the Heraion, see Tilton 1902; Amandry 1952: 239–54.
[11] On the buildings generally, see Tilton 1902; Caskey and Amandry 1952; Amandry 1952; Lauter 1973. On the South Stoa, see Coulton 1973.   [12] As argued by Hall (1995a).
[13] Thucydides IV.133.2.
[14] The chryselephantine statue is described by Pausanias II.17.4–5; Strabo, *Geography* VIII.6.10. For the surviving sculpture from the second temple of Hera, see Waldstein 1902: 139–76.

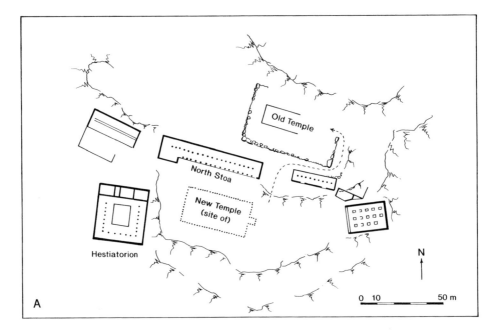

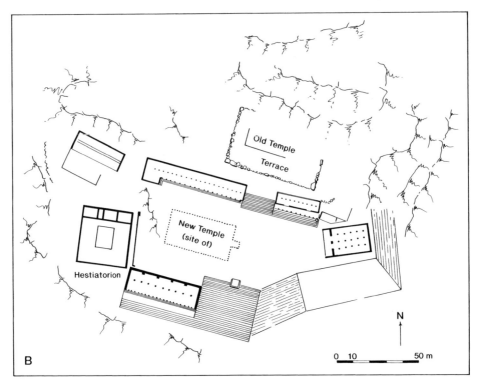

12.4 Plan of the Argive Heraion: (A) by 490 BC; (B) by *c.* 420 BC

destroyed nor rebuilt, but simply left as a ruin, rather like the older cathedral at Coventry bombed during the Second World War. Pierre Amandry and Hans Lauter, who have re-examined the areas excavated by American archaeologists at the turn of the nineteenth and twentieth centuries, have concluded that work was begun on the new temple well before 423 BC.[15] It was the Argives' original intention to have two temples to Hera: one old, to house the older, portable wooden cult image; and a new temple, specifically to house the new gold and ivory statue of their patron deity. Parallels for such 'double' temples can be found in other sites for which new temples were constructed in the fifth century to house new, chryselephantine cult images: the sanctuary of Zeus at Olympia and the sanctuary of Athena on the Acropolis of Athens. 'Double' temples and 'double' cult images present us with a much less familiar picture of Classical temples and cult than the one we are used to. If sanctuaries had two cult images, which one was real? Or do 'double' cult images necessarily reflect different aspects of the deity herself? And why are all these 'double' temples constructed in the latter part of the fifth century BC?

Clearly, many of the new temples of the fifth century were something more than simple enlargements or improvements on what had been there before. This fact comes into sharper focus when we consider the phenomenon of new cults. There is, for example, a much greater interest in cults to (named) heroes in Classical times than there had been before. Considerable effort went into the architectural embellishment of heroa, such as the Amphiareion at Oropos and the shrine to Hippolytos near Troizen. An important aspect of many hero cults in the Classical period was their role in healing. Visitors came to these places as much to get well as to worship. Of all the heroes credited with powers of healing, Asklepios was pre-eminent, and of all the sanctuaries of Asklepios that came into prominence in the fifth and fourth centuries BC, that at Epidauros was the most important.

Epidauros is a small city on the south-eastern shores of the Saronic gulf, and Asklepios is a minor hero, almost unknown in Epic, credited with healing powers. How and why it is that the sanctuary of Asklepios should become one of the largest sites of its kind in Greece during Classical times is certainly a question worth asking. The sanctuary itself is situated in an area of limestone hills, about 10 kilometres inland from the city itself. There had been a shrine of Apollo Maleatas in the hills nearby since the seventh century BC, and it is presumed that the cult of Asklepios was originally merely a minor aspect of the worship of Apollo. The first known dedication to Asklepios from Epidauros is a bronze phiale dedicated by one Mikylos, dated by Jeffery to between 500 and 475 BC.[16] Throughout the fifth century, the buildings in the Asklepion were far from prepossessing. There was, it is true, an altar, and a large building with an internal

---

[15] Amandry 1952: 273–4; Lauter 1973.
[16] Jeffery 1990: 182 no.10. See also discussion in *ibid.*: 180–1.

colonnade, building E, may have served as kind of 'cult complex' for the worship of both Apollo and Asklepios (fig. 12.5).[17] It was only from the early fourth century, from about 370 BC onwards, that building began in earnest. A largely Doric temple of Asklepios was constructed, a structure which, like the temple of Apollo Bassitas in Arcadia, had engaged Ionic columns within the cella. The temple itself was of modest proportions (11.76×23.06 m), and was built largely of limestone. Pentelic marble, imported from Attica, was used only for the pedimental sculpture, the akroterion, and the metopes within the pronaos.[18] Much more imposing was the tholos or 'Thymele' (figs. 11.10 and 11.11). This too, though not particularly large (about 20 m in diameter) was extremely carefully executed and elaborately decorated. An exterior Doric colonnade of limestone columns was surmounted by metopes with black rosettes, crowned in turn by an akroterion of Pentelic marble. The interior consisted of a colonnade of fourteen Corinthian columns, its floor being decorated with an elaborate geometric pattern made from black Argive limestone and white Pentelic marble. It may strike many readers as odd that, although this building was thoroughly excavated and minutely described by Pausanias, we have no clear idea what this was for.[19] None the less, the practice of combining the different 'orders' in one building seems to be a particular feature of the Epidaurian building programme. Different combinations of Doric, Ionic and Corinthian also occur in three smaller structures built during the major building phase of the site: the small temples of Artemis and Aphrodite; and the monumental entranceway, or propylaia.[20]

We are unusually well informed about the building programme undertaken at Epidauros, because, even if the structures themselves are not particularly well preserved, the building contracts have survived. These contracts are in the form of inscriptions on stone, which go into some detail concerning the craftsmen, the materials, the workmanship and the cost. From these we learn, for example, that the ceiling and roof of the temple of Asklepios were made of silver fir, and that the coffering beneath the roof and the door into the cella were made of a number of costlier, rarer woods (boxwood, cypress, elm and nettle-tree wood) and inlaid with ivory and gold.[21] It is from such inscriptions that we can infer that the temple itself cost 23 talents, the theatre 10, but that by far the most expensive item was the chryselephantine statue of Asklepios, costing 50 talents.[22] The building programme was then a considerable undertaking for a small state. When one considers that the city of Epidauros was also engaged in the refurbishment of the nearby

[17] For these buildings, see Tomlinson 1983: 72–6; Burford 1969: 47–52. The original report is by Kavvadias 1900.

[18] For the temple of Asklepios, see Kavvadias 1900: 34–48; Tomlinson 1983: 54–60.

[19] For the tholos of 'Thymele' see Kavvadias 1900: 48–71; Tomlinson 1983: 60–7. For the building accounts, see Burford 1966: 275–81; 1969: 63–8.

[20] See Burford 1969: 69–74; Tomlinson 1983: 76–9.

[21] On the detailed accounts for the temple of Asklepios, see Burford 1966: 256–63; 1969: 54–9.

[22] On the comparative costs of each item of building or construction, see Burford 1969: 81–5. On the chryselephantine statue of Asklepios, see Pausanias II.27.2. On its cost, Burford 1966: 263–74; 1969: 59–61.

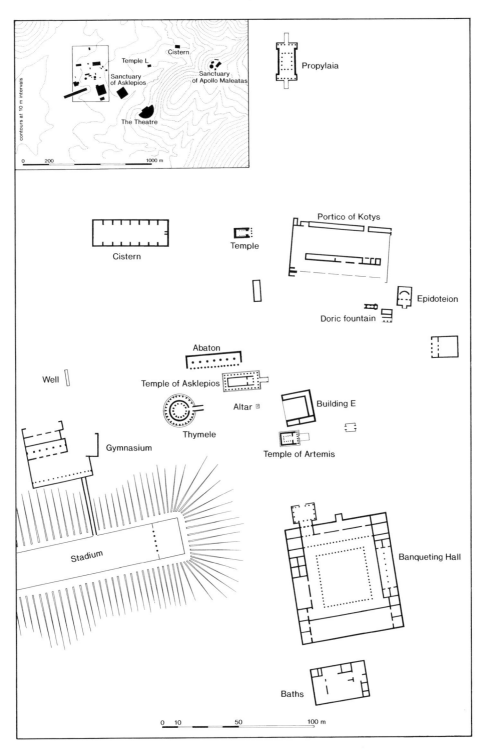

12.5 Simplified plan of sanctuary of Epidauros

sanctuary of Apollo Maleatas, and that the whole sanctuary complex, when completed in the early years of the third century BC, contained a banqueting hall (or
large hestiatorion), a hostel (katagogeion), a stadion, and the largest and most
acoustically sophisticated theatre in Classical Greece, then we must pause to
wonder what made such an undertaking worthwhile.[23]

Undoubtedly, a sanctuary of this kind attracted pilgrims in large numbers, and
many inhabitants of Epidauros would have benefited economically from their
coming there. Many scholars have suggested that, after the mysterious plague that
swept Athens in the early years of the Peloponnesian war, Greeks in general
would be especially concerned with their health, and that this helps to explain the
rise in healing cults.[24] Were then the citizens of Epidauros just responding to a new
'demand' for the ancient equivalent of hospitals? The Athenian plague may have
been a traumatic memory for many for quite some time, but we must remember
that building work at Epidauros did not begin in earnest until sixty years had
elapsed since the plague came to Athens. Rivalry with other states to have a large
and beautiful sanctuary, 'peer-polity interaction', was certainly a factor. But it
seems likely, for several reasons, that the city of Epidauros tried to involve other
parties in the project. It was simply too small a community to cover the costs of
the building by itself, and to think that the Epidaurians looked upon such a programme as an 'investment' is to think anachronistically. Instead, the city of
Epidauros engaged in a species of fund-raising. We know that the late Archaic
temple of Apollo at Delphi had been financed in part by an Athenian family, the
Alkmaionidai.[25] Epidauros aspired to create a sanctuary, like Delphi, of international significance, and it seems likely that they adopted a similar strategy.
Building work was undertaken, not after funds had been secured, but in order to
arouse interest from other states and individuals, by showing that Epidauros had
a project that was worthy of their support. Then as now, 'fund-raising' involved
both small contributions (an obol or two) from pilgrims, and much larger dona-
tions from wealthy individuals or friendly states.

These sanctuaries then were each something more than bigger and better versions of what had preceded them in the Archaic period. There must too have been
a reason for particular architectural trends, such as the vogue for circular buildings or the fashion for dining rooms (or hestiatoria), even if these reasons are difficult for us to understand. In each case there are subtle changes which betray a
change not only in emphasis, but in function. At Perachora, the obsession with
water supply has yet to be adequately explained. At the Argive Heraion, we are at

---

[23] On these other buildings, see Kavvadias 1900: 71–118; Tomlinson 1983: 39–47, 78–92. On the
theatre in particular see Kavvadias 1900: 71–96; Tomlinson 1983: 85–90; Von Gerkan and Müller-
Wiener 1961.

[24] E.g. Tomlinson 1983: 24; Burford 1969: 20–1. For the plague itself, see Thucydides II.49–54.

[25] The arrangement between Delphi, other donors (such as Amasis of Egypt) and the Alkmaionidai is
described in Herodotos. II.180.1 and V.62.2–3. It appears to have been a contract. For a discussion
of contracts outside of Epidauros (including Delphi), see Burford 1969: 93–5, and 109–18. On
Epidauros' international connections generally, see discussion in Burford 1969: 21–39.

a loss to explain the need for a 'doubling' of both temple and cult statue. Nor can we fully account for the new-found popularity of hero cults, even if the hero is a healer. It may be worth investigating whether any of these developments constitutes a trend, and if so whether they are evident in the larger, panhellenic sanctuaries of Classical Greece, particularly those with a long and distinguished history: Delphi and Olympia.

12.3 Panhellenic sanctuaries

In 480 BC the sanctuary of Zeus and Hera at Olympia, although of considerable size, was still relatively compact. The stadion, where most of the games were held, was only a few yards to the east of the altars of Zeus and Hera, and was overlooked by a series of 'treasuries' which contained the trophies and possessions of those western colonies (such as Gela, Metapontum or Syracuse) that maintained a special link with Olympia.[26] The rites of sacrifice and of athletic competition were still intimately connected with one another (fig. 7.10). But as the quadrennial festival lengthened to a full five days and as the number of visitors increased, so these arrangements came to seem inadequate. The construction of the second temple, the temple of Zeus, between 470 and 457 BC, must have made the sacred area seem even more cramped (see chapter 11, section 11.3). Hence, sometime around 450 BC, a decision was made to build a larger stadium, further to the east. In the course of its construction, many old votives that had stood on the stadium's embankment (including a Persian helmet, possibly captured at Marathon and set up by the Athenian victors) had to be removed to disused wells and other pits within the sacred area or altis.[27]

The obvious consequence of all this new building was an increase in the spatial segregation between sacrificial and athletic activities. Whether or not this effect was intended it is difficult to say. It does seem to have been part of a trend. One could argue, for example, that the decision to build an entirely new temple to Zeus entailed an increased separation between the cults of Zeus and of Hera. Against this is the fact that the 'temple of Hera' remained, in some sense, a temple of Zeus, since it continued to house a small, portable Archaic cult statue (mentioned by Pausanias) and sacrifices to Zeus continued to be made on an altar which remained much closer to the 'temple of Hera' than it did to the 'temple of Zeus'.[28] This raises the question of what the new temple, and the gold and ivory statue it was built to contain, was for. Gigantic chryselephantine statues were clearly not cult statues in the old sense, if by that we mean statues which could embody the

---

[26] On the state of Olympia in 480 BC, see Drees 1968: 111–21. On the treasuries in particular, see Adler *et al.* 1892: 40–56.

[27] On the excavation of the stadium, see Adler *et al.* 1892: 63–8; Kunze and Schleif 1938: 5–27; 1939: 5–29; Kunze 1967: 16–82. The most convincing reconstruction of the location of the early stadia (I and II), however, is by Brulotte 1994. For the finds from well 34, including the captured Persian helmet, see Kunze 1961: 129–37; 1967: 25–7.

[28] For the earlier statue of Zeus in the 'temple of Hera', see Pausanias V.17.1.

deity on all occasions, and so could be carried in sacred processions. In so far as chryselephantine statues 'presenced' the god within the sanctuary, that presence was fixed and immovable. In this sense, chryselephantine statues represent a radically new form of imagining the divine.

Why then did fifth-century Greeks expend so much time, skill and effort in creating these statues? Pausanias, who describes all of them in some detail, is little help here. He seems to take the purpose of these objects as read – he cannot imagine a future audience (such as ourselves) who might be perplexed as to what purpose they served. This is a classic problem of hermeneutics. Our situation, with regard to Pausanias (and Pausanias' understanding of these statues), is exactly comparable to that of the Moorish (Spanish Muslim) philosopher Averroes, who (as imagined by Jorge Luis Borges) is engaged in writing a commentary, for a Muslim audience, on Aristotle's *Poetics*.[29] Averroes is puzzled by the terms 'comedy' and 'tragedy', terms which are clearly crucial to the *Poetics* and whose meaning Aristotle takes for granted. Aristotle cannot imagine a culture where drama is unknown. Averroes on the other hand lives in a world – Islam – which has no use for drama, and where the very idea of telling a story through a dramatic performance seems absurd. As such, he has no purchase on the terms 'tragedy' and 'comedy'. No amount of philological ingenuity can resolve this question for him. Archaeologists, coming from a culture which no longer has much use for cult statues, have, perforce, to fall back on the available material evidence. Here at least we have better information for the statue of Zeus than for any other chryselephantine image. The statue itself does not survive, and no trace of it was found in the excavations of the temple itself.[30] But Pausanias does mention one other building associated with the statue: the workshop wherein it was constructed. This has been located and excavated.[31] The building itself was clear of debris, but nearby, under 'building G', excavators found a mass of waste material that included parts of ivory tusks and clay matrices for the gold leaf.[32] All this information allows us to make a more accurate reconstruction of what the statue looked like (even if it gets us no closer to explaining what it was for). We can at least say, however, that, to judge by the accounts for the much smaller chryselephantine statue of Asklepios at Epidauros, this image of Zeus must have been the single most expensive item of all the building works undertaken at Olympia in the Classical period. Work on the statue must have begun sometime after 438 BC, and continued for several years (if not decades) thereafter.[33]

[29] On 'Averroes' Search', see Borges 1998: 235–41.

[30] For the temple, see Adler *et al.* 1892: 4–27. For a description of the chryselephantine statue, see Pausanias V.10.2 and V.11.1–11; Strabo, *Geography* VIII.3.30. For a discussion of the relationship between statue and temple, see Coulton 1977: 111–15.

[31] On description of the workshop, see Pausanias V.15.1. On the excavation of the workshop itself, see Mallwitz and Schiering 1964; Snodgrass 1987: 24–7.

[32] On the workshop debris, see Schiering 1991.

[33] See again Pausanias V.11.1–11. For an idea of the cost of the statue, compare the cost of the much smaller chryselephantine statue of Asklepios: Pausanias II.27.2; Burford 1966: 263–74.

Developments in the fourth century were further to separate the cultic from the athletic (figs. 12.6 and 7.10). Such was the popularity of the festival that, some-time after 350 BC, an even grander stadium (stadium III) was constructed. This is the one that visitors can see today. Although, in principle, the stadium remained within the altis, and was connected to the sanctuary proper by means of a barrel-vaulted tunnel (one of the first of its kind in Greece), effectively athletics and acts of sacrifice had been separated off from one another.[34] This segregation was under-lined by the construction of a new stoa – the 'Echohalle' – over what had been the western part of stadium II.[35] As athletics were finally removed from the sight of the altars, so shrines within the altis proper multiplied. Major additions of the fourth century include a Doric temple of the Mother of the Gods (Rhea), and Olympia's only circular structure, the Philippeion, placed suggestively close to the mound of Pelops as a permanent reminder of who, in Greece after the battle of Chaironeia, was now calling the shots.[36]

If developments at Olympia indicate a trend towards the increased separation of activities in Classical times, the same cannot be said of the sanctuary of Apollo at Delphi (fig. 12.7). Here changes seem more modest. There may be several reasons for this. For one thing, the topography of Delphi makes it extremely unlikely that the Pythian games could ever have been held within the temenos of Apollo itself. The slopes are just too steep, and the games must have taken place elsewhere.[37] Of course, new stoas were built within the temenos during the fifth century, notably the portico of the Athenians.[38] But no great impulse to construct a new and more splendid temple of Apollo can be discerned. Indeed when, in the fourth century, the temple itself had to be rebuilt, it was as a faithful copy of its Archaic predecessor.[39] There are two other major structures built in Classical times. One is the Knidian Lesche, whose walls were painted by Polygnotos. This is situated right at the northern edge of the temenos. It is almost certainly a 'double' banqueting room or hestiatorion, similar in plan and purpose to the one at Perachora (fig. 12.8).[40] The other major addition is the theatre, built sometime in the fourth century just to the north-west of the temple itself. Whether or not plays were performed here (this was, after all, a shrine to Dionysos as well as to Apollo) or just choral odes in honour of Apollo it is difficult to say – as it is in general difficult to explain the popularity of theatres well beyond the bounds of sanctuaries of Dionysos. Delphi remained an important oracular shrine and

---

[34] On the third stadium, see Adler *et al.* 1892: 63–8; Kunze and Schleif 1938: 5–27; 1939: 5–29; Kunze 1967: 6–82. On the date of vaulted constructions generally in Greece (including the tunnel), see Boyd 1978.   [35] Adler *et al.* 1892: 70–2; Koenigs 1984.

[36] On the Metröon, see Adler *et al.* 1892: 37–40; on the Philippeion, *ibid.*: 129–33; Miller 1973.

[37] On the stadium generally, see Aupert 1979. The earliest phase of the stadium is Hellenistic, and Aupert (1979: 54) argues that the Pythian games must, from 590 BC until the late fourth century, have taken place elsewhere, 'dans la pleine alluviale de Pleistos, à un endroit non encore localisé entre Krisso et Itea'.   [38] Amandry 1953: 37–121.   [39] Courby 1927: 2–91.

[40] On the foundations of the Knidian Lesche, see Pouilloux 1960: 120–39. On its being a 'hestiatorion', see Tomlinson 1980: 224–8.

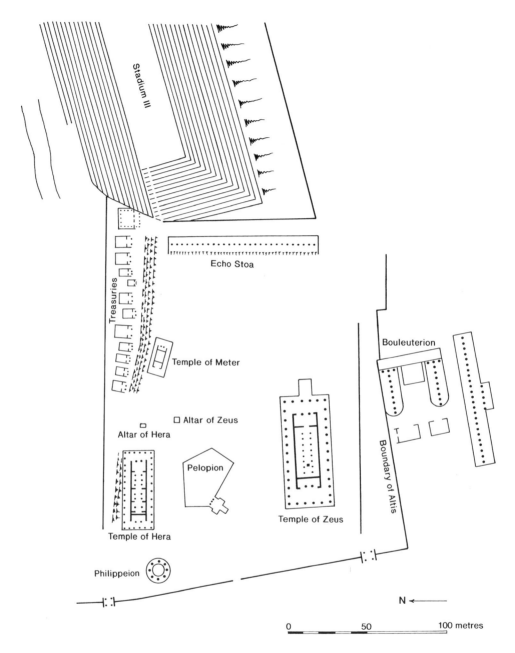

12.6 Plan of Olympia, *c.* 350 BC

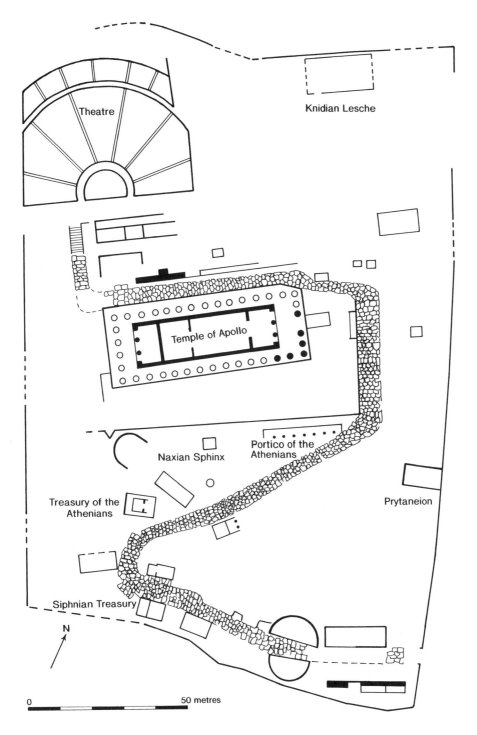

12.7 Plan of Delphi, *c.* 350 BC

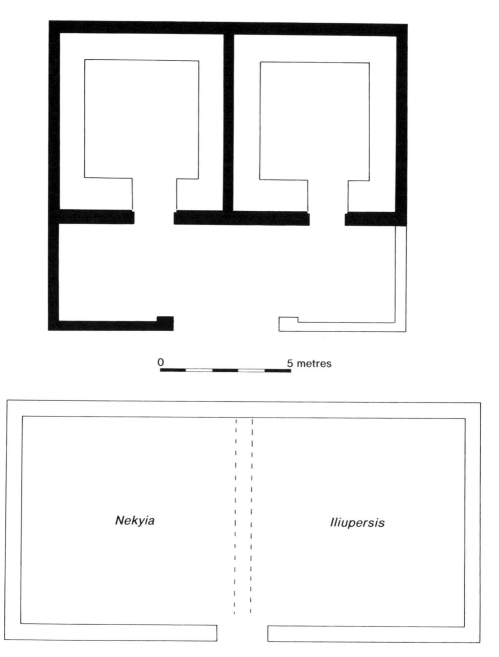

0 ___ 5 metres

12.8 Comparative plans of hestiatoria at Perachora and Delphi

Table 12.1 *Numbers of bronze objects deposited in the sanctuary of Poseidon at Isthmia (from information provided by Raubitschek 1998)*

Date range BC	Sculpture	Vases	Jewellery	Tripods	Total
1000–800	0	0	3	0	3
800–700	1	1	7	6	15
700–600	4	32	26	20	82
600–500	12	58	34	9	113
500–400	11	21	7	1	40
400–300	6	10	13	0	29

Table 12.2 *Numbers of lead figurines deposited in the sanctuary of Artemis Orthia near Sparta (information from Wace 1929, according to the chronology of Boardman 1963b)*

Date range BC	Period	Number
800–650	Lead 0	23
650–620	Lead I	5719
620–560	Lead II	9548
560–500	Lead III and IV	68,822
500–425	Lead V	10,617
425–250	Lead VI	4773

Delphi's Pythian games remained a key event in the 'festival circuit' of Classical times, but this led to few major architectural changes, certainly nothing to compare to the radical shifts we can see at Olympia.

But there is one area where we can detect a radical break with past practice. One of the most striking features of the excavation of Archaic sanctuaries had been the mass of votives uncovered. Votive offerings are mentioned less frequently in discussions of Classical sanctuaries. Is this because there were fewer of them? It would seem so. Snodgrass has noted a marked decline in the deposition of small, portable metal objects from the early fifth century onwards. Table 12.1 shows the number of bronze objects deposited in the sanctuary of Poseidon at Isthmia. By anyone's reckoning, there is a sharp fall in Classical times. Furthermore, far fewer Classical as opposed to Archaic lead figurines were recovered from the shrine of Artemis Orthia near Sparta (table 12.2), and there does seem to have been a spectacular fall in the number of small bronzes dedicated at Olympia.[41] But there

---

[41] For the argument, see Snodgrass 1990b: esp. 288–9. For the data from Artemis Orthia, see Wace 1929; for discussion, see Hodkinson 1998: esp. 107. For the data from Olympia, see Philipp 1981. For the bronzes from Isthmia, see Raubitschek 1998.

seems to have been no let up in the practice of setting up trophies of captured armour. Fifth-century helmets and shields at Olympia seem to be as common as those of the sixth.[42] There are too at Olympia numerous stone bases for bronze statues of athletic victors, most probably of Classical date, statues which have since been lost. And both Delphi and Olympia, as Pausanias notes, had been full of bronze chariot groups, almost none of which have survived. The archaeological record then gives a very poor picture of the number, ostentation and variety of Classical votives. If, however, we were still inclined to read the archaeological record as a direct transcription of social or behavioural reality, we might take note of the huge increase in Classical as compared to Archaic terracottas. Exact figures are hard to come by, but both the British Museum and the Louvre have many more Classical than Archaic examples, both of terracotta plaques and of figures in the round.[43] We might then be inclined to infer that Greeks had again changed their depositional practices, preferring in Classical times cheap terracotta to expensive metal. But there would be several objections to such an inference. For one thing, terracottas are not necessarily votive. Many have been found in houses. As with many objects collected for museums long ago, we do not know their contexts, and cannot really tell what any individual object was for.[44]

From all this we might be inclined to infer that the changes between the Archaic and Classical periods were small, and reflect nothing more than minor shifts in fashion, exacerbated through post-depositional factors. Ostentatious Classical bronzes have been melted down; smaller, portable objects have simply been buried in pits or wells. But this very observation underlines a crucial difference between Archaic and Classical practices. For, if Classical Greeks did dedicate small metal objects in large numbers, why have these not survived in later pits or wells? The most economical answer must be that personal possessions (at least if made of metal) had ceased to be thought of as appropriate gifts to the gods. This represents a shift from 'raw' to 'converted' offerings. In earlier times, Greeks dedicated the small objects that they owned, objects whose primary function was unrelated to their place in a sanctuary (a 'raw' object). In Classical times, votives offered seem increasingly to have been made primarily to be used as dedications (a 'converted' one). In earlier times too, masses of smaller votives were regularly cleared away. From the fifth century onward, the more expensive votives (partic-

---

[42] On the assumption that most of the Corinthian and the bulk of the 'Illyrian' and 'Chalcidian' helmets from Olympia are stylistically late Archaic and later, many must be of Classical date. The only really closely datable helmet is the Miltiades helm, which must have been made shortly before 490 BC; see Kunze 1956: 69–74. On the finds of helmets generally, see Kunze 1958: 125–51; 1961: 56–128; 1967: 116–83; 1994: 27–100. For the finds contexts, see in particular Kunze and Schleif 1938: 5–27; Kunze 1967: 25–7. On the date and significance of these finds, see discussion in Snodgrass 1990b: 289.

[43] On terracottas in the British Museum, see Higgins 1954; on those in the Louvre, see Mollard-Besques 1954; 1972.

[44] On Classical terracottas generally, see Higgins 1967: 57–94. On those from domestic contexts, see Robinson 1933b (Olynthos) and Wiegand and Schrader 1904: 330–66 (Priene). Most of the terracottas from Priene, however, are Hellenistic in date.

ularly those dedicated by states) tended to remain where they were. As Snodgrass says, the shift

> can be explained by reference to a change of preference, from 'raw' to 'converted' dedications . . . With a state offering to commemorate a victory, for example, the 'raw' offering of captured arms has its 'converted' counterpart in the form of an inscribed statue or group. A woman who dedicates an ornate female statuette, where her grandmother would have offered her personal jewelry, exemplifies the same change.[45]

This does seem to represent a fundamental shift in votive behaviour. It is not a shift that is quite so straightforward as the statistics themselves would imply. It is one, however, that has created a strange disjunction between the literary and archaeological record. Pausanias clearly had little or no knowledge of the vast quantities of 'raw' offerings to be found in the pits and wells of Olympia. What he saw were the ostentatious, 'converted' offerings made by the major political players of Classical Greece, offerings which, for the most part, have not survived. It is the states which have become the principal dedicants of major offerings. Individuals of course continued to make dedications, but these seem increasingly to have been of cheaper materials, such as terracotta.

Terracottas, however, are objects which regularly cross the boundary between the domestic and the sacred, between the city and its sanctuaries. It is a paradox of the Classical period that, while settlements come to be better defined as cities, so too cities increasingly come to resemble sanctuaries. Classical sanctuaries were, more and more, defined by a temenos wall. Classical cities too were walled. A city wall is a kind of temenos. Just as the temenos separated the sacred from the profane, so Classical Greeks had very firm ideas as to what should be inside the walls (houses, marketplaces, certain sanctuaries) and what outside (burials and cemeteries). It is time to take a closer look at Classical cities.

12.4 The shape of the city

When we think of a Greek city, we think of a city with walls, streets, sanctuaries and public spaces, located often on steep ground with an acropolis above. This kind of city, however, is a late development. It is, of course, quite possible that some cities, notably Corinth, had been surrounded by walls at some point in the Archaic period.[46] It was only in Classical times that walls were built around other Greek cities. Athens, for example, seems to have been unwalled before 478 BC.[47] It is hard to get a clear picture of how these older cities, such as Athens and Corinth, developed during the Classical period. Athens is something of a special case (see chapter 13 below). Our picture from Corinth is patchy. We can at least be sure that the great enceinte enclosing the Acrocorinth, the Potters' Quarter and

---

[45] Snodgrass 1990b: 292. The terminology of 'raw' and 'converted' offerings is borrowed from Walter Burkert (1987), adapted in turn from Lévi-Strauss.   [46] See Williams 1982.
[47] According to Thucydides I.90–3.

the agora had been completed in Classical times, though what proportion of this area was densely settled is not quite so clear. We can be reasonably sure that the production of terracottas and pottery from the Potters' Quarter was at more or less the same level it had been in Archaic times.[48] We can probably infer that the population of older cities also increased during Classical times. This seems to be the picture we gain from the 'urban surveys' undertaken in recent years. Occupation at Phlius (Phleious) in the north-west Peloponnese, and at Thespiai and Haliartos in Boeotia, does seem denser – at the very least, the Classical inhabitants of these cities seem to have produced more finds.[49] But we have a very poor idea of the internal structure of these older cities. For this, we have to turn to communities which only become prominent in the later fifth and fourth centuries BC.

Halieis in the Argolid, Olynthos in Chalkidiki, Messene in the south-west Peloponnese and Priene in Ionia were all relatively new foundations. But they were all autonomous communities (poleis), and had to look the part. They had to have walls, walls which would impress upon visitors the fact that these were the centres of independent states. By about 350 BC each one of these cities had been surrounded by fortifications, consisting of long walls interspersed with towers. These walls were not mortared, but were put together using a variety of drystone techniques. The word 'drystone' perhaps implies a crudity of construction that would be the very opposite of the truth. All of these walls were very carefully built from large blocks, blocks which were made to fit one another almost perfectly. Unlike Mycenaean or Minoan walls, not a gap can be seen in Classical Greek masonry. A standard of drystone wall construction was reached which was not equalled by anyone else apart from the Incas.

Walls have been a neglected subject of late. The best place to study them is the sanctuary of Eleusis in Attica, a site which provides us with a continuous sequence of walling types from the Geometric period onwards.[50] Here we can see that by the middle of the sixth century the crude stone foundations of Geometric times, intended to provide simply a base for a mudbrick superstructure, had been replaced by something much grander. The foundations of walls now consisted of large trapezoidal blocks. The superstructure of even large fortification walls remained mudbrick for much of the fifth century, and at Eleusis a few such walls survive. During the latter part of the Classical period walls built entirely of stone became more common. Traditionally, polygonal styles of masonry have tended to be dated earlier than ashlar or other isodomic styles, including trapezoidal.[51] In fact, there is no such neat pattern to the development of walls. Though many polygonal walls are clearly early in date, polygonal styles of masonry, including

[48] For Corinth, see Stilwell 1948: 3–62, 82–113; Stilwell and Benson 1984. For a general discussion of pottery production at Corinth, see Arafat and Morgan 1989.

[49] For Phlius (Phleious), see Alcock 1991b; for Haliartos and Thespiai, see Bintliff and Snodgrass 1988.

[50] For Eleusis, see Noack 1927. For walls generally, see Scranton 1941.

[51] For the traditional 'evolutionary' dating of walls, see Scranton 1941: 43–4 (Lesbian), 68 (polygonal), 98 (trapezoidal) and 99–136 (ashlar).

the 'Lesbian' used in the portico of the Athenians at Delphi, continued to be used well into the Hellenistic period.[52] Ashlar, polygonal and trapezoidal were alternative styles, used for a variety of reasons both aesthetic and practical. The aesthetic dimension should not be underestimated, since ashlar and trapezoidal masonry in particular could be decorated in many different ways. In fortification walls, the face could be left rough, though the edges were carefully drafted. This is called 'quarry face'. In other circumstances, a 'chisel face' might be preferred, or the ashlar wall could be dressed to an almost flat surface.

The sophistication achieved in Greek walling is best illustrated at Messene. This city, on the slopes of Mt Ithome, was founded in 369 BC, after the Thebans and their allies had defeated the Spartans at the battle of Leuctra, so freeing the Messenians from their centuries-long servitude to their Spartan masters.[53] The new city's first priority was strong defence, to protect against any Spartan revanche. For this reason, the area was enclosed with large walls by Messenians, Thebans and their allies at some speed. Yet the walls and towers themselves show little signs of haste, still less of carelessness. Indeed the walls are continuously bonded. That is, every tower is firmly fixed to the walls around it, and every stretch of wall to each of its two towers (fig. 14.7). There are no gaps which could be exploited by an attacking force. The gates too show great refinement. The Arcadian gate, facing west and north, forms a circle. Any hostile force that had made its way through the first gate would find itself surrounded. It is also highly decorated. Whilst the outside wall is in 'quarry face', the higher courses of walling on the inside of the gate are in 'chisel face'. The walls too are interspersed with niches, presumably to hold statues.[54] This gate was built as much to impress visitors as to provide a means of defence.

Unfortunately we know little about the internal layout of Messene. We know it had a theatre, and the Asklepion (which Pausanias describes) has been thoroughly explored.[55] But to understand urban space in more detail we have to turn to other sites. Chief amongst these is Olynthos, which was thoroughly explored by American archaeologists in the 1920s, 1930s and 1940s.[56] In Archaic times Olynthos had been a small hilltop town, no larger or more important than any other town in the area. After 479 BC, population began to increase, particularly after Olynthos was chosen to be the capital of the Chalcidian league in 432 BC. This 'synoecism' resulted in a large influx of new people who had to be accommodated. A new settlement was built on the 'North hill' (fig. 12.9). This new area was laid out on a strict grid plan: houses and streets in regular blocks, and of uniform size.[57] A similar principle, on this occasion using a regular block size of 100 by 600 ft, which could be subdivided into 24 units of about 50 by 50 feet, was

---

[52] Amandry 1953: 37–58.   [53] Lawrence 1979: 382–5; Alcock 1998: 179–83.
[54] Lawrence 1979: 318, 395–6.   [55] Pausanias IV.31.10; Alcock 1998: 187–9.
[56] For excavations at Olynthos, see Robinson 1930; 1933a; 1946; 1950; Robinson and Graham 1938.
[57] See especially Robinson and Graham 1938: 1–17, 42–4; Jameson 1990b: 95–7; Hoepfner and Schwandner 1994: 68–113.

OLYNTH

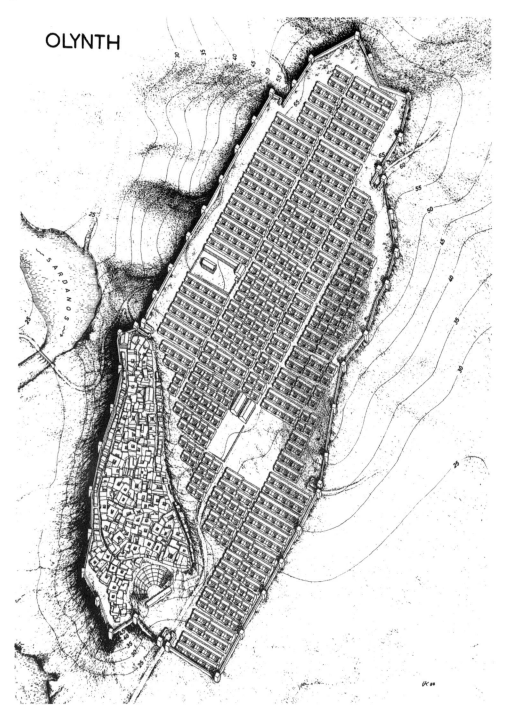

12.9 Overall plan of Olynthos, *c.* 350 BC

used at Halieis. Here though there is no single alignment to the grid. Different grids were applied to the eastern and western parts of the city, a compromise partly dictated by topography.[58]

The 'grid plan' has often been seen as the brainchild of the architect Hippodamos of Miletos, who was active around 478 BC. Certainly, many new cities of the early fifth century, such as Piraeus, Miletos and Rhodes, were built on strict orthogonal principles.[59] Archaeology however has shown that this idea goes back much earlier. Megara Hyblaia, founded in the late eighth century, had been laid out on some kind of a grid, albeit not one that was strictly rectilinear.[60] The houses at Vroulia on Rhodes (fig. 8.2) had been built in regular lines.[61] Rectangular blocks of houses, or 'insulae', had formed the basis for Greek town plans in Sicily and on the coast of the Black Sea in the late sixth century BC.[62] Even the Etruscan city of Marzobotto, founded in the sixth century, seems to have been arranged according to strict 'Hippodamian' principles.[63] Rather than trying to locate the origins of this idea in a particular personality or presiding genius, it may be more productive to note the similarities between urban and rural land division. The layout of house lots in the city and agricultural plots in the country around seems to have been arrived at using the same techniques of surveying and according to the same principles. Each citizen would be entitled to both a plot of land in the country and a house in the city – both were necessary conditions of citizenship. Of course, agricultural plots were invariably larger, but Jameson's observation still holds: 'the Greeks viewed a town as a common area of housing for all participants in the life of the community: a new town was one where approximately equal plots of land could be measured out and assigned to the members of the community'.[64] In other words, the city represented an ideal. The urban core of the polis, the asty, represented in microcosm the social arrangements and divisions of the territory of the polis as a whole. Some scholars have gone further, and seen in the fact of land division the essential principle of the Classical Greek polis: the polis was a community of (male) equals, each entitled to his share of land and housing.[65]

The city as the physical embodiment of the principle of the polis was however a development that only really became apparent in the fourth century. Perhaps the best example of the Classical city is Priene in Asia Minor (modern western Turkey) (fig. 12.10). The new city of Priene was founded on an entirely new site sometime after 352 BC.[66] The city sits in a splendidly defensible location. Its impressive walls enclose an acropolis and a lower town, built on a gentle slope.

---

[58] For Halieis, see Jameson 1990b: 95–7; 1969; Boyd and Rudolph 1978. For the principles of urban and rural land division, see Boyd and Jameson 1981.

[59] Hoepfner and Schwandner 1994: 17–67.

[60] Vallet *et al.* 1983: 144–9; Hoepfner and Schwandner 1994: 4–5.   [61] Kinch 1914.

[62] Hoepfner and Schwandner 1994: 6–16.   [63] Mansurelli 1979.   [64] Jameson 1990b: 95–6.

[65] As argued by Jameson 1990a; on land division see Boyd and Jameson 1981.

[66] On the siting and foundation of 'new' Priene, see Wiegand and Schrader 1904: 7–34; Hoepfner and Schwandner 1994: 188–9. No one knows where 'old' Priene may have been.

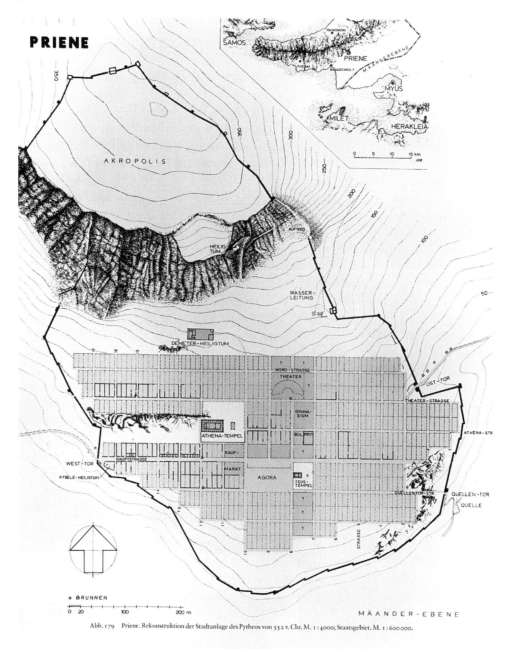

Abb. 179   Priene. Rekonstruktion der Stadtanlage des Pytheos von 352 v. Chr. M. 1 : 4000; Staatsgebiet. M. 1 : 600 000.

12.10 Overall plan of Priene, *c.* 350 BC

The city now overlooks a flat plain that, in ancient times, was an arm of the sea, over which the neighbouring city of Miletos could be seen to the south-west. Inside were houses, built on strong stone foundations, and laid out on a strict grid plan. Care was taken to provide the city with an adequate water supply, with many streets having their own public fountains.[67] At the centre of the city is a marketplace, or agora, and a fine temple of Athena.[68] The city is provided with every amenity that any of its citizens might want – from a gymnasium, where he could exercise, to a council house or bouleuterion, where the city's fate was decided. All these are splendid examples of their types.[69] Priene clearly was an independent Greek city designed to look like an independent Greek city. Still, there is a certain irony for the modern visitor who looks around Priene. To be sure, its building was begun when the independent city-state was still a practical reality throughout most of Greece, and historians may be quite right to link it to a 'democratic revival' in the middle of the fourth century. But it cannot have been completed that quickly, and its real heyday was in Hellenistic times, when Priene was a dependency first of the Seleucids of Antioch and then of the Attalids of Pergamon. It may seem at first to be the very model of a democratic social order, but in reality it came to represent a purely cultural ideal of 'Greekness' which was soon to be exported throughout the Near East.

Still at least Priene, together with Olynthos and Halieis, seems to represent the Classical ideal of the city-state – even if, in the case of Olynthos, Philip of Macedon was to bring that ideal to an abrupt close in 348 BC. The space within the walls represents in microcosm the space of the whole polis and its territory. Aristotle had gone further, and claimed that the city was like a household writ large.[70] Was then the Greek house the Greek city in miniature? Certainly, some scholars have been inclined to see in the houses starker evidence of the essential class and gender inequalities of the ancient polis. Are the same cultural principles at work in the household as in the city? It is time to look at the physical evidence at greater magnification and closer up.

12.5 The Classical house and the Classical household

There is a curious gap in the record of ancient Greek houses. We have a fairly good impression of what an eighth- or seventh-century house looked like from excavations at Vroulia on Rhodes or Zagora on Andros. But sixth-century houses are very

---

[67] On the layout of streets, see Wiegand and Schrader 1904: 35–67, 300–3; Hoepfner and Schwandner 1994: 190–8. On the water supply, see Wiegand and Schrader 1904: 68–80; Hoepfner and Schwandner 1994: 201–2.

[68] On the Agora at Priene, see Wiegand and Schrader 1904: 185–218. On the temple of Athena, see *ibid.*: 81–136; on the sculptures from this temple, Carter 1983.

[69] On the various other buildings at Priene, see Wiegand and Schrader 1904: 219–84. On the stoas in the agora, see Coulton 1976: 277–9. A clearer picture of which public buildings are Classical and which Hellenistic is given by Hoepfner and Schwandner 1994: 198–208, 222–5.

[70] Aristotle, *Politics* 1,252–3.

hard to come by. There may be a few from Corinth or Athens, but these seem to belong to the earlier part of that century.[71] The Classical 'courtyard house' seems to appear, without obvious forerunners, in the second half of the fifth century BC. Our best evidence once more comes from Olynthos, where the excavators made a particular study of the 'Hellenic House'.[72] The grid plan of this city enforces a degree of uniformity on house size (though there are some large houses which seem to occupy not one, but two house plots) (fig. 12.11). Though the plans of houses, however, are by no means identical, they do seem to conform to some general principles of design. They are all courtyard houses, where the main wall of the house separates it from the street outside. All the rooms faced inwards – these were rooms without a view. Or, as Jameson puts it: 'the court is not a front yard, separated by a fence or low wall from the street and accessible to view and to conversation from a passer-by, a transitional element between the outside and the inside, as in most modern Greek villages. It is entirely interior.'[73] The Classical Greek house then was a fine and private place. Its construction was traditional. Mud brick walls were generally built on a stone socle. A house generally had a timber frame, to support the second storey and the roof, which in turn was generally covered with terracotta tiles. Where a courtyard house has an internal porch, with columns, it is often referred to as a 'pastas' house.[74]

Though no two houses are identical, each house at Olynthos shared common features. Many had latrines and bathrooms, sometimes equipped with clay bathtubs.[75] As at Priene, attention had to be given to the public water supply. Some water was channelled from springs, though some houses did have their own cisterns. Most had storage rooms for pithoi (large clay storage jars), a method of keeping grain that goes back to the Bronze Age. It is clear too that the courtyard, though cut off from the street, was not purely domestic in the way that we would understand the term. The courtyard was a working area, as the numerous finds of saddle querns, mortars and olive presses testify. Houses, even in cities, were centres for agricultural activity.[76]

Not every house excavated had every one of these features. Each did however have its own 'oikos-unit', a living space equipped with a cooking area and (sometimes) a bathroom. Oikos means house, and the term 'oikos-unit' implies that here is the physical heart of the household. But surprisingly few of these 'oikos units' had a stone-built hearth. Indeed only seven out of the forty-two houses excavated

---

[71] For sixth-century buildings in Athens, see Wycherley and Thompson 1972: 25–9. For those in Corinth, see Williams and Fisher 1971: 3–10; 1972: 145–9; Williams *et al.* 1974: 14–24. For a general discussion, see Morris 1998a: 33–5.

[72] Nevett 1995a; 1995b; Robinson and Graham 1938. See now Nevett 1999: 53–79.

[73] Jameson 1990b: 97.

[74] Robinson and Graham 1938: 214–19, 223–303; Hoepfner and Schwandner 1994: 104–6.

[75] Robinson and Graham 1938: 135–7, 199–203 (bathrooms); *ibid.*: 205–6 (latrines). The Classical latrines (such as they are) of Olynthos are of the simplest type. See also Hoepfner and Schwandner 1994: 96–103.

[76] Robinson and Graham 1938: 207–8, 312–16 (storage rooms and pithoi); *ibid.*: 91, 307–11 (water supply); *ibid.*: 128–9, 326–43 (quernstones, mortars, olive presses, etc.).

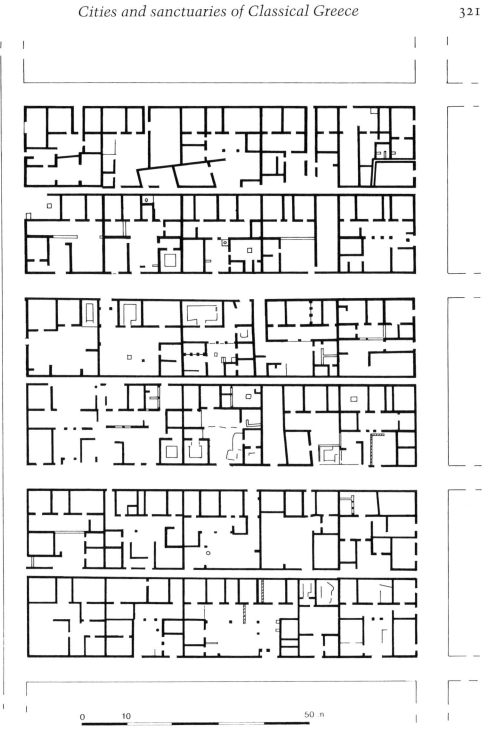

12.11 Blocks of houses at Olynthos

at Olynthos were equipped with this feature, which literary sources had led archae-ologists to expect in every home. Here literary ideals of 'hearth and home' are at variance with social and archaeological reality.[77] This has led many to disbelieve the archaeology, and suggest that stone hearths may have been the particular target of stone robbers. But it is clear that kitchens and 'oikos-units' could function per-fectly well without a hearth. Food could be cooked on portable braziers, of which several examples in both terracotta and bronze have been found on the site.[78]

As well as a kitchen, most houses at Olynthos seem to have been furnished with a dining room. This room seems to be the *andron* of Classical literature. 'Andron' means 'men's room', a space reserved for men to dine and drink together in a sym-posion. As in Archaic times, the symposion was a largely male affair, vividly illus-trated on many fifth-century Attic pots. These andrownes are, in a sense, smaller versions of the hestiatoria found in Classical sanctuaries. But, whereas the hestia-toria at Perachora or the Knidian Lesche at Delphi could accommodate eleven to fifteen symposiasts (assuming one symposiast per couch), only seven or eight could have comfortably been fitted into an andron in a typical house at Olynthos.[79] A dinner party at one of the smaller andrownes at Olynthos might have been very far from the aristocratic sympotic ideal, at least as represented on pots painted by the Brygos painter. There would be few gold and silver vessels, and no flute girls for entertainment. None the less, the andron was clearly regarded as a particularly important room in the house. If any room in the house was plastered, it would be the andron. Sometimes it was painted too, and frequently had to be entered through an anteroom, which in turn was often richly decorated.[80] Many of the houses at Olynthos – and not merely the grander ones such as the 'Villa of Good Fortune' (fig. 12.12) or the 'House of the Comedian' – had andrownes whose floors were decorated with pebble mosaics.[81] The attention paid to this room in Greek houses parallels the richness with which hestiatoria in sanctuaries, such as the Knidian Lesche, were decorated. In both city and sanctuary, it is sympotic space which is most deserving of a good painter or a good mosaicist.

Mention of either the kitchen or the andron inevitably raises questions of male and female space. Gender relations have become something of a preoccupation of

---

[77] Robinson and Graham 1938: 185–99; Mylonas 1946. What Robinson and Graham identified as a kitchen in 1938 was called an 'oikos-unit' by Mylonas in 1946. The room with the hearth (if there was one) was the 'oikos', and what had been called a 'flue' was reinterpreted as the cooking area. For stone-built hearths, see Robinson and Graham 1938: 114–16. See also discussion in Jameson 1990b: 105–6.

[78] For example, the bronze brazier in house A.xi.10; Robinson and Graham 1938: 128–9. For terracotta braziers, see Robinson 1930: 46, 65–6, 111; Robinson and Graham 1938: 63 n.9, 186.

[79] On hestiatoria in sanctuaries, see Tomlinson 1969: 164–72; 1980: 224–8. On the andron at Olynthos, see Robinson and Graham 1938: 171–85; Jameson 1990b: 98–9.

[80] Robinson and Graham 1938: 171–85, 291 (wall plaster). For the image of the symposion created by the Brygos painter, see Robertson 1992: 93–100.

[81] On the 'Villa of Good Fortune' and the 'House of the Comedian', see Robinson and Graham 1938: 55–68. On mosaics at Olynthos, see Robinson 1933: 1–14; 1946: 323–68. On the development of mosaics generally, see Robertson 1965; Salzmann 1982: esp. 98–104 for Olynthos. On mosaics in context, see now Westgate 1998.

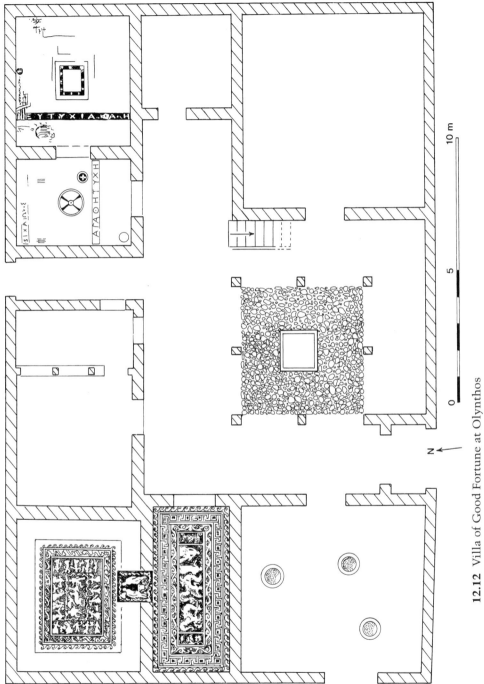

12.12 Villa of Good Fortune at Olynthos

10 m

5

0

N

Classical scholars ever since the publication of Sarah Pomeroy's *Goddesses, Whores, Wives and Slaves* in 1975.[82] And there are indeed some Greek terms (notably *andronitis*, 'man's' or 'husband's space'; and *gynaikonitis*, 'woman's' or 'wife's space') which imply that space within the Greek household was separated into male and female spheres. Certainly, it is likely that the dining room – the andron – was reserved for the man of the house and his male guests; it is more than probable too (though not certain) that cooking in the kitchen was undertaken largely by women. But archaeological evidence to support a notion of the rigid segregation of male and female space is hard to find. Take weaving as an example. Images on pots indicate that this was regarded as women's work. If there were a clearly defined female space, we should then be able to detect this by the distribution of loomweights. But loomweights at Olynthos do not seem to have been found in any one particular area. Looms seem to have been moved around the courtyard to make the best use of the light, or the shade. There seems in practice to have been little rigid division of space according to gender in the Classical household.[83]

Greek men none the less seem to have had very firm ideas about where women (and their wives in particular) should and should not be, judging by the sentiments expressed in the speeches of fourth-century Athenian orators. Men should be seen in public, and not allow strangers to intrude too much on their wives; women should stay and look after hearth and home. Here, as in the case of hearths, literary ideals may be at variance with practical reality.[84] Rigid segregation may not in fact have been practised. But, it is not unreasonable to suppose that women may have been secluded within the home, rather as women are in some Islamic countries today. Nevett has pointed out that the widespread adoption of the 'single entrance courtyard house' is something archaeologists have to explain, and a part of the explanation may be that it is a house plan designed to achieve a measure, not only of privacy, but of seclusion.[85] How popular then was this house type in Classical Greece? And what has happened to the marked differences between regions evident in the Archaic period?

Courtyard houses are certainly common enough in the Greek world of the fourth century BC. They are found everywhere from Thasos in the north Aegean to Sicily. There are none the less some regional differences. The andron seems to be much less easy to detect in Sicily and Magna Graecia.[86] Sometimes, houses were built on the same general plan as at Olynthos but on a larger scale. The 'House of the Mosaics' at Eretria for example is much grander than any contemporary house at Olynthos, and its andron is much more richly decorated.[87] At

---

[82] Pomeroy 1975. See also Walker 1993.   [83] On looms, see Robinson and Graham 1938: 167–9.

[84] For suggestions in literature of a segregation of 'male' and 'female' space, see Lysias III.6. For the origins of the terms andronitis and gynaikonitis, see Lysias I.9–10. For a discussion of this evidence, see Nevett 1995b: 363–4; Jameson 1990b: 104.

[85] For arguments in favour of 'seclusion' see Pomeroy 1975: 79–82; Walker 1993. For Nevett's interpretation, see Nevett 1994; 1995a; 1995b; and now Nevett 1999.   [86] Nevett 1995a: 102–7.

[87] Ducrey *et al.* 1993: 31–48, 85–96.

Kassope in western Greece, courtyards seem to have been very small, whereas the central living space or oikos was comparatively spacious.[88] Even in those areas of Greece where the 'pastas' form was not adopted, the principle of the internal courtyard was retained. At Priene, houses were built to a distinctive, local plan (fig. 12.13). One set of rooms faced another across a courtyard. On one side there was a four-room set with a porch (or prostas), two living rooms and a small andron; on the other a set of smaller and meaner structures. The andron here was much smaller even than those at Olynthos – rarely could more than two guests be accommodated at once.[89] The particular plan – and distinctive asymmetry – of these houses may seem to indicate that a more rigid pattern of gendered space may have prevailed at Priene. Gender division may not however be the reason for this particular house plan. Houses at Priene were built on a south-facing slope. They seem to have been designed to allow winter light to penetrate the furthest corners of the living area, while providing maximum shade in summer. The only designated 'female space' seems to have been on the first floor.[90]

It is clear none the less that at Priene, as at Olynthos, the 'internal courtyard' principle is being adhered to. Only on Crete do we see a different pattern. Of course, few Classical houses on Crete have been excavated, and fewer still with any regard to the distribution of finds within. Still, rock-cut features which formed a major part of houses on the First and Second Acropoleis of Praisos have been planned in some detail (figs 12.14 and 12.15).[91] Here the layout of the houses seems to be dictated by natural topography – there is no orthogonal grid plan. Moreover, the haphazard arrangement of rooms, basins, cisterns, cellars and wells is difficult to reconcile with any principle of privacy or seclusion. There is no andron, nor any sign of internal courtyards. Even the grandest of houses at Praisos, the so-called 'Almond Tree House', seems to have been built on quite different principles from those of Olynthos or Priene.[92] At Praisos, as elsewhere on Crete, a more open arrangement of space seems to have prevailed, with each house being accessible to its neighbour. The layout of Cretan Classical houses seems to resemble much more closely the pattern seen in a modern Greek village than it does the plans of Classical houses on the mainland or in Ionia.

Crete aside, the impression one gains from this brief survey of Classical house types is that there is much less regional variation than there had been in Archaic times. Just as the internal courtyard house is the most popular house form, so the orthogonal grid is the city plan most prevalent in the 'new towns' of Classical times. One could argue that both the grid and the courtyard house embody similar 'structuring principles'. The courtyard house separates women from public gaze and public life; the grid plan, in creating units of equal size,

---

[88] Hoepfner and Schwandner 1994: 145–61.
[89] Wiegand and Schrader 1904: 285–97, 319–28; Hoepfner and Schwandner 1994: 208–19.
[90] Hoepfner and Schwandner 1994: 210–19, 318–30.   [91] Whitley *et al.* 1995: 416–27; 1999: 253–6.
[92] Bosanquet 1902: 259–70. Recently more Classical and later houses have been excavated on Crete. But the ones at Eleutherna, for example, seem to be largely of Hellenistic date.

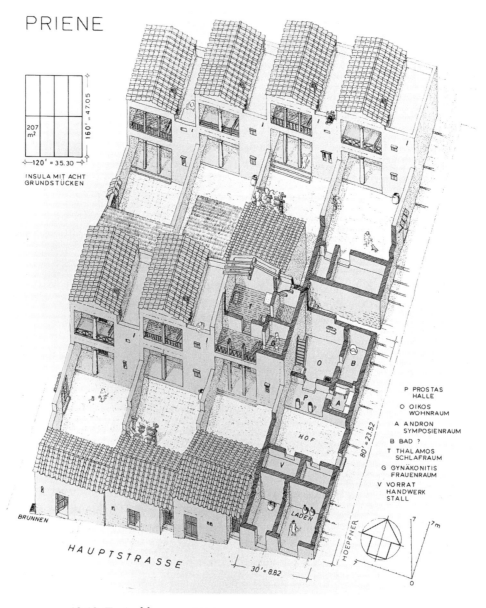

PRIENE

INSULA MIT ACHT
GRUNDSTÜCKEN

207 m²

160' = 47.05

120' = 35.30

80' = 23.52

30' = 8.82

BRUNNEN

HAUPTSTRASSE

HOF

LADEN

HOEPFNER

P PROSTAS
  HALLE

O OIKOS
  WOHNRAUM

A ANDRON
  SYMPOSIENRAUM

B BAD ?

T THALAMOS
  SCHLAFRAUM

G GYNÄKONITIS
  FRAUENRAUM

V VORRAT
  HANDWERK
  STALL

7m

12.13 Typical houses at Priene

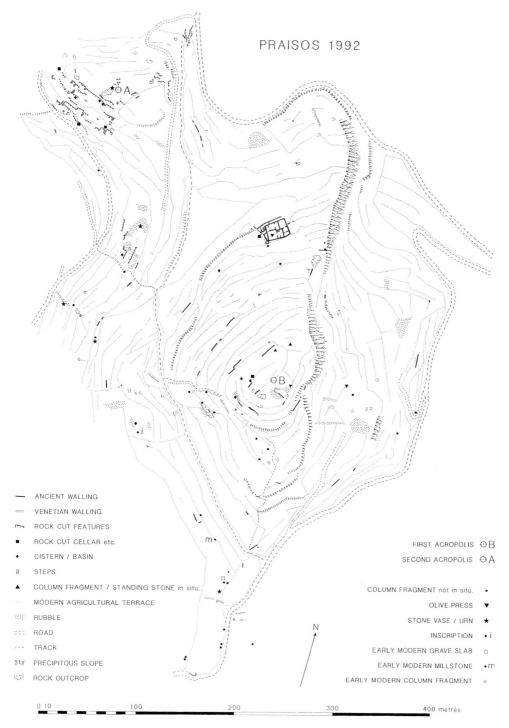

PRAISOS 1992

— ANCIENT WALLING
⹀ VENETIAN WALLING
⌐⌐ ROCK CUT FEATURES
■ ROCK CUT CELLAR etc.
◆ CISTERN / BASIN
⫫ STEPS
▲ COLUMN FRAGMENT / STANDING STONE in situ.
— MODERN AGRICULTURAL TERRACE
⠿ RUBBLE
⠿ ROAD
--- TRACK
ⱦⱦ PRECIPITOUS SLOPE
ⓦ ROCK OUTCROP

FIRST ACROPOLIS ⊖B
SECOND ACROPOLIS ⊖A

COLUMN FRAGMENT not in situ. •
OLIVE PRESS ▼
STONE VASE / URN ★
INSCRIPTION • i
EARLY MODERN GRAVE SLAB □
EARLY MODERN MILLSTONE • m
EARLY MODERN COLUMN FRAGMENT ○

N

0 10   100   200   300   400 metres

12.14 Overall plan of Praisos

STEPS

ANCIENT WALLING

ROCK CUT FEATURE

STONE/RUBBLE SPREAD

MODERN AGRICULTURAL TERRACE

ROCK OUTCROP

PRECIPITOUS SLOPE

PRAISOS 1994   2nd ACROPOLIS

0   10   50 metres

12.15 Detail of rock-cut houses on Second Acropolis of Praisos

exemplifies the principle of equality between citizen males. Seclusion of women and the assertion of male equality were the two principles upon which the Classical polis was built. This was particularly true of the democratic polis. If ideology underlies architectural expression, perhaps we should seek the beginnings of such ideas in that city which, above all others, came to represent the principles of Classical democracy – namely Classical Athens.

CHAPTER 13

THE ARCHAEOLOGY OF DEMOCRACY: CLASSICAL ATHENS

13.1 Archaeology and democracy

Of all Greek cities, Athens is the one we know most about. Athenians were the most articulate of Greeks. Whereas the literature produced by Athenians of the Archaic period is meagre, even in comparison to a small state like Mytilene, for the fifth and fourth centuries almost all of the more celebrated Greek dramatists, historians and philosophers were, in some sense, Athenian.[1] Moreover it was Athenian culture that later Greeks most valued, whatever regime they happened to live under. Just as the Athenian literary legacy was highly prized, so was Athenian art and architecture. Pheidias, Alkamenes and Praxiteles were all Athenian, and the Parthenon remained a paradigm of the Classical long after Athens as a city had lost all power and influence. If one wanted to define the Classical by demonstration, one could do much worse than describe Athenian literature and art. Such an undertaking, however, might well serve as a kind of belle-lettrist culture history, but it would not be archaeology. For archaeology's principal concern must always be to relate material culture to culture in general.

It was in the Classical period that the 'Greek city' took shape both as an ideal and as a practical reality. Such a city necessarily represented certain ideas about urban and domestic space. Athens may not have been the first Greek state to have become a democracy, but it was certainly the most influential polis in Classical times. In the late sixth century, this city received a new, democratic, constitution. Many historians have seen the literary and artistic achievements of fifth- and fourth-century Athens as intimately connected to this new political order. Athens was, in this view, not simply a polis that happened to have a democratic constitution. Athenian art and literature were the products of a democratic *culture*. Other scholars have noted that many Greek cities in Classical times, such as Olynthos and Priene, seem to have been designed on 'democratic' principles. The material culture of these communities seems to express certain democratic, or at

---

[1] Fifth- and fourth-century Athenians included the dramatists Aeschylus, Sophocles, Euripides, Aristophanes and (much later) Menander; the historians Thucydides and Xenophon; the orators Aeschines and Demosthenes; and the philosophers Socrates and Plato. There are, to be sure, major figures of these centuries who were not Athenian by birth; the lyric poets Pindar and Bacchylides, the sophists Protagoras and Gorgias, the historian Herodotos and the philosopher Aristotle. But of these last two, the former was markedly pro-Athenian, and the latter effectively became an Athenian resident (if not a citizen).

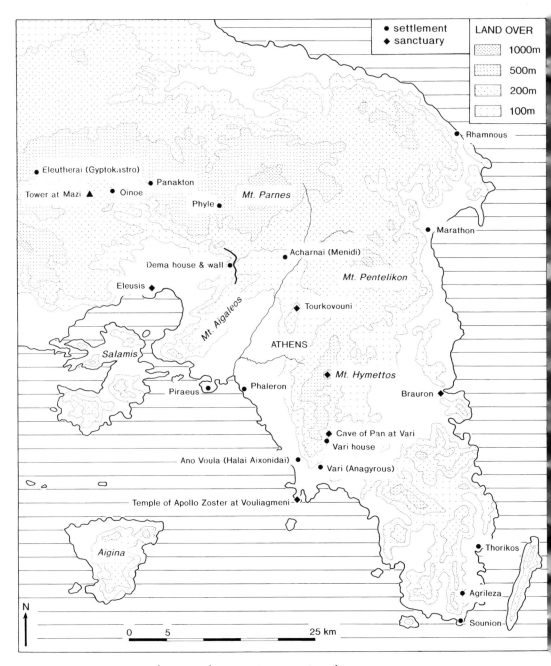

13.1 Map of Attica, showing sites mentioned in text

least civic and egalitarian, norms. Is it not then possible that the humblest of its artefacts, as well as the grandest of its buildings and the noblest of its sculptures, may have expressed the same ideals? Might it not be that Athenian houses, Athenian urban design, Athenian epigraphic habits and the manner in which Athenians buried and commemorated their dead were in some deep sense 'democratic'? If so, would not the study of Classical Athens then truly be an 'archaeology of democracy'?

Here a little caution must be exercised. Part of archaeology's task is to describe, and to assume that every aspect of Athenian life in the fifth and fourth centuries was 'democratic' is to prejudge the issue. As prehistorians are wont to tell us, societies are not 'sutured wholes'. Literary ideals and practical reality may conflict. Moreover, like any other Greek city, Athens was heir to the material forms of a deep-rooted aristocratic culture, a culture in which the symposion played a crucial role. Athenian fineware pottery bore a particularly close relationship to this institution. Literature too makes it clear that the aristocratic ideal remained a lively source of intellectual dissent.[2] Furthermore, democracy and the Classical period do not coincide exactly. Certain democratic forms seem to have been prevalent elsewhere in Greece in Archaic times.[3] The Athenian democratic constitution was only fully formulated by the statesman Cleisthenes in 507 BC. This constitution certainly empowered the 'common man' – that is, a free man of Athenian descent, whether rich or poor. But in some ways it came to set new and harder boundaries between citizens and non-citizens – that is between Athenian men on the one hand, and Athenian women, resident foreigners and slaves on the other. Democracy was in some ways a culture of exclusion. But if Athens was a 'democratic culture', it was one with roots in the constitutional innovations of the late Archaic period.

13.2 Democracy and public building: the Agora and the Pnyx

The civic and commercial centre of Classical Athens was its agora, or marketplace. While the Acropolis, being the seat of Athena and her cult, remained the most important of the city's shrines, most of Athens' public business was conducted in and around this large open space. The space itself was relatively new. Before the middle of the sixth century it must have appeared singularly unprepossessing. There is evidence for domestic activity until quite a late date, and it has been suggested that an earlier 'agora' may have existed in the saddle between the Areopagus and the Acropolis.[4] Some embellishments had taken place in late

---

[2] Both Plato and Xenophon had markedly undemocratic sympathies, for example.
  'Culture' is of course a tricky concept. For a recent discussion, see Sahlins 1999. On the distinctiveness of Athenian culture and material culture, see Morris 1998b: 64–70. Morris argues that, far from being unique, Athenian practices were representative of a wider 'central Greek' pattern.
[3] Evidence for this includes the law from Chios, discussed by Jeffery (1956).
[4] For arguments to this effect, see Wycherley 1978: 27; Thompson and Wycherley 1972: 19.

Archaic times. A fountain house had been built in the south-east corner, and an altar to the twelve gods erected, probably under the tyrant Peisistratos.[5] It was only at the end of the sixth century that boundaries of the agora were marked out by horos stones (figs. 8.12 and 8.13).[6] A number of other public buildings seem to date to this time. Most obviously, Cleisthenes' new constitution required a site for the new council of Five Hundred, the boule, which consisted of fifty members chosen by lot from each of the new ten tribes. This resulted in Greece's first bouleuterion, or council house, built just below the hill of Kolonos Agoraios on the western side of the Agora (fig. 13.2).[7] The first of the Agora's colonnaded porticoes or stoas, a type of building previously reserved for sanctuaries, was also constructed in the years just before 500 BC. This was the so-called stoa basileios, or 'Royal Stoa', built as a place where the 'king archon' or basileus could conduct his business.[8] The first of these stoas was a modest structure, with a single internal colonnade. More ambitious buildings were to come.

Construction in the Agora was inevitably interrupted by the Persian invasion of 480 BC.[9] However, if the so-called 'oath of Plataia' prevented those Greek allied states which had fought against Persia from rebuilding their sanctuaries, no such inhibition seems to have applied to public spaces. A new prytaneion or small council chamber was constructed in the south-west corner of the Agora sometime around 470–460 BC. Its proximity to the bouleuterion was deliberate, since it was designed to accommodate the fifty councillors or *prytaneis* who had charge of the 'executive business' of Athens for one of the ten months of the year. Circular in shape, it is often referred to as the tholos.[10] A further stoa built in the north-west corner of the Agora was considerably larger than the Royal Stoa, perhaps because its purpose was different. This was the famous Painted Stoa or stoa poikile.[11] It contained the wall paintings by Polygnotos, which celebrated the Athenian victory at Marathon. The stoa was also used to display arms and armour captured in other Athenian victories, notably the shields taken from the Spartans after

---

[5] For these developments, see Camp 1992: 39–44; Thompson and Wycherley 1972: 117–19. For the location of the late Archaic public buildings in Athens (including the prytaneion) that lay outside the Agora, see now Shear 1994.

[6] Lalonde 1991: 27; see also Thompson and Wycherley 1972: 117–19.

[7] Thompson and Wycherley 1972: 29–38; Thompson 1937: 115–217; 1940: 148–51; Camp 1992: 52–3. Like a number of other American authors, Camp (1992) constantly calls the boule the 'Senate', and the bouleuterion the 'Senate House'. This nomenclature is, to say the least, misleading, if not downright inaccurate. In both the Roman and American systems, senators are elected. In Rome, all elected magistrates above the rank of quaestor became senators, once their year of office was over. The councillors who made up the boule, however, were chosen by lot; they were not magistrates, nor need they have been ex-magistrates. Indeed, in a sense, Athens did have its own Senate, which resembled the Roman system quite closely: the Council of the Areopagus. This council too consisted of ex-magistrates, and it functioned rather like the Roman Senate until the mid-fifth century BC. If any body in democratic Athens should be called a Senate, this (and not the boule) is it.

[8] For the stoa basileios, see Thompson and Wycherley 1972: 83–90; Shear 1971: 243–55; 1973b: 382–5; 1975: 365–70.   [9] See Shear 1993; Camp 1995: 231–4.

[10] For the tholos, see Thompson and Wycherley 1972: 41–6; Thompson 1940: 44–105, 126–37.

[11] Shear 1984: 5–19; Castriota 1992: 127–30. For a summary of earlier conjectures, see Thompson and Wycherley 1972: 83–90.

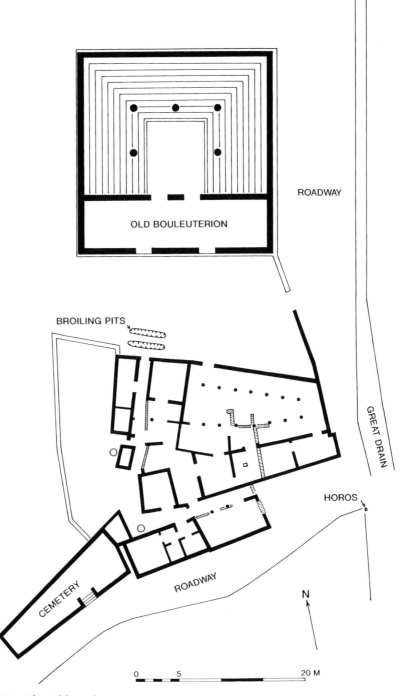

ROADWAY

OLD BOULEUTERION

BROILING PITS

GREAT DRAIN

HOROS

CEMETERY

ROADWAY

N

0   5   20 M

13.2 The Old Bouleuterion, *c.* 490 BC

Sphakteria in 425 BC. In celebrating and commemorating Athenian victories in war, its function differed hardly at all from stoas or porticoes in sanctuaries – notably the portico of the Athenians at Delphi which, Pausanias says, contained the arms captured after Athenian naval victories in the gulf of Corinth.[12]

These last were victories in the Peloponnesian war (431–403 BC), a war which, one might have thought, would have slowed down building activity a little. But there is no sign of this. A yet more splendid stoa, the Stoa of Zeus Eleutherios, was constructed between 430 and 420 BC. This had two wings, and, like the Painted Stoa, was decorated with pictures. Such a fine building, one would have thought, would have a suitably dignified function. But no – it seems to have been used simply as an all-purpose public amenity, there just for the pleasure and convenience of Athenian citizens.[13] A new bouleuterion was also built, just to the west of the old, which seems to have been retained as a kind of state archive.[14] The 'royal stoa' too was refurbished. On its two new wings, a complete code of laws was inscribed and set up towards the end of the fifth century BC, a code which, in theory, every citizen could consult.[15]

The publication, and monumentalisation, of a city's laws may seem to us a natural development in a democracy. Publication of the law made law accessible, equally available to every literate citizen. Such monumentalisation is part of a wider trend. Thousands of public inscriptions in stone seem to have been produced in Classical Athens, more than in any other city.[16] These range from things such as leases of public land (usually found in the Agora) to the tribute lists from allied states erected on the Acropolis.[17] Such inscriptions were not so much administrative as monumental: the tribute lists, inscribed with ostentatious regularity in a new style known as *stoichedon* and with the letters painted in red, were meant to be seen. Moreover, this trend is a marked break from Archaic Athenian practice, where informal inscriptions had been common but public inscriptions were few in number. The sudden rise in the number of these inscriptions seems to coincide with the inception of democracy.[18] So was democracy then the cause of this new 'epigraphic habit'? In a sense yes, but it would be to misinterpret these inscriptions if we were to see them as simply conveying information to the public at large. They were rather monuments to a democratic idea, their erection and inscription a performance of public accountability – an outward, durable and visible sign of the public character of the Athenian state.

[12] For the portico of the Athenians at Delphi, see Amandry 1953: 37–121. For the captured arms taken by the Athenians at Sphakteria and displayed in the Painted Stoa, see Camp 1992: 71–2.
[13] Thompson 1937: 5–77; Thompson and Wycherley 1972: 96–103. On stoas in the Agora generally, see Coulton 1976: 39–54.
[14] Thompson and Wycherley 1972: 29–38; Thompson 1937: 115–217; 1940: 148–51; Camp 1992: 90–4.
[15] Camp 1992: 100–2; Shear 1971: 243–55; 1975: 365–70. Thompson and Wycherley 1972: 83–90.
[16] For recent figures, see Hedrick 1999. Public inscriptions are collected by Lewis (1981).
[17] For the Athenian tribute lists, see Merritt *et al.* 1939; 1949; 1950; 1953. For public inscriptions in the Agora (including leases), see Lalonde *et al.* 1991.
[18] For Archaic Athens, see Whitley 1997b: 640–5. For a general consideration of the uses of public inscriptions in Classical Athens, see Hedrick 1999; Thomas 1989; 1992: 128–57.

Inscriptions such as the law code outside the stoa basileios are only one of many signs of a functioning democracy to be found within the Agora. Such range from the numerous ostraka, potsherds reused as ballots inscribed with the names of politicians whom someone had proposed for the kind of honourable exile known (appropriately) as ostracism, found both here and in the Kerameikos,[19] to the foundations of further public buildings. These last include lawcourts, containing ballot boxes, and the city's mint.[20]

So far, the buildings I have mentioned are all public or civic in character. But one of the meanings of 'agora' in both ancient and modern Greek is marketplace, and we know from written sources that goods were indeed bought and sold in the area.[21] Where then are the agora's stalls or shops? It could be that excavation has concentrated in those areas where archaeologists are most likely to find the buildings that Pausanias describes; or it may simply be that a 'shop' is an unprepossessing structure, and so difficult to identify. A few shops have been found on the north-east edge of the agora.[22] To a modern visitor, it might seem odd that none of the stoas was used as a shopping arcade. One of them, the South Stoa or (more precisely) South Stoa I, built in the last years of the fifth century, may at first sight seem a likely candidate for such a use. This is no simple portico with an open front and an internal colonnade. It has a row of more or less square rooms at the back. One may be inclined to interpret these as shops. But many of these rooms have an off-centre door, of a kind we find in andrones in houses and hestiatoria in sanctuaries. These rooms are moreover of a size and shape that could accommodate seven or so diners. There is other evidence to suggest that it was in the South Stoa that the metronomoi, officials charged with regulating Athenian weights and measures, met.[23] This stoa then was a public building with commercial interests.

Commerce and the 'public interest' are matters we have little difficulty in understanding. Other activities of ancient Greek state officials may strike us as a little strange. One of the ways in which Socrates perhaps hastened his own death was to suggest that, as a punishment for the 'impiety' for which he had just been convicted, he be dined at public expense in the prytaneion for the rest of his life

---

[19] The Agora evidence is collected by Lang (1990); see now Camp 1999: 268–74. For the Kerameikos evidence see Peek 1941: 51–89; Willemsen and Brenne 1991; Brenne 1994.

[20] For the mint, Thompson and Wycherley 1972: 78–9; Thompson 1954: 45–8. For the lawcourts in general, Thompson and Wycherley 1972: 52–72; Boeghold 1995. For the architectural evidence from the Agora, see Boeghold 1995: 10–16; Camp 1995. For the associated small finds, see Boeghold 1995: 53–90. Detailed evidence for laws and lawcourts in the eastern and north-eastern areas of the Agora has now been published by Townsend (1995a; 1995b). Relatively simple structures of the fifth century (buildings A–E) seem to have been replaced by something grander with an internal peristyle court in the fourth century. [21] The evidence is collected by Wycherley (1978: 91–103).

[22] For finds in the north-east corner of the Agora, see Townsend 1995a: 107–12; Shear 1973a: 122–34, 138–44. There may be other commercial buildings in the vicinity of the Agora; for evidence from the north-west corner, see Shear 1984: 43–50; Camp 1996: 236–41. Further evidence for commercial activity (particularly retailing) comes in the form of graffiti on reused wine amphoras, all dating to the latter part of the fifth century BC (Lawall 2000).

[23] On the South Stoa, see Thompson 1954: 39–45; Thompson and Wycherley 1972: 74–8; Camp 1992: 122–6; Wycherley 1978: 44–5.

(Plato, *Apology* 36d). Dining at public expense, however, was a common activity in and around the agora. Athenian officials did not have committee meetings, they had symposia. The fifty prytaneis dined together in the tholos, and the metronomoi in the South Stoa. The best evidence for these activities comes from a pit just behind the stoa basileios. This was full of drinking cups, from a minimum of about 840 vessels, 21 of which were inscribed with the ligature DE, meaning '*demosion*' (public property). The bulk of these vessels date to between 475 and 425 BC. They are the debris from the symposia of officials, who probably dined together in the stoa basileios.[24] Similar finds have come from an area under the restored Stoa of Attalos, and from the area of the tholos.[25] There can be no better archaeological illustration than these finds of how closely, for the Athenian citizen, democratic duty and democratic privilege were connected (fig. 13.3).

Athenian democracy however was not run solely by officials, whether elected or chosen by lot. Major decisions – both 'executive' and 'legislative' – were taken by the citizen body, meeting together in an assembly (*ekklesia*). There had then to be a place where several thousand citizens could meet. Perhaps the earliest assemblies were held in the Agora itself, but from about 500 BC onwards it seems that the ekklesia met on the north-east slopes of the Pnyx hill. This assembly area seems to have gone through three phases of construction, the last of which can be fixed to the latter part of the fourth century BC.[26] Like the Agora, the Pnyx hill had stoas, perhaps provided for the convenience of citizens who had to travel to Athens from 'out of town' to vote. The Pnyx was a kind of natural theatre, and certainly some of the decisions made here (the decision to raze Mytilene to the ground after Mytilene revolted in the middle of the Peloponnesian war, and the almost immediate reversal of that decision in 427 BC) were dramatic enough.[27] Athens could be described as a 'theatre culture', and it is perhaps time to look at the archaeological evidence behind this remarkable development.

13.3 Theatre and democracy

The comedies and tragedies performed in Athens in the fifth and fourth centuries BC are part of the enduring legacies of Greek civilisation. Drama, as we understand it, began here (though drama was also invented, quite independently, elsewhere, such as in Yuan China). Early Greek dramas, however, would strike us as very odd. They were not mere entertainments which one paid good money to see; they were ceremonies in which Athenian citizens participated. Used as we are more to the naturalistic conventions of film and television than to live theatrical

---

[24] On these finds, see Rotroff and Oakley 1992. On the ligatures in particular, see *ibid.*: 41–6; on the context of the finds, *ibid.*: 3–8; Shear 1973b: 382–5.

[25] Rotroff and Oakley 1992: 41–6; Thompson 1940: 126–37; Talcott 1936: 352–4.

[26] Thompson and Wycherley 1972: 48–52; Kouroniotis and Thompson 1932; Thompson 1936; Rotroff and Camp 1996.

[27] On the high drama of the Mytilenean debate, see Thucydides III.36.4–50. On the stoas of the Pnyx, see Thompson and Scranton 1943: 269–301.

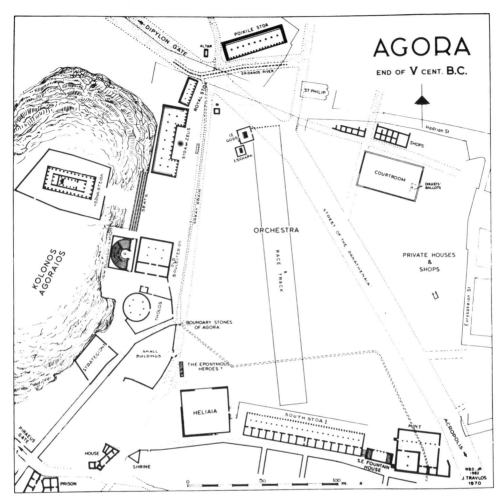

13.3 The Agora *c.* 400 BC

performances, Greek drama, with its masks, high boots, choruses and company
of no more than three actors, is very difficult for us to understand. (The nearest
thing in the modern world is Japanese Noh drama, which is not easily appreciated
by Western audiences.) This cultural gulf has, however, not prevented Greek
drama from inspiring modern artists. In the nineteenth century in particular,
Greek drama was seen as not merely a participatory but a moral art form, one that
did not simply provide a spectacle but involved the audience in ethical debate.
Greek tragedy's combination of consummate, lyrical poetry with insoluble moral
conundrums (which is more important, duty towards one's family, or obedience
to the state?) came to seem the very essence of High Art. Other critics have seen
the participation of the citizen audience in the drama as a means whereby the
community as a whole reaffirms its identity, even as it questions its own values.

Some modern artists have tried to emulate these ideals. Wagner's operas were conceived on such a vast scale and were (originally) intended to be performed only at festivals precisely in order to emulate the effects of Greek tragedy. Wagner wanted to create a mythical, operatic drama that would involve the whole German Volk, just as the Dionysia brought together all the citizens of Athens to witness both its comedies and its tragedies.[28]

Freighted with such expectations, the archaeological evidence for the physical setting in which the earliest dramas were performed was bound to disappoint. There is some literary evidence to suggest that some early plays were performed in the Agora, but, if so, all evidence for the portable wooden ikria used to provide seats has entirely disappeared.[29] Most of our ancient sources agree that nearly all the plays of Aeschylus, Sophocles, Euripides and Aristophanes were performed in the Theatre of Dionysos. This was located on the south-east slopes of the Acropolis, just to the north-east of the earliest, Archaic temple of Dionysos Eleutheros.[30] But evidence for the earliest phase of this theatre, usually dated to the very end of the sixth century, is exiguous in the extreme. It consists of little more than a semi-circular cutting into the slope of the hill. The only building, as such, was a curved wall built to create a terrace and so a flat space for the orchestra (the area where the chorus and actors performed). There is no evidence of seating – seats, such as they were, must have been of wood. Just as the Olympic games, in the early part of the fifth century, were played within sight of the temples and altars of the gods, so the earliest Greek dramas were performed within the sanctuary and within sight of the temple of Dionysos Eleutheros.[31]

Despite its modesty, the date of the first theatre confirms its democratic credentials. At some time later it was enlarged, being provided with a proper auditorium with stone seats, a stone (conglomerate) base on which to place the background and the scenes (literally, skenai), and a properly circular orchestra (fig. 13.4).[32] The dating of this second phase is hotly contested. It is based, not on closely datable and stratified finds, but on circumstantial details such as the liking of fourth-century architects for conglomerate rather than limestone. Earlier writers thought this second phase 'Periclean', i.e. dating to the latter part of the fifth century BC, but the available archaeological evidence is perfectly consistent with a date in the early fourth century, which is where more recent writers have wanted to place it.[33] This is well after the heyday of the great tragedians, though not of Middle and New Comedy. It was only towards the end of the fourth century

---

[28] Both tragedies and comedies were performed in the festival of the Great Dionysia (Goldhill 1987). But whether plays performed at the festival of the Lenaia were performed in the theatre of Dionysos is far from certain.

[29] For performances in the Agora, see Thompson and Wycherley 1972: 126–9; Camp 1992: 46.

[30] On the theatre and its location, see Travlos 1971: 537–52; Wycherley 1978: 203–13. On recent evidence, see Calligas 1994.   [31] On the first theatre, see Wycherley 1978: 206–7; Gebhard 1974.

[32] Wycherley 1978: 207–11.

[33] For earlier views, see Pickard-Cambridge 1946: 1–29. For the later down-dating, Travlos 1971: 537–52; Hammond 1972; Wycherley 1978: 210–13; Townsend 1986.

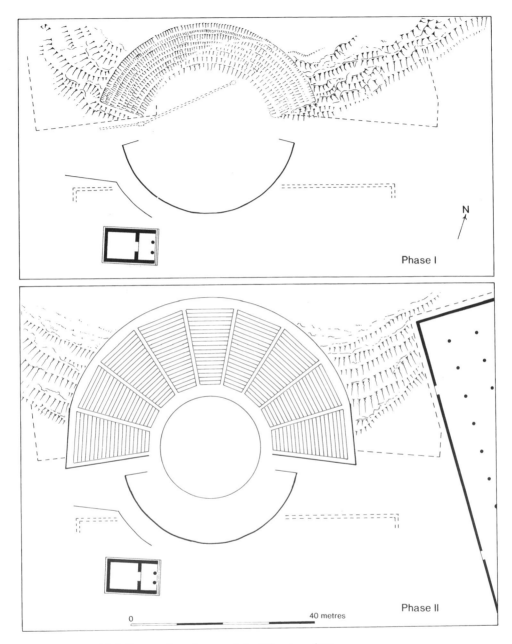

13.4 Successive phases of the Theatre of Dionysos

that the grandest of these theatres of Dionysos was built. A much larger auditorium, which could accommodate 14,000 people, was constructed (fig. 13.5). A stone skene or stage, backing onto a newly constructed stoa, now separated the theatre from the sanctuary of Dionysos, thus divorcing the god from the festivals held in his honour. As if in compensation, the sanctuary was equipped with a temenos wall and a second, slightly grander temple, which held a gold and ivory image of the god, crafted by Alkamenes.[34] Athens now finally had an architectural setting worthy of her reputation as the home of the great dramatists, even if most of their number had now passed away, and even if this latest theatre of Dionysos could not quite rival the even grander theatre at Epidauros.

It is sobering to reflect that, in all probability, not only Aeschylus' *Oresteia* and Sophocles' *Antigone*, but even Aristophanes' *Frogs* would have been performed in the earliest and least imposing of these theatres. The surviving remains of the Theatre of Dionysos therefore give a very misleading impression of the original setting of the plays. To gain some sense of what an early dramatic performance might have been like we have to go out of Athens, to the deme site of Thorikos in south-east Attica. Thorikos, though an integral part of the Athenian state, was also a small town. It had its own theatre, which probably dates to the early fifth century BC. Its orchestra is a curious elongated oval, and its stone seats could have accommodated all the inhabitants of Thorikos.[35] Here the relationship between Dionysos and theatrical performances seems even closer than in Athens. Plays must have been performed actually within the space between the temple and altar of Dionysos.

By the end of the Classical period, theatres were to be found in a number of Attic demes. There is a notable example in the Piraeus, on the western slopes of the hill of Mounychia. Such theatres were on occasion used for the meetings of the assembly as well as for theatrical performances.[36] Regardless of theatre's democratic credentials, Athens was never a 'theatre state' in Clifford Geertz's sense of the term, where only participation in common rituals kept the community together.[37] Despite Greek drama's cultural importance for later generations, and despite its crucial role in the political life of the city, it seems that Athenians in Classical times did not lavish much attention on the elaboration of the architectural setting of their most significant art form. Their efforts were directed elsewhere, towards more traditional forms of the polis' self-assertion and ornamentation – towards its shrines and its temples. One sanctuary in particular was the object of great effort, trouble and expense – Athena's shrine, in the heart of Athens, on the Acropolis.

---

[34] Wycherley 1978: 212–14; Townsend 1986.   [35] Hackens 1965; Gebhard 1974.
[36] Thucydides VIII.93.1; Travlos 1988: 340–63; Wycherley 1978: 263–4.
[37] For the whole notion of the 'theatre state', see Geertz 1980. A theatre state is one where political solidarity is maintained primarily through spectacle and ritual, rather than through some overarching bureaucracy. But to call any Greek state a 'theatre state' is to underestimate the role of military participation in the creation of social solidarity.

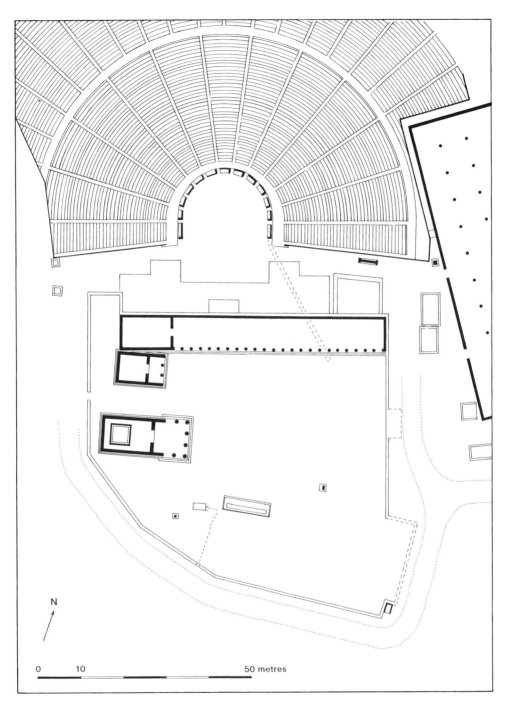

13.5 Theatre of Dionysos, final phase

N

0   10   50 metres

13.4. Athens embodied: the Acropolis and the Periclean building programme

There was certainly no shortage of imposing temples in late sixth-century Athens. The Acropolis contained at least one impressive temple of Athena, and, outside Athens, the sanctuary of Demeter at Eleusis had been much embellished in the century before 500 BC.[38] After Athens' victory at Marathon, work began on an even grander temple of Athena on what may have been a new site on the Acropolis. This was the older Parthenon and, though the limestone foundation platform was completed by 480 BC, the Persian sack of that year put a stop to any further building work.[39] Few, if any, temples were built in Athens or Attica in the years between 480 and 460 BC. The reason usually given for this is the 'oath of Plataia', the vow that the allied Greek states are thought to have made not to rebuild their temples until they had taken revenge on the Persians who had destroyed them. But if, as many historians believe, a peace treaty had been signed between Athens and Persia after Athens' decisive victory at Eurymedon (the so-called Peace of Callias), then there was no further obstacle to building.[40] From around 450 BC onwards Athens embarked on a whole series of large-scale temple building projects, a programme which coincides with the period of pre-eminence of the Athenian general/statesman Pericles.

Attica was a region already littered with cult sites before this 'programme' began. The peak sanctuaries of Zeus on Mt Hymettos and at 'Tourkovouni' (possibly ancient Mt Anchesmos) continued to be visited in Classical times, as did other small sanctuaries such as that of Artemis Mounychia.[41] There was something of a popular upsurge of devotion to the god Pan, to whom cave shrines were established at Vari (Anagyrous) and on Mt Parnes.[42] Still, though many early shrines existed, it is striking how many temples were built in the course of the fifth and fourth centuries BC. The preferred location for many Classical Attic sanctuaries seems to be on or near the coast. Certainly the remains of the temple of Apollo Zoster at Vouliagmeni, the temple of Demeter at Thorikos, the shrine

---

[38] Quite how many temples there were on the Acropolis before 490 BC is a matter of dispute. For a variety of views, see Plommer 1960; Hurwit 1985: 236–48; 1999: 99–121.

[39] Hurwit 1999: 129–36.

[40] For the 'oath of Plataia', see Lycurgus, *Against Leokrates* 80–1. The 'Peace of Callias' is discussed by Meiggs (1972: 128–51, 487–95). This 'Peace' used to be a perennial topic of discussion for several generations of ancient historians, who have reached no consensus on the subject. Our fifth-century sources (particularly Thucydides) make no explicit mention of it, and later sources differ as to what might have occasioned such a 'Peace'. I prefer Meiggs' date, but this is little more than an (uninformed) opinion. The most likely date for the battle of Eurymedon, however, is 466 BC (see Miller 1997: 12–13).

[41] On the temple of Artemis at Mounychia, see Palaiokrassa 1989. On 'peak sanctuaries' to Zeus, particularly the one on Mt Hymettos, see Langdon 1976: 100–6; on Tourkovouni, see Lauter 1985. The volume of Classical votive offerings from these shrines is small (see Langdon 1976: 71–2). That they continued to be visited and known is inferred from Pausanias' description (I.32.2).

[42] For caves to Pan at Marathon and Parnes, see Travlos 1988: 217–18, 319–28. For the cave of Pan near Vari, see Weller *et al.* 1903; Travlos 1988: 447–65. The cult of Pan is discussed by Osborne (1987a: 191–2). It seems to have been introduced into Attica only after 490 BC.

of Artemis at Brauron and the temple of Athena at Sounion all seem to date to the Classical period, although their exact date of construction is often unclear.[43] A number of other temples, however, are sufficiently well preserved to be dated more precisely: the temple of Poseidon at Sounion; the Hephaisteion on the small hill of Kolonos Agoraios just to the west of the Athenian Agora; the temple of Nemesis at Rhamnous; and the so-called temple of Ares at Acharnai (modern Menidhi). Such is the close similarity between at least three of these temples that one scholar at least has seen the hand of a single architect in their design.[44] Whatever one thinks of this suggestion, they are close enough in style, plan and execution to be of roughly similar date, and similar enough to the Parthenon to be dated around the middle of the fifth century BC. It is their similarity to the Parthenon (where we know Pericles did play a decisive role) that has led scholars to talk of a 'Periclean building programme'.

Such a programme, involving the construction of five temples in the space of thirty years, must have been a major undertaking. Their builders cut no corners, using only the best materials. The Hephaisteion, being the best preserved of them (indeed of all Greek temples), deserves careful scrutiny (figs. 13.6 and 13.7).[45] It was built almost entirely of marble quarried from the slopes of Mt Pentelikon (Pentelic marble), and brought in large blocks to the site. At first it seems a standard Doric temple, with six columns along the front and thirteen along the flanks. It has a typical pronaos and opisthodomos, and probably contained an interior colonnade of superimposed Doric columns within the cella. But its sculptural decoration is unusual. It was, to be sure, decorated with metopes, showing (in the front) the labours of Herakles and (along part of the sides) the deeds of Theseus – as if to suggest that the Athenian hero was the equal of his Peloponnesian counterpart. But odd for a Doric temple is the continuous frieze over both the pronaos and the opisthodomos, showing (respectively) a battle watched by the gods and the fight between Lapiths and Centaurs. This is an Ionic feature, very much out of place in this 'Doric' temple.

The Hephaisteion may have been conceived and begun earlier than many other Classical temples in Attica. There is nothing to indicate that there was an earlier shrine on this site, and therefore the 'oath of Plataia' would have been no inhibition to building here.[46] Its design clearly shows a willingness to innovate, to bend

---

[43] Travlos 1988.

[44] As argued by Plommer (1950). On the temple of Nemesis at Rhamnous, see now Miles 1989; on the so-called 'temple of Ares', Dinsmoor 1940. This temple is now thought to be, in fact, the temple of Athena at Pallene, moved to the Agora in Roman times. On the temples at Sounion, Travlos 1988: 404–29. On the whole question of the architect or architects of these temples, see Miles 1989: 239–42. On the Hephaisteion, see below. 'Periclean Doric' is characterised by slender columns and a specific proportion of column height to intercolumniation; see Coulton 1984.

[45] On the Hephaisteion, see Plommer 1950: 67–78; Dinsmoor Sn. 1941; 1968; Dinsmoor Jn. 1976; Camp 1992: 82–7; Reber 1999. On the fragmentary remains of pedimental sculpture, see Thompson 1949.

[46] Dinsmoor Sn. 1941: 125–7; Thompson and Wycherley 1972: 140–9; Miles 1989: 221–35. Coulton (1984) has put forward strong arguments for the Parthenon being the earliest of all these temples.

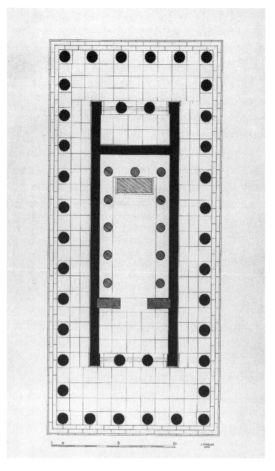

13.6 Plan of the Hephaisteion

if not to break the severe constraints of Doric design. The same impulse can be seen in the Parthenon itself, probably the first of these temples to be built (figs. 13.8 and 13.9). This great structure was built with remarkable speed between 447 and 438 BC.[47] Responsibility for its construction was shared by its architect, Iktinos, and its artist/designer-in-chief, Pheidias.[48] Like the Hephaisteion, it was built entirely of Pentelic marble, and, like the Hephaisteion too, it was a Doric temple with marked Ionic inclinations. These Ionic features are more than decorative; they are in part outcomes of a major innovation in temple design. The deepening of the opisthodomos and the relatively short length of the naos have the combined effect of putting the cult statue at the very centre of the building. Unlike the statue of Zeus in Olympia, the temple and the cult statue seem to have

---

[47] On the date and circumstances of the Parthenon's construction, see Wycherley 1978: 105–39; Plutarch, *Pericles* 12.1–13.5.   [48] Plutarch, *Pericles* 13.4.

13.7 Photo of Hephaisteion, from the south-west

been conceived and designed together. Temple and statue are all of a piece. Many of the other unusual features of the Parthenon – including its singular arrangement of columns (eight along the front, seventeen along the flanks) – arise from this central design imperative. Other innovations are harder to explain in purely architectural terms. Like any other Doric temple, the Parthenon contains major sculpture in its pediments and has an outer frieze of triglyphs and metopes. But no other Doric temple has an inner continuous frieze, running around cella, opisthodomos and pronaos (the entranceway).[49]

The Parthenon has fascinated scholars of every generation since the eighteenth century, though sometimes for different reasons. Earlier writers, being often professional architects, were particularly interested in its 'refinements'. Oddities such as the slight upward curvature of the stylobate, and the curving taper (entasis) of the columns, were intended, we are told by Vitruvius, to deceive the eye, and to make the building seem 'squarer' than it actually was.[50] Whether these refinements actually worked in any real optical sense may be questioned, but the fact that Greek architects bothered with them at all (as they undoubtedly did) at least shows the degree of mathematical and engineering skill that had been attained by the mid-fifth

---

[49] On the design of the Parthenon, see Carpenter 1970; and in particular Coulton 1984. On the placing of friezes, see now Coulton 2000. On the ornamentation of the Parthenon as a whole, see Brommer 1979; Ashmole 1972: 90–146; Boardman 1985: 96–145; Korres 1994b; Osborne 1998: 174–84; Hurwit 1999: 169–88.

[50] On refinements, see Vitruvius III.3.11; III.4.5; III.5.13. See also discussion in Lawrence and Tomlinson 1996: 125–8; Coulton 1977: 108–11; Hurwit 1999: 167–8.

13.8 View of western part of the Parthenon

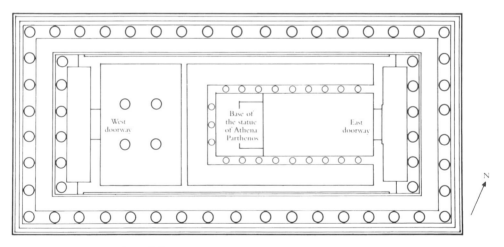

13.9 Plan of the Parthenon

century BC. In recent years, commentators have taken a greater interest in the Parthenon's decoration, that is in its iconography. Like a prehistorian pondering over the meaning of Scandinavian rock art, modern scholars have attempted new, bold interpretations of what the Parthenon 'meant' to fifth-century Athenians. Does its imagery have a message? And do the subjects of the cult statue, pediments, metopes and frieze have any common thread that tells us how fifth-century Athenians viewed themselves, their patron goddess and their place in the world?

The idea that public art and public architecture must relate in some way to civic ideology is, in many ways, an attractive one. The Parthenon was an expensive building, and, even if some of the funds came from Athens' allies (who had no real say in the matter) such a gigantic enterprise must in some way reflect public feeling in order to command public support. After all, the Parthenon is by far the largest structure to be built entirely of marble, marble which had to be quarried in Mt Pentelikon some 20 kilometres away and brought to Athens on wooden rollers.[51] But we cannot assume that iconography simply reflects ideology; we have to understand how the one relates to the other, and do so by taking a detailed look at the sculpture itself. In order to interpret the Parthenon's sculptures, we have first to identify their subjects. One might have thought that, in a fully historical period, this would be a straightforward matter. Plutarch, Pausanias and even Thucydides all discuss the Parthenon. Pausanias does indeed give us some useful details on the imagery of the huge chryselephantine cult statue of Athena (now only known through much smaller copies), and mentions that the west pediment shows the contest of Athena and Poseidon, and the east the goddess' remarkable birth (Pausanias I.24.5–7).[52] But that is it. He says nothing about either the metopes or the frieze, and neither does any other ancient source. For these we have to rely on archaeology alone.

The subjects of many, if not all, of the metopes at least can be identified fairly easily. These are entirely conventional. On the west, most seem to be of Greeks and Amazons; on the north, the sack of Troy, and other scenes involving the watchful gaze of the gods; on the east, the battle of Gods and Giants; and on the south, the fighting between Lapiths and Centaurs (fig. 13.10).[53] Their precise arrangement may still occasion difficulties, but the same applies to the much better documented Pedimental sculptures.[54] Problems arise with the frieze. It was

---

[51] See the discussion in Plutarch, *Pericles* 12. Castriota (1992: 226–9) is of the opinion that the iconography of the Parthenon, and the frieze in particular, was intended not merely to impress but also to engage the sympathies of the allied states. The idea of a processional frieze comes from Ionia and eastern Greece, and was thus intended as a nod in the direction of Ionic sensibilities. I am not convinced.

[52] Pausanias (I.24.5–7) mentions the pedimental sculpture only in passing, but devotes several sentences to the cult statue. On this see also Boardman 1985: 110–12; Brommer 1979: 59–61; and contributions in Berger 1984: 177–97.

[53] On the metopes, see Boardman 1985: 103–5; Ashmole 1972: 90–115; and contributions in Berger 1984: 202–8.

[54] On the pediments generally, see Boardman 1985: 98–103; Palagia 1993; and contributions in Berger 1984: 260–83. On the the arrangement of sculpture in the crucial eastern pediment, see Brommer 1979: 52–8; Palagia 1993: 18–39; Harrison 1967.

once thought that we knew what it represented: the Panathenaic procession, a major part of the festival of the Greater Panathenaia that brought the new peplos home to the Acropolis once every four years. This interpretation rests on the position of the so-called peplos scene, which shows the folding of a garment thought to be the peplos woven to cover the image of Athena Polias.[55] Certainly, the positioning of this scene, placed as it is over the pronaos, would suggest a close relationship to the cult of Athena (figs. 13.12 and 13.13). For it is this scene on the frieze that an observant worshipper would notice, between glancing at the birth of Athena on the east pediment and just before glimpsing the full splendour of the gold and ivory image of the goddess within.[56] Certainly too the frieze as a whole appears to be a procession. The whole of the western side and the western half of both the north and south sides are full of horsemen, usually identified as the Athenian cavalry or hippeis (fig. 13.11).[57] Then come, on both the north and south sides, chariots then carriers then elders and then sacrificial animals (fig. 13.14). The eastern side appears to show, moving in from both north and south ends, women, then heroes then gods; in the very centre is the folding of the peplos itself.

Most scholars still accept this identification, though sometimes with misgivings. For if the frieze depicts the Panathenaia, it leaves a lot out. Where are the maiden basket carriers, the bearers of tribute from allied states, and the Athenian hoplites themselves, whom we know from literary evidence formed an important part of the Panathenaic procession? Where is the wheeled ship, which transported the new peplos from the Pompeion along the sacred way to the Acropolis?[58] Too much space seems to be devoted to horsemen. Moreover, if the frieze depicts the Panathenaia, it is unique in Classical Greek temple decoration in portraying a contemporary event. Most temples are ornamented with scenes from myth, as, for example, on the slightly later frieze from the temple of Apollo Epikourios at Bassai, with its conventional scenes of Lapiths and Centaurs. One possible way around this problem is to suggest that the frieze represents the first, the original Panathenaia, an event which took place sometime in the mythical past. The difficulty here is that the Panathenaia proper was founded in 566 BC, well within historical memory. Or, perhaps since the Panathenaia is a recurrent event, a ritual, it partakes somehow of the timeless world of myth.

Such sophistries underscore the weakness of the traditional interpretation. A bolder approach has been to say that the frieze does indeed portray a story from

---

[55] That the frieze represents the Panathenaic procession was a suggestion of Stuart and Revett (1787: 12). It is one that most other authors have followed. Good accounts of the frieze are numerous. Ashmole 1972: 116–46; Robertson and Frantz 1975; Boardman 1985: 106–9; Jenkins 1994. For the peplos scene in particular, see Jenkins 1994: 35–42.   [56] A point emphasised by Jenkins (1994).

[57] The whole frieze has recently been republished by Jenkins (1994). Boardman (1977; 1984) is of the opinion that the horsemen represent, not the Athenian cavalry as such, but the heroised dead who fell at the battle of Marathon. He counts 192 horsemen, the number of the Athenian dead. The Parthenon is then as much an heröon as a temple to Athena. Unfortunately, no one else's arithmetic quite matches Boardman's (see Jenkins 1994: 29–30, 44).

[58] Points made by Boardman 1977; 1984; Connelly 1996: 54.

13.10 Metope of Lapith fighting Centaur, south side of the Parthenon

13.11 West side of Parthenon frieze (slab II, west frieze)

13.12 Drawing showing position of 'peplos' scene

13.13 Peplos scene from east frieze of Parthenon (slab V, figures 32–57)

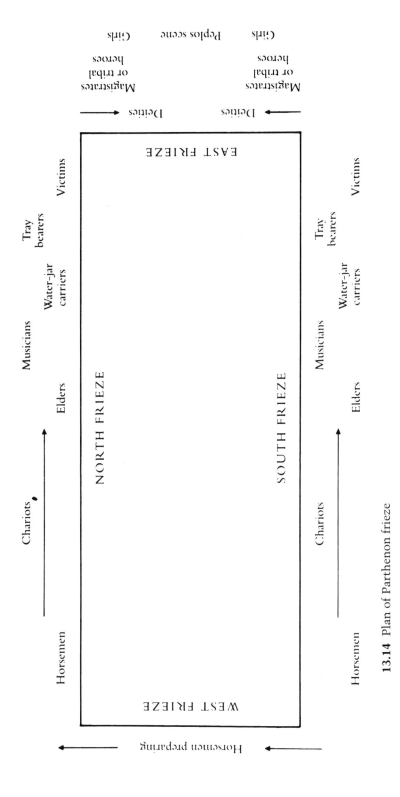

13.14 Plan of Parthenon frieze

the mythical past. Joan Connelly has recently suggested that the central, eastern part of the frieze at least represents a mythical scene involving ritual sacrifice.[59] The 'peplos scene' and the figures around allude to, but, like the best Athenian tragedy, do not actually show the legendary Athenian king Erechtheus sacrificing his daughters in order to save the city from destruction (figs. 13.12 and 13.13). The name of the temple, Parthenon, alludes not to the supposed cult of Athena Parthenos (Athena the Virgin) but to the virgins (*parthenoi*) whose supreme sacrifice guaranteed the safety of the city. Needless to say, this interpretation too has its own difficulties. For what does one do with the rest of the frieze, with the horsemen, chariots and elders? Are these merely onlookers, or are they supposed to represent the whole of the people of Athens, for whose sake Erechtheus' daughters were sacrificed?

Even if one simply accepts the idea that the frieze represents the Panathenaic procession, one is still left with the problem of relating its imagery to that of the Parthenon as a whole. Today it is easier to play iconographic games of guess-the-message than it would have been soon after the sculptures were put in place. The frieze is now displayed at eye level in the British Museum (and elsewhere), and photographs enable scholars to compare things that, in their original context, would be almost impossible to see side by side. If the frieze has a subtle message, it is one the ancient viewer would have great difficulty in perceiving. For to follow the 'procession' in its original setting by eye from start to finish would involve quite some strain on one's neck. In this light, Robin Osborne's suggestion that notional ancient viewers would try to engage closely with the sculpture of the frieze by following it round from west to east seems unlikely.[60] Perhaps the search for a 'hidden message' in sculpture with such a firmly architectural setting as that from the Parthenon is a mistake. It is not the particular meanings one could (in principle) derive from a close reading but the overall theme, the metanarrative, that is important. Athens is a great city, protected by its patron deity. Athena's worship involves everyone. Athenian men, unlike the half-human centaurs or the barbarous Amazons, are manly and strong. It is considerations such as these that have led several scholars to see, in all Athenian fifth-century public sculpture and painting, a deliberate set of allusions to Athens' victory in the Persian wars.[61] The Parthenon is a celebration of Athenian superiority, of *aristeia*. Begun after Marathon and completed after Eurymedon, the Parthenon makes a splendid victory monument.

Much ink has been spilt on the question of the Parthenon frieze. The frieze indeed looms much larger in modern scholarly debates (and in modern politics) than it probably did to contemporaries. Such minute attention to one part of the Parthenon has tended to obscure a more fundamental question about this building. What

---

[59] Connelly 1996; for criticisms see Jenkins 1994: 29; Hurwit 1999: 222–8; Harrison 1996.

[60] Osborne 1987b; see also Osborne 1994b; 1998: 174–84. For criticisms, see Jenkins 1994: 17–18.

[61] Castriota 1992: 17–32, 134–229. Athenian attitudes to Persia were, however, probably more complex than Castriota implies; see Miller 1997; Hölscher 1998.

exactly was it for? Like the temple of Zeus at Olympia, it must have been designed with the intention of housing a gigantic, chryselephantine cult statue. As at Olympia, it seems to have supplemented rather than replaced an older temple alongside it, a temple which had housed the venerable image of Athena made of olive-wood, the very one for which the new peplos was woven every four years (fig. 13.15).[62] It was this older temple, which had faced the altar of Athena's cult, which the Persians destroyed.[63] In 421 BC work began on a replacement. This was the Erechtheion, an Ionic temple which brought together in one structure all the ancient cults on the Acropolis. In one sense it functioned simply as a temple of Athena: it housed her cult image, and looked towards her altar (fig. 13.16). But it also served as a kind of 'cult complex'. Like its sister temple, it is built almost entirely of Pentelic marble, but it is much smaller. It may strike one as odd then that it took until 409 BC to complete. This may be because of its unusual plan and decoration. For the Erechtheion must be one of the strangest temples in all of Greece. It has an interior divided into two rooms; on its outside it has two porches, one (to the north) a simple Ionic tetrastyle, the other (to the south) holding the caryatids. It is built on two levels, and the Ionic frieze on its east and north sides is of dark Eleusinian limestone, on to which white marble figures had been pinned.[64] A wish to accommodate many if not all of the venerable cults and sacred places on the Acropolis (including that of the eponymous Erechtheus) may in part explain these peculiarities, but one cannot exclude another motivation: the simple wish to experiment.

It is perhaps a fitting irony that it was only by the time of Athens' defeat in 404 BC that all the major buildings on the Acropolis had been completed.[65] In addition to the Parthenon and Erechtheion, these comprised two other major structures. The Propylaia of Mnesikles had a Doric façade, interior Ionic columns and two wings, and was aligned on an axis almost parallel to that of the Parthenon. It provided the Acropolis with a suitably grand entrance.[66] The temple of Athena Nike was built in the 420s to replace the earlier naiskos (a small shrine) on the south-west bastion of the Acropolis. This is a little gem of an Ionic temple, ornamented with not only a frieze but an exterior parapet, whose sculptures would have been one of the first things that caught one's eye as one approached the Acropolis.[67] It was all in all a most impressive ensemble, and one that has, through numerous vicissitudes, lasted for over two thousand years. It must have been the

---

[62] On an instructive comparison between the Parthenon and the temple of Zeus, see Coulton 1977: 111–15.

[63] The evidence for this is summarised by Wycherley 1978: 143–6; Hurwit 1985: 236–48; 1999: 121–36.

[64] On the Erechtheion generally, see Wycherley 1978: 146–54; Hurwit 1999: 200–9. On the question of Athena's cult, see Hurwit 1999: 20–1, 25–6. On the architecture of the Erechtheion, Stevens *et al.* 1927. Pausanias' account (I.26.5–7) is confusing, but any reconstruction of the various cults and objects in the Erechtheion that does not place the statue of Athena in its eastern part (facing the altar) is not, to my mind, credible.

[65] For dating, see Dinsmoor 1913a; 1913b; also chapter 4, section 4.3 above.

[66] Hurwit 1999: 192–7; Tanoulas 1994a; 1994b; 1994c.

[67] Mark 1993: 69–92; Hurwit 1999: 209–15. For the sculpture, see Carpenter 1929.

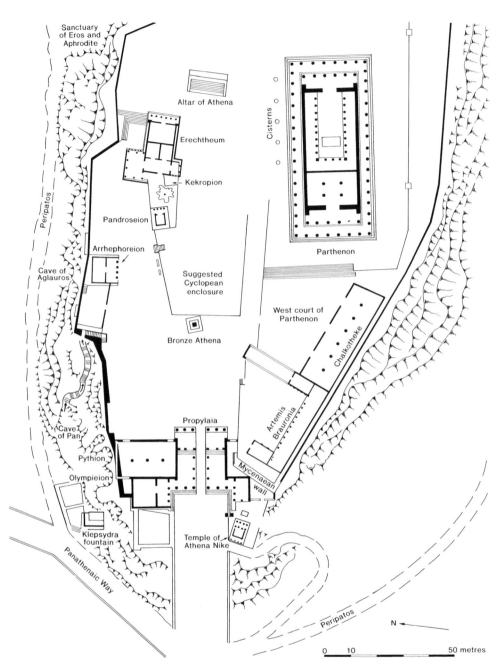

13.15 The Acropolis *c.* 400 BC

ERECHTHEION

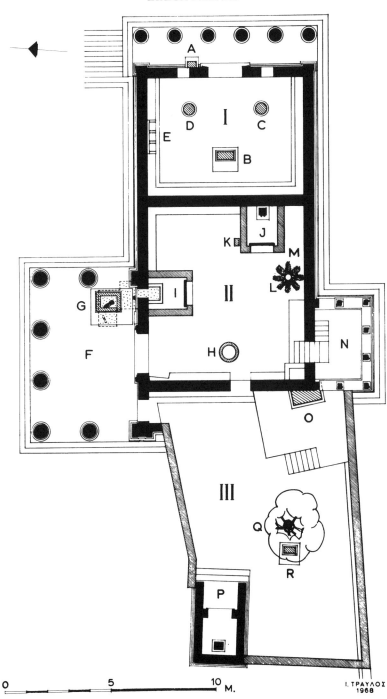

13.16 Plan of Erechtheion, showing conjectural position of various statues mentioned in Pausanias

Acropolis that was at the back of Thucydides' mind when he made his comparison between Sparta and Athens: that if one judged each city purely by its material remains, one would think the former little more than a village, but would considerably overestimate the wealth and military might of the latter.[68] Still, it was not the Acropolis alone that made Athens seem such an important city. In both its fortifications and its plan it conformed closely to the Aristotelian ideal of what a city ought to look like. It is time to take a closer look at the city's shape and the city's limits, its walls.

13.5 The shape of the democratic city: Athens and Piraeus

Whether or not Athens was fortified in Archaic times is a vexed question. The Acropolis certainly was, and there are suggestions that something known as the 'Pelasgian wall' surrounded much of the inhabited area below the Acropolis and the Areopagus. But no trace of any such wall has ever been found.[69] We do know however that, immediately after the Persian wars, whatever fortifications Athens may have had were thought to be inadequate. At the urging of the statesman Themistocles the people of Athens hurriedly erected a wall around their city. It had a stone socle (sometimes incorporating earlier grave monuments) but its superstructure, like many earlier fortification walls, was of mud brick.[70] Though the wall often had to be refurbished and, at times, rebuilt, it was this 'Themistoclean' wall that remained the basic line of defence for Athens for centuries to come. But it could not, of itself, ensure the safety of all the inhabitants of Attica, particularly those who were to live in the newly established port city of Piraeus, fortified in the 490s but, apparently, only established as a settlement sometime after 478 BC.[71] This city, built on an entirely new site, was laid out on a Hippodamian grid plan, whose features archaeologists are beginning to uncover. The Piraeus too had to be walled. A few decades later the two cities were to be linked by the Long Walls, fortifications built for the sole purpose of protecting communications between Athens and its port[72] (fig. 13.17).

The importance of the Piraeus to Athens, of course, lay in its harbours. The main harbour (the Kantharos) was used primarily for commercial shipping; the two smaller harbours of Zea and Mounychia were reserved as bases for Athens' powerful fleet of triremes. Some traces of this naval activity have survived, both in the form of actual ship-sheds (neoria, better rock-cut examples of which can be seen at Sounion) but also in the form of a large store-house for naval equipment, the skeuotheke of Philon, a long hall with double columns. Even this entirely

---

[68] Thucydides I.10.2; for discussion, see Cook 1955.
[69] Thucydides I.89.3; Wycherley 1978: 7–11.
[70] Thucydides I.90–3; Wycherley 1978: 11–16; Wrede 1933. For actual excavated parts of the Long Walls, see Travlos 1988: 288–300.
[71] Garland 1987; Wycherley 1978: 261–6; Hoepfner and Schwandner 1994: 22–31.
[72] Wycherley 1978: 15–16; Scranton 1938.

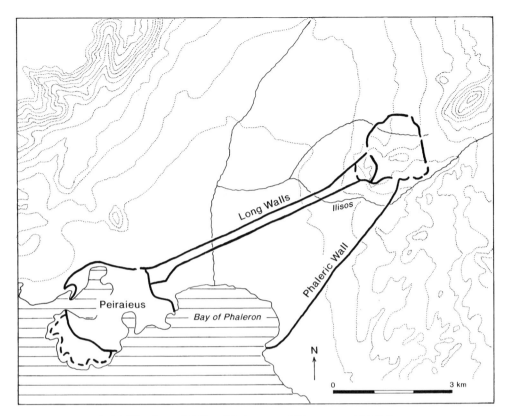

13.17 The Long Walls of Athens and Piraeus, *c.* 430 BC

functional building was decorated, albeit minimally, with a Doric frieze of triglyphs and metopes.[73]

Perhaps the most striking feature of the new city, however, was its houses.
Enough of these have turned up in rescue excavations in recent years to give us a
good idea, not only of the overall grid plan with its insulae (blocks), but also of
what an individual house was actually like. Many of these appear to have shared
a similar, if not quite identical, ground plan. They seem to have been quite small
'prostas' houses. Each had its own internal courtyard, a cistern and an andron that
could accommodate no more than seven diners. The plans and dimensions of
these houses are surprisingly similar to examples from Priene, built around one
hundred years later.[74] They are also remarkably unlike the (slightly later) courtyard houses that have been found in Athens itself. These are much less regular in

---

[73] Hoepfner and Schwandner 1994: 44–50.
[74] Hoepfner and Schwandner 1994: 23–43 (Piraeus) and 208–18 (Priene). For Priene, see also Wiegand
and Schrader 1904: 285–97. Not everyone agrees, however, that the average house in the Piraeus
was of more or less uniform size. Larger houses have been found, which have often been interpreted
as 'hotels' (Westgate pers. comm.).

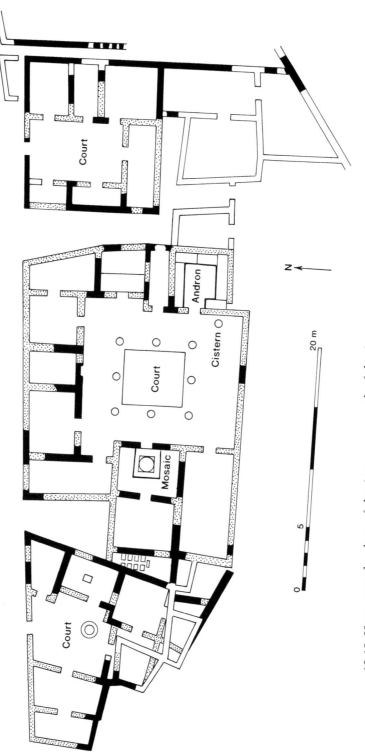

13.18 Houses on the slope of the Areopagos, south of the Agora

plan, and vary greatly in size. Examples include those houses excavated on the slopes of the Areopagus, just south of the Agora. One of these (which must be dated to the latter part of the fourth century) was quite large, having an internal peristyle court, and andron and mosaic floors[75] (fig. 13.18). Even larger houses, with much more impressive pebble mosaics, have been found on the outer edges of Athens, close to the Themistoclean wall.[76]

Though Piraeus may then seem to be the epitome of fifth-century political correctness, an embodiment of the ideal of isonomia (equal rights) and demokratia (rule by the people), where every free man has his plot, the same cannot be said for Athens itself. The irregular plans of houses in Athens is due, of course, to the fact that Athens was already an old city in 478 BC, and so had been built up in a haphazard fashion. But this fact alone cannot explain the wide disparities in the sizes of Athenian houses, nor in their degree of internal decoration. In some private houses, ostentation does not seem to have been frowned upon at all. Clearly there were great differences in wealth in Classical Athens, differences reflected in the houses themselves. The aristocracy survived the transition to democracy. Their values survived too. Perhaps the most effective means of examining how such a conflict of values may have affected Athens' material culture, would be to take a closer look at the evidence for that quintessential aristocratic institution: the symposion.

13.6 Public dining, private drinking: democratic and aristocratic symposia

There was no diminution in the scale of the production of Athenian fineware pottery in the fifth century BC. The pottery industry continued to employ several hundred people at any one time, and Athenian pots continue to be found all over the Mediterrannean.[77] Archaeological investigation has confirmed that pots were for the most part produced in the Potters' Quarter, the deme of the Kerameikos, just north and west of the Agora.[78] As in Archaic times, most fineware shapes, such as kraters (e.g. fig. 11.13), cups, amphoras and hydrias (e.g. fig. 2.2), were more suited to drinking than eating. This fundamental continuity is also reflected in pot imagery. Symposion and mythological scenes continue to dominate, as they had in the 'aristocratic' past. There are few, if any, images which could be seen as

---

[75] Shear 1973a: 146–56. For general discussion of Athenian houses, see Wycherley 1978: 237–52; Jones 1975; Nevett 1999: 86–7.   [76] Wycherley 1978: 243–4; Graham 1974; Jones 1975: 93–7.

[77] For discussion of the organisation of the pottery industry, see Beazley 1989b; Arafat and Morgan 1989; Cook 1972: 270–4. Cook's estimates are based on information given in Beazley 1963; 1971; summarised by Boardman 1989. Recent discoveries (summarised by Bazianopoulou-Valavani 1994) indicate that most of the kilns and workshops were located in the Outer Kerameikos (that is, outside the walls), in the direction of the Academy and the Kolonos Hippios (that is, to the north-west)

[78] Oakley 1992: esp. 203. Oakley infers, rightly, that much workshop activity must have taken place within the walls. But see the recent summary by Bazianopolou-Valavani 1994 (and note 77 above). Workshops may have had to have been relocated inside the walls because of the disturbed conditions of the Peloponnesian war.

reflecting a new, democratic point of view.[79] Is then the introduction of democracy less of a profound cultural change than some have supposed? Why are there not more 'democratic' images? What other reasons might there be for this continuity in shape and iconography?

One is that the overseas market for Athenian pots seems to have remained much the same. Works of major 'vase painters' continued to reach Italy. The overwhelming number of pots painted by the Berlin painter for example (active around 490 BC) have come from Italian contexts.[80] In the later fifth century, many of the pots attributed to the Meidias painter too have an Italian provenance.[81] There is nothing to indicate that any Etruscan, Latin, Campanian or Greek city in Italy became 'democratic'. Athenian shapes and imagery continued much as before because the tastes and circumstances of Athens' Italian customers remained much the same. Still, many are not satisfied that Athenian pots were made partly with Italian customers in mind, and so have come up with other explanations. The most forcefully argued of these is Michael Vickers' suggestion that the real democratic revolution only happened in the middle of the fifth century.[82] It was this revolution that led to a change in taste, and ultimately to a shift in iconography. Vickers' explanation however requires that we believe in a large number of auxiliary hypotheses: that the red-figure technique was invented only after the Persian wars; that red-figure expressly imitates the overall effect of gold on tarnished silver; that pottery was nothing more than a poor man's silver, whose decoration was a dim (if sometimes exact) reflection of the lost glory of metal vessels.[83] We are also required to believe that there was a Chinese-style 'cultural revolution' in the mid-fifth century, a revolution led by the Athenian politician Ephialtes, a revolution responsible (amongst other things) for the destruction of the Archaic buildings and dedications on the Acropolis by Ephialtes' 'red guards', an act of vandalism usually (and more plausibly) attributed to the Persians.[84]

In its extreme form, Vickers' hypothesis is untenable. But he is right to point out that there is, at some level, a relationship between the shapes of metal vessels and those of pots. Some fineware shapes do seem to derive from metal prototypes, even if the best examples are not 'red-figure' but 'black-glazed'.[85] He is right too to insist that the richer members of Athenian society would, in all probability,

[79] See generally Robertson 1992; Boardman 1989. For a few images with possible democratic overtones, see Spivey 1994.

[80] For the Berlin painter, see Beazley and Kurtz 1983; Beazley 1963: 196–214. For the distribution of his wares, see Sparkes 1996: 164–6.   [81] Burn 1987; Beazley 1963: 1,312–32.

[82] Vickers 1990b. For changes in iconography, see Himmelmann 1994: 23–48. If anything 'banausic' scenes become less common in the latter half of the fifth century.

[83] For arguments to this effect, see Vickers 1985a; 1990a; Vickers and Gill 1994: 105–53.

[84] Vickers 1990b. Ephialtes is however known to us only from relatively late sources; Aristotle's *Constitution of Athens* and Plutarch's *Pericles*. He is not mentioned by the only contemporary source we have for the mid-fifth century, the historian Thucydides. Sources mention nothing that could be construed as a revolution – merely a number of constitutional changes known as 'Ephialtes' reforms'.

[85] For black-glazed wares, see Sparkes and Talcott 1970; for discussion, see Sparkes 1996: 29–33, 145–51.

have used metal vessels in their symposia. There are some Classical houses in Athens which are large enough and splendid enough to have been the scene of such occasions. The house in Menander street, for example, has an exceptionally large andron which could seat at least fifteen symposiasts. The andron itself, and its anteroom, were both decorated with pebble mosaics of very high quality.[86] It may have been in such a room that Plato imagined the setting for his *Symposium*.

How far down the social scale did the use of metal vessels extend? Direct archaeological evidence for metal vessels is not to be found. Finds of pottery in houses have been less informative than one might have hoped. Excavations of houses in the Attic countryside have uncovered only meagre finds, mainly of 'black-glazed' pottery. Still, fragments of red-figure kraters were found at both the Vari House (fig. 13.19) and the Dema House, suggesting that symposia of some kind must have taken place there.[87] The pottery from houses around the Agora has yet to be fully published.[88] More informative are the finds from a small house in the Piraeus. A black-glazed skyphos, and other sherds not out of place in a symposion, have been recovered from a room next to the house's very small andron.[89] The evidence is scanty, but, given that metal vessels are more likely to have been used in houses with a large and well-decorated andron than in smaller and meaner dwellings, then the following hierarchy can be proposed. At the bottom rung was the small 'citizen's house' like the one in the Piraeus, with an andron that could only fit three couches and direct evidence only for the use of black-glazed pottery. Above this are the Vari House, the Dema House and the houses found near the Agora, with larger androones. The quantity of red-figured pottery, particularly kraters, found in and around the Agora strongly suggests that many must have been used in private as well as public symposia.[90] At the top end of the scale is the house like the one at Menander street, where metal vessels must surely have been used.

But what of public dining? Dining at public expense was one of the privileges (and duties) of Athenian officials. Hestiatoria (dining rooms) were attached to a

---

[86] Graham 1974. For mosaics in houses generally, see Westgate 1998; Salzmann 1982: 85–8. In my figures here (as elsewhere) I have been assuming that there was only one symposiast per couch. Iconographic evidence seems to show that this was the general rule, though there are also scenes (such as the tomb of the diver from Paestum) which show two symposiasts sharing the same couch.

[87] For these, see Jones 1975: 100–17; Jones *et al.* 1962: 87–100 (Dema House); Jones *et al.* 1973: 373–96 (Vari House). The Dema House is a late fifth-, the Vari House a late fourth-century structure. However it is remarkable how the proportions of types of pottery from these deposits remain (roughly) the same. Of the 98 sherds catalogued from the Dema House, four are red-figure and two of these are kraters; of the 195 catalogued from the Vari House, three are red-figure, of which two again are kraters.

[88] Most published pottery, both black-glazed (Sparkes and Talcott 1970) and red-figure (Moore 1997), seems to come from secondary or even tertiary deposits, such as filled-in wells, rather than primary ones such as house floors.

[89] Hoepfner and Schwandner 1994: 34–8; for the dating criteria, see Sparkes and Talcott 1970.

[90] There is now good statistical evidence to demonstrate that the krater was much more of a red-figure than a black-glazed shape. Of the 2,040 black-glazed vessels catalogued by Sparkes and Talcott (1970: 54–5), only ten are kraters. Of the 1,684 red-figure pots catalogued by Moore however (Moore 1997: 157–221), 420 are kraters. This strongly suggests that red-figure had a higher value than black and plain wares. See also discussion in Rotroff 1996.

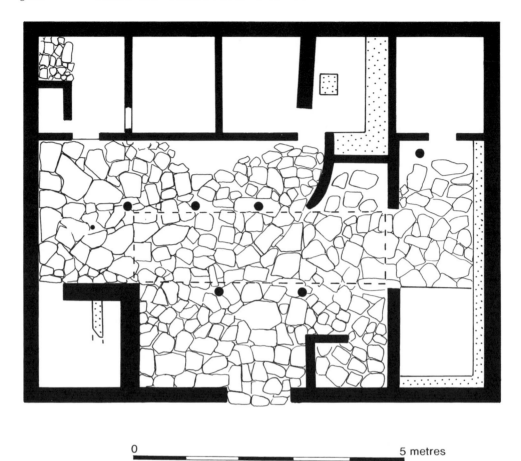

0 ———————————————————————— 5 metres

13.19 Plan of Vari house

number of public buildings, including the Pompeion in the Kerameikos, the start-ing point of the Panathenaic procession.[91] Dining seems to have taken place in several buildings in the Agora; the South Stoa; the stoa basileios; and the tholos. The size and shape of the tholos is such that the fifty prytaneis could never have dined there all together, all reclining on couches. They must have taken their communal meals sitting down.[92] Was dining while sitting then quintessentially democratic, whilst reclining remained 'aristocratic'? Since the South Stoa seems to have been designed to accommodate symposia, where the metronomoi dined on couches, no such inference can be made.[93] But it is unlikely that the symposia of public officials involved the use of very expensive metal vessels. Indeed the

---

[91] Hoepfner 1976. There are other 'hestiatoria' close to other public buildings and shrines in Athens, notably the Asklepeion; see Wycherley 1978: 181–2.
[92] See arguments in Cooper and Morris 1990.
[93] Thompson and Wycherley 1972: 74–8; Camp 1992: 122–6; Wycherley 1978: 44–5.

quantity of kraters, amphoras and cups found in the vicinity indicates that pots, not metal, were thought suitable for public dining. Perhaps the best indication of the kinds of vessels used comes from the deposit behind the stoa basileios. The deposit included a whole range of drinking shapes, both red-figure and black-glazed.[94]

Now vessels used in public dining can hardly have been the most expensive available; but nor are they likely to have been the cheapest. The stoa basileios deposit compares favourably with pots known to have come from private houses, and may give us our best impression of the pottery thought good enough to dine and drink with by an Athenian family (or drinking club) of the 'middling sort'. By 450 BC the symposium had clearly ceased to be an exclusively aristocratic affair. Indeed, the popularity of androns in most houses in both Athens and the Piraeus indicates clearly that this custom had 'trickled down' to the citizen population at large. The symposion had been democratised, and, as the fifth century wore on, the images on symposium pots changed too. Scenes with satyrs and Dionysos, and of aristocratic gatherings with fairly explicit sexual overtones, diminish in number, though myths remain as popular as ever.[95]

There were none the less areas of Athenian ceramic production that had little to do with drinking. Coarse household wares continued to be used in the kitchen and for storage. Athenian potters produced other kinds of fineware pottery for special occasions. Panathenaic amphoras continue in the black-figure style well into the fourth century BC.[96] A shape known as the chous (plural choes) was made specifically for use during the spring Festival of Flowers, the Anthesteria.[97] Varieties of white-ground vessels, particularly lekythoi, seem to have been made solely for use in funerals.[98] Social archaeologists have always taken a particular interest in the ways in which mortuary practices reflect either the structure or the values of past societies. The same interest applies to Classical Athens. Were Athenian graves then, in any sense, 'democratic'? Is there a direct relationship between a society's ideology and the ways in which it chose to bury or commemorate its dead?

13.7 Everyman's hero, everyman's tomb: burial in democratic Athens

In 490 BC the young Athenian democracy faced its first major test. The Persians had sent an expeditionary force to punish those Greek states, Eretria and Athens, which had supported the Ionian revolt. When the Persians landed at Marathon,

---

[94] Rotroff and Oakley 1992: 41–6; Talcott 1936: 352–4.

[95] See in general Robertson 1992; Boardman 1989. Himmelmann (1994: 23–48) notes a decline in scenes of everyday life, including symposion scenes.
  The whole question of the relationship between image and society is, of course, more complex than I have indicated here. Images do not directly 'reflect' anything, they comment upon them in oblique ways. For recent contributions to debates, see Csapo and Miller 1998 (on the kinds of narrative that appear in Classical times); Shapiro 1998 (on the question of autochthony and Athenian identity).   [96] Beazley 1986: 81–92; Bentz 1998.   [97] Hamilton 1992.   [98] Kurtz 1975.

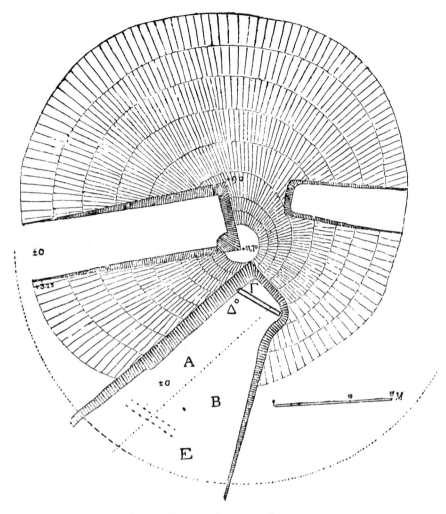

13.20 Plan of the Marathon tumulus

however, they were defeated. The victors, following recent practice, buried their dead (192 in all) where they fell, under a great mound or tumulus. This polyandrion (communal tomb) has been identified and excavated (fig. 13.20). The dead were cremated, and offerings of black-figure lekythoi placed in a clay-lined trench alongside.[99] The manner of burial resembles nothing so much as those aristocratic graves of the seventh century. Cremation beneath a tumulus has been taken as a deliberate allusion to the manner in which heroes were buried in the *Iliad*. The Athenians who buried their dead in this manner were then appropriating an aristocratic set of values that had likened the *kaloikagathoi* (beautiful and good) to

---

[99] For the excavation of the tumulus, see Stais 1893; for a summary in English, Hammond 1968: 14–17. The mound is noted by Pausanias I.32.3.

Homeric heroes, and used it to honour the war dead of the new democracy. Aristocratic symbols and values had been hijacked for democratic ends.[100]

At some later time, the 'Marathonomachai' (the Athenian hoplites who fought and died at Marathon) were treated as heroes. We do not know exactly when this happened, but it certainly fits in with a pattern of new hero cults that was characteristic of the new democracy.[101] One of Cleisthenes' reforms was to elevate ten *archegetai* (it is not entirely clear what this word means) to act as the ten Eponymous heroes for the ten tribes of the new order. Much later, in the fourth century, a monument to these figures was erected in the Agora.[102] Hero cults of many kinds flourished in Classical Athens; but some of the older tomb cults, notably the one at Menidhi, declined into insignificance.[103] Aristocratic forms which could serve the new democracy were transformed; others, whose significance was perhaps too closely tied to local, aristocratic kin groups, gradually disappeared. It may then be that the practice of tumulus burial was still too closely associated with the older and richer families of Attica to remain the preferred mode of burial for the war dead; or it may be that burying the dead where they fell in those foreign fields where Athenians found themselves in the earlier fifth century proved impractical. In any case, from about 460 BC, the war dead were brought back to Athens to be buried. Throughout Greece in the fifth century, the dead were normally buried outside the walls. In Athens, a special place, the *demosion sema*, was reserved for the war dead in the deme of the Kerameikos. The term demosion sema seems to refer to all public grave monuments, erected in the course of the fifth and fourth centuries along the road that leads from the Dipylon gate to the Academy.[104] The dead were commemorated individually as well as collectively, their names being inscribed in vertical rows on stone stelai.

These stelai are sometimes misleadingly referred to as 'casualty lists', as if they were issued by some Athenian Ministry of Information, intent that the public be kept abreast of Athens' wars abroad.[105] Lists of the war dead, however, convey more than information. The ranks of the dead on the Vietnam War memorial in Washington, or those to be found on monuments naming those who fell in the Great War in towns and villages all over England, Scotland and Wales, are more than 'lists'; they are memorials, there to perpetuate the memory of the fallen in the minds of later generations, and to hold up the dead as examples of valour and patriotism. That a similar purpose may be inferred for the 'casualty lists' is clear

---

[100] For arguments to this effect, see Whitley 1994b.

[101] Pausanias I.32.4; Whitley 1994b: 215–17, 226–30. See also Kearns 1989 for the literary and epigraphical evidence for Classical hero cults.

[102] Shear 1970; Kron 1976; Mattusch 1994. Cleisthenes' actions are noted in Aristotle's *Constitution of the Athenians* 21.6. There may have been an earlier monument to the Eponymous heroes, but if so no one has found it yet.

[103] For tomb cults of Classical date around the Agora, see Lalonde 1980. For the Menidhi tholos tomb, see Wolters 1899 and discussion in Antonaccio 1995: 104–9.

[104] Thucydides II.34.1–8. For discussion, see Clairmont 1983: esp. 7–15.

[105] This is the impression given by Bradeen 1969; 1974: 3–34. For discussion, see Clairmont 1983: esp. 46–59.

from another democratic practice instituted at the same time: the funeral speech, which set out to honour and commemorate the war dead.[106] Epigraphers have referred to these inscriptions as 'lists' because of their apparent plainness. But the adoption of a 'plain style' to commemorate the common warrior (and common man) is characteristic of democracies. A plain style is an effective means of stressing the essential equality of those who died in war, fighting for their city or their country. It is also in keeping with other changes in mortuary practice in early democratic Athens.

Plainness is the keynote of the early fifth century. The 'plain style' even extended to the tombs of distinguished foreigners. Pythagoras of Selymbria, a proxenos (a sort of ambassador) who seems to have died around 450 BC, was commemorated by nothing grander than a marble stele (fig. 13.21), set up over an inscription on a limestone plinth.[107] This is a monument fully in keeping with the spirit of the time and the place. The elaborate marble grave markers – the stelai, kouroi and korai – which had been so characteristic of late sixth-century Attica come to an abrupt end around 490 BC.[108] As overt signs of aristocratic kalokagathia diminish, so the number of actual graves uncovered increases dramatically. As in the late eighth century, the rate at which Athenians seem to be burying their dead undergoes something of a 'quantum leap', rising from around three per annum in 500 BC to around nine per annum in 450 BC (see fig. 8.10). At the same time, the number and quality of grave goods remains, to say the least, unspectacular.[109] The greater inclusiveness of graves, and the marked lack of wealth differences between them, has lent support to the idea that burial practices in this instance reflect an ideology of equality. Democracy acted as a kind of 'levelling ideology', which made it imprudent for anyone unduly to stress any superiority in wealth or birth. Everyone, in death at least, was equal; parsimony in grave goods, and plainness in sculptural expression, therefore came into favour.

This apparent uniformity, however, may mask other differences. Children's graves, as ever in Athens, were slightly different from those of adults. But any serious discussion of age and gender would rely on information supplied by osteologists. Only Classical graves from the Eckterrasse in the Kerameikos have been studied in this way, and no social analyses have yet been produced. One can say, however, that differences between adult male and adult female burials are far from pronounced.[110] This situation began to change subtly after 460 BC. Black-figure and red-figure grave goods are gradually replaced by white-ground vessels, particularly lekythoi. Such pots tend to have a distinctive iconography. They frequently show scenes of parting, or of mourning/commemoration beside grave markers

---

106 The most famous example of which is Pericles' funeral speech, Thucydides II.35–46. For discussion see Loraux 1986: 15–76.
107 Hoepfner 1973. See discussion in Morris 1992: 141–2; Knigge 1991: 97–9.
108 There are, I think, no kouroi or grave stelai in Richter's catalogues (Richter 1961: 53–5; 1970) which can be dated to after 490 BC.   109 For figures, see Morris 1987: 72–5, 220–1; 1992: 103–44.
110 On the Eckterrasse, see Kovasovics 1990; and discussion in Morris 1991b.

13.21 Drawing of the grave monument of Pythagoras of Selymbria

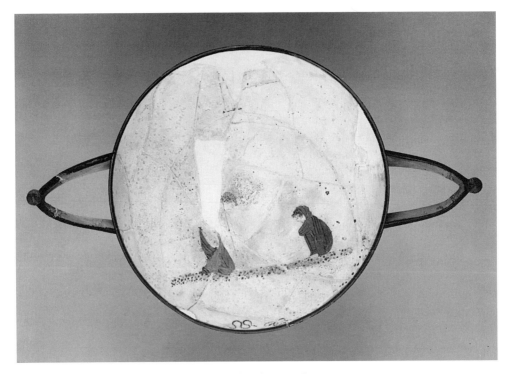

13.22 A white-ground cup by the Sotades painter

whose counterparts in the archaeological record have yet to be found.[111] Sometimes their imagery seems to relate directly to beliefs in an afterlife; Hermes Psychopompos, Hermes the bearer of souls, is often to be seen, escorting the dead to their place in Hades.

These white-ground vessels were, for the most part, made and painted by the same craftsmen who were responsible for red-figure. Some potters however seemed to excel in the medium of white-ground. One such was Sotades (see chapter 11 above), an innovator and experimenter with difficult shapes such as the rhyton.[112] Sometimes pots from Sotades' workshop are found in groups, groups which, in all probability, came from a single grave. A number of scholars have suggested that images on pots from one of these groups, now in the British Museum, relate to one another in quite a specific way (fig. 13.22). Taken together, they tell a story, or rather several stories with a common theme. The imagery thus provides us with important clues to Classical Athenian attitudes to death and the afterlife, clues which we do not find in the literary record.[113] Pots were probably not expensive grave items, but they do seem to have been carefully chosen to suit the

---

[111] Beazley 1989c; Kurtz 1975; Boardman 1989: 129–43.
[112] Hoffmann 1997; Robertson 1992: 185–90; Beazley 1963: 763–73.
[113] Burn 1985; Osborne 1988; Griffiths 1986. For a recent discussion of imagery on white-ground pots generally, see Sourvinou-Inwood 1995: 303–61.

circumstances of a particular man or woman. There are specific meanings to be uncovered beneath a general pattern of parsimony. This pattern is none the less the single most important fact of fifth-century Athenian burial practices. Differences between 'rich' and 'poor' graves are, statistically speaking, insignificant. The aristocratic and heroic connotations of cremation seem to have resonated hardly at all in fifth-century Athens – both cremation and inhumation were practised, and cremations are only slightly 'richer' than inhumations.[114] When this overall pattern changes we should take note.

Sometime after the beginning of the Peloponnesian war, Athenians began erecting sculptured grave monuments once more. These sculptures are often of considerable skill and quality, and it has been suggested that such stelai came back into fashion partly as a means of employing sculptors left idle after the completion of the Parthenon.[115] This may have been a factor, but something else is needed to account for such a sharp break with earlier fifth-century practice. A clue may lie in the revival of the peribolos or family grave enclosure. Such enclosures become more and more elaborate from the late fifth century onwards. Eventually, some manage to contain the remains of four generations of one particular family (fig. 13.23).[116] This emphasis on family may help to explain why a more ostentatious form of funerary display was accepted after 430 BC. Let us take a closer look at two monuments in detail, both from family periboloi. The first, dating to around 400 BC, shows Hegeso, wife of Proxenos (fig. 13.24). She is shown in profile, framed by a pediment with antae, and seated on a high-backed chair. She appears to be examining a box of jewellery being presented to her by her maid (a slave, most likely).[117] It is not possible to infer anything about Hegeso's age and circumstances from the inscription. (Attic funerary inscriptions rarely give such details). In the sculpture, she appears young, but somehow indistinct. Apart from her hairpiece, there is little that sets her apart from any other respectable wife or mother shown on grave monuments. 'Hegeso' closely resembles 'Ampharete', on another grave stele, and indeed an image of a seated woman from an earlier white-ground lekythos by the Achilles painter.[118] She is, in short, a specimen of a type, the very image of what an Athenian wife ought to look like: she attends to the duties of the house; while seeming 'young' and pretty, her drapery does not cling with the erotic suggestiveness of one of the victories from the parapet of Athena Nike. Wives and mothers had become more important to

[114] Morris 1992: 108–18; 1998b: 64–7.

[115] On this suggestion, see Richter 1961: 54–5; Boardman 1985a: 183–5. On tombstones generally, see Meyer 1993; Clairmont 1993a: 1993b.

[116] On periboloi, see Garland 1982. On family tomb plots, Humphreys 1980; Morris 1992: 128–49. For the evidence on which these discussions are based, see especially Kovasovics 1990; Knigge 1976; 1991: 111–48.

[117] Clairmont 1993b: 95–8; Osborne 1998: 195–201. For a general discussion of gender and the representation of women, see Stears 1995.

[118] On Ampharete, see Clairmont 1993a: 404–8. On this (Athens NM 1818; Beazley 1963: 998 no. 161) and other lekythoi by the Achilles painter, see Robertson 1992: 198–210; Oakley 1997: esp. 65–6.

13.23 Restored elevation drawing of precinct of Koroibos showing position of Hegeso's grave stele

Athenian identity after the reforms of the mid-fifth century. These stated, quite unequivocally, that to be an Athenian citizen one had to have, not only an Athenian father, but an Athenian mother too.[119] What better way then to affirm one's own (or one's children's) status as a good citizen than to put up a stele for your wife or mother?

The stele of Hegeso shows one way in which the competing demands of democratic ideology and family sentiment could be accommodated. The monument to Dexileos (figs. 13.25 and 13.26) on the other hand shows how such ideals could actually reinforce one another. Dexileos was an Athenian cavalryman who died in battle, serving his city, in 394/3 BC. Dexileos' actual body was laid to rest with the other war dead, but his family chose to erect a monument to him in their peribolos in the Kerameikos none the less. His monument was then an empty tomb,

[119] For this legislation, see Plutarch, *Pericles* 37.3; Aristotle, *Constitution of the Athenians* 26.4.

13.24 Grave stele of Hegeso

13.25 Drawing showing grave precinct of Dexileos

a cenotaph. It shows a young cavalryman with his horse trampling his enemy underfoot. The sculpture is not really realistic – the horse is too small for his rider, the billowing cloak is a little theatrical, and the faces of both Dexileos and his fallen enemy are more or less identical. Still, the monument makes its point quite effectively. For not every member of the wealthy 'cavalry class' fought for the democracy in the years around 400 BC. The inscription, uniquely, gives Dexileos' date of birth. This information conspicuously dissociates Dexileos from other members of his class who had been less than supportive of democracy in the preceding decades.[120] Dexileos is shown as a good soldier, cavalryman and democrat, someone of whom his family could be proud.

---

[120] Clairmont 1993b: 143–5; Osborne 1998: 13–16. On the iconography of 'state burials' generally, see Stupperich 1994.

13.26 Grave stele of Dexileos, in the Kerameikos, Athens

This may all seem obvious and rather natural. But family sentiment had never before been so conspicuous in Athenian grave monuments. Those of the Archaic age had emphasised individual arete, and often the grave goods accentuate forms of association (such as the symposion) other than the family. It is the fourth century in particular which is the heyday of Attic funerary sculpture, peribolos tombs and the sentiments of 'democracy and family' that underscored such ostentation. The sequence of monuments, however, comes to an abrupt end around 317 BC. The legislation of the new Athenian puppet ruler, Demetrios of Phaleron, outlawed such lavish sculptural display. Athenian citizens had henceforth to be commemorated in one of two ways: either by a monument known as a *trapeza*, or by a *kioniskos*, a small marble or limestone cylinder. These monuments could only be inscribed with a person's name, his father's name and his deme.[121] We appear here to be faced with a contradiction. Demetrios was no democrat; some later authors call him tyrant. His patrons were the new Hellenistic monarchs, Cassander in Macedon and Ptolemy in Egypt. But he was a philosopher, and, like many philosophers given political power, saw Athens as a kind of laboratory for the creation of the 'ideal state'. The fact that Athens, by this time, was no power to be reckoned with made his task that much easier. His promulgation in favour of the plain style of commemoration can therefore be seen as an extreme, philosophical expression of the polis ideology of isonomia, of the essential equality of all citizens. That this innovation outlasted Demetrios' rule, that it was maintained through various restorations of 'democracy' in Hellenistic times, testifies to the continued appeal of the polis idea. It is, of course, ironic that this 'plain style' flourished when Athens had ceased to count for much. But it may be a general rule of history that ideologies are most emphasised when the social order they represent is most threatened, and identities most cherished once the cause with which they are most closely associated has been lost.

Still we are left with a paradox: the burial record of Athens seems most 'democratic' when Athens had in fact ceased to be so. But it should not surprise us too much that there is no perfect match between political structure, ideology and material expression. Athenian culture had never been wholeheartedly democratic. Aristocratic symposia continued in Classical times, and there is indirect evidence to suggest that such symposia made more and more use of metal vessels towards the end of the fourth century.[122] Athenian public art may have wished to suggest that the Athenian common man was very much superior to the effeminate, barbarian Persians, but Persian luxury continued to have a positive appeal for many richer Athenians. How else can we explain the popularity of the rhyton, a vessel modelled on Persian metal prototypes?[123] True, the most democratic of

---

[121] For the effect of this legislation, see Knigge 1991: 42. See also discussion in Houby-Nielsen 1997. For the career of Demetrios of Phaleron, see Green 1990: 36–51.

[122] Rotroff 1996. The evidence is indirect.

[123] For rhyta, see Hoffmann 1961. For other aspects of fifth-century 'Persianising' iconography, see Hoffmann 1988. For a general discussion of the phenomenon, see Miller 1997: 135–52, 256–8.

Greek states was probably the most literate, to judge by the number of Athenian inscriptions that have been found.[124] Literacy played a crucial role in many democratic practices, such as ostracism. Still, many aspects of literacy and literary culture remained recondite. How many Athenians would ever read the inscriptions on book rolls which appear on a small number of red-figure pots?[125] Classical Athens remained an unequal society – less equal, in some respects, than Archaic Athens. For Classical Athens was also a slave economy. Our best material evidence for this, however, comes, not from the city but from the countryside.

---

[124] Classical Athens is rich in graffiti and inscriptions of every kind. It also boasts three out of the ten fourth-century personal letters written on lead which have been found (Jordan 2000). For the evidence from the Agora, see Lang 1976; for a selection of other inscriptions, Immerwahr 1990: 98–127.   [125] Immerwahr 1964; 1973.

CHAPTER 14

BEYOND THE POLIS: THE COUNTRYSIDE OF CLASSICAL GREECE

14.1 The Greek countryside

The Greek countryside has not traditionally been a principal object of the Classical archaeologist's attention. After all, ancient writers on ancient art concentrated on towns and sanctuaries; for Pausanias, the country was something one passed through between one shrine (whether urban or rural) and the next. For those scholars then for whom Pausanias is not merely a source but an inspiration, the countryside and its remains was hardly a dignified object of study. This does not quite mean that the archaeology of the Greek countryside has been neglected, but rather that its study was peripheral to 'Classical Archaeology' as traditionally understood. It has been not so much archaeologists as historians, particularly those with a strong interest in social or economic history, who have made the countryside their study. This is in spite of the usual philological inhibitions of classically trained historians, in this case the lack of a Greek equivalent for our term 'countryside'. To be sure, 'chora' (that is land or country) in ancient Greek is often opposed to 'asty' or 'polis' (town or city), but the term has none of the pleasurable connotations that 'countryside' has in English. It takes a Romantic, or at least a leisured, sensibility to look at rural Greece as 'countryside' or 'landscape'. This was not because ancient Greeks were insensitive to the beauty of springs, mountains and sea. Far from it. But any ancient 'phenomenology of landscape' focussed on certain locales, usually considered sacred, such as springs, groves or mountain peaks.[1] They had no sentimental attachment to the 'countryside' as such. The reason for this is simple. In ancient times, the country was no Arcadia. It was not a place of leisure or of *fêtes champêtres*, but a place of toil. Another Greek term for the country was *oikoumene*, the place where one lived and worked. The oikoumene was opposed to the *eschatia*, the (often mountainous) borderlands.[2] The oikoumene was where food was grown, animals were tended and goods – whether raw materials such as metals, or finished products such as pottery – were produced. It was a working landscape, one with no clear-cut distinction between the rural and the industrial.

That the study of the countryside may confound our romantic notions of the 'Classical' is not, however, a sufficient reason for paying it close attention. The

---

[1] For the concept of 'phenomenology', see Tilley 1994.   [2] Snodgrass 1987: 67–92.

chora of an ancient Greek polis was every bit as important to its citizens as its urban core. Indeed, recent studies have underlined quite how interdependent town and country were. Houses at Halieis in the southern Argolid, for example, which were located well within the perimeter of the city's walls, were (in the fourth century at least) equipped with olive presses and *koprones*. These last were pits for rubbish, not so much manure as mulch piles or rubbish heaps. Material from these koprones would (it is argued) later be used to increase the fertility of a householder's plot of agricultural land.[3] Archaeological traces in the countryside then represent patterns of human activity that relate directly to the life of the Greek polis, however distorted they may be by a variety of post-depositional factors. These patterns in turn are fundamental to our reconstruction of Greek society – or rather of the differences and similarities between the societies of Sparta, Athens, Boeotia, Crete or any other region of Greece. The countryside is the rural obverse of the polis. In more developed regions of Greece, the country-side was populated as much by (usually foreign) slaves as by (invariably Greek) cit-izens. Nowhere is this more evident than in Attica in Classical times.

14.2 Classical Attica: a working countryside

Unlike neighbouring Boeotia, there has been no large-scale intensive survey of the Attic countryside. Only the extremities of Attica have been explored using intensive methods: the Skourta plain to the north, an upland border area lying between Boeotia and Attica, whose status remained unclear throughout Antiquity; and the far south-east of the Attic peninsula, the area corresponding to the ancient deme of Atene.[4] Attica has however been thoroughly explored by generations of travellers, historians and archaeologists. Their accumulated lore has, in recent years, been supplemented by rescue excavations undertaken by the Greek Archaeological Service, in advance of such major developments as the con-struction of the new Athens airport at Spata.[5] All of this should, in principle, give us a reasonably good picture of the Attic settlement pattern. But in fact it has not. There are now two radically different views of how Attica was settled, and what the Attic countryside was used for. The first, which may be called the 'nucleated settlement model', has been championed by Robin Osborne; the second, which we could call the 'dispersed farmstead model', has been put forward by Hans Lohmann.

In the first view, most of Attica's inhabitants (outside of Athens and the Piraeus) lived in villages, villages which for the most part correspond to the ancient demes.[6] In the area around modern Vouliagmeni, for example, settle-ment seems to be densely concentrated in two areas, which seem to correspond

---

[3] Ault 1999.
[4] For the Skourta plain survey, see Munn and Zimmermann Munn 1989. For the Atene survey, Lohmann 1992; 1993a.   [5] E.g. Steinhauer 1994.
[6] This is the general argument of Osborne 1985: 37–42, 192–3.

to the demes of Halai Aixonidai (Ano Voula) and Anagyrous (Vari). Recent excavations have confirmed that these demes at least were nucleated villages, rather than dispersed groups of hamlets or isolated farmsteads.[7] Of course, Osborne does acknowledge that single farmsteads or dwellings did exist: the Dema House, in western Attica, is one, and the Vari House, just north of Anagyrous (fig. 13.19), another.[8] But these farmhouses seem to have been occupied for only brief periods of time, and may not have been intended as places of permanent residence. The Dema House seems to have been built during a lull during the Peloponnesian war, a war whose final stages rendered it uninhabitable.[9] The Vari House on the other hand was constructed later, in the fourth century, and seems to have been built for a special purpose. The lower slopes of Mt Hymettos are ideal for bee keeping, and it is at the Vari House that large quantities of combed coarseware pots (of a type similar to those used to make modern beehives) have been found.[10] Osborne's views have however been strongly countered by Hans Lohmann, who bases his own interpretations on his one-man survey of the deme of Atene in south-east Attica (fig. 13.1). We know from literary evidence that this area was one of the Attic demes, but one that appears to have no nucleated centre or major deme settlement.[11] Instead Lohmann found a dispersed pattern of isolated farmsteads, sixteen in all, nine of which had towers.[12] Some of these farmhouses, particularly those at Palaia Kopraisia, are of a size and complexity that suggest they were places of permanent residence. Site LE17 has a whole complex of structures, including a threshing floor and a sheepfold, and site LE16 was furnished with an andron with room for seven couches (figs. 14.1 and 14.2).[13] The area of Atene moreover seems to have been extensively terraced in Classical times. Terracing is a labour-intensive activity and a costly one. There would have to be some special reason beyond the need to intensify in this manner. Lohmann argues that the terraces are in fact indirect evidence for extensive rural slavery, and that only emphasis on a cash crop (such as the olive) could have justified such investment.[14]

Now of course one could argue that Atene is an atypical deme. Certainly, it is an unusual one in that it has no signs of occupation dating to the eighth and seventh centuries, and only the slightest indications of any sixth-century activity. Osborne has argued that it was a 'new deme', unlike most deme sites which

---

[7] For recent excavations at Halai Aixonidai (Ano Voula), see Andreou 1994; Lohmann 1992: 35–9; 1993a: 129–36. See also Osborne 1985: 22–9, 192–5.

[8] On the Dema House, see Jones *et al.* 1962; on the Vari house, Jones *et al.* 1973. For a partial catalogue of isolated farmsteads in Attica, see Osborne 1985: 190–1.

[9] Jones *et al.* 1962: 100–1. There may, however, be other reasons for the short 'life-span' of rural houses; see now Foxhall 2000.

[10] Jones *et al.* 1973: 397–414. There are similar finds from other sites in Attica: Trachones (Jones *et al.* 1973: 443–8); the Princess tower near Sounion (Jones *et al.* 1973: 448–52); and on the top of the hill of Velatouri, above Thorikos (Jones 1990).   [11] Lohmann 1992: 35.

[12] Lohmann 1993a: 126–248.   [13] Lohmann 1992: 42–9; 1993a: 513–17.

[14] Lohmann 1992: 51–6. See in particular the evidence found around PH33 (Lohmann 1993a: 431–3). On terraces generally, see Rackham and Moody 1992; on olive cultivation, Forbes 1992.

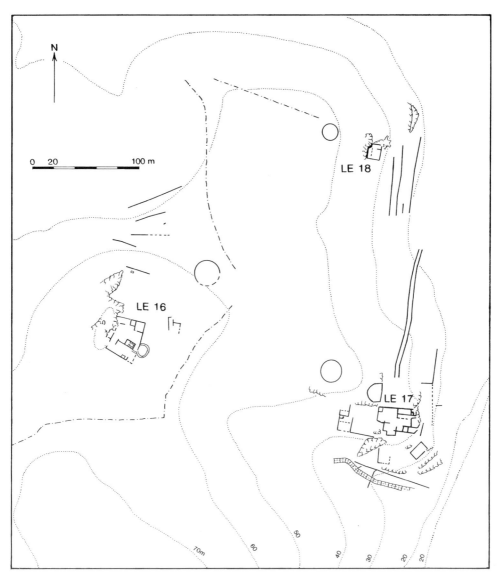

14.1 Farm complexes at Palaia Kopraisia (sites LE16 and LE17) in the area of the Atene survey

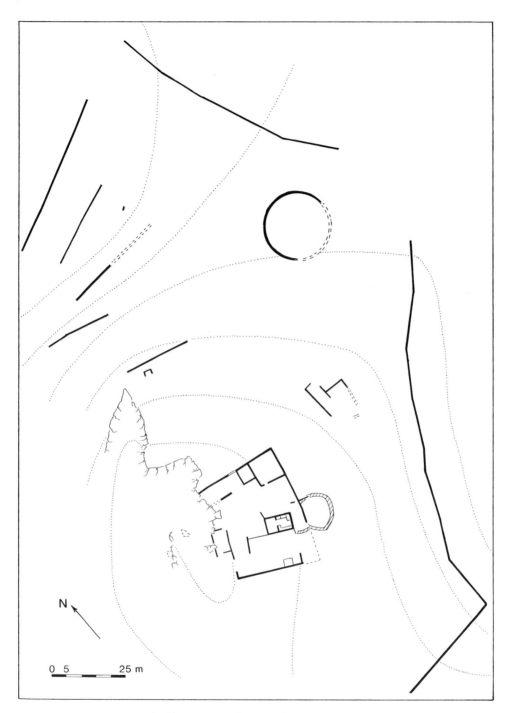

14.2 Detail of house complex at Palaia Kopraisia (site LE16)

go back to Geometric times.[15] But even if this is conceded, how 'atypical' was it? Clearly, settlement pattern may well have been different in the central Attic plain and other areas better suited to large-scale arable farming, such as the present-day Mesogeia. It may then be more instructive to compare Atene with the deme areas immediately adjacent to it, areas which shared the same basic topography of small, bare hills and small, coastal plains – namely Laurion.

The Laurion region was famed in Antiquity for its silver mines, and archaeological signs of this activity are everywhere. The largest settlement in the region was the deme of Thorikos, which, since 1963, has been thoroughly investigated by a Belgian team. Thorikos was a densely packed settlement (occupied since Geometric times), with numerous houses, whose amenities (particularly its theatre) are those of a town rather than a village.[16] But if the settlement can be called urban, it was also industrial. Mining for copper and silver had been going on there since the Bronze Age, and silver production continued in Classical times. The most striking testimony of this activity is the washeries.[17] These are sites where the silver ore was crushed, and then the heavier (silver) particles were progressively separated from the lighter (non-metallic) material by a process akin to panning for gold. Crushing, washing and separating had to be undertaken before the ore could be smelted and turned eventually into ingots or coins. This must have been hard and dirty work, work well beneath the dignity of citizens. Much of this work, and almost all the actual mining, must have been undertaken by slaves, as much of our literary sources and numerous inscriptions seem to imply.[18]

Thorikos then, like many industrial towns since, must have been a place where social inequalities were at their starkest. But if Thorikos was the Merthyr Tydfil of Classical Attica, then the Laurion area further south was its Rhondda. Here, around modern Agrileza, mines, washeries and other installations are strung out along the edge of the hillside, following the seams of silver ore beneath. At Agrileza itself three washeries, associated with a single ancient mine shaft, have been excavated by J.E. Jones.[19] Washery C was particularly large and well preserved. It was probably much larger indeed than the average Athenian ceramic workshop, which rarely employed more than five people at once. Much of the area of washery C is full of basins lined with waterproof hydraulic cement, and the

---

[15] As argued by Osborne 1996: 302–3.

[16] For the theatre at Thorikos, see Hackens 1965; 1967. For excavations of Classical houses and other installations, see Mussche 1965: 31–5; 1967; Mussche and Donnay 1967; Mussche 1969; Spitaels 1978. For an overview of all this evidence, see Mussche 1990.

[17] For the washeries at Thorikos, see Mussche 1965: 35–8. For evidence of mining activity (mostly pre-Classical), see Waelkens 1990.   [18] Osborne 1985: 111–12.

[19] For evidence from the Laurion area as a whole, see Jones 1982. For the washeries in the southern Agrileza valley, see Jones 1976; 1985. For furnaces and washeries elsewhere in Laurion, see Mussche and Conophagos 1973.

  Those outside Britain may be puzzled by these references to South Wales. Merthyr Tydfil is a large town, which grew up as a result of two phases of industrialisation, first of ironworking and then of coal mining. The Rhondda is (or used to be) an area of coal mining, where mines and associated settlements, instead of being concentrated in one large urban area, were strung out along the valley, following the coal seam.

modern visitor may well find himself a little perplexed as to what all this was for. One must remember that, unlike early industrial development in Northern Europe, which could rely on a copious flow of water from streams or rivers, production in southern Attica took place in an environment which was arid in the extreme. In such conditions water from springs (such as there was) was too precious to be wasted on washing. These waterproof basins and cisterns have thus been interpreted as a complex system for collecting, storing, using and then recycling rainwater. This system used gravity to good advantage, but in the end relied on the muscle power of slaves.

The picture we gain of the Attic countryside is then a rich and variegated one. Most of the sanctuaries, from the ill-frequented altars of Zeus on the peaks of hills and mountains to the caves of Pan on the slopes of Hymettos and Parnes, have surely been found. We know too that some of the inhabitants lived in villages, whilst others in other parts of Attica resided permanently in isolated farmhouses on the land. The countryside, far from being a rural retreat from the pressures of the town, was a region of production, a place of toil. Grain was grown on the plains around Eleusis and Athens itself; sheep, goats and bees were kept in the hills; terraces were built by slaves for olive cultivation; and silver was mined from Laurion. But this picture is essentially derived from haphazard bits of information. We can, for example, infer from various sources that the population of Classical Attica must have numbered several hundred thousand by the fourth century BC.[20] This is clearly a high figure for pre-industrial times. But since there seems to have been no single 'Attic settlement pattern', direct comparisons with other regions are fraught with difficulty. Fortunately many other regions of Greece have now been covered by intensive survey. Enough has now been done to draw conclusions in a systematic way. What kind of picture emerges?

14.3 Survey, settlement and population: regional patterns

In the past few decades, survey has become almost as popular as excavation as a means of uncovering information about the ancient world. Surveys have been undertaken in Messenia, Laconia, the Nemea valley, the southern Argolid, Methana, Boeotia, the islands of the Cyclades and many parts of Crete. Surface survey has many rationales; one is better to understand not so much the landscape as land use. Anyone who walks over the Greek landscape will be struck by the sheer number of surface sherds, many apparently unrelated to sites of human habitation or to sanctuaries. The densities of these sherds are extremely variable. One explanation for the volume of 'off-site' material is that it represents agricultural 'manuring'. Rubbish from koprones (rubbish tips) – both broken pottery (see table 14.1) and mulch – was put on arable land far away from any home or farmstead. This hypothesis remains controversial, and other explanations for the volume of

---

[20] For various population estimates, see Osborne 1985: 42–5; Morris 1987: 99–101.

Table 14.1 *Combined inventory of objects from two koprones (rubbish pits) from house 7 and house D at Halieis in the Peloponnese (after Ault 1999: appendix 1)*

Type of vessel (function)	Sherds (raw count)	Minimum number of vessels (MNV)	Percentage of MNV count (of sherds, excluding tile, etc.)
Cooking	116	86	28.3%
Food consumption (fineware)	96	43	14.1%
Drinking (fineware)	141	87	28.6%
Serving and pouring liquids (fine, plain and coarse ware)	169	38	12.5%
Storage (coarse)	391	37	12.2%
Undefined	1537	13	4.3%
	—	—	—
Total	2450	304	100%
Other objects:			
Lamps	7		
Loomweights	7		
Miniatures	7		
Tile	1309		
Metal	23		

'off-site' material have been put forward.[21] Many survey directors too see intensive fieldwalking as a species of rescue or salvage archaeology, undertaken in order to record all that there is to see today before it is bulldozed into oblivion tomorrow. Still, the principal aim of survey is to understand rural settlement; to determine how densely settled, and so how densely populated an area was. Archaeologists do not simply want to know how many sites there were, but whether there are many small sites (a dispersed pattern) or only a few large ones (a nucleated one). In general too, archaeologists have been keen to confirm (or at least to test) the impression given by our literary sources that Greece was a very populous place, more so perhaps in Classical times than in any other period before 1850.

The initial results from survey do tend to confirm this view. Preliminary results from the Boeotia survey, for example, indicate that in a small corner of Boeotia (an inverted L whose corners are Mt Helicon and the cities of Thespiai and Haliartos) there are over sixty-six sites datable to between 600 and 200 BC. This is a much higher density than for the preceding Bronze and Early Iron ages, and much higher too than for the Hellenistic or Roman periods. Though there is

---

[21] For the 'manuring' controversy, see Alcock *et al.* 1994: 143–70; Snodgrass 1994. Snodgrass' calculations are based on information now published by Ault (1999).

always some uncertainty in dating from surface remains alone, it seems that the great majority of these sites date to the fifth and fourth centuries BC. Most of the sites are small, covering an area of half a hectare or less – too small indeed to be villages.[22] But if not villages, do they represent isolated farmsteads or slightly more substantial hamlets? As yet we cannot tell, as none has been excavated. But there are enough of these sites to show that Boeotia at least was a densely popu- lated area in Classical times. Is then a high density of rural settlement character- istic of Greece as a whole? Or are both Attica and Boeotia unique, and is there no such norm to be found? These kinds of questions can only be answered by an empirical 'survey of surveys'. For convenience, I will begin with the Peloponnese and then move east and south.

Messenia, the westernmost part of the Peloponnese, has been surveyed twice; first extensively, by the Minnesota Messenia Expedition (MME); and latterly, a smaller area around Pylos has been investigated intensively, by the Pylos Regional Archaeology Project (PRAP). Results from the earlier survey (MME) seemed to show that there was a large number of Classical sites, particularly compared to those sites datable to the Early Iron Age.[23] Preliminary indications from the second survey (PRAP) do not appear to confirm this picture. PRAP noted only eight Archaic to Classical as opposed to eighteen Hellenistic sites, and com- mented upon the area's apparent 'lack of dispersed farmstead settlement', which they held to be characteristic of other regions of Greece in Classical times.[24] Of course, the Pylos region is hardly ideal for surface survey. Geomorphological biases of one kind or another are probably more pronounced here than for other regions, and much of the soft marls of the area has been completely transformed (not to say destroyed) in recent years through agricultural bulldozing.[25] Still, it is difficult to see how such biases would affect Archaic and Classical sites but not Hellenistic ones. There may be a particular historical reason for this anomaly. Messenia was, after all, a region of Greece that was, throughout Archaic and Classical times, in thrall to its neighbour, Laconia. It was only liberated from Spartan control after 370 BC, after which it became a normal Greek polis. If then dispersed rural settlement is characteristic of free, citizen states (that is either the more inclusive oligarchies or the democracies), states where every citizen had his plot of land, then this change in settlement pattern can be readily explained. The evidence from other surveys, however, makes it far from certain that such a general relationship between political structure and rural settlement did in fact exist.

Laconia too has been surveyed in the past decade or so. Though there seem in general to be more Classical than Archaic sites in the region as a whole, the detailed picture from the area of the Laconia survey, east of Sparta itself, is

---

[22] Bintliff and Snodgrass 1985a; 1985b; Snodgrass 1987: 104–15.
[23] For the results of MME (Minnesota Messenia Expedition), see McDonald and Rapp 1972: 94–6, 144–6. For PRAP (Pylos Regional Archaeological Project) results, Davis *et al.* 1997: 455–7; 1998: 158–62, 300.   [24] Davis *et al.* 1997: 456.   [25] Davis *et al.* 1998: 280–3.

harder to interpret.[26] Preliminary results from the Nemea valley survey indicate a relatively high density of Classical rural settlement, which seems to have increased from Archaic times.[27] But this pattern is not replicated further to the east. Here, in the area of the Southern Argolid Survey, Classical rural sites are not thick on the ground. The density of settlement is little different from Archaic times (fig. 14.3). There is, however, a sharp increase in the number of rural sites from about 350 BC onwards, a pattern strikingly similar to that from Messenia.[28] But if the patterns are similar the political circumstances of the two areas could hardly be more different. The southern Argolid was a region divided between several independent poleis, which had no need of a liberator. In these two cases we may be dealing with the archaeological problem of equifinality, where essentially different historical processes produce similar observable outcomes. Moreover these micro-regional patterns seem to be extremely localised. The pattern found in the southern Argolid is not replicated in the nearby Methana peninsula. This area seems not to have been densely settled in the Archaic period.[29] Settlement density however increases markedly in the Classical period, jumping from eight to forty-eight sites, and remains high during Hellenistic times.[30]

Results from surveys in the Cyclades present us with yet further subtle variations. In northern Keos, the territory of the small polis of Koressos, there do appear to be many more Classical than Archaic sites – 40 as against 29 (fig. 14.4). The number of Classical finds in general also greatly exceeds those of Archaic date.[31] However a degree of caution must be exercised here. Most Archaic finds date from the sixth century BC. There exists the strong possibility that the growth in rural settlement in northern Keos dates from only 600 BC or so onwards. 'Archaic' sites are then, for the most part, sixth-century sites. Since the Classical period spans two centuries, in contrasting 'Archaic' with 'Classical' settlement pattern we are not really comparing like with like. A fairer comparison would be between finds from different centuries, and here the evidence seems to indicate that a relatively dense, if dispersed pattern of rural settlement is an Archaic development, that simply continues into Classical times. Still, as elsewhere in Greece, the year 400 BC seems to represent a peak in the density of rural settlement, since there is a noticeable drop in the Hellenistic period.[32] The picture from Melos is different again. Here there seem to be fewer Classical rural sites than Archaic ones.[33] However, since Melos was surveyed using methods that were less intensive (or at least less sophisticated) than those employed in Keos, direct comparisons of numbers of sites may be misleading.

---

[26] Cavanagh *et al.* 1996: 263–438, esp. 270. For the more detailed picture closer to Sparta, see now Mee and Cavanagh 1998.   [27] Wright *et al.* 1990: 617.

[28] Jameson *et al.* 1994: 381–94, 548–53; Van Andel and Runnels 1987: 101–10.

[29] Gill and Foxhall 1997.   [30] Gill *et al.* 1997.

[31] Cherry *et al.* 1991: 247–55, 328–40; Osborne 1987a: 59–62.

[32] Cherry *et al.* 1991: 322 figs. 17.3 and 17.4.   [33] Cherry 1982: 21–3; Sparkes 1982: 49–50.

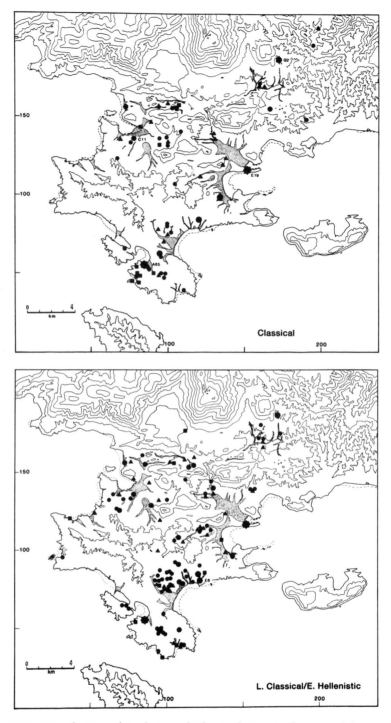

14.3 Distribution of Archaic and Classical sites in the area of the southern Argolid survey

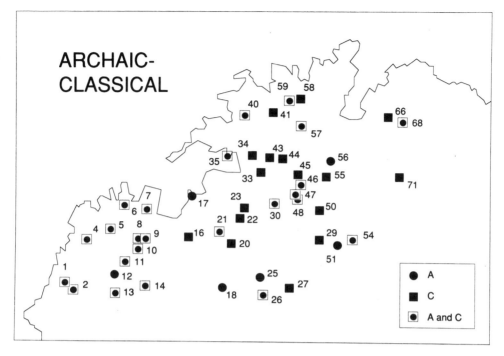

14.4 Distribution of Archaic and Classical sites in the area of the Keos

Still, the evidence from the Cyclades does underscore the possibility that marked variations in settlement patterns may have existed not only between regions, but also within them. This observation applies with even greater force to Crete. In Crete, of course, it is extremely hard to identify any pottery of sixth-century date, and the situation for the succeeding centuries hardly improves very much, if at all. A particular degree of caution must be exercised when interpreting the results of Cretan surveys. Starting in the east of the island, about five or so rural sites of Classical date have been found in the immediate vicinity of the city of Praisos (fig. 14.5), whilst there are no certain indications of any sixth-century habitation outside of the city itself.[34] Further to the west however, in the Kavousi area, the Classical period seems to be a complete blank. Donald Haggis, the survey director, even suggested that the region was simply abandoned.[35] Here, however, the absence of evidence may not be incontrovertible evidence of absence. Kavousi formed part of the territory of Hierapytna, a city with a reputation for being populous and powerful in Classical and Hellenistic Greece. Two possibilities seem more likely than total abandonment: either settlement underwent an exceptional degree of nucleation in the territory of Hierapytna; or here, as elsewhere in Crete for the sixth century, there is a particular problem of archaeological visibility, which we do not yet fully understand. Certainly, the picture

---

[34] Whitley *et al.* 1999: 253–6.   [35] Haggis 1996: 415.

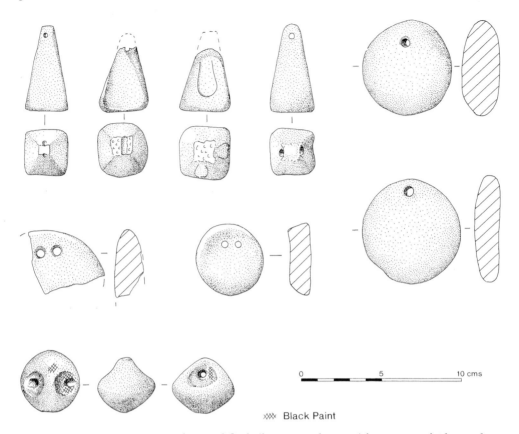

14.5 Drawing of typical finds (loom weights etc.) from sites of Classical date in the Praisos survey

from the neighbouring area to be surveyed, around Vrokastro, is ambiguous. There are, it seems, a large number of 'Greco-Roman' sites, but how many of these are Classical in date is almost impossible to say.[36] This is all in marked contrast to the pattern revealed by the survey of the western Mesara. From the thirteen sites which seem to have been occupied in Orientalising and Archaic times, the number of rural sites 'almost doubles' in the Classical period. Unlike some other areas of Greece however, there is no decline in the Hellenistic period. Rather the reverse. As in Messenia and the southern Argolid, rural settlement density continues to increase throughout the third century and after.[37]

What inferences can be drawn from this survey of surveys? For one thing, Classical Attica hardly represents the norm. Nowhere else, it seems, was settlement principally concentrated in nucleated villages. Indeed there seems to be no 'norm' at all. Instead at least two patterns, or models, can be discerned. The first of these is the 'Boeotia model'. This is where settlement is dense, but dispersed in

[36] Hayden *et al.* 1992: 329–33.   [37] Watrous *et al.* 1993: 230–1.

a constellation of small farmsteads or hamlets. In this model, the density of settlement reaches its zenith in the years around 400 BC, falling off slightly thereafter. Both northern Keos and, less certainly, the Nemea valley seem to conform to this pattern. Against this there is the 'Messenia model'. Here there is no particularly dense pattern of rural settlement in Classical times, and no obvious increase from the Archaic period. Dispersed, rural settlement seems to take off only in the years after 350 BC, and continues to increase, or at least remain high, through much of the Hellenistic period. Both the southern Argolid and, to a lesser extent, the western Mesara seem close to this Messenian pattern. Not all regions, of course, conform to either type, and there are subtleties of variation between each case that inevitably escape easy categorisation. It would moreover be naive to suppose that, because we have two models, we therefore need only two explanations. The examples of the southern Argolid and Messenia should suffice to confound this easy assumption.

Survey has produced much reliable, quantifiable data, data of a kind that is usually lacking in the literary record. These data have, however, their own difficulties of interpretation. Even when surveys use more or less identical methods, variations in such things as geomorphology, topography and land use make direct comparisons that much more problematic. The low density of sites in, for example, the Pylos area may be due to the background geology. The soft marls of Messenia are easily eroded, and the surface archaeology just as easily obliterated through bulldozing.[38] The low rolling hills of Boeotia are less easily destroyed. Final survey reports are able to take these factors into account, and weigh the evidence accordingly, but they cannot entirely eliminate the biases that arise from a fieldwalker's eye for certain details and his or her blindness to others.[39] These difficulties do not invalidate the enterprise however. Survey archaeology has thrown up some strange cases, but these are no less worthy of the historian's attention than the problems inherent in our literary sources. Understanding patterns of rural settlement remains a more important historical problem than solving the conundrum of the 'Peace of Callias'.

Still, for many scholars, settlement is but one aspect of land use, a better understanding of which is the real aim of survey. Hence the animated debate as to whether high densities of off-site material represent the residue of ancient manuring.[40] Hence too the concern with finding evidence for particular kinds of agricultural activity. This can be sought in many places; the Vari house provides us with direct evidence for bee keeping, in the form of combed pottery.[41] Anyone who has walked through the Greek countryside cannot fail to notice that spolia are everywhere. Often these spolia (fragments of stone buildings or installations) relate to past agricultural activity. Millstones and mortars can be seen built into later

---

[38] Zangger 1997; 1998.
[39] I know from personal experience that I have a good eye for Early Iron Age pottery, but a poor one for obsidian. Similarly, a less experienced fieldwalker will pick up fewer sherds than an experienced one.   [40] Alcock *et al.* 1994; Snodgrass 1994.   [41] Jones *et al.* 1973: 397–414; Jones 1990.

14.6 Olive-presses from Praisos (examples of spolia)

terrace walls; rock-cut cisterns and olive presses (e.g. fig. 14.6) are often encountered at the edge of fields. Though much of this material looks ancient, less than
you might think actually relates to agricultural activity of Classical date. Most
millstones date to the eighteenth or nineteenth centuries of our era. No systematic study has been made of agricultural cisterns or stone mortars.[42] A recent
study of rock-cut olive presses in Methana concluded that only the earliest of
these were of late Classical date, and most seem to be associated with sites of
Hellenistic or Roman agricultural activity.[43] The production of olive oil does not

[42] That is, not in an originally rural context (excepting Foxhall 1997b). For cisterns in a
Classical/Hellenistic city site, see Whitley *et al.* 1995: 416–27.
[43] Foxhall 1997b; Forbes 1992. For comparable examples from Keos, see Cherry *et al.* 1991: 293–7. For
the southern Argolid, see Ault (1999: 559–66) who argues that olive presses were only installed in
the fourth century. Lohmann (1992) has of course argued that the extensive terracing found in the
deme of Atene indicates that intensive olive production had begun there in Classical times.

seem to have been a major concern of the Classical farmer. Olives, it seems, only became a cash crop in later times. Still, this does not mean that the countryside was not worth protecting. Towers of one kind or another are to be found in many parts of the Greek countryside. The distribution of these, and other signs of violence, conflict or warfare, remains something of a mystery. It is to these problems that we now turn.

14.4 A fortified country? Island towers and defended borderlands

The mainland of Greece is full of walls and fortifications of one kind and another. Fortifications date to a number of different periods, and it does not take great skill to distinguish between masonry styles of different dates. Often, several phases can be traced on one site. Someone who has taken the trouble to climb the acropolis of Argos, for example, would have little difficulty in tracing the earliest, 'Cyclopean' walls, and in distinguishing these from the (Archaic or Classical) polygonal styles, whose drystone technique is in turn quite distinct from the Frankish and Venetian curtain walls which can be seen there. The walls of the acropolis at Argos indeed correspond to the three major periods in which fortifications have been built on the Greek mainland. The first of these is, of course, the Mycenaean period, and the last the later medieval, when the invading Franks established castles for themselves all over the Peloponnese and central Greece. Roman defensive walls, outside of a few sites such as Thessaloniki and Nicopolis, are something of a rarity in Greece, and no great stone defences seem to have been built in Early Iron Age or Archaic times. It is in Classical and Hellenistic times that the Greeks themselves seem to have devoted most energy to the construction of fortifications. Why is this?

The obvious answer is warfare. Both in Frankish/Late Byzantine and in Classical times, Greece was a mosaic of small states, states which were, more often than not, at war with one another. Both were periods of instability and shifting alliances, when your ally of one year would be your enemy the next. Such instability encourages people to put their faith in fortifications. The difficulty with this argument is that Greeks seem to have been no more warlike in Classical times than they had been in previous centuries. If Herodotos is to be believed, states such as Argos and Sparta regularly engaged in hoplite battles on disputed territory in the years before and after the Persian wars. One possible answer to this mystery is not that Greeks had become more warlike, but that the nature of warfare had changed. The classic hoplite clash of arms became less frequent, and the importance of the citizen-hoplite consequently diminished. Mobile light infantry, cavalry and sieges became more significant components in Greek warfare.[44] The Peloponnesian war, after all, ended with what amounted to a siege

---

[44] For a summary of these military developments, see Snodgrass 1999: 98–130, 138–41. On the importance of siege warfare and its effects, see Garlan 1974.

on a massive scale. The increasing importance of siege warfare provided a powerful stimulus for effective counter-measures. Hence the appearance of larger and better-built fortifications.

Certainly, these changes are a part of the picture. They help to explain the trouble taken by the newly liberated Messenians and their allies to provide their new city, Messene, with a thick wall of continuously bonded solid masonry, strengthened with frequent towers equipped for the use of defensive artillery (fig. 14.7).[45] But it is less clear whether siege warfare helps to explain the appearance of forts on the coasts of Attica and Laconia, and in the mountainous borderlands of Boeotia, Attica and the Megarid. Still less do they help to account for one of the most peculiar features of the Classical Greek landscape: the frequency of isolated towers, particularly in the islands.

In many islands of the Aegean, the foundations of ancient towers are a common sight. Most are square, some round, and almost all are built of isodomic masonry, usually cut from the local limestone. These towers are, on average, about 8–9 m by 8–9 m (when square) or 8–9 m in diameter (when round). Such towers are notoriously difficult to date, since few have been excavated. Masonry styles and associated finds point to a general range of dates between 600 and 200 BC; that is, some seem late Archaic, many Hellenistic, but most appear to be Classical.[46] Particularly dense concentrations of towers are to be found on the islands of Amorgos, Lesbos, Siphnos and Thasos. Towers are much rarer on other islands, though they are also to be found on parts of the mainland. What could account for such a strange distribution?

Two principal explanations have been put forward. First, many scholars have noted that towers are particularly common on those islands (Amorgos, Keos and Lesbos) which were divided into a number of different polities. Towers may therefore have served as part of a defensive network, or at least an 'early warning' system, to guard against a surprise attack from a neighbouring state. But a detailed examination of the location of towers on Keos and Lesbos does not seem to confirm this hypothesis. Towers are rarely intervisible, nor are they commonly placed with a good view over a neighbour's territory. They do not seem to have formed a network.[47] Other scholars have emphasised the frequency of towers in Thasos and Siphnos, both areas known for their mining and ore-processing, activities usually undertaken by slaves. Slave labourers need to be controlled, and those doing the controlling need to protect themselves.[48] These scholars have also noted that the silver working installations of the Laurion region are also closely associated with towers. The 'Golden Pig tower' for example is built right next to

---

[45] Lawrence 1979: 240–3, 382–5; Ober 1987a: 572–7; Adam 1982: 171–5.
[46] See discussion in Cherry *et al.* 1991: 285–98; Osborne 1986; 1987a: 67–81.
[47] For towers on Keos, see Cherry *et al.* 1991: 285–98 (esp. 293). For those on Lesbos, see Spencer 1995a. Spencer argues that many of the Lesbian towers are of Archaic date.
[48] For towers on Siphnos, see Young 1956a; Ashton 1991; for those on Thasos, Osborne 1986; 1987a: 76–81.

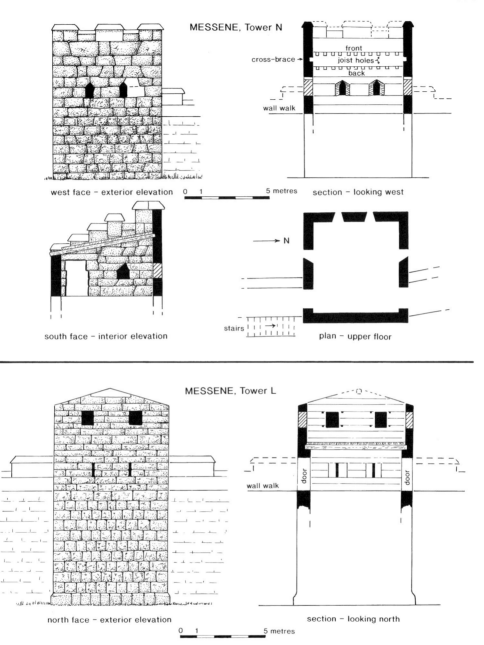

14.7 Elevations of towers from Messene

the three washeries at Agrileza.[49] But a detailed study of the towers of Thasos has revealed that not all towers seem to have performed this function. Some circular towers were built right on headlands on the coast, and seem to have served, if not as lighthouses exactly, then at least to signal that here there was a hazard to coastal shipping.[50] Other towers, such as those on Siphnos situated on high ground close to but not on the coast, might have better served as watchtowers.[51] One generalisation that does seem to hold good for all towers is that they are almost invariably rural. A study of their distribution in the Laurion region seemed to show that towers were almost always associated with other structures, buildings which were used for agriculture or other kinds of production. Young argued that the towers were a means of protecting valuables, particularly movables and farm equipment.[52] Certainly, many towers elsewhere are closely associated with agricultural property. The Vari house has its own small tower, as do many rural sites in the deme of Atene.[53] Many towers on Keos too seem to be closely linked to agricultural activities such as olive pressing.[54] We need not however view these agricultural towers in narrowly functional terms. Towers in Attica may have been the visible, monumental expression of a citizen's right to farm his land and 'protect his property'. Such deliberate monumentality need not imply actual residence on the land. Indeed, it may be that the greater the distance from the place of normal residence, the greater the need to make an unambiguous architectural statement of ownership.

Such an interpretation, though, seems to work best for Attica (if it works at all). Elsewhere there seems to be no general explanation for the location, distribution or shape of towers. Different towers in different locations served different functions. Nor is there any consistent relationship between the shape of a tower and its function. Circular towers may have been better suited for coastal signals, but otherwise both square and round towers were built for a variety of reasons. But if there is no general explanation for the distribution of island towers, there must be one for the appearance of border defences in the late fifth and fourth centuries BC. Border defences seem to have been of two kinds. First, the high ground that often divided one region or one polis from another was guarded by forts, often of remarkably solid construction. Second, coastal sites were often fortified, to protect sea routes, naval installations or ports. Such at least seems to have

---

[49] For towers in the Laurion area, see Young 1956b: esp. 126 for the 'Golden Pig' tower. See Jones 1976 for installations close to the tower. For a circular tower closely associated with the 'industrial quarter' of Thorikos, see Spitaels 1978.

[50] The Pyrgos tower on Thasos has an inscription which has led many to think it a lighthouse; see discussion in Osborne 1986; Cherry et al. 1991: 292.

[51] For the Siphnos towers, see Young 1956a; Ashton 1991. The most recent discussion of the location of towers in relation to their function is Cherry et al. 1991: 291-3.

[52] For the argument that towers served an agricultural purpose, see Young 1956b: 121-43; see comments in Cherry et al. 1991: 293-7.

[53] For the Vari House, see Jones et al. 1973: 438-43. For towers in the Atene area, see in particular the tower at Thimari (Th1), Lohmann 1993a: 459-61; 1993b. Finds from here included black-glazed pots and loomweights.   [54] For towers and agriculture on Keos, see Cherry et al. 1991: 296-7.

been the motivation behind the fortification of Sounion and Rhamnous during the latter part of the Peloponnesian war. The defensive walls of Sounion enclose both the temple of Poseidon and some ship sheds, which indicates that Athens kept a small force of triremes here.[55] Athens was not the only state that felt the need to fortify its coasts. So too did Sparta. The perioecic communities of Epidauros Limera and Zarax in south-east Laconia were also fortified sometime in the fourth century BC. Fortifications like these may have been built in response to the weakness and political isolation of the Spartan state after its defeat at Leuktra.[56]

Still, it is not these coastal defences, but border forts, particularly those along the frontiers of Boeotia, the Megarid and Attica, which have received most attention. Some of these fortifications are particularly impressive. The fort of Gyptokastro (almost certainly ancient Eleutherai) has a circuit of walls strengthened with square towers, enclosing an area of some 1.8 hectares (fig. 14.9). The walls are of isodomic masonry, consisting of carefully shaped limestone blocks with drafted edges.[57] Its location, overlooking the Kaza pass over Mt Kithairon, a route that links western Attica to Thebes, might at first sight seem adequately to explain its purpose: to guard the pass, and control the movement of troops from Boeotia to Attica. Eleutherai indeed seems to be the westernmost point of Attica's defence network. Though the neighbouring border fort of Oinoe cannot be seen from Eleutherai, there is at least one very high tower at Mazi that links the two sites. Similar towers, positioned so as to be intervisible, have been found further to the east.[58] A network of this kind makes sense in fourth-century political conditions, when it was Thebes, not Sparta, that represented the greatest threat to Athens. A similar motivation may lie behind the construction of a fort at Aigosthena, which lies in the north-west corner of the territory of the neighbouring state of Megara (fig. 14.8). Like Eleutherai, Aigosthena is a large and well-built fort, just by the sea at the westernmost end of the Kithairon range.[59] Though not located just above a pass, its situation makes it likely that, like Eleutherai, it was intended to guard one of the north–south routes over the isthmus of Corinth.

There is then a perfectly clear political logic behind the construction of these forts, for it was in the fourth century in particular that armies were constantly on

---

[55] On Sounion, see Travlos 1988: 404–29; on the fortifications in particular, Adam 1982: 208–9. These should date to near the end of the Peloponnesian war on the testimony of Thucydides VIII.4.

[56] On Epidauros Limera, see Wace and Hasluck 1908: 179–82; on Zarax, Wace and Hasluck 1909: 167–73. I have assumed here that the fortifications date to the fourth century. There is no positive evidence either way, but they could easily be later. Many believe that the walls of Zarax in particular were constructed in early Hellenistic times, when the site briefly became a possession of Argos (Pausanias III.24.1).

[57] On Gyptokastro (Eleutherai), see Stikas 1939; Travlos 1988: 170–6; Adam 1982: 216–17. The most recent discussion of the site and its finds is by Ober 1987a: 582–5; 1987b: 213–20. For its place in Attica's defensive network, see Ober 1985.

[58] On the Mazi tower, see Ober 1985: 155–7; 1987a: 589–91. On intervisibility generally, Ober 1985: 110: 196–7, 201–2. Ober believes that Oinoe and Eleutherai were directly intervisible, but this does not agree with my own direct observations.

[59] On Aigosthena, see Benson 1895; Ober 1987a: 586–9; Travlos 1988: 260–1; Adam 1982: 217–19.

AIGOSTHENA, Tower A

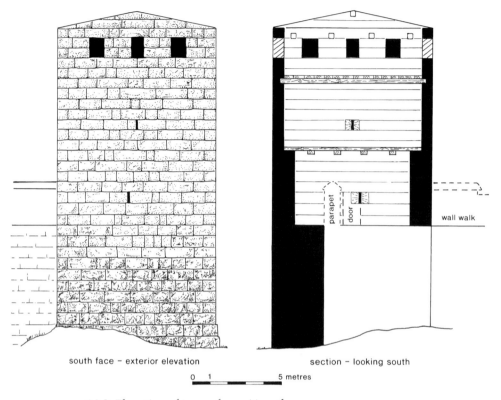

south face – exterior elevation   section – looking south

0   1   5 metres

14.8 Elevation of tower from Aigosthena

the move between Boeotia and the Peloponnese. But this fact also raises a question about the effectiveness of such fortifications. For neither Eleutherai nor Aigosthena seems to have been a major impediment, either to Theban armies moving south, or to Spartan armies moving north. Perhaps it is a mistake to see a purely military explanation for such monumental structures. The Attic border forts remained an imperfect frontier defence. In the west, to be sure, there was a network of forts and towers, but further east, a fort such as Phyle, high on the slopes of Mt Parnes, was not directly connected to any other.[60] Communication between a line of forts in such mountainous country must always have been difficult. Some scholars have therefore sought to find a social or symbolic dimension for the building of such structures. In Athens in the late fourth century, the institution known as the ephebeia assumed a much greater importance. An 'ephebe' was a young man, or rather a male in the process of becoming a young man, somewhere between irresponsible adolescence and responsible citizenship. In the fourth century 'ephebes' had to undertake military service in the wild 'border

---

[60] On Phyle, see Wrede 1924; Adam 1982: 206–7; Ober 1987b: 205–7.

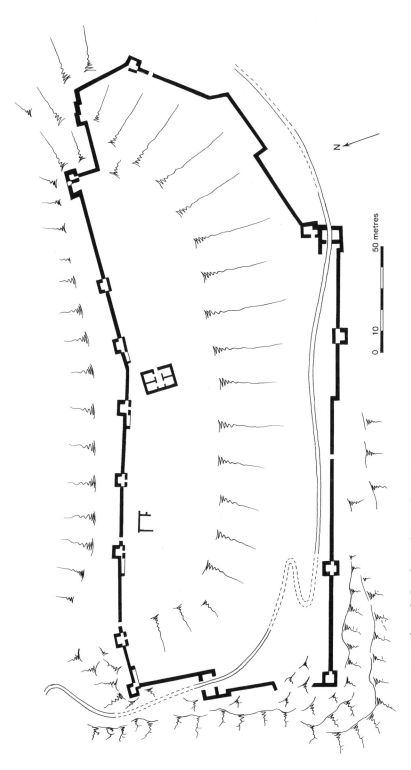

14.9 Plan of Eleutherai (Gyptokastro)

country' in forts such as Phyle. 'Ephebic service' was then a classic *rite de passage.*[61] A force composed of such inexperienced young men can hardly have been of the greatest military value, nor the most effective means of defence. The growth of frontier forts in the high country may be as much related to social changes of this kind as an outcome of a purely rational policy of military defence. Similarly, the care taken to construct these forts – in particular the attention paid to isodomic masonry with drafted edges – indicates that these structures are in no sense purely functional. They are deliberately and, one might almost say, ostentatiously monumental, and deliberately placed on the furthest bounds of a state's territory. They are, in a sense, monumental land markers, and the yearly cycle of an ephebe's military service in such places serves as a constant reaffirmation of the inviolability of a state's territory. In late Classical times, frontier forts may have performed a function similar to that proposed by de Polignac for border sanctuaries in the early Archaic period.[62]

Now I am not saying that these border forts had no military value; they do seem to have been part of a genuine defensive network (see fig. 13.1). Nor am I suggesting that Athens did not have what amounted to a defence policy. How else can we explain that other unique fourth-century fortification, the Dema wall? This wall guards the major route into Attica from the Peloponnese and Boeotia, running between the mountains of Parnes and Aigaleos. It is not continuous, but consists of a series of small walls, interrupted by sally ports. It is designed not then as a perfect barrier, but as a change to the terrain that tips the balance in favour of the defending army.[63] Still, the border country between the major powers of Classical Greece is not the only area dotted with fourth-century and early Hellenistic fortifications. Each of the small towns (or large villages) in western Boeotia and Phokis seems to have been fortified at this time. Large numbers of small fortified sites seem to have been characteristic of western Greece, particularly in those areas where major political units took the form of a federation of small towns, the ethnos. Some scholars have attributed this vogue for fortification to the persistence of an earlier, pre-hoplite pattern of warfare in these parts. Raiding and skirmishing between neighbours, it is argued, remained common practice well into Classical times.[64] But unless we see such fortified enceintes as corrals for sheep and goats on a colossal scale, it is hard to see the persistence of raiding as a plausible explanation. As in the Attic border forts, the care taken in the construction of these walls is much more than is required as an adequate protection against raids. Often the only really impressive feature of these small towns is their walls. Pausanias, for example, describes one of them, Panopeus, whose pretensions to be a polis he derides. Panopeus had no fountains, no agora, and no public buildings

---

[61] Vidal-Naquet 1981.

[62] De Polignac 1995: 32–88. Spencer (1995a) has argued that the 'Archaic' towers on Lesbos had as much a symbolic purpose as a practical one; that they were a means of 'marking' or 'monumentalising' the landscape.   [63] On this, see Jones *et al.* 1957; Munn 1993: 37–125.

[64] As argued by Osborne 1987a: 138–45.

as such.[65] Its fortifications however, at least as they survive today, are some of the best in Greece.[66] Panopeus took obvious pride in remaining an autonomous member of the Phokian ethnos. It may be that its fortifications were as much a mark of civic pride – and a sign of Panopeus' autonomy – as they were an effective measure against raids.

Whatever the reasons for this late Classical vogue for walls and towers, the fortifications themselves remind us that the Greek landscape was always a field of contest. The countryside of Greece was as far from the literary idyll of Arcadia as can be imagined. It was a place not of ease but of work. Some parts of the landscape were industrial. Many areas of Greece were densely settled in Classical times, settlement which must have been directly related to agricultural production. Much agricultural land was dotted with towers, whose functions were various, but were, more often than not, connected to an owner's need to guard himself or his property. By the late fourth century large parts of the countryside were fortified. This vogue for fortification persists into Hellenistic times, one among many late Classical developments that look forward to the changed political circumstances of the third century. This was a time when the whole of the eastern Mediterranean was dominated by powerful monarchies, monarchies which constantly interfered in the affairs of smaller Greek states. Whether or not the material culture of late Classical times in any way reflects these changes is a matter for the next chapter.

[65] Pausanias X.4.1.   [66] Osborne 1987a: 117–18.

CHAPTER 15

EPILOGUE: TOWARDS HELLENISTIC ARCHAEOLOGY

15.1 Periphery and centre

Classical archaeology has always displayed a strong belief in evolution; not, to be sure, evolution in the strict Darwinian sense of change through natural selection, but rather in the older, humanistic sense of evolution as progress. For many nineteenth-century scholars, Classical Greece represented the cultural pinnacle to which all societies should aspire. Even though modern attitudes have changed, no one would deny that Classical Greece represents a remarkable flowering of civilisation. Such cultural evolution as did take place did not affect all parts of Greece equally however. While many communities, both poleis and ethne, engaged in building yet more splendid temples and public buildings, communities on the fringes of the Greek world remained much as they had been in the middle of the Early Iron Age.

High in the Pindos mountains, in modern-day Epeiros (Epirus), is the site of Vitsa Zagoriou. This was a hamlet continuously inhabited from the ninth century until the fourth. Excavations have revealed a settlement with accompanying cemeteries. The finds show clearly that this settlement, though remote, was not isolated; the inhabitants had access to pottery and metalwork produced by Greek-speaking communities further south. They were quite as capable as anyone of being dedicated followers of Greek fashions. It is then remarkable how little many aspects of their lives changed in the five centuries of the site's history. Their burial practices in particular show tremendous consistency. Men were being buried with two spears and perhaps one sword in the ninth century and with the same grave goods in the fourth. The 'Molossian' inhabitants never tried to erect any temples or other public buildings. Greek civilisation (if not Greek material culture) seems to have passed them by.[1]

Vitsa Zagoriou, however, is to be found in an upland and peripheral region of Greece. Its situation alone, some might argue, would make its inhabitants highly resistant to change. Yet it is precisely those regions which, in the sixth and fifth centuries, had been peripheral to Classical Greek civilisation which were to become the innovating centres of the late fourth century. Developments in the peripheral regions of Caria and Macedon in particular were to shape the material

---

[1] Votokopoulou 1986.

practices of the Hellenistic world. It is to the first, and apparently more advanced, of these areas that we now turn.

15.2 Mausolus

The Carians were one of the many peoples of western Asia Minor (modern Turkey) who, for centuries, had been gradually if selectively adopting Greek ways. By the beginning of the fourth century, a Carian town like Mylasa might look altogether Greek, though, as Thucydides notes, Carians maintained a number of decidedly un-Greek customs, such as burial with arms.[2] The Carians were, however, Persian subjects, and the confederation of (nominally free) Carian towns was controlled by a ruler or dynast, who acted as a Persian satrap. The size of the Persian empire was such that the Carian dynast had considerable freedom of action. In the early part of the fourth century BC, one such dynast, Mausolus, had used this freedom to enlarge his realm by annexing the neighbouring region of Lycia.[3] He also moved his capital from Mylasa to the coastal Greek city of Halikarnassos. Late fourth-century Halikarnassos was a walled city laid out on a Hippodamian grid plan. In most respects it resembled any other Classical Greek city on the coast of Asia Minor, such as Miletos or Priene.[4] It differed in only two respects: it boasted a palace, and, at its very centre, set up on a vast rectangular terrace over 25,500 m² in extent, was, not any grand Ionic temple such as we might find in Ephesos or Samos, but a gigantic tomb: the Mausoleum.[5]

The Mausoleum (or Mausolleion), as its name suggests, was built to commemorate Mausolus. Begun in his reign, it was completed by his wife Artemisia after his death in 353 BC. Ostentatiously positioned where no grave would be allowed in any other Greek city, the Mausoleum is more than just a large tomb – though with a stylobate of 126 by 105 feet (38.4 × 32 m) it was certainly that.[6] Later writers considered it to be one of the seven wonders of the ancient world. What impressed them was not so much its size as the richness and the quality of its sculptural decoration. Vitruvius and the elder Pliny mention four sculptors (Skopas, Leochares, Bryaxis and either Praxiteles or Timotheus) who were said to be responsible for the sculptural decoration of each of the four sides.[7] Much of this

[2] Thucydides I.8.1.

[3] On Mausolus' career generally, see Hornblower 1982. Some might think that it would be more correct to spell Mausolus 'Maussollos', and the Mausoleum 'Maussolleion'. I do not. Most of our sources for Mausolus and the Mausoleum are Roman. Mausolus was a Carian, not a Greek, and we simply do not know how his name would have been spelt or should be transliterated.

[4] On the location of Halikarnassos, see Vitruvius II.8.11; Strabo, *Geography* XIV.2.16; Newton 1862b: 265–79. For the plan of the fourth-century city, see Hoepfner and Schwandner 1994: 226–34.

[5] On the terrace, see Pedersen 1991a: 9–114; 1991b.

[6] For excavations at the base of the Mausoleum, see Newton 1862b: 122–56; Jeppensen *et al.* 1981. Dimensions (incredible ones) are also given by Pliny, *Natural History* XXXVI.30–1.

[7] Pliny, *Natural History* XXXVI.30–1; Vitruvius, *On Architecture* VII, Praefatio 12–13. Vitruvius and Pliny disagree on the identity of the sculptors – where Pliny names Timotheus, Vitruvius gives us Praxiteles. Vitruvius also names Pytheos as architect, who may be the Pythis mentioned in Pliny. See discussion in Waywell 1978: 79–84. For another general discussion of the sources, see Jeppesen 1978.

sculpture was recovered in excavations conducted by Charles Newton in the mid-nineteenth century, and is now in the British Museum.[8] All the sculptures are of imported Pentelic marble, and recent estimates have put the total number of free-standing pieces at between 314 and 330.[9] It would have taken one sculptor 704 years to complete all of this work, which casts doubt on the accuracy of the ancient testimony. This fact may help to explain why attempts to 'attribute' individual sculptures to one of four hands have consistently failed. The easiest way to accommodate the ancient testimony with the archaeological evidence is to suppose that Pliny and Vitruvius were referring to four teams of sculptors, workshops headed by a 'master' such as Praxiteles, since: 'Taking eighteen years as the time scale for the building of the Mausoleum, the number of skilled craftsmen who have been required to carve all the sculptures in the round, working continuously, is forty.'[10] The free-standing sculpture seems to have been made to three (perhaps four) sizes. There were a number of 'colossal' sculptures (one-and-two-thirds life-size, i.e. 2.7–3 m), including the so-called figure of Mausolus himself (fig. 15.1); 'heroic' sculptures, one-and-one-third life-size (about 2.4 m); and life-size sculptures, generally 1.8 m.[11] Though the exact reconstruction of the Mausoleum remains controversial (since it was used as a quarry in the Middle Ages), we can be reasonably sure of the arrangement of this sculpture (figs. 15.2 and 15.3).[12] At the very top was a chariot group; then, at the base of the roof, at least 56 lions; then a portico of 36 (eleven by nine) Ionic columns, between which were 36 portraits of Mausolus and his family. Below this was the main frieze, whose subject was the perennial Classical favourite, Greeks fighting Amazons. Other sculptural groups decorated the podium and the base.[13]

There are no Greek precedents for a building of this type. To any citizen of the independent poleis of central Greece, the Peloponnese or Crete, a tomb of this size would have been quite out of place in the middle of a city. Its position would have been more appropriate for a temple. Indeed, some of the features of the Mausoleum have more in common with Greek sanctuaries than with Greek tombs. The large terrace resembles a temenos; and the sacrificial deposit of cattle, sheep, goats and lambs recently uncovered by Danish excavations has more in common with finds from Greek sanctuaries than with anything normally found in Greek tombs.[14] Large and richly ornamented tombs had, however, been characteristic of the peoples of western Asia Minor. The Nereid monument from neighbouring Lycia is a case in point. Not only is the overall design of the building, as many commentators have

---

[8] On the find spots of the sculpture, see Newton 1862b: 102–7, 110–12, 128–9; Waywell 1978: 1–15; Ashmole 1972: 147–91.   [9] Waywell 1978: 57.   [10] Waywell 1978: 81.

[11] Waywell 1978: 35–9. On Mausolus, see also Krischen 1925.

[12] There have been numerous attempts at (paper) reconstructions of the Mausoleum, the most influential of which is probably Krischen 1923; 1927. I have followed the reconstruction proposed by Jeppesen (1976).

[13] On the reconstruction of the free-standing sculpture, see Waywell 1978: 54–62; on the Amazonomachy, Ashmole 1972: 147–91; Boardman 1995: 27–9.

[14] On the sacrificial deposit, see Newton 1862b: 91–3; Jeppesen et al. 1981: 81–3; Sørensen 1981.

15.1 Colossal statue from the Mausoleum, thought to be a portrait of Mausolus

15.2 Reconstruction of Mausoleum long side, showing position of sculpture

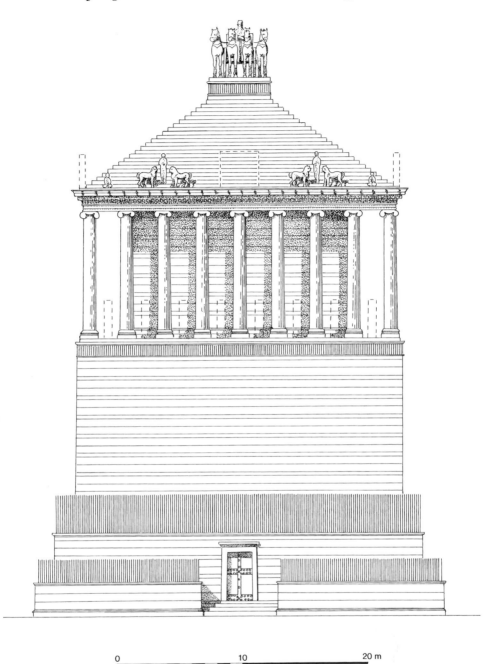

15.3 Reconstruction of Mausoleum, short side, showing position of sculpture

pointed out, 'Eastern (or Anatolian) in conception', the subject matter of the sculptures also owes little to the Greek mainland. As the most authoritative study of the sculpture puts it:

The origins of much of the sculptural decoration of the Mausoleum lie east of the Aegean in the funerary art of Ionia and Western Asia Minor. From this art derive the types of the chariot horses and standing lions; the hunting and sacrificial groups; the presence of many figures in Persian dress, some of whom fight with Greeks; and the hairstyles and dress-styles of many of the portrait statues.[15]

The Mausoleum then put Greek art and Greek artists to work to serve utterly un-Greek ends. It is then perverse, in my view, to see the Mausoleum as an example of the 'hellenisation' of Asia Minor. Rather the reverse. The Mausoleum foreshadows the more ostentatious, dynastic monuments of the Hellenistic and Roman worlds. Within a few years it had found imitators, notably the Lion tomb from the nearby city of Knidos.[16] More interesting than these indications of direct imitation, however, are the parallel, and apparently unrelated developments in quite a different part of the Aegean world: Macedon.

15.3 Macedon

Macedonia had always been an odd region of Greece. There are few indications that the density of rural sites increased in Macedonia in Classical times, in marked contrast to the situation elsewhere in Greece.[17] There are few if any signs of Macedonians making use of the Greek alphabet in late Archaic times, and there is virtually nothing epigraphic from the fifth century apart from a few inscribed coins.[18] Macedonian burial practices, such as those in evidence at the large cemetery of Sindos, seem to have had more in common with those of places like Vitsa Zagoriou than they did with the poleis of central Greece or even neighbouring Chalkidiki.[19] As in Vitsa, the Macedonian 'weapon burial ritual' persisted into the fourth century. It is evident in the tombs at Derveni, just north of Thessaloniki. Derveni is chiefly famed for its 'Orphic' papyrus and elaborate bronze volute-krater, with its Dionysiac imagery (fig. 15.4). It is not often remembered that this krater was used as a container for the ashes of a dead man of middling years and a younger woman, and that this cist grave (grave B) and two others nearby (graves A and gamma) were all 'warrior graves', i.e. burials with weapons.[20] Elaborate metal vessels survive from Macedonia (as they do not elsewhere) because Macedonians

---

[15] Waywell 1978: 77. For general discussion of its relationship to other contemporary sculptures, see *ibid.*: 67–78.   [16] On the Lion tomb at Knidos, see Newton 1863: 480–511.

[17] This statement is based on the initial results of the Langadas survey. There seems to have been a fall in the number of late Archaic/Classical sites compared to those datable to the Early Iron Age. See Andreou and Kotsakis 1994; 1995; forthcoming.   [18] Jeffery 1990: 364–5, 370, 479.

[19] Votokopoulou *et al.* 1985.

[20] On the context of the Derveni krater, see Picard 1963: 179–87; Makaronas 1963. On the osteological evidence, Musgrave 1990: 310–21. On the krater itself, Yiouri 1978. On Macedonian burial practices generally, see Morris 1998b: 75–80.

15.4 Bronze volute-krater from Derveni, tomb II

remained wedded to the ancient practice of placing large numbers of valuables in tombs. No fourth-century Athenian was buried in a bronze krater like this one. Just as Macedonians were inclined to give lavishly to the dead, so they remained reluctant to devote much energy to the gods. Neither expensive dedications nor large temples are common in Classical Macedon. Fourth-century temples do exist, to be sure. Some have been found at royal sites, such as Vergina (probably ancient Aigai). Such temples tend to be small. The temple of Eukleia at Vergina, for example, is only 8 m by 4 m overall, and does not have much in the way of votive offerings.[21] Macedonians lavished their attention not on their temples, but on their tombs.

These tombs became considerably more sophisticated in the course of the fourth century. The turn of the fourth and third centuries was the heyday of the

---

[21] Andronikos 1994a: 49–51. Not all scholars however are happy with the identification of Vergina with ancient Aigai. See Faklaris 1994.

Macedonian 'chamber tomb', a tumulus with a large funerary chamber beneath. A chamber could either be a large cist, or have a vaulted roof. Such tombs have been known for some time. One was excavated in the early years of this century near Langadas, north-east of Thessaloniki.[22] The tumulus was huge, 19.5 m high and 76 m in diameter. At its centre was a vaulted chamber, 9.5 m by 4.75 m. This consisted of an outer chamber or anteroom, entered through a wooden door; and an inner chamber or burial vault, entered via a door made out of marble. The antechamber had a painted façade, with pediment and Ionic pilasters. This tomb, like the vast majority of the 51 Macedonian tumuli excavated before 1977, had been robbed. Only an iron spearhead gave any hint of the kind of person who might have been buried within it.

Earlier this century, archaeologists were inclined to date these tombs to the Hellenistic period (that is, after 323 BC). Since the vast majority of tombs had been plundered, they could only be dated by the style of their façades and the techniques of their construction. Ionic and Doric façades could date to any period in the fourth and third centuries BC, and it was thought impossible that a major advance in architectural technique – the barrel vault – could have been independently developed in such a backwater as Macedon. It must have been one of those Oriental ideas that trickled back into Greece after Alexander's conquest of the Persian empire. The idea that tumulus burial must have provided a tremendous stimulus for the development of the barrel vault was not seriously entertained.

All this was changed by Andronikos' excavations of the great tumulus at Vergina. Within this great mound were three burial chambers. One of these (which was little more than a large cist tomb, of the type found at Derveni), the so-called tomb of Persephone, had been largely plundered in Antiquity, but contained perhaps the best-preserved surviving example of all Greek wall paintings.[23] The largest of these tombs, tomb II, measuring 7.82 m by 4.46 m, was both vaulted and unplundered (fig. 15.5). It contained a totally unparalleled quantity of bronze, silver and gold objects. It is this tomb which has attracted most controversy, ever since its identification by Andronikos (and others) as the tomb of Philip II of Macedon, who was assassinated and then buried at Aigai in 336 BC.[24] It was not merely the richness of the grave goods, but also their nature and their implicit symbolism, that Andronikos pointed to in support of his hypothesis. Though it resembles any other Macedonian tomb with chamber and antechamber, it has a particularly impressive Doric façade, with a painted hunting scene above. Its contents include arms (sword and spearhead) and armour (helmet, greaves, iron cuirass and ceremonial shield) – all the accoutrements in fact of a Macedonian 'warrior grave', and ones particularly appropriate for the career of a 'warrior king' such as Philip. Other items, however, relate more directly to the symposion.

---

[22] Macridy 1911; on Macedonian tombs generally, see Gossel 1980. Another fine example (probably Hellenistic in date) is published by S.G. Miller (1993).   [23] Andronikos 1994a: 86–95; 1994b.

[24] For the discovery of the tombs, see Andronikos 1994a: 55–83; for arguments in favour of its identification as that of Philip II, *ibid.*: 218–35; Hammond 1978.

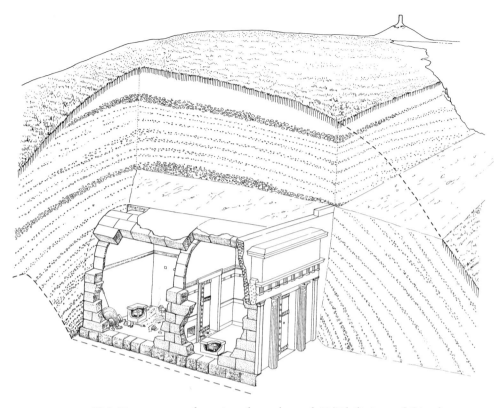

15.5 Reconstructed section through tomb II ('Philip's tomb') in the great mound at Vergina

These include an ivory couch or kline, and silver vessels for storing, mixing and drinking wine, such as amphorai, oinochoai, one krater, kylikes and skyphoi. In the very centre of the inner chamber was a marble sarcophagus; in the sarcophagus was a gold larnax, decorated with the 'star of Vergina'; and in the larnax were the cremated remains of a man of between 35 and 55 years of age, decorated with a golden wreath of oak leaves.[25]

That this is a royal tomb of some kind can hardly be doubted. But its exact identification remains controversial. American scholars in particular have championed the idea that this is the tomb, not of Philip II, but of his son, Philip III Arrhidaios, the idiot half-brother of and nominal successor to Alexander the Great. Arrhidaios was killed in 317 BC, and buried in 316.[26] The controversy has focussed on three points: whether a diadem or crown could have been in use in Greece before Alexander's conquests; whether the barrel vault could have been developed independently in Macedon; and whether the imported pottery found in the tomb, particularly the 'spool salt cellar', is consistent with a dating in 336 BC.

[25] Andronikos 1994a: 97–197.   [26] Lehmann 1980; 1982.

The point is more simply than one of correct identification. If Andronikos' critics are right, the whole sequence of Macedonian tombs should be down-dated to the early Hellenistic period, and their development becomes just another example of the 'Eastern influence' which resulted from Alexander's conquests. If Andronikos and his supporters are right, then the vast majority of Macedonian tombs of this type must be fourth century in date, and thus represent a remarkable indigenous artistic and architectural achievement. Let us deal with the objections to Andronikos' view in turn.

Of all the points raised by Andronikos' critics, the one concerning the 'diadem' carries the least weight. The 'diadem' in the grave is in fact a stephanos, a version in gold of the wreaths of various plants won by victors in the games or any other of the many agones (competitions) held in ancient Greece. It bears no relation to the diadem, a symbol of royal authority offensive to many Greeks, worn by the Great King.[27] As regards the barrel vault, there is plenty of evidence that the Greeks of the fourth century knew of some kind of vault. It is unclear however whether this was a barrel vault or a sophisticated form of corbelling. Still, one can see how the requirements of Macedonian aristocratic 'warrior graves' might have encouraged such innovation. An impressive tomb had to have both a chamber (to contain the grave goods) and a tumulus (to serve as a reminder of the importance of the person buried there). The chamber had to support the weight of the vast tumulus on top. Macedonians seem to have learnt from experience that a simple cist or lintel structure could not bear this kind of weight. Vaulted structures could; and the simplest kind of vault is the barrel vault.[28] This leaves the presence of 'spool salt cellars' as the only real obstacle to Andronikos' identification. Either Andronikos is wrong, or there is something fundamentally flawed about the accepted chronology of fourth-century deposits in the Athenian Agora.[29] The weakness of most of these objections does not mean that Andronikos is right; but if we can trust the facial reconstructions proposed on the basis of osteological examination, then there is another powerful point in favour of the burial being that of Philip II.[30]

Whatever one's view on the precise question of the identification of the tomb, two things stand out about Macedonian royal burials. One is that burials are of individuals. No more than two persons are generally found in any Macedonian chamber tomb, even when these chambers may be grouped together under one tumulus. The Mausoleum at Halikarnassos is by contrast a dynastic monument. The sculptural groups celebrate the whole Hektomnid dynasty, not merely

[27] Fredericksmeyer 1981; 1983.

[28] On fourth-century Greek knowledge of vaults, Plato, *Laws* 947d. For arguments in favour of an indigenous, Macedonian development of the vault, see Andronikos 1987; Tomlinson 1987.

[29] On 'spool salt cellars', see Rotroff 1984: esp. 349–51. For the early Hellenistic deposits in the Agora generally, Rotroff 1997.

[30] On the osteological evidence from the golden casket in the main chamber of tomb II ('Philip's tomb') see Xirotiris and Langenscheidt 1981: 144–54. On the facial reconstruction, Prag *et al.* 1984; Prag 1990.

Mausolus himself. The sacrificial deposit outside the monument must be seen as a sacrifice to the ruling group as a whole. Secondly, royal Macedonian tombs are clearly warrior graves writ large, bigger and better versions of the kind of burial any Macedonian male aristocrat might receive. In this respect, Macedonian burial practices have more in common with the Anglo-Saxon royal tombs at Sutton Hoo than they do with contemporary Anatolian tombs or the citizens' graves of a central Greek polis such as Athens.[31] Though the institution of kingship may help to explain why in both Macedon and Caria so much effort was lavished on royal tombs, differences in the particulars of cultural practices provide intriguing clues as to how Macedonian society differed from Carian. But if the arms and armour of 'Philip's tomb' link Macedon to a set of symbolic practices widely encountered in barbarian Europe in the Iron Age, the style of the tomb's façade, and the symposium vessels found within it, speak eloquently of the hellenising aspirations of the Macedonian ruling class. Macedonians desperately wanted to be seen as Greeks. They enthusiastically took up the Greek institution of the symposium, but in so doing changed it into something quite different from what it was before. This can be seen most clearly in that other Macedonian innovation – the palace.

Little is known about the houses of the average inhabitants of Macedon proper in early Classical times. But by the late fourth century Macedonians were clearly building houses that owed little to the vernacular traditions of a site like Kastanas. The luxurious late fourth-century houses excavated in the Macedonian capital, Pella, are in fact larger and more opulent versions of the kind of courtyard house one finds at Olynthos. Two of these, the 'house of Dionysos' and the 'house of the Rape of Helen', have now been published in detail. Both are large houses with a central peristyle courtyard (the house of Dionysos has two of these), and both are richly furnished with pebble mosaics (after which both houses are named).[32] One of these mosaics, showing the end of a stag hunt, gives us the mosaicist's name – 'Gnosis'. It is no surprise that this mosaic should decorate the floor of an andron. But whereas a rich man's house at Olynthos would have one, perhaps two, androness, with at most four mosaic floors, the house of Dionysos has at least two, and the house of the 'Rape of Helen' at least five, most of which have their own mosaics. This is more androness than one actually needs for the purposes of normal Greek male sociability.

---

[31] It is worth noting that the third chamber tomb in the great tumulus at Vergina, the 'Prince's tomb', was also a warrior grave (Andronikos 1994a: 198–217). The cremated remains in the silver larnax seem to be those of an adolescent male of between 13 and 16 years of age (Xirotiris and Langenscheidt 1981: 157–60). It is none the less a fallacy to argue that because someone was buried with weapons, these attributes accurately reflect what that man or woman did and suffered in life – and this is one of the weak points in Andronikos' arguments. Grave goods are not quasi-biographical facts. They are rather material metaphors for a whole host of cultural ideas that link masculinity, military prowess and kingly authority. Kings ought to be great warriors, and that is what the grave goods tell us. They have no bearing on whether the king was the ineffectual Arridhaios or the very effectual Philip. For a discussion of the parallel case of Anglo-Saxon warrior graves, see Härke 1990. For the implications of this argument for Greek archaeology, see Whitley 1995: 47–9.

[32] Makaronas and Yiouri 1989. See discussion in Westgate 1998: 104–6; Salzmann 1978: 104–8 (nos. 94–105); and Morris 1998b: 80–1.

The houses at Pella are part of an architectural trend which culminates in the palace at Vergina. This is a large building (104.5 m by 88.5 m) with a monumental entrance hall, built in the years around 300 BC. Like the houses at Pella, rooms are arranged around an internal peristyle courtyard, and like these houses too the palace has many andrones. In fact it has at least four fifteen-couch rooms (two with mosaics), at least two and more probably six rooms for nineteen couches, and three huge banqueting halls, each of which could easily accommodate thirty couches around its sides (fig. 15.6). These large rooms do not have mosaics; they are paved with irregular pieces of marble set in red mortar. The palace then appears to be not so much a residence as a building which could accommodate large numbers of banqueters, on a scale well beyond that of the average Greek house.[33] The palace at Vergina might then at first sight seem to be a triumphant affirmation of the symposium idea. But such gigantism could equally be seen as the death knell of the true, Greek symposion. It is time to look in more detail at other changes in drinking and dining as they manifest themselves in the material culture of other parts of the Greek world.

15.4 Drinking and dining at the close of the fourth century

The end of the fourth century, and the beginning of the Hellenistic era, is marked by a whole series of changes in the material culture of Greek lands. These changes affect everything from pots to houses. In many of the arts and crafts, such as gem engraving, the Hellenistic period is one of innovation. There is simply a much greater variety, in both material and type, of engraved gems in Hellenistic times than there had been in the Classical period.[34] Pot forms too show a decisive break with what had gone before. New techniques, such as the use of moulds, are introduced in pot production and decoration, and the Archaic and Classical tradition of figured drawing comes to an abrupt close.[35] Both Hellenistic pottery and Hellenistic engraved gems have more in common with material from the Roman world than with most of what the Classical Greeks produced in these fields. It is often extremely difficult to tell a Roman from an Hellenistic gem, and the technique used to produce the Hellenistic 'Megarian bowls' is, in essentials, the same as that later employed in the production of Roman Arretine or *terra sigillata*. Only the colour is different.

There has been an understandable temptation to link these changes in material forms to the enormous political and social changes that resulted first from the

---

[33] On the Vergina palace, see Rhomaios 1955; Andronikos 1994a: 38–46; Hoepfner 1996: 9–17. For the mosaics, see Salzmann 1978: 114–15 (nos. 130–1). For discussion, see Westgate 1998: 106–8. It should be noted however that, although most of the 'palace' seems to have been used for dining, there was a small 'west wing' (area L) which seems to have been a residence; see Hoepfner 1996: 17.

[34] On Hellenistic engraved gems, see Boardman 1970: 359–65; Henig 1994: 44–57; Boardman and Vollenweider 1978: 66–114; Plantzos 1999: esp. 35–41.

[35] On Hellenistic pottery generally, see Hayes 1991. On mould-made vessels, particularly 'Megarian bowls', see Rotroff 1982.

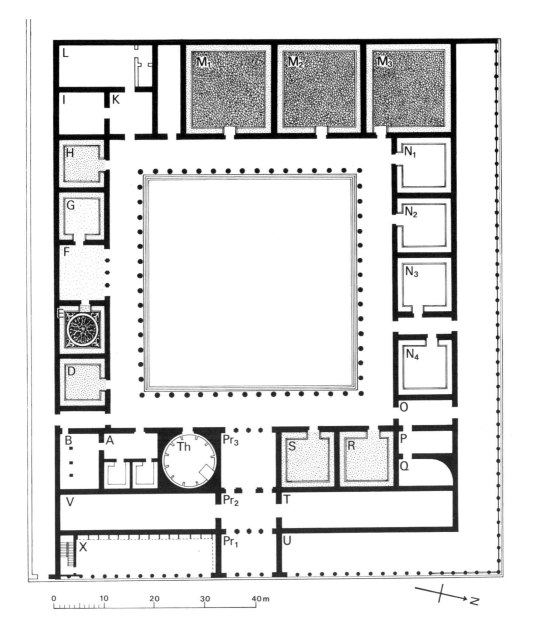

15.6 Plan of Palace at Vergina

domination of Macedon and then from Alexander's conquest of the East. These new material forms are somehow the expression of a new spirit. Whether this 'new spirit' is one of submission to monarchical authority, and the consequent withering of the polis ideal; or whether it is a spirit of 'individualism' arising from the opening up of possibilities in the East, or merely of new fields of opportunity for the unscrupulous willing to attach their fortunes to that of a more powerful man; these questions will find very different answers, depending on your political beliefs. Certainly the old communal bonds of the polis were loosening, and in this light the revival of tomb cults which becomes apparent at the very end of the fourth century has been plausibly interpreted as an expression of Hellenistic 'individualism'.[36] Scholars have also looked for material indices of the decline of ideals of citizenship and the polis. That there is a caesura in politics, pots and other material forms is not in doubt. The difficulty has always lain in specifying quite how political and social change is reflected or expressed in the material realm.[37] With the single exception of portraiture (see below), there seems to be no traceable causal link. How can, for example, the rise of the Macedonian monarchies have led to the decline of Attic red-figure ware? I would argue that the two are related, but, as always, the relationship is indirect.

One of the most striking differences between Classical and Hellenistic deposits in the Athenian Agora is the comparative rarity of the krater in the later period.[38] In the heyday of the Archaic and Classical symposium, the krater had always been the centrepiece, the place where wine, poetry and song were mixed.[39] Kraters can only perform such a role in relatively intimate surroundings. Literary evidence seems to suggest that seven was the ideal number of participants for a really successful symposium, one where the symposiasts were at ease, could enjoy themselves, and 'bond'.[40] Seven indeed seems to be the average number of couches in Classical Athenian andrones. Even dining rooms in public places such as the South Stoa seem to have had seven couches. The Classical polis was a network of private and public clubs, where no one was encouraged to pretensions of superiority over the other symposiasts.

The Macedonians turned the informal Greek symposium into an ostentatious public banquet. The 'symposia' that took place in the larger rooms of the palace at Vergina were hardly intimate occasions. Quite the opposite. It is difficult to see how any krater, metal or ceramic, could have served as a centre piece in a room designed for thirty or more people. Of course, a large krater, like the one from

---

[36] Alcock 1991a. A fine example of this revival is the construction of an altar within the 'Treasury of Minyas', the large Mycenaean tholos tomb at Orchomenos in Boeotia. For this see Antonaccio 1995: 127–30.

[37] See discussion in Pollitt 1986: 1–18: where he argues that Hellenistic culture was characterised by 'an obsession with fortune', a 'theatrical mentality', 'individualism' and a 'cosmopolitan outlook', all expressed in both art and literature.   [38] See the brilliant discussion by Rotroff 1996.

[39] Lissarrague 1990b: 19–46.

[40] The principal literary source is, of course, Plato's *Symposium*, where there seems to have been over seven (but not many more than seven) diners (not counting gatecrashers like Alcibiades).

Derveni, could still be an impressive ornament. Banquets at Vergina must, to be sure, have been magnificent, if the quality of the silver vessels from the Vergina tombs is anything to go by. But they could also be tests of endurance for the king's companions. As stories of Alexander the Great's drinking bouts make clear, a wrong word at a Macedonian symposium could cost you your life.[41]

A ceramic krater was clearly out of place in this new environment. A pot, however well decorated, was insufficiently ostentatious, and would easily be dwarfed by the scale of a large room. But Vergina is a long way from Athens. What do Macedonian drinking practices have to do with Athenian kraters? There is no direct connection. But by the end of the fourth century it was clear to everyone that, in political terms, Athens was of little account. Macedonians had established a trend towards larger and larger houses with larger and more opulently decorated andro"nes, such as the ones at Pella. Many late fourth-century Athenian houses seem to be following this lead. The late phase of one of the houses on the Areopagos slope (fig. 13.18) saw the house refurbished with an internal peristyle court, just like the ones at Pella. The house on Menander street has a fifteen-couch andron decorated with a rich pebble mosaic, and dates to the very end of the fourth century BC.[42] Ostentation seems to be replacing intimacy as the defining feature of late fourth-century Attic symposia.

Large houses, with internal peristyle courtyards and with rooms with mosaic floors, were to become much more common in the Hellenistic world. Just as 'Megarian bowls' anticipate Roman *terra sigillata*, so the form and decoration of Hellenistic houses foreshadow the Roman houses of Pompeii and Herculaneum. Larger Roman villas would often be decorated with, among other things, copies of famous Greek sculptures, including portraits of famous Greek poets, philosophers and statesmen. One of the most popular portraits, to judge from the number of surviving copies, was that of the Greek statesman Demosthenes, the inveterate opponent of all things Macedonian (fig. 15.8).

15.5 Portraits and politics

It is the Hellenistic, and not the Classical period that is the great age of Greek portraiture. Portraiture, in the sense of images intended to represent particular persons, was confined to sculpture in Classical times. Compared to, say, pedimental sculpture it was a minor feature of Classical art. Hellenistic portraits by contrast were produced in a whole variety of media, from full-length sculpture and portrait busts to images on engraved gems and coins.[43] The major impetus behind

---

[41] See Plutarch's *Alexander*, or indeed any account of Alexander's life. The victims of Alexander's anger were invariably killed at a symposion. On Macedonian symposia generally, see Tomlinson 1970.

[42] On the houses on the Areopagos slope, see Shear 1973a: 146–56. On the house in Menander street, Graham 1974. For a general discussion of this trend, see Walter-Karydi 1996.

[43] On Hellenistic portraits generally, see Smith 1988; 1991: 19–50. On portraits on gems, see Plantzos 1999: 42–65.

this development was the desire of Hellenistic rulers to create and disseminate effective images of themselves and their authority. The impetus can in fact be traced back to Alexander himself. Alexander was only too well aware that his rule depended on his reputation. Greek portraits were nothing if not the embodiment of reputation, a representation, that is, of the qualities thought to inhere in a person, a representation of what they represented. When therefore Alexander prevailed upon the celebrated artist Lysippos to sculpt Alexander's portrait, and decreed that no one else was allowed to do so, it is highly unlikely that Lysippos produced anything resembling a simple likeness. Our sources speak of Lysippos conveying Alexander's 'leonine' features and 'melting gaze', and it may not be that these terms refer simply to his appearance.[44] He may not have looked like that, but these were the features of his image that he wished to be widely conveyed. No actual original portraits of Alexander by Lysippos in fact survive; we have to infer the appearance of the portrait from a number of later Hellenistic and Roman copies that have. Many fit Plutarch's description in general terms, but the portrait from Yannitsa near Pella (fig. 15.7) is closer in time and space to Alexander and Lysippos than any other 'copy', and so may be closest to the original.[45] Such was Alexander's reputation that his successors continued to make use of his image for propaganda purposes after his death. It is they who are most probably responsible for producing and reproducing, in both coins and gems, the profile of Alexander wearing the horns of Zeus Ammon. Paradoxically, it is this, rather than the celebrated statue by Lysippos, that has proven to be Alexander's most enduring image.[46]

Hellenistic rulers were understandably keen on portraits. A favoured type was one that portrayed the ruler as an heroic, nude, muscled warrior-athlete, like the one that survives from Terme.[47] Such sculpture has a simple message – 'I'm a powerful man – follow me' (or at the very least, don't cross me). Images of rulers were, however, not the only type of portrait popular in the Hellenistic world. Statues of statesmen, poets and philosophers gained genuine popularity as well. One of these demands our closest attention. This is the bronze full-length statue of Demosthenes by Polyeuktos, which survives in over fifty Roman marble copies (e.g. fig. 15.8). This was set up by the Athenians in the agora in 280/79 BC, at a time when the Hellenistic kingdoms momentarily appeared weak. Made over forty years after Demosthenes' death, it can in no sense be a likeness. Rather it represents what Demosthenes represented – the qualities of an orator-politician,

[44] Plutarch, *Alexander* 4.1; *On the Fortune and Virtue of Alexander the Great* II.2.3 (= Plutarch *Moralia* 335b). See discussion in Pollitt 1986: 20–2.

[45] For the portraits of Alexander by Lysippos, see Pollitt 1986: 20–2; Smith 1988: 58–62, 155–6; 1991: 21–2; Richter and Smith 1984: 225–8. On Lysippos and his 'school', see Pollitt 1986: 47–58.

[46] Pollitt 1986: 24–8; on this particular gem, see Boardman and Vollenweider 1978: 76–8 (no. 280). On early coins with images of Alexander issued by his Successors (Ptolemy I, Seleukos I and Lysimachos), see Smith 1988: 60–1.

[47] Rome, Terme museum 1049; Smith 1988: 164 (no. 164); on the type, see generally Smith 1991: 19–20.

15.7 Marble head found at Yannitsa, near Pella,
thought to be of Alexander

who had to urge an unpopular course of action on his people in difficult times. It
stands for a certain kind of troubled republican virtue, a virtue that survives
despite the odds. As such it necessarily serves as an antithesis to other portrait
types. Not only is this old and anxious face, this unathletic stance and less than
impressive torso a deliberate contrast to the muscle-bound Hellenistic ruler, it
also acts as a more subtle commentary on other images of orator-statesmen. Fifth-
and fourth-century portraits of politicians, such as the famous bust of Pericles,
had a detached, Olympian air about them. The statesman was pursuing a noble
cause, and this was conveyed in the portrait. This tradition is continued in portraits of Demosthenes' great opponent and contemporary, Aischines. Of course,
Aischines' pragmatic policy of appeasement was the one that ultimately prevailed. Any student of *Realpolitik* would have condemned Demosthenes' consistent opposition to Macedon as little more than a futile gesture.[48] Demosthenes

---

[48] On the Demosthenes type, see Smith 1991: 37–8; Pollitt 1986: 59–63; Richter and Smith 1984:
108–13. On the 'Aischines' type, see *ibid.*: 73–5.

15.8 Roman marble copy of the Demosthenes of Polyeuktos, now
in Copenhagen Glyptothek

was a 'loser'. Like the city-state ideal to which he devoted his life, he ultimately failed. His portrait is a study in anxious, heroic integrity. Yet Demosthenes' oratory, his politics and his portrait are an integral (and inextricable) part of the legacy that has come down to us from ancient Greece. There can be no better image with which to close any book that seeks a better understanding of the Greek achievement.

FURTHER READING FOR EACH CHAPTER

Chapter 1

Further reading for the particulars of the Nessos amphora and the Delphi Charioteer appears in the notes. Of the general histories of Greek art referred to, Beazley and Ashmole, *Greek Sculpture and Painting* (1932) is the platonic original of which many other histories of Greek art are copies. Other surveys which can be recommended for background reading include Robertson, *A Shorter History of Greek Art* (1981), Boardman, *Greek Art* (1973) and Pedley, *Greek Art and Archaeology* (1993). There is also a new book on *Greek Art* by Nigel Spivey. For a useful summary of most of the literary evidence for ancient art, see Pollitt, *The Art of Ancient Greece: Sources and Documents* (1990); Robertson, *A History of Greek Art* (1975) remains the standard work of reference on the subject. For a prehistorian's view of Classical Archaeology, see Childe in *Antiquity* (1958). For other views as to why Classical Archaeology appears to be so odd to other archaeologists, see Shanks, *Classical Archaeology of Greece* (1995) and Snodgrass, *An Archaeology of Greece* (1987), esp. 1–35.

Chapter 2

There is, unfortunately, no general history of Classical Archaeology or of Classical Archaeology in Greece. Shanks, *Classical Archaeology of Greece* (1995) is not really a history, and Morris, 'Archaeologies of Greece' (1994a) concentrates mostly on more recent developments. Morris' article is none the less eminently worth reading. The early period of exploration is very well covered by Stoneman, *Land of Lost Gods* (1987). For Winckelmann see especially Potts, *Flesh and the Ideal* (1994). It is more difficult than one would think to obtain an English translation of Winckelmann's great work. For the history of the study of vase painting (and early work on vases) see Cook, *Greek Painted Pottery* (2nd edition 1972), 287–327. There is now a third edition of this indispensable book (1997). For William Hamilton, see Jenkins and Sloan, *Vases and Volcanoes* (1996). For early travellers and antiquarians in Greece from 1700 onwards see Stoneman, *Land of Lost Gods* (1987), 110–236 and Tsigakou, *The Rediscovery of Greece* (1981); for Lord Elgin see St. Clair, *Lord Elgin and the Marbles* (1967); for the build up of the British Museum see Jenkins, *Archaeologists and Aesthetes* (1992). There is no clear account in English of the work of Greek archaeologists, but see again Stoneman, *Land of Lost Gods* (1987), 237–64. For the history of German archaeology, see the brilliant book by Marchand, *Down from Olympus* (1996). For Beazley, see Kurtz, 'Beazley and the connoisseurship of Greek vases' (1985a) and Whitley, 'Beazley as theorist' (1997a) in *Antiquity*. Beazley rarely explained his method himself, except in 'Citharoedus' (1922) in the *Journal of Hellenic Studies*, which ought to be consulted by anyone interested. Beazley's clearest account of Greek 'vases' is *The Development of Attic Black Figure* (1951). For Vickers' and Gill's criticisms, see especially Vickers and Gill, *Artful Crafts* (1994).

Chapter 3

Hoffmann, *Sexual and Asexual Pursuit* (1977) and Snodgrass, *Archaeology and the Rise of the Greek State* (1977) are essential reading. As for early travellers, Stoneman, *Land of Lost Gods* (1987), 136–64 is a good introduction, though one should try to get the flavour of Dodwell and Leake for oneself. There are fortunately several good introductions to survey archaeology: Osborne, *Classical Landscape with Figures* (1987); Van Andel and Runnels, *Beyond the Acropolis* (1987); and Snodgrass, *An Archaeology of Greece* (1987), 67–131. There is no such easy introduction to petrology and the chemical analysis of pottery fabrics. Cook, *Greek Painted Pottery* (1972 or 1997) remains a very useful introduction to pottery and regionalism; Jones *et al.*, *Greek and Cypriot Pottery* (1986) is essential for the serious student but very difficult for the beginner. The clearest exposition of chemical analysis is Liddy (1996) in Coldstream and Catling, *Knossos North Cemetery*. For new iconographic approaches, see especially Bérard *et al.*, *A City of Images* (1989) and now Hoffmann, *Sotades* (1997). For social and contextual approaches it is perhaps best first to read Snodgrass, *Archaic Greece* (1980); then one can go on to the slightly partisan summary of 'rudiments of a social archaeology' in Shanks, *Classical Archaeology of Greece* (1995), 128–63, before consulting the works themselves (if you have time). Morris, *Classical Greece* (1994) contains a number of examples of social/contextual archaeology. For environmental archaeology (such as it is) see now Rackham and Moody, *The Making of the Cretan Countryside* (1996) and Rackham, 'Ancient landscapes' in Murray and Price, *The Greek City* (1990).

Chapter 4

The best introduction to chronology is Biers, *Art, Artefacts and Chronology in Greek Archaeology* (1992), though the most lucid explanation of seriation I have come across recently is Rotroff, *Agora XXIX: Hellenistic Pottery* (1997), 3–10 and 18–36. Cook, *Greek Painted Pottery* (1972), 259–69 and Cook, 'The Francis/ Vickers chronology' in the *Journal of Hellenic Studies* (1989) provide the best summation of the fixed points. Coldstream, *Greek Geometric Pottery* (1968), 302–31 discusses the eighth-century evidence in some detail, and Pollitt, *The Art of Ancient Greece* (1990) provides useful summaries of some of the literary sources for the later periods. The best of Francis and Vickers' articles remains 'Signa priscae artis' (1983) in the *Journal of Hellenic Studies*.

Chapter 5

The best account of the Dark Ages as a whole remains Snodgrass, *The Dark Age of Greece* (1971). Desborough, *The Greek Dark Ages* (1972) and Coldstream, *Geometric Greece* (1977) provide more detailed accounts of the earlier and later periods respectively. It should be remembered, however, that all these works were written before the full publication of finds from Nichoria and Lefkandi and the recent excavation of the North Cemetery at Knossos; excavation reports are always worth consulting. More up-to-date overviews of the evidence are provided by Hurwit, *The Art and Culture of Early Greece* (1985), 33–124 and Snodgrass, *An Archaeology of Greece* (1987), 170–210, and articles in two volumes edited by Langdon: *From Pasture to Polis* (1993) and *New Light on a Dark Age* (1997). For more specialised studies, Desborough, *Protogeometric Pottery* (1952) and Coldstream, *Greek Geometric Pottery* (1968) remain the near-definitive pottery studies; architecture and settlement have recently been given a very thorough treatment by Mazarakis Ainian, *From Rulers' Dwellings to Temples* (1997); for interpretation of burial evidence see Morris, *Burial and Ancient Society* (1987) and my *Style and Society in Dark Age Greece* (1991). The best recent account of the significance of the 'eighth-century revolution' is Hurwit, 'Art, poetry and the polis' in Langdon (1993), 14–42.

Chapter 6

The Orientalising period (or rather phenomenon) has recently been the subject of several books: Burkert, *The Orientalizing Revolution* (1992); Sarah Morris, *Daidalos* (1992); and, indirectly if implicitly, Bernal, *Black Athena* (1991). All of these make for stimulating reading, but all equally should be taken with a large pinch of salt (or scepticism). For the traditional view of the 'Orientalising' as a temporary, necessary, but ultimately unimportant phase in the glorious history of Greek art, see Robertson, *A Shorter History of Greek Art* (1981), 4–8. Aubet, *The Phoenicians and the West* (1993) is the best and most up-to-date treatment of the Phoenicians, though she does not really discuss Phoenician impact on the Greeks. There is as yet no detailed discussion of regional variations in response to Oriental 'influence', outside of specialised treatments of Attic, Corinthian, Euboean or Knossian pottery and art (for which see the bibliography), though there is an interesting discussion by Morris, 'The art of citizenship' in Langdon, *New Light on a Dark Age* (1997). Some indication of such regional variations is, however, provided by Coldstream, *Geometric Greece* (1977) and by Boardman, *The Greeks Overseas* (3rd edition 1980), which also remains the best introduction to the history of early Greek colonisation and trade. For the earliest Greek colonies and the establishment of Pithekoussai, there is the excellent book by Ridgway, *The First Western Greeks* (1992), which also discusses the 'Euboean trading network'. Serious students of the Greek alphabet should, of course, read Jeffery, *The Local Scripts of Archaic Greece* (2nd edition 1990), but the most stimulating introduction to the whole question of the introduction of the alphabet is Powell, *Homer and the Origin of the Greek Alphabet* (1991).

Chapter 7

The best introduction to the subject of Greek Religion is Burkert, *Greek Religion: Archaic and Classical* (1985). On the question of continuity see Morgan, 'From palace to polis' in Hägg, *The Role of Religion in the Early Greek Polis* (1996) and de Polignac 'Mediation, competition and sovereignty' in Alcock and Osborne, *Placing the Gods* (1994), 3–18. There is only one general book on votive offerings: Rouse, *Greek Votive Offerings* (1902), and it is very out of date; see also the articles in Linders and Nordquist, *Gifts to the Gods* (1987) and Hägg *et al.*, *Early Greek Cult Practice* (1988). On the spatial dimension of Greek cult, see Scully, *The Earth, the Temple and the Gods* (1979), de Polignac, *Cults, Territory and the Origins of the Greek City State* (1995) and articles in Alcock and Osborne, *Placing the Gods* (1994). On early panhellenic sanctuaries, see Morgan, *Athletes and Oracles* (1990); and for early sanctuaries generally, articles in Marinatos and Hägg, *Greek Sanctuaries: New Approaches* (1993). On developments in the eighth century, see Coldstream, *Geometric Greece* (1977), 317–40. On the 'uses of the past', see in particular Antonaccio, *An Archaeology of Ancestors* (1995), but also criticisms in de Polignac (1995), 128–49. For the development of early Greek temples, see Mazarakis-Ainian, *From Rulers' Dwellings to Temples* (1997) and Lawrence and Tomlinson, *Greek Architecture* (5th edition, 1996), 58–89. For architectural terracottas, and notes on more recent scholarship, see Winter, *Greek Architectural Terracottas* (1993).

Chapter 8

The best introduction to the question of polis formation and urbanism remains Snodgrass, *Archaic Greece: The Age of Experiment* (1980a). There are some useful articles in Rich and Wallace Hadrill, *City and Country in the Ancient World* (1991), especially Morris, 'The early polis as city and state'. For a comparative perspective, see articles in Renfrew and Cherry, *Peer Polity Interaction and Socio-Political Change* (1986). On Geometric settlements, see Mazarakis-Ainian, *From Rulers' Dwellings to Temples* (1997); on Archaic, see Lang, *Archaische Siedlungen in Griechenland* (1996). Though this is in German, it has excellent plans, and is easy to consult. On production and trade in the Greek city (particulary for pottery), see articles in Rasmussen and Spivey, *Looking at Greek Pottery* (1991) and Sparkes,

Greek Pottery: An Introduction (1991), though Boardman's article 'Trade in Greek decorated pottery' (1988a) remains particularly stimulating. On the development of armour and weapons, see Snodgrass, *Early Greek Armour and Weapons* (1964); on the hoplite reform see Snodgrass, 'The hoplite reform and history' (1965) in the *Journal of Hellenic Studies* and Salmon, 'Political hoplites?' (1977) in the same journal. On the question of burials and citizenship, see Morris *Burial and Ancient Society* (1987); many of Morris' ideas are expressed more clearly in his *Death Ritual and Social Structure in Classical Antiquity* (1992). For the Athenian Agora, see Camp, *The Athenian Agora* (2nd edition 1992). For other aspects of polis development (coinage, laws and literacy) see articles in Mitchell and Rhodes, *The Development of the Polis in Archaic Greece* (1997), and in Fisher and Van Wees, *Archaic Greece: New Approaches and New Evidence* (1998). Many of the same topics are also intelligently discussed in Osborne, *Greece in the Making* (1996a).

Chapter 9

Schnapp, 'Are images animated? The psychology of statues in Ancient Greece', in Renfrew, *The Ancient Mind* (1994), 40–4, has some very interesting thoughts on this problem, if on a rather philosophical level. On early imagery see Coldstream, 'Birth of the picture', in Rasmussen and Spivey, *Looking at Greek Vases* (1991), 37–56, and discussion in Hurwit, *The Art and Culture of Early Greece* (1985), 93–124. Hurwit's book is also a very useful guide to many of the issues discussed in this chapter. For the question of narrative art and mythological representation, see Snodgrass, *An Archaeology of Greece* (1987), 132–69; for what made Greek narrative special, see now, B. Powell 'From picture to myth: from myth to picture', in Langdon, *New Light on a Dark Age* (1997), 154–93. On the symposium the best work is undoubtedly Lissarrague, *The Aesthetics of the Greek Banquet* (1990), but articles in Murray, *Sympotica: A Symposium on the Symposion* (1990) are also worth looking at. Boardman, *Athenian Black Figure Vases* (1974) and *Athenian Red Figure Vases: The Archaic Period* (1978) remain very useful, though chiefly for their pictures. Boardman, *Greek Sculpture: The Archaic Period* (1976) provides a good summary of the available evidence, but is perhaps less stimulating in general than Ridgway, *The Archaic Style in Greek Sculpture* (1977). Richter, *Kouroi* (1970) and *Korai* (1968) remain the fundamental catalogues one should consult on these subjects. A more considered view of these genres is given by Stewart 'When is a kouros not an Apollo', in del Chiaro, *Corinthiaca* (1986), 54–70 and Stewart, *Art, Desire and the Body in Ancient Greek Culture* (1997), esp. 63–70. On later developments in temple architecture, see in particular Lawrence and Tomlinson, *Greek Architecture* (1996).

Chapter 10

Coldstream, *Geometric Greece* (1977) provides useful summaries of regional patterns in the eighth century. Virtually any synthetic work on the archaeology of

Archaic Greece touches on regionalism. One has only to glance at Cook, *Greek Painted Pottery* (1972), Jeffery, *The Local Scripts of Archaic Greece* (2nd edition 1990) and Winter, *Greek Architectural Terracottas* (1993) to appreciate this fact. It is only recently however that archaeologists have begun to treat these regional patterns as regional cultures, in the sense meant by Clarke, *Analytical Archaeology* (2nd edition 1978), 245–327. See in particular the article by Morris, 'Archaeology and Archaic Greek history', in Fisher and Van Wees, *Archaic Greece* (1998), 1–91. The most sophisticated attempt to quantify degrees of stylistic similarity within a region is Morgan and Whitelaw, 'Pots and politics' (1991), in the *American Journal of Archaeology*. For seventh-century Attica, Osborne, 'A crisis in archaeological history?' (1989), in the *Annual of the British School at Athens* provides a good introduction to the evidence, but to understand the controversy one should read S.P. Morris, *The Black and White Style* (1984) against the arguments put forward in I. Morris, *Burial and Ancient Society* (1987). My own views are given in Whitley, 'Protoattic pottery: a contextual approach' in Morris, *Classical Greece* (1994), 51–70. The evidence from Archaic Crete is usefully summarised by Boardman in the *Cambridge Ancient History* III.3 (1932), 222–33. It is only recently that the 'gap' has begun to be treated with any degree of seriousness (e.g. Prent 1997), but see my 'Cretan laws and Cretan literacy' (1997), in the *American Journal of Archaeology*. A vivid impression of Archaic Cretan metalwork is given in Hoffmann, *Early Cretan Armorers* (1972), including a discussion of the Spensithios decree. The publication of Coldstream and Catling, *Knossos North Cemetery* (1996) presents lots of new evidence for the seventh century. There is no good synthetic work on Archaic Macedonia, apart from remarks in Morris' (1998) article. Votokopoulou *et al.*, *Sindos* (1985) has many pictures which give a vivid impression of Macedonian burial practices. There are plenty of good works on sixth-century Athens. The later chapters of Hurwit, *The Art and Culture of Early Greece* (1985a) provide the best introduction. Shapiro, *Art and Cult under the Tyrants in Athens* (1989) provides a good discussion of the iconographic evidence, usefully summarised by Boardman in *Athenian Black Figure Vases* (1974) and *Athenian Red Figure Vases: The Archaic Period* (1978). The evidence for early Athenian writing is given in Immerwahr, *Attic Script* (1990) and discussed in my 'Cretan laws and Cretan literacy' (1997), 640–5. The best discussion of the burial evidence is now Houby-Nielsen, 'Burial language in the Archaic and Classical Kerameikos' (1995), in the *Proceedings of the Danish Institute at Athens*.

Chapter 11

The best introduction to the art of Classical Greece remains Pollitt, *Art and Experience in Classical Greece* (1972). Pollitt's source book, *The Art of Ancient Greece* (1990), is extremely useful when it comes to lost works. Classical sculpture is well covered by handbooks and guides: Boardman, *Greek Sculpture: The*

Classical Period (1985) and *Greek Sculpture: The Late Classical Period* (1995) both provide good, factual overviews. A more lively account is given in Ridgway, *Fifth Century Styles in Greek Sculpture*. The best account, however, of how sculpture and architecture are linked together remains Ashmole, *Architect and Sculptor in Classical Greece* (1972). For architecture generally, Lawrence and Tomlinson, *Greek Architecture* (1996) remains a good introduction. The subject of Athenian red-figure and white-ground 'vase painting' receives near-comprehensive treatment in Robertson, *The Art of Vase Painting in Classical Athens* (1992). Cook, *Greek Painted Pottery* (1972) provides useful summaries of other regional styles of red-figure.

Chapter 12

There are unfortunately no good general books on Greek sanctuaries in the Classical period. Some idea of how sanctuaries developed can none the less be gleaned from Lawrence and Tomlinson, *Greek Architecture* (1996), and Coulton, *Greek Architects at Work* (1977) provides a useful 'problem orientated' account of how temples were built. For the English reader, the best general accounts of a Classical sanctuary are of Epidauros; both Tomlinson, *Epidauros* (1983) and Burford, *The Greek Temple Builders of Epidauros* (1969) provide a vivid picture of what a Greek sanctuary was like, and how it was built. For panhellenic sanctuaries, there is the good general overview in Drees, *Olympia* (1968). For Classical cities, there is little that can be recommended in English; but for those who can persevere with a little German, Hoepfner and Schwandner, *Haus und Stadt im klassischen Griechenland* (1994) gives a vivid picture of how Classical cities were planned, as well as providing insights into Classical housing. We are better served when it comes to the study of houses and domestic space. There is first the excellent article by Jameson, 'Domestic space in the Greek city state', in Kent, *Domestic Architecture and the Use of Space* (1990); and several good articles by Nevett, notably 'Gender in the Classical household' (1995), in the *Annual of the British School at Athens*; and now her book, *House and Society in the Ancient Greek World* (1999).

Chapter 13

The best overview of the archaeology of Classical Athens remains Wycherley, *The Stones of Athens* (1978). For the Agora there is Camp's excellent *The Athenian Agora* (2nd edition 1992). There is now too an excellent overview of all the Acropolis finds, in Hurwit, *The Athenian Acropolis* (1999). The 'standard' view of the Parthenon frieze is given by Jenkins, *The Parthenon Frieze* (1994), but those who relish controversy should not miss Connelly, 'Parthenon and *parthenoi*: a mythological interpretation of the Parthenon frieze' (1996), in the *American Journal of Archaeology* or Castriota, *Myth, Ethos and Actuality* (1992). For a variety of views on numerous aspects of public and private art in fifth-century Athens, see also Osborne, *Archaic and Classical Greek Art* (1998). Wycherley, *Stones of Athens* (1978) remains the best guide to the overall structure of the city of Athens and to the theatre of Dionysos, but Travlos, *Pictorial Dictionary of Ancient Athens* (1971) and his *Bildlexikon des antiken Attika* (1988) remain invaluable sources for all kinds of sanctuary and other sites in both Athens and Attica. On Attic houses, Jones' article, 'Town and country houses in Attica in Classical times', in Mussche *et al.*, *Thorikos and the Laurion Area in Classical Times* (1975), remains the best overview. It is a pity it is published in such an obscure series. For the symposion, many items in Murray, *Sympotica* (1990) are extremely enlightening, but the best recent discussion (ostensibly only about the Hellenistic period) is Rotroff, *The Missing Krater and the Hellenistic Symposium* (1996). For burials and the Kerameikos, see Morris, *Death Ritual and Social Structure in Classical Antiquity* (1992), 108–49, and Knigge, *The Athenian Kerameikos* (1991). For the ambiguous Athenian attitude towards Persia, see both Castriota, *Myth, Ethos and Actuality* (1992) and M.C. Miller, *Athens and Persia in the Fifth Century BC* (1997).

Chapter 14

The best general book on the Greek countryside remains Osborne, *Classical Landscape with Figures* (1987). For a completely different view of the Greek countryside, however, one has to turn to Lohmann's article, 'Agriculture and country life in Classical Attica', in Wells, *Agriculture in Ancient Greece* (1992). For a good overview of the evidence from Laurion, see Jones, 'The Laurion silver mines: a review' (1982), in *Greece and Rome* 29. The best introduction to survey is Snodgrass, *An Archaeology of Greece* (1987), esp. 67–131, though it is closely rivalled by van Andel and Runnels, *Beyond the Acropolis: A Rural Greek Past* (1987) and Davis, *Sandy Pylos* (1998). The most informative survey reports are those of Jameson *et al.*, *A Greek Countryside* (1994) and Cherry *et al.*, *Landscape Archaeology as Long-Term History* (1991). On fortifications generally, see Adam, *L'Architecture militaire grecque* (1982). On island towers, see the debate conducted between Young's views in 'Studies in south Attica: country estates at Sounion' *Hesperia* 25 (1956) and those in Cherry *et al.*, *Landscape Archaeology* (1991), 285–98. The border defences of Attica are thoroughly discussed in Ober, *Fortress Attica* (1985), supplemented by Ober, 'Early artillery towers', *American Journal of Archaeology* 91 (1987).

Chapter 15

The best account of the Mausoleum remains Ashmole, *Architect and Sculptor in Classical Greece* (1972), 147–91, though anyone seriously interested in the evidence should also look at Waywell, *The Free-Standing Sculptures of the*

Mausoleum at Halicarnassus (1978). Most of the best evidence from Macedon comes from Vergina, and is well discussed and illustrated in Andronikos, *Vergina: The Royal Tombs* (1994). There are excellent discussions of the changes in house and pot forms in two article-length pieces: Westgate, 'Mosaics in context', *Bulletin of the Institute of Classical Studies* 42 (1998) (for houses and mosaics) and Rotroff, *The Missing Krater and the Hellenistic Symposium* (1996) (for pottery and the symposion). On the culture of the Hellenistic age generally, see Pollitt, *Art in the Hellenistic Age* (1986). Pollitt also has very useful discussions on particular portraits. On Hellenistic sculpture in particular, see Smith, *Hellenistic Sculpture* (1991).

BIBLIOGRAPHY

Adam, J.P. 1982. *L'Architecture militaire grecque*. Paris: Picard.

Adam, S. 1966. *The Technique of Greek Sculpture in the Archaic and Classical Periods*. BSA Suppl. 3. London: Thames and Hudson.

Adler, F., Bormman, R., Dörpfeld, W., Graeber, F. and Graef, P. 1892. *Olympia II: Die Baudenkmaler von Olympia*. Berlin: A. Asher.

Adler, F., Curtius, E., Dörpfeld, W., Graef, P., Partsch, J. and Weil, R. 1897. *Olympia I: Topographie und Geschichte von Olympia*. Berlin: A. Asher.

Ahlberg, G. 1971a. *Prothesis and Ekphora in Greek Geometric Art*. Studies in Mediterranean Archaeology 32. Göteberg: Paul Åstroms Forlag.

1971b. *Fighting on Land and Sea in Greek Geometric Art*. Stockholm: Skrifter Utgivna av Svenska Institutet i Athen.

Ahlberg-Cornell, G. 1992. *Myth and Epos in Early Greek Art: Representation and Interpretation*. SIMA 100. Jonsered: Paul Åstroms Forlag.

Akurgal, E. 1983. *Alt Smyrna I: Wohnschichten und Athenatempel*. Ankara: Turk Tarik Kurumu Basimei.

Alcock, S.E. 1991a. Tomb cult and the post-Classical polis. *American Journal of Archaeology* 95: 447–67.

1991b. Urban survey and the *polis* of Phlius. *Hesperia* 60: 421–63.

1993. *Graecia Capta: The Landscapes of Roman Greece*. Cambridge: Cambridge University Pres.

1998. Liberation and conquest: Hellenistic and Roman Messenia. In J.L. Davis (ed.), *Sandy Pylos: An Archaeological History from Nestor to Navarino*, 179–91. Austin: University of Texas Press.

Alcock, S.E., Cherry, J.F. and Davis, J.L. 1994. Intensive survey, agricultural practice and the Classical landscape of Greece. In Morris 1994b: 137–70.

Alcock, S.E. and Osborne, R. (eds.) 1994. *Placing the Gods: Sanctuaries and Sacred Space in Ancient Greece*. Oxford: Clarendon.

Alroth, B. 1988. The positioning of Greek votive figurines. In Hägg *et al.* 1988: 195–203.

Amandry, P. 1952. Observations sur les monuments de l'Heraion d'Argos. *Hesperia* 21: 222–74.

1953. *Fouilles de Delphes II: Topographie et architecture: la Colonne des Naxiens et le Portique des Athéniens*. Paris: de Boccard.

1988. A propos de monuments de Delphes: questions de chronologie (I). *Bulletin de Correspondance Hellénique* 112: 591–610.

1992. Fouilles de Delphes et raisins de Corinthe: histoire d'un négociation. In Picard 1992: 77–128.

Amyx, D.A. 1988. *Corinthian Vase-Painting of the Archaic Period*. 3 volumes, catalogue, commentary and plates. Berkeley and Los Angeles: University of California Press.

Amyx, D.A. and Lawrence, P. 1975. *Corinth VII.ii: Archaic Corinthian Pottery and the Anaploga Well*. Princeton: American School of Classical Studies at Athens.

Andersen, H.D, Horsnaes, H.W., Houby-Nielsen, S. and Rathje, A. (eds.) 1997. *Urbanization in the Mediterranean in the 9th to 6th Centuries BC.* Acta Hyperborea 7. Copenhagen: Museum Tusculanum Press.

Anderson, J.K. 1959. Old Smyrna: the Corinthian pottery. *Annual of the British School at Athens* 53–4 [1958–9]: 138–51.

Andreadaki-Vlasaki, M. 1991. The Khania area, circa 1200–700 BC. In D. Musti, A. Sacconi, L. Rocchetti, M. Rocchi, E. Scafa, L. Sportiello and M.E. Gianotta (eds.), *La Transizione dal Miceneo all'Alto Arcaismo: Dal Palazzo alla Città*, 403–23. Rome: Consiglio Nazionale delle Ricerche.

Andhreou, I. 1994. O dimos ton Aixonidon Alon. In Coulson *et al.* 1994: 191–209.

Andreou, S. and Kotsakis, K. 1994. Prehistoric rural communities in perspective: the Langadas survey project. In P.N. Doukelis and L.G. Mendoni (eds.), *Structures rurales et sociétés antiques*, 17–25. Paris: Annales Littéraires de l'Université de Besançon.

1995. Epiphaneiki erevna Langada: periodos 1992. *To Archaiologiko Ergo sti Makedonia* 6 [1992]: 349–56.

(forthcoming). Counting people in an artifact poor landscape: the Langadas case, Macedonia, Greece. In J. Bintliff (ed.), *Ancient Demography and Field Surveys: The Populus Conference.*

Andronikos, M. 1969. *Vergina I: To Nekrotapheion ton Tymvon.* Athens: I en Athenais Archaiologiki Etaireia.

1987. Some reflections on the Macedonian tombs. *Annual of the British School at Athens* 82: 1–16.

1994a. *Vergina: The Royal Tombs and the Ancient City.* Athens: Ekdotiki Athenon.

1994b. *Vergina II: The 'Tomb of Persephone'.* Athens: I en Athenais Archaiologiki Etaireia.

Antonaccio, C.M. 1992. Temples, tombs and the early Argive Heraeum. *Hesperia* 61: 85–105.

1993. The archaeology of ancestors. In Dougherty and Kurke 1993: 46–70.

1994. Placing the past: the Bronze Age in the cultic topography of early Greece. In Alcock and Osborne 1994: 79–104.

1995. *An Archaeology of Ancestors: Tomb Cult and Hero Cult in Early Greece.* Lanham, MD: Rowman and Littlefield.

Appadurai, A. 1986a. Introduction: commodities and the politics of value. In Appadurai 1986b: 3–63.

Appadurai, A. (ed.) 1986b. *The Social Life of Things: Commodities in Cultural Perspective.* Cambridge: Cambridge University Press.

Arafat, K.W. 1990. *Classical Zeus: A Study in Art and Literature.* Oxford: Clarendon.

Arafat, K.W. and Morgan, C. 1989. Pots and potters in Athens and Corinth: a review. *Oxford Journal of Archaeology* 8: 311–46.

Argoud, G. and Roesch, P. (eds.) *La Béotie antique.* Paris: Editions du Centre National de la Recherche Scientifique.

Ashmole, B. 1962. Some nameless sculptors of the fifth century BC. *Proceedings of the British Academy* 48: 213–33.

1970. Sir John Beazley (1885–1970). *Proceedings of the British Academy* 56: 443–61.

1972. *Architect and Sculptor in Classical Greece: The Wrightsman Lectures.* London: Phaidon.

Ashmole, B. and Yalouris, N. 1967. *Olympia: The Sculptures of the Temple of Zeus.* London: Phaidon.

Ashton, N.G. 1991. *Siphnos: Ancient Towers BC.* Athens: privately published.

Asquith, H.H. 1900. Address to the annual meeting of subscribers. *Annual of the British School at Athens* 6 (1899–1900): 135–7.

Auberson, P. 1968. *Eretria: fouïlles et recherches I: Temple d'Apollon Daphnéphoros.* Berne: Editions Francke.

1974. La reconstitution du Daphnéphoreion d'Erétrie. *Antike Kunst* 17: 60–8.

Aubet, M.E. 1993. *The Phoenicians and the West.* Translated from the Spanish by Mary Turton. Cambridge: Cambridge University Press.

Ault, B. 1999. *Koprones* and oil presses at Halieis: interactions of town and country and the integration of domestic and regional economies. *Hesperia* 68: 548–73.

Aupert, P. 1979. *Fouilles de Delphes II: topographie et architecture: le Stade.* Paris: de Boccard.

Bammer, A. 1984. *Das Heiligtum der Artemis von Ephesos.* Graz: Akademische Durch.

1991. Les sanctuaires des VIIIe et VIIe siècles à l'Artemision d'Ephèse. *Revue Archéologique* 1991: 63–83.

1998. Sanctuaries in the Artemision of Ephesus. In R. Hägg (ed.), *Ancient Greek Cult Practice from the Archaeological Evidence*, 27–47. Stockholm: Paul Åstroms Forlag.

Bankel, H.G. 1993. *Der spätarchaische Tempel der Aphaia auf Aegina.* Berlin: Walter de Gruyter.

Barrett, W.S. 1973. Pindar's twelfth Olympian and the fall of the Deinomenidai. *Journal of Hellenic Studies* 93: 23–35.

Barron, J.P. 1972. New light on old walls. *Journal of Hellenic Studies* 92: 20–45.

Baxandall, M. 1985. *Patterns of Intention: On the Historical Explanation of Pictures.* New Haven: Yale University Press.

Bazant, J. 1990. The case for a complex approach to Athenian vase painting. *Metis: Revue d'Anthropologie du Monde Grec Ancien* 5: 94–112.

Bazianopoulou-Valavani, E. 1994. Anaskaphes se athenaika keramika ergasteria archaikon kai klasikon chronon. In Coulson *et al.* 1994: 45–54.

Beazley, Sir J.D. 1911. The master of the Berlin amphora. *Journal of Hellenic Studies* 31: 276–95.

1918. *Attic Red-Figured Vases in American Museums.* Cambridge, MA: Harvard University Press.

1922. Citharoedus. *Journal of Hellenic Studies* 42: 70–98.

1926. Introduction. In Pfuhl 1926: vi.

1932. Little-Master cups. *Journal of Hellenic Studies* 52: 167–204.

1943. The training of archaeologists: university training. *Conference on the Future of Archaeology*, 42–4. University of London, Institute of Archaeology, Occasional Paper 5. London.

1944 Groups of early Attic black-figure. *Hesperia* 13: 38–57.

1951. *The Development of Attic Black-Figure.* Berkeley and Los Angeles: University of California Press.

1956. *Attic Black-Figure Vase Painters.* Oxford: Clarendon.

1963. *Attic Red-Figure Vase Painters.* 3 volumes, 2nd edition. Oxford: Clarendon.

1971. *Paralipomena.* Oxford: Clarendon.

1986. *The Development of Attic Black-Figure.* Revised edition, edited by D. von Bothmer and M.B. Moore. Berkeley and Los Angeles: University of California Press.

1989a. Attic black-figure: a sketch. In Beazley and Kurtz 1989: 1–25.

1989b. Potter and painter in ancient Athens. In Beazley and Kurtz 1989: 39–65.

1989c. Attic white lekythoi. In Beazley and Kurtz 1989: 26–38.

1989d. Spina and Greek pottery. In Beazley and Kurtz 1989: 60–5.

Beazley, Sir J.D. and Ashmole, B. 1932. *Greek Sculpture and Painting to the End of the Hellenistic Period.* Cambridge: Cambridge University Press.

Beazley, Sir J.D. and Kurtz, D.C. 1983. *The Berlin Painter.* Oxford: Clarendon.

Beazley, Sir J.D. and Kurtz, D.C. (ed.) 1989. *Greek Vases: Lectures by J.D. Beazley*. Oxford: Clarendon.

Becker, C. 1986. *Kastanas: Ausgrabungen in einerm Siedlungshügel der Bronze- und Eisenzeit Makedoniens 1975–9: Die Tierknochenfunde*. Prähistorische Archäologie in Südosteuropa 5. Berlin: Wissenschaftverlag Volker Spiess.

Benson, E.L. 1895. Aegosthena. *Journal of Hellenic Studies* 15: 314–24.

Benson, J.L. 1970. *Horse, Bird and Man: The Origins of Greek Painting*. Amherst: University of Massachusetts Press.

    1989. *Earlier Corinthian Workshops: A Study of Geometric and Protocorinthian Stylistic Groups*. Scripta Minora 1. Amsterdam: Allard Pierson Museum.

    1995. Human figures, the Ajax painter, and narrative scenes in earlier Corinthian vase painting. In Carter and Morris 1995: 335–62.

Benton, S. 1935. Excavations in Ithaca III: the Polis cave I. *Annual of the British School at Athens* 35 [1934–5]: 45–73.

Bentz, M. 1998. *Panathenäische Preisamphoren: Eine athenische Vasengattung und ihre Funktion vom 6–4 Jahrhundert v.Chr*. Basel: Beihefte 'Antike Kunst'.

Bérard, C. 1970. *Eretria: fouïlles et recherches III: l'Hérön à la Porte d'Ouest*. Berne: Editions Francke.

Bérard, C., Bron, C., Durand, J.L., Frontisi-Ducroux, F., Lissarrague, F., Schnapp, A. and Vernant, J.P. 1984. *La Cité des images: religion et société en grèce antique*. Paris and Lausanne: Fernand Nathan.

    1989. *A City of Images: Iconography and Society in Ancient Greece*. Translated from the French by Deborah Lyons. Princeton: Princeton University Press.

Bérard, C., Bron, C. and Pomari, A. (eds.) 1987. *Images et société en Grèce ancienne: l'iconographie comme méthode d'analyse*. Lausanne: Institut d'Archéologie et d'Histoire Ancienne.

Berger, E. (ed.) 1984. *Parthenon-Kongress Basel: Referate und Berichte 4. bis 8. April 1982*. 2 volumes. Mainz: Philipp von Zabern.

Bergquist, B. 1967. *The Archaic Greek Temenos: A Study of Structure and Function*. Skrifter Utgivna av Svenska Institutet i Athen 4, XIII. Lund: C.W.K. Gleerup.

    1988. The archaeology of sacrifice: Minoan-Mycenaean versus Greek. In Hägg *et al.* 1988: 21–34.

    1990. Sympotic space: a functional aspect of Greek dining rooms. In Murray 1990: 27–65.

Bernal, M. 1987. On the transmission of the alphabet to the Aegean before 1400 BC. *Bulletin of the American Schools of Oriental Research* 267: 1–20.

    1991. *Black Athena: The Afroasiatic Roots of Classical Civilization*. 2nd edition. London: Vintage Books.

Besques, S., *see* Mollard-Besques, S.

Betancourt, P.P. 1977. *The Aeolic Style in Architecture: A Survey of Its Development in Palestine, the Halikarnassos Peninsula and Greece, 1100–500 BC*. Princeton: Princeton University Press.

Biers, W.R. 1992. *Art, Artefacts and Chronology in Classical Archaeology*. London: Routledge.

    1994. Mass production, standardized parts and the Corinthian 'plastic' vase. *Hesperia* 63: 509–16.

Binford, L.R. 1972. Mortuary practices: their study and their potential. In L.R. Binford, *An Archaeological Perspective*, 208–43. New York and London: Academic Press.

Bintliff, J.L. and Snodgrass, A.M. 1985a. The Cambridge/Bradford Boeotia expedition: the first four years. *Journal of Field Archaeology* 12: 123–61.

    1985b. The development of settlement in south-west Boeotia. In Argoud and Roesch 1985: 49–70.

1988. Mediterranean survey and the city. *Antiquity* 62: 57–71.

Blegen, C.W. 1937. Post-Mycenaean deposits in chamber tombs. *Archaiologiki Ephemeris* 100: 377–90.

    1952. Two Athenian grave groups of about 900 BC. *Hesperia* 21: 279–94.

Blegen, C.W., Palmer, H. and Young, R.S. 1964. *Corinth XIII: The North Cemetery*. Princeton: American School of Classical Studies at Athens.

Blome, P. 1982. *Die figürliche Bildwelt Kretas in der geometrischen und früharchaischen Periode*. Mainz: Philipp von Zabern.

Blondé, F. and Perreault, J.Y. (eds.) 1992. *Les Ateliers de potiers dans le monde grec aux époques géométrique, archaïque et classique*. Bulletin de Correspondance Hellénique Supplément 23. Paris: de Boccard.

Blondé, F., Perreault, J.Y. and Peristeri, C. 1992. Un atelier de potier archaïque à Phari (Thasos). In Blondé and Perreault 1992: 11–40.

Blouet, A., Ravoisié, A., Poirot, A., Trézel, F. and de Gournay, F. 1831. *Expédition scientifique de Morée ordonée par le gouvernement français: architecture, sculptures, inscriptions et vues du Peloponese, des Cyclades et de l'Attique*. Vol. I. Paris: Firmin Didot Frères.

    1833. *Expédition scientifique de Morée ordonée par le gouvernement français: architecture, sculptures inscriptions et vues du Peloponese, des Cyclades et de l'Attique*. Vol. II. Paris: Firmin Didot Frères.

    1838. *Expédition scientifique de Morée ordonée par le gouvernement français: architecture, sculptures, inscriptions et vues du Peloponese, des Cyclades et de l'Attique*. Vol III. Paris: Firmin Didot Frères.

Boardman, Sir J. 1952. Pottery from Eretria. *Annual of the British School at Athens* 47: 1–48.

    1955. Painted funerary plaques and some remarks on prothesis. *Annual of the British School at Athens* 50: 51–66.

    1956. Chian and Naucratite. *Annual of the British School at Athens* 51: 55–62.

    1957. Early Euboean pottery and history. *Annual of the British School at Athens* 52: 1–29.

    1961. *The Cretan Collection in Oxford: The Dictaean Cave and Iron Age Crete*. Oxford: Clarendon.

    1962. Archaic finds at Knossos. *Annual of the British School at Athens* 57: 28–34.

    1963a. *Island Gems: A Study of Greek Seals in the Geometric and Early Archaic Periods*. Journal of Hellenic Studies Supplementary Paper 10. London: Society for the Promotion of Hellenic Studies.

    1963b. Artemis Orthia and chronology. *Annual of the British School at Athens* 58: 1–7.

    1965. Tarsus, Al Mina and Greek chronology. *Journal of Hellenic Studies* 85: 5–15.

    1966. Evidence for the dating of Greek settlements in Cyrenaica. *Annual of the British School at Athens* 61: 149–62.

    1967a. *Excavations in Chios 1952–55: Greek Emporio*. British School at Athens Supplementary Volume 6. London: Thames and Hudson.

    1967b. The Khaniale Tekke tombs, II. *Annual of the British School at Athens* 62: 57–75.

    1967c. *Archaic Greek Gems: Schools and Artists in the Sixth and Early Fifth Centuries BC*. London: Thames and Hudson.

    1970. *Greek Gems and Finger Rings: Early Bronze Age to Late Classical*. London: Thames and Hudson.

    1972. Herakles, Peisistratos and sons. *Revue Archéologique* 1972: 57–72.

    1974. *Athenian Black Figure Vases*. London: Thames and Hudson.

    1975a. *Athenian Red Figure Vases: The Archaic Period*. London: Thames and Hudson.

    1975b. Herakles, Peisistratos and Eleusis. *Journal of Hellenic Studies* 95: 1–12.

1977. The Parthenon frieze: another view. In U. Hückmann and A. Krug (eds.), *Festschrift für Frank Brommer*, 39–49. Mainz: Philipp von Zabern.

1978. *Greek Sculpture: The Archaic Period*. London: Thames and Hudson.

1979. Betwixt and between. *Classical Review* n.s. 29: 118–20.

1980. *The Greeks Overseas: Their Early Colonies and Trade*. 3rd edition. London: Thames and Hudson.

1981. Askoi. *Hephaistos* 3: 23–5.

1982. Crete. In Boardman and Hammond 1982: 222–33.

1983. Symbol and story in Geometric art. In Moon 1983: 15–36.

1984. The Parthenon frieze. In Berger 1984: 210–15.

1985a. *Greek Sculpture: The Classical Period*. London: Thames and Hudson.

1985b. Classical archaeology in Oxford. In Kurtz 1985b: 43–55.

1985c. *The Parthenon and Its Sculptures*. London: Thames and Hudson.

1987. Silver is white. *Revue Archéologique* 1987 (2): 207–13.

1988a. Trade in Greek decorated pottery. *Oxford Journal of Archaeology* 7: 27–33.

1988b. The trade figures. *Oxford Journal of Archaeology* 7: 371–3.

1988c. Classical Archaeology: whence and whither? *Antiquity* 62: 795–7.

1988d. Dates and doubts. *Archäologischer Anzeiger* 1988: 423–5.

1988e. Sex differentiation in grave vases. *Annali di Archeologia e Storia Antica* 10: 171–9.

1989. *Athenian Red Figure Vases: The Classical Period*. London: Thames and Hudson.

1990a. Al Mina and history. *Oxford Journal of Archaeology* 9: 169–90.

1990b. The Lyre Player group of seals: an encore. *Archäologischer Anzeiger* 1990: 1–17.

1990c. Symposion furniture. In Murray (1990): 122–31.

1995. *Greek Sculpture: The Late Classical Period*. London: Thames and Hudson.

1999. The Parthenon frieze: a closer look. *Revue Archéologique* 1999 (2): 305–30.

Boardman, Sir J. and Hammond, N.G.L. 1982. *The Cambridge Ancient History III.3: The Expansion of the Greek World, Eighth to Sixth Centuries BC*. 2nd edition. Cambridge: Cambridge University Press.

Boardman, Sir J. and Hayes, J. 1966. *Excavations at Tocra 1963–65: The Archaic Deposits I*. British School at Athens Supplementary Volume 4. London: Thames and Hudson.

1973. *Excavations at Tocra 1963–1965: The Archaic Deposits II and Later Deposits*. British School at Athens Supplementary Volume 10. London: Thames and Hudson.

Boardman, Sir J. and Schweizer, F. 1973. Clay analyses of Archaic Greek pottery. *Annual of the British School at Athens* 68: 267–83.

Boardman, Sir J. and Vollenweider, M.L. 1978. *Ashmolean Museum: Catalogue of the Engraved Gems and Finger Rings I: Greek and Etruscan*. Oxford: Clarendon.

Boeckh, A. 1828. *Corpus Inscriptionum Graecarum: Volumen Primum*. Berlin: Royal Prussian Academy of Letters.

Boedecker, D. and Raaflaub, K.A. (eds.) 1998. *Democracy, Empire and the Arts in Fifth-Century Athens*. Cambridge, MA: Harvard University Press.

Boeghold, A.L. 1962. The Nessos amphora – a note on the inscription. *American Journal of Archaeology* 66: 405–6.

1995. *The Athenian Agora XXVIII: The Lawcourts at Athens: Sites, Buildings, Equipment, Procedure and Testimonia*. Princeton: American School of Classical Studies at Athens.

Boehlau, J. 1887. Frühattischen Vasen. *Jahrbuch des deutschen archäologischen Instituts* 2: 33–66.

Bohen, B. 1988. *Kerameikos: Ergebnisse der Ausgrabungen XIII: Die geometrischen Pyxiden*. Berlin: Walter de Gruyter.

1997. Aspects of Athenian grave cult in the Age of Homer. In Langdon 1997: 44–55.

Bol, Peter C. 1989. *Argivische Schilde: Olympische Forschungen XVII*. Berlin: Walter de Gruyter.

Bookidis, N. 1993. Ritual dining at Corinth. In Marinatos and Hägg 1993: 45–61.

Bookidis, N., Hansen, J., Snyder, L. and Goldberg, P. 1999. Dining in the sanctuary of Demeter and Kore at Corinth. *Hesperia* 68: 1–54.

Borea, E. (ed.) 1984. *Di Bronzi da Riace: Rinvenimento, Restauro, Analisi ed Ipotesi di Interpretazione*. Bolletino d'Arte Serie Speziale 3 (2 volumes). Rome: Ministero per i Beni Culturali e Ambientali.

Borell, B. 1978. *Attisch geometrische Schalen: Ein spätgeometrische Keramikgattung und ihre Beziehungen zum Orient*. Mainz: Philipp von Zabern.

Borges, J.L. 1998. *Collected Fictions*. Translated by Andrew Hurley. Harmondsworth: Penguin.

Bory de St Vincent, M. 1835. *Expédition scientifique de Morée: section des sciences physiques: atlas*. Paris and Strasburg: F.G. Levrault.

1836. *Expédition scientifique de Morée: section des sciences physiques: tome premier: relation*. Paris and Strasburg: F.G. Levrault.

Bosanquet, R.C. 1902. Excavations at Praesos: I. *Annual of the British School at Athens* 8 [1901–2]: 231–70.

Bottema, S. 1979. Palynological investigations in Thessaly (Greece). *Palaeohistoria* 21: 19–40

1982. Palynological investigations in Greece with special reference to pollen as an indicator of human activity. *Palaeohistoria* 24: 257–89.

Boyd, T.D. 1978. The arch and the vault in Greek architecture. *American Journal of Archaeology* 82: 83–100.

Boyd, T.D. and Jameson, M.H. 1981. Urban and rural land division in ancient Greece. *Hesperia* 50: 327–42.

Boyd, T.D. and Rudolph, W.W. 1978. Excavations at Porto Cheli and vicinity: preliminary report IV: the lower town of Halieis, 1970–77. *Hesperia* 47: 333–55.

Bowden, H. 1991. The chronology of Greek painted pottery: some observations. *Hephaistos* 10: 49–59.

Bradeen, D.W. 1969. The Athenian casualty lists. *Classical Quarterly* 19: 145–59.

1974. *The Athenian Agora XVII: Inscriptions: The Funerary Monuments*. Princeton: American School of Classical Studies at Athens.

Braun, K. 1996. Die korinthische Keramik. In Felsch 1996: 215–69.

Breitinger, E. 1939a. Die Skelette aus den submykenischen Gräbern. In Kraiker and Kübler 1939: 223–55.

1939b. Die Brandreste aus den protogeometrischen Amphoren. In Kraiker and Kübler 1939: 257–61.

Brenne, S. 1994. Ostraka and the process of ostrakophoria. In Coulson *et al.* 1994: 13–24.

Brijder, H.A.G. 1983. *Siana Cups I and Komast Cups*. 2 volumes, text and plates. Amsterdam: Allard Pierson Museum.

Brinkmann, V. 1985. Die aufgemalten Namensbeischriften an Nord- und Ostfries des Siphnierschatzhauses. *Bulletin de Correspondance Hellénique* 109: 77–130.

Brock, J.K. 1957. *Fortetsa: Early Greek Tombs near Knossos*. British School at Athens Supplementary Volume 2. Cambridge: Cambridge University Press.

Brommer, F. 1979. *The Sculptures of the Parthenon: Metopes: Frieze: Pediments: Cult Statue*. Translated from the German by Mary Whitall. London: Thames and Hudson.

Broneer, O. 1971. *Isthmia I: Temple of Poseidon*. Princeton: American School of Classical Studies at Athens.

Brookes, A.C. 1981. Stoneworking in the Geometric period at Corinth. *Hesperia* 50: 285–90.

Brown, A. 1993. *Before Knossos . . . Arthur Evans' Travels in the Balkans and Crete.* Oxford: Ashmolean Museum.

Brueckner, A. 1893. Ein attischer Grabfund der geometrischen Periode. *Mitteilungen des deutschen archäologischen Instituts, athenische Abteilung* 18: 414–15.

Brueckner, A. and Pernice, E. 1893. Ein attischer Friedhof. *Mitteilungen des deutschen archäologischen Instituts, athenische Abteilung* 18: 73–191.

Brulotte, E.L. 1994. The 'Pillar of Oinomaos' and the location of Stadium I at Olympia. *American Journal of Archaeology* 98: 53–64.

Buchner, G. and Ridgway, D. 1993. *Pithekoussai I: La Necropoli: Tombe 1–723 Scavate dal 1952 al 1961.* 3 volumes, text, plates and plans. Rome: Giorgio Bretschneider.

Bundgaard, J.A. 1946. A propos de la date de la péristasis du Mégaron B à Thermos. *Bulletin de Correspondance Hellénique* 70: 51–7.

Burford, A. 1966. Notes on the Epidaurian building inscriptions. *Annual of the British School at Athens* 61: 254–334.

  1969. *The Greek Temple Builders at Epidauros.* Liverpool: Liverpool University Press.

Burkert, W. 1985. *Greek Religion: Archaic and Classical.* Translated from the German by John Raffan. Oxford: Basil Blackwell.

  1987. Offerings in perspective: surrender, distribution, exchange. In Linders and Nordquist 1987: 43–50.

  1992. *The Orientalizing Revolution: Near Eastern Influence on Greek Culture in the Early Archaic Age.* Translated from the German by E. Pinder and W. Burkert. Cambridge, MA: Harvard University Press.

Burn, L. 1985. Honey pots: three white-ground cups by the Sotades painter. *Antike Kunst* 28: 93–105.

  1987. *The Meidias Painter.* Oxford: Clarendon.

Burnyeat, M.F. 1997. Postscript on silent reading. *Classical Quarterly* 47: 74–6.

Buschor, E. 1930. Heraion von Samos: Frühe Bauten. *Mitteilungen des deutschen archäologischen Instituts, athenische Abteilung* 55: 1–99.

Buschor, E. and Schleif, H. 1933. Heraion von Samos: Der Altarplatz der Frühzeit. *Mitteilungen des deutschen archäologischen Instituts, athenische Abteilung* 58: 146–73.

Busignani, A. 1981. *Gli Eroi di Riace: Daimon e Techne.* Florence: Sansoni.

Callaghan, P.J. 1978. KRS 1976: excavations at a shrine of Glaukos, Knossos. *Annual of the British School at Athens* 73: 1–30.

  1992. Archaic to Hellenistic pottery. In L.H. Sackett (ed.), *Knossos: From Greek City to Roman Colony: Excavations at the Unexplored Mansion II*, 89–136. BSA Supplement 21. London: Thames and Hudson.

Callaghan, P.J. and Jones, R.E. 1985. Hadra hydriae and central Crete. *Annual of the British School at Athens* 80: 1–17.

Calligas, P.G. 1988. Hero-cult in Early Iron Age Greece. In Hägg *et al.* 1988: 228–34.

  1994. I periochi tou ierou kai tou theatrou tou Dionysou stin Athina. In Coulson *et al.* 1994: 25–30.

Cambitoglou, A., Birchall, A., Coulton, J.J. and Green, J.R. 1988. *Zagora 2: Excavation of a Geometric Town on the Island of Andros.* 2 volumes, text and plates. Athens: I en Athenais Archaiologiki Etaireia.

Cambitoglou, A., Coulton, J.J., Birmingham, J. and Green, J.R. 1971. *Zagora I: Excavation of a Geometric Settlement on the Island of Andros.* Sydney: Sydney University Press.

Camp, J.M. 1979. A drought in the late eighth century BC. *Hesperia* 48: 397–411.

1992. *The Athenian Agora: Excavations in the Heart of Classical Athens*. 2nd edition. London: Thames and Hudson.

1995. Rectangular peribolos. In Boeghold 1995: 99–103.

1996. Excavations in the Athenian Agora: 1994 and 1995. *Hesperia* 65: 231–61.

1999. Excavations in the Athenian Agora: 1996 and 1997. *Hesperia* 68: 255–83.

Carpenter, R. 1929. *The Sculpture of the Nike Temple Parapet*. Cambridge, MA: Harvard University Press.

1969. A belated report on the Hermes controversy. *American Journal of Archaeology* 73: 465–8.

1970. *The Architects of the Parthenon*. Penguin: Harmondsworth.

Carpenter, T.H. 1986. *Dionysian Imagery in Archaic Greek Art: Its Development in Black-Figure Vase Painting*. Oxford: Clarendon.

Carter, J.B. and Morris, S.P. (eds.) 1995. *The Ages of Homer: A Tribute to Emily Townsend Vermeule*. Austin: University of Texas Press.

Carter, J.C. 1983. *The Sculpture from the Sanctuary of Athena Polias at Priene*. London: Society of Antiquaries/Thames and Hudson.

1994. Sanctuaries in the *Chora* of Metaponto. In Alcock and Osborne 1994: 161–98.

Caskey, J.L. and Amandry, P. 1952. Investigations in the Heraion of Argos, 1949. *Hesperia* 21: 165–221.

Castriota, D. 1992. *Myth, Ethos and Actuality: Official Art in Fifth-Century BC Athens*. Madison: University of Wisconsin Press.

Catling, H.W. 1964. *Cypriot Bronzework in the Mycenaean World*. Oxford: Clarendon.

1977. Excavations at the Menelaion, Sparta, 1973–76. *Archaeological Reports* 23 (1976–7): 24–42.

1981. 'Barbarian' pottery from the Mycenaean settlement at the Menelaion, Sparta. *Annual of the British School at Athens* 76: 71–82.

1984. Workshop and heirloom: prehistoric bronze stands in the East Mediterranean. *Report of the Department of Antiquities Cyprus* 1984: 69–91.

1990. A sanctuary of Zeus Messapeus: excavations at Aphyssou, Tsakona, 1989. *Annual of the British School at Athens* 85: 15–35.

1995. Heroes returned? Subminoan burials from Crete. In Carter and Morris 1995: 123–36.

1996a. The Subminoan pottery. In Coldstream and Catling 1996: 295–310.

1996b. The objects other than pottery in the Subminoan tombs. In Coldstream and Catling 1996: 517–37.

1996c. The Dark Age and later bronzes. In Coldstream and Catling 1996, 543–74.

Catling, H.W., Carington-Smith, J. and Hughes-Brock, H. 1983. The small finds. In McDonald *et al.* 1983: 273–315.

Catling, H.W. and Catling, E.A. 1980. Objects in bronze, iron and lead. In Popham *et al.* 1980a: 231–64.

Catling, H.W. and Cavanagh, H. 1976. Two inscribed bronzes from the Menelaion, Sparta. *Kadmos* 15: 145–57.

Catling, R.W.V. 1984. New archaeology. *Classical Review* n.s. 34: 98–103.

Catling, R.W.V. and Lemos, I. 1990. *Lefkandi II.1: The Protogeometric Building at Toumba: The Pottery*. London: British School at Athens.

Cavanagh, W.G. 1996. The burial customs. In Coldstream and Catling 1996: 651–75.

Cavanagh, W.G., Crouwel, J., Catling, R.W.V. and Shipley, G. 1996. *Continuity and Change in a Greek Rural Landscape: The Laconia Survey*, Vol. II. BSA Supplement 27. London: British School at Athens.

Cavanagh, W.G., Curtis, M., Coldstream, J.N. and Johnston, A.W. (eds.) 1998. *Post-Minoan*

Crete: Proceedings of the First Colloquium. British School at Athens Studies 2. London: British School at Athens.

Cavanagh, W.G. and Laxton, R.R. 1984. Lead figurines from the Menelaion and seriation. *Annual of the British School at Athens* 79: 23–36.

Chamoux, F. 1955. *Fouïlles de Delphes IV.5: Monuments figurés: sculpture: L'Aurige.* Paris: Editions de Boccard.

Charbonneaux, J., Martin, R. and Villard, F. 1972. *Classical Greek Art, 480–330 BC.* Translated from the French by James Emmons. London: Thames and Hudson.

Charles, R.P. 1958. Etude anthropologique des nécropoles d'Argos: contribution à l'étude des populations de la Grèce antique. *Bulletin de Correspondance Hellénique* 82: 268–313.

    1963. *Etude anthropologique des nécropoles d'Argos: contritubion à l'étude de la Grèce antique.* Paris: Ecole Française d'Athènes.

Cherry, J.F. 1982. A preliminary definition of site distribution on Melos. In Renfrew and Wagstaff 1982: 10–23.

    1983. Frogs round the pond: perspectives on current archaeological survey projects in the Mediterranean region. In D.R. Keller and D.W. Rupp (eds.), *Archaeological Survey in the Mediterranean Area*, 375–410. BAR International Series 155. Oxford: British Archaeological Reports.

Cherry, J.F., Davis J.L. and Mantzourani, E. 1991. *Landscape Archaeology as Long-Term History: Northern Keos in the Cycladic Islands.* Monumenta Archaeologica 16. Los Angeles: Institute of Archaeology, University of California, Los Angeles.

Childe, V.G. 1943. The unity of archaeology. *Conference on the Future of Archaeology*, 20–5. University of London, Institute of Archaeology Occasional Paper 5. London.

    1958. Retrospect. *Antiquity* 32: 69–74.

    1964. *What Happened in History.* 3rd edition, with foreword and notes by G. Clark. Harmondsworth: Penguin.

Clairmont, C. 1955. Greek pottery from the Near East. *Berytus* 11.2: 85–139.

    1983. *Patrios Nomos: Public Burial at Athens During the Fifth and Fourth Centuries BC.* 2 volumes. BAR International Series 161. Oxford: British Archaeological Reports.

    1993a. *Classical Attic Tombstones: Vol. I: Catalogue.* Kilchberg, Switzerland: Acanthus.

    1993b. *Classical Attic Tombstones: Vol. II: Catalogue.* Kilchberg, Switzerland: Acanthus.

Clark, J.D.G. 1943. The contribution of archaeology to the post-war world. *Conference on the Future of Archaeology*, 6–8. University of London, Institute of Archaeology, Occasional Paper 5. London.

Clarke, D. L. 1978. *Analytical Archaeology.* 2nd edition, revised by Bob Chapman. London: Methuen.

Clogg, R. 1992. *A Concise History of Greece.* Cambridge: Cambridge University Press.

Cockerell, C.R. 1860. *The Temples of Jupiter Panhellenius at Aegina and of Apollo Epicurius at Bassae near Phigaleia in Arcadia.* London: John Weale.

Coldstream, J.N. 1968. *Greek Geometric Pottery: A Survey of Ten Local Styles and their Chronology.* London: Methuen.

    1973a. Knossos 1951–61: Orientalizing and Archaic pottery from the town. *Annual of the British School at Athens* 68: 33–63.

    1973b. *Knossos: The Sanctuary of Demeter.* BSA Supplement 8. London: Thames and Hudson.

    1976. Hero cults in the age of Homer. *Journal of Hellenic Studies* 96: 8–17.

    1977. *Geometric Greece.* London: Methuen.

    1982. Greeks and Phoenicians in the Aegean. In H.G. Niemeyer (ed.) *Phönizier in Westen: Die Beiträge des Internationalen Symposiums über 'Die phönizische Expansion in westlichen Mittelmeerraum'*, 261–75. Mainz: Philipp von Zabern.

1983a. The meaning of the regional styles in the eighth century BC. In Hägg 1983b: 17–15.

1983b. Gift exchange in the eighth century BC. In Hägg 1983b: 201–6.

1984a. Dorian Knossos and Aristotle's villages. In C. Nicolet (ed.), *Aux Origines de l'Hellénisme: La Crète et La Grèce: hommage à Henri van Effenterre*, 311–22. Paris: Publications de la Sorbonne.

1984b. Cypriaca and Cretocypriaca from the North Cemetery of Knossos. *Report of the Department of Antiquities Cyprus 1984*: 122–37.

1991. The Geometric style: birth of the picture. In Rasmussen and Spivey 1991: 37–56.

1992. Early Hellenic pottery. In Sackett 1992: 67–87.

1993. Mixed marriages at the frontiers of the early Greek world. *Oxford Journal of Archaeology* 12: 89–105.

1994. Pithekoussai, Cyprus and the Cesnola Painter. *Annali di Archeologia e Storia Antica* n.s. 1: 77–86.

1996. The Protogeometric and Geometric pottery. In Coldstream and Catling 1996: 311–420.

Coldstream, J.N. and Sackett, L.H. 1978. Knossos: two deposits of Orientalizing pottery. *Annual of the British School at Athens* 73: 45–60.

Coldstream, J.N. and Bikai, P.M. 1988. Early Greek pottery in Tyre and Cyprus: some preliminary comparisons. *Report of the Department of Antiquities Cyprus* 1988 (2): 35–44.

Coldstream, J.N. and Catling, H.W. (eds.) 1996. *Knossos North Cemetery: Early Greek Tombs*. 4 volumes. British School at Athens Supplementary Volume 28. London: British School at Athens.

Coldstream, J.N. and MacDonald, C.F. 1997. Knossos: area of South-West Houses, early Hellenic occupation. *Annual of the British School at Athens* 92: 191–245.

Coldstream, J.N. and Huxley, G.L. 1999. Knossos: the Archaic gap. *Annual of the British School at Athens* 94: 289–307.

Connelly, J.B. 1993. Narrative and image in Attic vase painting: Ajax and Cassandra at the Trojan Palladion. In Holliday 1993: 88–129.

1996. Parthenon and *parthenoi*: a mythological interpretation of the Parthenon frieze. *American Journal of Archaeology* 100: 53–80.

Cook, J.M. 1935. Protoattic pottery. *Annual of the British School at Athens* 35: 165–219.

1953. Mycenae 1939–52 III: The Agamemnoneion. *Annual of the British School at Athens* 48: 30–68.

1959. Old Smyrna 1948–51. *Annual of the British School at Athens* 53–4 [1958–9]: 1–34.

1985. On the date of Alyattes' sack of Smyrna. *Annual of the British School at Athens* 80: 25–8.

Cook, J.M. and Nicholls, R.V. 1998. *Old Smyrna Excavations: The Temples of Athena*. British School at Athens Supplementary Volume 30. London: British School at Athens.

Cook, R.M. 1955. Thucydides as archaeologist. *Annual of the British School at Athens* 50: 266–70.

1959. Die Bedeutung der bemalten Keramik für den Griechischen Handel. *Jahrbuch des deutschen archäologischen Instituts* 74: 114–23.

1969. A note on the absolute chronology of the eighth and seventh centuries BC. *Annual of the British School at Athens* 64: 13–15.

1972. *Greek Painted Pottery*. 2nd edition. London: Methuen.

1989. The Francis-Vickers chronology. *Journal of Hellenic Studies* 109: 164–70.

Cook, R.M. and Dupont, P. 1998. *East Greek Pottery*. London: Routledge.

Cook, R.M. and Woodhead, A.G. 1952. Painted inscriptions on Chiot pottery. *Annual of the British School at Athens* 47: 159–70.

Cooper, F.A. 1996a. *The Temple of Apollo Bassitas I: The Architecture*. Princeton: American School of Classical Studies at Athens.

1996b. *The Temple of Apollo Bassitas III: The Architecture: Illustrations*. Princeton: American School of Classical Studies at Athens.

Cooper, F.A. and Morris, S.P. 1990. Dining in round buildings. In Murray 1990: 66–85.

Coulson, W.D.E. 1983a. The Dark Age: the architecture. In McDonald *et al.* 1983: 9–60.

1983b. The Dark Age: the pottery. In McDonald *et al.* 1983: 61–259.

1985. The Dark Age pottery of Sparta. *Annual of the British School at Athens* 80: 29–84.

1991. The 'Protogeometric' from Polis reconsidered. *Annual of the British School at Athens* 86: 43–64.

1998. The Early Iron Age on the Kastro at Kavousi in East Crete. In Cavanagh *et al.* 1998: 40–4.

Coulson, W.D.E., Palagia, O., Shear, T.L. Jr., Shapiro, H.A. and Frost, F.J. (eds.) 1994. *The Archaeology of Athens and Attica under the Democracy*. Oxford: Oxbow.

Coulton, J.J. 1964. The stoa by the harbour at Perachora. *Annual of the British School at Athens* 59: 100–31.

1967. The West Court at Perachora. *Annual of the British School at Athens* 62: 353–71.

1973. The columns and roof of the South Stoa at the Argive Heraion. *Annual of the British School at Athens* 68: 65–85.

1974. Lifting in early Greek architecture. *Journal of Hellenic Studies* 94: 1–19.

1976. *The Architectural Development of the Greek Stoa*. Oxford: Clarendon.

1977. *Greek Architects at Work: Problems of Structure and Design*. London: Paul Elek.

1984. The Parthenon and Periklean Doric. In Berger 1984: 40–4.

1993. The Toumba building: description and analysis of the architecture. In Popham *et al.* 1993: 33–70.

2000. Fitting friezes: architecture and sculpture. In Tsetskhladze *et al.* 2000: 70–9.

Courbin, P. 1957. Une tombe géométrique d'Argos. *Bulletin de Correspondance Hellénique* 81: 322–86.

1966. *La Céramique géométrique de l'Argolide*. Paris: Editions de Boccard.

1974. *Tombes géométriques d'Argos* I. Paris: Librairie Philosophique J. Vrin.

1983. Obeloi d'Argolide et d'ailleurs. In Hägg 1983b: 149–56.

Courby, M.F. 1927. *Fouilles de Delphes II: topographie et architecture: la Terrasse du Temple*. Paris: Editions de Boccard.

Crielaard, J.P. 1995. Homer, history and archaeology: some remarks on the date of the Homeric world. In J.P. Crielaard (ed.), *Homeric Questions: Essays in Philology, Ancient History and Archaeology*, 201–88. Amsterdam: J.C. Gieben.

1996. How the West was won: Euboeans vs Phoenicians. In Niemeyer 1996: 235–60.

1999a. Production, circulation and consumption of Early Iron Age Greek pottery (eleventh to seventh centuries BC). In Crielaard *et al.* 1999: 49–81.

1999b. Early Iron Age Greek pottery in Cyprus and North Syria: a consumption-oriented approach. In Crielaard *et al.* 1999: 261–90.

Crielaard, J.P., Stissi, V. and van Wijngaarden, G.J. (eds.) 1999. *The Complex Past of Pottery: Production, Circulation and Consumption of Mycenaean and Greek Pottery (Sixteenth to Early Fifth Centuries BC)*. Amsterdam: J.C. Gieben.

Cross, F.M. 1984. Phoenicians in Sardinia: the epigraphical evidence. In M.S. Balmuth and R.J. Rowland (eds.), *Studies in Sardinian Archaeology*, 53–65. Ann Arbor: University of Michigan Press.

Crowfoot, J.W. (ed.) 1957. *Samaria-Sebaste 3: The Objects from Samaria*. London: Palestine Exploration Fund.

Csapo, E. and Miller, M. 1998. Democracy, empire and art: towards a politics of time and narrative. In Boedeker and Raaflaub 1998: 87–125.

Cuozzo, M. 1996. Prospettive teoriche e metodologiche nell' interpretazione delle necropoli: la post-processual archaeology. *Annali di Archeologia e Storia Antica* n.s. 3: 1–37.

Curry, M. 2000. The export of Attic black figure pottery in the early sixth century BC. In Tsetskhladze *et al.* 2000: 80–8.

Danner, P. 1997. Megara, Megara Hyblaea and Selinus: the relationship between the town planning of mother city, a colony and a sub-colony in the Archaic period. In Andersen *et al.* 1997: 143–65.

Dassios, Ph. 1992. Les péripéties de la Convention vue de Grèce (1881–1891). In Picard 1992: 129–42.

Daux, G. 1962. Chroniques des fouilles et découvertes archéologiques en Grèce en 1961. *Bulletin de Correspondance Hellénique* 86: 629–904.

    1963 Chroniques des fouilles et découvertes archéologiques en Grèce en 1962. *Bulletin de Correspondance Hellénique* 87: 689–836.

Daux, G. and Hansen, E. 1987. *Fouilles de Delphes: tome II: Topographie et architecture: le Trésor de Siphnos*. Paris: Editions de Boccard.

Davies, J.K. 1997. The 'origins of the Greek *polis*': where should we be looking? In Mitchell and Rhodes 1997: 24–38.

Davis, J.L. (ed.) 1998. *Sandy Pylos: An Archaeological Investigation from Nestor to Navarino*. Austin: University of Texas Press.

Davis, J.L., Alcock, S.E., Bennet, J., Lolos, Y.G. and Sheldermine, C.W. 1997. The Pylos regional archaeological project: part I: overview and the archaeological survey. *Hesperia* 66: 391–494.

Dawkins, R.M. (ed.) 1929. *The Sanctuary of Artemis Orthia at Sparta*. Supplement to the Journal of Hellenic Studies 5. London: Macmillan.

Day, L.P. 1997. The Late Minoan IIIC period at Vronda, Kavousi. In Driessen and Farnoux 1997: 391–406.

de Angelis, F. 1994. The foundation of Selinous: overpopulation or opportunities? In Tsetskhladze and de Angelis 1994: 87–110.

Demargne, P. 1947. *La Crète dédalique: études sur les origines d'une renaissance*. Paris: Editions de Boccard.

Demargne, P. and Van Effenterre, H. 1937. Recherches à Dreros II. *Bulletin de Correspondance Hellénique* 61: 333–48.

Dentzer, J.M. 1971. Aux origines de l'iconographie du banquet couché. *Revue Archéologique* 1971: 215–58.

    1982. *Le Motif du banquet couché dans le Proche Orient et le monde grec du VIIIe au IVe siècle avant J.C.* Rome: Ecole Française de Rome.

de Polignac, F. 1984. *La Naissance de la cité grecque: cultes, espace et société VIIIe–VIIe siècles avant J.C.* Paris: Editions La Découverte.

    1992. Influence extérieure ou évolution interne? L'innovation culturelle en Grèce géométrique et archaïque. In Kopcke and Tokumaru 1992: 114–27.

    1994. Mediation, competition and sovereignty: the evolution of rural sanctuaries in Geometric Greece. In Alcock and Osborne 1994: 3–18.

    1995. *Cults, Territory and the Origins of the Greek City-State*. Translated from the French by Janet Lloyd. Chicago: University of Chicago Press.

    1996a. Entre les dieux et les morts. Statut individuel et rites collectifs dans la cité archaïque. In Hägg 1996: 31–40.

    1996b. Offrandes, mémoire et compétition ritualisée dans les sanctuaires grecs à l'époque géométrique. In Hellström and Alroth 1996: 59–66.

de Salvia, F. 1993. I reperti di tipo Egiziano. In Buchner and Ridgway 1993: 763–811.

Desborough, V.R.d'A. 1952. *Protogeometric Pottery*. Oxford: Clarendon.

1964. *The Last Mycenaeans and Their Successors: An Archaeological Survey c.1200 – c.1000 BC.* Oxford: Clarendon.

1972. *The Greek Dark Ages.* London: Ernest Benn.

1980. The Dark Age pottery (SM-SPGIII) from settlement and cemeteries. In Popham *et al.* 1980: 281–354.

Descœudres, J.P. (ed.) 1990. *Greek Colonists and Native Populations: Proceedings of the First Australian Congress of Classical Archaeology.* Oxford and Canberra: Clarendon.

Dickinson, O. 1994. *The Aegean Bronze Age.* Cambridge: Cambridge University Press.

Dilke, O.A.W. 1948. The Greek theatre cavea. *Annual of the British School at Athens* 43: 125–92.

1950. Details and chronology of Greek theatre caveas. *Annual of the British School at Athens* 45: 21–62.

Dinsmoor, W.B. Sn. 1913a. Attic building accounts I: the Parthenon. *American Journal of Archaeology* 18: 53–80.

1913b. Attic building accounts II: the Erechtheum. *American Journal of Archaeology* 18: 242–65.

1940. The temple of Ares at Athens. *Hesperia* 9: 1–52.

1941 *Observations on the Hephaisteion.* Hesperia Supplement 5. Baltimore: American School of Classical Studies at Athens.

1968. The internal colonnade of the Hephaisteion. *Hesperia* 37: 159–77.

Dinsmoor, W.B. Jn. 1974. The temple of Poseidon: a missing sima and other matters. *American Journal of Archaeology* 78: 211–38.

1976. The roof of the Hephaisteion. *American Journal of Archaeology* 80: 223–46.

Dittenberger, W. and Purgold, K. 1896. *Olympia: Die Ergebnisse der von dem deutschen Reich veranstalteten Ausgrabung V: Die Inschriften.* Berlin: A. Asher and Co.

Docter, R.F. and Niemeyer, H.G. 1994. Pithekoussai: the Carthaginian connection: on the archaeological evidence of Euboeo-Phoenician partnership in the 8th and 7th centuries BC. *Annali di Archeologia e Storia Antica* n.s. 1: 101–15.

Dodwell, E. 1819a. *A Classical and Topographical Tour through Greece During the Years 1801, 1805 and 1806.* Vol I. London: Rodwell and Martin.

1819b. *A Classical and Topographical Tour through Greece during the Years 1801, 1805 and 1806.* Vol II. London: Rodwell and Martin.

Donlan, W. 1985. The social groups of Dark Age Greece. *Classical Philology* 80: 293–308.

Donnay, G. 1969. L'insula 2. In Mussche *et al.* 1969: 131–4.

D'Onofrio, A.M. 1982. *Korai* e *kouroi* funerari attici. *Annali di Archeologia e Storia Antica* 4: 135–70.

1988. Aspetti e problemi del monumento funerario attico arcaico. *Annali di Archeologia e Storia Antica* 10: 83–96.

1997. The 7th century BC in Attica: the basis of political organisation. In Andersen *et al.* 1997: 63–88.

Dörpfeld, W. 1935. *Alt Olympia: Untersuchungen und Ausgrabungen zur Geschichte des ältestens Heiligtums von Olympia und deren älteren Griechischen Kunst.* 2 volumes. Berlin: E.S. Mittler and Sohn.

Dougherty, C. 1993. *The Poetics of Colonization: From City to Text in Archaic Greece.* New York: Oxford University Press.

Dougherty, C. and Kurke, L. (eds.) 1993. *Cultural Poetics in Archaic Greece: Cult, Performance, Politics.* Cambridge: Cambridge University Press.

Drees, L. 1968. *Olympia: Gods, Artists and Athletes.* Translated from the German. London: Pall Mall Press.

Driessen, J. 1997. Le palais de Cnossos au MRII–III: combien de destructions? In Driessen and Farnoux 1997: 113–34.

Driessen, J. and Farnoux, A. (eds.) 1997. *La Crète mycenienne: Actes de la Table Ronde Internationale*. Bulletin de Correspondance Hellénique Supplement 30. Athens: Ecole Française d'Athènes.

Droop, J.P. 1906. Dipylon vases from the Kynosarges site. *Annual of the British School at Athens* 12 [1905–6]: 80–92.

Ducat, J. 1971. *Les Kouroi du Ptoion: le Sanctuaire d'Apollon Ptoieus à l'époque archaïque*. Paris: Editions de Boccard.

Ducrey, P., Metzger, I.R. and Reber, K. 1993. *Eretria: fouilles et recherches VIII: le Quartier de la Maison aux Mosaïques*. Lausanne: Ecole Suisse d'Archéologie en Grèce.

Dugas, C. 1952. *Exploration archéologique de Delos XXI: les vase attiques à figures rouges*. Paris: Editions de Boccard.

Dunbabin, T.J. 1948. *The Western Greeks: The History of Sicily and South Italy from the Foundation of the Greek Colonies to 480 BC*. Oxford: Clarendon.

    1954. The chronology of Protocorinthian vases. *Archaiologiki Ephemeris* 92–3.2 [1953–4]: 247–62.

Dunbabin, T.J. (ed.) 1962. *Perachora: The Sanctuaries of Hera Akraia and Limenia II: Pottery, Ivories, Scarabs and Other Objects from the Votive Deposit of Hera Limenia*. Oxford: Clarendon.

Dunbabin, T.J. and Robertson, M. 1953. Some Protocorinthian vase painters. *Annual of the British School at Athens* 48: 172–81.

Durand, J.L. and Schnapp, A. 1984. Boucherie sacrificielle et chasses initiatiques. In Bérard *et al.* 1984: 49–66.

    1989. Sacrificial slaughter and initiatory hunt. In Bérard *et al.* 1989: 53–70.

Dyson, S.L. 1993. From new to new age archaeology: archaeological theory and classical archaeology – a 1990s perspective. *American Journal of Archaeology* 97: 195–206.

Economokakis, R. (ed.) 1994. *Acropolis Restoration: The CCAM Intervention*. London: Academy Editions.

Ehrenberg, V. 1937. When did the polis rise? *Journal of Hellenic Studies* 57: 147–59.

Eilmann, R. 1933. Frühe griechische Keramik im samischen Heraion. *Mitteilungen des deutschen archäologischen Instituts, athenische Abteilung* 58: 47–145.

Empereur, J.Y. and Garlan, Y. 1986. *Recherches sur les amphores grecques*. Bulletin de Correspondance Hellénique Supplément XIII. Paris: Editions de Boccard.

Etienne, R. 1996. L'Ecole française d'Athènes 1846–1946. *Bulletin de Correspondance Hellénique* 120: 3–22.

Faklaris, P.B. 1994. Aegae: determining the site of the first capital of the Macedonians. *American Journal of Archaeology* 98: 609–16.

Felsch, R.C.S. 1981. Mykenischer Kult im Heiligtum bei Kalapodi? In Hägg and Marinatos 1981: 81–9.

    1987. Bericht über die Grabungen im Heiligtum der Artemis Elaphebolos und des Apollon von Hyampolis 1978–82. *Archäologischer Anzeiger* 1987: 1–99.

    1991. Tempel und Altäre im Heiligtum der Artemis Elaphebolos von Hyampolis bei Kalapodi. In R. Etienne and M.T. Le Dinahet (eds.), *L'Espace sacrificiel dans les civilisations méditerrannées de l'antiquité*. Paris: Diffusion de Boccard.

    1996. *Kalapodi: Ergebnisse der Ausgrabungen im Heiligtum der Artemis und des Apollon von Hyampolis in der antiken Phokis* I. Mainz: Philipp von Zabern.

Ferrari, G. 1987. Menelas. *Journal of Hellenic Studies* 107: 180–2.

Finley, M. 1979. *The World of Odysseus*. 2nd revised edition. Harmondsworth: Penguin.

Fisher, N. and Van Wees, H. (eds.) 1998. *Archaic Greece: New Approaches and New Evidence*. London: Duckworth.

Fittschen, K. 1969. *Untersuchungen zum Beginn der Sagendarstellungen bei den Griechen*. Berlin: Bruno Hessling.

Forbes, H. 1992. The ethnoarchaeological approach to ancient Greek agriculture: olive cultivation as a case study. In Wells 1992: 87–101.

Fotiadis, M. 1995. Modernity and the past-still-present: politics of time in the birth of regional archaeological projects in Greece. *American Journal of Archaeology* 99: 59–78.

Foxhall, L. 1995. Bronze to iron: agricultural systems and political structures in Late Bronze Age and Iron Age Greece. *Annual of the British School at Athens* 90: 239–50.

    1997a. A view from the top: evaluating the Solonian property classes. In Mitchell and Rhodes 1997: 113–36.

    1997b. Ancient farmsteads, other agricultural sites and equipment. In Mee and Forbes 1997: 257–68.

    1998. Cargoes of the heart's desire: the character of trade in the Archaic Mediterranean world. In Fisher and Van Wees 1998: 295–309.

    2000. The running sands of time: archaeology and the short term. *World Archaeology* 31 (1999–2000): 484–98.

Francis, E.D. and Vickers, M. 1983. Signa priscae artis: Eretria and Siphnos. *Journal of Hellenic Studies* 103: 49–67.

    1985. Greek Geometric pottery at Hama and its implications for Near Eastern chronology. *Levant* 17: 131–8.

    1988. The Agora revisited: Athenian chronology c.500–450 BC. *Annual of the British School at Athens* 83: 143–67.

Fredericksmeyer, E.A. 1981. Again the so-called tomb of Philip II. *American Journal of Archaeology* 85: 330–5.

    1983. Once more the diadem and barrel vault at Vergina. *American Journal of Archaeology* 87: 99–102.

Frel, J. 1983. Euphronios and his fellows. In Moon 1983: 147–58.

French, E. 1981. Cult places at Mycenae. In Hägg and Marinatos 1981: 41–8.

Freyer-Schauenburg, B. 1966. *Elfenbeine aus dem samischen Heraion: Figürliches, Gefässe und Siegel.* Hamburg: Cram, de Gruyter and Co.

    1974. *Samos XI: Bildwerke der archaischen Zeit und des strengen Stils.* Bonn: Rudolf Habelt Verlag.

Freytag, B. 1974. Ein spätgeometrischer Frauengrab vom Kerameikos. *Mitteilungen des deutschen archäologischen Instituts, athenische Abteilung* 89: 1–25.

Frickenhaus, A. 1912. Die Hera von Tiryns. *Tiryns I: Die Ergebnisse der Ausgrabungen des Instituts,* 1–126. Athens: Deutsches archäologisches Institut in Athen.

Fried, M.H. 1967. *The Evolution of Political Society: An Essay in Political Anthropology.* New York: Random House.

Furtwängler, A. 1890. *Olympia Vol. IV: Die Bronzen und die übrigen kleineren Funde von Olympia.* Berlin: A. Asher.

Furtwängler, A., Fiechter, E.R. and Thiersch, H. 1906. *Aegina: Das Heiligtum der Aphaia.* 2 volumes, text and plates. Munich: Verlag der K.B. Akademie der Wissenschaften.

Furtwängler, A. and Reichhold, K. 1900. *Griechische Vasenmalerei: Auswahl hervorrangender Vasenbilder.* Vol. I. Munich: F. Bruckmann.

Furtwängler, A., Reichhold, K., Buschor, E., Watzinger, C. and Zahn, R. 1932. *Griechische Vasenmalerei: Auswahl hervorrangender Vasenbilder.* Vol. VI. Munich: F. Bruckmann.

Gagarin, M. 1986. *Early Greek Law.* Berkeley and Los Angeles: University of California Press.

Gale, Z.A.S. and Gale, N.H. 1992. New light on the provenience of copper ox-hide ingots found on Sardinia. In Tykot and Andrews 1992: 317–46.

Gallant, T.W. 1986. Background noise and site definition: a contribution to survey methodology. *Journal of Field Archaeology* 13: 403–18.

Garlan, Y. 1974. *Recherches de Poliorcétique grecque*. Paris: Editions de Boccard.

Garland, R.W. 1982. A first catalogue of Attic peribolos tombs. *Annual of the British School at Athens* 77: 125–76.

   1987. *The Piraeus: From the Fifth to the First Century BC*. London: Duckworth.

Gavrilov, A.K. 1997. Reading techniques in Classical Antiquity. *Classical Quarterly* 47: 56–73.

Gebhard, E. 1974. The form of the orchestra in the early Greek theater. *Hesperia* 43: 428–40.

   1993. The evolution of a pan-Hellenic sanctuary: from archaeology towards history at Isthmia. In Hägg and Marinatos 1993: 154–77.

   1999. The location of Early Iron Age activity. In Morgan 1999a: 195–221.

Gerhard, E. 1831. Rapporto intorno i vasi Volcenti. *Annali dell'Instituto di Correspondenza Archeologica di Roma* 3: 5–218.

Gergova, D. 1993. Common elements in the ritual behaviour of Thracians and Macedonians. *Ancient Macedonia: Fifth International Symposium*, 471–8. Thessaloniki: Institute for Balkan Studies.

Gesell, G., Coulson, W.D.E. and Day, L.P. 1985. Kavousi 1982–83: the Kastro. *Hesperia* 54: 327–55.

   1986. Kavousi 1983–1984: the settlement at Vronda. *Hesperia* 55: 355–88.

Gill, D. 1988a. Trade in Greek decorated pottery: some corrections. *Oxford Journal of Archaeology* 7: 369–70.

   1988b. Expressions of wealth: Greek art and society. *Antiquity* 62: 735–42.

   1994. Positivism, pots and long-distance trade. In Morris 1994b: 99–107.

Gill, D. and Foxhall, L. 1997. Early Iron Age and Archaic Methana. In Mee and Forbes 1997: 57–61.

Gill, D., Foxhall, L. and Bowden, H. 1997. Classical and Hellenistic Methana. In Mee and Forbes 1997: 62–76.

Gill, D. and Vickers, M. 1990. Reflected glory: pottery and precious metals in classical Greece. *Jahrbuch des deutschen archäologischen Instituts* 105: 1–30.

Ginzburg, C. 1990. Clues: roots of an evidential paradigm. In C. Ginzburg, *Myths, Emblems, Clues*, 96–125. London: Hutchinson Radius.

Given, M. 1998. Inventing the Eteocypriots: imperialist archaeology and the manipulation of ethnic identity. *Journal of Mediterranean Archaeology* 11: 3–29.

Goldhill, S. 1987. The Great Dionysia and civic ideology. *Journal of Hellenic Studies* 107: 58–76.

Goldhill, S. and Osborne, R. (eds.) 1994. *Art and Text in Ancient Greek Culture*. Cambridge: Cambridge University Press.

Goldman, H. 1963. *Excavations at Gözlu Kule, Tarsus, Vol. III: The Iron Age*. 2 volumes, text and plates. Princeton: Princeton University Press.

Gombrich, Sir E.H. 1962. *Art and Illusion: A Study in the Psychology of Pictorial Representation*. 2nd edition. London: Phaidon.

Gomme, A.W., Andrewes, A. and Dover, K.J. 1970. *A Historical Commentary on Thucydides IV: Books V–VII*. Oxford: Clarendon.

Goody, J. and Watt, I. 1963. The consequences of literacy. *Comparative Studies in Society and History* 5: 304–45.

Gossel, B. 1980. *Makedonische Kammergräber*. Berlin: Monath's Kopiedruck.

Graef, B. and Langlotz, E. 1925. *Die antiken Vasen von der Akropolis zu Athen*. Vol. I. 5 volumes, text [1925], plates [1909–25]. Berlin: George Reimer/Walter de Gruyter.

   1933. *Die antiken Vasen von der Akropolis zu Athen*. 4 volumes, text [1933] and plates [1929–33] Berlin: Walter de Gruyter.

Graham, A.J. 1978. The foundation of Thasos. *Annual of the British School at Athens* 73: 61–98.

1982a. The colonial expansion of Greece. In Boardman and Hammond 1982: 83–162.

1982b. The Western Greeks. In Boardman and Hammond 1982: 163–95.

1986. The historical interpretation of Al Mina. *Dialogues d'Histoire Ancienne* 12 [Annales Littéraires de l'Université de Besançon 349]: 51–65.

Graham, J.W. 1974. Houses of Classical Athens. *Phoenix* 24: 45–54.

Green, P. 1990. *Alexander to Actium: The Hellenistic Age*. London: Thames and Hudson.

Greig, J.R.A. and Turner, J. 1974. Some pollen diagrams from Greece and their archaeological significance. *Journal of Archaeological Science* 1: 177–94.

Griffiths, A. 1986. 'What leaf-fringed legend?' A cup by the Sotades painter in London. *Journal of Hellenic Studies* 106: 58–70.

Guarducci, M. 1935. *Inscriptiones Creticae I: Tituli Cretae Mediae Praeter Gortynios*. Rome: Libreria dello Stato.

1939. *Inscriptiones Creticae II: Tituli Cretae Occidentalis*. Rome: Libreria dello Stato.

1942. *Inscriptiones Creticae III: Tituli Cretae Orientalis*. Rome: Libreria dello Stato.

1950. *Inscriptiones Creticae IV: Tituli Gortynii*. Rome: Libreria dello Stato.

Guralnick, E. 1978. The proportions of kouroi. *American Journal of Archaeology* 82: 461–72.

1981. Proportions of korai. *American Journal of Archaeology* 85: 269–80.

Hackens, T. 1965. Thorikos 1963: rapport préliminaire sur la première campagne de fouïlles: le théâtre. *L'Antiquité Classique* 34: 39–46.

1967. Le théâtre. In Mussche *et al.* 1967b: 75–96.

Hägg, R. 1974. *Die Gräber der Argolis in submykenischer, protogeometrischer und geometrischer Zeit I: Lage und Form der Gräber*. Uppsala: Acta Universitatis Upsaliensis.

1982. Zur Stadtwerdung des dorischen Argos. In D. Papenfuss and V.M. Strocka (eds.), *Paläst und Hütte: Beiträge zum Bauen und Wohnen in Altertum*, 297–307. Mainz: Philipp von Zabern.

1983a. Burial customs and social differentiation in 8th century Argos. In Hägg 1983b: 27–31.

(ed.) 1983b. *The Greek Renaissance of the Eighth Century BC: Tradition and Innovation*. Stockholm: Paul Astrom.

1987. Gifts to the heroes in Geometric and Archaic Greece. In Linders and Nordquist 1987: 93–9.

(ed.) 1996. *The Role of Religion in the Early Greek Polis*. Stockholm: Skrifter Utgivna av Svenska Institutet i Athen.

Hägg, R. and Marinatos, N. (eds.) 1981. *Sanctuaries and Cults in the Aegean Bronze Age: Proceedings of the First International Symposium at the Swedish Institute in Athens, 12–13 May 1980*. Stockholm: Skrifter Utgivna av Svenska Institutet i Athen.

Hägg, R., Marinatos, N. and Nordquist, G.C. (eds.) 1988. *Early Greek Cult Practice: Proceedings of the Fifth International Symposium at the Swedish Institute at Athens, 26–29 June 1986*. Stockholm: Skrifter Utgivna av Svenska Institutet i Athen.

Haggis, D.C. 1993. Intensive survey, traditional settlement patterns and Dark Age Crete. *Journal of Mediterranean Archaeology* 6: 131–74.

1996. Archaeological survey at Kavousi, Crete: preliminary report. *Hesperia* 65: 373–432.

Hall, J.M. 1995a. How Argive was the 'Argive' Heraion? The political and cultic geography of the Argive plain, 900–400 BC. *American Journal of Archaeology* 99: 577–613.

1995b. Approaches to ethnicity in the Early Iron Age of Greece. In Spencer 1995: 6–17.

1997. Alternative responses within polis formation: Argos, Mykenai and Tiryns. In Andersen *et al.* 1997: 89–109.

Hamilakis, Y. and Yalouri, E. 1996. Antiquities as symbolic capital in modern Greek society. *Antiquity* 70: 117–29.

Hamilton, R. 1992. *Choes and Anthesteria: Athenian Iconography and Ritual.* Ann Arbor: University of Michigan Press.

Hamilton, R.W. 1935. Excavations at Tell Abu Hawam. *Quarterly of the Department of Antiquities in Palestine* 4: 1–69.

Hammond, N.G.L. 1968. The campaign and battle of Marathon. *Journal of Hellenic Studies* 88: 13–57.

1972. The conditions of dramatic production to the death of Aeschylus. *Greek, Roman and Byzantine Studies* 13: 387–450.

1978. 'Philip's tomb' in historical context. *Greek, Roman and Byzantine Studies* 19: 331–50.

Hanfmann, G.M.A. 1963. The Iron Age pottery of Tarsus. In Goldman 1963: 18–332.

Hänsel, B. 1989. *Kastanas: Ausgrabungen in einem Siedlungshügel der Bronze- und Eisenzeit Makedoniens 1975–9: Die Grabung und Baubefund.* Prähistorische Archäologie in Südosteuropa 7. 2 volumes, text and plates. Berlin: Wissenschaftsverlag Volker Spiess.

Härke, H. 1990. 'Warrior graves'? The background to the Anglo-Saxon weapon burial ritual. *Past and Present* 126: 22–43.

Harrison, E.B. 1967. Athena and Athens in the east pediment of the Parthenon. *American Journal of Archaeology* 71: 27–58.

1996. The web of history: a conservative reading of the Parthenon frieze. In J. Neils (ed.), *Worshipping Athena: Panathenaia and Parthenon,* 198–214. Madison: University of Wisconsin Press.

Haskell, F. and Penny, N. 1981. *Taste and the Antique: The Lure of Classical Sculpture 1500–1900.* New Haven: Yale University Press.

Hayden, B.J. 1983. New plans of the Early Iron Age settlement at Vrokastro. *Hesperia* 52: 367–87.

1995. Rural settlement of the Orientalizing through to Early Classical period: the Meseleroi area, Eastern Crete. *Aegean Archaeology* 2: 93–144.

Hayden, B.J., Moody, J.A. and Rackham, O. 1992. The Vrokastro survey project, 1986–89: research design and preliminary results. *Hesperia* 61: 293–353.

Hayes, J.W. 1991. Fine wares in the Hellenistic world. In Rasmussen and Spivey 1991: 183–202.

Haynes, D.E. 1968. The Arundel Marbles: the formation and dispersal of the first great collection of Classical sculpture in England. *Archaeology* 21: 85–91 and 206–11.

Hedrick, C.W. Jn. 1999. Democracy and the Athenian epigraphic habit. *Hesperia* 68: 387–439.

Heilmeyer, W.D. 1972. *Frühe Olympische Tonfiguren: Olympische Forschungen VII.* Berlin: Walter de Gruyter.

1979. *Frühe Olympische Bronzefiguren: Die Tiervotive: Olympische Forschungen XII.* Berlin: Walter de Gruyter.

Herbert, S. 1977. *Corinth VII.4: The Red-Figure Pottery.* Princeton: American School of Classical Studies at Athens.

Herrmann, H.V. 1966. *Die Kessel der Orientalisierenden Zeit: Erster Teil: Kessalattaschen und Reliefuntersätze: Olympische Forschungen VI.* Berlin: Walter de Gruyter.

1979. *Die Kessel der Orientalisierenden Zeit: Zweiter Teil: Kesselprotome und Stabdreifüsse: Olympische Forschungen XI.* Berlin: Walter de Gruyter.

(ed.) 1987. *Die Olympia Skulpturen.* Darmstadt: Wissenschaftliche Buchgesellschaft.

Herrmann, K. 1984. Spätarchaische Votivsaülen in Olympia. *Mitteilungen des deutschen archäologischen Instituts, athenische Abteilung* 99: 121–43.

Herzfeld, M. 1987. *Anthropology through the Looking Glass: Critical Ethnography in the Margins of Europe.* Cambridge: Cambridge University Press.

Heurtley, W.A. 1935. Note on fragments of two Thessalian Proto-Geometric vases found at Tell Abu Hawam. *Quarterly of the Department of Antiquities in Palestine* 4: 181.

Higgins, W.A. 1954. *Catalogue of Terracottas in the Department of Greek and Roman Antiquities, British Museum*. London: British Museum.

1967. *Greek Terracottas*. London: Methuen.

Himmelmann, N. 1967 Erzahlung und Figur in der archaischen Kunst. *Abhandlung der geistes- und socialwissenschaftlichen Klasse der Akademie der Wissenschaften und der Literatur in Mainz* 2: 259–346. Wiesbaden: Franz Steiner.

1994. *Realistische Themen in der griechischen Kunst der archaischen und klassischen Zeit*. Berlin: Walter de Gruyter.

1997. *Tieropfer in der griechischen Kunst*. (Nordrhein-Westfalische Akademie der Wissenschaften, Vorträge G 349). Opladen: Westdeutsche Verlag.

Hochstetter, A. 1987. *Kastanas: Ausgrabungen in einem Siedlungshügel der Bronze- und Eisenzeit Makedoniens: Die Kleinfunde*. Prähistorische Archäologie in Südosteuropa 6. Berlin: Wissenschaftsverlag Volker Spiess.

Hodder, I. 1982. *Symbols in Action: Ethnoarchaeological Studies of Material Culture*. Cambridge: Cambridge University Press.

Hodkinson, S. 1997. The development of Spartan society and institutions in the Archaic period. In Mitchell and Rhodes 1997: 83–102.

1998. Lakonian artistic production and the problem of Spartan austerity. In Fisher and Van Wees 1998: 93–117.

Hoepfner, W. 1973. Das Grabmonument des Pythagoras aus Selymbria. *Mitteilungen des deutschen archäologischen Instituts, athenische Abteilung* 88: 145–63.

1976. *Kerameikos: Ergebnisse der Ausgrabungen X: Das Pompeion und seine Nachfolgerbauten.* Berlin: Walter de Gruyter.

1996. Zum Typus der Basileia und der königlichen Andromes. In Hoepfner and Brands 1996: 1–43.

Hoepfner, W. and Brands, G. (eds.) 1996. *Basileia: Die Paläste der hellenistischen Könige: Internationales Symposion Berlin*. Mainz: Philipp von Zabern.

Hoepfner, W. and Schwandner, E.L. 1994. *Haus und Stadt im klassischen Griechenland.* Wohnen in der klassischen Polis 1. 2nd edition. Munich: Deutscher Kunstverlag.

Hoffman, G.L. 1997. *Imports and Immigrants: Near Eastern Contacts with Iron Age Crete*. Ann Arbor: University of Michigan Press.

Hoffmann, H. 1961. The Persian origin of Attic rhyta. *Antike Kunst* 4: 21–6.

1962. *Attic Red-Figured Rhyta*. Mainz: Philipp von Zabern.

1972. *Early Cretan Armorers*. Mainz: Philipp von Zabern.

1977. *Sexual and Asexual Pursuit: A Structuralist Approach to Greek Vase Painting*. Royal Anthropological Institute Occasional Paper 34. London: Royal Anthropological Institute.

1979. In the wake of Beazley: prolegomena to an anthropological study of Greek vase painting. *Hephaistos* 1: 61–70.

1988. The cicada on the omphalos: an iconological excursion. *Antiquity* 62: 744–9.

1997. *Sotades: Symbols of Immortality on Greek Vases*. Oxford: Clarendon.

Hogarth, D.G. 1900. The Dictaean Cave. *Annual of the British School at Athens* 6: 94–116.

1908. *Excavations at Ephesus: The Archaic Artemisia*. London: British Museum.

Hölkeskamp, K.J. 1992. Written law in Archaic Greece. *Proceedings of the Cambridge Philological Society* 38: 87–117.

Holliday, P.J. (ed.) 1993. *Narrative and Event in Ancient Art*. Cambridge: Cambridge University Press.

Hölscher, T. 1998. Images and political identity: the case of Athens. In Boedecker and Raaflaub 1998: 153–83.

Homolle, M. Th. 1909. *Fouilles de Delphes IV.1: Monuments figurés: sculpture*. Paris: Libraires des Ecoles Françaises d'Athènes et de Rome.

Homolle, M. Th. and Gottlob, K. 1925. *Fouilles de Delphes II: Topographie et architecture: la tholos du sanctuaire d'Athena Pronaia à Delphes*. Paris: de Boccard.

Hood, S. and Warren, P. 1966. Ancient sites in the province of Ayios Vassilios, Crete. *Annual of the British School at Athens* 61: 164–89.

Hood, S., Warren, P. and Cadogan, G. 1964. Travels in Crete, 1962. *Annual of the British School at Athens* 59: 50–99.

Hopkinson, J.H. and Baker-Penoyre, J. 1902. New evidence on the Melian amphorae. *Journal of Hellenic Studies* 22: 46–75.

Hornblower, S. 1982. *Mausolus*. Oxford: Clarendon.

Houby-Nielsen, S. 1992. Interaction between chieftains and citizens? 7th century BC burial customs in Athens. *Acta Hyperborea* 4: 343–74.

1995. 'Burial language' in Archaic and Classical Kerameikos. *Proceedings of the Danish Institute at Athens* 1: 129–91.

1997. Grave gifts, women and conventional values in Hellenistic Athens. In P. Bilde, T. Engberg-Pedersen, L. Hannestad and J. Zahle (eds.), *Conventional Values of the Hellenistic Greeks*, 220–62. Aarhus: Aarhus University Press.

Howgego, C. 1995. *Ancient History from Coins*. London: Routledge.

Humphreys, S.C. 1980. Family tombs and tomb cult in ancient Athens: tradition or traditionalism? *Journal of Hellenic Studies* 100: 96–126.

Hurwit, J.M. 1985a. *The Art and Culture of Early Greece, 1100–480 BC*. Ithaca, NY: Cornell University Press.

1985b. The Dipylon shield once more. *Classical Antiquity* 4: 121–6.

1990. The words in the image: orality, literacy and early Greek art. *Word and Image* 6: 180–97.

1993. Art, poetry and the polis in the age of Homer. In Langdon 1993: 14–42.

1999. *The Athenian Acropolis: History, Mythology and Archaeology from the Neolithic Era to the Present*. Cambridge: Cambridge University Press.

Iakovidis, S.E. 1969. *Perati: To Nekrotapheion*. 3 volumes. Athens: I en Athenais Archaiologiki Etaireia.

Immerwahr, H.R. 1964. Book rolls on Attic vases. In C. Henderson (ed.), *Classical, Medieval and Renaissance Studies in Honor of Berthold Louis Ullmann*, 17–48. Rome: Edizioni di Storia e Letteratura.

1973. More book rolls on Attic vases. *Antike Kunst* 16: 143–7.

1990. *Attic Script: A Survey*. Oxford: Clarendon.

Jackson, A.H. 1991. Hoplites and the gods: the dedication of captured arms and armour. In V.D. Hanson (ed.), *Hoplites: The Classical Greek Battle Experience*, 228–49. London: Routledge.

1999. Three possible dedications of arms and armor at Isthmia. In Morgan 1999a: 161–6.

Jacob-Felsch, M. 1996. Die spätmykenische bis frühprotogeometrische Keramik. In Felsch 1996: 3–213.

Jacobsthal, P. 1956. *Greek Pins and Their Connexions with Europe and Asia*. Oxford: Clarendon.

James, P., Thorpe, I.J., Kokkinos, N., Morkot, R. and Frankish, J. 1991a. *Centuries of Darkness*. London: Jonathan Cape.

1991b. Review feature: Centuries of Darkness. *Cambridge Archaeological Journal* 1: 227–53.

James, T.G.H. 1962. The Egyptian-type objects. In Dunbabin 1962: 461–516.

Jameson, M.H. 1969. Excavations at Porto Cheli and vicinity, preliminary report I: Halieis. *Hesperia* 38: 311–42.

1990a. Private space and the Greek city. In Murray and Price 1990: 171–95.

1990b. Domestic space in the Greek city-state. In S. Kent (ed.), *Domestic Architecture and the Use of Space: An Interdisciplinary Cross-Cultural Study*, 92–113. Cambridge: Cambridge University Press.

Jameson, M.H., Runnels, C.N. and van Andel, T.H. 1994. *A Greek Countryside: The Southern Argolid from Prehistory to the Present Day*. Stanford, CA: Stanford University Press.

Jarman, M.R. 1973. Preliminary report on the animal bones. In Coldstream 1973b: 177–9.

Jeffery, L.H. 1956. The courts of justice in Archaic Chios. *Annual of the British School at Athens* 51: 157–67.

1962a. Inscriptions on vases and small objects. In Dunbabin 1962: 393–402.

1962b. The inscribed gravestones of Archaic Attica. *Annual of the British School at Athens* 57: 115–53.

1964. Old Smyrna: inscriptions on sherds and small objects. *Annual of the British School at Athens* 59: 39–49.

1990. *The Local Scripts of Archaic Greece*. 2nd edition, revised with addenda by A. Johnston. Oxford: Clarendon.

Jeffery, L.H. and Morpurgo-Davies, A. 1970. *Poinikastas* and *poinikazen*: BM 1969:42.1: a new Archaic inscription from Crete. *Kadmos* 9: 118–54.

Jenkins, I. 1992. *Archaeologists and Aesthetes in the Sculpture Galleries of the British Museum 1800–1939*. London: British Museum Press.

1994. *The Parthenon Frieze*. London: British Museum Press.

Jenkins, I. and Sloan, K. 1996. *Vases and Volcanoes: Sir William Hamilton and His Collection*. London: British Museum Press.

Jenkins, R.J.H. 1936. *Dedalica: A Study of Dorian Plastic Art in the Seventh Century BC*. Cambridge: Cambridge University Press.

Jeppesen, K. 1976. Neue Ergebnisse zur Wiederherstellung des Maussolleions von Halikarnassos. *Istanbuler Mitteilungen* 26: 47–99.

1978. Zur Gründung und Baugeschichte des Maussolleions von Halikarnassos. *Istanbuler Mitteilungen* 27/28 [1977–8]: 169–211.

Jeppesen, K., Højlund, F. and Sørensen, K.A. 1981. *The Mausolleion at Halikarnassos I: The Sacrificial Deposit*. Copenhagen: Gyldendansk Boghandel, Nordisk Forlag.

Johansen, K. Friis. 1957. Exochi: Ein frührhodisches Gräberfeld. *Acta Archaeologica* 28: 1–192.

Johnston, A.W. 1978. Lists of contents: Attic vases. *American Journal of Archaeology* 82: 222–6.

1983. The extent and use of literacy: the archaeological evidence. In Hägg 1983b: 63–8.

1991. Greek vases in the marketplace. In Rasmussen and Spivey 1991: 203–31.

Johnston, A.W. and Andreiomenou, A.K. 1989. A Geometric graffito from Eretria. *Annual of the British School at Athens* 84: 217–20.

Johnston, A.W. and Jones, R.E. 1978. The 'SOS' amphora. *Annual of the British School at Athens* 73: 103–41.

Jones, J.E. 1975. Town and country houses of Attica in Classical times. In H. Mussche, P. Spitaels and F. Goemaen-De Poerck (eds.), *Thorikos and Laurion in Archaic and Classical Times*, 63–144. Miscellanea Graeca 1. Ghent: Belgian Archaeological Mission in Greece.

1976. Laveries (ergasteria) sur la pent nord de la haute Laurion. *L'Antiquité Classique* 45: 149–72.

1982. The Laurion silver mines: a review. *Greece and Rome* n.s. 29: 169–83.

1985. Laurion: Agrileza, 1977–1983: Excavations at a silver mine site. *Archaeological Reports* 31 [1984–5]: 106–23.

1990. Ancient beehives at Thorikos: combed pots from the Velatouri. In Mussche *et al.* 1990: 63–71.

Jones, J.E., Graham, A.J. and Sackett, L.H. 1973. An Attic country house below the Cave of Pan at Vari. *Annual of the British School at Athens* 68: 355–452.

Jones, J.E., Sackett, L.H. and Eliot, C.W.J. 1957. To Dema: a survey of the Aigaleos–Parnes wall. *Annual of the British School at Athens* 52: 152–89.

Jones, J.E., Sackett, L.H. and Graham, A.J. 1962. The Dema house in Attica. *Annual of the British School at Athens* 57: 75–114.

Jones, R.E., Boardman, J., Catling, H.W., Mee, C.B., Phelps, W.W. and Pollard, A.M. 1986. *Greek and Cypriot Pottery: A Review of Scientific Studies.* Fitch Laboratory Occasional Paper 1. Athens: British School at Athens.

Jones, S. 1974. *Men of Influence in Nuristan.* London: Seminar Press.

Jordan, D.R. 2000. A personal letter found in the Athenian Agora. *Hesperia* 69: 91–103.

Junker, K. 1998. Research under dictatorship: the German Archaeological Institute 1929–45. *Antiquity* 72: 282–92.

Kahil, L. 1977. L'Artemis de Brauron: rites et mystère. *Antike Kunst* 20: 86–98.

Kakridis, I. Th. 1978. *I Archaioi Ellines sti Neoelleniki Laiki Paradosi.* Athens: Morphotiko Idhryma Ethnikis Trapezis.

Kaletsch, H. 1958. Zur lydischen Chronologie. *Historia* 7: 1–47.

Kavvadias, P. 1890. *Deltion Archaiologikon Ekdidomenon tou Genikou Ephorou ton Archaiotiton kai Mouseion.* Athens: S.K. Vlastos.

1900a. *Istoria tis Archaiologikis Etaireias apo tis en etei 1837 Iddryseos aftis mechri tou 1900.* Athens: I en Athenais Archaiologiki Etaireia.

1900b. *To Hieron tou Asklepiou en Epidauroi kai I Therapeia ton Asthenon.* Athens: I en Athenais Archaiologiki Etaireia.

Kavvadias, P. and Kawerau, G. 1906. *I Anaskaphi tis Akropoleios apo tou 1885 mechri tou 1890/ Die Ausgrabung der Akropolis vom Jahre 1885 bis zum Jahre 1890.* Athens: I en Athenais Archaiologiki Etaireia.

Kawerau, G. and Soteriadis, G. 1908. Der Apollotempel zu Thermos. *Antike Denkmaeler herausgegeben vom kaiserlich deutschen archaeologischen Institut* II.5 [1902–8]: 1–8.

Kearns, E. 1989. *The Heroes of Attica.* BICS Supplement 57. London: Institute of Classical Studies.

Kearsley, R. 1989. *The Pendent Semi-Circle Skyphos: A Study in Its Development and an Examination of It as Evidence for Euboean Activity in Al Mina.* BICS Supplement 44. London: Institute of Classical Studies.

Keuls, E.C. 1983. Attic vase-painting and the home textile industry. In Moon 1983: 209–30.

Kilian-Dirlmeier, I. 1984. *Nadeln der frühhelladischen bis archaischen Zeit von der Peloponnes.* Praehistorische Bronzefunde XIII, 8. Munich: C.H. Beck.

1985. Fremde Weihungen in griechische Heiligtümern vom 8. bis zum Beginn des 7. Jahrhunderts V. Chr. *Jahrbuch des Römisch-Germanischen Zentralmuseums Mainz* 32: 215–54.

Kinch, K.F. 1914. *Vroulia: fouilles de Vroulia (Rhodes).* Berlin: Georg Reimer.

Klein, N.L. 1997. Excavation of the Greek temples at Mycenae by the British School at Athens. *Annual of the British School at Athens* 92: 247–322.

Klippel, W.E. and Snyder, L.M. 1991. Dark Age fauna from Kavousi, Crete: the vertebrates from the 1987 and 1988 excavations. *Hesperia* 60: 179–86.

Knigge, U. 1976. *Kerameikos: Ergebnisse der Ausgrabungen IX: Der Südhügel.* Berlin: Walter de Gruyter.

1991. *The Athenian Kerameikos: History, Monuments, Excavations.* Translated from the German by Judith Binder. Athens: Krene editions.

Koenigs, W. 1984. *Die Echohalle: Olympische Forschungen XIV*. Berlin: Walter de Gruyter.

Koenigs, W., Knigge, U. and Mallwitz, A. 1980. *Kerameikos: Ergebnisse der Ausgrabungen XII: Rundbauten in Kerameikos*. Berlin: Walter de Gruyter.

Kokkou, A. 1977. *I Merimna yia tis Archaiotites stin Ellada kai ta Prota Mouseia*. Athens: Ekdotiki Hermes.

Kopcke, G. 1967. Neue Holzfunde aud dem Heraion von Samos. *Mitteilungen des deutschen archäologischen Instituts, athenische Abteilung* 82: 101–48.

Kopcke, G. and Tokumaru, I. (eds.) 1992. *Greece between East and West: 10th–8th Centuries BC*. Mainz: Philipp von Zabern.

Kopytoff, I. 1986. The cultural biography of things. In Appadurai 1986b: 64–91.

Korres, M. 1994a. The construction of ancient Greek temples. In Economokakis 1994: 20–7.

1994b. The sculptural adornment of the Parthenon. In Economokakis 1994: 28–33.

1994c. The history of the Acropolis monuments. In Economokakis 1994: 35–51.

1995. *From Pentelicon to the Parthenon*. Athens: Melissa.

Koufa, A.P. 1996. Die Graffiti auf der Keramik. In Felsch 1996: 271–331.

Koukouli-Chrysanthaki, Ch. 1993. I proimi epochi tou Siderou stin anatoliki Makedonia. *Ancient Macedonia: Fifth International Symposium*, 679–735. Thessaloniki: Institute for Balkan Studies.

Kouroniotis, K. 1903. Anggeia Eretrias. *Archaiologiki Ephemeris* 1903: 1–38.

1913. Goldschmuck aus Eretria. *Mitteilungen des deutschen archäologischen Instituts, athenische Abteilung* 38: 289–328.

1928. To hieron tou Apollonos tou Zosteros. *Archaiologikon Deltion* 11 [1927–8]: 9–53.

Kouroniotis, K. and Thompson, H.A. 1932. The Pnyx in Athens. *Hesperia* 1: 90–217.

Kovacsocics, W.K. 1990. *Kerameikos: Ergebnisse der Ausgrabungen XIV: Die Ekterrasse an der Gräberstrasse des Kerameikos*. Berlin: Walter de Gruyter.

Kraiker, W. and Kübler, K. 1939. *Kerameikos: Ergebnisse der Ausgrabungen I: Die Nekropole des 12. bis 10. Jahrhunderts*. Berlin: Walter de Gruyter.

Krause, C. 1982. Zur stadtbaulichen Entwicklung Eretrias. *Antike Kunst* 25: 137–44.

Krischen, F. 1923. Jonische Bauten Kleinasiens und der Aufbau des Mausoleums von Halikarnass. *Bonner Jahrbucher* 128: 1–19.

1925. Die Statue des Maussollos. *Jahrbuch des deutschen archäologischen Instituts* 40: 22–8.

1927. Die Entwurf des Maussolleions von Halikarnass. *Archäologischer Anzeiger* 1927: 162–9.

Kron, U. 1976. *Die zehn attischen Phylenheroen: Geschichte, Mythos, Kult und Darstellungen*. Athenische Mitteilungen 5. Berlin: Gebr. Mann.

1996. Priesthoods, dedications and euergetism. What part did religion play in the political and social status of Greek women? In Hellström and Alroth 1996: 139–82.

Kübler, K. 1943. *Kerameikos: Ergebnisse der Ausgrabungen IV: Neufunde aus der Nekropole des 11. und 10. Jahrhunderts*. Berlin: Walter de Gruyter.

1954. *Kerameikos: Ergebnisse der Ausgrabungen V: Die Nekropole des 10. bis 8. Jahrhunderts*. 2 volumes, text and plates. Berlin: Walter de Gruyter.

1959. *Kerameikos: Ergebnisse der Ausgrabungen VI.1: Die Nekropole des späten 8. bis frühen 6. Jahrhunderts*. 2 volumes. Berlin: Walter de Gruyter.

1970. *Kerameikos: Ergebnisse der Ausgrabungen VI.2: Die Nekropole des späten 8 bis frühen 6 Jahrhunderts*. 2 volumes, text and plates. Berlin: Walter de Gruyter.

1973. Ein archaische Grabanlage vor dem heiligen Tor und ihre Deutung. *Archäologischer Anzeiger* 1973: 172–93.

1976. *Kerameikos: Ergebnisse der Ausgrabungen VII: Die Nekropole der Mitte des 6 bis Ende des 5 Jahrhunderts*. 2 volumes, text and plates. Berlin: Walter de Gruyter.

Kuniholm, P.I. 1996. The prehistoric Aegean: dendrochronological progress as of 1995. *Acta Archaeologica* 67: 327–35.

Kuniholm, P.I. and Striker, C.L. 1987. Dendrochronological investigations in the Aegean and neighbouring regions, 1983–86. *Journal of Field Archaeology* 14: 385–98.

Kunze, E. 1931. *Kretische Bronzereliefs*. Stuttgart: W. Kohlhammer.

  1950. *Archaische Schildbänder: Olympische Forschungen II*. Berlin: Walter de Gruyter.

  1956. *Bericht über die Ausgrabungen in Olympia V*. Berlin: Walter de Gruyter.

  1958. *Bericht über die Ausgrabungen in Olympia VI*. Berlin: Walter de Gruyter.

  1961. *Bericht über die Ausgrabungen in Olympia VII*. Berlin: Walter de Gruyter.

  1967. *Bericht über die Ausgrabungen in Olympia VIII*. Berlin: Walter de Gruyter.

  1991. *Beinschienen: Olympische Forschungen XXI*. Berlin: Walter de Gruyter.

Kunze, E., Mallwitz, A., Herrmann, K., Heilmeyer, W.D., Söldner, M. and Kyrieleis, H. 1994. *Bericht über die Ausgrabungen in Olympia IX*. Berlin: Walter de Gruyter.

Kunze, E. and Schleif, H. 1938. *Bericht über die Ausgrabungen in Olympia II*. Berlin: [no publisher named].

  1939. *Bericht über die Ausgrabungen in Olympia III*. Berlin [no publisher named].

Kurtz, D.C. 1975. *Athenian White Lekythoi: Patterns and Painters*. Oxford: Clarendon.

  1985a. Beazley and the connoisseurship of Greek vases. *Greek Vases in the J. Paul Getty Museum* 2: 237–50. Malibu, CA: J. Paul Getty Museum.

Kurtz, D.C. (ed.) 1985b. *Beazley and Oxford*. Oxford: Oxford University Committee for Archaeology.

Kyrieleis, H. 1979. Babylonische Bronzen im Heraion von Samos. *Jahrbuch des deutschen archäologischen Instituts* 94: 32–48.

  1993. The Heraion at Samos. In Marinatos and Hägg 1993: 125–53.

  1996. *Samos X: Der Grosse Kuros von Samos*. Bonn: Rudolf Habelt.

Kyrieleis, H. and Röllig, W. 1988. Ein altorientalischer Pferdeschuck aus dem Heraion von Samos. *Mitteilungen des deutschen archäologischen Instituts, athenische Abteilung* 103: 37–75.

Lalonde, G.V. 1980. A hero shrine in the Athenian Agora. *Hesperia* 49: 97–105.

  1991. Horoi. In Lalonde *et al.* 1991: 1–51.

Lalonde, G.V., Langdon, M.K. and Walbank, M.B. 1991. *The Athenian Agora XIX: Inscriptions: Horoi, Poletai Records, Leases of Public Land*. Princeton: American School of Classical Studies at Athens.

Lambrinoudakis, V.K. 1988. Veneration of ancestors in Geometric Naxos. In Hägg *et al.* 1988: 235–46.

Lambrinoudakis, V.K. and Gruben, G. 1987. Das neuentdeckte Heiligtum von Iria auf Naxos. *Archäologischer Anzeiger* 1987: 569–621.

Lang, F. 1996. *Archaische Siedlungen in Griechenland: Struktur und Entwicklung*. Berlin: Akademie Verlag.

Lang, M.L. 1976. *The Athenian Agora XXI: Graffiti and Dipinti*. Princeton: American School of Classical Studies at Athens.

  1990. *The Athenian Agora XXV: Ostraka*. Princeton: American School of Classical Studies at Athens.

Langdon, M.K. 1976. *A Sanctuary of Zeus on Mount Hymettus*. Hesperia Supplement 16. Princeton: American School of Classical Studies at Athens.

  1997. Cult in Iron Age Attica. In S. Langdon 1997: 113–24.

Langdon, S. 1987. Gift exchange in the Geometric sanctuaries. In Linders and Nordquist 1987: 107–13.

Langdon, S. 1995. The pottery of the Early Iron Age and Geometric periods. In Runnels *et al.* 1995: 57–73.

Langdon, S. (ed.) 1993. *From Pasture to Polis: Art in the Age of Homer*. Columbia: University of Missouri Press.

1997. *New Light on a Dark Age: Exploring the Culture of Geometric Greece*. Columbia: University of Missouri Press.

Langlotz, E. 1920. *Zur Zeitbestimmung der strengrotfiguren Vasenmalerei und der gleichzeitigen Plastik*. Leipzig: Verlag E.A. Seemann.

Lauter, H. 1973. Zur frühklassischen Neuplannung des Heraion von Argos. *Mitteilungen des deutschen archäologischen Instituts, athenische Abteilung* 88: 175–87.

1985. *Der Kultplatz auf dem Turkovuni*. Berlin: Gebr. Mann.

Lawall, M.L. 2000. Graffiti, wine selling, and the reuse of amphoras in the Athenian Agora. *Hesperia* 69: 3–90.

Lawrence, A.W. 1979. *Greek Aims in Fortification*. Oxford: Clarendon.

Lawrence, A.W. and Tomlinson, R.A. 1996. *Greek Architecture*. 5th edition (Pelican History of Art). New Haven and London: Yale University Press.

Leake, W.M. 1830a. *Travels in the Morea*. Vol. I. London. Reprinted 1968 by Adolf M. Hakkert, Amsterdam.

1830b. *Travels in the Morea*. Vol. II. London. Reprinted 1968 by Adolf M. Hakkert, Amsterdam.

1830c. *Travels in the Morea*. Vol. III. London. Reprinted 1968 by Adolf M. Hakkert, Amsterdam.

1835a. *Travels in Northern Greece*. Vol. I. London. Reprinted by Adolf M. Hakkert, Amsterdam.

1835b. *Travels in Northern Greece*. Vol. II. London. Reprinted by Adolf M. Hakkert, Amsterdam.

Lebessi, A. 1985. *To Iero tou Ermi kai tis Aphroditis sti Symi Viannou I.1: Chalkina Kritika Torefmata*. Athens: I en Athenais Archaiologiki Etaireia.

Lehmann, P.W. 1980. The so-called tomb of Philip II: a different interpretation. *American Journal of Archaeology* 84: 527–31.

1982. The so-called tomb of Philip II: an addendum. *American Journal of Archaeology* 86: 437–42.

Lemos, A.A. 1991. *Archaic Pottery of Chios: The Decorated Styles*. 2 volumes, text and plates. Oxford: Oxford University Committee for Archaeology/Oxbow.

Levi, D. 1931. Arkades: Una città cretese all'alba della civiltà ellenica. *Annuario della scuola italiana di Atene e della Missioni Italiane in Oriente* X–XII [1927–29].

Lévi-Strauss, C. 1972. *The Savage Mind*. 2nd edition, translated by E. Gellner. London: Weidenfeld and Nicholson.

Lewis, D.M. 1981. *Inscriptiones Graecae I:1: Inscriptiones Atticae Euclidis Anno Anteriores: Decreta et Tabulae Magistratuum*. 3rd edition (of IG). Berlin: Walter de Gruyter.

Lewis, D.M., Jeffery, L.H. and Erxleben, E. 1994. *Inscriptiones Graecae I:2: Inscriptiones Atticae Euclidis Anno Anteriores: Dedicationes, Catalogi, Termini, Tituli Sepulcrales, Varia*. 3rd edition. Berlin: Walter de Gruyter.

Liddy, D.J. 1996. A chemical study of decorated Iron Age pottery from the Knossos North Cemetery. In Coldstream and Catling 1996: 465–514.

Linders, T. and Nordquist, G. (eds.) 1987. *Gifts to the Gods: Proceedings of the Uppsala Symposium 1985*. Uppsala: Acta Universitatis Upsaliensis.

Lissarrague, F. 1990a. *The Aesthetics of the Greek Banquet: Images of Wine and Ritual*. Translated from the French by A. Szegedy-Maszak. Princeton: Princeton University Press.

1990b. Around the krater: an aspect of banquet imagery. In Murray 1990: 196–209.

1994. *Epiktetos egraphsen*: the writing on the cup. In Goldhill and Osborne 1994: 12–27.

Lohmann, H. 1992. Agriculture and country life in Classical Attica. In Wells 1992: 29–60.

1993a. *Atene: Forschungen zu Siedlungs- und Wirtschaftstruktur des klassischen Attika*. 2 volumes. Cologne and Weimar: Böhlar Verlag.

1993b. Ein Turmgehöft klassischer Zeit in Thimari (Attika). *Mitteilungen des deutschen archäologischen Instituts, athenische Abteilung* 108: 101–49.

Loraux, N. 1986. *The Invention of Athens: The Funeral Oration in the Classical City*. Translated from the French by Alan Sheridan. Cambridge, MA: Harvard University Press.

Lord, L.E. 1947. *A History of the American School of Classical Studies at Athens 1882–1942*. Cambridge, MA: Harvard University Press.

Lo Schiavo, F., Macnamara, E. and Vagnetti, L. 1985. Late Cypriot imports to Italy and their influence on local bronzework. *Papers of the British School at Rome* 53: 1–71.

Love, I.C. 1970. A preliminary report of the excavations at Knidos, 1969. *American Journal of Archaeology* 74: 149–55.

1972a. A preliminary report of the excavations at Knidos, 1970. *American Journal of Archaeology* 76: 61–76.

1972b. A preliminary report of the excavations at Knidos, 1971. *American Journal of Archaeology* 76: 393–405.

Luke, J. 1994. The nature of Greek contacts with the Levant in the Geometric period (with particular reference to ceramic evidence). Unpublished Ph.D. dissertation, University of Cambridge.

Lullies, R. 1940. Zur boiotisch rotfiguren Vasenmalerei. *Mittelungen des deutschen archäologischen Instituts, athenische Abteilung* 65: 1–27.

Maass, M. 1978. *Die geometrischen Dreifüsse von Olympia: Olympische Forschungen X*. Berlin: Walter de Gruyter.

1981. Die geometrischen Dreifüsse von Olympia. *Antike Kunst* 24: 6–20.

McClellan, A. 1994. *Inventing the Louvre: Art, Politics and the Origins of the Modern Museum in Eighteenth-Century Paris*. Cambridge: Cambridge University Press.

McDonald, W.A. 1972. The problems and the program. In McDonald and Rapp 1972b: 3–17.

McDonald, W.A., Coulson, W.D.E. and Rosser, J. 1983. *Excavations at Nichoria in Southwest Greece III: Dark Age and Byzantine Occupation*. Minneapolis: University of Minnesota Press.

McDonald, W.A. and Hope-Simpson, R. 1972. Archaeological exploration. In McDonald and Rapp 1972b: 117–47.

McDonald, W.A. and Rapp, G.R. (eds.) 1972a. *The Minnesota Messenia Expedition: Reconstructing a Bronze Age Regional Environment*. Minneapolis: University of Minnesota Press.

1972b. Perspectives. In McDonald and Rapp 1972a: 240–61.

MacGillivray, J.A. 1997. The re-occupation of Eastern Crete in the Late Minoan II–IIIA1/2 periods. In Driessen and Farnoux 1997: 275–9.

McPhee, I. 1983. Local red-figure from Corinth. *Hesperia* 52: 137–53.

1986. Laconian red-figure from British excavations at Sparta. *Annual of the British School at Athens* 81: 153–65.

Macridy, Th. 1911. Un tumulus Macédonien à Langaza. *Jahrbuch des deutschen archäologischen Instituts* 26: 193–215.

Maddin, R. 1983. Early iron technology in Cyprus. In Muhly *et al.* 1983: 303–12.

Madigan, B.C. 1992. *The Temple of Apollo Bassitas II: The Sculpture*. Princeton: The American School of Classical Studies at Athens.

Makaronas, Ch. 1963. Taphoi para to Derveni Thessalonikis. *Archaiologikon Deltion B Chronika* 18: 193–6.

Makaronas, Ch. and Yiouri, E. 1989. *I Oikies Arpagis tis Elenis kai Dionysou tis Pellas.* Athens: I en Athenais Archaiologiki Etaireia.

Malkin, I. 1996. The *polis* between myths of land and territory. In Hägg 1996: 9–19.

Mallwitz, A. and Schiering, W. 1964. *Die Werkstatt des Pheidias in Olympia I: Olympische Forschungen V.* Berlin: Walter de Gruyter.

Mansurelli, G.A. 1979. The Etruscan city. In D. Ridgway and F.R. Ridgway (eds.), *Italy Before the Romans: The Iron Age, Orientalizing and Etruscan Periods,* 353–71. New York: Academic Press.

Marchand, S.L. 1996. *Down from Olympus: Archaeology and Philhellenism in Germany, 1750–1970.* Princeton: Princeton University Press.

Marchand, S.L. and Grafton, A. 1997. Martin Bernal and his critics. *Arion* 3rd series 5.2: 1–35.

Marinatos, N. and Hägg, R. (eds.) 1993. *Greek Sanctuaries: New Approaches.* London: Routledge.

Mark, I.S. 1993. *The Sanctuary of Athena Nike in Athens: Architectural Stages and Chronology.* Hesperia Supplement 26. Princeton: American School of Classical Studies at Athens.

Markoe, G. 1985. *Phoenician Bronze and Silver Bowls from Cyprus and the Mediterranean.* University of California Classical Studies 26. Berkeley and Los Angeles: University of California Press.

Matthäus, H. 1985. *Metallgefässe und Gefassuntersätze der Bronzezeit, der geometrischen und archaischen Periode auf Cypern.* Prähistorische Bronzefunde II.8. Munich: C.H. Beck.

　　1988. Heirloom or tradition? Bronze stands of the second and first millennium BC. in Cyprus, Greece and Italy. In E.B. French and K.A. Wardle (eds.), *Problems in Greek Prehistory: Papers Presented at the Centenary Conference of the British School at Athens, Manchester, April 1986,* 285–300. Bristol: Bristol Classical Press.

Mattusch, C.C. 1977. Bronze- and ironworking in the area of the Athenian Agora. *Hesperia* 46: 340–79.

　　1988. *Greek Bronze Statuary: From the Beginnings through the Fifth Century.* Ithaca, NY: Cornell University Press.

　　1994. The Eponymous heroes: the idea of sculptural groups. In Coulson *et al.* 1994: 73–81.

Maurizio, L. 1998. The Panathenaic procession: Athens' participatory democracy on display? In Boedeker and Raaflaub 1998: 297–317.

Mazarakis-Ainian, A. 1987. Geometric Eretria. *Antike Kunst* 30: 3–24.

　　1988. Early Greek temples: their origin and function. In Hägg *et al.* 1988: 104–19.

　　1997. *From Rulers' Dwellings to Temples: Architecture, Religion and Society in Early Iron Age Greece.* SIMA 121. Jonsered: Paul Åstroms Forlag.

Mee, C. and Cavanagh, W.G. 1998. Diversity in a Greek landscape: the Laconia survey and rural sites project. In W.G. Cavanagh and S.E.C. Walker (eds.), *Sparta in Laconia: Proceedings of the 19th British Museum Classical Colloquium,* 141–8. London: British School at Athens.

Mee, C. and Forbes, H. (eds.) 1997. *A Rough and Rocky Place: The Landscape and Settlement History of the Methana Peninsula, Greece.* Liverpool: Liverpool University Press.

Meiggs, R. 1972. *The Athenian Empire.* Oxford: Clarendon.

Merritt, B.J., Wade-Gery, H.T. and McGregor, M.F. 1939. *The Athenian Tribute Lists.* Vol. I. Cambridge, MA: Harvard University Press.

　　1949. *The Athenian Tribute Lists.* Vol. II. Princeton: American School of Classical Studies at Athens.

　　1950. *The Athenian Tribute Lists.* Vol. III. Princeton: American School of Classical Studies at Athens.

1953. *The Athenian Tribute Lists.* Vol. IV. Princeton: American School of Classical Studies at Athens.

Meyer, E.A. 1993. Epitaphs and citizenship in Classical Athens. *Journal of Hellenic Studies* 113: 99–121.

Michaelis, A. 1882. *Ancient Marbles in Great Britain.* Translated from the German by C.A.M. Fennell. Cambridge: Cambridge University Press.

Miles, M.M. 1989. A reconstruction of the temple of Nemesis at Rhamnous. *Hesperia* 58: 137–249.

Miller, M.C. 1997. *Athens and Persia in the Fifth Century BC: A Study in Cultural Receptivity.* Cambridge: Cambridge University Press.

Miller, S.G. 1973. The Philippeion and Macedonian Hellenistic architecture. *Mitteilungen des deutschen archäologischen Instituts, athenische Abteilung* 88: 189–218.

1993. *The Tomb of Lyson and Kallikles: A Painted Macedonian Tomb.* Mainz: Philipp von Zabern.

Mitchell, L.G. and Rhodes, P.J. (eds.) 1997. *The Development of the Polis in Archaic Greece.* London: Routledge.

Moignard, E. 1996. The Orientalizing pottery. In Coldstream and Catling 1996: 421–62.

1998. Native wit: some Orientalising pottery from the Knossos North Cemetery. In W.G. Cavanagh and M. Curtis (eds.), *Post-Minoan Crete: Proceedings of the First Colloquium*, 80–6. London: British School at Athens.

Mollard-Besques, S. 1954. *Catalogue raisonné des figurines et reliefs en terre cuite grecs, étrusques et romaines I (Musée National du Louvre): époques préhellénique, géométrique, archaïque et classique.* Paris: Editions des Musées Nationaux.

1972. *Catalogue raisonné des figurines et reliefs en terre cuite grecs, étrusques et romaines III (Musée National du Louvre): époques hellénistiques et romaine, Grèce et Asie Mineure.* Paris: Editions des Musées Nationaux.

Mook, M.S. 1998. Early Iron Age domestic architecture: the Northwest building on the Kastro at Kavousi. In Cavanagh *et al.* 1998: 45–57.

Moon, W.G. (ed.) 1983. *Ancient Greek Art and Iconography.* Madison: University of Wisconsin Press.

Moore, M.B. 1997. *The Athenian Agora XXX: Attic Red-Figured and White-Ground Pottery.* Princeton: American School of Classical Studies at Athens.

Morelli, G. 1892. *Italian Painters: Critical Studies of their Works I: The Borghese and Doria-Pamfili Galleries in Rome.* London: John Murray.

Morgan, C. 1990. *Athletes and Oracles: The Transformation of Olympia and Delphi in the Eighth Century BC.* Cambridge: Cambridge University Press.

1991. Ethnicity and early Greek states: historical and material perspectives. *Proceedings of the Cambridge Philological Society* 37: 131–63.

1993. The origins of pan-hellenism. In Hägg and Marinatos 1993: 18–44.

1994. The evolution of a sacral 'landscape': Isthmia, Perachora, and the early Corinthian state. In Alcock and Osborne 1994: 105–42.

1996. From palace to polis? Religious developments on the Greek mainland during the Bronze Age/Iron Age transition. In Hägg 1996: 41–57.

1997. The archaeology of sanctuaries in Early Iron Age and Archaic *ethne*: a preliminary view. In Mitchell and Rhodes 1997: 168–98.

1999a. *Isthmia VIII: The Late Bronze Age Settlement and Early Iron Age Sanctuary.* Princeton: American School of Classical Studies at Athens.

1999b. Some thoughts on the production and consumption of Early Iron Age pottery in the Aegean. In Crielaard *et al.* 1999: 213–59.

Morgan, C. and Whitelaw, T. 1991. Pots and politics: ceramic evidence for the rise of the Argive state. *American Journal of Archaeology* 95: 79–108.

Morris, I. 1986. The use and abuse of Homer. *Classical Antiquity* 5: 81–138.

1987. *Burial and Ancient Society: The Rise of the Greek City-State*. Cambridge: Cambridge University Press.

1988. Tomb cult and the 'Greek renaissance': the past in the present in the 8th century BC. *Antiquity* 62: 750–61.

1989. Circulation, deposition and the formation of the Greek Iron Age. *Man* n.s. 24: 505–19.

1991a. The early polis as city and state. In Rich and Wallace Hadrill 1991: 25–57.

1991b. Review of Kovasovics 1990. *American Journal of Archaeology* 95: 750–1.

1992. *Death Ritual and Social Structure in Classical Antiquity*. Cambridge: Cambridge University Press.

1994a. Archaeologies of Greece. In Morris 1994b: 8–47.

(ed.) 1994b. *Classical Greece: Ancient Histories and Modern Archaeologies*. Cambridge: Cambridge University Press.

1996. The absolute chronology of the Greek colonies in Sicily. *Acta Archaeologica* 67: 51–9.

1997a. The art of citizenship. In Langdon 1997: 9–43.

1997b. An archaeology of equalities? The Greek city-states. In D.L. Nichols and T.H. Charlton (eds.), *The Archaeology of City-States: Cross-Cultural Approaches*, 91–105. Washington, DC: Smithsonian Institution Press.

1998a. Archaeology and Archaic Greek history. In Fisher and Van Wees 1998: 1–91.

1998b. Beyond democracy and empire: Athenian art in context. In Boedeker and Raaflaub 1998: 59–86.

1999. *Archaeology as Cultural History: Words and Things in Early Iron Age Greece*. Oxford: Blackwell.

Morris, S.P. 1984. *The Black and White Style: Athens and Aegina in the Orientalizing Period*. New Haven: Yale University Press.

1992. *Daidalos and the Origins of Greek Art*. Princeton: Princeton University Press.

1997. Greek and Near Eastern art in the age of Homer. In Langdon 1997: 56–71.

Mountjoy, P.A. 1988. LHIIIC late versus Submycenaean. *Jahrbuch des deutschen archäologischen Instituts* 103: 1–33.

Muhly, J.D., Maddin, R. and Karageorghis, V. (eds.) 1983. *Early Metallurgy in Cyprus, 4000–500 BC. Acta of the International Archaeological Symposium*. Larnaca: Pierides Foundation.

Munn, M.H. 1993. *The Defense of Attica: The Dema Wall and the Boiotian War of 378–375 BC*. Berkeley and Los Angeles: University of California Press.

Munn, M.H. and Zimmermann Munn, M.L. 1989. Studies on the Attic–Boiotian frontier: the Stanford Skourta plain project, 1985. In J.M. Fossey (ed.), *Boeotia Antiqua I: Papers on Recent Work in Boiotian Archaeology and History*, 73–127. Amsterdam: J.C. Gieben.

Murray, O. 1980. *Early Greece*. Glasgow: Fontana Collins.

1983. The symposion as social organisation. In Hägg 1983b: 195–9.

(ed.) 1990. *Sympotica: A Symposium on the Symposion*. Oxford: Clarendon.

1994. Nestor's cup and the origins of the Greek symposion. *Annali di Archeologia e Storia Antica* n.s. 1: 47–54.

Murray, O. and Price, S. (eds.) 1990. *The Greek City: From Homer to Alexander*. Oxford: Clarendon.

Muscarella, O.W. 1992. Greek and Oriental cauldron attachments: a review. In Kopcke and Tokumaru 1992: 16–45.

Musgrave, J.H. 1990. The cremated remains from tombs II and III at Nea Mihaniona and tomb Beta at Derveni. *Annual of the British School at Athens* 85: 301–25.

Mussche, H.F. 1965. Thorikos 1963: rapport préliminaire sur la première campagne de fouilles: le secteur industriel. *L'Antiquité Classique* 34: 30–8.

1967. Le quartier industriel. In Mussche *et al.* 1967b: 57–71.

1969. Le quartier industriel. In Mussche *et al.* 1969: 121–30.

1971. Le quartier industriel. In Mussche *et al.* 1971: 103–33.

1990. Insula 3. In Mussche *et al.* 1990: 12–62.

Mussche, H.F. and Conophagos, C. 1973. Ore washing establishments and furnaces at Megala Pevka and Demoliaki. In Mussche *et al.* 1973: 61–72.

Mussche, H.F., Bingen, J., de Geyter, J., Donnay, G. and Hackens, T. 1967a. *Thorikos II 1964: rapport préliminaire sur la deuxième campagne de fouilles*. Brussels: Comité des Fouilles Belges en Grèce.

Mussche, H.F., Bingen, J., Servais, J., de Geyter, J., Hackens, T., Spitaels, P. and Gautier, A. 1967b. *Thorikos III 1965: rapport préliminaire sur la troisième campagne de fouilles*. Brussels: Comité des Fouilles Belges en Grèce.

Mussche, H.F., Bingen, J., Servais, J., Paepe, R. and Donnay, G. 1969. *Thorikos IV 1966/67: rapport préliminaire sur la quatrième campagne de fouilles*. Brussels: Comité des Fouilles Belges en Grèce.

Mussche, H.F., Bingen, J., Servais, J., Paepe, R., Bussers, H. and Gasche, H. 1971. *Thorikos V 1968: rapport préliminaire sur la cinquième campagne de fouilles*. Brussels: Comité des Fouilles Belges en Grèce.

Mussche, H.F., Bingen, J., Conophagos, C., de Geyter, J., Paepe, R., Vandenten, G. and Deraymaekdr, D. 1973. *Thorikos VI 1969: rapport préliminaire sur la sixième campagne de fouilles*. Brussels: Comité des Fouilles Belges en Grèce.

Mussche, H.F., Bingen, J., Jones, J.E. and Waelkens, M. 1990. *Thorikos IX 1977/1982: rapport préliminaire sur les 13e, 14e, 15e et 16e campagnes de fouilles*. Ghent: Comité des Fouilles Belges en Grèce.

Mylonas. G.E. 1946. Excursus II: the oecus unit of the Olynthian house. In Robinson 1946: 369–98.

1957. *O Protoattikos Amphorefs tis Elefsinos*. Athens: I en Athenais Archaiologiki Etaireia.

Myres, J.L. 1943. The future of discovery: archaeology overseas I: Greek and Roman archaeology. *Conference on the Future of Archaeology*, 26–9. University of London, Institute of Archaeology Occasional Paper 5. London.

Nafissi, M. 1989. Distribution and trade. In C.M. Stibbe, *Laconian Mixing Bowls: A History of the Krater Lakonikos from the Seventh to the Fifth Century BC*, 68–88. Amsterdam: Allard Pierson Museum.

Napoli, M. 1970. *La Tomba del Tuffatore: La Scoperta della Grande Pittura Greca*. Bari: de Donato.

Naveh, J. 1962. The excavations at Mesad Hashavyahu: preliminary report. *Israel Exploration Journal* 12: 89–113.

1982. *Early History of the Alphabet*. Leiden and Jerusalem: Magnes Press.

1988. Semitic epigraphy and the antiquity of the Greek alphabet. *Kadmos* 27: 65–86.

Neeft, C.W. 1987. *Protocorinthian Subgeometric Aryballoi*. Amsterdam: Allard Pierson Museum.

Nevett, L. 1994. Separation or seclusion? Towards an archaeological approach to investigating women in the Greek household in the fifth to third centuries BC. In M. Parker Pearson and C. Richards (eds.), *Architecture and Order: Approaches to Social Space*, 98–112. London: Routledge.

1995a. The organisation of space in Classical and Hellenistic houses from mainland Greece and the western colonies. In Spencer 1995b: 89–108.

1995b. Gender relations in the Classical Greek household: the archaeological evidence. *Annual of the British School at Athens* 90: 363–81.

1999. *House and Society in the Ancient Greek World.* Cambridge: Cambridge University Press.

Newton, Sir C.T. 1862a. *A History of Discoveries at Halicarnassus, Cnidus and Branchidae. Vol. I: Plates.* London: Day and Son.

1862b. *A History of Discoveries at Halicarnassus, Cnidus and Branchidae. Vol. II. Part I.* [text] London: Day and Son.

1863. *A History of Discoveries at Halicarnassus, Cnidus and Branchidae. Vol. II. Part 2.* [text] London: Day and Son.

Nicholls, R.V. 1959. Old Smyrna: the Iron Age fortifications and associated remains on the city perimeter. *Annual of the British School at Athens* 53–4 [1958–9]: 35–137.

1983. Early monumental religious architecture at Old Smyrna. In D. Buitron-Oliver (ed.), *New Perspectives in Early Greek Art*, 151–71. Hanover, NH: University Press of New England.

Niemeyer, H.G. 1990. The Phoenicians in the Mediterranean: a non-Greek model for expansion and settlement in Antiquity. In Descœudres 1990: 469–89.

(ed.) 1996. *Die Akten des Internationalen Kolloquiums 'Interactions in the Iron Age: Phoenicians, Greeks and Indigenous Peoples in the Western Mediterranean'.* Hamburger Beiträge zur Archäologie 19/20. Mainz: Philipp von Zabern.

Noack, F. 1927. *Eleusis: Die baugeschichtliche Entwicklung des Heiligums.* 2 volumes, text and plates. Berlin and Leipzig: Walter de Gruyter.

Nowicki, K. 1987a. The history and setting of the town at Karphi. *Studi Micenei ed Egeo Anatolici* 26 (Rome): 257–79.

1987b. Topography of refuge settlement in Crete. *Jahrbuch des römisch-germanisch Zentralmuseums Mainz* 34: 213–34.

1999. Economy of refugees: life in the Cretan mountains at the turn of the Bronze and Iron Ages. In A. Chaniotis (ed.), *From Minoan Farmers to Roman Traders: Sidelights on the Economy of Ancient Crete*, 145–71. Stuttgart: Franz Steiner Verlag.

Nylander, C. 1962. Die sog. mykenischen Säulenbasen auf der Akropolis in Athen. *Opuscula Atheniensia* 4: 31–47.

Oakley, J. 1992. An Athenian red-figure workshop from the time of the Peloponnesian war. In Blondé and Perreault 1992: 195–203.

1997. *The Achilles Painter.* Mainz: Philipp von Zabern.

Ober, J. 1985. *Fortress Attica: Defense of the Athenian Land Frontier 404–322 BC.* Leiden: E.J. Brill.

1987a. Early artillery towers: Messenia, Boiotia, Attica, Megarid. *American Journal of Archaeology* 91: 569–604.

1987b. Pottery and miscellaneous artefacts from fortified sites in northern and western Attica. *Hesperia* 56: 197–227.

Ohly, D. 1953. *Griechische Goldbleche des 8. Jahrhunderts v. Chr.* Berlin: Deutsches archäologisches Institut.

1967. Neue Holzfunde aus den Heraion von Samos: Befund und Rekonstruktion der Herastatuette. *Mitteilungen des deutschen archäologischen Instituts, athenische Abteilung* 82: 89–99.

Osborne, R. 1985. *Demos: The Discovery of Classical Attika.* Cambridge: Cambridge University Press.

1986. Island towers: the case of Thasos. *Annual of the British School at Athens* 81: 166–78.

1987a. *Classical Landscape with Figures: The Ancient Greek City and Its Countryside.* London: George Philip.

1987b. The viewing and obscuring of the Parthenon frieze. *Journal of Hellenic Studies* 107: 98–105.

1988. Death revisited, death revised: the death of the artist in Archaic and Classical Greece. *Art History* 11: 1–16.

1989. A crisis in archaeological history? The seventh century BC in Attica. *Annual of the British School at Athens* 84: 297–322.

1994a. Looking on – Greek style. Does the sculpted girl speak to women too? In Morris 1994a: 81–96.

1994b Framing the centaur: reading fifth-century architectural sculpture. In Goldhill and Osborne 1994: 52–84.

1996a. *Greece in the Making, 1200–479 BC*. London: Routledge.

1996b. Pots, trade and the Archaic Greek economy. *Antiquity* 70: 31–44.

1998a. *Archaic and Classical Greek Art*. Oxford: Oxford University Press.

1998b. Inter-personal relations on Athenian pots: putting others in their place. In P. Cartledge, P. Millett and S. Von Reden (eds.), *Kosmos: Essays in Order, Conflict and Community in Classical Athens*, 13–36. Cambridge: Cambridge University Press.

1998c. Early Greek colonization? The nature of Greek settlement in the West. In Fisher and Van Wees 1998: 251–69.

Palagia, O. 1993. *The Pediments of the Parthenon*. Leiden: E.J. Brill.

Palaiokrassa, L. 1989. Neue Befunde aus dem Heiligtum der Artemis Munichia. *Mitteilungen des deutschen archäologischen Instituts, athenische Abteilung* 104: 1–40.

Papadopoulos, J.K. 1993. To kill a cemetery: the Athenian Kerameikos and the Early Iron Age in the Aegean. *Journal of Mediterranean Archaeology* 6: 175–206.

1996. Euboians in Macedonia? A closer look. *Oxford Journal of Archaeology* 15: 151–81.

1997. Phantom Euboians. *Journal of Mediterranean Archaeology* 10: 191–219.

Pariente, A. 1992. Le monument argien des 'Sept contre Thèbes'. In Piérart 1992: 195–225.

Pashley, R. 1837a. *Travels in Crete*. Vol I. London: John Murray.

1837b. *Travels in Crete*. Vol II. London: John Murray.

Payne, H.G.G. 1926. On the Thermon metopes. *Annual of the British School at Athens* 27 [1925–6]: 124–32.

1928. Early Greek vases from Knossos. *Annual of the British School at Athens* 29: 224–98.

1931. *Necrocorinthia: A Study of Corinthian Art in the Archaic Period*. Oxford: Clarendon.

1940. *Perachora: The Sanctuaries of Hera Akraia and Limenia I: Architecture, Bronzes, Terracottas*. Oxford: Clarendon.

Payne, H.G.G. and Mackworth-Young, G. 1950. *Archaic Marble Sculpture from the Acropolis*. Revised edition. London: Cresset Press.

Peatfield, A. 1994. After the 'Big Bang' – what? or, Minoan symbols and shrines beyond Palatial collapse. In Alcock and Osborne 1994: 19–36.

Pedersen, P. 1991a. *The Maussolleion at Halikarnassos 3.1: The Maussolleion Terrace and Accessory Structures: Text and Appendices*. Aarhus: Aarhus University Press.

1991b. *The Maussolleion at Halikarnassos 3.2: The Maussolleion Terrace and Accessory Structures: Catalogue*. Aarhus: Aarhus University Press.

Pedley, J.G. 1990. *Paestum: Greeks and Romans in Southern Italy*. London: Thames and Hudson.

1993. *Greek Art and Archaeology*. Englewood Cliffs, NJ: Prentice Hall.

Peek, W. 1941. *Kerameikos: Ergebnisse der Ausgrabungen III: Inschriften: Ostraka: Fluchtafeln*. Berlin: Walter de Gruyter.

Pendlebury, J.D.S. 1939. *The Archaeology of Crete: An Introduction*. London: Methuen.

Pendlebury, J.D.S., Pendlebury, H.W. and Money-Coutts, M.B. 1938. Excavations in the plain of Lasithi III: Karphi: a city of refuge of the Early Iron Age of Crete. *Annual of the British School at Athens* 38 [1937–8]: 57–145.

Pernier, L. 1914. Templi arcaici sulla Patela di Prinias in Creta. *Annuario della Scuola Italiana di Atene e della Missioni Italiane in Oriente* 1: 18–111.

Petit, Th. 1999. Eteocypriot myth and Amathusian reality. *Journal of Mediterranean Archaeology* 12: 108–20.

Petsas, Ph. 1978. *Pella: Alexander the Great's Capital.* Thessaloniki: Institute for Balkan Studies.

Pfuhl, E. 1926. *Masterpieces of Greek Drawing and Painting.* Translated from the German by J.D. Beazley. London: Chatto and Windus.

Philipp, H. 1981. *Bronzeschmuck aus Olympia: Olympische Forschungen XIII.* Berlin: Walter de Gruyter.

Picard, C. 1963. Usages funéraires grecs récemment révélés en Macédoine et Scythie Mineure. *Revue Archéologique* 1: 179–94.

Picard, O. (ed.) 1992. *La Redécouverte de Delphes.* Paris: Editions de Boccard.

Pickard-Cambridge, A.W. 1946. *The Theatre of Dionysus in Athens.* Oxford: Clarendon.

Piérart, M. (ed.) 1992. *Polydipsion Argos: Argos de la fin des palais mycéniens à la constitution de l'état classique.* Bulletin de Correspondance Hellénique Supplément 22. Athens: Ecole Française d'Athènes.

Plantzos, D. 1999. *Hellenistic Engraved Gems.* Oxford: Clarendon.

Plommer, W.H. 1950. Three Attic temples. *Annual of the British School at Athens* 45: 66–112.

1960. The Archaic Acropolis: some problems. *Journal of Hellenic Studies* 78: 127–59.

Plommer, W.H. and Salviat, F. 1966. The altar of Hera Akraia at Perachora. *Annual of the British School at Athens* 61: 207–15.

Pollitt, J.J. 1972. *Art and Experience in Classical Greece.* Cambridge: Cambridge University Press.

1986. *Art in the Hellenistic Age.* Cambridge: Cambridge University Press.

1990. *The Art of Ancient Greece: Sources and Documents.* Cambridge: Cambridge University Press.

Pomeroy, S.B. 1975. *Goddesses, Whores, Wives and Slaves: Women in Classical Antiquity.* London: Robert Hale and Company.

Popham, M.R. 1986. A late Minoan IIIC pyxis in the Andreades collection. *Oxford Journal of Archaeology* 5: 157–64.

1987. An early Euboean ship. *Oxford Journal of Archaeology* 6: 353–9.

1995. An engraved Near Eastern bronze bowl from Lefkandi. *Oxford Journal of Archaeology* 14: 103–7.

1997. The final destruction of the palace at Knossos: seals, sealings and pottery: a reconsideration. In Driessen and Farnoux 1997: 375–85.

Popham, M.R., Calligas, P.G. and Sackett, L.H. 1989. Further excavation of the Toumba cemetery at Lefkandi, 1984 and 1986, a preliminary report. *Archaeological Reports* 35 [1988–9]: 117–29.

1993. *Lefkandi II.2. The Protogeometric Building at Toumba: The Excavation, Architecture and Finds.* London: The British School at Athens.

Popham, M.R. and Lemos, I. 1995. A Euboean warrior-trader. *Oxford Journal of Archaeology* 14: 151–7.

1996. *Lefkandi III: The Toumba Cemetery* (plates). London: British School at Athens.

Popham, M.R., Sackett, L.H. and Themelis, P.G. 1980. *Lefkandi I: The Iron Age Settlement and Cemeteries.* 2 volumes, text and plates. British School at Athens Supplemenary Volume 11. London: Thames and Hudson.

Popham, M.R., Sackett, L.H. and Touloupa, E. 1982a. The hero of Lefkandi. *Antiquity* 56: 169–74.

1982b. Further excavations at Lefkandi in 1981. *Annual of the British School at Athens* 77: 214–48.

Porada, E. 1963. Seals. In Goldman 1963: 347–58.

Potts, A. 1982. Winckelmann's construction of history. *Art History* 5: 377–407.

1994. *Flesh and the Ideal: Winckelmann and the Origins of Art History.* New Haven: Yale University Press.

Pouilloux, J. 1960. *Fouilles de Delphes II: topographie et architecture: la région nord du sanctuaire (de l'époque archaïque à la fin du sanctuaire).* Paris: de Boccard.

Powell, B.B. 1991. *Homer and the Origin of the Greek Alphabet.* Cambridge: Cambridge University Press.

1992. Homer and the origin of the Greek alphabet. *Cambridge Archaeological Journal* 2: 115–26.

1997. From picture to myth, from myth to picture. In Langdon 1997: 154–93.

Prag, A.J.N. 1990. Reconstructing King Philip II: the 'nice' version. *American Journal of Archaeology* 94: 237–47.

Prag, A.J.N., Musgrave, J.H. and Neave, R.A.H. 1984. The skull from tomb II at Vergina: King Philip II of Macedon. *Journal of Hellenic Studies* 104: 60–78.

Preka-Alexandri, K. 1992. A ceramic workshop in Figareto, Corfu. In Blondé and Perreault 1992: 41–52.

Purcell, N. 1990. Mobility and the *polis*. In Murray and Price 1990: 29–58.

Qviller, B. 1981. The dynamics of Homeric society. *Symbolae Osloenses* 56: 109–55.

Raaflaub, K. 1998. A historian's headache: how to read 'Homeric society'? In Fisher and Van Wees 1998: 169–93.

Rackham, O. 1983. Observations on the historical ecology of Boeotia. *Annual of the British School at Athens* 78: 291–351.

1990. Ancient landscapes. In Murray and Price 1990: 85–111.

Rackham, O. and Moody, J. 1992. Terraces. In Wells 1992: 123–30.

1996. *The Making of the Cretan Landscape.* Manchester: Manchester University Press.

Radet, G. 1992. La Grande Fouille vue par un contemporain. In Picard 1992: 144–79.

Rapp, G. Jn. and Aschenbrenner, S.E. (eds.) 1978. *Excavations at Nichoria in Southwest Greece I: Site, Environs and Techniques.* Minneapolis: University of Minnesota Press.

Rapp, G. Jn., Jones, R.E., Cooke, S.R.B. and Henrickson, E.L. 1978. Analyses of the metal artifacts. In Rapp and Aschenbrenner 1978: 166–81.

Rasmussen, T. 1985. Etruscan shapes in Attic pottery. *Antike Kunst* 28: 33–9.

1991. Corinth and the Orientalizing phenomenon. In Rasmussen and Spivey 1991: 57–78.

Rasmussen, T. and Spivey, N. (eds.) 1991. *Looking at Greek Vases.* Cambridge: Cambridge University Press.

Rathje, A. 1979. Oriental imports in Etruria in the eighth and seventh centuries BC: their origins and implications. In D. and F. Ridgway (eds.), *Italy before the Romans: The Iron Age, Orientalising and Etruscan Periods,* 145–83. New York and London: Academic Press.

Raubitschek, A.E. 1949. *Dedications from the Athenian Acropolis: A Catalogue of the Inscriptions of the Sixth and Fifth Centuries BC.* Cambridge, MA: Archaeological Institute of America/Harvard University Press.

Raubitschek, I.K. 1998. *Isthmia VII: The Metal Objects (1952–1989).* Princeton: American School of Classical Studies at Athens.

Renfrew, C. 1972. *The Emergence of Civilisation: The Cyclades and the Aegean in the Third Millennium BC.* London: Methuen.

1973. *Social Archaeology: An Inaugural Lecture.* Southampton: University of Southampton.

1975. Trade as action at a distance: questions of integration and communication. In J.A. Sabloff and C.C. Lamberg-Karlovsky (eds.), *Ancient Civilization and Trade*, 3–59. Albuquerque: University of New Mexico Press.

1981. The sanctuary at Phylakopi. In Hägg and Marinatos 1981: 67–80.

1984. *Approaches to Social Archaeology*. Edinburgh: Edinburgh University Press.

1986. Introduction: peer polity interaction and socio-political change. In Renfrew and Cherry 1986: 1–18.

Renfrew, C. and Cherry, J.F. (eds.) 1986. *Peer Polity Interaction and Socio-Political Change*. Cambridge: Cambridge University Press.

Renfrew, C. and Wagstaff, M. (eds.) 1982. *An Island Polity: The Archaeology of Exploitation in Melos*. Cambridge: Cambridge University Press.

Rhomaios, K. 1916. Ek tou proistorikou Thermou. *Archaiologikon Deltion* 1 [1915]: 225–79.

1955. To anaktoron tis Palatitsas. *Archaiologiki Ephemeris 1953–4: Eis Mnimin Georgiou P. Oikonomou*. Vol. I: 141–50.

Rich, J. and Wallace-Hadrill, A. (eds.) 1991. *City and Country in the Ancient World*. London: Routledge.

Richter, G.M.A. 1961. *Archaic Gravestones of Attica*. London: Phaidon.

1968. *Korai: Archaic Greek Maidens*. London: Phaidon.

1970. *Kouroi: Archaic Greek Youths*. 3rd edition. London: Phaidon.

Richter, G.M.A. and Milne, M.J. 1935. *Shapes and Names of Athenian Vases*. New York: Metropolitan Museum of Art.

Richter, G.M.A. and Smith, R.R.R. 1984. *Portraits of the Greeks*. (Abridged and revised.) Ithaca, NY: Cornell University Press.

Ridgway, B.S. 1970. *The Severe Style in Greek Sculpture*. Princeton: Princeton University Press.

1977. *The Archaic Style in Greek Sculpture*. Princeton: Princeton University Press.

1981. *Fifth Century Styles in Greek Sculpture*. Princeton: Princeton University Press.

1984. *Roman Copies of Greek Sculpture: The Problem of the Originals*. Ann Arbor: University of Michigan Press.

Ridgway, D. 1992. *The First Western Greeks*. Cambridge: Cambridge University Press.

1994. Phoenicians and Greeks in the West: a view from Pithekoussai. In Tsetskhladze and de Angelis 1994: 35–46.

Ridgway, D. and Ridgway, F.R.S. 1992. Sardinia and history. In Tykot and Andrews 1992: 355–63.

Rizza, G. and Scrinari, V.S.M. 1968. *Il Santuario sull'Acropoli di Gortina*. Rome: Libreria dello Stato.

Robertson, M. 1965. Greek mosaics. *Journal of Hellenic Studies* 85: 72–89.

1975. *A History of Greek Art*. 2 volumes, text and plates. Cambridge: Cambridge University Press.

1981. *A Shorter History of Greek Art*. Cambridge: Cambridge University Press.

1985. Beazley and Attic vase painting. In Kurtz 1985: 19–30.

1992. *The Art of Vase Painting in Classical Athens*. Cambridge: Cambridge University Press.

Robertson, M. and Franz, A. 1975. *The Parthenon Frieze*. London: Phaidon.

Robinson, D.M. 1930. *Excavations at Olynthus II: Architecture and Sculpture: Houses and Other Buildings*. Baltimore: Johns Hopkins Press.

1933a. *Excavations at Olynthus V: Mosaics, Vases and Lamps of Olynthus found in 1928 and 1931*. Baltimore: Johns Hopkins Press.

1933b. *Excavations at Olynthus VII: The Terra-Cottas of Olynthus found in 1931*. Baltimore: Johns Hopkins Press.

1946. *Excavations at Olynthus XII: Domestic and Public Architecture.* Baltimore: Johns Hopkins Press.

1950. *Excavations at Olynthus XIII: Vases found in 1934 and 1938.* Baltimore: Johns Hopkins Press.

Robinson, D.M. and Angel, J.L. 1942. *Excavations at Olynthus XI: Necrolynthia: A Study in Greek Burial Customs and Anthropology.* Baltimore: Johns Hopkins Press.

Robinson, D.M. and Graham, J.W. 1938. *Excavations at Olynthus VIII: The Hellenic House: A Study of the Houses Found at Olynthus with a Detailed Account of Those Excavated in 1931 and 1934.* Baltimore: Johns Hopkins Press.

Robinson, H.S. 1976. Excavations at Corinth: Temple Hill, 1968–72. *Hesperia* 45: 203–29.

Rodenwaldt, G. 1939. *Korkyra: Archaische Bauten und Bildwerke II: Die Bildwerke des Artemistempels von Korkyra.* Berlin: Gebr. Mann.

1940. *Korkyra: Archaische Bauten und Bildwerke: Der Artemistempel: Architektur, Dachterrakoten, Inschriften.* Berlin: Gebr. Mann.

Roebuck, C. 1972. Some aspects of urbanization in Corinth. *Hesperia* 41: 96–127.

Roebuck, M.C. 1990. Archaic architectural terracottas from Corinth. *Hesperia* 59: 47–63.

Rolley, C. 1984. Delphes? Non! In Borea 1984: 327–330.

1990. En regardant L'Aurige. *Bulletin de Correspondance Hellénique* 114: 285–97.

1992. Argos, Corinthe, Athènes: identité culturelle et modes de développement. In Piérart 1992: 37–49.

Ross, L. 1855. *Archäologische Aufsätze.* Vol. I. Leipzig: B.G. Teubner.

1861. *Archäologische Aufsätze.* Vol. II. Leipzig: B.G. Teubner.

Rotroff, S.I. 1982. *The Athenian Agora XXII: Hellenistic Pottery: Athenian and Imported Moldmade Bowls.* Princeton: American School of Classical Studies at Athens.

1984. Spool saltcellars in the Athenian Agora. *Hesperia* 53: 342–54.

1996. *The Missing Krater and the Hellenistic Symposium: Drinking in the Age of Alexander the Great.* Broadhead Classical Lecture 7. University of Canterbury, Christchurch, NZ.

1997. *The Athenian Agora XXIX: Hellenistic Pottery: Athenian and Imported Wheelmade Table Ware and Related Material.* 2 volumes, text and plates. Princeton: American School of Classical Studies at Athens.

Rotroff, S.I. and Camp, J.M. 1996. The date of the third period of the Pnyx. *Hesperia* 65: 263–94.

Rotroff, S.I. and Oakley, J.H. 1992. *Debris from a Public Dining Place in the Athenian Agora.* *Hesperia* Supplement 25. Princeton: American School of Classical Studies at Athens.

Rouse, W.H.D. 1902. *Greek Votive Offerings: An Essay in the History of Greek Religion.* Cambridge: Cambridge University Press.

Runciman, W.G. 1990. Doomed to extinction: the *polis* as an evolutionary dead end. In Murray and Price 1990: 347–67.

Runnels, C., Pullen, D.J. and Langdon, S. 1995. *Artifact and Assemblage: The Finds from a Regional Survey of the Southern Argolid, Greece. Vol. I: The Prehistoric and Iron Age Pottery and the Lithic Artifacts.* Stanford: Stanford University Press.

Rupp, D.W. 1983. Reflections on the development of altars in the eighth century BC. In Hägg 1983b: 101–7.

Russell, J.M. 1993. Sennacherib's Lachish Narratives. In Holliday 1993: 55–73.

Russo, C.F. 1993. Appendice I: L'iscrizione della *kotyle* 168–9. In Buchner and Ridgway 1993: 743–59.

Rutkowski, B. 1987. The temple at Karphi. *Studi Micenei ed Egeo Anatolici* 26 (Rome): 257–79.

Sackett, L.H. (ed.) 1992. *Knossos: From Greek City to Roman Colony: Excavations at the Unexplored Mansion II.* London: Thames and Hudson.

Sackett, L.H., Hankey, V., Howell, R.J., Jacobsen, T.W. and M.R. Popham 1966. Euboea: contributions towards a survey. *Annual of the British School at Athens* 61: 33–112.

Sahlins, M. 1999. Two or three things I know about culture. *Journal of the Royal Anthropological Institute* 5: 399–421.

Said, E.W. 1995. *Orientalism: Western Conceptions of the Orient.* 2nd edition, with afterword. Harmondsworth: Penguin.

Sakellarakis, J.A. 1988. Some Geometric and Archaic votives from the Idaean Cave. In Hägg *et al.* 1988: 173–93.

Sallares, R. 1991. *The Ecology of the Ancient Greek World.* London: Duckworth.

Salmon, J. 1977. Political hoplites? *Journal of Hellenic Studies* 97: 84–101.

2000. Pots and profits. In Tsetskhladze *et al.* 2000: 245–52.

Salzmann, D. 1982. *Untersuchungen zu den antiken Kieselmosaiken von den Anfängen bis zum Beginn der Tessaratechnik.* Berlin: Gebr. Mann.

Schaber, W. 1982. *Die archaischen Tempel der Artemis von Ephesos.* Stiftland: Verlag Waldsassen.

Schaus, G.P. 1985. *The Extramural Sanctuary of Demeter and Persephone at Cyrene, Libya: Final Reports II: The East Greek, Island and Laconian Pottery.* Philadelphia: University Museum, University of Pennsylvania.

Schiering, W. 1991. *Die Werkstatt des Pheidias in Olympia II: Werkstattfunde: Olympische Forschungen XVIII.* Berlin: Walter de Gruyter.

Schleif, H. 1934. Der Zeusaltar in Olympia. *Jahrbuch des deutschen archäologischen Instituts, athenische Abteilung* 49: 139–56.

Schmitt-Pantel, P. 1992. *La Cité au banquet: histoire des repas publis dans les cités antiques.* Paris and Rome: de Boccard and Ecole Française de Rome.

Schnapp, A. 1984. Eros en chasse. In Bérard *et al.* 1984: 67–83.

1989. Eros the hunter. In Bérard *et al.* 1989: 71–88.

1994. Are images animated? The psychology of statues in Ancient Greece. In C. Renfrew and E. Zubrow (eds.), *The Ancient Mind: Elements of Cognitive Archaeology,* 40–4. Cambridge: Cambridge University Press.

1996. *The Discovery of the Past: The Origins of Archaeology.* Translated from the French by Ian Kinnes and Gillian Varndell. London: British Museum Press.

Schuller, W., Hoepfner, W. and Schwandner, E.L. (eds.) 1989. *Demokratie und Architektur: Der hippodamische Städtbau und die Entstehung der Demokratie.* Munich: Deutscher Kunstverlag.

Schwandner, E.L. 1985. *Der ältare Porostempel der Aphaia auf Aegina.* Berlin: Walter de Gruyter.

Schweitzer, B. 1917. *Untersuchungen zur Chronologie der geometrischen Stile in Griechenland I.* Karlsruhe: G. Braunsche Hofbuckdruckerei.

1918. Untersuchungen zur Chronologie und Geschichte der geometrischen Stile in Griechenland. *Mitteilungen des deutschen archäologischen Instituts, athenische Abteilung* 43: 1–152.

1971. *Greek Geometric Art.* Translated from the German by Peter and Cornelia Usborne. London: Phaidon.

Scranton, R.L. 1938. The fortifications of Attica at the opening of the Peloponnesian war. *American Journal of Archaeology* 43: 525–36.

1941. *Greek Walls.* Cambridge, MA: Harvard University Press.

Scully, V. 1979. *The Earth, the Temple and the Gods: Greek Sacred Architecture.* Revised edition. New Haven: Yale University Press.

Shanks, M. 1993. Style and the design of a perfume jar from an Archaic Greek city state. *Journal of European Archaeology* 1: 77–106.

1995. *Classical Archaeology of Greece: Experiences of the Discipline*. London: Routledge.

1999. *Art and the Early Greek State: An Interpretive Archaeology*. Cambridge: Cambridge University Press.

Shapiro, H.A. 1989. *Art and Cult under the Tyrants in Athens*. Mainz: Philipp von Zabern.

1998. Autochthony and the visual arts in fifth-century Athens. In Boedeker and Raaflaub 1998: 127–51.

Shaw, J. 1989. Phoenicians in southern Crete. *American Journal of Archaeology* 93: 165–83.

Shay, J.M. and Shay, C.T. 1978. Modern vegetation and fossil plant remains. In Rapp and Aschenbrenner 1978: 41–59.

Shear, T.L. Jn. 1970. The monument of the Eponymous Heroes in the Athenian Agora. *Hesperia* 39: 145–222.

1971. The Athenian Agora: excavations of 1970. *Hesperia* 40: 241–79.

1973a. The Athenian Agora: excavations of 1971. *Hesperia* 42: 121–79.

1973b. The Athenian Agora: excavations of 1972. *Hesperia* 42: 359–407.

1975. The Athenian Agora: excavations of 1973–4. *Hesperia* 44: 331–74.

1984. The Athenian Agora: excavations of 1980–82. *Hesperia* 53: 1–57.

1993. The Persian destruction of Athens: evidence from Agora deposits. *Hesperia* 62: 383–482.

1994. 'Isonomous t'Athenas epoiesatin': the Agora and the Democracy. In Coulson *et al.* 1994: 225–48.

Sherratt, E.S. 1994. Commerce, iron and ideology: metallurgical innovation in 12th–11th century Cyprus. In V. Karageorghis (ed.), *Cyprus in the 11th Century BC: Proceedings of the International Symposium*. Nicosia: University of Cyprus/A.G. Leventis Foundation.

Simon, E. 1983. *Festivals of Attica: An Archaeological Commentary*. Madison: University of Wisconsin Press.

Sloan, R.E. and Duncan, M.A. 1978. Zooarchaeology at Nichoria. In Rapp and Aschenbrenner 1978: 60–77.

Smith, A.H. 1892. *A Catalogue of Sculpture in the Department of Greek and Roman Antiquities, British Museum*. Vol. I. London: British Museum.

1900. *A Catalogue of Sculpture in the Department of Greek and Roman Antiquities, British Museum*. Vol. II. London: British Museum.

1916. Lord Elgin and his collection. *Journal of Hellenic Studies* 36: 163–372.

Smith, C. 1902. A Proto-Attic vase. *Journal of Hellenic Studies* 22: 29–45.

Smith, R.R.R. 1988. *Hellenistic Royal Portraits*. Oxford: Clarendon.

1991. *Hellenistic Sculpture*. London: Thames and Hudson.

Snodgrass, A.M. 1964. *Early Greek Armour and Weapons*. Edinburgh: Edinburgh University Press.

1965. The hoplite reform and history. *Journal of Hellenic Studies* 85: 110–22.

1971. *The Dark Age of Greece: An Archaeological Survey of the Eleventh to the Eighth Centuries BC*. Edinburgh: Edinburgh University Press.

1974. An historical Homeric society? *Journal of Hellenic Studies* 94: 114–25.

1977. *Archaeology and the Rise of the Greek State*. Cambridge: Cambridge University Press.

1980a. *Archaic Greece: The Age of Experiment*. Berkeley and Los Angeles: University of California Press.

1980b. Towards the interpretation of the Geometric figure scenes. *Mitteilungen des deutschen archäologischen Instituts, athenische Abteilung* 95: 51–8.

1982. *Narration and Allusion in Archaic Greek Art.* Eleventh J.L. Myres memorial lecture. London: Leopard's Head Press.

1983a. Cyprus and the beginnings of iron technology in the eastern Mediterranean. In Muhly *et al.* 1983: 285–94.

1983b. Two demographic notes. In Hägg 1983b: 167–71.

1985. The site of Askra. In Argoud and Roesch 1985: 87–95.

1986. Interaction by design: the Greek city state. In Renfrew and Cherry 1986: 47–58.

1987. *An Archaeology of Greece: The Present State and Future Scope of a Discipline.* Berkeley and Los Angeles: University of California Press.

1989. The coming of the Iron Age in Greece: Europe's earliest Bronze/Iron transition. In M.L.S. Sorensen and R. Thomas (eds.), *The Bronze Age–Iron Age Transition in Europe: Aspects of Continuity and Change in European Societies c.1200–500 BC*, 22–35. BAR IS 483(i). Oxford: British Archaeological Reports.

1990a. Survey archaeology and the rural landscape of the Greek city. In Murray and Price 1990: 113–36.

1990b. The economics of dedication at Greek sanctuaries. *Scienze dell'Antichità: Storia, Archeologia, Antropologia* 3–4 [1989–90]: 287–94.

1991. Archaeology and the study of the Greek city. In Rich and Wallace-Hadrill 1991: 1–23.

1994. Response: the archaeological aspect. In Morris 1994b: 197–200.

1996. Iron. In Coldstream and Catling 1996: 575–97.

1998. *Homer and the Artists: Text and Picture in Early Greek Art.* Cambridge: Cambridge University Press.

1999. *Arms and Armor of the Greeks.* 2nd edition. Baltimore: Johns Hopkins University Press.

Snycer, M. 1979. L'inscription phénicienne de Tekke, près de Cnossos. *Kadmos* 18: 89–93.

Sørensen, K.A. 1981. A zoological analysis of the osteological material from the sacrificial layer at the Maussolleion at Halikarnassos. In Jeppesen *et al.* 1981: 91–110.

Soteriadis, G. 1900. Anaskaphai en Thermo. *Archaiologiki Ephemeris* 3: 161–211.

Sourvinou-Inwood, C. 1993. Early sanctuaries, the eighth century and ritual space: fragments of a discourse. In Marinatos and Hägg 1993: 1–17.

1995. *'Reading' Greek Death: To the End of the Classical Period.* Oxford: Clarendon.

Sparkes, B. 1982. Classical and Roman Melos. In Renfrew and Wagstaff 1982: 45–53.

1991. *Greek Pottery: An Introduction.* Manchester: Manchester University Press.

1996. *The Red and the Black: Studies in Greek Pottery.* London: Routledge.

Sparkes, B. and Talcott, L. 1970. *The Athenian Agora XII: Black and Plain Pottery of the 6th, 5th and 4th Centuries BC.* 2 volumes, text and plates. Princeton: American School of Classical Studies at Athens.

Spencer, N. 1995a. Multi-dimensional group definition in the landscape of rural Greece. In Spencer 1995b: 28–42.

(ed.) 1995b. *Time, Tradition and Society in Greek Archaeology: Bridging the 'Great Divide'.* London: Routledge.

Spitaels, P. 1978. Insula 3: Tower compound 1. In P. Spitaels, J. Bingen, A. Uyttendaele, F. Blondé, K. Van Gelder, A. Cheliotis and A. Helsen, *Thorikos 1970–71: rapport préliminaire sur les septième et huitième campagnes de fouilles*, 39–110. Ghent: Comité des Fouilles Belges en Grèce.

Spivey, N. 1991. Greek vases in Etruria. In Rasmussen and Spivey 1991: 131–50.

1994. Psephological heroes. In R. Osborne and S. Hornblower (eds.), *Ritual, Finance,*

Politics: Athenian Democratic Accounts Presented to David Lewis, 39–51. Oxford: Clarendon.

1996. *Understanding Greek Sculpture: Ancient Meanings, Modern Readings*. London: Thames and Hudson.

Spratt, T.A.B. 1865a. *Travels and Researches in Crete*. Vol. I. London: John van Voorst.

1865b. *Travels and Researches in Crete*. Vol. II. London: John van Voorst.

Stais, V. 1890. O tymvos en Vourva. *Mitteilungen des deutschen archäologischen Instituts, athenische Abteilung* 15: 318–29.

1893. O en Marathoni Tymvos. *Mitteilungen des deutschen archäologischen Instituts, athenische Abteilung* 18: 46–63.

1917. Sounio anaskaphi. *Archaiologiki Ephemeris:* 168–213.

Stais, V. and Wolters, P. 1891. Amphora aus Athen. *Antike Denkmaeler herausgegeben vom kaiserlich deutschen archaeologischen Institut* 1.5: 46–8.

Stansbury-O'Donnell, M.D. 1989. Polygnotos' *Iliupersis*: a new reconstruction. *American Journal of Archaeology* 93: 203–15.

1990. Polygnotos' *Nekyia*: a reconstruction and analysis. *American Journal of Archaeology* 94: 213–35.

1999. *Pictorial Narrative in Ancient Greek Art*. Cambridge: Cambridge University Press.

St. Clair, W. 1967. *Lord Elgin and the Marbles*. Oxford: Oxford University Press.

Stears, K. Dead women's society: constructing female gender in Athenian funerary sculpture. In Spencer 1995b: 109–31.

Steinhauer, G. 1994. Paratiriseis stin oikistiki morphi ton attikon dimon. In Coulson *et al.* 1994: 175–89.

Stevens, G.P., Caskey, L.D., Fowler, H.N. and Paton, J.M. 1927. *The Erechtheum*. 2 volumes, text and plates. Cambridge, MA: Harvard University Press.

Stewart, A. 1986. When is a kouros not an Apollo? The Tenea 'Apollo' revisited. In M.A. del Chiaro (ed.), *Corinthiaca: Studies in Honor of Darell M. Amyx*, 54–70. Columbia: University of Missouri Press.

1987. Narrative, genre and realism in the work of the Amasis painter. In [no editor] *Papers on the Amasis Painter and His World*, 29–42. Malibu: J. Paul Getty Museum.

1990. *Greek Sculpture: An Exploration*. 2 volumes, text and plates. New Haven: Yale University Press.

1997. *Art, Desire and the Body in Ancient Greece*. Cambridge: Cambridge University Press.

Stikas, E.G. 1939. Anaskaphi 'Eleftheron' (Panaktou). *Praktika tis en Athinais Archaiologikis Etaireias* 1938 [1939]: 41–9.

Stillwell, R. 1969. The Panathenaic frieze: optical relations. *Hesperia* 38: 231–41.

Stilwell, A.N. 1948. *Corinth XV.i: The Potters' Quarter*. Princeton: American School of Classical Studies at Athens.

1952. *Corinth XV.ii: The Potters' Quarter: The Terracottas*. Princeton: American School of Classical Studies at Athens.

Stilwell, A.N. and Benson, J.L. 1984. *Corinth XV.iii: The Potters' Quarter: The Pottery*. Princeton: American School of Classical Studies at Athens.

Stoddart, S. and Whitley, J. 1988. The social context of literacy in Archaic Greece and Etruria. *Antiquity* 62: 761–72.

Stoneman, R. 1987. *Land of Lost Gods: The Search for Classical Greece*. London: Hutchinson.

Strøm, I. 1988. The early sanctuary of the Argive Heraion and its external relations (8th–early 6th century BC): the monumental architecture. *Acta Archaeologica* 59: 173–203.

1992. Evidence from the sanctuaries. In Kopcke and Tokumaru 1992: 46–60.

Stroud, R.S. 1968. *Drakon's Law on Homicide*. Berkeley and Los Angeles: University of California Press.

    1979. *The Axones and Kyrbeis of Solon and Drakon*. Berkeley and Los Angeles: University of California Press.

Stuart, J. and Revett, N. 1762. *The Antiquities of Athens*. Vol. I. London: John Haberkorn.

    1787. *The Antiquities of Athens*. Vol. II. London: John Nichols.

    1794. *The Antiquities of Athens*. Vol. III. London: John Nichols.

    1816. *The Antiquities of Athens*. Vol. IV. London: T. Bensley.

Stupperich, R. 1994. The iconography of Athenian state burials in the Classical period. In Coulson *et al.* 1994: 93–103.

Tainter, J.A. 1978. Mortuary practices and the study of prehistoric social systems. In M.B. Schiffer (ed.), *Advances in Archaeological Method and Theory* I, 105–41. New York and London: Academic Press.

    1988. *The Collapse of Complex Societies*. Cambridge: Cambridge University Press.

Talcott, L. 1936. Vases and kalos names from an Agora well. *Hesperia* 5: 333–54.

Tandy, D.W. 1997. *Warriors into Traders: The Power of the Market in Early Greece*. Berkeley and Los Angeles: University of California Press.

Tanner, J. 1999. Culture, social structure and the status of visual artists in Classical Greece. *Proceedings of the Cambridge Philological Society* 45: 136–75.

Tanoulas, T. 1994a. The Propylaea and the western access of the Acropolis. In Economokakis 1994: 52–67.

    1994b. The restoration of the Propylaea. In Economokakis 1994: 150–67.

    1994c. New discoveries at the Propylaea. In Economokakis 1994: 181–3.

Theodossiev, N. 1998. The dead with golden faces: Dasaretian, Pelagonian, Mygdonian and Boeotian funeral masks. *Oxford Journal of Archaeology* 17: 345–67.

Thomas, R. 1989. *Oral Tradition and Written Record in Classical Athens*. Cambridge: Cambridge University Press.

    1992. *Literacy and Orality in Ancient Greece*. Cambridge: Cambridge University Press.

    1995. Written in stone? Liberty, equality, orality and the codification of law. *Bulletin of the Institute of Classical Studies* 40: 59–74.

Thompson, H.A. 1936. Pnyx and Thesmophorion. *Hesperia* 5: 151–200.

    1937. Buildings on the west side of the Agora. *Hesperia* 6: 1–226.

    1940. *The Tholos of Athens and Its Predecessors*. Hesperia Supplement 4. Baltimore: American School of Classical Studies at Athens.

    1949. The pedimental sculpture of the Hephaisteion. *Hesperia* 18: 230–68.

    1954. Excavations in the Athenian Agora: 1953. *Hesperia* 23: 31–67.

    1966. Activity in the Athenian Agora, 1960–1965. *Hesperia* 35: 37–54.

Thompson, H.A. and Scranton, R.A. 1943. Stoas and city walls on the Pnyx. *Hesperia* 12: 269–383.

Thompson, H.A. and Wycherley, R.A. 1972. *The Athenian Agora XIV: The Agora of Athens: The History, Shape and Uses of an Ancient City Center*. Princeton: American School of Classical Studies at Athens.

Tilley, C. 1994. *A Phenomenology of Landscape*. Oxford and Providence, RI: Berg Publications.

Tilton, E.L. 1902. The architecture of the Argive Heraeum. In Waldstein 1902: 105–36.

Tomlinson, R.A. 1969. Perachora: the remains outside the two sanctuaries. *Annual of the British School at Athens* 64: 155–258.

    1970. Ancient Macedonian symposia. In B. Laourdas and Ch. Makaronas (eds.), *Ancient Macedonia: Papers Read at the First International Symposium Held in Thessaloniki, August 1968*, 308–15. Thessaloniki: Institute of Balkan Studies.

1980. Two notes on possible hestiatoria. *Annual of the British School at Athens* 75: 221–6.

1983. *Epidauros*. London and St Albans: Granada Publishing.

1987. The architectural context of the Macedonian vaulted tombs. *Annual of the British School at Athens* 82: 305–12.

1988. Water supplies and ritual at the Heraion, Perachora. In R. Hägg, *et al.* 1988: 167–71.

1990. The chronology of the Perachora *hestiatorion* and its significance. In Murray 1990: 95–101.

Tosto, V. 1999. *The Black-Figure Pottery Signed 'NIKOSTHENESEPOIESEN'*. 2 volumes, text and plates. Amsterdam: Allard Pierson Series.

Townsend, R.F. 1986. The fourth-century skene of the Theater of Dionysos at Athens. *Hesperia* 55: 421–38.

1995a. *The Athenian Agora XXVII: The East Side of the Agora: Remains beneath the Stoa of Attalos*. Princeton: American School of Classical Studies at Athens.

1995b. The square peristyle and its predecessors. In Boeghold 1995: 104–13.

Travlos, J. 1971. *Pictorial Dictionary of Ancient Athens*. London: Thames and Hudson.

1988. *Bildlexikon zur Topographie des antiken Attika*. Tübingen: Ernst Wasmuth.

Trendall, A.D. 1967. *The Red-Figured Vases of Lucania, Campania and Sicily*. 2 volumes, text and plates. Oxford: Clarendon.

1989. *Red Figure Vases of South Italy and Sicily*. London: Thames and Hudson.

Trendall, A.D. and Cambitoglou, A. 1978. *The Red-Figured Vases of Apulia I: Early and Middle Apulian*. Oxford: Clarendon.

1982. *The Red-Figured Vases of Apulia II: Late Apulian*. Oxford: Clarendon.

Treu, G. 1897. *Olympia: Die Ergebnisse der von dem deutschen Reich veranstalteten Ausgrabung III: Die Bildwerke in Stein und Thon*. 2 volumes, text and plates. Berlin: A. Asher & Co.

Trigger, B.G. 1984. Alternative archaeologies: nationalist, colonialist, imperialist. *Man* n.s. 19: 355–70.

1989. *A History of Archaeological Thought*. Cambridge: Cambridge University Press.

1998. Archaeology and epistemology: dialoguing across the Darwinian chasm. *American Journal of Archaeology* 102: 1–34.

Tsetskhladze, G.R. and de Angelis, F. (eds.) 1994. *The Archaeology of Greek Colonisation: Essays Dedicated to Sir John Boardman*. Oxford: Oxford University Committee for Archaeology.

Tsetskhladze, G.R., Prag, A.J.N.W. and Snodgrass, A.M. (eds.) 2000. *Periplous: Papers on Classical Art and Archaeology Presented to John Boardman*. London: Thames and Hudson.

Tsigakou, F.M. 1981. *The Rediscovery of Greece: Travellers and Painters of the Romantic Era*. London: Thames and Hudson.

Tykot, R.H. and Andrews, T.K. (eds.) 1992. *Sardinia in the Mediterranean: A Footprint in the Sea: Studies in Sardinian Archaeology Presented to Miriam S. Balmuth*. Sheffield: Sheffield Academic Press.

Vagnetti, L. 1989. A Sardinian askos from Crete. *Annual of the British School at Athens* 84: 355–60.

Vallet, G. and Villard, F. 1952. Les dates de fondation de Megara Hyblaea et de Syracuse. *Bulletin de Correspondance Hellénique* 76: 289–346.

1958. La date de fondation de Sélinonte: les données archéologiques. *Bulletin de Correspondance Hellénique* 82: 16–26.

1964. *Mégara Hyblaea 2: la céramique archaïque*. 2 volumes, text and plates. Paris: Editions de Boccard.

Vallet, G., Villard, F. and Auberson, P. 1976. *Mégara Hyblaea 1: le quartier de l'agora archaïque*. 2 volumes, text and plates. Rome: Ecole Française de Rome.

  1983. *Mégara Hyblaea 3: guide des fouilles: introduction à l'histoire d'une cité coloniale d'occident*. Rome: Ecole Française de Rome.

Van Andel, T.H. and Runnels, C. 1987. *Beyond the Acropolis: A Rural Greek Past*. Stanford: Stanford University Press.

Van Straten, F.T. 1981. Gifts for the gods. In H.S. Versnel (ed.), *Faith, Hope and Worship: Aspects of Religious Mentality in the Ancient World*, 65–151. Leiden: E.J. Brill.

  1988. The god's portion in Greek sacrificial representations: is the tail doing nicely? In Hägg *et al.* 1988: 51–68.

Van Wees, H. 1992. *Status Warriors: War, Violence and Society in Homer and History*. Amsterdam: J.C. Gieben.

  1998. Greeks bearing arms: the state, the leisure class, and the display of weapons in Archaic Greece. In Fisher and Van Wees 1998: 333–78.

Varoufakis, G.J. 1983. The origin of Mycenaean and Geometric iron on the Greek mainland and the Aegean islands. In Muhly *et al.* 1983: 315–22.

Vickers, M. 1985a. Artful crafts: the influence of metalwork on Athenian painted pottery. *Journal of Hellenic Studies* 105: 108–28.

  1985b. Persepolis, Vitruvius and the Erechtheum Caryatids: the iconography of medism and servitude. *Revue Archéologique* 1985: 3–28.

  1987a. Value and simplicity: eighteenth-century taste and the study of Greek vases. *Past and Present* 116: 98–137.

  1987b. Dates, methods and icons. In Bérard *et al.* 1987: 19–25.

  1990a. Golden Greece: relative values, minae and temple inventories. *American Journal of Archaeology* 94: 613–25.

  1990b. Attic symposia after the Persian wars. In Murray 1990: 105–21.

Vickers, M. and Gill, D. 1994. *Artful Crafts: Ancient Greek Silverware and Pottery*. Oxford: Clarendon.

Vidal-Naquet, P. 1981. The Black Hunter and the origin of the Athenian *ephebeia*. In R.L. Gordon (ed.), *Myth, Religion and Society: Structuralist Essays by M. Detienne, L. Gernet, J.P. Vernant and P. Vidal-Naquet*, 147–62. Cambridge: Cambridge University Press.

Vink, M.C.V. 1997. Urbanization in late and Sub-Geometric Greece: abstract considerations and concrete case studies of Eretria and Zagora c. 700 BC. In Andersen *et al.* 1997: 111–41.

Viviers, D. 1992. *Recherches sur les ateliers de sculpteurs et la cité d'Athènes à l'époque archaïque: Endoios, Philergos, Aristoklès*. Brussels: Académie Royale de Belgique.

Von Bothmer, D. (ed.) 1985. *The Amasis Painter and His World: Vase Painting in Sixth-Century BC Athens*. Malibu, CA: J. Paul Getty Museum.

Von Gerkan, A. and Müller-Wiener, W. 1961. *Das Theater von Epidauros*. Stuttgart: W. Kohlhammer.

Von Reden, S. 1997. Money, law and exchange: coinage in the Greek polis. *Journal of Hellenic Studies* 117: 154–76.

Votokopoulou, I. 1986. *Vitsa: Ta Nekrotapheia Mias Molossikis Komis*. 3 volumes. Athens: Ekdhosi tou Tameiou Arkhaiologikon Poron kai Apallotriseon.

  1993. Archaiko iero stin Sani, Chalkidikis. In *Ancient Macedonia: Fifth International Symposium*, 471–8. Thessaloniki: Institute for Balkan Studies.

Votokopoulou, I., Despini, A., Michailidou, V. and Tiverios, M. 1985. *Sindos: Katalogos tis Ekthisis*. Thessaloniki: Archaiologiko Mouseio Thessalonikis.

Wace, A.J.B. 1929. The lead figurines. In Dawkins 1929: 249–84.

Wace, A.J.B. and Hasluck, F.W. 1908. Laconia II: topography: south-eastern Laconia. *Annual of the British School at Athens* 14: 161–82.

1909. Laconia II: topography: east central Laconia. *Annual of the British School at Athens* 15: 158–76.

Waelkens, M. 1990. Tool marks and mining techniques in mine nr 3 (Thorikos). In Mussche *et al.* 1990: 114–43.

Walcot, P. 1966. *Hesiod and the Near East.* Cardiff: University of Wales Press.

Waldbaum, J.C. 1978. *From Bronze to Iron: The Transition from the Bronze Age to the Iron Age in the Eastern Mediterranean.* SIMA 54. Göteberg: Paul Åstroms Forlag.

Waldbaum, J.C. and Magness, J. 1997. The chronology of early Greek pottery: new evidence from seventh-century BC. destruction levels in Israel. *American Journal of Archaeology* 101: 23–40.

Waldstein, C. 1902. *The Argive Heraeum.* Vol. I. Boston and New York: Houghton, Mifflin & Co.

1905. *The Argive Heraeum.* Vol. II. Boston and New York: Houghton, Mifflin & Co.

Walker, S. 1993. Women and housing in Classical Greece: the archaeological evidence. In A. Cameron and A. Kuhrt (eds.), *Images of Women in Antiquity,* 81–91. 2nd edition (first published 1983). London: Routledge.

Walter, H. 1990. *Das griechische Heiligtum dargestellt am Heraion von Samos.* Stuttgart: Vrachaus J.M. Mayer.

Walter-Karydi, E. 1996. Die Nobilitierung des griechischen Wohnhauses in der spätklassischen Zeit. In Hoepfner and Brands 1996: 56–61.

Wardle, K.A. 1980. Excavations at Assiros, 1975–9. *Annual of the British School at Athens* 75: 229–67.

1987. Excavations at Assiros Toumba 1986: a preliminary report. *Annual of the British School at Athens* 82: 313–29.

1988. Excavations at Assiros Toumba 1987. *Annual of the British School at Athens* 83: 375–87.

1989. Assiros Toumba. *Annual of the British School at Athens* 84: 447–63.

Watrous, L.V. 1980. J.D.S. Pendlebury's excavations in the plain of Lasithi: the Iron Age sites. *Annual of the British School at Athens* 75: 269–83.

1982a. *Lasithi: A History of Settlement on a Highland Plain in Crete.* Hesperia Supplement 18. Princeton: American School of Classical Studies at Athens.

1982b. The sculptural program of the Siphnian Treasury at Delphi. *American Journal of Archaeology* 86: 159–72.

Watrous, L.V., Chatzi-Vallianou, D., Pope, K., Mourtzas, N., Shay, J., Shay, C.T., Bennet, J., Tsoungarakis, D., Angelomati-Tsoungarakis, E., Vallianos, C. and Blitzer, H. 1993. A survey of the western Mesara plain in Crete: preliminary report of the 1984, 1986 and 1987 field seasons. *Hesperia* 62: 191–248.

Waywell, G.B. 1978. *The Free-Standing Sculptures of the Mausoleum at Halicarnassus in the British Museum: A Catalogue.* London: British Museum Publications.

Weinberg, S.S. 1943. *Corinth VII.i: The Geometric and Orientalizing Pottery.* Cambridge, MA: Harvard University Press.

Weller, C.H., Dunham, M.E., Thallon, I.C., King, L.S., Baldwin, A. and Bassett, S.E. 1903. The cave at Vari. *American Journal of Archaeology* n.s. 7: 263–349.

Wells, B. 1983. *Asine II: Results of the Excavations East of the Acropolis 1970–72. Fasc. 4. The Protogeometric Period 2: An Analysis of the Settlement.* Stockholm: Skrifter Utgivna av Svenska Institutet i Athen.

(ed.) 1992. *Agriculture in Ancient Greece: Proceedings of the Seventh International Symposium at the Swedish Institute, Athens.* Stockholm: Paul Åstroms Forlag.

West, M.L. (ed.) 1980. *Delectus ex Iambis et Elegis Graecis*. Oxford Classical Texts. Oxford: Clarendon.

Westgate, R. 1998. Greek mosaics and their architectural and social context. *Bulletin of the Institute of Classical Studies* 42 [1997/8]: 93–115.

Whitbread, I.K. 1995. *Greek Transport Amphorae: A Petrological and Archaeological Study*. Fitch Laboratory Occasional Paper 4. Exeter: British School at Athens.

Whitley, J. 1988. Early states and hero cults: a re-appraisal. *Journal of Hellenic Studies* 108: 173–82.

   1991a. *Style and Society in Dark Age Greece: The Changing Face of a Pre-literate Society 1100–700 BC*. Cambridge: Cambridge University Press.

   1991b. Social diversity in Dark Age Greece. *Annual of the British School at Athens* 86: 341–65.

   1993. The explanation of form: towards a reconciliation of archaeological and art-historical approaches. *Hephaistos* 11/12 [1992–3]: 7–33.

   1994a. Protoattic pottery: a contextual approach. In Morris 1994b: 51–70.

   1994b. The monuments that stood before Marathon: tomb cult and hero cult in Archaic Attica. *American Journal of Archaeology* 98: 213–30.

   1995. Tomb cult and hero cult: the uses of the past in Archaic Greece. In Spencer 1995b: 43–63.

   1997a. Beazley as theorist. *Antiquity* 71: 40–7.

   1997b. Cretan laws and Cretan literacy. *American Journal of Archaeology* 101: 635–61.

   1998. From Minoans to Eteocretans: the Praisos region, 1200–500 BC. In Cavanagh *et al.* 1998: 27–39.

   2000. Gender and hierarchy in early Athens: the strange case of the disappearance of the rich female grave. *Metis: Revue d'Anthropologie du Monde Grec Ancien* 11 [1996]: 209–31.

Whitley, J., O'Conor, K. and Mason, H. 1995. Praisos III: a report on the architectural survey undertaken in 1992. *Annual of the British School at Athens* 90: 405–28.

Whitley, J., Prent, M. and Thorne, S. 1999. Praisos IV: a preliminary report on the 1993 and 1994 survey seasons. *Annual of the British School at Athens* 94: 215–64.

Wide, S. 1899. Geometrische Vasen aus Griechenland. *Jahrbuch des deutschen archäologischen Instituts* 14: 26–43, 78–86 & 188–215.

   1900. Geometrische Vasen aus Griechenland. *Jahrbuch des deutschen archäologischen Instituts* 15: 49–58.

Wiegand, Th. and Schrader, H. 1904. *Priene: Ergebnisse der Ausgrabungen und Untersuchungen in den Jahren 1895–98*. Berlin: Georg Reimer.

Willemsen, F. 1957. *Dreifusskessel von Olympia: Alte und neue Funde: Olympische Forschungen III*. Berlin: Walter de Gruyter.

Willemsen, F. and Brenne, S. 1991. Verzeichnis der Kerameikos Ostraka. *Mitteilungen des deutschen archäologischen Instituts, athenische Abteilung* 106: 147–56.

Williams, C.K. II 1982. The early urbanization of Corinth. *Annuario della Scuola Archeologica di Atene* 60: 9–19.

Williams, C.K. II and Fisher, J.E. 1971. Corinth 1970: Forum area. *Hesperia* 40: 1–51.

   1972. Corinth 1971: Forum area. *Hesperia* 41: 143–84.

Williams, C.K. II, MacIntosh, J. and Fisher, J.E. 1974. Excavations at Corinth, 1973. *Hesperia* 43: 1–76.

Williams, D. 1991. The drawing of the human figure on early red-figure vases. In D. Buitron (ed.), *New Perspectives in Early Greek Art*, 285–301. Hanover, NH and London: University Press of New England.

1996. Re-figuring Attic red figure: a review article. *Revue Archéologique* 1996.2: 227–52.

Willkomm, H. 1989. Radiokohlensoffdatierungen des Siedlungshügels Kastanas. In Hänsel 1989: 395–411.

Winckelmann, J.J. 1764. *Geschichte der Kunst des Alterthums*. Dresden: Waltherische hof-Buchhandlung.

1850. *The History of Ancient Art among the Greeks*. Translated from the German by G. Henry Lodge. London: John Chapman.

Winter, I.J. 1976. Phoenician and North Syrian ivory carving in its historical context: questions of style and distribution. *Iraq* 38: 1–22.

1988. North Syria as a bronzeworking centre in the early first millennium BC: luxury commodities at home and abroad. In J.C. Curtis (ed.), *Bronzeworking Centres of Western Asia c.1000–539 BC*, 193–225. London and New York: Keegan Paul International.

Winter, N.A. 1990. Defining regional styles in Archaic Greek architectural terracottas. *Hesperia* 59: 13–32.

1993. *Greek Architectural Terracottas from the Prehistoric to the End of the Archaic Period*. Oxford: Clarendon.

Wolters, P. 1899. Vasen aus Menidi II. *Jahrbuch des deutschen archäologischen Instituts* 14: 103–35.

Woodford, S. 1971. Cults of Heracles in Attica. In D.G. Mitten, J.G. Pedley and J.A. Scott (eds.), *Studies Presented to George M.A. Hanfmann*, 211–25. Mainz: Philipp von Zabern.

Wrede, W. 1924. Phyle. *Mitteilungen des deutschen archäologischen Instituts, athenische Abteilung* 49: 153–224.

1933. *Attische Mauern*. Athens: Deutsches archäologisches Institut.

Wrede, W., Gerkan, A. von, Hampe, R. and Jantzen, U. 1937. *Bericht über die Ausgrabungen in Olympia*. Berlin: Walter de Gruyter.

Wright, H.E. 1972. Vegetation history. In McDonald and Rapp 1972: 188–99.

Wright, H.T. 1977. Recent research on the origin of the state. *Annual Review of Anthropology* 6: 379–97.

Wright, J.C. 1982. The old temple terrace at the Argive Heraeum and the early cult of Hera in the Argolid. *Journal of Hellenic Studies* 102: 186–201.

Wright, J.C., Cherry, J.F., Davis, J.L., Mantzourani, E., Sutton, S.B. and Sutton, R.F. 1990. The Nemea valley archaeological project: a preliminary report. *Hesperia* 59: 579–645.

Wycherley, R.E. 1978. *The Stones of Athens*. Princeton: Princeton University Press.

Xirotiris, N.I. and Langenscheidt, F. 1981. The cremations from the Royal Macedonian tombs at Vergina. *Archaiologiki Ephemeris* 1981: 142–60.

Yiouri, E. 1978. *O Kratiras tou Derviniou*. Athens: I en Athenais Archaiologiki Etaireia.

Yoffee, N. 1993. Too many chiefs? (or safe texts for the 90s). In N. Yoffee and A. Sherratt (eds.), *Archaeological Theory: Who Sets the Agenda?*, 60–78. Cambridge: Cambridge University Press.

Young, J.H. 1956a. Ancient towers on the island of Siphnos. *American Journal of Archaeology* 60: 51–5.

1956b. Studies in south Attica: country estates at Sounion. *Hesperia* 25: 122–46.

Young, R.S. 1939. *Late Geometric Graves and a Seventh-Century Well in the Agora*. Hesperia Supplement 2. Athens: American School of Classical Studies at Athens.

1951. Sepulturae intra urbem. *Hesperia* 20: 67–134.

1981. *Three Great Early Tumuli: Gordion Excavations Final Report I*. Philadelphia: University Museum Publications.

Zangger, E. 1998. The environmental setting. In Davis 1998: 1–9.

Zangger, E., Timpson, M.E., Yazvenko, S.B., Kuhnke, F. and Knauss, J. 1997. The Pylos regional archaeological project part II: landscape evolution and site preservation. *Hesperia* 66: 549–641.

Zimmermann, J.L. 1989. *Les Chevaux de bronze dans l'art géométrique grec*. Mainz: Philipp von Zabern.

INDEX

Note: Alternative names and spellings are given in brackets. Words transliterated from the Greek are in italics.